The Persuasive Portrayal of David and Solomon in Chronicles

McMaster Divinity College Press
McMaster Biblical Studies Series, Volume 3

The Persuasive Portrayal of David and Solomon in Chronicles

A Rhetorical Analysis of the Speeches and Prayers in the David-Solomon Narrative

SUK-IL AHN

Foreword by Mark J. Boda

◆PICKWICK *Publications* · Eugene, Oregon

THE PERSUASIVE PORTRAYAL OF DAVID AND SOLOMON IN CHRONICLES
A Rhetorical Analysis of the Speeches and Prayers in the David-Solomon Narrative

McMaster Biblical Studies Series, Volume 3
McMaster Divinity College Press

Copyright © 2018 Suk-il Ahn. All rights reserved. Except for brief quotations in critical publications or reviews, no part of this book may be reproduced in any manner without prior written permission from the publisher. Write: Permissions, Wipf and Stock Publishers, 199 W. 8th Ave., Suite 3, Eugene, OR 97401.

Pickwick Publications
An Imprint of Wipf and Stock Publishers
199 W. 8th Ave., Suite 3
Eugene, OR 97401

McMaster Divinity College Press
1280 Main Street West
Hamilton, Ontario, Canada
l8s 4k1

www.wipfandstock.com

PAPERBACK ISBN: 978-1-5326-0492-8
HARDCOVER ISBN: 978-1-5326-0494-2
EBOOK ISBN: 978-1-5326-0493-5

Cataloguing-in-Publication data:

Names: Ahn, Suk-il, author | Boda, Mark J., foreword.

Title: Book title : The persuasive portrayal of David and Solomon in chronicles : a rhetorical analysis of the speeches and prayers in the David-Solomon narrative / Suk-il Ahn ; foreword by Mark J. Boda.

Description: Eugene, OR: Pickwick Publications, 2018 | McMaster Biblical Studies Series | Includes bibliographical references and index.

Identifiers: ISBN 978-1-5326-0492-8 (paperback) | ISBN 978-1-5326-0494-2 (hardcover) | ISBN 978-1-5326-0493-5 (ebook).

Subjects: LCSH: Bible. Chronicles, 1st—Criticism, interpretation, etc. | Bible. Chronicles, 2nd—Criticism, interpretation, etc. | David, King of Israel | Solomon, King of Israel | Bible. Old Testament—Prayers.

Classification: BS1345.52 A28 2018 (paperback) | BS1345.52 (ebook).

Manufactured in the U.S.A.   02/01/18

Contents

Foreword by Mark J. Boda / vii

Preface / ix

Abbreviations / xi

1 Introduction / 1

2 Rhetorical Situation / 33

3 Rhetorical Unit / 64

4 Speeches and Prayers in David's Narrative / 82

5 Speeches and Prayers in Solomon's Narrative / 212

6 Conclusion / 273

Bibliography / 283

Index of Modern Authors / 301

Index of Ancient Sources / 305

Foreword

It is my delight to write this foreword to Suk-il Ahn's new contribution to the field of Chronicles study. Dr. Ahn joined the Divinity College at a time when three of us in the Old Testament department at McMaster were all working intensely in 1 and 2 Chronicles (Drs. Boda, Evans, and Konkel) and so he was a welcome conversation partner for our own ideas on these fascinating books even as he pursued his own direction. My own study of Chronicles has been enhanced through the interaction I have had with Dr. Ahn over the past decade, for which I am truly thankful (also for the many Tim Hortons' coffees).

When I did my own work on Chronicles I relied upon the fine work of Mark Throntveit arising from his doctoral work at Union under Patrick Miller in the early 1980s and so it was a delight to host Professor Throntveit for the review of Dr. Ahn's dissertation. Of course, much has happened in the three decades between the two works and Dr. Ahn's work seeks after a more wholistic narrative reading of the speeches and moves the discussion to the level of rhetorical persuasion, seeking to discern the ways in which the Chronicler uses these speeches to shape the audience's response. Rather than replacing Dr. Throntveit's fine work, it builds on that foundation and provides new insights.

So I recommend Dr. Ahn's contribution to all who find in Chronicles, not merely the "things omitted" (ΠΑΡΑΛΕΙΠΟΜΕΝΩΝ) as the Old Greek considered it, but rather the exciting "accounts of the days" (דברי הימים) of the Masoretic tradition. As we listen to these ancient royal voices we hear echoes of the Chronicler's passion for a generation emerging from centuries of crisis and in need of renewed vision for life as the people of God.

Mark J. Boda, Ph.D. (Cantab.)
Hamilton, Ontario, Canada

Preface

THIS STUDY BEGAN WITH puny expectations: My study of Chronicles would serve some students in South Korea who might want to study Chronicles. It seemed to be a good opportunity for me to study the book of Chronicles in the Hebrew Bible since, as far as I know, only a few have studied in Chronicles in South Korea. I was also eager to participate in the Old Testament scholarly world through McMaster Divinity College since I have met many colleagues and well-known scholars through McMaster Divinity College and my time there has helped me understand how the scholarly world works. This was an awesome experience for me, and greatly expanded the horizon of my knowledge of the Old Testament.

The book of Chronicles has been ignored by many readers, who have regarded it as an unnecessary repetition and as a supplement to Samuel-Kings. This atmosphere has drastically changed in the last two decades. Recently, a number of studies on Chronicles have appeared in the Old Testament scholarly world. Most of them understand Chronicles not as a supplement to Samuel-Kings, but as a work with its own integrity and message. This study reflects this sort of recent interest.

This study examines the speeches and prayers in the David-Solomon narrative in Chronicles and seeks to demonstrate that the Chronicler's portrayal of David and Solomon attempts to establish the Yehudite community identity by arguing that the Jerusalem temple is the sole worship place of Israel in the Persian period and by asserting that as a commitment to YHWH accompanied by the worship of YHWH through the Jerusalem temple, the covenantal relationship between YHWH and Israel continues even into the Persian period. This study employs Kennedy's rhetorical method with some modifications of his concept of rhetorical situation: the narrative situation and the Chronicler's situation. The former reflects the narrative world, while the latter reflects the Chronicler's own time in Persian Yehud. Although we cannot know the original situation and audience, we may determine approximately the boundaries of the Chronicler's time by dating Chronicles. Thus, the Chronicler's portrayal of David and Solomon through speeches and prayers serves to persuade his audience of the significance of the Jerusalem temple, reformulating the Yehudite community identity as a cultic community in the Persian period by pointing to the continuity of the covenantal relationship between YHWH and Israel through the Jerusalem temple in the Persian era.

I am grateful to those who have helped in the writing of my dissertation. First of all, I am grateful to my supervisors, Dr. Mark J. Boda and Dr. Paul S. Evans, for their instruction and encouragement with which they helped me write this dissertation. Their careful guidance and encouragement have greatly enhanced my understanding of the scholarly world. In particular, my supervisor, Dr. Mark Boda, has been a model scholar of teaching and encouraging students throughout my time studying at McMaster Divinity College. I am also grateful to Dr. Stanley E. Porter who taught me methodologies and linguistics in biblical study and to Dr. Mark A. Throntveit, as an external examiner, who gave me his useful comments on my dissertation.

Special thanks go to my wife Jaesoon Lee who supported me throughout my study in the U.S. and Canada. She faithfully handled all the challenges and difficulties during my study. Furthermore, I am thankful to my mother, mother-in-law, brother-in-law (Sunho Lee), and mother-church (Seoul-Nam Presbyterian Church). Without their prayers and help, my dissertation would never have been completed. Furthermore, I would like to thank my two sons, Junhwan and Soohwan, who have made me happy and our home joyful during these years of my study. Finally, I am grateful to my God that this dissertation has been brought to completion. I praise my God who has always been good to me.

I hope that this study would convey to the readers both the purpose of the Chronicler as the author and the intention of God as the ultimate author, and I pray that this study would help and galvanize others who might want to study the Old Testament, especially the book of Chronicles.

Abbreviations

AB	Anchor Bible
ABD	*The Anchor Bible Dictionary*
AOTC	Apollos Old Testament Commentary
BBR	*Bulletin for Biblical Research*
BEATAJ	Beiträge zur Erforschung des Alten Testaments und des Antiken Judentums
BETL	Biblotheca Ephemeridum Theologicarum Lovaniensium
Bib	*Biblica*
BibInt	*Biblical Interpretation: A Journal of Contemporary Approaches*
BN	*Biblische Notizen*
BS	*Bibliotheca Sacra*
BWANT	Beiträge zur Wissenschaft vom Alten und Neuen Testament
BZAW	Beihefte zur Zeitschrift für die Alttestamentliche Wissenschaft
CBC	The Cambridge Bible Commentary on the New English Bible
CBQ	*Catholic Biblical Quarterly*
CBR	*Currents in Biblical Research*
CTM	*Concordia Theological Monthly*
ET	*Expository Times*
FAT	Forschungen zum Alten Testament
FOTL	The Forms of the Old Testament Literature
FRLANT	Forschungen zur Religion und Literatur des Alten und Neuen Testaments
FTS	Freiburger Theologische Studien
HAR	*Hebrew Annual Review*
HAT	Handbuch zum Alten Testament
HBM	Hebrew Bible Monographs
HBT	*Horizons in Biblical Theology*
HCOT	Historical Commentary on the Old Testament
HS	*Hebrew Studies*
HSM	Harvard Semitic Monographs

Abbreviations

HTR	*Harvard Theological Review*
HUCA	*Hebrew Union College Annual*
ICC	International Critical Commentary
Int	*Interpretation*
JAOS	*Journal of the American Oriental Society*
JBL	*Journal of Biblical Literature*
JBQ	*Jewish Bible Quarterly*
JETS	*Journal of the Evangelical Theological Society*
JHNES	Johns Hopkins Near Eastern Studies
JHS	*Journal of Hebrew Scriptures*
JJS	*Journal of Jewish Studies*
JSS	*Journal of Semitic Studies*
JSNTSup	Journal for the Study of the New Testament Supplement Series
JSOT	*Journal for the Study of the Old Testament*
JSOTSup	Journal for the Study of the Old Testament Supplement Series
JTS	*Journal of Theological Studies*
LHBOTS	The Library of Hebrew Bible/Old Testament Studies
LS	*Louvain Studies*
LSTS	The Library of Second Temple Studies
LTQ	*Lexington Theological Quarterly*
MSJ	*The Master's Seminary Journal*
NCB	New Century Bible Commentary
NIDOTTE	*New International Dictionary of Old Testament Theology and Exegesis*
NIVAC	NIV Application Commentary
OS	*Oudtestamentische Studiën*
OTE	*Old Testament Essays*
OTG	Old Testament Guides
OTL	Old Testament Library
OtSt	*Oudtestamentische Studiën*
PR	*Philosophy and Rhetoric*
RQ	*Restoration Quarterly*
RR	*Rhetoric Review*
RSQ	*Rhetoric Society Quarterly*
RTR	*Reformed Theological Review*
RThP	*Revue de Théologie et de Philosphie*
SBL	Society of Biblical Literature

Abbreviations

SBLDS	SBL Dissertation Series
SJOT	*Scandinavian Journal of the Old Testament*
SSN	Studia Semitica Neerlandica
STDJ	Studies on the Texts of the Desert of Judah
TDOT	*Theological Dictionary of the Old Testament*
TLOT	*Theological Lexicon of the Old Testament*
TOTC	Tyndale Old Testament Commentaries
TynBul	*Tyndale Bulletin*
VT	*Vetus Testamentum*
VTSup	*Vetus Testamentum*, Supplements
WBC	Word Biblical Commentary
WMANT	Wissenschaftliche Monographien zum Alten und Neuen Testament
WTJ	*Westminster Theological Journal*
WW	*Word and World*
ZAW	*Zeitschrift für die Alttestamentliche Wissenschaft*

1

Introduction

THE PRESENT STUDY ATTEMPTS to examine the persuasive portrayal of David and Solomon in Chronicles and its contribution to the Chronicler's purpose. In particular, the speeches and prayers in Chronicles are seen as the Chronicler's key strategy for presenting the early history of Israel to those who were living in the Persian era. In fact, speeches and prayers occupy a large portion of Chronicles. Thus, the persuasive portrayal of David and Solomon will be explored in terms of the speeches and prayers in the David-Solomon narrative.

Many scholars have claimed that the Chronicler portrays David and Solomon as idealized kings in the narrative of the temple building.[1] However, if they were idealized in Chronicles, why does the Chronicler include David's census and his initial failure to bring the ark to Jerusalem? It seems that the Chronicler's purpose in portraying David and Solomon does not simply lie in idealizing the reign of David and Solomon in order to glorify YHWH.

How then does the Chronicler depict David and Solomon? What is the primary purpose of the Chronicler in portraying David and Solomon? What do David and Solomon say about themselves in their speeches and prayers, and what do others say about David and Solomon? What roles do they play in the persuasive purpose of the Chronicler? Previous studies on David and Solomon in Chronicles took into account David as the founder of the cultic system and the one who prepared for the building of the temple and Solomon as one who completed the establishment of the cult and the

---

1. For example, McConville says, in relation to Solomon, "The Chronicler's aim in his portrayal of Solomon is to show how God governed the events of history to impart to the kingdom of Israel, at least once, a splendour that was fit to symbolize his own" (McConville, *I & II Chronicles*, 110). Williamson, focusing more on the promises made to David, states, "The Chronicler wished to present Solomon as one man who fulfilled the conditions of obedience to the will of God that were necessary for the permanent establishment of the dynasty" (Williamson, *1 and 2 Chronicles*, 236). Duke also concludes, "As with the portrayal of David, that of Solomon is positive and idealistic" (Duke, *Persuasive Appeal*, 66). According to Throntveit, this idealized Solomon was for the glorification of God. See Throntveit, "Idealization," 411–27. On the other hand, Kelly identifies the contention that Solomon in Chronicles was idealized as "a subjective interpretation," and he thinks the Chronicler has a balanced view of Solomon by citing verses critical of Solomon such as 2 Chr 10:4, 10–11, 14. See Kelly, "Messianic Elements," 257–58.

building of the temple.² However, the Chronicler's portrayal of David and Solomon goes beyond these themes.

In this study, I will examine the persuasive portrayal of David and Solomon, based on speeches and prayers in the narrative framework with the assumption that the David-Solomon narrative is a sub-rhetorical unit within the whole book of Chronicles. I will argue that the Chronicler's persuasive portrayal of David and Solomon is designed to help reconstruct the identity of the Yehudite community as a cultic community through the Jerusalem temple, revealing the continuity of the covenantal relationship between YHWH and the Judahites in the Persian era. Even if the images of David and Solomon are as the preparer of the temple building and builder of the temple, their primary roles in the Chronicler's presentation are to re-establish the identity of the Yehudite community in Persian Yehud on the basis of the Jerusalem temple, pointing to the continuity of the covenantal relationship in the Persian period,³ which was expressed by the Davidic covenant regarding temple building. In this study, the covenant relationship in the Persian era is defined as a commitment to YHWH through the Jerusalem temple with a dedication to the worship of YHWH.⁴

In effect, the rhetorical situation is an identity crisis in the Persian era. The identity of Israel as God's people was challenged by the destruction of Jerusalem (587/86 BCE) since their identity markers such as king, temple, and worship disappeared.⁵ However, Cyrus's edict changed the deportees' situation in Babylon, leading to their return to their homeland. As part of the reformation of their identity in the Persian era, some groups of the returnees from Babylon to Jerusalem, including those who remained in Yehud later, would feel the need to reformulate their identity as God's people in the Persian period and to confirm their covenantal relationship with YHWH, since the relationship seems to have been broken during the exile. In their eyes, it would be doubtful whether or not YHWH's covenants with Israel were still valid in the Persian era. Thus, the Chronicler's persuasive portrayal of David and Solomon serves to reconstruct the community identity through the Jerusalem temple,

---

2. De Vries describes David as a cult founder, indicating that David "ordained the Levites to their office who brought the worship of Yahweh to its highest perfection and its true fulfillment" (De Vries, "Moses and David," 639). Braun holds that the Chronicler's purpose is "to portray Solomon as the divinely chosen temple builder" (Braun, "Chosen Temple Builder," 590).

3. For discussion of covenant in Chronicles, see Boda, "Reenvisioning the Relationship," 391–408. For the relationship of the Davidic dynasty and the future hope, see Boda, "Gazing through the Cloud of Incense," 217–47.

4. I agree with Boda's view. Boda indicates that covenant in Chronicles reveals not "a shift from vital reciprocal relationship between Yahweh and the people, to a sterile unilateral relationship mediated by law and stripped of its reciprocal immediacy" but "rather a shift away from covenant with general commitment to the statutes of law as the dominant idiom for expressing the relationship between Yahweh and the people to a commitment to Yahweh expressed through the Chronicler's idiom of immediate relationship with general and particular commitments to the renewal of cult and worship" (Boda, "Reenvisioning the Relationship," 404).

5. Boda, 1–2 Chronicles, 8.

Introduction

revealing the continuity of the covenantal relationship between YHWH and Israel in the Persian period.

HISTORY OF RESEARCH

Until the nineteenth century Chronicles was regarded as a reliable historical source of pre-exilic Israel. However, this was challenged with the advent of the historical-critical method, so that Chronicles was seen as a tendentious alteration, and its historical reliability was underlined.[6] When the new century came, the tendency of studies of Chronicles has gradually shifted from the discussion of historical reliability to literary approaches.

Studies of Chronicles Since the Twentieth Century

Studies of the book of Chronicles since the twentieth century, while continuing the discussion of historical reliability, have been focused on its literary aspects. Three key issues can be discerned: the composition of the book of Chronicles,[7] the relationship of Chronicles and Ezra-Nehemiah,[8] and the messages of Chronicles or the purpose of the Chronicler (as the author of the book of Chronicles).

Some scholars, regarding the book of Chronicles as a literary product and not as a historical source, have examined the themes of Chronicles and the purpose of the Chronicler.[9] For example, von Rad, stressing the unique materials in Chronicles,

---

6. For the discussion, see Graham, *Utilization*, 76–95. Recently, due to the discovery of the Dead Sea Scrolls (DSS), specifically 4QSam^a, the view that the Chronicler's *Vorlage* is tantamount to the Masoretic text (MT) was doubted. Text-critical examination showed that the Chronicler's sources were more akin to the Lucianic version of the LXX and some sections of Samuel found in 4QSam^a than to the MT. See Tiňo, *King and Temple*, 22–23.

7. For instance, Noth identified Chronicles primarily as a single composition with the Chronicler's theological additions, based on Samuel–Kings (Noth, *The Chronicler's History*, 29–50). Rudolph could not identify any patterns of specific editions (Rudolph, "Problems of the Books of Chronicles," 402). Cross proposed three stages of composition of the book of Chronicles (Cross, "Reconstruction of the Judean Restoration," 4–18). Ackroyd proposed that the literary history of Chronicles was an ongoing process that was settled at a significant point in time (Ackroyd, "Historical Literature," 307). On the other hand, Japhet—against redaction theories— identified the book of Chronicles as a unified work (Japhet, *I & II Chronicles*, 3–7). Recently, Person has contended, based on Auld's common source hypothesis, that the Deuteronomistic History and the Chronicler's History were contemporaneously edited by two scribal guilds in the Persian era. In Person's view, the broader oral traditions enable various ideologies to be incorporated into the two texts, so that these ideological texts are merely different expressions of the same tradition. See Person, *Deuteronomic History*.

8. Chronicles and Ezra-Nehemiah have been regarded as a single book since Zunz's view has been dominant until recently from his 1832 study (Zunz, *Die gottesdienstlichen Vorträge*). See Japhet, "Historical Reliability," 88. However, Nachmanides and Gersonides in earlier literature already took into account Chronicles and Ezra-Nehemiah as a single work. See Kalimi, *Retelling*, 6–7. This view has now been challenged and the separate authorship of Chronicles and Ezra-Nehemiah has been acknowledged, even if still there are ongoing debates. See Japhet, "Supposed Common Authorship," 330–71; Williamson, *Israel*, 5–70.

9. The literary devices of Chronicles have been noted from the medieval era: "The literary device

examines the history of Israel rewritten by the Chronicler.[10] Welch, investigating the Chronicler's message and theology, seeks to "concentrate attention on what the author had to say, and through the study of what he did say discover, if possible, the purpose he had in writing his book."[11] Other literary studies of Chronicles have followed such as those of Myers, Braun, Schaefer, Willi, Ackroyd, Japhet, Mosis, and Williamson.[12] Some central themes were recognized including Davidic dynasty, temple, cult, and true Israel.[13]

Studies of the relationship between the Davidic dynasty and temple have been performed by McKenzie, Riley, Dyck, Schweitzer, Tiňo, and Hwang.[14] According to Riley, the situation of the postexilic community without a monarch required a re-valuation of previous history and former kings of Israel. Riley dealt with the relationship between the king and worship in Chronicles, stating that cultic fidelity results in dynastic prosperity, whereas cultic unfaithfulness results in dynastic disaster. Riley contends that "the net result of the Chronistic intertwining of endorsement and threat centered on the cultus is that the cultus emerges as a principal reason for the monarchy's very existence and takes precedence over the Davidic monarchy as the real concern of the Chronicler."[15] In Riley's view, the Davidic covenant is still valid in that the liturgical life of the Yehudite community fulfilled God's call for his people even though Judah as a political entity did not exist anymore. He holds that "the Chronicler placed the dynastic promise into the larger context of the Temple as the major effect of the Davidic covenant, and thus demonstrated through his narrative that the days of the dynasty had ended while the covenant with David remained."[16] Thus, Riley concludes that the kingship existed for the cult and that the Davidic promise was incorporated into the cult.

---

of resumptive repetition (*Wiederaufnahme*) was noted already by the medieval Jewish commentators Rashi, Ibn Ezra, Kimchi, and the commentary on Chronicles that is ascribed to Rashi." See Kalimi, *Retelling*, 7.

10. Von Rad, *Das Geschichtsbild*.

11. Welch, *Work of the Chronicler*, 6.

12. Those literary and theological works of Chronicles are: North, "Theology of the Chronicler," 369–81; Myers, "Kerygma of the Chronicler," 259–73; Engler, "Attitude of the Chronicler"; Braun, "Significance of 1 Chronicles 22, 28 and 29," 581–90; Schaefer, "Significance of Seeking God"; Willi, *Die Chronik*; Ackroyd, "Theology of the Chronicler," 101–16; Chang, "*Tendenz* of the Chronicler"; Japhet, *Ideology*; Mosis, *Untersuchungen*; Newsome, "The Chronicler's View"; Rigsby, "Historiography"; Williamson, *Israel*; Osborne, "Genealogies of I Chronicles 1–9"; and Im, *Das Davidbild*.

13. As for the meaning of true Israel, Noth and Rudolph thought that Chronicles was an anti-Samaritan work that only legitimated the cult of Jerusalem and the kingdom of Judah, whereas Japhet and Williamson, against the view that the Chronicler speaks of the concept of 'Israel' only for the kingdom of Judah, proposed a broader concept of Israel. See Noth, *The Chronicler's History*; Rudolph, *Chronikbücher*; Japhet, *Ideology*; Williamson, *Israel*; and Oeming, *Das wahre Israel*.

14. McKenzie, *The Chronicler's Use*; Riley, *King and Cultus*; Dyck, *Theocratic Ideology*; Schweitzer, *Reading Utopia*; Tiňo, *King and Temple*; Hwang, "Hope for the Restoration."

15. Riley, *King and Cultus*, 155–56.

16. Ibid., 201.

Introduction

McKenzie claims that Chronicles legitimated the dominion of the Davidic dynasty over Israel, showing the kingship of YHWH is granted to the Davidic dynasty.[17] Dyck also suggests that Chronicles represents the reign of YHWH as the reign of the priests, displaying the Chronicler's purpose—that only Jerusalem is the legitimate center of the whole Israel.[18] Recently, Schweitzer has examined the genealogies, policies, and temple cult through the lens of literary theories, identifying the Davidic dynasty as the political utopia and the cult and the administrators of the temple as the cultic utopia. He identifies the two themes of Chronicles as the Davidic dynasty and the cult of the temple.[19] Tiňo investigates palace-temple relations in Chronicles in the theology of Chronicles, interacting with the previous and contemporary traditions of Judah.[20] According to Tiňo, the identification of David as a second Moses led the Chronicler to represent David as a mediator and as a king that functioned as a priestly king, displaying a manifest link with the ideology of ANE kingship, in which the realms of palace and temple were not strictly distinguished.[21] More recently, Hwang, viewing the Davidic covenant as the basis of the hope for a restoration of the Davidic kingdom in Chronicles, has raised questions about both the un-conditionality and conditionality of the Davidic covenant. In Hwang's view, the dynastic promise is conditional in that the Davidic kings are disciplined and punished and the kingdom can disappear when it does not meet the conditions given by YHWH. On the other hand, it is unconditional in that YHWH's *hesed* will never depart from the Davidic kingdom. Thus, Hwang regards the two characteristics of the Davidic covenant as complementary.[22]

Two further studies of Chronicles are noteworthy. Jeon, in his study of Solomon in Chronicles, challenges the assumption that Solomon was portrayed as an ideal king, and contends that Solomon in Chronicles was not impeccable. The focus of his study is on three elements: the law for the king prohibiting many horses and wives (Deut 17:16–20); Solomon's Egyptian wife as a foreigner (2 Chr 8); and the division of the united kingdom (2 Chr 10).[23] According to Jeon, these elements are indicators to the

---

17. McKenzie, *The Chronicler's Use*.

18. Dyck, *Theocratic Ideology*, 227–28. In his book, Dyck tries to examine "the relationship between the Chronicler's theocratic ideas and the sociohistorical context" (*Theocratic Ideology*, 1) by employing an ideological approach to the social-scientific methods, in order to reveal the social force of the Chronicler's rhetoric. In particular, Dyck wishes to show that the theocracy in the Second Temple period was an ideological achievement and significantly contributed to the Chronicler's presentation of the history of Israel.

19. Schweitzer, *Reading Utopia*.

20. Tiňo, *King and Temple*, 33.

21. Ibid., 160–61.

22. Hwang, "Hope for the Restoration," 5. See also Hwang, "Coexistence."

23. Jeon, *Impeccable Solomon*, 270–78.

readers of Chronicles that Solomon is not an ideal king. He employs a reader-sensitive approach, which depends on how familiar the readers are with the history of Israel.[24]

Lynch in his study of monotheism in Chronicles investigates "the interrelation of divine and institutional reality in Chronicles as a backdrop for understanding the coordination of claims about the sole divinity and the exaltation of Israel's central institutions."[25] He contends that monotheism and the exaltation of YHWH are part of a bilaterally reinforcing dynamic between YHWH and Israel's focal institutions (the temple, priesthood, and kingship), indicating that the exaltation of Israel's focal institutions is a principal means by which the Chronicler exalts Yahweh and, more often than not, expresses the sole divinity of Yahweh. Thus, Chronicles, according to Lynch, recasts the early history of Israel from the perspective of sincere commitments to Israel's institutions, drawing out diverse ways that they mediate God's power and urge national unity.

With respect to the studies of the nature of the book of Chronicles and the Chronicler, we can categorize them into four views.[26] The first view, which was held by scholars like Wellhausen, Benzinger, Kittel, and Welch, treats Chronicles as midrash.[27] Wellhausen, for instance, argues, "Whether one says Chronicles or Midrash of the Book of Kings is on the whole a matter of perfect indifference; they are children of the same mother, and indistinguishable in spirit and language, while on the other hand the portions which have been retained verbatim from the canonical Book of Kings at once betray themselves in both respects."[28] Welch, taking the same position of Wellhausen, notes that "the Chronicler was not writing history" but the core of Chronicles is midrash.[29] However, although the book of Chronicles is midrashic, it is not appropriate for Wellhausen and his followers to regard the whole book as midrash.[30] Wellhausen and his followers rejected Chronicles as a historical source for the

---

24. However, the real readers of Chronicles cannot be certainly defined. We cannot know how sensitive they were to the Chronicler's presentation. Accordingly, Jeon's assumption that the readers were sensitive to these allusions appears to have been overestimated. Jeon also overlooks, focusing on Solomon's Egyptian wife, that the mother of Rehoboam, another of Solomon's wives was a foreigner, an Ammonite (2 Chr 12:13, her name was Naamah).

25. Lynch, *Monotheism*, 16.

26. See Kalimi, "Was the Chronicler a Historian?" 74–85; Kalimi, *Ancient Israelite Historian*, 20–33.

27. Wellhausen, *Prolegomena*; Benzinger, *Die Bücher der Chronik*; Kittel, *Die Bücher der Chronik*; Welch, *Work of the Chronicler*. For the discussions of David and Solomon in Samuel-Kings, see Gunn, *Story of King David*; Fokkelman, *Narrative Art*; Brueggemann, *David's Truth*; Knoppers, *Two Nations under God*; Polzin, *David and the Deuteronomist*; Eslinger, *House of God*; Noll, *Faces of David*; Linafelt et al, *Fate of King David*.

28. Wellhausen, *Prolegomena*, 227.

29. Welch, *Work of the Chronicler*, 54.

30. Kalimi, "Was the Chronicler a Historian?" 75–76; Kalimi, *Ancient Israelite Historian*, 20–23.

pre-exilic history of Israel.[31] As Kalimi indicates, it is obvious that their views were based on Ranke's definition of historicism.[32]

The second view sees the author of Chronicles, the so-called Chronicler (henceforth, the Chr), as an exegete.[33] Willi, for instance, describes the nature of the book of Chronicles as a commentary, writing, "When the Chronicler intended to surrender to the compulsion to write a history of the pre-exilic period, for this very reason he had but one option, namely, an interpretation of the material of tradition passed on to him, and that meant an interpretation of the Deuteronomistic History."[34] Thus, Willi sees the Chr as an exegete interpreting Samuel-Kings. Willi's influence can be seen in Smend's work, which claims that the Chr employed the Deuteronomistic History as a canonical text.[35] In other words, the work of the Chr was to interpret previous canonical texts. However, the Chr's purpose was not simply to exegete previous books. Rather, the Chr attempted to adapt and supplement earlier books, omitting some descriptions in them and inserting his own theological viewpoint.[36]

The third view understands the Chr as a theologian.[37] It treats the book of Chronicles as theological discourse. Ackroyd, for instance, proposes that the Chr's purpose was to represent "a unifying concept of the nature of the Jewish religious community and hence of its theology and the meaning of its rich and varied traditions."[38] Ackroyd contends:

> It points forward to other attempts at unification to be found in later Jewish and Christian writings, and while it would be straining the evidence to describe it as the first 'theology of Old Testament,' it nevertheless, in its endeavour to be comprehensive and yet true to the tradition, anticipates some more modern essays which have sought the essential centre of Old Testament theological thought . . .[39]

Later, Coggins independently arrives at the same understanding so that he describes the Chr's presentation as "basically theological," noting, "More important, therefore,

---

31. Kalimi, "Was the Chronicler a Historian?" 76.

32. Ranke's dictum is "how it really was" (*wie es eigentlich gewesen ist*) and it overshadowed the work of historians in the nineteenth century.

33. Kalimi, *Ancient Israelite Historian*, 23–27.

34. Willi, *Die Chronik*, 54, quoted in and translated by Kalimi, "Was the Chronicler a Historian?" 77.

35. Smend, *Entstehung*, 228.

36. For more critiques of the Chr as an exegete, see Kalimi, "Was the Chronicler a Historian?" 79–81.

37. Kalimi, *Ancient Israelite Historian*, 27–29.

38. Ackroyd, "Theology of the Chronicler," 108.

39. Ibid., 108. See also Ackroyd, "The Chronicler as Exegete," 2–3, 24.

than asking questions about historicity, is the attempt to discover the underlying theological purpose of the Chronicler."[40]

The fourth view depicts the Chr as a historian.[41] For instance, Kalimi indicates that Chronicles appeared as a historical book after the books of Kings in the LXX.[42] He writes, "The inclusion of the work among the historical books in the LXX and the fact that the book deals with the monarchical era and is based largely on Samuel-Kings (which all regard as historical books) points to the identification of Chronicles as an example of historiography."[43]

Chronicles was thus regarded as biblical historiography although some considered the book an unreliable source of history. In Kalimi's view, however, even bad history is still historiographical.[44] Interestingly, Jonker understands the book of Chronicles as "reforming history," regarding it as "an attempt to reformulate and sanitize the older traditions about the past, as well as an attempt to reformulate the identity of God's people in the changed socio-historical circumstances of the last Persian era."[45]

In my judgment, the book of Chronicles has some characteristics of each of these: midrash, exegesis, theology, and history. Of these characteristics, the book is dominantly historical in that it deals with the early history of Israel. Significantly, Kalimi indicates why Chronicles is history: "the author deals with the past; he collects material from the earlier book and perhaps additional sources; he selects from the sources, evaluates, and interprets them; he makes connections between the sources; and above all his work as a whole is imprinted with a unique historiography."[46] The book of Chronicles is history, more specifically a historical narrative as composed of lists, poetry, and narration. Thus, it is presumed in this study that the Chr as a historian retells the history of Israel.

The book of Chronicles was written in the form of historical narrative with some lists and poetry, so it has the nature of historical narrative. Narratives are rhetorical passages that communicate meaning to the implied audience in order to persuade them.[47] In this regard, historical narrative, like any communicative act, functions rhetorically. According to White, historical narrative is defined as "a verbal structure in the form of a narrative prose discourse that purports to be a model, or icon, of past

---

40. Coggins, *The First and Second Books of the Chronicles*, 5–6.

41. See Kalimi, *Ancient Israelite Historian*, 29–33.

42. Kalimi, "Was the Chronicler a Historian?" 82.

43. Ibid., 83. Kalimi provides features of historiography found in Chronicles: "the author deals with the past; he collects material from the earlier books and perhaps additional sources; he selects from the sources, evaluates, and interprets them; he makes connections between the sources; and above all, his work as a whole is imprinted with a unique 'philosophy' of history" ("Was the Chronicler as a Historian?" 83).

44. Kalimi, "Was the Chronicler a Historian?" 85.

45. Jonker, "Reforming History," 24–25.

46. Kalimi, *Ancient Israelite Historian*, 30.

47. See Duke, "Rhetorical Approach," 114–15.

Introduction

structures and processes in the interest of *explaining what they were by representing them*."[48] The implied author (or the narrator) intends to persuade the implied audience to accept his/her story. Accordingly, historical narrative provides the implied audience with information about the past and forces it to make decisions.[49] The degree to which the implied audience accepts the story depends on the rhetorical effectiveness of the narrative.[50] As Duke argues, each historical narrative has a rhetorical function and can be examined by means of "its persuasive artistry."[51] Thus, if we accept White's definition of historical narrative and its rhetorical function, the book of Chronicles, as historical narrative, needs to be investigated by rhetorical analysis. Before turning to the rhetorical method to examine the speeches and prayers in the David-Solomon narrative in Chronicles, we need to review the previous studies on kings' speeches and prayers in Chronicles, which play rhetorically significant roles in the Chr's retelling of the history of Israel.

Studies of Kings' Speeches and Prayers in Chronicles

One key issue in reference to the Chr's retelling of the history of Israel is kings' speeches and prayers in Chronicles. Those speeches and prayers, occupying a large portion of the narrative, contribute to the Chr's persuasive portrayal of those kings. In fact, speech and dialogue play a key role in Hebrew narrative. They move the plot of narrative forward.[52]

According to Boda, speeches legitimate the actions of a character by providing the reason for those actions.[53] Dialogue emphasizes the core of a story, indicating "key turning points or climaxes in the structural framework of a narrative."[54] Furthermore,

---

48. White, *Metahistory*, 2. Duke in his rhetorical study of Chronicles employs White's definition of historical narrative. For a discussion of the rhetorical nature of historical narratives, see Duke, *Persuasive Appeal*, 31–33.

49. The decisions that the implied audience make are the judgment of a past event, the evaluation of praise or blame, the acceptance of some coherent laws among events, and the belief in the ultimate end of history. See Duke, *Persuasive Appeal*, 33.

50. It is a rhetorical matter whether a historical narrative effectively makes itself accepted as "realistic" representation or "objective" account. White states, "In realistic narrative representation—as against mythic or legendary representations—the narrator is both present and absent: present as a means of communication, absent as a means of communication that is transparent and does not block access to the segment of experience whose organization it is his purpose to reveal to us. It is the presence of an identifiable narrative voice that permits us to credit such as 'realistic' representations as a history and a certain kind of novel as 'objective' accounts." See White, "Structure," 13.

51. Duke, *Persuasive Appeal*, 33.

52. Dialogue and speech are important elements of narrative plot. In this regard, it is noteworthy that Alter refers to Hebrew narrative as "narration-through-dialogue" (Alter, *Art of Biblical Narrative*, 69). Furthermore, the narrator employs dialogue to control "the pace of the plot, at times delaying the advancement of the action and/or focusing on a particular character to accentuate the narrative moment or character" (Boda, "Prayer as Rhetoric," 286).

53. Boda, "Prayer as Rhetoric," 286.

54. Ibid., 286.

speeches reveal "the ideological message of the narrator."⁵⁵ A character's speeches express thoughts, motives, desires, and beliefs. Thus, the narrator, by a speech, can convey "the inner psychology and ideology of a character."⁵⁶ The narrator (or the implied author) utilizes speeches to contribute to the liveliness of the passage and to provide information in an artistic way.⁵⁷ Accordingly, kings' speeches and prayers in Chronicles are rhetorical passages that the Chr has created in his own way.

Early studies on speeches and prayers in Chronicles should be noted. For instance, Driver in his analysis of speeches in Chronicles reveals that those speeches provide significant evidence of the Chr's particular usage and style.⁵⁸ Von Rad, in his study, regards the Chr's speeches as Levitical sermons with sermon-like character.⁵⁹ Plöger also contends that the Chr employed these speeches to emphasize what he thought were significant periods of time, such as the reigns of David and Solomon and the construction of the temple.⁶⁰

These studies of the Chr's speeches have been followed by the work of scholars such as Braun, Rigsby, Throntveit, Duke, and Mason.⁶¹ For instance, Braun in his study of the significance of 1 Chr 22, 28 and 29, deals with David's speeches, focusing on the concept of rest and Solomon's election. Then, Braun contends that the primary purpose of the Chr was to portray Solomon as the chosen temple builder by YHWH.⁶²

Rigsby examines the speeches employed by the Chr that are parallel to those in Samuel-Kings in their content and functions. These speeches make the narrative proceed and reveal similar religious concerns.⁶³ In respect to the religious speeches, Rigsby concludes that the speeches in Samuel-Kings reveal the so-called "Chronistic

---

55. Ibid., 286.

56. Ibid., 286.

57. Ibid., 286.

58. Driver, "The Speeches in Chronicles," 1:241–56; 2:286–308. Driver has concluded with this statement: "It would have been interesting to point out how the speeches peculiar to the Chronicler reflect, in almost every case, the interests and point of view of the Chronicler himself" ("The Speeches in Chronicles," 255).

59. Von Rad, "Levitical Sermon," 267–80.

60. Plöger, "Reden und Gebete," 54–60.

61. For the royal speeches and prayers, see Rigsby, "Historiography"; Braun, "Significance of 1 Chronicles 22, 28, and 29"; Throntveit, *When Kings Speak*; Duke, *Persuasive Appeal*; Mason, *Preaching*. For the prophetic speeches in Chronicles, see Newsome, "The Chronicler's View"; Macy, "Sources" (esp. 64–75); De Vries, "Forms of Prophetic Address"; Schniedewind, *Word of God* (esp. 80–108).

62. Braun, "Significance of 1 Chronicles 22, 28, and 29"; Braun, "Chosen Temple Builder," 581–90.

63. Rigsby, "Historiography," 80–141. According to Rigsby, the speeches that make the narrative proceed are 1 Chr 10:1–14 (1 Sam 31:1–13); 1 Chr 11:4–9 (2 Sam 5:6–10); 1 Chr 11:15–19 (2 Sam 23:13–17); 1 Chr 19:1–15 (2 Sam 10:1–14); 2 Chr 9:1–12 (1 Kgs 10:1–13); and the speeches that reveal similar religious concerns are 1 Chr 13:5–14 (2 Sam 6:1–11); 1 Chr 14:10–17 (2 Sam 5:19–25); 1 Chr 17:1–27 (2 Sam 7:1–29); 1 Chr 21:1–27 (2 Sam 24:1–25); 2 Chr 1:7–13 (1 Kgs 3:5–15); 2 Chr 6:1–39 (1 Kgs 8:12–53); 2 Chr 7:11–22 (1 Kgs 9:1–9); 2 Chr 24:4–6 (2 Kgs 12:4–7); 2 Chr 25:4 (2 Kgs 14:6); 2 Chr 33:2–9 (2 Kgs 21:2–9); 2 Chr 34:14–28 (2 Kgs 22:8–20).

Tendenz" to a greater degree than the parallel texts in Chronicles.[64] In respect to other speeches, Rigsby claims that they were transformed in Chronicles; their contents are actually identical but their functions are distinct from those in Samuel-Kings. In Rigsby's view, the speeches in Samuel-Kings emphasize more political and military aspects, whereas those in Chronicles are more manifestly related to cultic and theological aspects.[65]

Duke points to the functions of speeches in relation to enthymeme in Aristotle's rhetoric.[66] According to Duke, of twenty-one royal speeches, ten exhibit the enthymeme in its positive or negative ways,[67] and nine royal prayers present the enthymeme implicitly because they are to seek YHWH.[68] Thus, Duke concludes that the Chr employed speeches to address his audience effectively, indicating that the Chr used "the ethos of the characters who spoke to give an authoritative tone to the themes he wished to inculcate in his audience."[69] However, unfortunately, Duke does not expound upon these speeches and prayers in Chronicles because Duke's focus is on the application of the enthymeme of Aristotle's rhetoric to the book of Chronicles.

Mason, providing his assessment and expansion of von Rad's argument about the Levitical sermons, investigates main themes and rhetorical devices in thirty addresses in Chronicles.[70] The focus of his study is on the addresses that have no parallels to Samuel-Kings. Mason concludes his analysis of speeches in Chronicles by stating that "any king of the Davidic line who is given an address is usually showing concern for the temple or its worship—he is, in fact, acting in a David-like way."[71]

---

64. Ibid., 140.

65. Ibid., 142–82. These speeches are 1 Chr 11:1–3 (2 Sam 5:1–3); 2 Chr 2:1–12 (1 Kgs 5:1–12); 2 Chr 10:1—11:4 (1 Kgs 12:1–24); 2 Chr 16:1–6 (1 Kgs 15:17–22); 2 Chr 18:1–34 (1 Kgs 22:1–40); 2 Chr 23:1–15 (2 Kgs 11:4–16); 2 Chr 25:17–24 (2 Kgs 14:8–14); 2 Chr 32:9–17 (2 Kgs 18:17–25 plus 19:9–13).

66. Duke, *Persuasive Appeal*, 119–35 (esp. 128–30).

67. Ibid., 129. Duke identifies twenty-one royal speeches in relation to enthymeme: 1 Chr 12:17; 13:2–3; 22:7–16; 22:18–19; 28:2–8; 28:9–10; 28:20–21; 29:1–5; 2 Chr 2:3–10; 2:11–16; 6:1–11; 9:5–8; 13:4–12; 14:7; 19:6–7; 19:9–11; 20:20; 29:5–11; 30:6–9; 32:7–8; 35:3–6. Of these speeches, Duke regards 1 Chr 22:7–16; 22:18–19; 28:20–21; 2 Chr 13:4–12; and 14:7 as implicit enthymeme and 1 Chr 28:2–8; 28:9–10; 2 Chr 20:20; 29:5–11; and 30:6–9 as explicit enthymeme (171–72).

68. Ibid., 128. Nine prayers that Duke has identified are 1 Chr 17:16–27; 21:8; 21:17; 29:10–19; 2 Chr 6:14–42; 14:11; 20:6–12; 24:22; 30:18–19 (169).

69. Duke, *Persuasive Appeal*, 134. He also states that the enthymematic communication "developed from a relatively safe and subtle presentation to a direct and repeated proclamation" (*Persuasive Appeal*, 134).

70. Mason, *Preaching*, 13–122. The addresses in Chronicles that he has investigated are 1 Chr 12:18[19]; 13:2–3; 15:2, 12–13; 22:6–16; 22:17–19; 28:2–10; 28:20–21; 29:1–5, 20; 2 Chr 12:5–8; 13:4–12; 14:7[6]; 15:1–7; 16:7–9; 19:1–3; 19:6–7, 9–11; 20:14–17; 20:20; 20:37; 21:12–15; 24:20–2; 25:7–9; 25:15–16; 26:17–18; 28:9–11; 28:12–13; 29:5–11, 31; 30:6–9; 31:10; 32:7–8; 35:3–6.

71. Mason, *Preaching*, 124. Mason also says that "All we can say is that there is a certain broad fitness in the themes of the addresses given to kings, priests, or the prophetic figures. Beyond that we can say only that the Chronicler sees them all as 'messengers' (II 36:15f). They are those through whom God has spoken to his people at every stage of their history" (137).

Throntveit examines royal speeches and royal prayers in Chronicles, focusing on their role in revealing the ideology of the Chr and the structure of Chronicles.[72] Throntveit's work must receive special attention in that he dealt with how both royal speeches and royal prayers play key roles in displaying the Chr's purpose. His definition of *royal speech* is that it was a speech spoken by a king, not as part of a conversation, significantly altered from the source and unique to the Chr.[73] Throntveit's analysis of royal speeches is based on Braun's categories of speeches such as rationales, edicts, and orations, as classified by means of form and content.[74] According to Throntveit, royal prayer has the same definition with one more criterion—prayer as "reported in direct discourse."[75] Throntveit's analysis of the royal prayers is analogous to that of the royal speeches. The difference between the two is "to whom the utterance is addressed," that is, royal speech is addressed to a human addressee, whereas royal prayer is addressed to God.[76]

Throntveit then claims that the orations particularly have a specific audience, use imperatives, and report the response of the addressees when compared with rationales. Those orations are longer than the edicts and include historical retrospect.[77] Throntveit considers that the royal speeches might "be used to determine the structural framework of the Chronicler's work," indicating that the royal speeches occurred at the turning points in the narrative.[78] According to Throntveit, the royal prayers also have the same characteristics when compared with the royal speeches. The longer prayer included historical retrospects and the royal prayers, not in poetic style but in prose, frequently contained rhetorical questions. In content, the royal prayers contained laments with the emphasis on both Yahweh's power and his people's dependence.[79] Throntveit concludes that both the royal speeches and prayers have the same form.

According to Throntveit's examination, the periodization of the history of Israel is divided into three units: (1) the united monarchy of David and Solomon; (2) the divided monarchy from Abijah to Hezekiah; and (3) the reunited monarchy, Hezekiah and Josiah, in which Hezekiah is portrayed as a new David and a new Solomon.[80] This periodization depicts the monarchy in three eras—unity, disunity, and back to unity

---

72. Throntveit, *When Kings Speak*.
73. Ibid., 11.
74. Ibid., 20; Braun, "Significance of 1 Chronicles 22, 28, and 29," 225–49 (esp. 228).
75. Throntveit, *When Kings Speak*, 51.
76. Ibid., 75.
77. Ibid., 50.
78. Ibid., 50.
79. Ibid., 75.
80. Ibid., 109–25.

Introduction

respectively.⁸¹ In these divisions, Throntveit contends that royal speeches were placed at determining points in the whole narrative.⁸²

However, Throntveit's study has a few shortcomings. First of all, with respect to his criteria of royal speech⁸³ Throntveit only considers the royal speeches that are not found in Samuel-Kings. As a result, other royal speeches in conversations and dialogues as found in Samuel-Kings are not included in his analysis. In Throntveit's view, the Chr rarely employed conversations and dialogues to advance his narrative when compared to Samuel-Kings. This contention is simply based on the observation of the frequent use of the verb אמר, so that Throntveit excludes twenty-four royal speeches by his criterion that royal speech is not part of conversation or dialogue.⁸⁴ In my judgment, conversation or dialogue can be a literary context of royal speech and the royal prayer. Accordingly, the speech and prayer as a part of dialogues can be well understood in a communicative context in which the speech or the prayer is located.

Second, Throntveit's study attempts to understand the royal speeches as a distinct form of speech, which was to extend Braun's three classifications of royal speeches (that is, rationales, edicts, and orations).⁸⁵ For this reason, Throntveit does not take into account the significance of speeches and prayers in a broader narrative unit in the final form of the text as a broader literary context.

In addition, Throntveit, in another article, examines the idealization of Solomon in Chronicles by David's speeches and Solomon's prayer.⁸⁶ He indicates that "the Chronicler's crucial reinterpretation of the promises contained in Nathan's oracle" has three significant moments in the narrative: "the dynastic oracle itself; David's recalling of the promises made in the oracle at various junctures in his final addresses; and Solomon's allusions to the oracle at the time of the dedication of the newly built temple."⁸⁷ Throntveit describes the idealization of Solomon as the glorification of God, based on the dynastic oracle (1 Chr 17), David's speeches of encouragement (1 Chr 22, 28, 29), and Solomon's prayer (2 Chr 6:40–42).⁸⁸ Thus, he concludes that Solomon is portrayed as an idealized king in order to glorify God. However, Solomon's image is not just for the glorification of God. The Chr's purpose goes beyond that portrayal of Solomon for it also intends to showcase David and Solomon, based on the building

---

81. Ibid., 125. Cf. Knoppers, "Reunited Kingdom," 74–88.

82. The determining points are 1 Chr 13:2a, 3; 15:2; 12–13; 22:1, 5, 7–13; 28:2–3, 6–7, 9–10; and 29:20 in David's narrative and 2 Chr 2:3–10 and 6:2–11 (// 1 Kgs 18:12–21) in Solomon's. See Throntveit, *When Kings Speak*, 113.

83. Ibid., 11. Throntveit's four criteria are that the speech is (1) "on the lips of king"; (2) "not part of conversation or dialogue" (3) "though paralleled in the *Vorlage* [Samuel-Kings], has been significantly altered"; and (4) "unique to the Chronicler."

84. Ibid., 12.

85. Ibid., 20–21; Braun, "Significance of 1 Chronicles 22, 28, and 29," 225–49.

86. Throntveit, "Idealization," 411–27.

87. Ibid., 414.

88. Ibid., 411–27.

of the temple, as the bearers of the covenantal relationship between God and Israel. In this regard, Throntveit, focusing on Solomon's image for the glorification of God, did not display the images of David and Solomon as the bearers of the covenantal relationship between YHWH and the Judahites, which would contribute to the reconstruction of the covenantal relationship in the Persian period by reminding the Yehudite community of God's covenant with Israel.

Most of these studies of the Chr's speeches concentrated on the form-critical classifications or thematic interpretations,[89] which resulted in a fragmentary understanding of the text, especially the Chr's narrative itself. Form-critical analysis, even if it has proved itself as a useful method in the study of Psalms, tends to lead to a fragmented understanding of the text by neglecting the literary context of its final form. Although Throntveit notes the role of the speech in the structure of the whole book, his study tends to neglect the final form of the whole text by breaking it into parts and by focusing on the forms and contents of these sections. Thus, the Chr's speeches have not been examined in the whole context of Chronicles with a broader narrative frame.[90] In effect, speech in a narrative is deliberately selected as a *"reported direct speech"* by the implied author (or the narrator) in order to give special voice to a certain character at a certain time and space.[91] Accordingly, the Chr's speeches need to be investigated in the narrative context. In this regard, Japhet rightly noted that the speeches spoken by kings are connected with the historical background and narrative development, concluding that "added speeches and prayers therefore provide a clear and unequivocal expression of the writer's views."[92]

A king's prayer as a king's speech to YHWH contributes to the persuasive portrayal of David and Solomon in Chronicles. The previous approaches to biblical prayer were mostly form-critical studies such as those of Gunkel, Mowinckel, and Westermann.[93] As a result, the study of biblical prayer has not been distinguished from that of Psalms. The narrative context in which the prayers were placed has been neglected. Balentine properly indicates this situation, stating "a significant body of

---

89. For example, Plöger has classified kings' speeches such as Abijah's and Hezekiah's (2 Chr 13:4–12; 30:6–9) as "call to return" (*Umkehrreden*). See Plöger, "Reden und Gebete," 57–58. Mason has placed a few royal speeches such as David's (1 Chr 15:2, 12–13; 22:6–16; 22:17–19; 28:2–10; 28:20–21), Asa's (2 Chr 14:7), Jehoshaphat's (2 Chr 19:6–7, 9–11), and Hezekiah's (2 Chr 29:5–11; 32:7–8), under the heading of "Encouragement for a Task" (Mason, *Preaching*, 18).

90. Bar-Efrat points out that the speeches of characters are the most important and extensive part in biblical narratives, which occupy the largest space and carry a substantial part of character's action. See Bar-Efrat, "Die Erzählung in der Bibel," 104–5.

91. Jonker states, "Direct speech in narrative remains reported direct speech," investigating the self-understanding of the community in the Persian Period through the direct speeches as the *Sondergut* passages in 2 Chr 10–36. Jonker, "Who Constitutes Society," 705.

92. Japhet, *Ideology*, 10.

93. See Gunkel and Begrich, *Introduction to Psalms*; Mowinckel, *Psalms*; Westermann, *Praise and Lament*.

Introduction

prayer texts—namely those in prose narratives—receives little attention on their own."[94] Greenberg contends that the specificity of the prayers, which were embedded in narrative context, signifies "that they play a part in the argument of a narrative and its depiction of character."[95] In particular, it is noteworthy that Balentine underscores the function of prayer in the narrative context of the Hebrew Bible, writing:

> [P]rayer as a literary vehicle for providing characterization (of both prayer and God), for addressing certain themes (e.g., divine justice), and for conveying and promoting certain postures or attitudes (e.g., penitence and contrition) . . . also concerned to attend to the use of prayer as a means of conveying ideological and theological perspectives, again in relation to both God and human partner.[96]

Thus, these scholars emphasized the investigation of the prose prayers in the narrative context, indicating the shortcoming of the form-critical studies of prayer.[97] Accordingly, royal prayers in Chronicles in line with royal speeches need to be examined in the final form of the text as a broader narrative frame.

When a character speaks to God, he or she will often employ "rhetorical techniques to try to persuade God to his or her point of view."[98] In this regard, a prayer can be seen as a speech spoken to God. Thus, we can understand the Chr's persuasive portrayal of David and Solomon by the rhetorical effects on the narrative audience and the Chr's audience as being expressed in their speeches and prayers and other characters' speeches.

Therefore, in this study I will argue that the Chr's persuasive portrayal of David and Solomon is designed to reformulate the identity of the Yehudite community through the Jerusalem temple, revealing the continuity of the covenantal relationship between YHWH and Israel in the Persian period. In order to demonstrate this persuasive portrayal, I will examine the speeches and prayers in the David-Solomon narrative, focusing on rhetorical effect in the original context and considering the Chr's main purpose in his retelling of Israelite history in the Persian period. Now, we

94. Balentine, *Prayer*, 18.

95. Greenberg, *Biblical Prose Prayer*, 17–18.

96. Balentine, *Prayer*, 29.

97. According to Greenberg, study of the narrative technique of the Bible "has something to gain from attention to the embedded prose prayers" (*Biblical Prose Prayer*, 46). Because they are adjusted to their situations, the embedded prose prayers can serve to describe character (*Biblical Prose Prayer*, 47). Corvin, applying what he describes as "functional criticism," examines prose prayers in the Old Testament (OT). He classifies them into two categories in relation to their literary context, of which most of the prayers are assigned to "contextual prayers" (Corvin, "Stylistic and Functional Study of the Prose Prayers," 156). Staudt, examining seventeen prayers in the Deuteronomistic History, concludes that the prayers were tailored to strategic places in the narrative context between crisis and its resolution, residing in the "hiatus" between God's word and its fulfillment. Accordingly, prayer functions theologically as "the instrument for the participation of the people with their God in the unfolding history of Israel's covenantal relationship" (Staudt, "Prayer and the People," 338–9).

98. Walsh, *Old Testament Narrative*, 36.

turn to the methodology to examine the speeches and prayers in the David-Solomon narrative.

RESEARCH METHODOLOGY

The interest in the text itself led some scholars to employ rhetorical analysis, which "uses our knowledge of the conventions of literary composition practiced in ancient Israel and its environment to discover and analyze the particular literary artistry found in a specific unit of Old Testament text."[99] Text itself provides a certain meaning for a word in the text from within its own language.[100] We need to deal with the text itself, focusing on narrative as rhetoric in that Chronicles as historical narrative functions rhetorically.

Narrative as Rhetoric

Narrative is rhetoric because it occurs when someone tells a story for an audience in a special situation for a particular purpose.[101] Accordingly, narrative as rhetoric conveys a certain message to its audience in order to evoke a fitting response from them. In this kind of rhetorical analysis of narrative, two literary concepts—the implied author and the implied reader—should be noted. In effect, for this study, the Chr could be identified as the implied author since we cannot know the real author of the book of Chronicles. In the same way, the Chr's audience can be considered as the implied reader (or the implied audience) since we cannot reconstruct the real reader either.

Booth sought to develop a kind of rhetorical criticism in his study of narratives.[102] Booth's examination of narrative rhetoric isolates two concepts necessary for a detailed model of narrative analysis: the first is the implied author, which designates "the core of norms and choices" of the narrative,[103] and the second is the implied reader, which designates the norms and values necessary for an interpretation of a narrative guided by the author.[104] According to Booth, "From the real author's viewpoint, a successful reading of his book must eliminate all distance between the essential norms of his implied author and the norms of the postulated [implied] reader."[105] For Booth the implied author is separated from both the real author and the narrator,[106] and the

---

99. Watson and Hauser, *Rhetorical Criticism*, 4.

100. See Groom, *Linguistic Analysis*, xvii–xxii.

101. The reading of narrative has multiple dimensions in that when we read a narrative, we use our intellects, emotions, ideologies, and ethics. See Phelan, *Narrative as Rhetoric*.

102. Booth, *Rhetoric of Fiction*.

103. Ibid., 74–75.

104. Ibid., 138.

105. Ibid., 157.

106. Ibid., 73. He defines the narrator as "the speaker in the work who is after all only one of the elements created by the implied author and who may be separated from him by large ironies" (*Rhetoric of Fiction*, 73).

Introduction

implied reader is distinguished from the real reader. Following Booth's examination of narrative rhetoric, Chatman applies his insights to the specific situation of a narrative, writing, "A narrative is a communication; hence, it presupposes two parties, a sender and a receiver. Each party entails three different personages. On the sending end are the real author, the implied author, and the narrator . . . on the receiving end, the real audience (listener, reader, viewer), the implied audience, and the narratee."[107] Thus, Chatman represents his model of narrative communication as a diagram:[108]

> Real → | Implied author → Narrator → Narratee → Implied reader | → Real →
> author reader

This diagram has some implications. (1) The implied author and the implied reader are structural principles.[109] (2) The narrator and narratee are narrative devices of the implied author. Both of them are rhetorical devices, and they are created by the implied author. Narrator and narratee are part of the narrative itself.[110] (3) The real author and the real reader are outside of the narrative; the vertical slashes before the implied author and behind the implied reader indicate that "the real author and real reader are outside of the narrative transaction."[111] (4) Although Chatman does not say so manifestly, the direction of the arrows gives a primacy to the sender in narrative communication.[112] Thus, Booth and Chatman develop a model of narrative analysis, employing useful concepts, that is, the implied author and the implied reader (or implied audience). In this study, the two concepts will be discussed in relation to the Chr and his audience below.

Rhetorical Analysis

Methodologies related to the rhetorical dimension have been used on OT literature in the past few decades, especially after the call of James Muilenburg to move beyond form criticism.[113] Since Muilenburg's proposal of rhetorical criticism, two different understandings of rhetoric have appeared: the art of composition and the art of

---

107. Chatman, *Story and Discourse*, 28.
108. Ibid., 151.
109. Ibid., 149.
110. Ibid., 149–50.
111. Ibid., 150-1.
112. Literary critics, emphasizing a primary locus for the generation of meaning other than at the sender end of the narrative transaction, challenge his model seriously. Iser, for instance, represents a challenge to Chatman's model by emphasizing that narrative communication "take[s] into account not only the actual text but also, and in equal measure, the actions involved in responding to that text" (Iser, "The Reading Process," 279). Thus, Iser stresses that readers can interact with the perspectives of the text in a way that the real author cannot predict ("The Reading Process," 279–99).
113. Muilenburg, "Form Criticism," 1-18.

persuasion.[114] Accordingly, it is necessary to summarize briefly rhetorical analysis of the OT.

Rhetorical criticism in biblical studies can be traced back to the address of Muilenburg, published as "Form Criticism and Beyond,"[115] in which he defined rhetorical criticism, explaining:

> What I am interested in, above all, is in understanding the nature of Hebrew literary composition, in exhibiting the structural patterns that are employed for the fashioning of a literary unit, whether in poetry or in prose, and in discerning the many and various devices by which the predications are formulated and ordered into a unified whole. Such an enterprise I should describe as rhetoric and the methodology as rhetorical criticism.[116]

Rhetorical criticism practices a close reading that "a responsible and proper articulation of the words in their linguistic patterns and in their precise formulations will reveal to us the texture and fabric of the writer's thought, not only what it is that he thinks, but as he thinks it."[117] Accordingly, Muilenburg gave the priorities in rhetorical criticism to the definition of the limits of the literary unit[118] and the determination of the structure of the composition, that is, the discernment of "the configuration of its component parts."[119] For Muilenburg, rhetorical criticism means the art of composition.

Even though Muilenburg did not reject Gunkel's form criticism, he thought it should be supplemented by rhetorical criticism. Trible points out that Muilenburg's interest was in "Hebrew composition: discerning structural patterns, verbal sequences, and stylistic devices that make a coherent whole."[120] Thus, Kennedy's methodological insights have a significant effect on the following rhetorical studies, which really go beyond what Muilenburg has proposed.

Since Muilenburg's proposal, some scholars have followed his methodology, understanding rhetoric as the art of composition. For example, Kessler and Greenwood performed synchronic literary study, investigating the literary characteristics of the text.[121] This is also found in OT studies. Hauser defines rhetorical criticism as

---

114. See Trible, *Rhetorical Criticism*, 32–48. There have been a number of rhetorical studies of the OT. For the studies of the art of composition, see Lundbom, *Jeremiah*, and Ceresko, "Rhetorical Analysis of David's 'Boast.'" For the art of persuasion, see Gitay, *Prophecy and Persuasion*; Clifford, *Fair Spoken and Persuading*; Barton, "History and Rhetoric," 51-64; Clines, "Deconstructing the Book of Job," 65-80; and Patrick and Scult, *Rhetoric*.

115. Muilenburg, "Form Criticism," 1–18.

116. Ibid., 8.

117. Ibid., 7.

118. Ibid., 8–9.

119. Ibid., 10.

120. Trible, *Rhetorical Criticism*, 26.

121. Kessler, "Methodological Setting," 35–36; Greenwood, "Rhetorical Criticism," 418–26.

Introduction

"a form of literary criticism which uses our knowledge of the conventions of literary composition practiced in ancient Israel and its environment to discover and analyze the particular literary artistry found in a specific unit of Old Testament text."[122] From this analysis, we can discuss the message of the text and its impact on the audience. Accordingly, these scholars follow Muilenburg's primary proposal "that rhetorical criticism should be the study of stylistics of composition in Hebrew prose and poetry, and that a study of stylistics will underscore the unity of biblical texts."[123]

On the other hand, other scholars employed rhetorical criticism in different ways. They have understood rhetoric as the art of persuasion. For instance, Wuellner argues that the core of rhetorical criticism should be argumentation and persuasion, criticizing Muilenburg and his school in that they restricted rhetoric to forms.[124] Howard also insists that the primary concern of rhetorical criticism in OT studies be for its speech and persuasion.[125] According to Howard, rhetorical criticism in OT studies has been focused on the surface structures and forms of texts, so that Muilenburg and his followers did not pay attention to "the suasive or oral aspects of biblical literature."[126] Consequently, these scholars understand rhetorical criticism as the art of persuasion.

Patrick and Scult, indicating that Muilenburg and his followers have been focused on stylistic analysis, contend that rhetorical criticism should be "a fuller understanding of rhetoric as the way a text manages its relationship with its audiences."[127] Thus, Patrick and Scult broadly extended the concept of rhetoric "as the means by which a text establishes and manages its relationship to its audience in order to achieve a particular effect."[128]

Modern rhetoric also has given attention to the argumentative nature of discourse for the purpose of persuading the audience. In this context, Perelman and Olbrechts-Tyteca's new rhetoric appeared.[129] The new rhetoric, following classical rhetoric, tried

---

122. Watson and Hauser, *Rhetorical Criticism*, 4. Hauser considers the primary task of rhetorical criticism as finding "integrating devices" to determine the limits of the literary unit of the text (*Rhetorical Criticism*, 9–14). These devices "bind the unit together and help set its boundaries," possibly including "a word, a phrase, or even a longer cluster of words that appears near the beginning and near the end of the literary unit, and perhaps also intermittently in the middle" (*Rhetorical Criticism*, 9).

123. Dozeman, "OT Rhetorical Criticism," 714.

124. Wuellner, "Where is Rhetorical Criticism," 448–63 (esp. 453).

125. Howard, "Rhetorical Criticism," 87–104. Howard points out, "Old Testament rhetorical criticism has been more properly a literary enterprise, its methodology more akin to the approaches found within Prague structuralism, Anglo-American formalism (or 'New Criticism'), or Russian formalism. These three schools all have been relatively independent of each other, but a common concern is their emphasis upon the forms and surface structures of texts" (99–100).

126. Ibid., 102.

127. Patrick and Scult, *Rhetoric*, 8.

128. Ibid., 12. According to Patrick and Scult, the range of the extended concept "includes stylistic devices, but goes beyond style to encompass the whole range of linguistic instrumentalities by which a discourse constructs a particular relationship with an audience in order to communicate a message" (12).

129. Perelman and Olbrechts-Tyteca, *New Rhetoric*.

to establish rhetoric as a theory of argumentation. Perelman defines the New Rhetoric as "a theory of argumentation that has as its object the study of discursive techniques and that aims to provoke or to increase the adherence of men's minds to the theses that are presented for their assent. It also examines the conditions that allow argumentation to begin and be developed, as well as the effects produced by this development."[130]

Perelman and Olbrechts-Tyteca do not intend to deny that argumentation always begins with prerequisites assumed to be held generally. Actually, this issue comprises a significant section of their book's discussion.[131] However, argumentation is closely related to the audience. They argue that a variety of audiences can be seen to hold different "arguments" generally. Even a "universal audience" as conceived by one person or group will be different from that conceived by others. It is this relativism that they laud as providing "meaning to human freedom," defining it as "a state in which a reasonable choice can be exercised."[132]

Perelman and Olbrechts-Tyteca also attempt to analyze literary argumentation. In their analysis they often employ a different approach than ancient rhetoric, rejecting the division of rhetoric into three genres: forensic, deliberative, and epideictic,[133] of which the epideictic is regarded as the most important one in contrast to the theory of ancient rhetoric. While ancient rhetoric tends to describe the epideictic genre as a speech for an audience's enjoyment that consists of praise or blame, Perelman and Olbrechts-Tyteca contend that there is much more to it than this. This argument is devised to reinforce "the disposition toward action by increasing adherence to the values it lauds."[134] Accordingly, "the purpose of an epidictic [sic] speech is to increase the intensity of adherence to values held in common by the audience and the speaker."[135]

In general, Perelman and Olbrechts-Tyteca are not concerned with rhetorical form or genre, that is, structural rhetoric. Rather, they are concerned with argumentation techniques and their effectiveness. It is in this respect that they discuss stylistics, writing, "We refuse to separate the form of a discourse from its substance, to study stylistic structures and figures independently of the purpose they must achieve in the argumentation."[136] Perelman and Olbrechts-Tyteca precisely state that their work is not concerned with forms of expression only devised to accomplish an aesthetic effect.[137] Thus, the New Rhetoric is a rhetorical study focused on argumentation for the

---

130. Sloan and Perelman, "Rhetoric," 808; Perelman and Olbrechts-Tyteca, *New Rhetoric*, 4.

131. Perelman and Olbrechts-Tyteca, *New Rhetoric*, 63–114.

132. Ibid., 514.

133. Ibid., 21.

134. Ibid., 50. They also say, "Unlike deliberative and legal speeches, which aim at obtaining a decision to act, the educational and epidictic speeches create a mere disposition toward action, which makes them comparable to philosophical thought" (54).

135. Ibid., 52.

136. Ibid., 142.

137. Ibid., 142–43.

Introduction

purpose of persuading audience. Mack summarizes the goals of the New Rhetoric, explaining:

> By linking the persuasive power of a speech not only to its logic of argumentation, but to the manner in which it addresses the social and cultural history of its audience and speaker, Perelman and Olbrechts-Tyteca demonstrated the rhetorical coefficient that belongs to every human exchange involving speech, including common conversation and the daily discourse of a working society. This takes rhetoric out of the sphere of mere ornamentation, embellished literary style, and the extravagances of public oratory, and places it at the center of a social theory of language.[138]

However, it should be noted that Lenchak indicates that the New Rhetoric neglects stylistics in favor of argumentation, arguing, "Style is another means of persuasion, another way of promoting or increasing adherence to proposed theses."[139] In Lenchak's judgment, rhetorical criticism should consider style as a means of persuasion, seeking to achieve the adherence of an audience by means of both persuasion and style.

In any case, Perelman and Olbrechts-Tyteca primarily focused on the so-called art of persuasion instead of the art of composition which has dominated the rhetorical study of the OT since Muilenburg.[140] Accordingly, in this study, the Chr's art of persuasion will be investigated in relation to the speeches and prayers in the David-Solomon narrative. I will argue that the Chr's persuasive portrayal of David and Solomon is designed to contribute to reconstruct the covenantal relationship between YHWH and the Judahites in the Persian era. For this study, I will employ Kennedy's method with some modifications. Kennedy proposed rhetorical criticism as a methodology in a definitive way.[141] According to him, the goal of rhetorical analysis is "the discovery of the author's intent and of how that is transmitted through a text to an audience."[142] In this way, rhetorical analysis focuses on what the author's intention is and how the author achieves his/her goal.

There have been rhetorical studies of the OT that have employed Kennedy's method.[143] For instance, Renz in his study of the book of Ezekiel attempts to demonstrate that the prophetic book can be understood as a single rhetorical unit displaying some similarities between form criticism and rhetorical criticism. He argues that it

---

138. Mack, *Rhetoric*, 16.

139. Lenchak, *"Choose Life!"* 68.

140. Muilenburg, "Form Criticism," 1–18. Muilenburg asserts "a responsible and proper articulation of the words in their linguistic patterns and in their precise formulations will reveal to us the texture and fabric of the writer's thought, not only what it is that he thinks, but as he thinks it" (7).

141. According to Black, Kennedy's method embodies "an articulated procedure" as "truly a method, not merely an interpretive perspective." See Black, "Rhetorical Criticism," 255–56.

142. Kennedy, *New Testament Interpretation*, 12.

143. For example, Renz, *Rhetorical Function*; Möller, *Prophet in Debate*; Barker, *From the Depths of Despair*.

is not merely a patchwork of various traditions; its diverse parts work together to build up a coherent argument.[144] In his rhetorical study of the book of Amos, Möller seeks to "demonstrate that the presentation of the debating prophet is the primary rhetorical means" used by the author of the prophetic book in order to achieve their communicative purposes.[145] He argues that the prophetic book presents the exchange between the prophet Amos and his audience, the eighth-century Israelites, in order to warn its readers of the consequences of disobedience.[146] Recently, Barker, focusing on Joel's rhetoric, attempts to demonstrate that the book of Joel shifts from devastation to promises of restoration through its persuasive appeal of divine and human responses, in order to pronounce the necessity of crying out in a time of crisis and relying on YHWH in any situation.[147]

There are other rhetorical studies of Hebrew narrative. For example, by making use of Kennedy's rhetorical method, Lenchak examines the third address of Moses (Deut 28:69–30:20); he argues that the rhetorical features were to lead the implied audience of the address to choose YHWH and to obey his covenantal regulations.[148] Eslinger, partially employing Kennedy's method, investigates the rhetoric and persuasion of 2 Sam 7 and asserts that what YHWH has done with Solomon was no more than to make somewhat manifest what has been hidden in the Davidic covenant. Eslinger believes that there is no retrospective conditionalization because the conditions of the Sinaitic covenant are embedded in the core of the Davidic covenant.[149] On the other hand, employing Aristotle's enthymeme and three modes of persuasion in Aristotle's rhetoric (logos, ethos, pathos), Duke examines the book of Chronicles as mentioned above.[150] Kang argues that the persuasive portrayal of Solomon in 1 Kgs 1–11, revealing the inevitability of Solomon's failure by using Aristotle's ethical, rational, and emotional appeal, "functions to persuade the reader in the exile to realize the fact that the continuity of the nation's covenant relationship with Yahweh does not depend on the Davidic kingship, the temple, and the land, but on Yahweh's mercy and their repentance."[151] In sum, these scholars have carried out rhetorical studies of the prophetic books and Hebrew narrative using Kennedy's method.

Thus, in order to examine the speeches and prayers of David and Solomon within their narrative context, Kennedy's method can be summarized in four steps: rhetorical

---

144. See Renz, *Rhetorical Function*, 249–51.

145. Möller, *Prophet in Debate*, 2.

146. See Möller, *Prophet in Debate*, 294–96.

147. See Barker, *From the Depths of Despair*, 34–36.

148. Lenchak, *"Choose Life!"* esp. 233–42.

149. Eslinger, *House of God*, xi, 1–20.

150. Duke contends that the Chr intends "to persuade his audience by the example of Israel's (Judah's) history that they should 'seek Yahweh' and uphold the proper temple cultus in order to receive blessing" (Duke, *Persuasive Appeal*, 51). However, he does not analyze in detail the speeches and the prayers of David and Solomon, even if he provides those lists in the appendix of his book.

151. Kang, *Persuasive Portrayal*, 301–2.

Introduction

unit, rhetorical strategy (rhetorical genre, invention, arrangement, and style), rhetorical situation (especially with the focus on audience),[152] and rhetorical effectiveness.[153]

Rhetorical Unit

A rhetorical unit has a beginning, middle, and end. Kennedy indicates that a rhetorical unit must have "within itself a discernible beginning and ending, connected by some action or argument."[154] Wuellner defines a rhetorical unit as "an argumentative unit affecting the reader's reasoning or the reader's imagination."[155] Accordingly, a rhetorical unit is "either a convincing or a persuasive unit"[156] in that it challenges the implied audience to respond to its argument appropriately. In this step, the first thing to do is to determine the rhetorical units. The range of a rhetorical unit can be identified in various ways from a few verses to the whole text of a book. It depends on various rhetorical devices of delimiting a rhetorical unit such as repetition, inclusio, and chiasmus. Once the rhetorical units are determined, the diverse rhetorical features within these units can be articulated, and we would assess their persuasive effect on the implied audience, especially in relation to the speeches and prayers in the narrative of David and Solomon.

Rhetorical Strategy

Ancient rhetoric is classified into the five parts: invention (*inventio*); arrangement (*dispositio*); style (*elocutio*); memory (*memoria*); and delivery (*actio* or *pronuntiatio*).[157] The last two parts were neglected since the rhetoric of written discourses has been stressed with the invention of printing. Memory is concerned with the memorizing of speeches, and delivery is the rules for the voice and the use of gestures.[158] Thus, in this study dealing with written discourse, only the first three parts will be employed. First, invention (*inventio*) is a planning of discourse and argumentation. It includes "the discovery of material suitable to the occasion."[159] *Inventio* is a part of rhetorical process in that it seeks to discover potent arguments. By means of invention, the speaker attempts to determine the issue at stake, assessing the nature of the issue,

---

152. In the rhetorical situation of a discourse, the most significant component would be the audience of the discourse. Although we cannot reconstruct the real audience, we need to assume the implied audience in order to assess the rhetorical effectiveness of the discourse. For this reason, I will more deeply discuss audience in the rhetorical situation.

153. Kennedy, *New Testament Interpretation*, 33–38.

154. Ibid., 34.

155. Wuellner, "Where is Rhetorical Criticism," 455.

156. Ibid., 455.

157. Kennedy, *New Testament Interpretation*, 13–14.

158. Lenchak, *"Choose Life!"* 56–57.

159. Trible, *Rhetorical Criticism*, 8; Möller, *Prophet in Debate*, 41.

and then seeks to find proper techniques and arguments to support his/her position.[160] Thus, the purpose of a discourse is to draw its audience to the resolution proposed by the speaker. In the process of argumentation, the audience should be persuaded to accept the speaker's view, and they should be also dissuaded from other views.[161]

Second, rhetorical arrangement (*dispositio*) attempts to "determine the rhetorically effective composition of the speech and mold its elements into a unified structure."[162] This is about "what subdivisions it falls into, what the persuasive effect of these parts seems to be, and how they work together to some unified purpose in meeting the rhetorical situation."[163] In order to carry out this evaluation, "line-by-line analysis of the argument" (or verse-by-verse), including assumptions, topics, and rhetorical features, is needed in order to delineate "their function in context."[164] Möller defines *dispositio* more thoroughly, explaining:

> [I]nterest in a text's *dispositio*, its structure or the organization of its argument, goes beyond the mere delineation of its rhetorical units referred to as the first step of rhetorical-critical enquiry. The focus at this point is on the persuasive effect of the textual units. To uncover this effect, the critic asks whether and how these units work together to achieve some unified purpose, or indeed fail to do so.[165]

Accordingly, the arrangement is indispensable for effective argumentation. If an argument has no order or structure, it would be ineffective in persuading the audience. A well-structured argument can effectively draw the audience's attention and elicit fitting responses. In this context, the arrangement of an argument can reinforce positively or weaken negatively the audience's adherence to what the speaker argues. As the discourse proceeds, it changes the audience's situation, resolving the rhetorical problem. It does not leave its audience the same. There is a great difference between before and after their hearing of the discourse. Thus, the arrangement of an argument is especially significant "because the changes in the audience are both effective and contingent."[166]

Third, style (*elocutio*) is the style of written discourse. Rhetorical analysis views stylistic features not as simply embellishments of discourse but as instruments of a

---

160. Lenchak, "*Choose Life!*" 57; Brandt, *Rhetoric of Argumentation*, 14.
161. Lenchak, "*Choose Life!*" 57.
162. Kennedy, *New Testament Interpretation*, 23.
163. Ibid., 37.
164. Kennedy, *New Testament Interpretation*, 37. Kennedy writes, "It should be kept in mind that a speech or a text read aloud is presented linearly: the audience hears the words in progression without opportunity to review what has been said earlier, and an orally received text is characterized by a greater degree of repetition than is a text intended to be read privately" (*New Testament Interpretation*, 37).
165. Möller, *Prophet in Debate*, 42.
166. Perelman and Olbrechts-Tyteca, *New Rhetoric*, 491.

Introduction

rhetor using them in order to intensify certain parts of discourse. Thus, stylistic features are an effective means to persuade the audience in order to achieve the expected consequences.[167]

The rhetorical strategy of the Chr is concerned with the three aspects—invention (*inventio*), structure (*dispositio*) and style (*elocutio*), which will be examined in relation to speeches and prayers in the David-Solomon narrative. In this study, the issue at stake and appropriate arguments to support the speaker's position will be considered in the rhetorical units (invention), and I will examine the speeches and prayers in each rhetorical unit of the David-Solomon narrative by their arrangements with their rhetorical features (arrangement and style), which will be tied in to determining the rhetorical effects of the speeches and prayers.

In addition, Kennedy's method has three possible rhetorical genres: (1) judicial (or forensic) rhetoric attempts to induce the audience to judge events of the past; (2) deliberative rhetoric seeks to influence the audience's decision about immediate or future action; and (3) epideictic rhetoric views the audience as those who pursue the goal of reinforcing certain values.[168] Each contains its own features. For instance, in judicial, the primary argument includes "the question of truth or justice"; in deliberative, it comprises "the question of self-interest and future benefits"; in epideictic, it involves "a change of attitude or deepening of values such as the honorable and the good."[169] The three genres further have their positive and negative forms, which are for judicial rhetoric prosecution and defense, for deliberative rhetoric exhortation and dissuasion, and for epideictic rhetoric encomium and invective respectively.[170]

Even if the three genres especially speak of the circumstances of classical oratory, these can be applied to any discourse—when the author tries to persuade the audience to judge events of the past (judicial); when the author tries to persuade them to take action in the future (deliberative); or when the author tries to persuade them to hold some view-point in the present (epideictic).[171] In the case of epideictic rhetoric, it is sometimes understood as being laudatory or polemical. However, Perelman and Olbrechts-Tyteca emphasize epideictic rhetoric, viewing it as basically educational in nature.[172] In this study, the characteristics of the speeches and prayers in the David-Solomon narrative will be briefly mentioned in each unit according to the rhetorical genres.

---

167. Möller, *Prophet in Debate*, 42.
168. Kennedy, *New Testament Interpretation*, 36.
169. Ibid., 20.
170. Ibid., 20.
171. Ibid., 19.
172. Perelman and Olbrechts-Tyteca, *New Rhetoric*, 47–54.

Rhetorical Situation

The rhetorical situation is the situation that led to the utterance. An exploration of rhetorical situation investigates audience, events, objects, relations, time, and place, etc. Lloyd F. Bitzer first introduced the concept of rhetorical situation.[173] He defines rhetorical situation as "a complex of persons, events, objects, and relations presenting an actual or potential exigence which can be completely or partially removed if discourse, introduced into the situation, can so constrain human decision or action as to bring about the significant modification of the exigence."[174] A rhetorical study investigates the persons, events, objects, and the relations involved, for they have an effect on what the speaker says and the reason for what is said.

According to Bitzer, "Rhetorical discourse comes into existence as a response to [a] situation, in the same sense that an answer comes into existence in response to a question, or a solution in response to a problem."[175] Rhetorical situation controls rhetorical discourse. In Bitzer's view, "discourse is rhetorical insofar as it functions (or seeks to function) as a fitting response to a situation which needs and invites it."[176] Thus, the rhetorical situation controls the answer and solution of the rhetorical problem.

Bitzer classifies the three components of rhetorical situation: the exigence, the audience, and the constraints.[177] First, an exigence is "an imperfection marked by urgency; it is a defect, an obstacle, something waiting to be done, a thing which is other than it should be."[178] According to Bitzer, every rhetorical situation has "at least one controlling exigence which functions as the organizing principle: it specifies the audience to be addressed and the change to be effected."[179] Bitzer's statement proposes that an exigence is a discernible thing that calls for a speech to be given, indicating that an exigence occurs at a point in time and that the nature of it confines what the rhetor may do or speak. Interestingly, Miller contends that "the ultimate character of an exigence is a conclusion in the mind of its perceiver," developing "the proposition that within the limits specified by each exigence, the *ultimate* or *perceived* nature of the exigence depends upon the constraints *of the perceiver*."[180] According to Miller,

---

173. Kennedy, *New Testament Interpretation*, 34.

174. Bitzer, "Rhetorical Situation," 6.

175. Ibid., 5. Bitzer views rhetoric as "a mode of altering reality, not by the direct application of energy to object, but by the creation of discourse which changes reality through the mediation of thought and action" (4).

176. Ibid., 6.

177. Ibid., 6. Bitzer indicates that "the second and third are elements of the complex, namely the *audience* to be constrained in decision and action, and the *constraints* which influence the rhetor and can be brought to bear upon the audience" (6).

178. Ibid., 6.

179. Ibid., 7.

180. Miller, "Rhetorical Exigence," 111–2 (italics Miller's).

Introduction

"the antecedent of every rhetorical situation is the exigence from which the situation derives its significance."[181]

Second, rhetoric always needs an audience because rhetorical discourse brings about change by affecting hearers' decisions and actions.[182] The audience consists of those persons "capable of being influenced by the discourse and of being mediators."[183] For Bitzer, the audience is involved in a rhetorical situation only to the extent that it is "capable of being constrained in thought or action in order to effect positive modification of the exigence."[184] Interestingly, Garret and Xiao consider "the audience as the active center of the rhetorical situation."[185] According to them, the audience as "the pivotal element" links "the rhetorical exigency (the audience's unsolved questions), the constraints (the audience's expectations), and the rhetor (as a member of the audience)."[186]

Every discourse presumes an audience. If the audience does not exist, the speaker does not have to make discourse.[187] A speaker would take into account a specific audience before his/her communicative act. In particular, the necessity of the audience is manifestly revealed in persuasive argument because one aspect of rhetoric is "its nature as *addressed*, since persuasion implies an audience."[188] As an argument proceeds, it must draw attention from the audience to whom it is directed. It becomes the necessary condition for performing any kind of argumentation.[189] Thus, in order to produce an effective argument, it is important for the speaker to adapt to the audience. In effect, "every persuasive discourse is an adaptation to the audience."[190]

More significantly, the role of the audience is not simply passive. Every discourse can be seen as an interaction between the speaker and the audience.[191] The interaction

---

181. Ibid., 118.

182. Bitzer, "Rhetorical Situation," 7.

183. Ibid., 8.

184. Bitzer, "Functional Communication," 23.

185. Garret and Xiao, "Rhetorical Situation Revisited," 39.

186. Ibid., 39. They address here that with this emphasis (on the audience) "the debate over the facticity of the exigency loses much of its force since the important question becomes whether the audience accepts that an exigency exists" (39).

187. Culley indicates that the audience "act as censors in that the audience will only listen to what it wants to listen to," so that the speaker should be "very sensitive to the standards of audience" (Culley, "Approach," 121).

188. Burke, *Rhetoric of Motives*, 38.

189. Perelman and Olbrechts-Tyteca, *New Rhetoric*, 18.

190. Perelman, *New Rhetoric and the Humanities*, 57. It means that the speaker can begin only with premises already approved by the audience (Perelman and Olbrechts-Tyteca, *New Rhetoric*, 286). Accordingly, argumentation reinforces those premises, introduces acceptable ideas, and makes an audience intellectual and emotional. In order to this, the author seeks to draw from the audience their attention and goodwill, association with the speaker. See Booth, *Rhetoric of Fiction*, 124; Kennedy, *New Testament Interpretation*, 45.

191. Arnold, "Oral Rhetoric," 194.

makes the speaker's utterance effective. In this regard, it is worth quoting Aristotle's statement: "no analysis of communication can be complete without a thorough study of the role of the receptors of a message."[192] Accordingly, if we understand the significance of the audience's role, how can we define the audience? Even if the audience cannot be identified with certainty, an audience can be defined "as *the ensemble of those whom the speaker wishes to influence by his argumentation*."[193] Kennedy, stressing the author's intention, defines an audience as "an immediate and universal audience."[194]

In effect, rhetorical analysis extends the concept of audience. An argument is for "the universal audience," based on a specific audience in a specific context.[195] Interestingly, Lenchak, employing Polzin's categories, identifies two sorts of audiences: "the text-world audience" and "the original real audience of the narrator/author."[196] Thus, the audience is not limited to those who the speaker addresses, and the effect of a discourse also is not limited to its intended audience.[197] The audience can be extended to all persons who may hear a discourse in the future.

Third, rhetorical situation always comprises certain constraints. They are "made up of persons, events, objects, and relations which are parts of the situation because they have the power to constrain decision and action needed to modify the exigence."[198] According to Bitzer, general sources of constraint involve "beliefs, attitudes, documents, facts, traditions, images, interests, motives," etc., and when the rhetor joins the situation, the discourse of the rhetor "not only harnesses constraints given by the situation but provides additional important constraints" such as the personal character, the logical proofs, and the style of the rhetor.[199] Thus, Bitzer concludes that the three components include "everything relevant in a rhetorical situation."[200]

Bitzer's definition of rhetorical situation has been criticized and modified by scholars. For instance, Vatz indicates that Bitzer's rhetorical situations are predetermined and prescribe the fitting response, making meaning inherent in the situation. In Vatz's view, situations cannot be separated from rhetors, who respond to the exigencies and constraints in their own ways. They initiate both text and situation. In this way, the rhetor, not the situation, controls the meaning. Thus, Vatz holds, modifying

---

192. Aristotle, *Rhetoric*, I.9.1367b.

193. Perelman and Olbrechts-Tyteca, *New Rhetoric*, 19.

194. Kennedy, *New Testament Interpretation*, 35.

195. For the discussion of "the universal audience," see Perelman and Olbrechts-Tyteca, *New Rhetoric*, 31–34.

196. Lenchak, *"Choose Life!"* 87; Polzin, *Moses and the Deuteronomist*, 72, 92.

197. Fox, "Rhetoric of Ezekiel's Vision," 4.

198. Bitzer, "Rhetorical Situation," 8.

199. Ibid., 8. Bitzer also indicates that two main classes of constraints are: "(1) those originated or managed by the rhetor and his method (Aristotle called these 'artistic proofs') and (2) those other constraints, in the situation, which may be operative (Aristotle's 'inartistic proofs')" (8).

200. Ibid., 8.

Introduction

Bitzer's concept of rhetorical situation, that "meaning is not discovered in situations, but *created* by rhetors."[201]

Consigny takes a middle way between Bitzer and Vatz. Consigny, as Vatz has done, indicates that Bitzer neglects the rhetor's role in his construction of the rhetorical situation. On one hand, he disagrees with Bitzer's view of rhetorical situation as "determinate and predetermining a 'fitting' response."[202] On the other hand, he disagrees with Vatz's view of the rhetor "as completely free to create his own exigence at will and select his subject matter in a manner of 'pure arbitration.'"[203] Accordingly, the rhetorical situation cannot totally control the rhetor's acts, and even the rhetor cannot independently create the situation. It is noteworthy that Consigny claims that the rhetor "must transform the indeterminacies into a determinate and coherent structure."[204] Between Bitzer and Vatz, Consigny's proposal centers around the traditional topics, which have been understood as "an essential *instrument* for discovery or invention" and as "a *realm* in which the rhetor thinks and acts."[205] In Consigny's view, the topics control the rhetor, not to invent exigence, audience, and constraints, but to discover the specificities of new situations. Thus, the art of topics allows the rhetor to engage in a particular situation.[206] Gorrell appropriately summarizes Consigny's view: "The art of using the topics allows the rhetor both the integrity that he sees missing in Bitzer's paradigm and the receptivity that he sees missing in Vatz's. Bitzer's rhetor enters problem; Vatz's rhetor invents problems; Consigny's rhetor solves problems."[207] Thus, the rhetor is not only affected by the rhetorical situation passively but also invents in part the rhetorical situation actively. Even the rhetor is controlled by the topics and solves the rhetorical problems. In this regard, the rhetorical situation is significantly connected to the author and the audience.

In addition, Stamps, proposing a synchronic reading of rhetorical situation, highlights "the rhetorical situation embedded in the text and created by the text which contributes to the rhetorical effect of the text."[208] According to him, in order to be an effective argument, the construction of the situation should be at least accorded with the situation of some audience, even if it is a partial accordance. So the persuasive effectiveness of the argument is closely connected to the literary exhibition of the situation.[209] When there is accordance with some of the audience, the speaker can

201. Vatz, "Myth," 157 (italics Vatz's). For Vatz, rhetoric is "a *cause* not an *effect* of meaning. It is antecedent, not subsequent to a situation's impact" (160).
202. Consigny, "Rhetoric," 178.
203. Ibid., 178.
204. Ibid., 178.
205. Ibid., 182.
206. Ibid., 185.
207. Gorrell, "Rhetorical Situation," 398.
208. Stamps, "Rethinking," 199.
209. Ibid., 200.

elicit a fitting response from the audience. In Stamps' view, the text presents its situation, on which the argument of the whole discourse and its rhetorical units are built. To determine rhetorical situation, the text operates as the conditions of the speaker and the audience.[210] Thus, Stamps stresses the significance of the text as a primary constraint of rhetorical situation.

In line with this discussion, the Chr is closely linked to the rhetorical situation of Chronicles. The rhetorical situation (exigence, audience, constraints) significantly influences the Chr, whereas it is also affected by the Chr. Accordingly, in presenting the early history of Israel, the Chr tries to solve the rhetorical problems in the rhetorical situation. In particular, the Chr employs a number of kings' speeches and prayers in presenting the early history of Israel. The Chr's message is conveyed by the mouth of the Davidic kings. As Bitzer indicates, speech is given rhetorical importance by the situation.[211] The role of a speaker is to influence the audience in terms of his discourse in order to persuade them to respond to the exigence appropriately.[212] The speaker sometimes frames a rhetorical situation by means of discourse and shapes the exigence that needs a fitting response from the audience. As the argument of a discourse proceeds, the situation is changed by the nature of response.[213] Thus, in this study, the rhetorical situation of Chronicles, apart from the rhetorical situation in each rhetorical unit of the David-Solomon narrative, will be examined according to Bitzer's three components.

In particular, my approach to the audience in this study draws on the two levels of audience: the narrative audience and the Chr's audience. The narrative audience is detected in the narrative so that we may recognize them in the narrative itself, yet the Chr's audience as the implied audience is not easily detected. Some clues could be recognized in the narrative that testifies to an anticipated response from the implied audience.[214] If we determine the boundaries of the composition date of the book of Chronicles, we may to some degree discern the Chr's audience.[215] In a broad way, we may say that the Chr would feel the need to retell the early history of Israel. In doing so, the Chr would decide to include the speeches and prayers as his rhetorical devices in order to convey his intention and message. Thus, in this study, I will examine the rhetorical situation of each unit in the David-Solomon narrative, considering both the

---

210. Ibid., 210.

211. Bitzer, "Rhetorical Situation," 5.

212. See Patrick and Scult, *Rhetoric*, 34.

213. Perelman and Olbrechts-Tyteca, *New Rhetoric*, 491. Perelman and Olbrechts-Tyteca employ "argumentative situation," instead of rhetorical situation, which dynamically shifts to accord the audience's responses to the advancement of the discourse (96).

214. See Powell, *Narrative Criticism*, 19–20. Powell indicates properly that the concept of the implied reader (i.e., the reader in the text) "moves narrative criticism away from being a purely reader-centered (pragmatic) type of criticism and makes it a more text-centered (objective) approach" (20).

215. It will be more specifically considered in Chapter 3.

Introduction

narrative audience in the narrative itself and the Chr's audience based on the textual evidences of Chronicles with the composition date of the book of Chronicles.

Rhetorical Effectiveness

The last stage of a rhetorical analysis is to assess the rhetorical effectiveness of the rhetorical discourse, which is to examine the argumentative effectiveness in relation to the exigence. Rhetorical effectiveness is to "review its success in meeting the rhetorical exigence and what its implications may be for the speaker or audience."[216] The primary concern in the rhetorical effectiveness evaluates whether "the utterance is a fitting response to the exigency that occasioned it" or not.[217] It should be noted that the actual effectiveness of a discourse cannot be detected. The potential effectiveness of the discourse, however, can be considered by whether the rhetorical utterance succeeded in modifying the exigence or not, bringing a fitting response from the audience. Accordingly, the rhetorical effectiveness focuses on what the rhetorical utterance accomplished, providing certain solutions for the rhetorical problems. For this reason, the effectiveness of a rhetorical utterance (or discourse) is closely connected to the rhetorical situation and the audience. According to how the rhetorical situation and the audience are defined, the rhetorical effectiveness would be quite different. In this step, thus, the possible effectiveness of the speeches and prayers in the David-Solomon narrative will be identified by the two levels of audience, that is, the narrative audience and the Chr's audience. I will consider whether or not the possible effectiveness of the speeches and prayers as the rhetorical utterances draw out the fitting responses from the two sorts of audiences and whether or not the rhetorical problems are effectively resolved by the speeches and prayers.

In sum, I will carry out a rhetorical study of the speeches and prayers in the David-Solomon narrative in Chronicles with Kennedy's methodology. In this study, I will examine speeches by other characters as well as the speeches and prayers by David and Solomon in the David-Solomon narrative. First, I will delimit the rhetorical units in the David-Solomon narrative by some criteria, and then I will examine the speeches and prayers in the rhetorical units by the Chr's rhetorical strategy, identifying the rhetorical features and techniques, the Chr's intention or purpose, etc. Next, I will focus on constructing the rhetorical situation by the two layers of audience. Finally I will evaluate the possible rhetorical effectiveness of the speeches and prayers and then provide some implications. By this process, I will argue that the Chr's persuasive portrayal of David and Solomon is designed to serve to reconstruct the identity of the Yehudite community as a cultic community through the Jerusalem temple in Persian Yehud, revealing the continuity of the covenantal relationship between YHWH and Israel in the Persian era.

---

216. Kennedy, *New Testament Interpretation*, 38.
217. Möller, *Prophet in Debate*, 42.

OUTLINE OF THIS STUDY

Chapter 1 has discussed the topic and the methodology of this study, in which the purpose of this study and the nature of rhetorical analysis are summarized. Chapter 2 discusses the rhetorical situation of Chronicles, apart from the rhetorical situation in each unit of the David-Solomon narrative. Three components of the rhetorical situation will be dealt in relation to the narrative situation and the Chr's rhetorical situation. Chapter 3 delimits the rhetorical units in the David-Solomon narrative. Each unit will be determined by criteria such as the beginning and ending markers of a discourse. Chapter 4 performs a rhetorical analysis of the speeches and prayers in each rhetorical unit of David's narrative; their rhetorical strategy, situation, and effectiveness will be treated. Chapter 5 carries out a rhetorical analysis of the speeches and prayers in each rhetorical unit of Solomon's narrative; their rhetorical strategy, situation, and effectiveness will also be treated. Finally, chapter 6 summarizes the rhetorical analysis of the speeches and prayers in each unit of the David-Solomon narrative and then evaluates the Chr's persuasive portrayal of David and Solomon, which serves to reformulate for the Chr's audience the identity of the Yehudite community as a cultic community based around the centrality of the Jerusalem temple in the Persian Yehud, revealing that the covenantal relationship between YHWH and Israel still continues through the Jerusalem temple in the Persian period.

2

Rhetorical Situation

THE RHETORICAL SITUATION IS the context from which the rhetorical discourse arises. The rhetorical act depends on the rhetorical situation.[1] The rhetorical situation of Chronicles can be traced by using the three components Bitzer suggested: exigence, audience, and constraints. However, we need to modify Bitzer's concepts of rhetorical situation in that, as Vatz mentions, the rhetor can create exigencies and constraints, not merely controlled by the rhetorical situation.[2] Accordingly, the rhetor as the author, which Bitzer has neglected, must be emphasized in the three components. In line with this, a rhetorical discourse may be understood from the relationship between the author and the audience.

The rhetorical situation of a discourse has two levels: one is the text-world and the other is the author's real world. However, we cannot know the actual author and the actual world of ancient texts like narrative discourse in the OT. Thus, the implied author as a literary construct is employed. If we presume the Chr is the implied author of Chronicles, the Chr's own time can be traced by determining the date of the book of Chronicles. Accordingly, the determination of the composition date of Chronicles leads us to the Chr's own time and audience. In this context, we need to recognize that there are two layers of audience in relation to a narrative discourse. Polzin refers to two types of audience in his study on Deuteronomy: the text-world audience and the original audience. The former is the audience to which Moses speaks on the plains of Moab and the latter the real audience of the author of Deuteronomy.[3] It seems that Polzin did not clearly distinguish two layers of the text-world audience, that is, narrative audience and the implied audience. However, it should be noted that the concept

---

1. Reflecting Bitzer's view, Brinton classifies the relation between rhetorical act and rhetorical situation into three distinct aspects: (1) the rhetorical act arises from the rhetorical situation ("a *causal* connection"); (2) the characteristic of the rhetorical act relies on the rhetorical situation ("'*meaning-dependence*'"); and (3) the rhetorical situation requires a fitting response ("a *normative* connection"). See Brinton, "Situation," 234.

2. See "Rhetorical Situation" in the Introduction and Vatz, "Myth."

3. See Polzin, *Moses and the Deuteronomist*, 72, 92. Polzin proposes that the author of Deuteronomy gradually destroys the distinction between Moses and the narrator in order to increase the authority of his narrator (*Moses and the Deuteronomist*, 57).

of audience drawn from some insights of narrative analysis can be more complicated than we might initially think.

If we accept Chatman's narrative model as mentioned in chapter 1, there would be three levels of sender and receiver: (1) the narrator and the narrative audience; (2) the implied author and the implied audience; and (3) the real author and the real audience.[4] In this scheme, the levels of rhetoric would be that of the implied author and the implied audience and that of the narrator and the narrative audience. Accordingly, the implied author conveys messages to the implied audience through the narrator and narrative audience as part of the narrative itself.[5] In general, the narrator delivers the messages of the implied author. It means that the implied author speaks through the narrator in a narrative. As the narrative advances, the narrative audience is further extended to the implied audience.[6] It can be diagramed as follows:

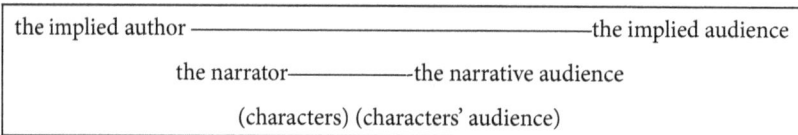

If we differentiate between the narrator and the implied author, the former tells what is going on (the event) and who speaks at a certain time (the characters' speeches), whereas the latter conveys its intention through the narrator's telling.[7] Booth indicates that the narrator is "the speaker in the work who is after all only one of the elements created by the implied author."[8] Accordingly, the implied author speaks through what the narrator describes and tells. This being so, what is the difference between the implied audience and the narrative audience? In a narrative, the implied audience is the addressee(s) of the implied author, and the narrative audience is the hearer(s) of the narrator. Both the implied audience and the narrative audience constitute two kinds of audiences within a narrative world.

These two layers of audience are related to our study of speeches and prayers in the David-Solomon narrative in Chronicles. The Chr as the implied author conveys his message to his audience through the narrative discourse, and the narrator deploys the story through the characters' speeches and acts.[9] The implied audience is the ad-

---

4. See above, "Narrative as Rhetoric"; Chatman, *Story and Discourse*, 149–51; Booth, *Rhetoric of Fiction*, 137–38, 151–52, 421–31; Eslinger, *Into the Hands*, 4–15; Iser, *The Implied Reader*, 274–94.

5. Chatman, *Story and Discourse*, 149–50.

6. For this reason, Chatman considers, stressing the implied author and the implied reader, that "the narrator and narratee are optional" (*Story and Discourse*, 151). Contra Chatman, Rimmon-Kenan contends that the narrator and narratee are "constitutive, not just optional, factors in narrative communication" (*Narrative Fiction*, 91). He also regards only four of Chatman's categories (the real author, the real reader, the narrator, the narratee) as relevant conception of narration, excluding the concept of the implied author and implied audience. Rimmon-Kenan, *Narrative Fiction*, 90–92.

7. Bar-Efrat, *Narrative Art*, 14.

8. Booth, *Rhetoric of Fiction*, 73.

9. Schmid distinguishes the characters' discourse from the narrator's discourse in the narrative

Rhetorical Situation

dressee of the Chr's retelling of Israelite history, while the narrative audience is the addressee(s) of the narrator (or characters). The Chr cannot always be separated from the narrator because in some cases the implied author speaks as the narrator. Thus, we need to recognize two levels of author, audience, and situation in the narrative discourse. In what follows, we will discuss the narrative situation and the Chr's rhetorical situation, considering the two layers of audience in Chronicles.

THE NARRATIVE SITUATION OF THE DAVID-SOLOMON NARRATIVE

The narrative situation comprises the urgent situation of the narrative, the narrative audience, and the narrative constraints. The urgent situation of the narrative is the motivation of the rhetorical discourses of the characters in the narrative. The urgent narrative situation might be indicated in the David-Solomon narrative itself. David and Solomon as the major characters in the narrative make speeches to their audience (the narrative audience) in order to draw fitting responses from them.

Urgent Situations of the David-Solomon Narrative

There are a variety of urgent situations in the David-Solomon narrative. For instance, in the David narrative, the urgent narrative situations are David's becoming king over Israel after the demise of Saul (1 Chr 11–12), the bringing of the ark to Jerusalem (1 Chr 13–16), the Davidic covenant regarding the building of the temple (1 Chr 17), the reinforcement of David's kingship (1 Chr 18–20), David's census-taking (1 Chr 21), the preparation for the building of the temple (1 Chr 22), David's appointment of the temple personnel (1 Chr 23–27), and David's urging Solomon and the Israelites to build the temple (1 Chr 28–29). In the Solomon narrative, the urgent narrative situations are Solomon's worship at Gibeon (2 Chr 1), Solomon's preparation of the building of the temple (2 Chr 2), the transfer of the ark to the Jerusalem temple, and the dedication of the temple (2 Chr 5–7). Thus, these sorts of the urgent situations of the narrative are reflected in the David-Solomon narrative in Chronicles.

The urgent situation of the narrative is closely related to the Chr's exigence because the Chr as the implied author has the final authority to choose the rhetorical situation of Chronicles, even though he would be influenced by the situation. The Chr, using the narrator as his agent in the narrative, indirectly conveys his messages to the implied audience. This being so, the urgent narrative situation arises from certain problems of the characters in the narrative, whereas the Chr's exigence originates from the rhetorical problems of his own time. The Chr ultimately chooses and arranges the urgent situation of the narrative and brings the narrator's description to his

---

text. According to him, "the *narrative text* is made up of two components, the *narrator's discourse* and the *characters' discourse*. Whereas the narrator's discourse is produced only in the act of narration, the characters' discourse is represented as having existed before the act of narration, and as being merely reproduced in the performance of that act" (Schmid, *Narratology*, 118, 121).

own time in order to convey his message to his audience. Thus, the narrative situation is closely connected to the Chr's own exigence.

The narrative situation is also related to the narrative audience as the first audience and, at the same time, the Chr's exigence to the implied audience as the second audience. The speeches and prayers in the David-Solomon narrative are addressed to the narrative audience (e.g., the assembly of Israel and YHWH). Furthermore, the speeches and prayers affect the narrative audience since the goal of the rhetorical discourses is to persuade the narrative audience (or the hearers of their speeches and prayers).

The Narrative Audience in the David-Solomon Narrative

The narrative audience is the addressee(s) of the characters' speeches and prayers in the narrative. The narrator tells his story through the characters' acts and speeches. The narrative audience as the first audience is the addressees of the characters' speeches and prayers. The major characters in Chronicles are YHWH, prophets (e.g., Nathan and Gad), and kings (e.g., David, Solomon, Huram and the queen of Sheba). In this context, the narrative audience is the addressee(s) of the characters' speeches and prayers in the David-Solomon narrative.

Accordingly, we can enumerate the narrative audience in the David-Solomon narrative. In David's ascension to the throne (1 Chr 11–12), the narrative audience is the followers of David in the wilderness, including the Benjaminites and Judahites (1 Chr 12:16). In the ark narrative (1 Chr 13–16), the narrative audience is the assembly of Israel, including the leaders of Israel (1 Chr 13:1–2). In the Davidic covenant (1 Chr 17), the narrative audience is David, Nathan, and YHWH, since YHWH's speech was given to David through Nathan and David prayed to YHWH in response. In David's war (1 Chr 18–20), the narrative audience is David's messengers (1 Chr 19:2) and Hanun (1 Chr 19:3). In the census narrative (1 Chr 21), the narrative audience is Joab and David's officials (1 Chr 21:2) and David and Ornan with his four sons (1 Chr 21:20–21). In David's organization of the temple personnel and civil officials (1 Chr 23–27), the narrative audience is the leaders of Israel, the priests and Levites. In David's final speeches (1 Chr 28–29), the narrative audience is various leaders of Israel (1 Chr 28:1), Solomon (1 Chr 28:9, 20) and the whole assembly of Israel (1 Chr 29:1).

Furthermore, in YHWH's appearance to Solomon (2 Chr 1), the narrative audience is Solomon and possibly those who came to Gibeon with him. In the exchange of Solomon's message and Huram's responding letter (2 Chr 2), the narrative audience is Huram and Solomon (2 Chr 2:3, 11). In the dedication of the temple (2 Chr 5:2—7:22), the narrative audience is all the assembly of Israel (2 Chr 6:3, 13), YHWH as the addressee of Solomon's prayer (2 Chr 6:14–42), and Solomon as the addressee of YHWH's speech (2 Chr 7:12–22). In Solomon's achievements (2 Chr 8), the addressee of Solomon's speech regarding Pharaoh's daughter is not clear since his speech seems be a monologue. In the speech of the queen of Sheba (2 Chr 9:5–8), the narrative audience is Solomon and his officials.

The narrative audience as the first audience constitutes a crucial component of the narrative situation. In effect, the David-Solomon narrative itself could be understood through the interaction of the narrative audience and the characters' speeches and prayers in the narrative situation. Furthermore, the narrative audience leads us to the Chr's audience as the second audience. The Chr as the implied author chooses and arranges the characters' speeches and prayers as his rhetorical devices. In this context, the addressee(s) of the speeches and prayers would be the Chr's audience, who is obviously hinted at in the text although not always easily identified.

The Narrative Constraints of the David-Solomon Narrative

Narrative constraints are the elements in the rhetorical discourses of a narrative that may impact the achievement of its rhetorical goal. Both David and Solomon, as the major characters in the David-Solomon narrative, utter their rhetorical discourses when urgent narrative situations (such as crucial events) occur. In this context, the preceding events function as the narrative constraint, and the geographical setting would be a key narrative constraint of the rhetorical discourses. Thus, we will consider David's ascension to the throne (1 Chr 11–12) and Solomon's dedication of the temple (2 Chr 6:1—7:11) as two examples of narrative constraints.

First, the narrative constraints of David's speech in his ascension to the throne (1 Chr 11–12) are the events such as the demise of Saul and the Israelites' joining to David; the geographical setting, such as strongholds and Hebron, constrain the rhetorical discourses. Accordingly, the rhetorical discourses, such as David's speech and his dialogue, are limited by various events and the geographical setting.

Second, the narrative constraints of the speech and prayer in Solomon's dedication of the temple (2 Chr 6:1—7:11) are the events such as the completion of the temple building and the transfer of the ark to the temple, and the geographical setting is the Jerusalem temple. These events and the place constrain Solomon's speech and prayer in the rhetorical unit. When Solomon completes the construction of the temple, he brings the ark of the covenant of YHWH into the temple (2 Chr 5:2–10) and dedicates it (2 Chr 6). At that time, Solomon makes a speech to the assembly of Israel (2 Chr 6:3–11) and prays to YHWH (2 Chr 6:12–42). YHWH answers him with his glory (2 Chr 7:1). In this context, the constraints of the rhetorical discourse (Solomon's speech and prayer) are the events of the completion of the temple and the transfer of the ark to the temple in Jerusalem. Accordingly, the preceding events of the dedication of the temple constrain Solomon's rhetorical discourse.

In this regard, the narrative constraints in the rhetorical discourse of the narrative are the crucial events in the narrative context. In particular, the preceding events in the rhetorical unit of the David-Solomon narrative constrain David's and Solomon's rhetorical discourses. Thus, the speeches and prayers in the David-Solomon narrative are affected by the narrative constraints.

THE CHR'S RHETORICAL SITUATION

The Chr's rhetorical situation is comprised of three components: the Chr's exigence, audience, and constraints. The Chr conveys his messages to his audience, initiating the rhetorical situation, and is affected by the situation. Accordingly, the rhetorical situation of the Chr can be constructed by the dynamics of these three components. Before we turn to the Chr's rhetorical situation, the date of the book of Chronicles needs be determined since his rhetorical situation can be reconstructed by the date of the book's composition. It is after determining the date of the book of Chronicles that we can describe the possible rhetorical situation of the Chr.

The Date of the Book of Chronicles

There has been a range of proposals for the date of the composition of the book of Chronicles.[10] The range of the proposed dates spans about 400 years, from the sixth century BCE to the second century BCE.[11] Some evidence in Chronicles narrows down the range of the date.[12] For instance, the reference to "the first year of Cyrus king of Persia" in 2 Chr 36:22 points to the beginning of the Persian Empire (539 BCE),[13] and the reference to the Persian coin, *darics* in 1 Chr 29:7 clarifies the time when the book was composed in that this coin was minted after 515 BCE.[14] As some scholars claim, the Chr's language displays features of Late Biblical Hebrew,[15] not revealing

---

10. Klein summarizes scholars' discussion on the dates of the composition of Chronicles. According to him, the earliest date, the late sixth century, is argued by Braun, Dillard, Freedman (515 BCE); McKenzie, Newsome (525–515 BCE); Throntveit (527 BCE). The advocates of a fourth-century BCE date are Albright and Myers. Noth advocates a third-century date (300–200 BCE), and so does Welten (300–250 BCE) (Klein, *1 Chronicles*, 13–14). See also Braun, *1 Chronicles*, xxiv; Dillard, *2 Chronicles*, xix; Freedman, "The Chronicler's Purpose," 436-42; McKenzie, *The Chronicler's Use*, 25–26; Newsome, "Toward a New Understanding," 201-17; Throntveit, *When Kings Speak*, 97–107; Albright, "Date and Personality," 119–21; Myers, *I Chronicles*, lxxxvii–lxxxix; Noth, *The Chronicler's History*, 73, 83–87; and Welten, *Geschichte*, 199–200.

11. Williamson refers to "'the establishment of the kingdom of Persia' in 2 Chr 36:20, which precludes a date earlier than 539 BC, and on the other hand by textual attestation of the existence of Chronicles before the middle of the second century BC, namely the citation of LXX of Chronicles by Eupolemos" (Williamson, *1 and 2 Chronicles*, 15). Klein views the range as covered from 520–515 BCE to the Maccabean era (ca. 160 BCE). See Klein, *1 Chronicles*, 13.

12. See Klein, *1 Chronicles*, 14–16.

13. See Briant, *From Cyrus to Alexander*, 40–44.

14. Williamson, *1 and 2 Chronicles*, 15. Klein indicates that the coin was "first minted by Darius I (522–486 BCE)." See Klein, *1 Chronicles*, 15.

15. See Polzin, *Late Biblical Hebrew*, 12–15, 27–84. Klein indicates that although the language of Chronicles had the features of Late Biblical Hebrew, "the present state of typological linguistic investigation does not allow a more specific identification of time within the postexilic period." Klein, *1 Chronicles*, 16. According to Japhet, the Chr's language "is clearly 'Late Biblical Hebrew', with features

Greek influence.[16] The Hellenistic effect on Judah seems to have functioned from the third century BCE. This testifies to the date of the book of Chronicles being before the influx of Greek influence, no earlier than the Persian era, in determining the date of Chronicles.[17] However, Knoppers points out that many features of the Chr's language in the genealogies can be understood by analogy to Greek historiography and then he contends that Hellenistic influence had been in Palestine before Alexander the Great arrived.[18] For Knoppers, the composition of Chronicles shows certain signs of direct or indirect contact with historiographical traditions, which were confirmed in the ancient Aegean world, even though it is acknowledged that most of the influences on Chronicles can be traced to earlier biblical works.[19] In my judgement, Knoppers' assertion does not open up the possibility of a Hellenistic date of Chronicles. It simply indicates a certain relation between the composition of the Chr's genealogies and Greek historiography. In effect, Knoppers' assertion focuses on the influence of Greek historiography on Chronicles. However, the Chr's work in the late Persian period could have conversely influenced Greek historiography. Knoppers also does not point to the possibility that Chronicles could have been more influenced by earlier biblical writings.

Boda summarizes the evidence for determining the date of the book of Chronicles: the extensive use of Samuel-Kings proposes that Chronicles must have been written after the final event (2 Kgs 25:27–30); the final verses of Chronicles (2 Chr 36:22–23); the *darics* (1 Chr 29:7); the absence of details on the building project of Solomon and much emphasis on the cultic systems propose that Chronicles was recorded in a period when the temple was functional, not in the period when the temple was being built;[20] and the genealogy concerning the Davidic line (1 Chr 3:17–24) continues at least two generations after Zerubbabel.[21]

According to Boda, the evidence suggests that Chronicles was written in 425 BCE as the earliest date. As for the latest possible date, Chronicles seems to have been used in some books such as 1 Maccabees, Sirach, and the DSS in the Second Temple

---

common to late biblical and extra-biblical works such as Ezra-Nehemiah, Esther, Daniel, etc., on the one hand, and the Dead Sea Scrolls and the Samaritan Pentateuch on the other" (Japhet, *I & II Chronicles*, 25). However, recently, some scholars have observed that only very few features of Late Biblical Hebrew are confirmed in all the texts of Late Biblical Hebrew. For instance, Young, Rezetko, and Ehrensvärd state, "It is often difficult to determine which feature in which book would represent truly late language" (Young et al., *Linguistic Dating*, 1:86). See Young et al., *Linguistic Dating*, 1:86–87.

16. Williamson, *1 and 2 Chronicles*, 16. Interestingly, Peltonen considers that Persian influence on the book of Chronicles was quite insufficient ("A Jigsaw Without a Model," 238).

17. Japhet, *I & II Chronicles*, 25.

18. See Knoppers, "Greek Historiography," 627–50.

19. Ibid., 647.

20. See Dillard, *2 Chronicles*, 31; Knoppers, *I Chronicles*, 111.

21. Boda, *1–2 Chronicles*, 7–8, 52–57. Boda, following Klein, dates "the final generation in this genealogy to the latter half of the fifth century BC" (8). See also Klein, *1 Chronicles*, 113.

period.[22] This indicates a date prior to the mid-third century for Chronicles,[23] which is supported by the fact that the LXX contains Chronicles. Therefore, it can be said that the book of Chronicles was written between 425 and 250 BCE.[24]

Most scholars hold to a fourth-century date for the book's composition,[25] which points to the late Persian era and the beginning of the Hellenistic era. In line with this view, I consider the date of the composition of Chronicles as the middle of the fourth century BCE, which will be presumed in this study. Now, we turn to the Chr's exigence as the first one among the three components of the rhetorical situation.

The Chr's Exigence

Exigence, as the first component of the rhetorical situation, is the motivation of the rhetorical discourse, which can be shown by raising a set of questions: what the rhetorical discourse intends to accomplish; what the goal of the rhetorical act is; and how the audience of the rhetorical discourse is supposed to respond to it.[26] In fact, the rhetorical goal is a part of the exigence for the rhetorical act since the attempt to resolve the exigence would be a strong motive of the rhetor.[27] Broadly speaking, the rhetorical purpose is to persuade its audience to respond fittingly to the discourse.

The Chr's exigence is primarily related to community-identity formation in the Persian period, which inherently contains the conflicts between some groups in the Yehudite community. The rhetorical problem of the Chr seems to be these conflicts, which raise a question about the identity of Israel as God's people in the Persian period. The rhetorical need provides its answer to the Yehudite community. Thus, the Chr, answering this rhetorical problem and responding to the rhetorical need, presents the early history of Israel to his audience in order to draw fitting responses and change the situation.

The Judahite identity as God's people was seriously challenged by the destruction of Jerusalem (587/86 BCE). Unfortunately, their key identity markers such as a king, the temple, and cultic worship disappeared with the destruction of their capital.[28] In this context, some Judahites were deported from their homeland and were moved

---

22. For instance, Sirach (47:9–10), which can generally be dated 200–180 BCE, appears to presume the Chr's description of David. Additionally, Eupolemos, who was a Jewish historian in Judea (ca. 150 BCE), appears to have known a Greek version of Chronicles. See Kalimi, "History of Interpretation," 14–17; Klein, *1 Chronicles*, 13; Knoppers, *I Chronicles*, 105–11. In addition, Oeming views 350–250 BCE as the most probable date of Chronicles (*Das wahre Israel*, 44–45).

23. Knoppers, *I Chronicles*, 111.

24. Boda, *1–2 Chronicles*, 7–8; Kalimi, *Ancient Israelite Historian*, 41–65.

25. For instance, those scholars are Klein, Boda, Japhet, De Vries, and Williamson. See Boda, *1–2 Chronicles*, 7–8; Klein, *1 Chronicles*, 13–16; Japhet, *I & II Chronicles*, 23–28; De Vries, *1 and 2 Chronicles*, 16; Williamson, *1 and 2 Chronicles*, 15–17; Curtis and Madsen, *Chronicles*, 6.

26. Grant-Davie, "Rhetorical Situations," 268–69.

27. Ibid., 269.

28. Boda, *1–2 Chronicles*, 8.

Rhetorical Situation

to Babylonia. Seventy years later, YHWH's word spoken by Jeremiah was fulfilled (2 Chr 36:21–22). Cyrus,[29] the king of Persia, pronounced an imperial decree, which led some of the deportees to return to the land of Judah. This returning was another fulfillment of YHWH's word (2 Chr 36:23; cf. Isa 44:28). In this regard, the decree of Cyrus serves as a catalyst for the Chr's rewriting of the history of Israel. Thus, the return of exiles from Babylonia raised the question about community identity in Persian Yehud, which led to the conflicts between the returnees and the remainees in Yehud. As a result, the question of community identity became one of the key issues in the Persian period.

Community Identity in Persian Yehud

One of the most interesting features of the Judahite history in the Persian period is the rise of various communities in diverse places, like Mesopotamia, the Levant, and Egypt. Recently, scholars have given special attention to the issues regarding population, borders, the socio-political structure in Persian Yehud, and the effect of the Persian imperial policy on Yehud.[30] More recently, some scholars have given more attention to the issue of community identity in Persian Yehud, focusing on the relationship between the community in Yehud and the outside community.[31] For instance,

29. Briant indicates that Cyrus's accession is "the point of departure for the first territorial empire that brought political unification to the immense area from the Aegean to the Indus" (*From Cyrus to Alexander*, 13). See also Kuhrt, *Persian Empire*, 1:47–53.

30. During the last decade, scholarly works produced a new image of Yehud with some shared assumptions: (1) The Babylonian aggressions of the early sixth-century BCE did not deport the whole population of Jerusalem. (2) Only a few descendants of the deportees returned from Babylon to Yehud in 539 BCE, and returns from Babylonia occurred over several decades. (3) The Jerusalem population in the Persian period was much smaller than earlier assessments (these assessments have continuously declined from ten thousand to a few thousand). (4) The Yehudite community was not incorporated and experienced substantial social conflict. This conflict included clashing views on the construction of the temple and its function as well as cultic practice. (5) Yehud was strongly affected by Persian imperial policies. The Persian government used methods of social control in Yehud analogous to those that the empire employed in other colonial provinces. (6) The economic situation of Yehud as a Persian province is significant in understanding the Yehudite society under the Persian rulers. (7) Yehud was a place of ethnic conflict and ethnic clarity, laying the foundation of later understanding. See Berquist, *Approaching Yehud*, 3–4.

31. As for how the socio-political structure of Yehud was affected by Persian imperial policies, Hoglund contends that the Persian Empire made Jerusalem into a place to collect and store imperial incomes (*Achaemenid Imperial Administration*, 224). Berquist also argues that the Persian rulers made the Jerusalem temple central storage for the revenue for Yehud (*Judaism in Persia's Shadow*, 131–46). Furthermore, Schaper maintains that the temple in Jerusalem was a financial center for Yehud, operating as a bank. He claims that the imperial purpose of the Babylonian temples is parallel to that of the Jerusalem temple, which also functioned as the mint of king and as the agency of collection ("Jerusalem Temple," 528–39; "Temple Treasury," 200–206). In addition, there are a number of topics that scholars have begun to address with the new perspectives on Yehud: "(1) imperialism and its effects, including postcolonial interpretation sensitive to the multiple encodings of agency and resistance; (2) bodies and sexualities as constructed in the Persian period; (3) economics, including food, migration, trade, and class; (4) identity, in particular ethnicity and perceptions of the other in the setting of pluralism; (5) scribalism and canonization, as well as the proliferation of texts; (6) regional differences

there were conflicts between the deportees in Babylonia (the so-called "*golah* community") and the remainees in homeland. In this context, the discussion of community identity in Yehud firstly leads us to note recent archaeological and demographic studies on the Persian era that reflect the tension between the tribes of Judah and Benjamin. Significantly, this tension is also reflected in Chronicles, forming one of key exigencies of the Chr. Thus, recent studies on the Persian Yehud provide the backdrop of the Chr's exigence.

Tension between the Tribes of Judah and Benjamin

Recent archaeological data in Persian Yehud reveals that after the fall of Jerusalem the land was not empty.[32] For instance, Schniedewind claims that the land of Judah was not empty but merely depopulated.[33] Stern contends that after the fall of Jerusalem, even though large sections of the towns and villages in Judah were completely or partly destroyed, "only two regions appear to be have been spared this fate, the north of Judah, i.e., the region of Benjamin . . . and probably the land of Ammon."[34] All evidence of the archaeological data reveals that the land was not empty during the exile.[35] This means that the territory of Benjamin was not destroyed.[36] It might explain Benjamin's status as a leading tribe alongside Judah in Chronicles.

---

between Yehud and its neighbors, within the imperial context; (7) relations and influences between Yehud and its not-Persian contacts, including peoples of the Mediterranean; (8) the reintegration of social history with religious practices of the period; and (9) understanding the production and uses of texts within the period, including the history of different writings now extant and the intertextual relations between texts" (Berquist, *Approaching Yehud*, 4–5).

32. Faust, *Judah*, 184–5. For recent archaeological studies on Yehud, see Faust, "Settlement Dynamics," 23–51; Edelman, "Settlement Patterns in Persian-Era Yehud," 52–64; Finkelstein, "Persian Period Jerusalem and Yehud," 2–13; Lipschits, "Persian Period Finds from Jerusalem," 2–30; Grabbe, "They Shall Come Rejoicing to Zion," 116–27; Meyers, "Exile and Restoration," 166–73.

33. Schniedewind, *How the Bible Became a Book*, 143.

34. Stern, *Archaeology of Land*, 350. See also Faust, *Judah*, 187.

35. For the discussion of the myth of empty land, see Barstad, "After the 'Myth of the Empty Land,'" 3–20; Carroll, "Exile! What Exile?" 62–79; Davies, "Exile! What Exile? Whose Exile?" 128–38; Fried, "The Land Lay Desolate," 21–54; Oded, "Where is the 'Myth of the Empty Land,'" 55–74.

36. For instance, Mizpah in Benjaminite territory was "the new administrative center in which Gedaliah was established by the Babylonians," and "the nearby venerable shrine of Bethel probably served as the imperially sanctioned religious center after the deliberate and systematic destruction of the Jerusalem temple under the direction of Nebuzaradan" (Blenkinsopp, *David Remembered*, 51). Bethel, founded as a rival sanctuary of northern tribes to Jerusalem, "survived the Assyrian conquest in 722 B.C.E (2 Kgs 17:26–28)" (Blenkinsopp, *David Remembered*, 50–51; "Benjamin Traditions," 629–45). Knoppers also refers to "the northern Israelites who survived the Assyrian invasion and remained within their ancestral territories" (*Jews and Samaritans*, 8). Knoppers holds that Samaria had a relatively stable economy with a stable population in the seventh and sixth centuries. It means that while Samaria remained stable, Judah was devastated. This imbalanced situation would cause a sort of tension between the two provinces in the Persian period ("Revisiting the Samaritan Question," 265–90).

Yehud as a province of the Persian Empire also experienced a severe decline in its population, economy, and culture due to the Babylonian destruction in 587 BCE. Recent demographic studies showcase that the population of Yehud is estimated to have been 30,000 people, around a 70 percent decrease from the end of the Iron II period.[37] Most of the population after the Babylonian destruction lived in small, unwalled settlements. There seem to have been only three walled settlements—Mizpah, Ramat Rahel, and Jerusalem.[38] Lipschits notes an 89 percent decrease in the number of settlements from the end of Iron Age to the Persian period in the sites nearby Jerusalem (within three kilometers), stating that in the Benjaminite area there was a somewhat stable population.[39]

Furthermore, the borders and the territory of Yehud were reduced when compared with the previous state of Judah. Interestingly, even though the northern border of the kingdom of Judah in the last years before the fall of Jerusalem cannot be reconstructed, as Lipschits points out, "the border of the kingdom of Judah in its last years expanded slightly northward" (to Bethel-Oprah), which means that the border of the kingdom of Judah included some parts of the Benjaminite area (the cities such as Gibeah, Gibeon, Mizpah and Bethel).[40] This is another example that explains Benjamin's status as a leading tribe alongside Judah in the Persian era.

These archaeological and demographic studies on the Persian period indicate that after the fall of Jerusalem the Benjaminite areas were not totally destroyed and that they had a relatively stable population. In this context, there would be a question about who would take the leadership of Yehud after the exile. The Benjaminites who dwelt in a relatively stable area without any severe destruction would compete with the Judahites who had had the leadership of Israel through the Davidic monarchs. According to Blenkinsopp, Benjaminite-Judean hostility was a primary feature of the half-century history: "between the fall of Jerusalem [587/586 B.C.E.] and the fall of

---

37. Lipschits, "Demographic Changes in Judah," 323–76. For more discussion of demographic changes in Yehud, see Carter, *Emergence of Yehud*.

38. See Carter, *Emergence of Yehud*, 214–15. Carter represents Yehud as being based in the central hills of Palestine, using archaeological data. He provides full discussion of the social demographic study of Yehud.

39. Lipschits, "Demographic Changes in Judah," 332–33; "Achaemenid Imperial Policy," 19–52. Regarding the demographic changes in Judah between the end of the Iron Age and the Persian period, "it appears that the destruction of Jerusalem and the end of the kingdom of Judah brought about the gravest demographic crisis in the history of the kingdom of Judah, with much more severe results than the Sennacherib campaign of 701 B.C.E. The Babylonians concentrated their effort on Jerusalem and its environs, while the region of Benjamin and the northern Judean hills were hardly touched and continued almost unchanged in terms of settlement patterns and demography" (Lipschits, *Fall and Rise of Jerusalem*, 270, 267–71).

40. Lipschits, *Fall and Rise of Jerusalem*, 146. For the recent discussion of the tribe of Benjamin and the Benjaminite area, see Na'aman, "Saul, Benjamin, Part 1," 211–24; "Saul, Benjamin, Part 2," 335–49; Hentschel, "Der Bruderkrieg zwischen Israel und Benjamin," 17–38; Davies, "Trouble with Benjamin," 93–111; Blenkinsopp, "Benjamin Traditions," 629–45; Levin, "Joseph, Judah and the 'Benjamin Conundrum,'" 223–41.

Babylon in 539 B.C.E. and probably on into the early Persian period."[41] In effect, the Benjaminites seem to have sought primacy, struggling for political superiority over the Judahites and striving to establish Gibeon within the tribe of Benjamin as the central cultic place.[42] Edelman suggests that the rivalry of Saul and David resurfaced in the early Persian Yehud, claiming that there was tension between the non-*golah* group in Benjamin and the *golah* community over both the appointment of governor (Saul's descendants or David's) and the place of the temple rebuilding (Gibeon or Jerusalem).[43] According to her, the genealogies of Saul (1 Chr 8:29–40; 9:35–44) indirectly verify this tension.[44] Furthermore, this tension between the Judahites and Benjaminites was implicitly reflected in 1 Chr 9:3 ("In Jerusalem there lived . . .") and 1 Chr 9:35 ("In Gibeon there lived . . ."). In this context, the Judahites would advocate that Jerusalem be the cultic center, whereas the Benjaminites would support Gibeon as the center. Thus, the Benjaminites appear to have competed with the Judahites, striving for making Gibeon, the city related to their own tribe, as the cultic city.[45]

The conflicts of this period and the final resolution are found in the Chr's presentation. After the separation of the northern tribes, Rehoboam prepares to fight against the northern tribes with the army of Judah and Benjamin, but the fight is prevented by the intervention of Shemaiah, a man of God (2 Chr 11:1–5). For this reason, Rehoboam simply reinforces the defense of Judah-Benjamin against the northern tribes, appointing his sons as governors in the territories of Judah and Benjamin, obviously regarded as one territory (2 Chr 11:5–12, 23). This situation continues in Judah until the fall of Jerusalem.[46]

The final settlement of this conflict is manifest in terms of "the frequent allusion in Chronicles and Ezra-Nehemiah to 'Judah and Benjamin' as a single entity."[47] Judah and Benjamin also settled together in Jerusalem.[48] Blenkinsopp summarizes appropriately that "while the twelve-tribal Israel was never lost from sight, its sole

---

41. Blenkinsopp, *David Remembered*, 30.

42. See Edelman, "Saulide-Davidic Rivalry," 69–91; "Gibeon and Gibeonites," 153–67; Knoppers, "Israel's First King," 187–213 (esp. 206–10); Amit, "Saul Polemic," 647–61; Jonker, "Revisiting the Saul Narrative," 283–305. For the early discussion of the relation between Saul and Gibeon, see Blenkinsopp, "Did Saul Make Gibeon His Capital?" 1–7; Walters, "Saul of Gibeon," 61–76.

43. Edelman, "Saulide-Davidic Rivalry," 90. For the *golah* community, see below.

44. First Chronicles 8:29–40 represents Saul's descendants of Benjamin before the exile, and 1 Chr 9:35–44 repeats as a link between the resettlement of Jerusalem in the Persian period (1 Chr 9:1–35) and the Saul-David narrative. Edelman, "Saulide-Davidic Rivalry," 78.

45. Finally, it was the Judahites who had the priority to the Benjaminites, making kings and integrating the royal city, the ark, and the temple. See Berger, "Chiasm and Meaning," 12.

46. Blenkinsopp, *David Remembered*, 35. In addition, Judah and Benjamin promise to observe the conditions of Josiah's covenant (2 Chr 34:32). Both of them are said to have been "involved in the rebuilding of the temple and the resolution of the intermarriage crisis (Ezra 1:5; 4:1–4; 10:9)" (35).

47. Ibid., 35.

48. Ibid., 35.

surviving representatives were the conjoined tribes of Judah and Benjamin."[49] Thus, this observation points to the socio-political situation of the Yehudite community in relation to the frequent references to Judah and Benjamin.

Jonker also confirms this characteristic in the genealogical section in Chronicles, maintaining that the genealogies are designed to "claim equal status between Judah and Benjamin."[50] As a matter of fact, Benjamin or the Benjaminites are frequently referred to in Chronicles. Even the section of genealogies (1 Chr 1–9) contains two lists for Benjamin (1 Chr 7:6–12; 1 Chr 8:1–40). More significantly, the genealogical section begins with Judah (1 Chr 2:3—4:23) and closes with Benjamin (1 Chr 8:1–40),[51] in which the Chr stresses the settlement of some Benjaminites in Gibeon (1 Chr 8:29–32).[52] Knoppers appropriately argues, "In an era in which kinship relations and the question of ancestry were of great consequence for determining status and self-identity, the prominence of Benjamin is striking," stating that three tribes in the genealogies were predominant in comparison with others: the Judahites (1 Chr 2:3—4:23), the Levites (1 Chr 5:37—6:66), and the Benjaminites (1 Chr 8:1–40).[53] In line with these views, it is noteworthy that Giffone recently argues for Benjamin and the Benjaminites in Chronicles, writing:

> The tribes of Judah, Levi and Benjamin were the primary constituent tribes of the people of Yehud during the Persian period, and these distinctions appear to have had continued relevancy in Jewish communities for centuries afterward. After Benjamin came to be associated with the Southern Kingdom and the Northern Kingdom was captured by Assyria, the people of the Judahite and Benjaminite tribal regions (including the Levites associated with the Jerusalem cult) constituted the kingdom of Judah that was subdued by the Babylonians between 598 and 582 BCE. These three tribes are prominent in the Chronicler's genealogies (1 Chr 2:3—4:23; 6:1–81; 8:1—9:1), and the returnees from Babylon were primarily (or perhaps exclusively) members of these tribes (1 Chr 9:2–44).[54]

---

49. Ibid., 36.

50. Jonker, "Of Jebus, Jerusalem and Benjamin," 86.

51. Klein indicates that Judah and Benjamin, as two principal tribes, "made up the province of Yehud" (*1 Chronicles*, 86).

52. Jonker, "Revisiting the Saul Narrative," 300.

53. Knoppers, "Israel's First King," 207.

54. Giffone, "Sit at My Right Hand," 4. He summarizes his analysis of Benjamin in Chronicles as follows: (1) "After the division of the kingdom, the Northern tribes collectively retreat from the Chronicler's purview—but Benjamin remains a relevant collective identity, as evidenced by the numerous references to 'Benjamin' and 'Benjaminites' in 2 Chronicles. Benjamin remains the primary constituent tribe of 'all Israel' beside Judah and Levi"; (2) "Benjaminites are prominent in all sections of Chronicles, serving in important administrative and military positions"; (3) "Uniquely Benjaminite locations receive less attention because they have no cultic significance for the Chronicler"; (4) "It is implied that the Jerusalem temple belongs equally to Judah, Benjamin and Levi, being located on the border between the territories of the first two tribes and administered by the third" (*Sit at My Right*

Thus, these scholars emphasize that Judah and Benjamin, including the Levites who served at the Jerusalem temple, were the primary tribes in Yehud.[55] Their superiority over other tribes seems to have characterized Yehud throughout the following centuries. Even though the priority of the two tribes of Benjamin and Judah in the postexilic era was apparent, the socio-political situation of Yehud was more complicated. It can be seen in the issue of community identity in Persian Yehud, which needs to be explained further.

The Issue of Community Identity in Persian Yehud

In recent Persian-period scholarship, community identity in Persian Yehud is one of the most important topics. Kessler proposes a variety of Jewish communities in the Persian period: "(1) *golah* returnees in Yehud; (2) *golah* remainees in Babylonia; (3) Yehudite remainees; (4) Israelite/Judean residents in Egypt; (5) Israelite/Judean inhabitants in the province of Samaria, and (6) other Israelite/Judeans in the various regions of the Levant."[56] The emergence of these communities can be traced to the Jehoiachin exile (597 BCE, 2 Kgs 24:8–17), which divided the Judahites into two communities, the deportees with Jehoiachin into Babylonia and those who remained in the homeland with Zedekiah (Jer 40:6).[57]

Of the communities of Kessler's division, the first three groups are our concern in relation to the issue of community identity in the Persian Yehud since they seem to have reflected the identity of the Yehudite community with their conflicts about who would be God's people in the Persian period.[58] Accordingly, on the basis of the three groups, we will discuss the relationship between the returnees from Babylon to Yehud

---

Hand, 167).

55. The prominence of the three tribes, including Levi, is shown in 1 Chr 9:33–34. In this summary of the Levites and other dwellers in Jerusalem, the Chr seems to have made the clause "these dwelt in Jerusalem" (יָשְׁבוּ בִירוּשָׁלָם אֵלֶּה) in 1 Chr 9:34b correspond to the clause "in Jerusalem they dwelt" (וּבִירוּשָׁלַם יָשְׁבוּ) in 1 Chr 9:3, which summarizes "the whole account of the population of Jerusalem" (Johnstone, *1 and 2 Chronicles*, 1:128). According to Johnstone, the genealogies (1 Chr 1:1—9:34) culminate in the weekly presentation of the twelve loaves to God by the Levites of Korah (1 Chr 9:32). In his discussion of the genealogies, Johnstone writes: "All is prepared: the land is fully settled by God's people; the Levites dwell in the midst to guide and instruct and serve at the gates of the sanctuary to ensure the scrupulous fulfilment of every duty to God and so to protect the sanctity of Israel's relationship with God from any defilement because of carelessness, neglect or wilful [sic] error" (*1 and 2 Chronicles*, 1:128–9).

56. Kessler, "Diaspora and Homeland," 141.

57. Rom-Shiloni, *Exclusive Inclusivity*, xvi. She contends that the Jehoiachin exile is the starting point of the emergence of various communities in Persian Yehud.

58. With respect to the fourth and fifth groups, for the relation between the deportees who returned to Yehud and the population in Samaria to the north, see Ben Zvi, "Inclusion in and Exclusion," 95–149; Knoppers, *Jews and Samaritans*; "Revisiting the Samarian Question," 265–89. For the relationship between the Egypt diaspora community and the communities in Jerusalem and Babylon, see Bar-Kochva, *Pseudo-Hacataeus, On the Jews*; Garbini, *History and Ideology*, 133–50. See also Cataldo, *Theocratic Yehud*, 12. He provides useful discussion of the socio-political situation of Yehud.

(the *golah* community) and those who remained in Judah, including the relationship between the returnees and the Babylonian remainees, which will be followed by our discussion of the community-identity formation and the characteristics of Yehudite community.

First, Kessler analyzes the relationship between the returnees to their homeland and those who remained in Judah. Kessler argues that the Judahites in Babylonia controlled the *golah* community and Yehud.[59] It meant that the remainees in Babylonia had authority over the returnees. According to Kessler, the *golah* community, as a founding group or a released elite, were placed in Yehud by the Babylonian diaspora and ultimately by the Persian rulers.[60] Persian Yehud seems to have enjoyed some autonomy due to the Persian imperial carelessness, and the *golah* community, as the central authority over Yehud, subsequently regulated this autonomy.[61] Accordingly, Kessler summarizes his arguments as follows:

> The Golah returnees functioned as a Charter Group—that is, an elite who moved into a new territory, as representative both of the imperial Crown and the home religious community ... the installation and effective functioning of the Golah as an elite may have been a critical and decisive element in the emergence of Yehud as a center in the mid-fifth century. The Golah's role generated a number of dynamics, of which questions of identity and self-definition and the exclusion and inclusion of other groups and communities were an integral part.[62]

In Kessler's view, the *golah* returnees as a charter group were governed by the Babylonian diaspora community with the approval of the Persian rulers. The *golah* group continuously maintained its authority over Yehud. However, Kessler's argument assumes that both the Persian Empire and the Judahites in Yehud approved the authority of the *golah* community for religious legitimation.[63] Kessler's model seems to be heavily based on Porter's sociological study, which deals with power relations between the elite group and non-elite group in the colonial region.[64] Following this model, Kessler considers a charter group as "*a geographically transplanted elite*,"[65] who moves into a depopulated territory and then establishes itself as a social force with hegemony in the region.[66] In the case of the *golah* community, however, it consists of some elite groups. They were moved into Babylonia and were established as the *golah*

---

59. Kessler, "Persia's Loyal Yahwists," 103.

60. Ibid., 99–100.

61. Ibid., 105–7.

62. Ibid., 112.

63. See Cataldo, *Theocratic Yehud*, 26.

64. Porter's book, *Vertical Mosaic: An Analysis of Social Class and Power in Canada* was first published in 1965. The fiftieth-anniversary edition was published by University of Toronto Press in 2015.

65. Kessler, "Diaspora and Homeland," 142.

66. See Kessler, "Persia's Loyal Yahwists," 98–101.

community. Accordingly, they did not move into a depopulated area, but they were moved into Babylonia as deportees from their homeland after the fall of Jerusalem.

Similarly, Bedford examines the relationship between the returnees to Yehud and the remainees in Babylonia. Bedford contends that the *golah* community in Yehud continuously relied on the Babylonian diaspora community for its leadership, appointing Sheshbazzar, Zerubbabel, Ezra, and Nehemiah as the leaders of the community.[67] Bedford states, "With the homeland devoid of Judeans, the first generation of repatriates is sent as a colony of Judeans from the Babylonian diaspora to re-inhabit the homeland (Ezr. ii)."[68] According to Bedford, the return of the *golah* community and their construction of the temple in Jerusalem are just the beginning of restoration. The Persian rulers, supporting the Babylonian diaspora community, legitimized their request for authority over the *golah* community in Yehud. The Babylonian diaspora community sustained their decisive traditions, whereas the homeland community was "undermining its identity through intermarriage with non-Judeans, whose only claim to legitimacy lies in residence in the homeland."[69] The diaspora community in Babylonia, going on the relationship between themselves and the *golah* community in Yehud, governed the homeland community. Thus, the socio-political authority lay in the Babylonian diaspora community.[70] However, Bedford does not provide any real discussion regarding the governing structure in Persian Yehud, stressing the authority of the Babylonian diaspora community. Furthermore, he considers the *golah* community simply as a subordinate group. As a result, the *golah* community is described as a sort of passive community. For Bedford, the active aspect of the *golah* community is not the main concern.[71]

Second, community identity in Persian Yehud must be understood as a process of identity formation, not as a fixed and static category. Berquist argues that community identity should be sought in the processes of imperialization and decolonization. Identity is a pattern formed by multiple forces such as religion, nationality, and ethnicity, all of which are imperializing and decolonizing. Berquist contends, "National identity is both Persian and Yehudite; what this combination means to each individual is highly fluid and always a product of internal conflict."[72] Accordingly, the questions of ethnicity, nationality, and religion are transformed into those of identity forma-

---

67. Bedford, "Diaspora," 151, 158.
68. Ibid., 153.
69. Ibid., 156.
70. Ibid., 158.
71. Cataldo also appropriately points out the deficiency of Bedford's view; in Bedford's argument, "the *golah* community did not belong to a society unique to Yehud but was a sort of satellite society of the Babylonian diaspora—the diaspora being, for Bedford, a Judean community living within a Babylonian-Persian (Elamite) society. Bedford reduces the *am ha'aretz* to Samarians and other non-Judeans, while defining 'Judean' as the Babylonian-Elamite diaspora" (Cataldo, *Theocratic Yehud*, 25–26).
72. Berquist, "Constructions of Identity," 63.

tion "as continuing *processes*," not "as fixed and static categories."[73] In this context, it would be more relevant to "speak not of identity but of identity formation."[74] Berquist concludes:

> Understanding Judean identity formation involves a complex analysis of multiple social levels with attention to numerous processes in which people internalize the forces of imperialization and decolonization. As social agents, these self-identifying Judeans together constructed a story of the development of Judah during the Achaemenid Period, as they turned their role scripts into social action and deployed themselves in patterns of ethnicity, politics, and religion, as well as myriad other complex social patterns. Such attention to identity formation necessitates deeper and more critical understandings of the forces of imperialization and decolonization and the way that these forces shape identity and difference within societies.[75]

Similarly, Jonker, noting the flexibility and complexity of ethnic and national identity in Yehud, emphasizes the multidimensional aspects of identity formation in Yehud.[76] According to Jonker, the Judahite history in the Persian period reflects a process of identity formation within multiple levels—such as the Persian imperial, regional provincial, inner-Yehudite, and cultic context, not a single socio-historical level.[77] Except for cultic context, the three dimensions are fitting to ethnic and national identity. After considering the evidence of this process in Chronicles, Jonker argues: "It is important to emphasize that these levels never functioned in isolation. The inhabitants of Yehud, and particularly the literati who were responsible for the writing of another historiography, the books of Chronicles, were exposed to all these contexts, and were active participants in all of them."[78] Thus, in Jonker's view, the focus of national and ethnic identity is on its flexibility and complexity.

Furthermore, Jonker argues for "textual identities" regarding the community identity formation in the Persian Yehud.[79] The idea of "textual identities" is related to the interaction among the social identities reflected in texts, which is based on the presupposition that "a close relationship between literature and self-understanding could be envisaged."[80] In this framework, Jonker examines the textual reflections of

---

73. Ibid., 63.
74. Ibid., 63.
75. Ibid., 64–65.
76. Jonker, "Engaging with Different Contexts," 63–93.
77. Ibid., 64–74.
78. Ibid., 73–74.
79. Jonker, "Who Constitutes Society," 703–24.
80. Ibid., 703-4. Jonker provides three insights, writing: "The notion 'textual identities' emphasizes the fluid, dynamic, and discursive nature of processes of identity formation . . . It emphasizes the close interrelationship between the social environment within which a group exists, the textual resources that are available in the given culture, and the role that renewed textual construction plays in the process of identity formation . . . It cautions us not only to take into account multiple motivational

the self-understanding in 2 Chr 10–36,⁸¹ and then he concludes that although we cannot know the actual self-understanding in the real situation at that time, this sort of study on textual identities might reveal at least the self-identity of one community within that society in the Persian era.⁸² However, Berquist's and Jonker's views do not clearly reveal the conflicts between inner communities, such as the *golah* community and the remainees in Yehud, although they indicate properly that the process of the identity formation of the Judahite community had multiple dimensions in the Persian period.

Third, community identity in Persian Yehud must be considered according to broader sociological dynamics. The social structure in Yehud has been understood as a sort of citizen-temple community. Weinberg's model of the citizen-temple community tries to explain the socio-political structure of the Levant in Yehud between the sixth and fourth centuries BCE.⁸³ According to Weinberg, the Jerusalem temple was a dominant institution; the priests of the Jerusalem temple possessed the central authority over the citizen-temple community,⁸⁴ and they even occupied significant amounts of private property in Yehud. Accordingly, the priests as a dominant ruling group governed the social, economic, and political structures in Yehud.⁸⁵

In particular, Weinberg argues that the *bet abot* ("the fathers' house") was a social structure in the Persian period, based on the *bet ab* in the pre-exilic period.⁸⁶ After the exile, the *bet abot* came to define the social identity of Yehud.⁸⁷ The Yehudite groups, which were a part of the Babylonian *golah* as the returnees to their homeland, were larger than the pre-exilic groups. In Weinberg's view, the *bet abot* group displayed a social unit or a communal unity in the Persian era.⁸⁸ However, as Levin appropriately indicates, a slight semantic change, from *bet ab* to *bet abot*, cannot prove the difference between the social-structure of pre-exilic Judah and the *golah* community in the Persian Yehud.⁸⁹

---

factors that could have contributed to the self-categorization of the Yehudite community in the late Persian period but also to view those motivational factors within a discursive framework" (704).

81. Ibid., 707–14. Jonker elsewhere suggests that in the narrative of Jehoram (2 Chr 21:2—22:1), "we see a Jerusalemite temple community in the process of negotiating a new identity" ("Textual Identities," 211, 197–217).

82. Jonker, "Who Constitutes Society," 718.

83. Weinberg, *Citizen-Temple Community*.

84. Ibid., 111–13.

85. For critiques of Weinberg's view, see Carter, *Emergence of Yehud*, 294–307; Cataldo, "Persian Policy," 240–52.

86. Weinberg, *Citizen-Temple Community*, 49–61. Weinberg defines the concept of *bet abot* as an "agnatic band which came into existence in the peculiar situation of the exile and repatriation" (61).

87. Ibid., 49 (esp. table 1).

88. Ibid., 54–55. Weinberg proposes that the terms, *bet abot* or *bet ab* do not strictly express a blood-relation but can speak of social groups which have separated from a parent group.

89. Levin, "Who Was the Chronicler's Audience," 240. See also Dyck, *Theocratic Ideology*, 188–98.

Smith-Christopher, expanding Weinberg's model, argues that the structural identity of Yehud was a survival mechanism of the Babylonian diaspora.[90] He suggests in his model that "Fourth World" people are a dominated minority[91] and that such a community develops survival mechanism and strategies. Smith-Christopher selected four cases to examine survival mechanisms of a social group in its subordinate situation: structural adaptation, the rise of new leadership, ritual, and the folklore.[92] According to him, the social structure of the Babylonian diaspora continuously affected Persian Yehud,[93] which was a social context of the *golah* community. On the basis of this understanding, he provides a possible way to understand the ideological backdrop for the exclusivist proclivities of the *golah* community. Smith considers that the exclusivism of Haggai and Ezra-Nehemiah reflects the survival mechanism.[94] Thus, he concludes, "The preservation of an identity under threat calls for 'defensive structure.' If, as we have suggested, 'ethnic identity' is preserved by conscious choice in circumstances of intercultural contact . . . then an analysis of the social mechanisms of the Judean exiles in Babylon ought to reveal creatively structured identities in order to be 'the people of God' in a foreign land."[95]

However, survival mechanism is much more diverse than the four cases he suggests. In particular, his view, based on the people of the "Fourth World" as a subordinate minority, seems to be quite oriented to helpless people. Furthermore, Smith-Christopher, arguing for the functionalist view in a frame of the materialist view, does not note that in a sociological study the functionalist view does not blend with the materialist view.[96]

In sum, the issue of community identity in Persian Yehud may be summarized by the relationship between the returnees from Babylonia to Yehud (the *golah* community) and those who remained in Yehud, the relationship of the *golah* community and the Babylonian diaspora community, community identity formation, and broad sociological dynamics in a community. These relationships between the communities reflect the struggles or conflicts between them, on which the Persian policies had influence. Accordingly, there were a variety of struggling groups in Yehud. Of the three issues of the community identity in the Persian period, I will consider the community identity formation as the Chr's key exigence since the Persian era was a transitional period from a monarchical nation to a cultic community.

---

90. Smith-Christopher, *Religion of the Landless*, 93–126.
91. Ibid., 8.
92. Ibid., 61–90.
93. Ibid., 119–20.
94. Ibid., 197.
95. Ibid., 93.
96. Ibid., 116, 144.

Possible Exigencies of the Chr

This being so, what is the Chr's exigence? It is the identity crisis of Israel after the exile, which led to the conflicts between some communities in the Persian period, especially between Judah and Benjamin. The exile seriously affected the life of the Israelites. As a result of the exile, their key identity markers disappeared and they were primarily divided into two separate communities: the *golah* community in Babylonia and the remainees' community in Judah. As time went on, the separated communities established themselves in their living places. Yet, Cyrus' edict opened a new era and affected both the *golah* community in Babylonia and the remainees in Yehud. Some of the *golah* community returned to Yehud, which brought about conflicts between the returnees from Babylonia and the remainees in Yehud. As a result, the *golah* community competed with the remainees. This competition appears to have continued until the Chr's own time.

Accordingly, the Chr would have felt the rhetorical need to present the early history of Israel to the Yehudite community in order to resolve this problem in this Persian context. In particular, the Chr would wish to resolve the conflict between the Judahites and the Benjaminites by his presentation. The Chr's rhetorical discourses reflect this conflict, which constitutes the Chr's rhetorical situation as a key exigence. In effect, as Jonker indicates it well, the Chr points to the tabernacle in Gibeon (1 Chr 16:39; 21:29; 2 Chr 1:3). The Chr appears to have intended to emphasize the close link between the Benjaminites and the Gibeon sanctuary. In comparison to Gibeon, Jerusalem as the city of David is the center of David's power, on which the first temple was built. Furthermore, it seems to be located on the border between Judah's and Benjamin's territories.[97] It meant that Jerusalem was surrounded by the Benjaminite area, which probably reflects the presence of the Benjaminites in Jerusalem in the Persian period.[98] However, the Chr's exigence goes beyond this, pointing to the essential problem in the Yehudite community.

The Yehudite community raised questions about their identity within the Persian Empire. The identity formation of the Yehudite community would have been a significant issue in the Persian era, since they experienced an identity crisis after the destruction of Jerusalem. Their identity as God's people was challenged by the exile. The Chr's contemporaries struggled with the discrepancy between their historical-theological traditions and their present situation. In the Persian era, they had to make efforts to reconstruct their community identity, shifting from a monarchical nation to a cultic community.[99] In this context, the Chr emphasizes the temple and its worship. The Chr's rhetorical problems were who should be included in the worship of YHWH, where should the place of worship be located, and who or which group

---

97. For the discussion of the border between Benjaminite and Judahite areas, see Lipschits, *Fall and Rise of Jerusalem*; "Achaemenid Imperial Policy," 19–52.

98. Jonker, "Revisiting the Saul Narrative," 300.

99. See Jonker, "Rhetorics of Finding a New Identity," 396–412 (esp. 411).

should lead the worship of YHWH.[100] The Chr attempts to provide the answers to these problems by presenting an early history of Israel. Accordingly, the Chr reveals the issue of community-identity formation in Persian Yehud. He might wish to gather the scattered people around the Jerusalem temple as the sole worship place in Israel. The Chr's rhetorical need was to reformulate their identity as marked by their worship of YHWH in the Jerusalem temple. This concern over the centrality of Jerusalem constitutes one of the most crucial rhetorical situations of the Chr. In this context, the Chr's description of the David-Solomon narrative seems to have been focused on the building of the Jerusalem temple.

Thus, the Yehudite community in the Persian period needs to be further examined through the book of Chronicles itself since the Chr retells the early history of Israel to those who lived in the Persian period. The book of Chronicles itself reflects the identity of the Yehudite community. This will be dealt with in the analysis of the speeches and prayers in the David-Solomon narrative. Now we turn to the question of who the Chr's audience was.

The Chr's Audience

As the second component of the rhetorical situation, the audience is those to whom a discourse is addressed and those who can be influenced by the discourse. If the audience is easily identified, the effectiveness of a discourse can be clearly recognized. However, we cannot know the real audience of a discourse. Rather, we can reconstruct the implied audience to some degree on the basis of the implied author's presentation. In the same way, the Chr's audience can be traced on the basis of the Chr's presentation. Thus, if the Chr's audience can be specifically defined, the effectiveness of the Chr's rhetorical discourses can be assessed to some degree. In order to discern the Chr's audience, we need to examine the textual evidences about the Chr's audience as reflected in Chronicles.

The Chr's audience was related to the Yehudite community after Cyrus had announced his decree (2 Chr 36:22–23). However, the Yehudite community in the Persian period had complicated traits, revealing conflicts among some groups in the community as mentioned above. The Chr's audience may be traced on the basis of biblical evidences.

The list of the returnees in the Chr's genealogies (1 Chr 1–9) implicitly alludes to the audience to be persuaded by the Chr's retelling of the early history of Israel (as mentioned above in the two lists for Benjamin [1 Chr 7:6–12, 1 Chr 8:1–40]). The list of the returnees (1 Chr 9:1b–34)[101] begins with a summary note (1 Chr 9:1b–3),

---

100. Langston, *Cultic Sites in the Tribe of Benjamin*, 180–200.

101. This section depicts the restored Jerusalem and its major inhabitants. As Ackroyd indicates, "The lists of names run very closely parallel to those found in Neh. 11, where the same basic material has been used to provide a picture of the Jerusalem to which Nehemiah brought a fuller population after his restoring of the city walls. The differences suggest that two forms of the same original list have

in which it is noteworthy that the Chr's unique phrase, "the first dwellers" (וְהַיּוֹשְׁבִים הָרִאשֹׁנִים, 1 Chr 9:2), alludes to the Yehudite community.[102] The summary note is followed by lists of laity in Judah (vv. 4–6), Benjamin (vv. 7–9), and clergy (vv. 10–34), distinguishing between Levites, gatekeepers, and musicians.[103] The summary note reflects a social situation of the Yehudite community in Persian Yehud.

The Chr recapitulates the genealogical section, stating that Judah was taken into exile to Babylonia due to their unfaithfulness (1 Chr 9:1b).[104] The reference to the exile in this verse at the end of the Chr's genealogies (1 Chr 1–9) predicts the reference to exile in 2 Chr 36:20 in the closing statement of the Chr's narrative section (1 Chr 10—2 Chr 36).[105]

In 1 Chr 9:2, the Chr describes "the first dwellers" in their homeland as four categories of people: Israel (probably ordinary people), the priests, the Levites, and the temple servants. According to Johnstone, 1 Chr 9:2 introduces the Chr's intention to provide "a suprahistorical interpretation"[106] of the Israelites' existence. The Chr already has employed diverse lists from different historical periods in the genealogies in 1 Chr 2-8 as though all of them were on the same time line. The Chr now provides a list of the dwellers in Jerusalem (1 Chr 9:2–17; cf. Neh 11:3–19) in the Persian period. As a result, the effect of this presentation is that the individuals of broadly different historical eras are related to one another.[107] Johnstone concludes that the Chr's purpose is "to gather together in a global manner the fullness of Israel past and present in timeless contemporaneity" and to portray "an ideal Israel in all-inclusive terms."[108] Even though his conclusion seems to be exaggerated, Johnstone provides one aspect of the nature of Israel's restoration in Chronicles. Thus, the genealogical lists (1 Chr 1-9) advance the following narrative sections, alluding to the Chr's audience.

In addition, 1 Chr 3:17–24 implicitly alludes to the Chr's audience. These verses include the genealogies of the sons of Jehoiachin (Jeconiah) after the exile, in which special attention is given to Jehoiachin by using the phrase, "the captive" (1 Chr 3:17). In particular, Jehoiachin's grandson Zerubbabel is stressed among his descendants.

---

been used in the two places; we may compare this double use with that of Ezra 2 and Neh. 7, where the same list has been used equally for two quite distinct purposes. Both these double usages are a pointer to the original independence of the Nehemiah material from the main work of the Chronicler" (Ackroyd, *I and II Chronicles*, 43).

102. See Japhet, *I & II Chronicles*, 207.

103. See Boda, *1-2 Chronicles*, 98–101.

104. The term "מַעַל," as one of the favorite words of the Chr, occurs in 1 Chr 9:1, 10:13, and 2 Chr 21:11, 13.

105. Klein, *1 Chronicles*, 265.

106. Johnstone, "Guilt and Atonement," 94.

107. It can be said that "these men of Nehemiah's time in vv. 3–17 rub shoulders with David and Samuel's appointees (the inversion of the historical Samuel and David is further evidence of the Chr's suprahistorical thinking!) in vv. 18–22" (Johnstone, "Guilt and Atonement," 94).

108. Johnstone, "Guilt and Atonement," 94.

The name of Zerubbabel, meaning "seed of Babel," reflects the state of the exiled Judahites. The genealogy after Zerubbabel is written for six generations (1 Chr 3:19–20), in which it is noteworthy that the names of Zerubbabel's sons and daughter signal the new era of restoration: "Meshullam (meaning 'recompensed' or 'restored'), Hananiah (Yahweh is gracious), Shelomith (peace), Hashubah (consideration), Ohel (tent [of Yahweh]), Berekiah (Yahweh has blessed), Hasadiah (Yahweh has shown loyalty), Jushab-hesed (let covenant loyalty be restored)."[109] Interestingly, the Chr does not mention any historical events after the genealogical list of Zerubbabel's descendants. In this regard, Zerubbabel and his genealogies indirectly describe a social situation of the early Yehudite community. Thus, the references to the list of returnees and Zerubbabel's genealogies in Chronicles allude to the Chr's audience, indicating that the Yehudite community would come to include the descendants of the returnees from Babylonia and the remainees in Yehud. The Yehudite community as the audience of the Chr needs to be considered further.

The Chr's audience was the Yehudite community, including the descendants of both those who returned from Babylonia to Yehud (of the Babylonian *golah*, 2 Chr 36:23) and those who had lived in Yehud after the exile.[110] Probably, his audience was a community that dealt with the reality of life in Persian Yehud after the fall of their nation.[111] The reconstruction of the Jerusalem temple, without the Davidic line, shows that the temple and the priestly orders would be the only hope for the community of faith in the Persian period. Nevertheless, the Yehudite community would have experienced much loss and would have been in need of future hope as the Judahites would have the experienced enduring Persian occupation of Judah.[112]

This being so, who were the returnees from Babylonia, and who were those who had remained in Judah and Jerusalem? Rom-Shiloni argues that both the *golah* community in Babylonia and the remainees in Judah developed exclusivist ideologies in the process of self-understanding by reconstructing social conflict between the communities for almost 150 years (597–432 BCE).[113] The conflict between the *golah* community and the remainees in the homeland finally came to an end with the *golah* returnees' superiority over the remainees. Her study might shed light on the

---

109. Boda, *1–2 Chronicles*, 56; Klein, *1 Chronicles*, 121. The latter five sons in the list of Zerubbabel were possibly born after his return to Jerusalem (Willi, *Die Chronik*, 117). Boda argues, "If Zerubbabel was born in approximately 575 BC, counting 20 years for each generation from that point would place the birth of the generation of Anani (3:24) in approximately 455 BC. This date would confirm the evidence of the Elephantine papyri, which are dated to 407 BC and mention the name of Anani, who would have been 48 years old at that time" (Boda, *1–2 Chronicles*, 57). See also Klein, *1 Chronicles*, 113.

110. For the situation of these two communities, see Albertz, *History of Israelite Religion*, 371–74; *Israel in Exile*, 98–111.

111. Boda, *1–2 Chronicles*, 10.

112. Ibid., 10.

113. Rom-Shiloni, *Exclusive Inclusivity*.

Chr's rhetorical situation since the descendants of these two communities would have formed the Chr's audience.

According to Rom-Shiloni, Haggai, Zechariah, and Ezra-Nehemiah significantly provide biblical evidence regarding the identity of the Yehudite community. Haggai and Zechariah (chapters 1–8) prophesied during a very short time between 522 and 520 BCE, and addressed the *golah* community, those who had returned from Babylonia to Yehud.[114] In Haggai and Zechariah, Zerubbabel and Jeshua as the leaders of the community (Hag 1:1, Zech 3–4) are the primary addressees of Zechariah's prophecies (Zech 3–4) and Heldai, Tobijah, Jedaiah, and Josiah, the son of Zephaniah, in Zech 6:9–14 are referred to as the persons who belong to the *golah* community, those "who have come from Babylon" (Zech 6:10).[115] In Ezra and Nehemiah, the returnees are mentioned as "the sons of the exile" (Ezra 4:1; 6:19, 20; 8:35) or those "who came from captivity" (Ezra 3:8), "who returned from exile" (Ezra 6:21), and "who escaped from captivity" (Neh 1:2, 3, 8:17).[116] Accordingly, the returnees from Babylonia (the *golah* community) were those who had experienced the exile, and the descendants of the *golah* community would become the Yehudite community in Persian Yehud. In this context, the posterity of the *golah* community, mentioned in Haggai, Zechariah, and Ezra-Nehemiah, would have constituted a main part of the Chr's audience.

More significantly, the book of Chronicles contains a few phrases that provide a glimpse into the identity of the Chr's audience. It is noteworthy that the Chr refers to the remnant in Chronicles. As Japhet indicates, the term שאר occurs twelve times in the book of Chronicles: שאר: 1 Chr 11:8; 16:14; 2 Chr 9:29; 24:14; שארית: 1 Chr 4:43; 12:38[39]; 2 Chr 34:9; 36:20; the *Niphal* form: נשארת: 1 Chr 13:2; 2 Chr 21:17; 30:6; 34:21, and these occurrences have no parallels in Samuel-Kings.[117] Even though the list of the term is mostly not about the remnant, Japhet considers that the idea of the remnant is a viable concept in Chronicles.[118]

According to her, the remnant idea is effectively expressed in Hezekiah's speech (2 Chr 30:6–9), in which Hezekiah begins, "O people of Israel, return to YHWH . . . so that he may return to the remnant of you who have escaped (הַפְּלֵיטָה הַנִּשְׁאֶרֶת) from the land of the kings of Assyria" (2 Chr 30:6), and ends, saying, "For as you return to YHWH, your kindred and your children will find compassion with their captors and return to this land. For YHWH your God is gracious and merciful . . ." (2 Chr 30:9). In

---

114. In particular, Zechariah employs three phrases to refer to the people: "all the people of the land" (Zech 7:5); "my people" (Zech 8:7); and "the remnant of this people" (Zech 8:6, 8). Haggai also uses these designations in 1:12–14; 2:1–4. Rom-Shiloni, *Exclusive Inclusivity*, 55.

115. Rom-Shiloni, "From Ezekiel to Ezra-Nehemiah," 137. For the discussion of the conflicts between the two communities in Haggai and Zechariah, see Rom-Shiloni, *Exclusive Inclusivity*, 48–81.

116. Rom-Shiloni, *Exclusive Inclusivity*, 9, 33–47. See also Rom-Shiloni, "From Ezekiel to Ezra-Nehemiah," 131.

117. Japhet, "Concept of the 'Remnant,'" 446.

118. Ibid., 448. She also indicates that the Chronicler clings to "hopes for their return to God through their return to the Davidic authority and the temple in Jerusalem" (448).

this context, Hezekiah refers to two distinctive groups among the people of northern Israel: the people who were exiled by the Assyrians and "the remnant of you who have escaped" (2 Chr 30:6)—the people comprising "those who survived the Assyrian assault and remained in the land."[119] In this case, the remnant means the northern Israelites who avoided the Assyrian assault (cf. 2 Chr 34:9).

The remnant also refers to "the inhabitants of Jerusalem" who were exiled from their homeland to Babylonia after the fall of Jerusalem and: "He [the king of the Chaldeans] took into exile in Babylon those who escaped from the sword" (וַיֶּגֶל הַשְּׁאֵרִית מִן־הַחֶרֶב אֶל־בָּבֶל, 2 Chr 36:20).[120] In this context, the remnant means the Judahites in Jerusalem who constituted the Babylonian *golah* after the exile, not the remnant of northern Israel. Furthermore, the phrase "those who are left in Israel and Judah" (הַנִּשְׁאָר בְּיִשְׂרָאֵל וּבִיהוּדָה, 2 Chr 34:21), which is parallel to the phrase "for the people and for all Judah" (2 Kgs 22:13), includes both the remnants of northern Israel and southern Judah.[121] It leads us to note the Chr's frequent use of the phrase "all Israel" (כָּל־יִשְׂרָאֵל) in Chronicles.

The phrase "all Israel" occurs around twenty times in the *Sondergut* passages of Chronicles.[122] Japhet points to three meanings of phrase: the whole people (2 Chr 29:24; 30:5; 35:3), northern Israel (2 Chr 11:13; 13:4, 15; 30:1, 6), and Judah as the southern kingdom (2 Chr 12:1; 24:8; 28:23).[123] Interestingly, this phrase is often found in the context of the David-Solomon narrative, stressing that the two kings ruled over the whole people (e.g., 1 Chr 11:10; 12:39; 13:5; 28:4, 8; 29:23, 25, 26).[124] Probably, the Chr's intention was to unite the scattered tribes as Israel—especially centered on Jerusalem—the united monarchy at the time of David and Solomon. Thus, the term "all Israel" in the *Sondergut* passages reveals its various dimensions and aspects. For the Chr, "all Israel" seems to have meant Israel's continuity as God's people. Japhet contends, "'Israel' is anything but a remnant. Israel in Chronicles is the people of God, who never lost his providence and grace; their existence in their land is conceived in the broadest dimensions—geographical, ethnic, political, and religious, and their history is marked by undisturbed continuity. Israel is 'all Israel' in the most comprehensive terms."[125] Accordingly, the Chr's audience was the descendants of both the Babylonian *golah* who returned to their homeland and those who were left in Judah after the exile. The phrase "all Israel" may implicitly point to all of these audiences.

---

119. Ibid., 446.

120. Ibid., 447.

121. Ibid., 448.

122. Japhet, *Ideology*, 276. Japhet points out that the most significant feature about Israel in the Chr's view is the concept of 'all Israel' in its greatest dimensions and in its various aspects (267–93).

123. Ibid., 276–77.

124. Ibid., 276.

125. Japhet, "Concept of the 'Remnant,'" 449.

The Chr's presentation depended on his audience. In this context, it can be said that Chronicles is defined as a "reforming history."[126] It means that Chronicles is an attempt to retell the early history of Israel and "an attempt to reformulate the identity of God's people in the changed socio-historical circumstances of the Late Persian era."[127] Thus, the Chr, considering the Yehudites as his audience, presents the early history of Israel, recalling the past and anticipating a hopeful future of them in the Persian period.

In sum, the Chr's audience was the Yehudite community, the cultic community, comprised of the descendants of both the returnees from Babylonia to their homeland (of the Babylonian *golah*, 2 Chr 36:23) and the Judahites who had remained in the provincial district Yehud in the Persian Empire.[128] More significantly, the Chr's audience was the Yehudite community that experienced the reality of life under the Persian ruler.

The Chr's Constraints

As the third component of the rhetorical situation, the constraints are all elements of the situation: persons, events, objects, and relations, etc. These constraints originate from the immediate (or broader) contexts of the rhetorical discourse, generally including the geographical and historical backdrop of the discourse.[129] They are capable of constraining decisions and actions necessary to change the exigence. In Chronicles, there are a number of elements that serve as constraints for the Chr. These elements not only serve as the Chr's constraints but also are able to constrain his audience's decisions and actions to change the urgent situation. In this regard, the constraints might be the limitations on the author's discourse and the audience's comprehension.[130] The Chr would have considered his and his audience's limitations when presenting something like Israelite history, in order to achieve the rhetorical purpose of his presentation. In accordance with it, the audience would understand more easily something familiar to them.

The key constraint of the Chr was Persian Yehud as a provincial district of the Persian Empire, not an independent nation. The Persian government ultimately controlled Yehud as a vassal state, which constrains the Chr's presentation and his audience's comprehension. In this context, the Chr's retelling of the early history of Israel is constrained by his audience, while the understanding of the audience is affected by the Chr's presentation. Accordingly, the constraints of the Chr and his audience appear to work together. In what follows, two examples of the Chr's constraints will be

---

126. Jonker, "Reforming History," 21–44.

127. Ibid., 24–25.

128. See Ackroyd, *The Chronicler in His Age*, 131.

129. Grant-Davie, "Rhetorical Situations," 273.

130. When we say that constraints mean limitations, they can be closely related to exigence. In effect, exigence takes place in the rhetor's constraints. See Grant-Davie, "Rhetorical Situations," 276.

Rhetorical Situation

discussed: the fulfillment of Jeremiah's prophecy for the seventy years of Sabbath rest (2 Chr 36:21) and Cyrus' decree (2 Chr 36:22–23).[131]

The Chr's constraints are the elements of the Chr's situation that may impact the achievement of his rhetorical goals. The Chr's retelling of the early history of Israel may be constrained by persons, events, objects, and relations in the Chr's situation of the Persian period. On the basis of the book of Chronicles, we might say that the fulfillment of Jeremiah's prophecy and the Cyrus' edict were key events in Israelite history that constrain the Chr's presentation, because they serve as the catalyst for the Chr's presentation. When the Chr reviews the early history of Israel, the events appear to have created his contemporary situation and have affected the life of the Yehudite community in the Persian period. Thus, we will consider Jeremiah's prophecy for the seventy years of Sabbath rest (2 Chr 36:21) and Cyrus' decree (2 Chr 36:22–23) as the main constraints of the Chr.

First, Jeremiah's prophecy of the seventy years functions as a constraint of the rhetorical discourse of the Chr. The fulfillment of Jeremiah's prophecy of the seventy-year exile is emphasized in 2 Chr 36:21. YHWH's word given to Jeremiah ("seventy years" in Jer 25:11–12 and 29:10) is fulfilled. The seventy years provide the land with the Sabbath years that had not been kept, which meant that for seventy cycles—490 years—the Sabbath years had been missed.[132]

It is noteworthy that Lev 26 assumes that Israel had not kept the Sabbath years for a long time. The consequences for breaking YHWH's commandments of the land's Sabbath are written in 26:14–33, and the final penalty meant exile and devastation (v. 34).[133] In effect, the reference to the exile as a punishment for Sabbath-breaking is mentioned in Jeremiah's (Jer 17:19–27) and Ezekiel's prophecies (e.g., Ezek. 20:1–32).[134] Accordingly, the Chr's rhetorical discourse is constrained by the reference to the fulfillment of Jeremiah's prophecy, even though the Chr looks back on the exile.

Second, the edict of Cyrus (2 Chr 36:22–23)[135] functions as a constraint of the rhetorical discourse of the Chr. Second Chronicles 36:17–21 includes the disaster of

---

131. There are other citation sources in the Chr's constraints. For instance, The Book of Kings of Israel (1 Chr 9:1; 2 Chr 20:34), The Events of the Kings of Israel (2 Chr 33:18), The Commentary on the Book of the Kings (2 Chr 24:27), The Book of the Kings of Judah and Israel (2 Chr 16:11; 25:26; 28:26; 32:32), and The Book of the Kings of Israel and Judah (2 Chr 27:7; 35:27; 36:8). In relation to these designations, Boda indicates that "none of these names match the names of the sources cited throughout Kings" (Boda, *1–2 Chronicles*, 13–15).

132. Klein, *2 Chronicles*, 545.

133. Ibid., 545.

134. Tuell, *First and Second Chronicles*, 245.

135. The edict of Cyrus is referred to three times, in 2 Chr 36:22–23; Ezra 1:1–3; and Ezra 6:1–5. Most scholars think that the edict of Cyrus was added to Chronicles later (Curtis and Madsen, *Chronicles*, 3, 525; Williamson, *1 and 2 Chronicles*, 419; De Vries, *1 and 2 Chronicles*, 423; Tuell, *First and Second Chronicles*, 9, 246; Thompson, *1, 2 Chronicles*, 392). Only Keil considers that 2 Chr 36:22–23 was repeated by the Chr himself (Keil, *Chronicles*, 515–16). See Kalimi, *Ancient Israelite Historian*, 145. In this study, I consider 2 Chr 36:22–23 as the final verses fixed in Chronicles.

Jerusalem, the destruction of the temple, and the exile; whereas, 2 Chr 36:22–23 contains Cyrus' decree of the Judahites' return to their homeland, showing a reversal of the previous two verses. These final verses, as drawn from Ezra 1:1–3,[136] stress the time of restoration and conclude the book of Chronicles with hope, serving to guide the audience's attention to the sequence.[137]

According to Kelly, the reference to Cyrus's edict is not quoted merely to provide a positive ending to the book of Chronicles (cf. 2 Chr 36:20–21). The Chr appears to emphasize that the conditions for restoration exist. In the final verses, the verb "let him go up" (וְיָעַל, the jussive form of עלה) points to an invitation to return to homeland and to worship YHWH and functions as an appeal to the Yehudite community of the Chr.[138] Thus, Cyrus's decree gives the *golah* community his permission to return to Jerusalem and to rebuild the temple. The concluding verses indicate that the *golah* community came to return to their homeland, which is "grounded in Yahweh's redemptive activity."[139]

Interestingly, the decree of Cyrus in the final verses (2 Chr 36:22–23) is expressed as direct discourse:

> . . . all the kingdoms of the earth the Lord, the God of heaven, has given to me
> (כָּל־מַמְלְכוֹת הָאָרֶץ נָתַן לִי יְהוָה אֱלֹהֵי הַשָּׁמַיִם)
>
> and he has charged me to build him a house at Jerusalem, which is in Judah
> (וְהוּא־פָקַד עָלַי לִבְנוֹת־לוֹ בַיִת בִּירוּשָׁלַם אֲשֶׁר בִּיהוּדָה)
>
> Whoever is among you of all his people, may the Lord his God be with him.
> Let him go up (מִי־בָכֶם מִכָּל־עַמּוֹ יְהוָה אֱלֹהָיו עִמּוֹ וְיָעַל)[140]

This speech of Cyrus verifies and reinforces the Chr's view of "exile as something that was overcome or bridged straightaway in the interests of the on-going story of Israel

---

136. Williamson claims that 2 Chr 36:22–23 was taken from Ezra 1:2–3 due to liturgical reasons (*1 and 2 Chronicles*, 419), whereas Redditt considers 2 Chr 36:22–23 to have been moved to Ezra 1 ("Dependence of Ezra-Nehemiah," 229–31). On the other hand, Japhet, suggesting the third source, contends that the two texts drew from the third (*I & II Chronicles*, 1076–77). I follow Williamson's view.

137. Ackroyd, *I and II Chronicles*, 209–10.

138. Kelly, *Retribution*, 188–89. Walters states the importance of this concluding word, explaining: "It is a word which, in the Chronicler's typological understanding, opens expansively towards the future in many ways: וְיָעַל intimates the great pilgrim festivals at which devout Israelites go up to Jerusalem; it expresses the wistful longing of God's people in diaspora for Jerusalem; it asserts in every age the divine presence with God's people, and calls for them to participate in 'building the LORD'S house'. Above all, it links God's gift of hope for the future with divine worship, and with human participation in it" (Walters, "Saul of Gibeon," 68).

139. Kelly, *Retribution*, 190.

140. Japhet, *I & II Chronicles*, 1076. Japhet writes, "The reversal of historical fortunes is also expressed by close affinity of literary detail. In the same way that the destruction was brought about by a foreign king, Nebuchadnezzar king of Babylon, so its reversal initiated by a foreign king, Cyrus the king of Persia. The work of these world powers is part of the divine plan in the history of Israel" (1076–77).

in its land," so that the audience "is not left to ponder the catastrophe of 587/6 and the seventy year exile but is rather hurried along into the Persian period and the restoration beyond exile."[141] According to Boda, the last verses in Chronicles represent "a proclamation that identifies the building of the temple with Cyrus, not the people. The *golah* is merely invited to 'go up.' This suggests that the implied reader is not to be associated with the community in the early Persian period, the phase in which the temple was rebuilt, but with the postconstruction community."[142] Accordingly, it indicates that the exiled community accepted imperial rule, which justifies "the present imperial reality of the Chronicler's readers, affirming the constitution (golah), activities (temple building), and polity (colony) of the Persian-period Yehudite community."[143] Thus, the decree of Cyrus is a sign of a new beginning in Israelite history.

Probably, after this proclamation of Cyrus, there would have been questions about the identity of the Judahites in the Persian period[144] now that they could return to their homeland: how could they explain the event of the exile that they had already experienced, how could they reformulate their identity in the Persian era, and how could they understand their present situation? This exigence would lead them to ask what would indeed be the relationship between God and Israel in the Persian period.

In particular, the Chr's reference to Cyrus' edict in the final verses functions as the fulfillment of God's word, especially given to Jeremiah regarding the seventy-year exile, the following destruction of Babylon (Jer 51:11), and the restoration of the Judahites (Jer 29:10; 25:11–12; 27:6–7).[145] Furthermore, Isaiah's references to Cyrus' release of the deportees (Isa 45:13) and the rebuilding of Jerusalem and the temple (Isa 66:13–14) are fulfilled.[146] Thus, the Chr, emphasizing God's will through Cyrus as God's agent, attests to many prophecies being fulfilled in the Persian era, and the edict of Cyrus functions as a constraint of the Chr by causing the deportees to return to their homeland even though he looks back on this event.

CONCLUSION

I have examined the rhetorical situation of Chronicles by the three components (exigence, audience, and constraints), indicating two layers of audience. I have dealt with the narrative situation (urgent narrative situation, the narrative audience and the narrative constraints) and the Chr's rhetorical situation (the Chr's exigence, audience, and constraints). In the narrative context, the urgent narrative situation is the motivation of the speeches and prayers of the characters in the David-Solomon narrative.

---

141. Dyck, *Theocratic Ideology*, 83.
142. Boda, "Identity and Empire," 255, n. 21.
143. Boda, "Identity and Empire," 270.
144. For the discussion of different modes of Judean identity in the Achaemenid period, see Berquist, "Constructions of Identity," 53–66.
145. Kalimi, *Ancient Israelite Historian*, 149; Williamson, *1 and 2 Chronicles*, 417–18.
146. Kalimi, *Ancient Israelite Historian*, 150–51.

The narrative audience is the addressee of the speeches and prayers. The narrative constraints are the elements in the rhetorical discourse of a character that impact on the achievement of its goal. In this context, the constraints are the limitations of the rhetorical discourses, which are the preceding events and the geographical setting. Thus, the narrative situation comprises the urgent narrative situation, the narrative audience, and the narrative constraints. Furthermore, the narrative situation as the creation of the Chr is closely related to the Chr's rhetorical situation. The Chr, through the narrative discourse, conveys his message to his audience, reflecting his concern and intention in the Persian period. Thus, we need to be familiar with the Chr's rhetorical situation in order to comprehend more clearly the Chr's retelling of the early history of Israel through the speeches and prayers in the David-Solomon narrative.

In the Chr's rhetorical situation, the possible exigencies of the Chr are the tension between the Judahites and the Benjaminites and the issue of community identity in Persian Yehud. There were struggles among the specific groups or communities (e.g., the returnees from Babylonia and the remainees in Yehud) in the late Persian period. The postexilic community, the Chr's audience, is comprised of the *golah* community and the remainees in Yehud. As the key constraint of the Chr, the Persian Yehud as a provincial district of the Persian Empire was emphasized. The references to Jeremiah's prophecy as the fulfillment of YHWH's word and the decree of Cyrus as a direct speech of the king of Persia were also offered as the examples of the Chr's constraints.

In order to respond to the urgencies in the Persian period, the Chr attempts to persuade the Yehudite community to comprehend that God made the *golah* community (the early generation of the Chr's audience) return to their homeland and rebuild the temple in Jerusalem. In particular, the Chr presents the early history of Israel, employing a number of speeches and prayers as his rhetorical devices. For instance, Cyrus' decree is also a speech as a direct discourse of the king of Persia. In this situation, the Judahites in Persian Yehud would have experienced a sort of identity crisis as God's people and the Chr would have felt the need to redefine their identity by his presentation. Accordingly, the Chr attempts to redefine the identity of the Yehudite community in the Persian era. In this regard, Gerstenberger properly states that the Chr presents to the Yehudite community under the Persian Empire "the way in which their predecessors had established and ordered their shared community of faith. The rules, rites, and structures valid now were considered to have originated mostly in the time of David and Solomon."[147] In effect, the Chr's retelling of Israelite history is focused on the David-Solomon narrative, in which the speeches and prayers are dominant rhetorical devices of the Chr to convey his messages to his audience.

---

147. Gerstenberger, *Israel in the Persian Period*, 158. He also points out that although the king functions as military commander, as was his historical role, the role does not go far. It is also diminished for the sake of the Lord's effectiveness in conflicts of foreign affairs. A king's task as an organizer of the community is much more significant (158). Furthermore, in Gerstenberger's view, "the worship-related forms of speech (prayers, speeches, oracles, sermons, etc.)," which are predominantly employed in Chronicles, "point to the early Jewish community life" (159).

Rhetorical Situation

Therefore, the Chr's rhetorical situation concerns the problems that the Yehudite community faced under Persian rule. These problems are reflected in the Chr's exigence, audience, and constraints. The Judahites in Persian Yehud wished they were still God's people, although their identity as God's people seems to have gone away after the exile. Thus, the Chr, responding to this situation, presents the early history of Israel, and he expects fitting responses from his audience, the Yehudite community.

3

Rhetorical Unit

A RHETORICAL UNIT IS a part of a text or sometimes the whole text itself. Kennedy describes one rhetorical unit as containing those characteristics.

> One rhetorical unit may be enclosed within another, building up a structure which embraces the whole book. In rhetorical criticism it is important that the rhetorical unit chosen have some magnitude. It has to have within itself a discernible beginning and ending, connected by some action or argument. Five or six verses probably constitute the minimum text which can be subjected to rhetorical criticism as a distinct unit, but most will be longer, extending for the better part of a chapter or for several chapters.[1]

A rhetorical unit is also an "argumentative unit affecting the reader's reasoning or the reader's imagination."[2] In this regard, a rhetorical unit functions as a persuasive unit, influencing or convincing the implied audience.

DETERMINATION OF A RHETORICAL UNIT

It is important to provide criteria for determining rhetorical units at the outset. We can appeal to various beginning markers and ending markers in the Hebrew Bible. These markers can be considered as one element of criteria in order to trace the author's persuasive purposes. Callow writes, "The progression of the author's thought is best seen in the light of his own grouping of his material. As the author moves towards his communicative goal, he does not do so in an undifferentiated string of clauses. The clauses will be grouped and that grouping will be controlled by the author's purpose."[3] Dorsey's beginning markers and ending markers will be employed in the present study as the criteria for determining a rhetorical unit. According to Dorsey, those markers are as follows:[4]

---

1. Kennedy, *New Testament Interpretation*, 34.
2. Wuellner, "Where is Rhetorical Criticism," 455.
3. Callow, "Units and Flow," 464.
4. Dorsey, *Literary Structure*, 22–23. See also Muilenburg, "Form Criticism," 9, 14–16; Pickering, *Framework*, 279–80; Berlin, *Poetics and Interpretation*, 102–3, 107; Bar-Efrat, "Some Observations,"

Rhetorical Unit

Beginning markers (BM)	Ending markers (EM)
1. Title	1. Summary
2. Introductory formula (e.g., "there are three things..., four things... [Prov 30:15, 18, 21, 29]; "these are the generations..." as frequently repeated in Genesis)	2. Concluding formula (e.g., "and it was evening, and it was morning..." in Gen 1, "and the land had peace for x years" in Judg 3:11, 30; 5:31; 8:28)
3. Common beginning word or phrase (e.g., "thus says YHWH," "hear," "behold," "woe," "therefore," "and now," "in that day" or "in those days" or "the days are coming," "for" or "surely"[A])	3. Conclusion (e.g., tension resolved, action completed, major character's death, and final result, etc.)
4. Vocative	4. Poetic refrain
5. Rhetorical question	5. Flashback
6. Imperative	6. Association with audience's own time (e.g., "to this day")
7. Orientation (e.g., clauses setting the stage for the upcoming narrative)	7. Poetic climactic lines or concluding exclamation
8. Abstract (narrative clauses summarizing the whole upcoming story)	8. Closing prophetic speech (e.g., "says YHWH")
9. First part of an *inclusio* or a chiasmus	9. Last part of *inclusio* or chiasmus
10. Various shifts and discourse markers[B] (e.g., time, place, characters or speaker, theme or topic, genre, narrative techniques—like shift from dialogue to narrative summary, speed of action,[C] from prose to poetry or vice versa, tense and mood or person of the verbs, etc.)	10. Various shifts and discourse markers (e.g., time, place, characters or speaker, theme or topic, genre, narrative techniques, speed of action, from prose to poetry or vice versa, tense and mood or person of the verbs, etc.)

A. Muilenburg, "Linguistic and Rhetorical Usages," 135–60.
B. For the discourse markers, see van der Merwe et al., *Biblical Hebrew*, 328–33.
C. Bar-Efrat, "Some Observations," 159–60.

Thus, by employing these markers, the range of a discourse as a rhetorical unit can be determined. I will determine several sub-rhetorical units in the Chr's description of David and Solomon by using the beginning and ending markers, noting the internal structure of the narrative of David and Solomon as a key factor to delimiting a rhetorical sub-unit in it. Before we turn to it, however, the book of Chronicles as a large rhetorical unit will be considered. In line with it, the narrative of David and Solomon will be examined as a rhetorical unit in the whole book of Chronicles below.

THE BOOK OF CHRONICLES AS A RHETORICAL UNIT

The book of Chronicles in itself functions as an argumentative unit to persuade the implied audience, constituting the large context of its sub-units. The book of Chronicles has quite a clear structure, which can be divided into three larger units by using the beginning markers and the ending markers. The first unit (1 Chr 1–9) is distinct

158–61; Kang, *Persuasive Portrayal*, 153–55.

from the second (1 Chr 10—2 Chr 9) by the change of its genre from lists (genealogies) to narrative; the second unit is separated from the third (2 Chr 10–36) by the main character's death (Solomon's death), the summary statement (forty-year reign of Solomon), and the final result (divided nation). Accordingly, it can be displayed as follows:

> 1 Chr 1–9 Genealogies from Adam to Saul's Family
> 1 Chr 10–2 Chr 9 David's and Solomon's Reign[5]
> 2 Chr 10–36 Subsequent Davidic Kings' Reign

First, 1 Chr 1–9 deals with genealogies from Adam to Saul's family, including the descendants of the twelve tribes of Israel and even the returnees from the exile. In his study on the Chr's genealogies, Sparks proposes the chiastic structure of 1 Chr 1–9,[6] in which special attention is given to the descendants of Levi (1 Chr 6:1–80, with more interest in the priesthood of Aaron and the temple musicians). In what follows, Judah and Benjamin are emphasized. The descendants of Judah (1 Chr 2:3—4:23, with the emphasis on the genealogy of David and the Davidic dynasty) and the descendants of Benjamin are placed in a symmetrical formation, surrounding the list of Levi. Interestingly, the lineage of Benjamin is displayed both in 1 Chr 7:6–12 and in 1 Chr 8:29–40 with a little variant pattern. This repetition functions to give attention to a tribe closely linked with Judah and to set up the narrative section.[7]

Second, with the Saul narrative (1 Chr 10), the narrative section begins. The backdrop of the Saul narrative is the genealogy of Saul's family (1 Chr 9:35–44), which

---

5. Even though David's narrative (1 Chr 10–29) is separated from Solomon's narrative (2 Chr 1–9) by his death notice (1 Chr 29), the two narratives are presented as a unit by the Chr's description of the temple building based on the Davidic covenant.

6. Even though Sparks' chiastic structure of 1 Chr 1–9 has subjective divisions, it shows clearly the importance of some tribes. Sparks (*The Chronicler's Genealogies*, 29) displays the structure as follows:

> A 1 Chr 1:1–53: The World before Israel
>   B 1 Chr 2:1–2: The sons of Israel
>   C 1 Chr 2:3—4:23: Judah—the tribe of King David
>   D 1 Chr 4:24—5:26: Tribes of Israel in victory and defeat
>   E 1 Chr 6:1–47: The descendant of Levi
>   F 1 Chr 6:48–49: The cultic personnel in their duties
> F^1 1 Chr 6:50–53: The cultic leaders
> E^1 1 Chr 6:54–81: The descendants of Levi in their land
> D^1 1 Chr 7:1–40: Tribes of Israel in defeat and restoration
> C^1 1 Chr 8:1–40: Benjamin—the tribe of King Saul
> B^1 1 Chr 9:1a: "All Israel" counted
> A^1 1 Chr 9:1b–34: Israel re-established

7. It is noteworthy that Ezra and Nehemiah refer to Judah and Benjamin as two key tribes in Jerusalem under the Persian rule. Ezra mentions both Judah and Benjamin together as two central tribes in Jerusalem: "When the adversaries of Judah and Benjamin heard that the returned exiles were building a temple to YHWH the God of Israel" (Ezra 4:1). Nehemiah also says that some Judahites and Benjaminites lived in Jerusalem (Neh 11:4). Nehemiah 11:7–9 contains the list of Benjaminites at that time. See Chapter 2, "Rhetorical Situation." Duke, *Persuasive Appeal*, 55.

is almost identical with the genealogy of Benjamin (1 Chr 8:29–40). David and Solomon (1 Chr 11–2 Chr 9) are portrayed as exalted kings of Israel, as many scholars have suggested that David and Solomon are idealized in the description of the Chr. However, in my judgment the David-Solomon narrative is presented as a single unit that is based on the Davidic covenant regarding temple building.

Third, the subsequent narratives (2 Chr 10–36) deal with the kings of Judah after Solomon, in which Josiah's death signals the end of the monarchial era and the beginning of exile.[8] David and Solomon provide a standard criterion for the subsequent kings of Judah. Of those kings, Jehoshaphat, Ahaz, Hezekiah and Josiah are obviously compared to David and Solomon (2 Chr 17:3; 28:1; 29:2; 34:2–3). If a king does right in the eyes of YHWH, walks in the way of righteousness, humbles himself, and seeks YHWH, the king will be blessed with military victory, wealth, prosperity, building projects, etc. However, if the king walks in the way of unrighteousness, relies upon a foreign king or nation, or forsakes YHWH, the king will be confronted by the opposite destiny.[9]

THE DAVID-SOLOMON NARRATIVE AS A RHETORICAL UNIT (1 CHR 10–2 CHR 9)

The David-Solomon narrative, as the second largest unit in the book of Chronicles contains a number of speeches and prayers. Since the focus of this study is on an analysis of the speeches and prayers in the David-Solomon narrative (1 Chr 10–2 Chr 9), the rhetorical shape of the David-Solomon narrative will be investigated, and then the speeches and prayers in this narrative will be considered.

Scholars have argued that David and Solomon's narrative should be considered as a unified one in Chronicles.[10] For instance, Williamson states that the Chr's interest is in presenting "the reign of David and Solomon as a single, united event within the divine economy for the life of the nation, in which the complementary nature of the two kings' functions plays an important role."[11] Japhet indicates that 1 Chr 10—2 Chr 9 deals with "the history of David and Solomon, presented as one period," which is depicted "as the climax of Israel's history, in which it reached its peak in both worldly

---

8. Ristau, "Reading and Rereading Josiah," 228–37. In this regard, 1 Chr 36, which begins after Josiah's death, can be regarded as a new rhetorical unit in the subsequent narratives, which also indicates that Israel became an imperial vassal kingdom after Josiah's death. In any case, the kings of Judah after Solomon can be summarized: Rehoboam (2 Chr 10–12), Abijah (2 Chr 13), Asa (2 Chr 14–16), Jehoshaphat (2 Chr 17–20), Jehoram (2 Chr 21), Ahaziah and Athaliah (2 Chr 22), Joash (2 Chr 23–24), Amaziah (2 Chr 25), Uzziah (2 Chr 26), Jotham (2 Chr 27), Ahaz (2 Chr 28), Hezekiah (2 Chr 29–32), Manasseh and Amon (2 Chr 33), Josiah (2 Chr 34–35), and three-month reign of Jehoahaz and three kings of Judah (Jehoiakim, Jehoiakin, Zedekiah) before the fall of Jerusalem (2 Chr 36).

9. See Duke, *Persuasive Appeal*, 66.

10. See Plöger, "Reden und Gebete," 56–57; Braun, "Solomonic Apologetic," 503–16; "Chosen Temple Builder," 581–90; "The Message of Chronicles," 502–14; Williamson, "Eschatology," 132, 140–1.

11. Williamson, "Eschatology," 140.

and spiritual achievements."[12] Why should David and Solomon be considered together? It can be seen by the Chr's description itself in Chronicles. In effect, David and Solomon are simultaneously referred to in some of the verses in Chronicles in comparison to those in Kings.[13]

Dual reference to David and Solomon is found first in 2 Chr 7:10 (cf. 1 Kgs 8:66). Second Chronicles 7:10 reads "... he sent the people to their tents, joyful and glad of heart for the goodness that the Lord had done *to David and to Solomon* and to Israel his people" (לְאׇהֳלֵיהֶם שְׂמֵחִים וְטוֹבֵי לֵב עַל־הַטּוֹבָה אֲשֶׁר עָשָׂה יְהוָה לְדָוִיד שִׁלַּח אֶת־הָעָם וְלִשְׁלֹמֹה וּלְיִשְׂרָאֵל עַמּוֹ); whereas, 1 Kgs 8:66 reads, "For all the good that the Lord had done *to David* his servant and to Israel his people" (עַל כָּל־הַטּוֹבָה אֲשֶׁר עָשָׂה יְהוָה לְדָוִד עַבְדּוֹ וּלְיִשְׂרָאֵל עַמּוֹ).[14] Thus, in Kings, the temple building and God's fulfilled promises are described as the Lord's goodness to David, who commences and prepares the building project; whereas, in Chronicles, David is linked with Solomon, who carries out the plan and builds the temple.

Another dual reference to David and Solomon occurs in 2 Chr 11:17: "Because they walked in the way of David and Solomon for three years" (כִּי הָלְכוּ בְּדֶרֶךְ דָּוִיד שָׁלוֹשׁ וּשְׁלֹמֹה לְשָׁנִים). In Kings, Judah's monarchs are compared with David alone; in Chronicles, David and Solomon are depicted as moral exemplars. In Japhet's view, the description in Chronicles is only possible when Solomon's faults are totally overlooked.[15]

Third, Solomon is referred to alongside David in the context of the temple building, although the Chr depicts Solomon as merely following his father David's instructions regarding temple building and organization. This is evident in 2 Chr 35:4: "And prepare by the house of your fathers according to your divisions, by the writing of David king of Israel and by the writing of Solomon his son" (וְהָכִינוּ לְבֵית־אֲבוֹתֵיכֶם יִשְׂרָאֵל וּבְמִכְתַּב שְׁלֹמֹה בְנוֹ כְּמַחְלְקוֹתֵיכֶם בִּכְתָב דָּוִיד מֶלֶךְ). Furthermore, in 2 Chr 35:3, the temple is uniquely depicted as "the house that Solomon the son of David king of Israel built" (יִשְׂרָאֵל בַּיִת אֲשֶׁר בָּנָה שְׁלֹמֹה בֶן־דָּוִיד מֶלֶךְ).[16]

Fourth, the David and Solomon narrative have the same patterns in the narrative framework. It is noticeable that Street, in his study of the literary artistry of the ark narrative in Chronicles, refers to the fact that there is a similar pattern between 1 Chr 15 and 2 Chr 5.[17] According to Street's observation, both David and Solomon

---

12. Japhet, "Postexilic Historiography," 159.

13. Japhet, *Ideology*, 375.

14. Ibid., 375. Italics Japhet's.

15. Ibid., 375.

16. Ibid., 375.

17. According to Street, the parallels between these two accounts are significant enough to be able to say that "the Chronicler was not merely interested in David as a royal political figure, but also as a king who was concerned for the cult. Such parallels show that the two passages draw upon the same elements, which ultimately reveal that the proper function of the cult is the primary concern of the Chronicler." See Street, *Significance*, 65.

first of all assemble various leaders of Israel to bring the ark of the covenant of YHWH from the house of Obed-edom (1 Chr 15:16) and then from the city of David (2 Chr 5:2). Second, the ark is transferred into the city of David (1 Chr 15:28–29) and then into the most holy place of the temple (2 Chr 5:7). Third, both of them, including all the assembly of Israel, sacrifice before the ark (1 Chr 15:26; 2 Chr 5:6). Fourth, music accompanies the transferring of the ark (1 Chr 15:28; 16:7–36; 2 Chr 5:11). Finally, the priests and the Levites sanctify themselves (1 Chr 15:14; 2 Chr 5:11).[18] Braun also notes that the Chr's description of Solomon is essentially similar to that of David: (1) both David and Solomon ascend to the throne of YHWH by "the divine choice"; (2) both of them gain "the unanimous consent of all Israel"; (3) and both give their wholehearted dedication to the temple and cult.[19] However, Street and Braun do not mention how this pattern works together in Chronicles. This pattern stresses two kings' key roles in the building of the temple in Jerusalem. Thus, the David-Solomon narrative must not be regarded as being separated from one another. Rather, the narrative of two kings should be considered as a large rhetorical unit in Chronicles.

Review of the Structure of the Narrative of David and Solomon

First of all, it is necessary to determine a few sub-rhetorical units as argumentative units in the David-Solomon narrative. The literary structure is "the network of relations among the parts of an object or a unit,"[20] which can be found by observing the patterns of a text (e.g., chiasm, motif, alternation, *inclusio*, etc.). Although the literary structure of a text is not identical to the arrangement of its arguments, it has some value for a rhetorical study. The structure of a text or discourse is rhetorical in that it can be one element that affects the implied audience.[21]

Past scholarship has analyzed the structure of the David-Solomon narrative. Some scholars suggest three divisions of the book of Chronicles, regarding the David and Solomon narrative as one time of the united monarchy in the history of Israel. For instance, Braun identifies the book of Chronicles as three parts: genealogical prologue (1 Chr 1–9), the united monarchy (1 Chr 10–2 Chr 9), and the divided monarchy (2 Chr 10–36), in which the united monarchy comprises the David-Solomon narrative, including the short narrative of Saul (1 Chr 10).[22] In the part of the united monarchy,

---

18. Ibid., 65.
19. Braun, "Solomonic Apologetic," 511.
20. Bar-Efrat, "Some Observations," 155.
21. Ibid., 172.
22. See Braun, *1 Chronicles*, xli. Braun divides 1 Chr 10–2 Chr 9 as follows:

A. The David history, chaps. 10–21
   1. The death of Saul, chap. 10
   2. The rise of David, chaps. 11–12
   3. David, the Ark, and the cult, chaps. 13–17
   4. David's wars, chaps. 18–21

1 Chr 13–17 is considered as one sub-unit, in which Braun includes the ark narrative (1 Chr 13–16) and God's covenant with David (1 Chr 17). First Chronicles 18–21, as another sub-unit, contains the census narrative (1 Chr 21) and David's wars (1 Chr 18–20). First Chronicles 22–29 is regarded as a transitional sub-unit to link David's narrative to the ensuing narrative of Solomon (2 Chr 1–9).[23] In Braun's view, David and Solomon's narrative are "presented as complementary, representing a single unit with its focus upon the temple."[24] It is noteworthy that Braun views 1 Chr 22–29 as a transitional part between the accounts of David and Solomon. Accordingly, 1 Chr 10—2 Chr 9 as the David-Solomon narrative shapes a large rhetorical unit in Chronicles. However, he does not distinguish the ark narrative (1 Chr 13–16) and the Davidic covenant (1 Chr 17). Probably, for Braun the Davidic covenant appears to be the final result of the ark narrative.

On the other hand, other scholars suggest four divisions of the book of Chronicles, considering the David narrative and the Solomon narrative as two sub-units. For instance, Klein divides the book of Chronicles into four parts, based on the genealogies of the kings of Judah: genealogies (1 Chr 1–9), the reign of David (1 Chr 10–29), the reign of Solomon along with the emphasis on the building of the temple (2 Chr 1–9), and the reigns of the kings of Judah (2 Chr 10–36).[25] In Klein's view, 1 Chr 21–29, beginning with the census narrative (1 Chr 21), comprises the narrative of David's preparations for the temple building (1 Chr 22–29).[26] Accordingly, Klein does not distinguish David's census and David's preparation for the building of the temple. He appears to regard the census narrative as an introduction of 1 Chr 21–29. Tuell also divides 1 Chr 10—2 Chr 9 as two narratives: the David narrative (1 Chr 10–29) with Saul's death as its prologue (1 Chr 10) and Solomon narrative (2 Chr 1–9). According to him, the David narrative has three crucial movements: the proclamation of David's kingship by all Israel (1 Chr 11:1—12:40); David's achievements and his failures (1 Chr 13:1—21:30); David's final act (1 Chr 22:1—29:30).[27] The Solomon narrative is

   B.   Transitional Unit, chaps. 22–29
       1.   David's first speech, chap. 22
       2.   Secondary arrangements, chaps. 23–27
       3.   David's speeches, blessing, and death, chaps. 28–29

   C.   The Solomon history, 2 Chr 1–9

On the other hand, Boda divides 1 Chr 10–2 Chr 9 into two parts: David's account (1 Chr 10–29) and Solomon's account (2 Chr 1–9), providing in detail almost chapter by chapter (*1-2 Chronicles*, 19–20).

23. Braun, *1 Chronicles*, xli.
24. Ibid., xli.
25. Klein, *1 Chronicles*, 49–50; *2 Chronicles*, 12–13.
26. Klein, *1 Chronicles*, 49.
27. Tuell, *First and Second Chronicles*, 42. Tuell, here, modifies Wright's view in a slightly different way. See Wright, "The Founding Father," 49–59.

divided into three parts: Solomon's becoming king (2 Chr 1:1–17); Solomon's building of the temple (2 Chr 2:1—7:22); Solomon's reign (2 Chr 8:1—9:31).[28]

In a slightly different way, Williamson divides the book of Chronicles into four parts, based on the characters: genealogies (1 Chr 1–9), the united monarchy (1 Chr 10–2 Chr 9), the divided monarchy (2 Chr 10–28), and Hezekiah to the Babylonian exile (2 Chr 29–36).[29] In Williamson's division, it is noteworthy that the subsequent narratives (2 Chr 10–36) are divided into two parts (2 Chr 10–28 and 29–36) by Hezekiah's era as a turning point in Israelite history. Williamson proposes an outline of the David–Solomon narrative as united monarchy, in which three sub-sections are identified by the three kings of Israel: Saul (1 Chr 10:1–14); David (1 Chr 11–29); and Solomon (2 Chr 1–9).[30] However, it is not clearly explained why he views 2 Chr 8:1–16 as the concluding appendix to the building of the temple.[31]

Interestingly, De Vries identifies the book of Chronicles as three parts. But, he leaves out the genealogical part (1 Chr 1:1—9:34) and emphasizes the ensuing two parts by noting the theological theme of YHWH's nation and the temple: the account of establishing YHWH's nation and temple (1 Chr 9:35—2 Chr 9:31) and the account of bringing wrath on YHWH's temple and nation (2 Chr 10—36:23).[32] He proposes an extended view on the David and Solomon narrative. It is interesting that the first part (1 Chr 9:35—2 Chr 9:31), comprised of the David-Solomon narrative, begins with Saul's genealogy (1 Chr 9:35–44).[33] In this first part, two sub-units are identified: the reinforcement of David rule (1 Chr 9:35—21:27) and the temple building (1 Chr 21:28—2 Chr 9:31).[34] Accordingly, De Vries views the structure of the David-Solomon narrative as characterized by a theological theme: YHWH's nation and temple. However, this division interferes with seeing the inner flow of the David-Solomon narrative.

Dorsey, on the other hand, suggests the outline of the David-Solomon narrative by appeal to two chiastic structures. The David narrative (1 Chr 10–29) is divided into two parts: the establishment of David's kingdom (1 Chr 10:1—22:1) and David's preparations for the building of the temple (1 Chr 22:2—29:30). According to Dorsey,

---

28. Tuell, *First and Second Chronicles*, 116.

29. Williamson, *1 and 2 Chronicles*, 34–35. He considers David and Solomon's narrative as the united monarchy like Braun.

30. Ibid., 35.

31. Ibid., 227.

32. De Vries, *1 and 2 Chronicles*, 96–97.

33. In line with it, Knoppers considers 1 Chr 9:35—10:14 as Saul's reign (Knoppers, *I Chronicles*, 515–16); Johnstone, identifying 1 Chr 9:35—10:14 as Saul's narrative, separates it from David's and Solomon's narratives (1 Chr 11–2 Chr 9) (Johnstone, *1 and 2 Chronicles*, 1:138–9). With respect to Solomon's narrative (2 Chr 1–9), Johnstone discerns two parts of twenty years: the first twenty years is concerned with the temple building (2 Chr 1–7) and the second with his international fame (2 Chr 8–9) (1:294–95).

34. De Vries, *1 and 2 Chronicles*, 96–97.

the first part ends with 1 Chr 22:1 and the second part begins with 1 Chr 22:2.³⁵ The first part is primarily composed of two accounts of the location of the temple.³⁶ This part is comprised of seven chiastic sub-units, placing David's bringing the ark to Jerusalem accompanied by the priests and the Levites as the center of the chiasm.³⁷ Thus, the focus in the first part is on the temple.³⁸ The second part also contains seven sub-units arranged symmetrically.³⁹ The focus in the second part is on the priests.⁴⁰ Thus, Dorsey concludes in the second part that the Chr again stresses "the importance of the temple, priests, and Levites by structuring the entire unit so that it begins, ends, and centers on this theme."⁴¹ However, Dorsey does not explain why the ark narrative (1 Chr 13–15), occupying the center in the first-part, is emphasized more than the

35. Dorsey (*Literary Structure*, 147) outlines 1 Chr 10:1—22:1 as follows:

a David becomes king and captures Jerusalem (where the future temple will be) from the Jebusites (10:1—11:9)
  b military exploits of David and his soldiers (11:10—12:40 [11:10—12:41])
    c David wishes to bring Yahweh's ark to Jerusalem but is prevented (13:1—14:17)
      d CENTER: ark brought to Jerusalem; role of Levites and priests in the celebration (15:1—16:43)
    c' David wishes to build Yahweh's house (בית) in Jerusalem but is prevented (17:1-27)
  b' military exploits of David and his soldiers (18:1—20:8)
a' David acquires the future temple mount from Araunah the Jebusite (21:1—22:1)

36. Ibid., 146. Street also considers that the David narrative has two sections, regarding 1 Chr 10 as an attachment to the David narrative: "the founding of the Davidic dynasty" (1 Chr 11—22:1) and "David's final organization of the cult, instructions regarding the temple, and the organization of the government" (1 Chr 22:2—29:30) (Street, *Significance*, 113).

37. Dorsey, *Literary Structure*, 146-7.

38. Dorsey concludes the first section with this statement: "The unit's overall symmetric arrangement serves to highlight the central importance of the temple. While David's other accomplishments are also recounted in the unit, David's activities involving the temple are emphasized by being placed at the beginning, in the middle, and at the end. This structural design reflects the author's agenda—to encourage the postexilic community to pay attention to the temple as King David did" (Ibid., 146).

39. Ibid., 146-7. Some beginning markers are recognized in the second section of David's reign: the appearance of Solomon; the shift in focal point (from an account of David's reign [1 Chr 10-21] to David's preparation for building of the temple [1 Chr 22-29]); the shifts in the speed of action (no action is actually shown in 1 Chr 22-29).

40. Dorsey (Ibid., 147) outlines 1 Chr 22:2—29:30 as follows:

a David assembles people and gives speech to Solomon and people concerning the temple (22:2-19)
  b civil ruler: David's appointment of Solomon as king (23:1)
    c Levites: their duties assisting the priests (23:2-32)
      d CENTER: priests and their duties (24:1-19)
    c' Levites: their duties as musicians and gatekeepers (24:20—26:32)
  b' civil rulers: David's appointment of government officials (27:1-34)
a' David assembles people and gives speech to Solomon and people concerning the temple; David's death (28:1—29:30)

41. Ibid., 147.

Rhetorical Unit

Davidic covenant (1 Chr 17). Recently, Berger proposes a chiastic structure of 1 Chr 17–29 as follows:[42]

> A Divine speech: David's successor must build temple; David's prayer (chapter 17)
>   B Bloodshed disqualifying David from building temple:
>   Wars
>   Fatal census (conducted over Joab's objection) (chapters 18–21)
>   X Citation of divine speech: Solomon must build temple,
>   for David "spilled much blood and waged many wars" (chapter 22)
>   B' David's preparations for building of temple:
>   Organization of cult
>   Proper census (fatal census now attributed to Joab) (chapters 23–27)
> A' Citation of divine speech: Solomon must build temple; David's speeches and prayer (chapters 28–29)

In the case of Berger's divisions, 1 Chr 17–29 is regarded as one rhetorical unit, and 1 Chr 17 seems to function as the introduction of the unit. Dorsey emphasizes the ark narrative in relation to the temple service; whereas, Berger stresses the divine speech in relation to the building of temple. Accordingly, it is not possible to clearly explain the discrepancy between the structures that scholars propose. We only recognize the criteria and reasons for their divisions.

Dorsey also views the Solomon narrative (2 Chr 1–9) as a chiastic structure with seven-fold symmetry,[43] in which Solomon's building of the temple is placed at the center. In this structure, the building of the temple is emphasized as the most significant achievement of Solomon.[44] Two further proposals of the structure of the Solomon narrative are noteworthy. Dillard and Selman also provide the literary structure of the Solomon narrative, focusing on building of the temple. Dillard suggests a chiastic structure of the Solomon narrative in its own unity, which can be briefly outlined as follows:[45]

> A Solomon's wealth and wisdom (1:1–17)

---

42. See Berger, "Chiasm and Meaning," 27.
43. According to Dorsey (Ibid., 148), 2 Chr 1–9 can be outlined as follows:

> a Solomon's wisdom and wealth (1:1–17)
>   b Solomon's foreign relations with Hiram of Tyre (2:1–18 [1:18—2:17])
>   c Solomon builds the temple (3:1—5:1)
>   d CLIMAX: dedication of the temple (5:2—7:10)
>   c' God accepts the temple (7:11–22)
>   b' Solomon's foreign relations with Hiram of Tyre and queen of Sheba (8:1—9:12)
> a' Solomon's wisdom and wealth (9:13–28)
> conclusion: Solomon's death (9:29–34)

44. Ibid., 148.
45. Dillard, "Literary Structure," 87–88.

B Recognition by gentiles/ dealings with Hiram (2:1–16)
      C Temple construction/ gentile labor (2:17—5:1)
         D Dedication of temple (5:2—7:10)
         D´ Divine response (7:11–22)
      C´ Other construction/ gentile labor (8:1–16)
   B´ Recognition by gentiles/ dealings with Hiram (8:17—9:12)
A´ Solomon's wealth and wisdom (9:13–28)

Selman proposes that the structure of the Solomon narrative is displayed in a brief outline as follows:[46]

A 1:1–17 Solomon's wisdom, wealth and fame
   B 1:18–2:17 Solomon prepares for the temple
      C 3:1—5:1 Construction of the temple
      C´ 5:2—7:22 Dedication of the temple
   B´ 8:1–16 Solomon completes the temple and other building works
A´ 8:17—9:28 Solomon's wisdom, wealth and fame

According to these scholars, the emphasis is on the dedication of the temple (2 Chr 5:2—7:22). In this regard, their views on the structure of the Solomon narrative are similar to Dorsey's. Thus, there seems to be a scholarly agreement regarding the structure of the Solomon narrative in Chronicles.

In sum, scholars' proposals of the structure of the David-Solomon narrative contain—to considerable degree—their own subjective divisions.[47] However, their analyses can be very helpful in determining a rhetorical unit, because any proposal of the structure of a text can be temporarily provided as a tool for understanding the text. Accordingly, as most scholars agree, the range of the David-Solomon narrative is 1 Chr 10–2 Chr 9.[48] This large rhetorical unit, comprising several sub-rhetorical units, can be divided into two parts by the main characters: the David narrative (1 Chr 10–29) and the Solomon narrative (2 Chr 1–9). In my judgment, the rhetorical units in a narrative can be identified by the beginning and ending markers in the narrative as mentioned above. Although those markers are not absolute criteria to delimit the boundaries of rhetorical units in the narrative, we can figure out several sub-units with the beginning and ending markers, since the internal structure is key to delimiting a rhetorical unit in the narrative.

46. Selman, *2 Chronicles*, 285–86.

47. Boda provides "a list of the most frequent errors of rhetorical analysts who have claimed chiastic structures in Hebrew compositions" ("Chiasmus in Ubiquity," 56), which includes errors in symmetry, subjectivity, probability, and purpose. See Boda, "Chiasmus in Ubiquity," 55–70.

48. First Chronicles 9 deals with the lists of the dwellers in Jerusalem after the exile (vv. 3–13), Levitical families (vv. 14–34), and Saul's family (vv. 35–44). Then the narrative section (1 Chr 10:1) begins with telling Saul's fighting against the Philistines and ends with referring to his death. Thus, the narrative flow in Chronicles shifts from the lists to narrative section. Accordingly, 1 Chr 10 can be a rhetorical unit. In this study, I consider it as the introduction of David's and Solomon's narratives, following Zalewski. See Zalewski, "Purpose of the Story of the Death of Saul," 449–67.

Rhetorical Unit

Sub-Rhetorical Units in the David-Solomon Narrative

The David narrative (1 Chr 10:1—29:30) begins with Saul's death (chapter 10). It is made of two disjunctive parts: the account of the establishment of David's kingdom (1 Chr 10:1—22:1) and his preparation for building the temple (22:2—29:30). Each part has several rhetorical sub-units. The account of the establishment of David's kingdom has eight rhetorical sub-units. First, David ascends the throne of Israel (chs. 11–12); David's ascension to the throne (11:1–3) functions as the beginning marker (BM 10, various shifts) and its celebration (12:38–40) as the ending marker (EM 3, conclusion). This sub-unit also forms an *inclusio* (BM 9 and EM 9), with an event occurring at Hebron (David becoming king over all Israel). Second, David brings the ark to Jerusalem (chs. 13–16); David's initiative to transfer the ark to Jerusalem (13:1–3) functions as the beginning marker (BM 7, orientation; BM 10), and all people and David going home after the ark is placed in a tent in Jerusalem (16:43) as the ending marker (EM 3). This sub-unit—the so-called ark narrative—has a clear narrative progression. Third, YHWH's promise to David is given through Nathan the prophet in connection with the temple (ch. 17). This sub-unit begins with the phrase "it came to pass . . ." (v. 1, BM 10, shift in time) and closes with the adverbial phrase "and now" (v. 27, EM 10, literally "and now" but "therefore" as the discourse marker). Fourth, David gains various materials for the building of the temple in his wars against the neighboring nations (chs. 18–20); in this pericope, another phrase "it came to pass . . ." (18:1), functions as the beginning marker (BM 10) and the complete action of David's wars (20:8) as the ending marker (EM 3, final result of event). Fifth, David obtains the temple site (21:1—22:1); David's census-taking (21:1) functions as the beginning marker (BM10, shift in theme), and David's announcement that "this shall be the house of YHWH God and the altar of burnt offering for Israel" after YHWH's choice of the temple site (22:1) functions as the ending marker (EM 3, the concluding remark of the census narrative). Sixth, David prepares for the temple building (22:2–19); his preparation of building materials (vv. 2–5) functions as the beginning marker (BM 10, shift in theme) and David's charging all the leaders of Israel to build the temple (vv. 17–19) as the ending marker (EM 3, the concluding remark of his preparation). Seventh, David organizes the temple personnel, who would attend to the temple service (chs. 23–27); the beginning marker (BM 10, shift in time) is the phrase "David is old and satisfied with days" (23:1) and the ending marker (EM 10, shift from narrative to list) is the list of David's counselors (27:32–34). Finally, David urges the people of Israel and Solomon to build the temple (chs. 28–29); David's assembling of all the officials of Israel (28:1) functions as the beginning marker (BM 10, shift from the list to narrative) and the summary statement of the reign of David (29:26–30) as the ending marker (EM 3, the summary statement and the death of the main character).

The Solomon narrative (2 Chr 1–9) is comprised of six rhetorical sub-units. First, Solomon's greatness in wisdom and wealth (ch. 1) is described; the summary statement (v. 1) functions as the beginning marker (BM 3, narrative clause summarizing the upcoming story) and the description of Solomon's wealth (vv. 16–17) as the ending marker (EM 3, conclusion). Second, Solomon actually prepares for the building of the temple (ch. 2); the same phrase "70,000 burden-bearers and 80,000 stonemasons in the mountain and 3,600 overseers" (1:18 [2:1] and 2:17[18]) forms an *inclusio*, BM 9 and EM 9. Third, Solomon constructs the temple (chs. 3–4); the temple building is begun and completed (3:1; 5:1). The whole event of building temple functions as the beginning and ending marker (BM3 and EM3, the building of the temple in theme). Fourth, Solomon dedicates the temple (chs. 5–7); Solomon's initiative to transfer the ark (5:2) functions as the beginning marker (BM 7) and God's acceptance of the temple (7:12–22) as the ending marker (EM 3). This unit deals with the first and last events in the account of the dedication of the temple. Fifth, Solomon's achievement is described (ch. 8). In this sub-unit, the phrase "it came to pass at the end of twenty years" (v. 1) functions as the beginning marker (BM 10), and the ending marker (EM 3) is the concluding statement, "The house of YHWH was completed" (v. 16). Finally, Solomon's great wealth is again emphasized along with his international fame (ch. 9); the depiction of Solomon's wealth forms an *inclusio* with that in the account of Solomon's reign (ch. 1). The depiction of his wealth (8:17) functions as the beginning marker (BM 10, shift in time) and the summary statement of Solomon's reign (9:29–31) as ending marker (EM 3, his forty-year reign and his death).

In particular, the Chr's depiction of Solomon is parallel to that of David. The account of David's reign ends with "a formulaic summary of David's reign, death, and burial, with a reference to further written sources about David (1 Chron. 29:26–30)."[49] Solomon's reign also ends with a similar summary statement of David's reign (2 Chr 9:29–31). Accordingly, these summary statements serve to frame the David and Solomon narrative as two sub-rhetorical units in the whole narrative of David and Solomon. Thus, the rhetorical unit of David's and Solomon's narrative can be summarized as below:

David's Reign (1 Chr 11–29)		
Chs. 11–12	David's ascension to the throne	Beginning: David's anointing as king of all Israel at Hebron (11:1–3)
[BM 9, 10] [EM 3, 9]		End: the celebration of making David king over all Israel at Hebron (12:39–41[Eng. 38–40])
		(an *inclusio* by an event at Hebron)
Chs. 13–16	David's transfer of the ark to Jerusalem	Beginning: David's initiative to transfer the ark to Jerusalem (13:1–3)
[BM 7, 10] [EM 3]		End: after the ark placed in the tent, all the people and David went home (16:43)
		(narrative sequence of the ark narrative)

---

49. Dorsey, *Literary Structure*, 148.

Rhetorical Unit

Ch. 17 [BM 10] [EM 10]	The Davidic covenant	Beginning: "It came to pass when David dwelt in his house" (17:1, וַיְהִי כַּאֲשֶׁר יָשַׁב דָּוִיד בְּבֵיתוֹ) End: "And now" (lit.) (17:27, וְעַתָּה) (וְעַתָּה also occurs in 17:7, 23, 26, 27)
Chs. 18–20 [BM 10] [EM 3]	David's wars	Beginning: "It came to pass after this" (וַיְהִי אַחֲרֵי־כֵן, 18:1) End: the descendants of giants in Gath fell by David and his commanders (20:8) (a complete action of David's wars)
21—22:1 [BM 10] [EM 3]	David's census and the temple site	Beginning: Satan incited David to take a census (21:1) End: "This shall be the house of YHWH God..." (זֶה הוּא בֵּית יְהוָה הָאֱלֹהִים..., 22:1)
22:2–19 [BM 10] [EM 3]	David's preparation for the temple building	Beginning: David preparation of building material (22:2–5) End: David's charge to all the leaders of Israel (22:17–19)
Chs. 23–27 [BM 10] [EM 10]	David's organization of clergy and other leaders	Beginning: "David is old and satisfied with days" (23:1, וְדָוִיד זָקֵן וְשָׂבַע יָמִים) End: the list of David's counselors (27:32–34) (time sequence and enumerating name list)
Chs. 28–29 [BM 10] [EM 3]	David's final speeches and actions	Beginning: David assembled all the leaders at Jerusalem (28:1) End: summary statement of David's reign (29:26–30)

Solomon's Reign 2 Chr 1–9		
1:1–17 [BM 3] [EM 3]	Solomon's wisdom and wealth	Beginning: summary statement of Solomon's greatness (1:1) End: Solomon's wealth (1:16–17)

1:18—2:17 [2:1–18] [BM 9] [EM 9]	Solomon's preparation for the temple building	Beginning: Solomon's building project (1:18[2:1]) וַיִּסְפֹּר שְׁלֹמֹה שִׁבְעִים אֶלֶף אִישׁ סַבָּל וּשְׁמוֹנִים אֶלֶף אִישׁ חֹצֵב בָּהָר וּמְנַצְּחִים עֲלֵיהֶם שְׁלֹשֶׁת אֲלָפִים וְשֵׁשׁ מֵאוֹת (Solomon counted 70,000 men burden-bearers and 80,000 men stonemasons in the mountain, and overseers over them 3,600; 2:1[2:2]) וַיַּעַשׂ מֵהֶם שִׁבְעִים אֶלֶף סַבָּל וּשְׁמֹנִים אֶלֶף חֹצֵב בָּהָר וּשְׁלֹשֶׁת אֲלָפִים וְשֵׁשׁ מֵאוֹת מְנַצְּחִים לְהַעֲבִיד אֶת־הָעָם (He made them 70,000 burden-bearers and 80,000 stonemasons in the mountain and 3,600 overseers to make the people work; 2:17[18]) End: Solomon's assignment of laborers (2:17[18]) (*inclusio*, 2:1[2] and 2:17[18])
3:1—5:1 [BM 3] [EM 3]	Solomon's building of the temple	Beginning: "Solomon began to build the house of YHWH . . . ." (3:1) (וַיָּחֶל שְׁלֹמֹה לִבְנוֹת אֶת־בֵּית־יְהוָה) End: "all the work that Solomon did for the house of YHWH was finished . . . ." (5:1) (וַתִּשְׁלַם כָּל־הַמְּלָאכָה אֲשֶׁר־עָשָׂה שְׁלֹמֹה לְבֵית יְהוָה)
5:2—7:22 [BM 7] [EM 3]	The dedication of the temple	Beginning: Solomon's initiative to transfer the ark to the temple (5:2) Ending: God's acceptance of the temple (7:12–22)

Rhetorical Unit

8:1–16 [BM 10] [BM 3]	Solomon's achievements	Beginning: "It came to pass at the end of twenty years that Solomon had built the house of YHWH and his house" (8:1) (וַיְהִי מִקֵּץ עֶשְׂרִים שָׁנָה אֲשֶׁר בָּנָה שְׁלֹמֹה אֶת־בֵּית יְהוָה וְאֶת־בֵּיתוֹ) End: "all the work of Solomon was prepared until the day of the foundation of the house of YHWH and until its completion, the house of YHWH was completed" (8:16) (וַתִּכֹּן כָּל־מְלֶאכֶת שְׁלֹמֹה עַד־הַיּוֹם מוּסַד בֵּית־יְהוָה וְעַד־כְּלֹתוֹ שָׁלֵם בֵּית יְהוָה) (time and concluding statement)
8:17—9:31 [BM 10] [EM 3]	Solomon's great wealth and international fame	Beginning: Solomon's wealth (8:17) End: summary statement of Solomon's reign (9:29–31)

Thus, we can see that David's narrative has eight sub-rhetorical units and Solomon's narrative six sub-rhetorical units from the beginning and ending markers, which can be categorized as *inclusio*, shift in time, and summary statements.[50] Altogether, the David-Solomon narrative entirely has fourteen sub-rhetorical units, in which there are a number of speeches and prayers.

Speeches and Prayers in the David-Solomon Narrative

The David-Solomon narrative comprises a number of speeches and prayers uttered by the characters. A number of scholars have addressed the speeches and prayers of David and Solomon.[51] For instance, Throntveit identifies the speeches of David and Solomon (1 Chr 11:17, 19; 13:2–3, 12; 14:11; 15:2, 12–13; 17:1; 19:2, 5; 22:1; 22:5; 22:7–13, 14–16; 22:17–19; 23:25–32; 28:2–10; 28:20–21; 29:1–5, 20; 2 Chr 2:2[3]–9[10]; 6:1–2, 4–11; 8:11)[52] and six prayers (1 Chr 14:10a; 17:16–27; 21:8; 21:17; 2 Chr 1:8–10; 6:14–42).[53] Duke identifies twelve speeches of David and Solomon (1 Chr 12:17; 13:2–3; 22:7–16;

---

50. Scholars have suggested slightly different divisions in the David-Solomon narrative. For instance, De Vries identifies the building of the temple (1 Chr 21:28—2 Chr 9:31) as three: 1 Chr 21:28—22:19; 23:1—29:30; 2 Chr 1:1—9:31 (*1 and 2 Chronicles*, 97). Japhet, considering 1 Chr 13–17 as one unit, divides 2 Chr 8–9 as four: 8:1–18; 9:1–12, 13–28, 29–31 (*I & II Chronicles*, 12–13). Hill also views 1 Chr 13–17 as one unit (*1 & 2 Chronicles*, 51). Klein considers 1 Chr 10–12 as one unit in that 1 Chr 10:14 and 29:26–30 "bracket the beginning and ending of David's reign" (*1 Chronicles*, 49).

51. See the Introduction for the history of research on kings' speeches and prayers.

52. Throntveit, *When Kings Speak*, 11–50; "The Chronicler's Speeches," 228–9. However, Throntveit does not deal with other speeches of David (1 Chr 21:8–13, 17, 24; 29:10–19).

53. Throntveit, *When Kings Speak*, 51–61. His four criteria of prayer are words on the lips of the king, directly reported discourse, unique to the Chr, and significantly changed in the case of the parallel in the *Vorlage* (51–52).

22:18–19; 28:2–8; 28:9–10; 28:20–21; 29:1–5; 2 Chr 2:3–10; 2:11–16; 6:1–11; 9:5–8)[54] and five prayers (1 Chr 17:16–27; 21:8; 21:17; 29:10–19; 2 Chr 6:14–42).[55] Mason only deals with eight addresses in the David-Solomon narrative (1 Chr 12:19[18]; 13:2–3; 15:2, 12–13; 22:6–16; 22:17–19; 28:2–10; 28:20–21; 29:1–5, 20).[56] However, they do not deal with any other speeches in the David-Solomon narrative. For instance, the divine speeches (e.g., 2 Chr 1:7, 11–12; 7:12–22) and foreign royal figures' speeches (e.g., Huram [2 Chr 2], the queen of Sheba [2 Chr 9]) are not examined. The divine speeches as well as the speeches and prayers of David and Solomon play significant roles in the Chr's portrayal of David and Solomon, and the foreign kings' speeches also serve to his portrayal of them. Thus, all speeches and prayers in the David-Solomon narrative will be examined in this study, which is outlined as below.

Rhetorical Unit	Speeches and Prayers
1 Chr 11–12	A speech of the Israelites to David (11:1–2)
	The Jebusites' and David's speech (11:5a, 6a)
	David's speeches in the account of the mighty warriors (11:17,19)
	David's speech and Amasai's response (12:17–19[16–18])
	The Philistine rulers' speech (12:20b[19b])
1 Chr 13–16	Speeches in David's first attempt to transfer the ark (13:2–3, 12)
	Speech in the first battle account (14:10–11, 14–15)
	Speeches in the second attempt to transfer the ark (15:2, 12–13)
	David's prayer: His psalm of praise (16:8–36)
1 Chr 17	David's speech and Nathan's response (17:1, 2)
	Nathan's oracle of the Davidic covenant (17:4–15)
	David's prayer (17:16–27)
1 Chr 18–20	David's speech and the Speech of Hanun's officials (19:2–3, 5b)
	Joab's speech (19:12–13)

---

54. Duke, *Persuasive Appeal*, 129.

55. Ibid., 128, 169. Balentine views the number of prayers of David and Solomon as eleven in Chronicles. According to Balentine, David's prayers are six (1 Chr 14:10; 16:8–36; 17:16–27; 21:8; 21:17; 29:10–19), while Solomon's prayer are five (2 Chr 1:8–10; 5:13; 6:14–42; 7:3, 6) (Balentine, "'You Can't Pray a Lie,'" 252). Furthermore, Balentine indicates that the Chr has surrounded the narrative of David and Solomon with the most focused prayers, regarding 2 Chr 5:13 as the psalmic prayer (262). On the other hand, Beentjes identifies nine prayers of David's and Solomon. According to Beentjes, David utters six prayers (1 Chr 14:10; 17:16–27; 21:8, 17, 26; 29:10–20) and Solomon three prayers (2 Chr 1:8–10; 6:3–11; 6:14–42). Of these prayers, 1 Chr 21:26 has no wording of the prayers and the Chronicler only refers to the fact that people are praying. In other words, the David-Solomon narrative contains eight of their prayers (Beentjes, "Psalms and Prayers," 10).

56. Mason, *Preaching*, 13–122.

1 Chr 21–22:1	Dialogue between David and Joab (21:2–3)
	Dialogue between David and Gad as God's agent (21:8, 9–13, 17)
	Dialogue between David and Ornan (21:22–24)
	David's speech (22:1)
1 Chr 22:2–19	David's speech (22:5)
	David's speech to Solomon (22:7–16)
	David's speech to all the leaders of Israel (22:18–19)
1 Chr 23–27	David's speech (23:25–26, 28–32)
1 Chr 28–29	David's speech to the Leaders (28:2–8)
	David's speech to Solomon (28:9–10)
	David's final speech to Solomon (28:20–21)
	David's speech to the assembly (29:1–5)
	David's prayer to YHWH (29:10–19)
2 Chr 1	Solomon's speech (1:8–10) and God's speech to him (1:7, 11–12)
2 Chr 2	Solomon sent words to Huram (2:2[3]–9[10])
	Huram sent a letter to Solomon (2:10[11]–15[16])
2 Chr 5:2–7:22	Solomon's speech (6:1–11)
	Solomon's prayer (6:14–42)
	The divine speech to Solomon (7:12–22)
2 Chr 8:1–18	Solomon's speech (8:11b)
2 Chr 9:1–31	The speech of the queen of Sheba (9:5–8)

The speeches and prayers in the David-Solomon narrative as the Chr's key rhetorical devices play significant roles in portraying David and Solomon as those who sought YHWH, David as the preparer of the temple building and Solomon as the temple builder. Accordingly, I will carry out a rhetorical study on the speeches and prayers in the David-Solomon narrative, focusing on the rhetorical strategy with the possible rhetorical situation and effectiveness. It will exhibit that the Chronicler's portrayal of David and Solomon serves to reformulate the identity of the Yehudite community in the Persian period as a cultic community centered on the Jerusalem temple and asserts that YHWH's covenant with Israel continues through the Jerusalem temple in the Persian era. Now we turn to the rhetorical analysis of the speeches and prayers in the David-Solomon narrative.

4

Speeches and Prayers in David's Narrative

DAVID'S NARRATIVE (1 CHR 10–29) is composed of a series of small narratives, which constitute sub-rhetorical units. After the introductory depiction of Saul's demise (1 Chr 10:13–14),[1] the David narrative begins with his ascension to the throne (1 Chr 11–12). The anointing of David as king of Israel provides an indispensable backdrop to the following narratives,[2] wherein the Chr's retelling of David's reign legitimizes the preparation of the temple building.

The following sub-rhetorical unit is the ark narrative (1 Chr 13–16), wherein David urges all Israel to bring the ark of the covenant of YHWH to Jerusalem. The transfer of the ark of YHWH succeeds on the second attempt as it is carried upon the Levites' shoulders according to God's instruction. In the next scene of the narrative, the Chr, employing the speeches and prayers of David and the divine speeches, describes the Davidic covenant regarding the temple building and the dynasty (1 Chr 17).

David's wars (1 Chr 18–20) are meant to establish a time of peace to build the temple. Even though David's census (1 Chr 21) provokes God's anger upon Israel, it

---

1. In 1 Chr 10:13–14, the Chronicler concludes Saul's reign (1 Chr 10) by stating that he did not seek YHWH: "Saul died for his unfaithfulness; he was unfaithful to YHWH in that he did not keep God's command." Seeking YHWH is one of the Chronicler's crucial themes. Recent interpretation of 1 Chr 10 can be summarized as three views. First, the function of the narrative is to see it as providing a past for David's kingdom. For example, Japhet insists that this chapter sets up a continuum between the reign of David and the past of Israel (Japhet, *I & II Chronicles*, 230). Second, this chapter is seen as an introduction to the story of David. For instance, Zalewski asserts that the Chronicler underscores the legitimacy of the transfer of Saul's kingship to David, recognizing that the core of Saul's story lies in 1 Chr 10:13–14 (Zalewski, "Purpose of the Story of the Death of Saul," 449–67). Third, Saul's story is seen as an independent unit that has nothing to do with the following narrative. (Ackroyd, *The Chronicler in His Age*, 313–23; Mosis, *Untersuchungen*, 17–43). See also Trotter, "Reading, Readers," 299–303. Of the three interpretations, there is no universal formula for drawing out the Chronicler's purpose, yet each interpretation has to some degree validity. In my judgment, 1 Chr 10 appears to function as an introduction to the David narrative, beginning with the summary statement: Saul did not seek YHWH (1 Chr 10:13–14).

2. For instance, military campaigns (1 Chr 11:4–9; 14:8–16; 18:1–17; 19:1–19; 20:1–8), two attempts to transfer the ark (1 Chr 13:1–14; 15:1—16:3), the appointment of the temple personnel (1 Chr 16:4–43; 23:1—26:32), YHWH's covenant with David (1 Chr 17:1–27), the census-taking (1 Chr 21:1—22:1), and the ensuing preparation of the building of the temple (1 Chr 22:2–19, 1 Chr 28–29).

leads to YHWH's election of the temple site. As a result, David prepares for the temple building (1 Chr 22) and organizes the temple personnel (1 Chr 23–27).[3] Finally, when David is old, he gives his last speeches to the leaders of Israel and Solomon (1 Chr 28–29), to prepare them for Solomon's accession and to urge them to build the temple.[4]

Thus, through speeches and prayers in David's narrative, the Chr describes David as the preparer of the building of the temple and as a king who observes God's laws and commandments.[5] However, the Chr's portrayal of David goes beyond this description. The Chr appears to have had more interest in describing David as the worship founder of the Jerusalem temple.[6] In accordance with this interest, the Chr's portrayal of David is "not so much idealized as *focused*, narrowly and precisely, on one aspect: David as worship leader and founder."[7] Thus, the Chr's portrayal of David is closely related to the preparation of the temple building, which is discussed via the speeches and prayers in the David narrative.

SPEECHES IN DAVID'S ASCENSION TO THE THRONE (1 CHR 11–12)

David's ascension to the throne (1 Chr 11–12) as a rhetorical unit includes several speeches by characters in the narrative: the Israelites' speech to David (1 Chr 11:1–2); the Jebusites' speech to David (1 Chr 11:4–5); David's speech to his army (1 Chr 11:6); David's speeches on account of the mighty warriors (1 Chr 11:17, 19); David's speech and Amasai's responding speech (12:17[16]–18[17]); and the Philistine rulers' speech (1 Chr 12:20[19]). These speeches as the Chr's rhetorical devices play significant roles in the narrative progression and the Chr's portrayal of David.

Rhetorical Unit

This rhetorical unit (1 Chr 11–12) deals with David's ascension to the throne and contains the list of his mighty warriors. The emphasis of this unit centers upon support for David from the mighty warriors at the strongholds, especially those who come to

---

3. See Schniedewind, *Word of God*, 143–44.

4. McCarthy claims that the principal purpose of 1 Chr 22–29 is to portray the "legitimate succession of one leader of all Israel for another" (McCarthy, "An Installation Genre," 37). Wright concludes David's narrative with the statement: "the Chronicler seems to portray David as organizing his governmental apparatus from aristocratic and temple personnel, a social/political structure from the Persian period that had slowly evolved throughout the Neo-Babylonian and Persian periods in the ancient Near East" (Wright, "The Founding Father," 58).

5. According to Wright, studies on 1 Chronicles have been focused on the ark narrative and the preparation of the temple building by a variety of typological approaches. In these studies, true worship is emphasized (Wright, "The Founding Father," 46–47). "The issue becomes the theological and liturgical practice of the postexilic Judean community, faced with existential decisions for the future of their community" ("The Founding Father," 47). For typological studies on Chronicles, see Mosis, *Untersuchungen*; Riley, *King and Cultus*; Duke, *Persuasive Appeal*; and Williamson, *1 and 2 Chronicles*.

6. Tuell, *First and Second Chronicles*, 42.

7. Ibid., 42.

join David from the northern tribes of Israel. Williamson proposes a chiastic structure for this rhetorical unit:[8]

> A. 1 Chr 11:1–9 David's ascension to the throne at Hebron and his acquiring Jerusalem
> > B. 1 Chr 11:10–47 David's mighty warriors at Hebron
> > > C. 1 Chr 12:1–7 The Benjaminites' support for David at Ziglak
> > > > D. 1 Chr 12:8–15 The Gadites' support for David at the stronghold
> > > > D'. 1 Chr 12:16–18 Some Benjaminites' and Judahites' support for David at the stronghold
> > > C'. 1 Chr 12:19–22 The Manassites' support for David at Ziglak
> > B'. 1 Chr 12:23–37 David's mighty warriors at Hebron
> A'. 1 Chr 12:38–40 David's ascension to the throne at Hebron

In this outline, the support of the Benjaminites and the Judahites for David occupy the center. Williamson's observation is appropriate, as both Benjamin and Judah became the core tribes in the Persian period, as mentioned above.[9] Japhet, suggesting a similar structure to Williamson's, divides 1 Chr 11:1–9 (A) into two parts: the enthronement of David (1 Chr 11:1–3) and the conquest of Jerusalem (1 Chr 11:4–9).[10] In my view, it seems appropriate that Japhet separates the capture of Jerusalem from 1 Chr 11:1–9. In effect, David's first act as king over Israel is the conquest of Jerusalem, which possibly indicates that the Chr's interest in Jerusalem is expressed from the outset of the narrative section in Chronicles. Klein summarizes the primary message of 1 Chr 11–12 as follows:[11]

1. A unanimous Israel made David king at Hebron (11:1–3; 12:38–40).
2. David's coronation was in accord with the word of Yahweh (11:10; 12:23).
3. David's first act as king was to make Jerusalem his capital (11:4–9).
4. Various military groups rallied to David's cause already at Hebron (11:10—12:41).

In 1 Chr 11, the Israelites ask David to be the king of Israel, and David ascends the throne of Israel at Hebron as the fulfillment of YHWH's words given through Samuel. David then captured Jerusalem from the Jebusites, which will later be called the city of David. It is mentioned that David becomes very great, for God is with him. In 1 Chr 12, a number of Israelites come to and join David in the stronghold to make David the king over all Israel. Thus, these two chapters deal with the early stages of

---

8. See Williamson, "We Are Yours," 168–70; Kalimi, *Reshaping*, 228. The structure of 1 Chr 11–12 suggests that in the early stage of David's ascension to the throne, the northern tribes willingly collaborate with David.

9. See chapter 2, "The Rhetorical Situation."

10. Japhet, *I & II Chronicles*, 233. Japhet's division is different from Williamson's in another point: Japhet regards 1 Chr 12:38 as the summary of the preceding sub-division (1 Chr 12:23–38), but Williamson views it as the introduction of the last sub-division (1 Chr 12:38–40).

11. Klein, *1 Chronicles*, 298.

Speeches and Prayers in David's Narrative

David's kingdom, focusing on David's ascension to the throne according to YHWH's word.

Several speeches in this rhetorical unit may be found in the narrative context,[12] among which three speeches of David (1 Chr 11:1–2; 11:7, 9; 12:17[16]–19[18]) seem to reinforce the Chr's argument that David's ascension to the throne is legitimate according to YHWH's words. This rhetorical unit shows that the northern tribes such as Benjamin and Manasseh come to join David at Hebron. It suggests that the support for David comes from all the tribes of Israel, including the Benjaminites, the tribe of Saul. Thus, with widespread support, David ascends the throne of Israel.

Rhetorical Strategy

Dispositio (disposition or arrangement) is the structure or the organization of a text's argument. The disposition of a text is focused on the persuasive effect of its rhetorical units, not simply the delineation of the units. How do these units work together to accomplish a certain purpose?[13] Rhetoricians also employ stylistic features (*elocutio*) in order to elaborate some parts of a discourse. In this regard, stylistic features are a means for accomplishing the expected effect.[14] Several speeches in David's ascension to the throne reveal their stylistic or rhetorical features.

The Israelites' Speech to David (1 Chr 11:1–2)

All Israel[15] asks David to be the king of Israel (1 Chr 11:1–2), and David becomes king at Hebron (1 Chr 11:3).[16] David's ascension to the throne is accomplished according to

---

12. Trible's features of a text are: beginning and ending, repetition of words, phrases and sentences, types of discourse, design and structure, plot development, and character portrayals (Trible, *Rhetorical Criticism*, 102–3).

13. Kennedy, *New Testament Interpretation*, 37.

14. Ibid., 37. Kennedy points out that the style of a text (*elocutio*) is another significant element of persuasive discourse in rhetorical analysis.

15. In effect, the Chr frequently refers to the designation of "All Israel" in the narrative of David and Solomon (1 Chr 11–29 and 2 Chr 1–9). For instance, all Israel joins the warriors to support David (1 Chr 11:10); the warriors make David king over all Israel at Hebron (1 Chr 12:39); David assembles all Israel from Egypt to Hamath to transfer the ark from Kiriath-jearim (1 Chr 13:5, 6, 8); the Philistines hears that David became king of all Israel (1 Chr 14:8); all Israel again gathers in Jerusalem to bring the ark to Jerusalem (1 Chr 15:3, 28); YHWH also mentions all Israel in the Davidic covenant regarding the dynasty (1 Chr 17:6); David's officials hold their appointment in all Israel (1 Chr 18:14); all Israel passes over the Jordan with David to fight against the Arameans (1 Chr 19:17); in David's census-taking, Joab goes throughout all Israel (1 Chr 21:4); all Israel takes part in Solomon's accession (1 Chr 29:21, 23, 25); and the summary statement points out that David reigns over all Israel (1 Chr 29:26). Furthermore, Solomon goes to Gibeon with the assembly of all Israel (2 Chr 1:2); all Israel participates in the dedication of the temple (2 Chr 7:6, 8); and the summary statement points out that Solomon reigns over all Israel in Jerusalem for forty years (2 Chr 9:30). See Flanagan, *David's Social Drama*, 219. For more discussion for the term "All Israel" in Chronicles, see Japhet, *Ideology*, 211–17.

16. In 1 Chr 11:3, the Chr quotes 2 Sam 5:3, "and they anointed David king over Israel," with the addition of the phrase, "according to the word of YHWH through the hand of Samuel" (כִּדְבַר יְהוָה בְּיַד־שְׁמוּאֵל). The Chr stresses God's choice of David as the king of Israel. See Kalimi, *Reshaping*, 201.

YHWH's word. In this context, the Chr legitimizes David's kingship after Saul's death by emphasizing the prophetic words of God's promise:

1 Chr 11:1–2	
¹וַיִּקָּבְצוּ כָל־יִשְׂרָאֵל אֶל־דָּוִיד חֶבְרוֹנָה	And all Israel gathered to David at Hebron,
לֵאמֹר	saying,
הִנֵּה עַצְמְךָ וּבְשָׂרְךָ אֲנָחְנוּ׃	"Behold, your bone and your flesh we (are)
²גַּם־תְּמוֹל גַּם־שִׁלְשׁוֹם גַּם בִּהְיוֹת שָׁאוּל מֶלֶךְ	In times past, even when Saul was king,
אַתָּה הַמּוֹצִיא וְהַמֵּבִיא	you (were) the one who led out and brought in
אֶת־יִשְׂרָאֵל	Israel,
וַיֹּאמֶר יְהוָה אֱלֹהֶיךָ לְךָ	and YHWH your God said to you,
אַתָּה תִרְעֶה אֶת־עַמִּי אֶת־יִשְׂרָאֵל	'You shall shepherd my people Israel,
וְאַתָּה תִּהְיֶה נָגִיד	and you shall be leader
עַל עַמִּי יִשְׂרָאֵל׃	over my people Israel.'"

This utterance (as deliberative rhetoric) is a short speech of the Israelites who come to David at Hebron. The issue at stake (*inventio*) is the demise of Saul. They feel the need to have a new king over Israel, and thus they reason that David could be the king of Israel instead of Saul. All Israel comes to David, and addresses him in order to make him king over Israel.[17] The arrangement of this speech betrays its rhetorical features. First Chronicles 11:1 is a verbless clause with the order predicate-subjective.[18] The first term "Behold" (הִנֵּה) is designed to draw the attention of the audience.[19] The two predicates, "your bone and your flesh," that follow הִנֵּה form the clause of classification by placing them in front of the subject (אֲנָחְנוּ). This kinship language (cf. Gen 2) shows the loyalty of the Israelites to David.[20] The Chr compares all Israel (the Israelites) to David's bone and flesh. Literally, all Israel cannot be David's bone and flesh. Rather, this is a *metaphor* that expresses an abstract aspect in terms of concrete objects.[21] Accordingly, the Israelites reveal their loyalty to David by expressing kinship language.

---

17. The phrase, "all Israel" (1 Chr 11:1) is an exaggerated expression as all Israel cannot realistically gather to David. In this regard, this speech would be addressed to certain leaders of the Israelites.

18. Waltke and O'Connor, *Biblical Hebrew Syntax*, 8.4.2.a.

19. Some scholars define הִנֵּה as an injection; whereas, others consider it as an adverb. However, it does not really fit in either of the two classifications. Rather, "it refers to a whole clause. In fact, it always precedes the clause upon which it has a bearing . . . It does involve the speaker in the content of the clause, but it does not refer to his opinion on the degree of probability of the events or state of affairs. It points to the content of the clause that follows it" (Van der Merwe et al., *Biblical Hebrew*, 329).

20. David utters this phrase ("you are my bone and flesh") when he encourages the elders of Judah to restore David's kingship after Absalom's death (2 Sam 19:12–13). See Klein, *1 Chronicles*, 299.

21. With respect to metaphor, Bar-Efrat states, "The word is used in a non-literal sense, there being similarity but no direct continuity between its literal and non-literal meanings" (Bar-Efrat, *Narrative Art*, 209).

First Chronicles 11:2a further indicates that the relationship between David and all Israel originates in the past, even when Saul was still the king of Israel. David had been the leader of Israel since the time of Saul's reign. In what follows (1 Chr 11:2b), the leaders of Israel will reinforce their argument, quoting YHWH's speech to David. YHWH has previously said to David that he should be the shepherd and leader of Israel. On the basis of YHWH's word, the people contend that David should be the next king of Israel after Saul's demise.

In the Israelites' utterance, two rhetorical features are noteworthy. First, the pronoun אַתָּה in 1 Chr 11:2 occurs three times; it emphasizes that it will be David who will be the king of Israel instead of Saul. Rhetorically, the repetition of the pronoun at the beginning of the verse forms an *anaphora*.[22] Second, the phrase, "my people Israel" (עַמִּי יִשְׂרָאֵל, אֶת־עַמִּי אֶת־יִשְׂרָאֵל) also occurs twice, although the two phrases are slightly different: one has the direct object marker and the other does not. The repetition of this phrase at the end of the verse rhetorically forms an *epiphora*.[23] The two features indicate that David was the ruler of Israel even when Saul was king, and that YHWH promises David that he will become king over Israel. The repetition of אַתָּה emphasizes that the speaker is YHWH. God's promise stresses that David plays a significant role even when Saul was still king, and that David's action is legitimate in comparison with Saul's. The Israelite speech appeals to David's role as the ruler of Israel in the past and YHWH's word given to David, reinforcing their argument in this utterance.

In sum, the speech of the Israelites indicates that David should be the king of Israel after Saul's death, appealing to: (1) the fact that David was the ruler of Israel even when Saul was king; and (2) what God has said to David. All Israel requests David to be the king of Israel. Thus, their speech reinforces the legitimacy of David's ascension to the throne after Saul's death by reminding David that he was once the ruler of Israel and what YHWH has said to him.

The Jebusites' and David's Speech in the Capture of Jerusalem (1 Chr 11:5a, 6a)

Although the Jebusites who have been dwelling in Jebus (Jerusalem) say to David, "You will not come in here" (1 Chr 11:5a as *epideictic* rhetoric), David conquers Jerusalem (the city of David). During the capture of Jerusalem, he makes a speech to his mighty warriors in order to conquer the Jebusites. It is very interesting that David's first act is the capture of Jerusalem after his ascension to the throne:[24]

---

22. *Anaphora* is defined as "repetition of the same word at the beginning of successive clauses and verses." See Lanham, *Handlist*, 11.

23. *Epiphora* (*conversio*) is "repetition of a closing word or words at the end of several (usually successive) clauses, sentences, or verses." See Lanham, *Handlist*, 16.

24. For the Chr's emphasis on Jerusalem, see Beentjes, "Jerusalem in the Book of Chronicles," 15–28; "Jerusalem," 115–27; Dennerlein, *Die Bedeutung Jerusalems*, 141–47; Kalimi, "The Capture of Jerusalem," 66–79; "Jerusalem," 189–205; "The View of Jerusalem," 556–62; Knoppers, "Jerusalem at War in Chronicles," 57–76; Selman, "Jerusalem in Chronicles," 43–56.

1 Chr 11:5a	
וַיֹּאמְרוּ יֹשְׁבֵי יְבוּס לְדָוִיד	And the inhabitants of Jebus said to David
לֹא תָבוֹא הֵנָּה	"You will not come in here."
1 Chr 11:6a	
וַיֹּאמֶר דָּוִיד	And David said,
כָּל־מַכֵּה יְבוּסִי בָּרִאשׁוֹנָה	"Whoever smites the Jebusite first
יִהְיֶה לְרֹאשׁ וּלְשָׂר	will become head and commander."

Following David's utterance, Joab the son of Zeruiah first goes up to smite them. As a result, he becomes a commander (1 Chr 11:6b as deliberative rhetoric). After David conquers Jerusalem, he makes it a stronghold as the city of David (1 Chr 11:7), which is broadly built and firmly repaired by Joab (1 Chr 11:8). The Chr summarizes that David becomes greater and greater, for God was with him (1 Chr 11:9). With respect to David's conquering of Jerusalem, Kalimi claims that the capture of Jerusalem is depicted "as the most remarkable and meaningful national goal in which all the Israelites participated and to which they contributed willingly, as a result of deep conviction."[25] Thus, David's speech contributes to the capture of Jerusalem as the first act of David as king of Israel.

David's Speeches in the Account of the Mighty Warriors (1 Chr 11:17, 19)

First Chronicles 11:10–47 contains the list of David's mighty warriors who have given him strong support.[26] First Chronicles 11:10 emphasizes that "according to the word of YHWH," the leaders of David's mighty warriors come to David to make him their king. The same phrase, "the word of YHWH," is also found repeatedly in 1 Chr 11:3 and 12:23, reinforcing YHWH's choice of David. In this respect, Klein states appropriately, "The human support of David proves valid because of divine authorization."[27] Accordingly, the phrase is repeated in the narrative of David's ascension to the throne at Hebron, functioning as an introduction to the list of David's mighty warriors and the leaders of the tribes.[28]

---

25. Kalimi, "The Capture of Jerusalem," 78–79.

26. In 1 Chr 11:10, the word חזק in the hithpael (המתחזקים) is one of the frequently used roots in Chronicles (1 Chr 11:10; 19:13; 2 Chr 1:1; 12:13; 13:7, 8, 21, 16:9; 17:1; 21:4; 27:6; 32:5) (Klein, *1 Chronicles*, 302). This verb often occurs in context that deals with king's establishment in power (Curtis and Madsen, *Chronicles*, 29–30; Williamson, *Israel*, 54).

27. Klein, *1 Chronicles*, 302.

28. Kalimi, *Reshaping*, 282–83. "The link between the two sections was strengthened by arranging the new introduction (v. 10b) in chiastic order compared with the previous conclusion (v. 3b)" (*Reshaping*, 283):

"And they anointed David king over Israel
according to the word of YHWH by the hand of Samuel."
(וַיִּמְשְׁחוּ אֶת־דָּוִיד לְמֶלֶךְ עַל־יִשְׂרָאֵל כִּדְבַר יְהוָה בְּיַד־שְׁמוּאֵל׃ 1 Chr 11:3b)

Speeches and Prayers in David's Narrative

First Chronicles 11:15–20 refers to an instance of the warriors' support for David, and contains two short speeches of David concerning three mighty warriors of the thirty (1 Chr 11:17 [as deliberative rhetoric] and 11:19 [as *epideictic* rhetoric]).

1 Chr 11:17	
מִי יַשְׁקֵנִי מַיִם	"Who would give me water to drink
מִבּוֹר בֵּית־לֶחֶם	from the well of Bethlehem
אֲשֶׁר בַּשָּׁעַר	that is by the gate?"
1 Chr 11:19	
וַיֹּאמֶר חָלִילָה לִּי	And said, "Far be it from me,
מֵאֱלֹהַי מֵעֲשׂוֹת זֹאת	by my God, to do this;
הֲדַם הָאֲנָשִׁים הָאֵלֶּה אֶשְׁתֶּה	the blood of these men can I drink
בְּנַפְשׁוֹתָם	with their lives?
כִּי בְנַפְשׁוֹתָם הֱבִיאוּם	for with their lives they have brought it";
וְלֹא אָבָה לִשְׁתּוֹתָם	and he was not willing to drink it;
אֵלֶּה עָשׂוּ שְׁלֹשֶׁת הַגִּבֹּרִים	these (things) did the three mighty ones.

David's three warriors who hear David's word draw water from the well of Bethlehem, breaking through the Philistine lines. When these three warriors come back with the water from the well, David realizes that he has placed them in a very dangerous situation. For this reason, he regards the water as comparable to their blood by David's speech, in which the phrase "the blood of these men" is emphasized by being placed first in the inquiry. He does not drink the water, but instead pours it out to YHWH.[29] This episode is an example of widespread support for David from all Israel. David's speech reveals the loyalty of the three warriors and David's character with a dramatic action, which reinforces his kingship. Thus, the Chr points to David's integrity and his recognition of his warriors' sacrifice.

David's Speech and Amasai's Response (1 Chr 12:17–19[16–18])

After the demise of Saul, a number of mighty warriors come to David and join him at the stronghold to make him king over all Israel. In 1 Chr 12, the list of mighty warriors demonstrates that the widespread support for David comes from all the tribes of Israel. In this chapter, David's speech and Amasai's responding speech play a significant role in the Chr's portrayal of David. The central issue is who will be the next king over

---

"Those who are strengthening themselves with him... to make him king, according to the word of YHWH, over Israel."
(הַמִּתְחַזְּקִים עִמּוֹ בְמַלְכוּתוֹ עִם־כָּל־יִשְׂרָאֵל לְהַמְלִיכוֹ כִּדְבַר יְהוָה עַל־יִשְׂרָאֵל: 1 Chr 11:10b)

29. In 2 Sam 23:17, David says, "Be it far from me, O YHWH, to do this; is it the blood of the men who went with their lives?" The water the three warriors drew from the well in Bethlehem is identified with their lives.

Israel after the demise of Saul. It stands to reason that the Benjaminites could have claimed that the next king of Israel should belong to the tribe of Benjamin; after all, the first king of Israel, Saul, was a Benjaminite.[30] It is initially unclear whether the Benjaminites' attitude to David will be positive or negative when they come to join him. However, the dialogue between David and Amasai reveals that both the Benjaminites and the Judahites support David's claim.

First Chronicles 12:17–19[16–18] contains the dialogue between David and Amasai (the head of the thirty). This exchange occurs when some Benjaminites and Judahites came to join David in the stronghold (1 Chr 12:17[16]).[31] At this time, David speaks to them as *deliberative* rhetoric (1 Chr 12:18[17]) and Amasai makes a responding speech as *epideictic* rhetoric (1 Chr 12:19[18]):

1 Chr 12:18[17]	
וַיֵּצֵא דָוִיד לִפְנֵיהֶם וַיַּעַן	And David went out before them And answered
וַיֹּאמֶר לָהֶם	and said to them
אִם־לְשָׁלוֹם בָּאתֶם אֵלַי לְעָזְרֵנִי	"if for peace you have come to me to help me,
יִהְיֶה־לִּי עֲלֵיכֶם לֵבָב לְיָחַד	I will have a heart to you for unitedness,
וְאִם־לְרַמּוֹתַנִי	but if (you have come) to betray me
לְצָרַי בְּלֹא חָמָס בְּכַפַּי	to my adversaries without violence in my hands.
יֵרֶא אֱלֹהֵי אֲבוֹתֵינוּ וְיוֹכַח: ס	(May) the God of our fathers see and decide."

David's speech (1 Chr 12:18[17]) is comprised of two opposite conditional clauses, which may be rhetorically labeled *antitheton* (antithesis).[32] This literary pattern frequently occurs in Chronicles (1 Chr 15:12; 19:12; 28:9). Japhet points out that it serves "to present a given situation in its two aspects, positive and negative, giving full expression to their respective consequences."[33] In the first conditional clause, the protasis (אִם־לְשָׁלוֹם בָּאתֶם אֵלַי לְעָזְרֵנִי) demonstrates that David wants to know if they are coming to him in order to help him. In this protasis, the two phrases, "for peace" (לְשָׁלוֹם) and "to help me" (לְעָזְרֵנִי) are noteworthy. The former phrase is emphatically placed in front of the verb, and the latter reveals that David wishes to know their intentions.[34] In the ensuing apodosis, the utterance, "I have a heart to you for unitedness" exhibits

---

30. See Chapter 2, "Rhetorical Situation."

31. For the Chr's concept of Judah and Benjamin, see Japhet, *I & II Chronicles*, 263–64; Klein, *1 Chronicles*, 319.

32. Lanham, *Handlist*, 16.

33. Japhet, *I & II Chronicles*, 264. Japhet indicates, "Stylistically, David's speech exemplifies a characteristic phenomenon of the poetic and semi-poetic sections of Chronicles, that is, the 'anthological style'" (*I & II Chronicles*, 265).

34. The latter phrase, "to help me" is omitted in the parallel texts (1 Sam 16:4 and 1 Kgs 2:13), both of which contain a similar clause, "Do you come peaceably," (שָׁלֹם בֹּאֶךָ, the difference between the two verses is that the latter has the interrogative הֲ (הֲשָׁלוֹם) in front of "peace"). Thus, this phrase "to help me" stresses the central motif ("help") in this rhetorical unit (Japhet, *I & II Chronicles*, 264).

that David will welcome their coming to help him, if their coming is for peaceful purposes. The first conditional clause indicates that if their coming is to help David, he will welcome them positively.

In the second conditional clause, the protasis, "if to betray me to my adversaries" reveals that David wishes to know if their intention was to come to betray him to his adversaries. In this protasis, an *ellipsis* is seen: "if (you have come) to betray me to my adversaries" (אִם־לְרַמּוֹתַנִי לְצָרַי). In particular, the following phrase, "without violence in my hand" (בְּלֹא חָמָס בְּכַפַּי) seems to have broken the valence of the protasis-apodosis, drawing out the audience's attention. The phrase stresses David's innocence in relation to his ascension to the throne.[35] The ensuing apodosis, "[May] the God of our fathers see and decide" also serves to reveal his innocence. David wishes YHWH God to see and decide their intentions. The second conditional clause indicates that if their coming is to betray David to his enemies, only God will decide what their intention to come to David was. This calling upon God is a request for God's justice upon them.

David's speech demonstrates that he needs to confirm why these Benjaminites and Judahites have come to join him. David has been staying at strongholds in the wilderness, avoiding the threat of Saul the Benjaminite. David considers that the threat has not been removed, even after the death of Saul. Owing to his suspicions, when they come to join him, David makes a speech in terms of two contrasting protases and apodoses. The Chr stresses the innocence of David's ascension to the throne by using this speech, in which David's concern over Benjamin is expressed by placing the Benjaminites before the Judahites:

1 Chr 12:19[18]	
וְרוּחַ לָבְשָׁה אֶת־עֲמָשַׂי רֹאשׁ הַשָּׁלִישִׁים	And the Spirit clothed Amasai, head of the thirty
לְךָ דָוִיד	"(peace) *to you*, O David
וְעִמְּךָ בֶן־יִשַׁי	And with you, O son of Jesse
שָׁלוֹם שָׁלוֹם לְךָ	Peace (be), peace *to you*[A]
וְשָׁלוֹם לְעֹזְרֶךָ	And peace to the one who helps you
כִּי עֲזָרְךָ אֱלֹהֶיךָ	For your God is the one who helps you"
וַיְקַבְּלֵם דָּוִיד	And David received them
וַיִּתְּנֵם בְּרָאשֵׁי הַגְּדוּד׃ פ	and made them the heads of the troop
A. Kalimi observes a chiastic arrangement in this verse ("*to you*"). Kalimi, *Reshaping*, 220.	

Amasai delivers his speech (1 Chr 12:19 [18])[36] after the Spirit comes upon him. His inspired speech is for David and David's kingship, addressed to David and all of

---

35. Japhet indicates that even though this phrase "disturbs the metrical balance of the verse and even the sequence of the idea," the second conditional clause provides "the basis for David's declaration of his innocence" (Japhet, *I & II Chronicles*, 264).

36. The backdrop of Amasai's speech is when David was at Ziklag (1 Sam 21:1–7). Interestingly, those who came to join David in Chronicles are different from those in Samuel-Kings. In 1 Sam 22:2,

Israel. Amasai's utterance of a wish of peace is given by the expression, "(peace) to you, O David and with you, O son of Jesse." This phrase presents strong support for David with a wish of peace. Significantly, the word, "peace" (שָׁלוֹם) is employed three times by Amasai, reflecting David's utterance in 1 Chr 12:18[17] (in which the key word, "help" is employed twice). In Amasai's speech, the pronoun suffix *ka* (ךָ) constitutes *rhyme*, repeating the sound six times at the ends of words.[37] This pronoun refers to David with a wish of peace. Amasai appeals to the relationship between God and David, which is also emphasized by the personal pronouns ("to you. . .the one who helps you. . .your God. . .helps you"). Accordingly, Amasai's utterance indicates that the ones that will join David to help him will also find peace.

Furthermore, this is a response to the preceding speech of David ("me. . .my adversaries. . .God of our fathers" in 1 Chr 12:18[17]). According to Japhet, a rhetorical feature of this dialogue between David and Amasai is "the inclusion of an apologetic or causal clause" to make the argument strong.[38] David refers to his reasons for turning to God for vindication ("without violence in my hands" in 1 Chr 12:18[17]). Amasai also legitimizes David's blessing with a causal clause ("For your God is the one who helps you" in 1 Chr 12:19[18]), which shows that David already has the help of YHWH. Thus, these two references exhibit David's innocence and God's favor to David,[39] especially assuming certain peace between the Benjaminites and the Judahites as the hearers of Amasai's speech.

Mason deals with this speech as the first in his study of the addresses in Chronicles.[40] As for the Chr's description of those who come to join David, Mason claims that "the 'all Israel' theme is being represented in an expression of loyalty in this early stage of David's career" (1 Chr 12:9[8]; 16[15]; 21[20]).[41] This suggests that the support for David broadly came from all the tribes of Israel. Mason concludes Amasai's speech with this statement:[42]

> It is not coincidental that the first of the addresses in Chronicles thus speaks of the divine choice of David from well before the time of his kingship. It acts as a summons to all true 'Israelites' to align themselves with the well-being of the Davidic line by showing that active support which places them within the divine purpose. Equally significantly, it associates 'peace' with David, that peace which later will characterise his continuing line and the temple.

"Everyone who was in distress, and everyone who was in debt, and everyone who was discontented gathered to him. . .," those who came to David are problematic people; whereas, in 1 Chr 12:17–19 [16–18], those who came to David are mighty warriors from the Benjaminites and the Judahites.

37. Bar-Efrat, *Narrative Art*, 201.
38. Japhet, *I & II Chronicles*, 265.
39. Ibid., 265–6.
40. Mason, *Preaching*, 13–16.
41. Ibid., 14.
42. Ibid., 16.

Unfortunately, Mason does not note that Amasai is speaking to David on behalf of both the Benjaminites and the Judahites. The Chr places the dialogue between David and Amasai at the center of this broader support of all Israel. The Chr seems to have presented a strategy for how the support of Benjamin and Judah for David is an example of the broader support from all Israel. Furthermore, Schniedewind argues that Amasai's speech in the narrative context "serves to encourage the people to help David become king."[43] In my judgment, Amasai's speech, responding to David's speech, serves to legitimize David's ascension to the throne after Saul's death by encouraging all the tribes of Israel to help David. The "help" motif is dominant in this rhetorical unit.[44] For instance, the key word, "help" (עזר) is used in 1 Chr 12:1, 18, 19, 20, 22, 23. Instead of עזר, the form עדר is also found in 1 Chr 12:34, 39.[45] Thus, the "help" motif is emphasized in this rhetorical unit in order to point out that widespread support for David comes from all the tribes of Israel.

In sum, as the climax in the narrative of David's ascension to throne, the dialogue between David and Amasai focuses on peace and help for David. Amasai's speech fits well within the theme of this unit, that is, that the support for David comes from all the tribes of Israel with the emphasis on the 'help' motif. The Chr's description of David's ascension to the throne shows that David after the demise of Saul, gains broader support from all Israel, among which the support of the Benjaminites and the Judahites is rhetorically emphasized by Amasai's speech.

The Philistine Rulers' Speech (1 Chr 12:20b[19b])

First Chronicles 12:20–22[19–21] contains the list of the warriors who come to join David at Ziklag from the Manassites. When they come to David, the Philistines are about to fight against Saul. David has demanded to participate in the battle, as he is staying at Ziklag under Achish of Gath. However, the Philistine rulers suspect that once the battle begins, David will desert to Saul. Thus, they send David away before the battle of Gilboa. At this time, the Philistine rulers make a speech as *epideictic* rhetoric (1 Chr 12:20b):

1 Chr 12:20b[19b]	
שִׁלְּחֻהוּ סַרְנֵי פְלִשְׁתִּים	The princes of the Philistines sent him away,
לֵאמֹר	saying
בְּרָאשֵׁינוּ יִפּוֹל	"At the cost of our heads he will desert
אֶל־אֲדֹנָיו שָׁאוּל	to his master Saul?"

---

43. Schniedewind, *Word of God*, 110.

44. According to Alter, the techniques of repetition are *leitwort*, motif, theme, sequence of actions, and type-scene (Alter, *Art of Biblical Narrative*, 95–6).

45. For the discussion for this key word, see Allen, "Kerygmatic Units," 26–27. Rudolph also observes that עזר plays a significant role in 1 Chr 12 (Rudolph, *Chronikbücher*, 105).

The rhetorical question asked by the Philistine rulers reveals their strong mistrust of David, implying that David indeed will desert to Saul since David was once a key official of Saul. As a result, David comes back to Ziklag. Klein suggests that David would have passed through the area of Manasseh when he travels back to Ziklag.[46] In this context, the Manassites come to join David. Significantly, the Manassites' coming to him appears to show that even northern tribes supported David from the early stages of David's reign. Thus, the widespread support for David from all the tribes in Israel is confirmed.

Rhetorical Situation

The rhetorical situation may be considered at two levels: the narrative situation and the Chr's rhetorical situation. The former is related to the narrative audience and the latter to the Chr's audience. Accordingly, the rhetorical situation of Chronicles contains two levels of contexts: the narrative context and the Chr's own context.

The narrative situation of 1 Chr 11–12 is the transitional period from Saul's death to David's ascension to the throne of Israel. The urgent situation in the narrative is the demise of Saul. After this event, the Israelites would have been interested in who would become the next king of Israel. Since Saul tries to kill him, David has been staying at strongholds in the wilderness. In this narrative context, some of the Israelites consider David (currently in the wilderness) as the next king. They gather to David at Hebron in order to make him king over Israel (1 Chr 11:1–3), appealing to the fact that YHWH has previously said to Samuel that David would be the king of Israel after Saul (1 Chr 11:3; cf. 1 Sam 16). After David is anointed as king over Israel at Hebron, his first act is the capture of Jerusalem (1 Chr 11:4–9). The Israelites provide their strong support for David (1 Chr 11:10–47). Even Benjamin and Manasseh (a northern tribe) come to join David when he is at Ziklag (1 Chr 12:1–7; 12:19–22; cf. 1 Sam 27). In this context, the speeches of the characters in the narrative are addressed to their audience, in which the narrative audience in 1 Chr 11–12 is multiple audiences such as the Israelites in Hebron, some Benjaminites and Manassites, and the Israelites who are dwelling in the strongholds with David. Each speech in 1 Chr 11–12 is addressed to its audience and the preceding event of Saul's death constrains the speeches in David's ascension to the throne.

These speeches in the narrative context are related to the Chr's own rhetorical situation. When the Chr retells the early history of Israel thorugh the narrative characters, especially through their speeches, he feels a rhetorical need to frame this unit as the first building block of his presentation. The rhetorical situation of the Chr reflects his own time.

In the Israelites' speech to David, the Chr seems to have brought all of Israel into relationship with David by using kinship language (1 Chr 11:1). In the Persian

---

46. Klein, *1 Chronicles*, 321.

period, it would be easy to create an "us" mentally as people who were comprised of the returnees from Babylonia and those remaining in Yehud.[47] The Chr appears to have underscored via this speech the kinship connection between all Israel, as well as between Israel and David. In the Jebusites' and David's speech, the Jebusites demonstrate their attitude to David, saying that David will not come to them (1 Chr 11:5a). David encourages his army to smite the Jebusites, saying that the one who smites them will be his commander (1 Chr 11:6a). So Joab smites them and captures Jerusalem. In this context, the stress on Joab's role might reflect the eminence of his family in the Persian era (1 Chr 4:14; cf. Ezra 2:6 // Neh 7:11; Ezra 8:9).[48] Klein contends that "the Chronicler attributes the capture to David and all Israel in order to lend more authority and prestige to this city and its temple."[49] Williamson believes, on the other hand, that "Jerusalem's significance is presented as a purely political focus for the nation; its religious significance as the site of the future temple is not mentioned here at all, and it developed only later."[50] It seems that Klein points to the Chr's intention in his own context, whereas Williamson to the narrator's intention in the narrative context. Accordingly, the Chr seems to have arranged the capture of Jerusalem in the early part of the David narrative in order to stress Jerusalem as the place of the future temple.

In David's speech, the Chr wishes to legitimize David's ascension to the throne, emphasizing the mighty warriors' support for David through an episode (1 Chr 11:17, 19). In the speeches of David and Amasai, the Chr underscores that David obtains the widespread supports from even the Benjaminites and Judahites. In line with this, Schniedewind contends that the Chr precisely elaborates on Amasai's speech (1 Chr 12:19[18]) in the immediate context by employing the verb "to help" as a central motif.[51] This verb frequently occurs in 1 Chr 11–12. Willi notes that a number of names are repetitively connected with עזר in 1 Chr 11–12.[52] Williamson claims that the recurring motif of this verb in these chapters is found in the three characteristic uses of the Chr: help from the Lord; help from the godly men who came to David; and the responsibility not to be helped by the ungodly men, nor to help them.[53] Thus, the Chr, using the help motif as a key concept in Amasai's speech, presents the widespread support for David from even the Benjaminites to the Chr's own audience in the Persian period. In the Philistine officials' speech, the Chr appears to convey to his audience that David does not help the Philistines and does not participate in the battle against Israel. Accordingly, the Chr portrays David as a faithful character that does not fight against Saul when he stays in a stronghold under the Philistine rulers.

47. Ibid., 299.
48. See Welten, *Geschichte*, 59–63; Oeming, "Eroberung Jerusalems," 417.
49. Klein, *1 Chronicles*, 300.
50. Williamson, *1 and 2 Chronicles*, 98.
51. Schniedewind, *Word of God*, 111.
52. Willi, *Die Chronik*, 224.
53. Williamson, "We Are Yours," 166–67.

The Chr's rhetorical problem is to reconstruct community identity as God's people in Persian Yehud. The Yehudite community, which was comprised of the returnees from Babylonia and those who had remained in Yehud, needs to rebuild its community identity. In the process of this identity (re)formation, one key aspect is the tension between Judah and Benjamin, while another aspect is to unite the scattered people of Israel around the Jerusalem temple in the Persian period.

In effect, the two tribes, Judah and Benjamin, frequently appear together in the Persian period. For instance, the settlement list (according to Ezra 2:20–35; Neh 7:25–38) exhibits an important characteristic of Benjamin in comparison with Judah during the Persian period. The Benjaminites (in the community who lived in Yehud after the exile) appear to have occupied the leadership in Yehud after the exile. When the Judahites (in the *golah* community) returned from Babylonia to their homeland, the Benjaminites had already assumed the leadership. Clearly, there would have been tension between the Benjaminites and the Judahites. Accordingly, in this situation, the Chr would have felt urgency to present the early history of Israel.

In line with this, the Chr's interest is in the scattered peoples after the exile. The Chr wishes to unite them into the Yehudite community, as the worship community, around the Jerusalem temple in the Persian period. This is reflected in the Chr's portrayal of David as faithful towards YHWH. The Chr emphasizes the widespread support for David from the mighty warriors and even the northern tribes in Israel. The Chr looks back on the united monarchy in the past, and looks forward to the formation of the worship community as a new identity of the Yehudites. This new identity will be like the united monarchy in the time of David and Solomon.

Thus, in order to rebuild the community identity of Israel like the united monarchy in the Persian era, the Chr, reflecting this tension between the two tribes, communicates to the Yehudite community that after the demise of Saul, David receives strong support from all Israel. This support includes Benjamin and Manasseh. These tribes were eager to make David king over all Israel. In addition, the Chr portrays David as the one who was eager for worship to YHWH, alluding to the future place of worship in Israel by describing David's capture of Jerusalem as his first act after David ascended the throne of Israel.

This being so, what is the Chr's intention in his presentation of this rhetorical unit? Scholars have indicated that 1 Chr 11–12 shows that David's ascension to the throne is the fulfillment of YHWH's word. For instance, Braun holds that 1 Chr 11–12 stresses that those warriors who came to David are "representatives of the fact that *all Israel* was enthusiastic in its support of David's kingship, which was of course according to God's plan."[54] Klein claims that the Chr displays "the complete correspondence

---

54. Braun, *1 Chronicles*, 162. In Braun's view, the list of the mighty warriors is not merely the names of individual, but has "the cumulative effect of their more than fifty names which points to God's pleasure and Israel's full participation in the rise of King David, whose chief task will be the construction of a house of rest for his God in Jerusalem" (*1 Chronicles*, 162).

between the rise of David and the will and word of Yahweh" (1 Chr 10:14; 11:3).[55] However, neither Braun nor Klein mentions the Chr's situation.

In effect, the two summary statements in this unit (1 Chr 12:24[23], 39[38]) point to the Chr's purpose. The two summary statements include the same key phrase. In 1 Chr 12:24[23], David's warriors came to David in order "to turn the kingdom of Saul to David" (לְהָסֵב מַלְכוּת שָׁאוּל אֵלָיו). In the same fashion, David's mighty men arrayed in battle line come to David at Hebron in order "to make him king over all Israel" (לְהַמְלִיךְ אֶת־דָּוִיד עַל־כָּל־יִשְׂרָאֵל) and "to make David king" (לְהַמְלִיךְ אֶת־דָּוִיד) in 1 Chr 12:39[38]. The text emphasizes three times that they come to David in order "to make David king over all Israel." By this phrase, the Chr, legitimizing the Davidic kingship, appears to imply a shift from Benjaminite hegemony to Judahite in Jerusalem in the Persian period.

The Chr's purpose in this unit is to legitimize David's ascension to the throne in accordance with YHWH's word. The Chr stresses the widespread support for David from all the tribes of Israel. The climactic scene of this legitimacy is shown in David's and Amasai's speeches, as mentioned above. In my judgment, by the speeches in 1 Chr 11–12, the Chr describes David as the king over Israel who gains widespread support from all Israel, including the northern tribes, which constitutes the first building block of his portrayal.

Rhetorical Effectiveness

The rhetorical effectiveness of a speech cannot be recognized only by internal elements (disposition, style, etc.). We do not have enough evidence to assess the actual effectiveness of the discourse in an ancient text. Accordingly, the rhetorical question is whether the speech had the *potentiality* that it would modify the exigence.[56] In this unit, the narrative situation is the transitional period from the demise of Saul to David's ascension to the throne. This originates from Saul's death. The Israelites might raise a question about who will be the next king of Israel instead of Saul. They may consider that David should be the king of Israel. As a result, all Israel comes to join David at strongholds in the wilderness and makes a speech to him (1 Chr 11:1–2), in which they appeal to David's career as the ruler of Israel even when Saul was king. They consider YHWH's word to him. In doing so, they effectively persuade David to become king over Israel. As a result, David, responding to their speech, makes a covenant with them before YHWH. They anoint him king over Israel at Hebron (1 Chr 11:3). The first act of David after the ascension to the throne is the capture of Jerusalem, in which the Jebusites' speech to David (1 Chr 11:4–5) and David's speech (1 Chr 11:6) help the narrative audience to understand the acquisition of the capital city as the city of David. In this unit, David makes speeches in the episode of his three

---

55. Klein, *1 Chronicles*, 298.
56. Möller, *Prophet in Debate*, 42–43.

mighty warriors (1 Chr 11:17, 19), in which David's integrity and his warriors' loyalty to him are well indicated. In this regard, David's speech seems to have impacted his followers, especially those who were dwelling at the strongholds, in the time of reinforcement of his kingship.

In the situation of the demise of Saul, some Israelites may have claimed that the next king should be one of the Benjaminites because Saul, the first king of Israel, belonged to Benjamin. In this context, when the Benjaminites and the Judahites come to join David, David doubts their intentions in coming to him. This is reflected in the speeches of David and Amasai (1 Chr 12:18–19[17–18]). David's speech, which is expressed by two contrasting conditional clauses, leads to Amasai's positive response. Following this, David makes the Benjaminites and the Judahites the commanders of his army. In this regard, David's and Amasai's speech will impact the hearers of their speeches who potentially might be the Benjaminites and the Judahites with David and Amasai. In addition, the Philistine rulers' speech (1 Chr 12:20[19]) emphasizes that David does not participate in the Philistine battle against Saul, reminding the narrative audience of David's innocence. Thus, these speeches serve to solve the urgent situation of the narrative, drawing a fitting response from the supporters for David as the narrative audience.

The Chr conveys his messages to his own audience through the characters' speeches in his presentation. The rhetorical effectiveness of the speeches and prayer is related to the Chr's situation. Accordingly, the Chr, through the speeches and prayer, persuades his own audience in the Persian era. For instance, the Israelites' speech to David would effectively persuade the Yehudite community using kinship language to understand that all of Israel supported David (1 Chr 11:1). The Chr's audience, through the speeches of the Jebusites and David, will recognize the capture of Jerusalem as the first act of David who becomes king over Israel. In David's speech, the Chr persuades the Yehudites to understand the widespread support for David by the episode of the mighty warriors (1 Chr 11:17, 19). In the speeches of David and Amasai, it should be noted that the Benjaminites and the Judahites are mentioned together. In this way, the Chr intends to emphasize Judah and Benjamin as the two leading tribes in the Yehudite community, reflecting the tension between them in the Persian period. This tension is implicitly reflected in the speeches between David and Amasai. In effect, this occurs when the Chr describes the coming together of Benjaminites and the Judahites to join David at the stronghold (1 Chr 12:17–19[16–18]). The Chr shows the Yehudites that both the Benjaminites and the Judahites came to join David. David's speech and Amasai's response will impact the Chr's audience, revealing that both tribes had supported the Davidic leadership from the early stage of the united monarchy. In this way, the Chr indicates that the two tribes of Judah and Benjamin are the two leading tribes in the Persian period. In the Philistine officials' speech, the Chr expresses to his audience that David does not help the Philistines and does not participate in the battle against Israel. The Chr portrays David as a faithful character who did not fight against Saul when he stayed in a stronghold under the Philistine rulers.

In the Persian era, the rhetorical problem of the Chr was the reformulation of community identity as God's people under the Persian rule. The Chr feels the need to rewrite this early history for the Yehudite community, comprised of the returnees from Babylonia and those who had remained in Yehud, in order to reconstruct their community identity under the Persian Empire. In this unit, the Chr, employing the speeches of characters (the speeches of the Israelites and David), persuades the Yehudite community to recognize that David's ascension was legitimate, as the accomplishment of YHWH's words, with the emphasis on the widespread support for David from all Israel. David's ascension will be the first building block in the Chr's persuasive portrayal of David. Thus, the speeches and prayer effectively communicated to the Yehudite community as the Chr's audience and reminded the Yehudites of David's portrayal in the early stage of the united monarchy. The Chr's message by the rhetorical devices (speech and prayer) would have been very persuasive to them with the hope for the future.

SPEECHES AND PRAYERS IN THE ARK NARRATIVE (1 CHR 13-16)

The ark narrative (1 Chr 13-16)[57] as a rhetorical unit contains several speeches and prayers: David's speeches in the first attempt to transfer the ark to Jerusalem (1 Chr 13:2-3, 14); David's inquiries in the battle against the Philistines (1 Chr 14:10-11; 14-15); David's speeches in the second attempt to bring the ark into Jerusalem (1 Chr 15:2, 12-13); and David's prayer as his psalm of praise (1 Chr 16:8-36). David's speeches and prayer serve as instruments that the ark narrative advances. The Chr conveys his message through the narrator's character. In this unit, David makes speeches and prayers in order to persuade the Israelites to bring the ark to Jerusalem. In line with this, the Chr, through David's speeches and prayer, wishes to persuade the implied audience as to the significance of Jerusalem in the Persian era.

---

57. For discussion of the ark narrative (1 Chr 13-16), see Mosis, *Untersuchungen*, 44-81; Welten, "Lade-Temple-Jerusalem," 169-83 (esp. 173-77); Eskenazi, "Literary Approach," 258-74; Dennerlein, *Die Bedeutung Jerusalems*, 38-67; Begg, "The Ark in Chronicles," 133-45; Street, *Significance*; Jonker, "The Ark of Covenant of the Lord," 409-31. For studies on the ark narrative in 1 Sam 4-6 and 2 Sam 6, see Jackson, "The Ark Narratives"; Campbell, *The Ark Narrative*; Miller and Roberts, *The Hand of the Lord*; Rost, *The Succession of the Throne of David*, 6-34; Eslinger, *Kingship of God in Crisis*; Gitay, "Reflection on the Poetics of the Samuel Narrative," 221-30; Polzin, *Samuel and the Deuteronomist*; Van der Toorn and Houtman, "David and the Ark," 209-31; Eynikel, "The Relation Between the Eli Narrative and the Ark Narrative," 88-106; Bodner, "Ark-eology," 169-97 (*The Artistic Dimension*, 59-85). See also Fretheim, "The Cultic Use of the Ark"; "The Ark in Deuteronomy," 1-14; Coats, "The Ark of the Covenant in Joshua," 137-57; Gutmann, "The History of the Ark," 22-30; von Rad, "The Tent and the Ark," 103-24; Seow, "The Designation of the Ark," 185-98; Woudstra, *The Ark of the Covenant*.

The Persuasive Portrayal of David and Solomon in Chronicles

Rhetorical Unit

This rhetorical unit displays a clear narrative progression. The unit begins with David urging the whole assembly of Israel to bring the ark to Jerusalem (1 Chr 13:1–3), and it ends with the statement that after the ark is moved into the tent at Jerusalem, all Israel departs to their home and David returns home to bless his household (1 Chr 16:43). Some scholars suggest that the rhetorical unit has four parts: the first attempt to bring the ark to Jerusalem (1 Chr 13:1–14); David's family and his battle against the Philistines (1 Chr 14:1–17); the second attempt to bring the ark to Jerusalem and its success (1 Chr 15:1—16:3); the Levites' leading worship before the ark (1 Chr 16:4–43).[58] Others propose slightly different structures of 1 Chr 13–16, especially 1 Chr 16. Their divisions seem to be based upon the parallel texts in Samuel-Kings. Japhet provides a chiastic structure for 1 Chr 15:25—16:43, which may be described as follows:[59]

> 1 Chr 16:1–3 their basics sources from 2 Sam 6:17–20a
>   1 Chr 16:4 permanent arrangements of the Levites
>   1 Chr 16:7 connecting link
>   1 Chr 16:8–36 psalm[60]
>   1 Chr 16:37 connecting link
>   1 Chr 16:38–42 permanent arrangements of the Levites
> 1 Chr 16:43 their basics sources from 2 Sam 6:17–20a

In her division, it is noteworthy that both of the connecting links (1 Chr 16:7, 37) are related to Asaph and his brothers. Probably, the reason would be their key roles as worship leaders. Similarly, Selman suggests a chiastic structure for 1 Chr 16:1–43.[61]

> a. 16:1–3, God's blessing for every Israelite
>   b. 16:4–7, Levites appointed for worship at Jerusalem
>   c. 16:8–36, Psalm of praise
>   b¹. 16:37–42, Levites and priests appointed for worship at Gibeon
> a¹. 16:43, Blessing for David's household.

---

58. Knoppers, *I Chronicles*, 578–661; Klein, *1 Chronicles*, 327–70; Boda, *1-2 Chronicles*, 125–51. De Vries in detail divides 1 Chr 15:1—16:3 as two sections: the preparation the clergy for bringing the ark (1 Chr 15:1–25) and the entrance ceremony of the ark (1 Chr 15:25—16:3). See De Vries, *1 and 2 Chronicles*, 97.

59. Japhet, *I & II Chronicles*, 312.

60. According to Hill ("Patchwork Poetry," 97–101), the Chr has made a new psalm with a chiastic structure, bringing three psalms into 1 Chr 16:
16:8 "Give thanks to YHWH" (הוֹדוּ לַיהוָה) (=Ps 105:1)
16:9 "Sing to him [YHWH]" (שִׁירוּ לוֹ) (=Ps 105:2)
16:23 "Sing to YHWH" (שִׁירוּ לַיהוָה) (=Ps 96:1)
16:34 "Give thanks to YHWH" (הוֹדוּ לַיהוָה) (=Ps 107:1)

61. Selman, *1 Chronicles*, 173.

Selman's division is also based on the fact that 1 Chr 16:1–3 (a) and 1 Chr 16:43 (a¹) are taken from 2 Sam 6:17–20.[62] However, although the outer sections (a, a¹) originate from the same source, the ark narrative in Chronicles has its own narrative context. In my judgment, 1 Chr 16:1–3 closes the transferring of the ark to Jerusalem (1 Chr 15:1—16:3) with God's blessing. First Chronicles 16:43 closes the celebration of the placement of the ark in Jerusalem (1 Chr 16:4–43) with blessing. Berger, following Selman's view, proposes a more detailed structure for the ark narrative (1 Chr 13–16):[63] the transfer of the ark to Jerusalem (1 Chr 13:1—16:1) and the Levites' appointment to the service of the ark (1 Chr 16:2–43), each of which reveals a chiastic structure.[64] In Berger's view similar to Selman, the two blessings (1 Chr 16:2, 43) function as the frame of the second part (1 Chr 16:2–43). The placement of the ark in a tent at Jerusalem (1 Chr 16:1) belongs to the first part. However, Berger does not explain why this verse belongs to the first part. His division also seems to interrupt the flow of the whole ark narrative by viewing two chiastic structures. Rather, the ark narrative is coherently composed of several parts in its narrative context without pause. Eskenazi suggests that the ark narrative, based on the goal of the transfer of the ark to Jerusalem, is composed of three parts: "Objective defined: to bring the ark to Jerusalem" (1 Chr 13:1–4); "Process of actualization: the transfer of the ark" (1 Chr 13:5—15:29); "Objective reached: celebration of the ark's arrival in Jerusalem" (1 Chr 16:1–43).[65] Eskenazi's division seems to have more coherence than Berger's.

In my view, this rhetorical unit is composed of four parts, as some scholars claim, by the clear sequences of the events in the narrative context: the first attempt to bring the ark to Jerusalem (1 Chr 13:1–14), which includes David's speeches (1 Chr 13:2–3, 14); David's exaltedness and his battle against the Philistines (1 Chr 14:1–17), which contains David's speeches (1 Chr 14:10–11; 14–15); the second attempt to bring the ark to Jerusalem (1 Chr 15:1—16:3), which includes David's speeches (1 Chr 15:2, 12–13); Levites' leading worship before the ark (1 Chr 16:4–43), which has David's prayer as his psalm of praise (1 Chr 16:8–36).

Rhetorical Strategy

David needs to reinforce his kingship after his ascension to the throne. David notes that the ark of YHWH had been neglected in the days of Saul. Accordingly, by transferring "the ark of the covenant of YHWH" as a symbol of YHWH's presence, David's kingship is strengthened. However, the ark narrative goes beyond that. The central role of Jerusalem is emphasized in the Chr's context. The Chr, in depicting the ark narrative, seems to have had more interest in the importance of Jerusalem as the

---

62. Selman, *1 Chronicles*, 173.
63. Berger, "Chiasm and Meaning," 17–22.
64. Ibid., 20, 22.
65. See Eskenazi, "Literary Approach," 264.

Speeches in David's First Attempt to Transfer the Ark (1 Chr 13:2–3, 12)

First Chronicles 13 begins with David's consultation with the leaders of Israel (1 Chr 13:1). Interestingly, David's plan to transfer the ark to Jerusalem is more focused on the people's decision, although he initiates the transfer of the ark, in comparison to the parallel text (2 Sam 6:1–11, which is focused on David's activities).⁶⁷ First Chronicles 13 describes David's rule as more democratized and shows "the balance between consultation and persuasion—that is, the openness to consult and the skill to persuade."⁶⁸ After consulting with the leaders of Israel, David makes a speech to the whole assembly of Israel as deliberative rhetoric, urging them to bring the ark (1 Chr 13:2–3):

1 Chr 13:2–3	
² וַיֹּאמֶר דָּוִיד לְכֹל קְהַל יִשְׂרָאֵל	And David said to all the assembly of Israel,
אִם־עֲלֵיכֶם טוֹב	"If it seems good to you
וּמִן־יְהוָה אֱלֹהֵינוּ	and (if it is) from YHWH our God,
נִפְרְצָה נִשְׁלְחָה עַל־אַחֵינוּ	let us send abroad to our brothers
הַנִּשְׁאָרִים בְּכֹל אַרְצוֹת יִשְׂרָאֵל	who remain in all the lands of Israel,
וְעִמָּהֶם הַכֹּהֲנִים וְהַלְוִיִּם	and with them the priests and the Levites
בְּעָרֵי מִגְרְשֵׁיהֶם	in the cities of their pasture,
וְיִקָּבְצוּ אֵלֵינוּ׃	that they may be gathered to us
³ וְנָסֵבָּה אֶת־אֲרוֹן אֱלֹהֵינוּ אֵלֵינוּ	and then let us bring back the ark of our God to us,
כִּי־לֹא דְרַשְׁנֻהוּ בִּימֵי שָׁאוּל׃	for we did not seek it in the days of Saul"

The phrase "If it seems good to you and (if it is) from YHWH our God" (1 Chr 13:2) suggests that David first of all takes heed of YHWH's will before he initiates the transfer of the ark. First Chronicles 13:3 is the key point of this speech, wherein David states that the people are responsible for the ark, not merely the king or the priests and the Levites. In the days of Saul, there had been a widespread neglect of this responsibility.⁶⁹ David believes that after his ascension to the throne his kingship may be reinforced by bringing the ark of the covenant of YHWH to Jerusalem. By employing conditional clauses (אִם־עֲלֵיכֶם טוֹב) and cohortative verb forms (נִשְׁלְחָה, נָסֵבָּה),⁷⁰ David makes a

---

66. Johnstone indicates properly that "Jerusalem's position at the heart of David's kingdom and nascent empire was to have been confirmed by the bringing in of the ark" (Johnstone, *1 and 2 Chronicles*, 1:180).

67. Japhet, *I & II Chronicles*, 274.

68. Boda, *1–2 Chronicles*, 127.

69. Begg, "The Ark in Chronicles," 136. Begg points out that 1 Chr 13:1–4 as a *Sondergut* emphasizes the peoples' responsibility for the ark.

70. In 1 Chr 13:2, the two consecutive verbs ("let us send abroad," נִפְרְצָה נִשְׁלְחָה) are adverbially

Speeches and Prayers in David's Narrative

speech to the assembly of Israel, by which the narrator conveys David's intention to gather the Israelites and bring the ark to Jerusalem.

In this speech, the protasis is verbless clauses, and the apodosis has the cohortative verbs, pointing to the rhetorical device of *cohortatio* (exhortation).[71] David says, "If it seems good to you and (if it is) from YHWH our God, let us send abroad to our brothers who remain in all the land of Israel, and with them the priests and the Levites in the cities of their pasture, that they may be gathered to us, and then let us bring back the ark of our God to us, for we did not seek it in the days of Saul." David's speech is full of exhortation. By this speech, David intends to persuade the assembly of Israel to gather their brothers and then to bring the ark back to them.

In particular, the phrase, "with them [brothers who remain in all the land of Israel] the priests and the Levites" (1 Chr 13:2) is noteworthy in that the rhetorical purpose of the Chr is shown through the narrator's character. Japhet, following Williamson's view, indicates that the term "who remain" (הַנִּשְׁאָרִים) merely refers to those who have not yet come to Hebron in line with 1 Chr 12:39[38].[72] However, the term's nuance goes beyond that. Boda suggests that this term originally refers to "the remainder of the community that was not present to David, but for the Chr, writing in the early Persian period with many Israelites still in 'exile' from the land, this term takes on the expanded nuance of the 'remnant.'"[73] Furthermore, it appears that the reference to both "the priests and the Levites" (1 Chr 13:2) is related to not only David's transfer of the ark but also his appointment of them to the cultic service after the installation of the ark at Jerusalem. Thus, David, through this speech, effectively encourages the assembly of Israel to gather their brothers, including the priests and the Levites, in order to bring back the ark to them.

In the following verse of the speech, David points out that the Israelites did not seek the ark during Saul's reign (1 Chr 13:4). It is this contrast between Saul's failure and David's success that the Chr intends to display with David's speech. Unlike Saul, David initiated the proper worship of YHWH. This is why David's first action after his ascension to the throne is the capture of Jerusalem, which is followed by the transfer of the ark to Jerusalem.[74] In this context, David's encouragement to seek the ark points to David's faithful attitude toward YHWH.

---

used in this speech. In the adverbial use of two consecutive verbs, "the principal idea is introduced only by the second verb, while the first contains the definition of the manner of the action" and "the *co-ordination* of the complementary verbal idea in the finite verb frequently occurs" (Gesenius, *Hebrew Grammar*, §120d). Japhet also indicates, following this, that the usage of נִפְרְצָה in 1 Chr 13:2 is unique (Japhet, *I & II Chronicles*, 275). On the other hand, Johnstone reads this verb, in contradiction with the adverbial reading, as "'let us *burst forth* and send to brothers'" (Johnstone, *1 and 2 Chronicles*, 1:169).

71. Lanham, *Handlist*, 36.
72. Japhet, *I & II Chronicles*, 275; Williamson, *1 and 2 Chronicles*, 114.
73. Boda, *1–2 Chronicles*, 128.
74. See Amit, "Saul Polemic," 652.

In particular, the cohortative verb "let us bring back" (נָסֵבָּה) in 1 Chr 13:3 is identified as a key word in the Chr's retelling of the early history of Israel, which is also used in the transfer of the kingship from Saul to David (1 Chr 10:14).[75] Eskenazi indicates further that in 1 Chr 13:1–4, the four key terms (שאול, דרשנהו, נסבה, נפרצה) are repeatedly used as *Leitwörter*.[76] According to her, these words frequently occur throughout the ark narrative, tying the narrative together. Their wordplay and themes link the ark narrative immediately, in terms of contrasting David's success with Saul's death (1 Chr 10:14).[77] Significantly, the verb פרץ (נפרצה) in 1 Chr 13:2) is a unifying motif in 1 Chr 13–15 dealing with the ark narrative (1 Chr 13:11; 14:11; 15:13).[78] Rhetorically, it may be called *multiclinatum*, which is "the repetition of verbal roots in succession."[79] Eskenazi contends that "the verb פרץ, a word out of place in the Chronicler's account of David's initial exhortation of the people (13:2), finds its full expression in this portion of the ark narrative."[80] In the text which follows, this verb is rhetorically used in the first battle against the Philistines (1 Chr 14:10–11).

Thus, David gathers the whole assembly of Israel after consulting with the leaders of Israel. He makes a speech to them to encourage them to bring the ark of the covenant of YHWH to Jerusalem. His speech is persuasive, and affects the whole assembly. As a result, they agree to the task of bringing the ark to Jerusalem.

However, the first attempt to transfer the ark fails due to an unexpected event. During the first transfer of the ark, Uzzah stretches out his hand to steady the ark as the oxen shake it (1 Chr 13:9). YHWH is angry with this, and Uzzah dies on account of his putting out his hand to the ark (1 Chr 13:10). The transfer of the ark is stopped there, and the ark therefore remains in the house of Obed-edom (1 Chr 13:14). This event makes David fear YHWH.

1 Chr 13:12	
וַיִּירָא דָוִיד אֶת־הָאֱלֹהִים בַּיּוֹם הַהוּא	And David feared God that day,
לֵאמֹר	saying,
הֵיךְ אָבִיא אֵלַי אֵת אֲרוֹן הָאֱלֹהִים׃	"How can I bring the ark of God to me?"

---

75. See Japhet, *I & II Chronicles*, 276; Williamson, *1 and 2 Chronicles*, 115; Boda, *1-2 Chronicles*, 128.

76. Eskenazi, "Literary Approach," 265.

77. Ibid., 265; Begg, "'Seeking Yahweh,'" 128–41.

78. Williamson, *1 and 2 Chronicles*, 114; Klein, *1 Chronicles*, 327; Allen, "Kerygmatic Units," 26–28.

79. Lundbom indicates that this rhetorical device occurs frequently in Jeremiah (Lundbom, *Hebrew Prophets*, 178; *Jeremiah*).

80. Eskenazi observes that "פרץ is repeated three times when God strikes Uzzah (13:11) and again four times in the victory over the Philistines (14:11). One final repetition interprets all the preceding ones. Speaking to the Levites, David says: 'Because you did not carry it [i.e., the ark] the first time, YHWH our God broke forth [פרץ] upon us' (15:13)" (Eskenazi, "Literary Approach," 266). Mosis also identifies the function of פרץ as a keyword (Mosis, *Untersuchungen*, 60–61).

Speeches and Prayers in David's Narrative

David utters a rhetorical question (1 Chr 13:12) as *epideictic* rhetoric, revealing his fear of God.[81] David comes to know that it is impossible for him to transfer the ark. The rhetorical question emphasizes David's inability in bringing the ark to Jerusalem because "the answer is self-evident or known to everybody and therefore not to be doubted or discussed."[82] David had not previously experienced any significant setbacks. However, as the first attempt to bring the ark to Jerusalem has been blemished by Uzzah's act, the task is stopped and the ark remains in the house of Obed-edom for three months (1 Chr 13:14). David utters his fear in accomplishing this task with a rhetorical question, which functions to emphasize David's inability to transfer the ark to Jerusalem.[83] So although this rhetorical question is designed to express David's lack of ability to complete the task, it is a question that needs answering which he does by reference to proper cultic instruction. The answer to the question is given in the second attempt to bring the ark to Jerusalem (1 Chr 15:11–13), wherein David explains that the first attempt failed since the people did not seek YHWH according to YHWH's ordinances. Through this speech, David emphasizes that they must keep the instructions YHWH had given to Moses at Sinai.

Speeches in the First Battle Account (1 Chr 14:10–11)

First Chronicles 14 is comprised of two sub-sections: David is established as king over Israel at Jerusalem (1 Chr 14:1–7), then he defeats the Philistines twice (1 Chr 14:8–17).[84] Of the two sub-sections, the second contains David's speech as his prayer and God's speech as the answer of his prayer. David inquires of God before he fights two battles against the Philistines; God positively replies to David's inquiry.

At the first battle in the valley of Rephaim (1 Chr 14:8–12), David inquires of God for the strategy to fight against the Philistines as deliberative rhetoric.

---

81. 1 Chr 13:12 is parallel to 2 Sam 6:9. Attention is given to the change of the subject from the ark of YHWH (2 Sam 6:9) to David (1 Chr 13:12). The verb form is also changed in accordance to the subject from יָבוֹא (*Qal* imperfect third person masculine singular) to אָבִיא (*Hiphil* imperfect first person common singular). In 2 Sam 6:9, we read "And David feared YHWH that day and he said, 'How can the ark of YHWH come to me?'" (וַיִּרָא דָוִד אֶת־יְהוָה בַּיּוֹם הַהוּא וַיֹּאמֶר אֵיךְ יָבוֹא אֵלַי אֲרוֹן יְהוָה). See Japhet, *Ideology*, 30–33.

82. Bar-Efrat, *Narrative Art*, 211. Lanham defines the rhetorical question as *erotesis* (Lanham, *Handlist*, 71).

83. Klein, *1 Chronicles*, 335.

84. For the political background of David's battles against the Philistines, see Garsiel, "David's Warfare against the Philistines," 150–64.

1 Chr 14:10–11	
ⁱ⁰ וַיִּשְׁאַל דָּוִיד בֵּאלֹהִים לֵאמֹר	And David inquired of God, saying,
הַאֶעֱלֶה עַל־פְּלִשְׁתִּים	"Shall I go up against the Philistines?
וּנְתַתָּם בְּיָדִי	And will you give them into my hand?"
וַיֹּאמֶר לוֹ יְהוָה	And YHWH said to him,
עֲלֵה וּנְתַתִּים בְּיָדֶךָ׃	"Go up and I will give them into your hand"
¹¹ וַיַּעֲלוּ בְּבַעַל־פְּרָצִים	And they went up to Baal-Perazim,
וַיַּכֵּם שָׁם דָּוִיד וַיֹּאמֶר דָּוִיד	and David smote them there, and David said,
פָּרַץ הָאֱלֹהִים אֶת־אוֹיְבַי	"God has broken through my enemies
בְּיָדִי כְּפֶרֶץ מָיִם	by my hand, like the breakthrough of waters,"
עַל־כֵּן קָרְאוּ	therefore they have called
שֵׁם־הַמָּקוֹם הַהוּא בַּעַל פְּרָצִים׃	the name of that place Baal-Perazim

YHWH brings about Saul's death and David's success. Saul consults a medium instead of inquiring of God (1 Chr 10:14), whereas David inquires of God as to how to fight against the Philistines (1 Chr 14:10, 14 are parallel to 2 Sam 5:19, 23).[85] Because Saul did not seek YHWH, he faced defeat and died. By contrast, David seeks God's guidance and thus, achieves great victories with divine assurance and he gains international fame, bringing the fear of him on all nations (1 Chr 14:7).[86] Klein points out appropriately that seeking YHWH (וַיִּשְׁאַל) "before the holy war is exactly what Saul failed to do (1 Chr 10:13, וְלִשְׁאֹל)."[87] By this speech, the Chr reveals a clear contrast between Saul and David, stressing the significance of "seeking YHWH." Accordingly, when David inquires of God how to fight the Philistines, God answers David's prayer. David defeats the Philistines.

In David's prayer and God's answer, the verb form עלה is frequently used (three times). This verb stresses that David and his army go up in order to fight against the Philistines according to God's word. In particular, when David smites them, he says, "God has broken through my enemies by my hand," in which the phrase "by my hand" constitutes *synecdoche*, a rhetorical device whereby a part substitutes the whole.[88] It emphasizes that God smites the Philistines through David as His agent (1 Chr 14:11; cf. 2 Sam 5:20).[89]

Furthermore, the wordplay involving פרץ in 1 Chr 14:11 is noteworthy. Baal-Perazim constitutes *epiphora*, repeating the word at the end of the first line and the last

---

85. The Chr employs the phrases "went up" (וַיַּעֲלוּ) and "by my hand" (בְּיָדִי) in 1 Chr 14:11 instead of the phrases "came to" (וַיָּבֹא) and "before me" (לְפָנַי) in 2 Sam 5:20 (Kalimi, *Reshaping*, 162–63).

86. Ibid., 329–30.

87. Klein, *1 Chronicles*, 341.

88. Lanham, *Handlist*, 148.

89. Klein says that in 1 Chr 14:11 "Divine and human cooperation is expressed" (Klein, *1 Chronicles*, 342).

line.⁹⁰ David's speech, "God has broken through (פָּרַץ) my enemies by my hand, like the breakthrough (פֶּרֶץ) of waters" utilizes a *simile*.⁹¹ The image is like a "sudden rush of water in the rainy season" in Israel.⁹² In this speech, the root of פרץ is employed four times in the form of the verb and its cognate noun.⁹³ Through these rhetorical devices in David's speech, the Chr stresses that David has followed God's guidance and that God surely has defeated the Philistines by David's hand. This military success contributes to the Chr's portrayal of David by showcasing David's attitude towards YHWH before the battles.

Speech in the Second Battle Account (1 Chr 14:14–15)

In the account of the second battle (1 Chr 14:13–17), David again inquires of God how to fight against the Philistines as deliberative rhetoric.

1 Chr 14:14–15	
¹⁴ וַיִּשְׁאַל עוֹד דָּוִיד בֵּאלֹהִים	And David again inquired of God
וַיֹּאמֶר לוֹ הָאֱלֹהִים	and God said to him,
לֹא תַעֲלֶה אַחֲרֵיהֶם	"Do not go up after them,
הָסֵב מֵעֲלֵיהֶם	turn round from them
וּבָאתָ לָהֶם מִמּוּל הַבְּכָאִים:	and come to them in front of the balsam trees
¹⁵ וִיהִי כְּשָׁמְעֲךָ אֶת־קוֹל	and it shall be when you hear the sound
הַצְּעָדָה בְּרָאשֵׁי הַבְּכָאִים	of the marching in the tops of the balsam trees,
אָז תֵּצֵא בַמִּלְחָמָה	then you shall go out to battle,
כִּי־יָצָא הָאֱלֹהִים לְפָנֶיךָ	for God will have gone out before you
לְהַכּוֹת אֶת־מַחֲנֵה פְלִשְׁתִּים:	to smite the camp of the Philistines"

In 1 Chr 14:14–15 (cf. 2 Sam 5:23–24),⁹⁴ the Chr seems to have made "a wordplay between David's going out and Yahweh's going out."⁹⁵ Through this second inquiry, David receives God's concrete instructions of how to battle against the Philistines, which is different from a simple affirmation of victory ("Go up and I will give them into your hand," 1 Chr 14:10) that he receives in the first inquiry regarding the battle. According to God's instructions David fights against them and, in turn, defeats them.

---

90. *Epiphora* as a rhetorical device is the repetition of a word at the end of two or more lines (Lanham, *Handlist*, 69).

91. Ibid., 140.

92. Boda, *1–2 Chronicles*, 135.

93. Kalimi observes that this word reveals the rhetorical device, paronomasia (pun), which is defined as "a collocation of words which resemble one another in their roots or consonantal sounds, but differ in meaning" (Kalimi, "Paronomasia," 27). For the paronomasia of פרץ in 1 Chr 14:11, see Kalimi, "Paronomasia," 40.

94. The Chr replaces the verb "act quickly" (תֶּחֱרָץ) in 2 Sam 5:24 as "go out" (תֵּצֵא) in 1 Chr 14:15.

95. Klein, *1 Chronicles*, 343.

As a result of David's victory over the Philistines, David gains his international fame among the nations (1 Chr 14:17), and David's kingship is further strengthened.

Interestingly, Kalimi argues that Isa 28:21 alludes to the narrative of David's battle against the Philistines in 1 Chr 14:8–16 (cf. 2 Sam 5:17–25).[96] According to Kalimi, in depicting the first battle against the Philistines, the Chr identifies "Baal-perazim" (2 Sam 5:20) with "Mount Perazim" (Isa 28:21). As a result, the Chr employs "went up" (וַיַּעֲלוּ) in 1 Chr 14:11 instead of "came to" (וַיָּבֹא) in 2 Sam 5:20. The verb עלה seems to have been more relevant in contexts related to high places such as mountains or hills.[97] Williamson also mentions that "the Chronicler may have thought that Baal-perazim was a hill or mountain, on the basis of Isa. 28:21."[98]

With respect to these two battles, the Chr elsewhere speaks of his main theme, which is "…if you seek him he will be found by you, but if you forsake him he will reject you forever" (אִם־תִּדְרְשֶׁנּוּ יִמָּצֵא לָךְ וְאִם־תַּעַזְבֶנּוּ יַזְנִיחֲךָ לָעַד, 1 Chr 28:9) and "…if you seek him, he will be found by you, but if you forsake you he will forsake you" (אִם־תִּדְרְשֻׁהוּ יִמָּצֵא לָכֶם וְאִם־תַּעַזְבֻהוּ יַעֲזֹב אֶתְכֶם, 2 Chr 15:2).[99] The Chr stresses the theme of seeking YHWH throughout. David's inquiry of God is in line with the theme of seeking YHWH. Accordingly, the description of the two battles against the Philistines represents David as the one who seeks out YHWH.[100] Thus, through this speech, the Chr emphasizes that David seeks out YHWH. By the Chr's description, the Yehudites should be further encouraged to take back their land by seeking YHWH.

---

96. Kalimi, *Reshaping*, 195. Allusion is defined as "intertextual structuring—directing the reader from one text to a second text by borrowing a word, phrase, or linguistic-literary devices from the first text and inserting it into the second text" (*Reshaping*, 194).

97. Ibid., 136. With respect to the second battle, he indicates here that the Chr, based on Isa 28:21, wrote "And they made a raid in the valley" (1 Chr 14:13, וַיִּפְשְׁטוּ בָעֵמֶק) instead of "And they spread themselves out in the valley of Rephaim" (2 Sam 5:22, וַיִּנָּטְשׁוּ בְּעֵמֶק רְפָאִים) and that the Chr used the name Gibeon, "And they smote the camp of the Philistines from Gibeon to Gezer" (1 Chr 14:16, וַיַּכּוּ אֶת־מַחֲנֵה פְלִשְׁתִּים מִגִּבְעוֹן וְעַד־גָּזְרָה) in place of the name Geba, "And he smote the Philistines from Geba to your coming to Gezer" (2 Sam 5:25, וַיַּךְ אֶת־פְּלִשְׁתִּים מִגֶּבַע עַד־בֹּאֲךָ גָזֶר).

98. Williamson, *1 and 2 Chronicles*, 118.

99. See Kalimi, *Reshaping*, 327.

100. Boda states that the emphasis in these two battles is "on David as inquirer of God the Lord as victorious Divine Warrior." See Boda, *1–2 Chronicles*, 134.

Speeches and Prayers in David's Narrative

Speeches in the Second Attempt to Transfer the Ark (1 Chr 15:2, 12-13)[101]

First Chronicles 15[102] begins with the statement that David builds his houses in the City of David and prepares a site for the ark of God (1 Chr 15:1).[103] David again attempts to transfer the ark to Jerusalem. At this time, David commands the Levites to carry the ark as *epideictic* rhetoric, recognizing the fact that God has chosen them to carry it (1 Chr 15:2):

1 Chr 15:2	
אָז אָמַר דָּוִיד	Then David said,
לֹא לָשֵׂאת אֶת־אֲרוֹן הָאֱלֹהִים	"No one is to carry the ark of God
כִּי אִם־הַלְוִיִּם	but the Levites,
כִּי־בָם בָּחַר יְהוָה לָשֵׂאת	for YHWH chose them to carry
אֶת־אֲרוֹן יְהוָה וּלְשָׁרְתוֹ עַד־עוֹלָם: ס	the ark of YHWH, and to serve him forever."

The second attempt to transfer the ark is carried out. At this time, David makes a speech, giving an answer to why the first attempt to transfer the ark was a failure. David's speech provides the answer for the rhetorical question (1 Chr 13:12), which is rhetorically called *hypophora*.[104] By answering the rhetorical question, David gives the instructions to transfer the ark properly to the Levites according to the word of YHWH, commissioning them to move the ark (1 Chr 15:1-15).

This speech reveals his faithfulness to the Deuteronomic law in the Pentateuch. In particular, 1 Chr 15:2 may be divided into two utterances. The first utterance, "No one is to carry the ark but the Levites," is equated with Deut 10:8 ("At that time YHWH separated the tribe of Levi to carry the ark of the covenant of YHWH..." בָּעֵת הַהִוא הִבְדִּיל יְהוָה אֶת־שֵׁבֶט הַלֵּוִי לָשֵׂאת אֶת־אֲרוֹן בְּרִית־יְהוָה), and the second utterance,

---

101. The second attempt to transfer the ark to Jerusalem in 1 Chr 15:1—16:3 is parallel to that in 2 Sam 6:12-19. These two versions seem to have different purposes. For the author of Samuel, the significance of the narrative is on the depiction of transferring the ark to Jerusalem; whereas, for the Chronicler the immediate preparations between the first attempt and the second attempt are most significant (Street, *Significance*, 13). For the discussion of the differences between the two versions, see Japhet, *I & II Chronicles*, 293-94; Williamson, *1 and 2 Chronicles*, 119-20, 126-27.

102. According to Selman, the primary purpose of 1 Chr 15 is not to depict the history of the Levites and their organization. The focal point seems to be on David's role in relation to the Levites and worship in Israel. David is portrayed as the one who is responsible for the changed role of the Levites (1 Chr 15:3, 11, 16). However, this point is supplementary to the main purpose that provides extraordinary encouragement for the personnel of Israelite worship (Selman, *1 Chronicles*, 161).

103. First Chronicles 15:1 is linked to 1 Chr 16:1: "David prepared a place for the ark of God and stretched out a tent for it" (1 Chr 15:1), and "they brought the ark of God and placed it in the midst of the tent that David stretched out for it" (1 Chr 16:1). According to Kalimi, "The individual parts that conclude the literary inclusio are presented in chiastic order relative to the same parts in the introduction: setting up the Tent, the Levites bearing the Ark, and the accompaniment by David and all Israel. Thus, 1 Chr 15:1, 3 take their content from 1 Chr 15:18, 16:1, which parallel 2 Sam 6:15, 17" (Kalimi, *Reshaping*, 307).

104. Lanham, *Handlist*, 87.

"YHWH chose them to carry the ark of YHWH and to serve him forever," is equated with Deut 18:5 ("For YHWH your God chose him from all your tribes..." כִּי בוֹ בָּחַר יְהוָה אֱלֹהֶיךָ מִכָּל־שְׁבָטֶיךָ).[105] As such, the Chr frequently emphasizes that the bearers of the ark are the Levites. We can clearly see it in 1 Chr 15:26–27, "And it came to pass when God helped the Levites who were bearing the ark of the covenant of YHWH (וַיְהִי בֶּעְזֹר הָאֱלֹהִים אֶת־הַלְוִיִּם נֹשְׂאֵי אֲרוֹן בְּרִית־יְהוָה)... and all the Levites who were bearing the ark (וְכָל־הַלְוִיִּם הַנֹּשְׂאִים אֶת־הָאָרוֹן)..."[106] Thus, the Chr reveals that David already has learned YHWH's ordinances regarding His election of the Levites as those who can convey the ark.

Furthermore, this short speech functions to persuade all of Israel and the Levites to bring the ark to Jerusalem again. David assembles all Israel and the descendants of Aaron and the Levites (1 Chr 15:3–4)[107] in order to transfer the ark to Jerusalem. Then, David summons the two priests Zadok and Abiathar and the Levites (1 Chr 15:11) who are about to carry the ark. David makes a speech to the priests and the Levites as deliberative rhetoric (1 Chr 15:12–13):

1 Chr 15:12–13	
12 וַיֹּאמֶר לָהֶם	And he said to them,
אַתֶּם רָאשֵׁי הָאָבוֹת לַלְוִיִּם	"You are the heads of the fathers of the Levites,
הִתְקַדְּשׁוּ אַתֶּם וַאֲחֵיכֶם	consecrate yourselves and your brothers,
וְהַעֲלִיתֶם אֵת אֲרוֹן יְהוָה אֱלֹהֵי יִשְׂרָאֵל	and bring up the ark of YHWH God of Israel
אֶל־הֲכִינוֹתִי לוֹ:	to the place I have prepared for it
13 כִּי לְמַבָּרִאשׁוֹנָה לֹא אַתֶּם	because at the first you did not (carry it),
פָּרַץ יְהוָה אֱלֹהֵינוּ בָּנוּ	YHWH our God broke forth upon us,
כִּי־לֹא דְרַשְׁנֻהוּ	for we did not seek him
כַּמִּשְׁפָּט:	according to the ordinance"

In 1 Chr 15:12, David commands the heads of the families of the Levites to consecrate themselves and to bring up the ark of YHWH. At this time, the narrative audience is the leaders of the Levites. It is noteworthy that the word קדש in 1 Chr 15:12 is for the first time employed in the narrative section, which is a typical word among the Chr's

---

105. Japhet contends that this is an example of "the Chronicler's anthological style: selecting ready-made elements from various texts, he weaves them into one fabric, and uses the whole to express his own attitudes" (Japhet, *I & II Chronicles*, 297). Williamson believes that "David's careful observance of the Deuteronomic law forms an important link in the Chronicler's claim for Levitical participation in the temple service" (Williamson, *1 and 2 Chronicles*, 122–23).

106. See Kalimi, *Reshaping*, 150.

107. Knoppers observes that 1 Chr 16:43 shows an *inclusio* with 1 Chr 15:3, indicating that the second section of the ark narrative (1 Chr 15–16) constitutes a rhetorical unit (Knoppers, *1 Chronicles*, 655). Johnstone also notices that a keyword "house" in 1 Chr 16 links the ark narrative to the following narrative of the promise of Davidic dynasty in 1 Chr 17 (Johnstone, *1 and 2 Chronicles*, 1:197).

terms.¹⁰⁸ According to David's command, the Levites consecrate themselves to transfer the ark (1 Chr 15:14). Some phrases in 1 Chr 15:12 are repeated in 1 Chr 15:14 (e.g., "consecrate themselves," "to bring up," "the ark of YHWH," "God of Israel"). Interestingly, the phrase "he has prepared a place for the ark of God" (וַיָּכֶן מָקוֹם לָאָרוֹן הָאֱלֹהִים) in 1 Chr 15:1, 3 is repeated in 1 Chr 15:12. This repetition conspicuously reveals the significance of the place (מָקוֹם). The ark of YHWH will be located in the place which David has prepared for it.¹⁰⁹

In 1 Chr 15:13, the Chr provides an explanation for the failure of the first attempt to transfer the ark (1 Chr 13:1–14). The phrase, "for we did not seek him according to the ordinance" (כִּי־לֹא דְרַשְׁנֻהוּ כַּמִּשְׁפָּט) points to not only the original tribe who are permitted to bear the ark but also how to bear the ark, reflecting the previous phrase "for we did not seek it in the days of Saul" (1 Chr 13:3, כִּי־לֹא דְרַשְׁנֻהוּ בִּימֵי שָׁאוּל). In the first attempt, the ark is carried by Uzzah and his brother (Ahio) and they transport the ark by putting it on a new cart (1 Chr 13:7); whereas, in the second attempt, the ark is carried by the Levites and they carry it upon their shoulders with poles (1 Chr 15:15; Num 7:9).¹¹⁰ Thus, the second attempt succeeds due to their observance of YHWH's ordinances.

In 1 Chr 15:13, the phrase, "YHWH. . . broke forth upon us" (פָּרַץ יְהוָה אֱלֹהֵינוּ בָּנוּ) is linked to the phrase, "YHWH had broken forth upon Uzzah" (פָּרַץ יְהוָה פֶּרֶץ בְּעֻזָּא) in 1 Chr 13:11. In these passages, the personal pronoun is changed from third person singular (Uzzah) to first person plural (us). Probably, this means that Uzzah's death is not merely a personal punishment but also a communal punishment. The focus is on the link of Uzzah's sin with the peoples' sin.¹¹¹ Accordingly, David, in the second attempt to bring the ark, is depicted as the one who is faithful to the Deuteronomic law.

In the Chr's description of the second attempt to transfer the ark, a stylistic feature of the Chr is noteworthy.¹¹² In 1 Chr 15:25–29, special attention is given to the term "the ark of the covenant of YHWH."¹¹³ The designation of the ark has been changed from "the ark of God" or "the ark of YHWH" in the preceding chapter to

---

108. Johnstone, *1 and 2 Chronicles*, 1:182–83.

109. Japhet indicates three conspicuous features of this speech: (1) David's speech in 1 Chr 15:12–13 is exactly repeated "in the execution of the orders," in 1 Chr 15:14–15; (2) אַתֶּם is emphasized in this speech; (3) The phrase, "the ark of the Lord" is repeated three times (1 Chr 15:12, 14, 15) (Japhet, *I & II Chronicles*, 300–301).

110. See Kalimi, *Reshaping*, 150–51.

111. It is appropriate that it is "an admission of sin and an acceptance of full responsibility" (Japhet, *I & II Chronicles*, 301).

112. For instance, the Levites only could carry the ark by rods on their shoulders (Num 4:1–15). In the Chr's view, the first attempt to bring the ark to Jerusalem failed because the law of carrying the ark was not kept. So, the second attempt, based on the law-keeping, succeeds by the Levites' carrying the ark (1 Chr 15:26).

113. It is noteworthy in the ark narrative that the Chr employs the term, "the ark of the covenant" (1 Chr 15:25, 26, 28, 29), whereas it is used as "the ark of God" or "the ark of YHWH" in 2 Sam 6:2, 3, 4, 6, 7, 9, 10, 11, 12, 13, 15, 17.

"the ark of the covenant of the YHWH" in 1 Chr 15. In this chapter, the term, "the ark of the covenant of YHWH" occurs four times (1 Chr 15:25, 26, 28, 29), which is not shown in the parallel text (2 Sam 6:12–19). In the context of 1 Chr 14 dealing with David's international fame, the designation of the ark is usually given by the term "the ark of God" or "the ark of YHWH"; whereas, it is given by the term "the ark of the covenant of YHWH" in 1 Chr 15, adding the significant word, "covenant" to the preceding designation of the ark.[114] Johnstone, noting the change of the designation of the ark, indicates that the Chr is:

> now concerned about the inner-Israel significance of the ark: at the formal moment of the final integration of symbol and reality at the centre of the nation's life, it is Israel in relation to the LORD, the name by which Deity has been made known to Israel alone, as the people of the LORD that stands now in the forefront of interest.[115]

For the Chr, the focus is on the meaning of the ark which the ark conveys. In effect, the ark is absent from the Judahites' life in the time of the Chr.[116] Much earlier, with the destruction of Jerusalem, the ark had disappeared and the Israelites had been deported to Babylon (2 Chr 36:15–20). After seventy years (2 Chr 36:21), due to the edict of Cyrus (2 Chr 36:22–23) they have returned to their homeland and the temple (though without the ark) is restored. Thus, as the symbol of YHWH's presence, the ark of the covenant of YHWH is significantly linked to the temple.

David commands the Levites, who have the responsibility for the task, to bring the ark of YHWH "according to the ordinance." At this time, they correctly carry the ark upon their shoulders and the second attempt to bring the ark to Jerusalem is successful. David's speech functions to persuade the assembly of Israel and the Levites to carry out the task of transferring of the ark according to YHWH's instructions given through Moses.

Furthermore, after the transfer of the ark to Jerusalem, David plays the role as a worship leader like the high priest on behalf of the Israelites (1 Chr 15:27), in which we read that David was clothed with a robe of fine linen (וְדָוִיד מְכֻרְבָּל בִּמְעִיל בּוּץ) and

114. For the designation of the ark, see Japhet, *Ideology*, 96–100. With respect to the function of the ark, the suggested functions of the ark are fetish-chest, bearer of God's image, a miniature temple, throne, footstool, a simple receptacle, war-palladium, or spatial center of amphictyony (Shin, *The Ark of Yahweh*, 32–44).

115. Johnstone, *1 and 2 Chronicles*, 1:186.

116. There have been various views about the disappearance of the ark. For instance, Jer 3:16 alludes to the disappearance of the ark; 2 Macc 2:47 states that Jeremiah concealed the ark; 2 Esd 10:20–22 indicates that the ark was taken by the Babylonians. Day provides a good summary of the views on the disappearance of the ark: it was hidden on Mt. Gerizim in Eli's time or Moses'; it was taken to Ethiopia in Solomon's time; it was eliminated by Shashak; it was removed by careful action after collapse of the united monarch; it was transferred by Jehoash, or Ahaz, or Hezekiah, or Manasseh; it was hidden by Josiah or by Jeremiah; and it was taken away or destroyed by the Babylonians under Nebuchadnezzar (Day, "Whatever Happened to the Ark," 250–70). See also Shin, *The Ark of Yahweh*, 148–49.

wore a linen ephod (וְעַל־דָּוִיד אֵפוֹד בָּד).¹¹⁷ Thus, David is portrayed as a worship leader who recognizes YHWH's ordinances.

David's Psalm of Praise (1 Chr 16:8–36)

David's psalm in 1 Chr 16 has been discussed by scholars. Butler suggests that the constitution of this psalm (1 Chr 16:8–36)¹¹⁸ concerns the Chr's theological intentions, especially based on YHWH's kingship, YHWH's sovereignty, and the Davidic covenant.¹¹⁹ Noting that Butler does not give attention to the inner structure of a new psalm, Hill contends that the Chr has made a new psalm in 1 Chr 16.¹²⁰ According to Hill, the new psalm has a cohesive structure and fits well into the primary context of 1 Chr 13–20.¹²¹ Shipp uses Hill's concept and suggests that the Levitical activities in 1 Chr 16:4 (such as "give thanks," "praise," "remember") shapes this psalm, providing a "connective echo"¹²² that fixes this psalm in its narrative context.¹²³ Kleinig proposes that the Chr had special interest in exhibiting the theological importance of choral music as a ritual activity before YHWH.¹²⁴ However, these studies have been heavily focused on the structure of the new psalm, in which scholars have divided it into several parts.¹²⁵ Yet, they minimally discuss why they divide it so. The narrative context likely provides a clue to figure out the structure of this psalm.

---

117. Although Johnstone asserts that "[i]t is through the power of the liturgy associated with the ark that the community is drawn into the significance of what the ark stands for–the dominion of God" (Johnstone, *1 and 2 Chronicles*, 1:183).

118. Williamson proposes that 1 Chr 16:8–36 is parallel to David's final prayer in 1 Chr 29:10–19. Both prayers refer to YHWH's covenant with the patriarchs and David's praise to YHWH's kingship. He concludes that these prayers have many similarities and provide a narrative framework to 1 Chr 17–19, in which special attention is given to David's preparations for the building of the temple (Williamson, *1 and 2 Chronicles*, 186).

119. See Butler, "A Forgotten Passage," 142–50.

120. See Hill, "Patchwork Poetry," 97–101. I agree with Hill's statement that "the composite psalm in 1 Chr. xvi is not 'patchwork poetry' but deliberate and artistically skillful 'reasoned verse'" (101). For the discussion of chiasmus in Chronicles, see Kalimi, *Reshaping*, 215–31.

121. According to Hill ("Patchwork Poetry," 97–101), this aspect was ignored in Butler's assertion. For Butler "the composite psalm does not fit the 'historical' context because the enemies of Israel have already been delivered into the hands of David (cf. xvi 35 with xiv 17)" (101). However, Hill indicates properly that "Butler fails to consider chap. xviii–xx which recount David's victories over the Philistines and Ammonites *after* the return of the ark of God and *before* he began the task of organizing the kingdom" (101). See also Butler, "A Forgotten Passage," 145.

122. Hill, "Patchwork Poetry," 99.

123. Shipp, "'Remember His Covenant Forever,'" 31–39. Shipp employs Hill's concept.

124. Kleinig, *The Lord's Song*, 133–48.

125. There are scholars who divide this psalm into two (1), three (2), four (3), five (4), and six (5) parts: (1) Johnstone, *1 and 2 Chronicles*, 1:175 (vv. 8–22; 23–36); Japhet, *I & II Chronicles*, 316 (vv. 8–33; 34–36); (2) De Vries, *1 and 2 Chronicles*, 151 (vv. 8–22; 23–33; 34–36a); (3) Williamson, *1 and 2 Chronicles*, 128–29 (vv. 8–13; 14–22; 23–33; 34–36a); Hill, "Patchwork Poetry," 100 (vv. 8; 9–22; 23–33; 34–36); Selman, *1 Chronicles*, 168–72; Balentine, "You Can't Pray a Lie," 255; (4) Kleinig, *The Lord's Song*, 143–44 (vv. 8; 9–22; 23–30; 31–33; 34); (5) Thompson, *1, 2 Chronicles*, 140–42 (vv. 8–13;

After the ark is placed in the tent at Jerusalem, David appoints the Levites as ministers before the ark and then makes a prayer to God. The last sub-unit of the ark narrative (1 Chr 16:4–43) contains the appointment of some Levites as ministers before the ark (1 Chr 16:4–7),[126] David's psalm of praise (1 Chr 16:8–36), and the maintenance of regular worship (1 Chr 16:37–43). Of these three parts, David's psalm of praise is his speech as deliberative rhetoric:[127]

1 Chr 16:8–36	
⁸ הוֹדוּ לַיהוָה	Give thanks to YHWH,
קִרְאוּ בִשְׁמוֹ	call on his name,
הוֹדִיעוּ בָעַמִּים עֲלִילֹתָיו׃	make known his deeds among the peoples
⁹ שִׁירוּ לוֹ זַמְּרוּ־לוֹ	Sing to him, sing praises to him,
שִׂיחוּ בְּכָל־נִפְלְאֹתָיו׃	speak of all his wonders
¹⁰ הִתְהַלְלוּ בְּשֵׁם קָדְשׁוֹ	Glory in his holy name
יִשְׂמַח לֵב מְבַקְשֵׁי יְהוָה׃	Let the heart of those who seek YHWH rejoice
¹¹ דִּרְשׁוּ יְהוָה וְעֻזּוֹ	Seek YHWH and his strength
בַּקְּשׁוּ פָנָיו תָּמִיד׃	Seek his face continually
¹² זִכְרוּ נִפְלְאֹתָיו אֲשֶׁר עָשָׂה	Remember his wonders that he has done,
מֹפְתָיו וּמִשְׁפְּטֵי־פִיהוּ׃	his signs, and the judgments of his mouth
¹³ זֶרַע יִשְׂרָאֵל עַבְדּוֹ	O seed of Israel, his servant,
בְּנֵי יַעֲקֹב בְּחִירָיו׃	sons of Jacob, his chosen ones
¹⁴ הוּא יְהוָה אֱלֹהֵינוּ	He (is) YHWH our God,
בְּכָל־הָאָרֶץ מִשְׁפָּטָיו׃	his judgments (are) in all the earth
¹⁵ זִכְרוּ לְעוֹלָם בְּרִיתוֹ	Remember his covenant forever,
דָּבָר צִוָּה לְאֶלֶף דּוֹר׃	The word he commanded to a thousand generations
¹⁶ אֲשֶׁר כָּרַת אֶת־אַבְרָהָם	which he made with Abraham,
וּשְׁבוּעָתוֹ לְיִצְחָק׃	and his oath to Isaac
¹⁷ וַיַּעֲמִידֶהָ לְיַעֲקֹב לְחֹק	and he established it to Jacob for a statute,
לְיִשְׂרָאֵל בְּרִית עוֹלָם׃	To Israel (as) a an everlasting covenant
¹⁸ לֵאמֹר לְךָ אֶתֵּן אֶרֶץ־כְּנָעַן	Saying, "to you I will give the land of Canaan,
חֶבֶל נַחֲלַתְכֶם׃	the portion of your inheritance."
¹⁹ בִּהְיוֹתְכֶם מְתֵי מִסְפָּר	When you (they) are few of number,

---

14–22; 23–29; 30–33; 34; 35–36a); Watts, *Psalm and Story*, 156.

126. 1 Chr 16:4–6 is unique in that it has no parallel in the Samuel narrative. It should be noted that the Chr has more interest in the development of the cult than the author of Samuel. See Japhet, *I & II Chronicles*, 314.

127. David's psalm should be regarded as his prayer or his speech, since it is written in a reporting speech form (e.g., imperatives). Actually, 1 Chr 16:7 reads "Then on that day David first gave orders to praise YHWH by the hand of Asaph and his brethren." Thus, David's psalm is an indirect speech.

כִּמְעַט וְגָרִים בָּהּ:	as a little thing, and sojourners in it
20 וַיִּתְהַלְּכוּ מִגּוֹי אֶל־גּוֹי	And they wandered from nation to nation,
וּמִמַּמְלָכָה אֶל־עַם אַחֵר:	and from one kingdom to another people
21 לֹא־הִנִּיחַ לְאִישׁ לְעָשְׁקָם	He allowed no man to oppress them,
וַיּוֹכַח עֲלֵיהֶם מְלָכִים:	and he reproved kings on account of them
22 אַל־תִּגְּעוּ בִּמְשִׁיחָי	"Do not touch my anointed ones,
וּבִנְבִיאַי אַל־תָּרֵעוּ:	and (to) my prophets do not evil"
23 שִׁירוּ לַיהוָה כָּל־הָאָרֶץ	Sing to YHWH, all the earth,
בַּשְּׂרוּ מִיּוֹם־אֶל־יוֹם יְשׁוּעָתוֹ:	proclaim his salvation from day to day
24 סַפְּרוּ בַגּוֹיִם אֶת־כְּבוֹדוֹ	Recount his glory among nations,
בְּכָל־הָעַמִּים נִפְלְאֹתָיו:	his wonders among all peoples
25 כִּי גָדוֹל יְהוָה	For great (is) YHWH,
וּמְהֻלָּל מְאֹד	and one who is praised greatly,
וְנוֹרָא הוּא עַל־כָּל־אֱלֹהִים:	and he is to be feared above all gods
26 כִּי כָּל־אֱלֹהֵי הָעַמִּים אֱלִילִים	for all the gods of the peoples are worthless gods,
וַיהוָה שָׁמַיִם עָשָׂה:	but YHWH made the heavens
27 הוֹד וְהָדָר לְפָנָיו	Splendor and majesty (are) before him,
עֹז וְחֶדְוָה בִּמְקֹמוֹ:	Strength and joy (are) in his place
28 הָבוּ לַיהוָה מִשְׁפְּחוֹת עַמִּים	Ascribe to YHWH, O families of peoples,
הָבוּ לַיהוָה כָּבוֹד וָעֹז:	Ascribe to YHWH glory and strength
29 הָבוּ לַיהוָה כְּבוֹד שְׁמוֹ	Ascribe to YHWH the glory of his name,
שְׂאוּ מִנְחָה וּבֹאוּ לְפָנָיו	Lift up an offering and come before him,
הִשְׁתַּחֲווּ לַיהוָה בְּהַדְרַת־קֹדֶשׁ:	Worship YHWH in the glory of holiness
30 חִילוּ מִלְּפָנָיו כָּל־הָאָרֶץ	Tremble before him, all the earth,
אַף־תִּכּוֹן תֵּבֵל	the world is firmly established,
בַּל־תִּמּוֹט:	it will not be moved
31 יִשְׂמְחוּ הַשָּׁמַיִם וְתָגֵל הָאָרֶץ	Let the heavens rejoice, and let the earth be glad,
וְיֹאמְרוּ בַגּוֹיִם	so that they may say among the nations,
יְהוָה מָלָךְ:	"YHWH reigns"
32 יִרְעַם הַיָּם וּמְלוֹאוֹ	Let the sea thunder and that it fills,
יַעֲלֹץ הַשָּׂדֶה וְכָל־אֲשֶׁר־בּוֹ:	let the field rejoice and all that is in it
33 אָז יְרַנְּנוּ עֲצֵי הַיָּעַר	Then the trees of the forest will sing for joy
מִלִּפְנֵי יְהוָה	before YHWH,
כִּי־בָא לִשְׁפּוֹט אֶת־הָאָרֶץ:	for he is coming to judge the earth

³⁴ הוֹדוּ לַיהוָה כִּי טוֹב	Give thanks to YHWH, for he is good,
כִּי לְעוֹלָם חַסְדּוֹ:	for his steadfast love is forever
³⁵ וְאִמְרוּ הוֹשִׁיעֵנוּ אֱלֹהֵי יִשְׁעֵנוּ	and say, "Save us, O God of our salvation,
וְקַבְּצֵנוּ וְהַצִּילֵנוּ מִן־הַגּוֹיִם	And gather us and deliver us from the nations,
לְהֹדוֹת לְשֵׁם קָדְשֶׁךָ	to give thanks to your holy name,
לְהִשְׁתַּבֵּחַ בִּתְהִלָּתֶךָ:	to laud your praise
³⁶ בָּרוּךְ יְהוָה אֱלֹהֵי יִשְׂרָאֵל	Blessed (be) YHWH, God of Israel,
מִן־הָעוֹלָם וְעַד הָעֹלָם	From everlasting to everlasting."
וַיֹּאמְרוּ כָל־הָעָם אָמֵן	And all the people said, "Amen"
וְהַלֵּל לַיהוָה:	and they praised YHWH

David's prayer contains a number of imperatives, which the Chr appears to have employed as a stylistic feature although this psalm is eclectically taken from some different psalms. For instance, the imperative verb forms are "give thanks," "call," "make known" (הוֹדוּ, קִרְאוּ, הוֹדִיעוּ) in 1 Chr 16:8, "sing," "speak" (שִׁירוּ, שִׂיחוּ) in 1 Chr 16:9, "glory" (הִתְהַלְלוּ) in 1 Chr 16:10, "seek" (דִּרְשׁוּ, בַּקְּשׁוּ) in 1 Chr 16:11, and "remember" (זִכְרוּ) in 1 Chr 16:12.

This psalm is comprised of several parts of three different psalms with some modifications (1 Chr 16:8–22 // Ps 105:1–15; 1 Chr 16:23–33 // Ps 96:1–13; 1 Chr 16:34–36 // Ps 106:1, 47–48). In particular, 1 Chr 16:8–22 concerns God's faithfulness to Israel (Ps 105).[128] First Chronicles 16:23–33 contains praise to God who comes in judgment (Ps 96), and 1 Chr 16:34–36 is a refrain and a doxology[129] (three verses in Ps 106 dealing with a confession of sins). Although this psalm consists of some parts of three different psalms, it has its unity in the Chr's presentation. In what follows, this psalm will be discussed by three sections: praise to God's faithfulness (1 Chr 16:8–22); immense praise to God (1 Chr 16:23–33); and a summary supplication (1 Chr 16:34–36).

First, 1 Chr 16:8–22[130] is a call to praise YHWH, which contains two subsections. The one is the call to praise YHWH (1 Chr 16:8–11) and the other is the remem-

---

128. 1 Chr 16:15–22 (// Ps 105:8–15) alludes to the patriarchs' narrative in Genesis: 1 Chr 16:15–18 (// Ps 105:8–11) alludes to the land promised to them (Gen 12:7; 15:17; 22:15–18; 26:2–5; 27:13–15; 35:9–13) and 1 Chr 16:19–22 (// Ps 105:12–15) to the patriarchs' wandering among the nations (Gen 12:10–20; 20:1–18; 26:7–11; 32:24, 29). See Kalimi, *Reshaping*, 195.

129. Japhet believes that 1 Chr 16:34 as the response of the people to the Levites' singing is an antiphon as well as a refrain, which begins and ends a few psalms (e.g., Pss 106:1; 107:1; 118:1–4, 29; 136) and that 1 Chr 16:35–36 is perhaps "uttered by the participants in the cult, at the end of prayer" (e.g., Pss 72:18–19; 89:53) (Japhet, *I & II Chronicles*, 316).

130. Some phrases in 1 Chr 16:8–22 are changed from the original, Ps 105:1–15: "O seed of Israel" (זֶרַע יִשְׂרָאֵל) in 1 Chr 16:13 instead of "O seed of Abraham" (זֶרַע אַבְרָהָם) in Ps 105:6; the change of the verb form from the indicative, "he remembered" (זָכַר) in Ps 105:8 to the imperative, "remember" (זִכְרוּ) in 1 Chr 16:15; and the phrase, "When you were few in number" (בִּהְיוֹתְכֶם מְתֵי מִסְפָּר) in 1 Chr 16:19 instead of "When they were few in number" (בִּהְיוֹתָם מְתֵי מִסְפָּר) in Ps 105:12.

brance of the covenantal relationship between YHWH and Israel (1 Chr 16:12–22). The first subsection begins with the phrase "give thanks to YHWH" (1 Chr 16:8), which forms an *inclusio* with the same phrase in 1 Chr 16:34.[131] Another phrase "sing to him [YHWH]" (1 Chr 16:9) also shows an *inclusio* with that in 1 Chr 16:23. These phrases invite the hearers to praise YHWH, emphasizing God's deeds, wonders, and holy name. The call to praise ends with the emphasis on seeking YHWH. In effect, the verb "to seek" is repeated three times (1 Chr 16:10–11) by using two different verbs (מְבַקְשֵׁי, דִּרְשׁוּ, בַּקְּשׁוּ). The theme of seeking YHWH is one of the Chr's favorite terms in retelling the early history of Israel.

The second subsection concerns the remembrance of YHWH's great work (1 Chr 16:12–14) and of YHWH's covenants with the patriarch (1 Chr 16:15–22), which is divided by the imperative "remember" (זִכְרוּ) in 1 Chr 16:12, 15. This imperative verb displays the rhetorical device *anaphora* by repeating it at the beginning of successive verses.[132] In 1 Chr 16:15 (cf. 1 Chr 16:17) the Chr emphasizes that YHWH makes an everlasting covenant with Israel on the basis of the covenants with the patriarchs (1 Chr 16:16–17: cf. Abraham [Gen 15; 22:15–18]; Isaac [Gen 26:2–5]; and Jacob [Gen 28:13–15; 35:11–12]). What is interesting is that the Chr employs the divine speeches as a quotation in this subsection: "to you I will give the land of Canaan, the portion of your inheritance" (1 Chr 16:18) and "Do not touch my anointed ones, and (to) my prophets do not evil" (1 Chr 16:22). The former phrase points to God's promise regarding the land as the inheritance of Israel; the latter, God's intervention in the case of the Israelites under the oppression of other nations. Accordingly, these direct discourses stress the covenantal God from the early history of Israel. In 1 Chr 16:19–20, the people of Israel are small in number "as a little thing" (כִּמְעַט), which displays the rhetorical device of *simile*. In the past, the people had been wandering sojourners among the nations and the peoples, which is stressed by the phrases "from nation to nation" (מִגּוֹי אֶל־גּוֹי) and "and from one kingdom to another people" (וּמִמַּמְלָכָה אֶל־עַם אַחֵר) with an *ellipsis* of the verb "they wandered" (וַיִּתְהַלְּכוּ) at the second line in 1 Chr 16:20. YHWH chooses a small people (1 Chr 16:13) and calls them as "my anointed ones" and "my prophets" (1 Chr 16:22). Accordingly, the covenantal God and His sovereignty are emphasized.

Second, 1 Chr 16:23–33[133] deals with immense praise to God, which can be divided into three subsections: praise of all the earth (1 Chr 16:23–27); praise of the

---

131. Klein, *1 Chronicles*, 364.

132. Lanham, *Handlist*, 11.

133. First Chronicles 16:23–33, which is parallel to Ps 96:1b–13a, has some modifications: 1 Chr 16:23 is combined with Ps 96:1b and 96:2b; the phrase, "in his place" (בִּמְקֹמוֹ) in 1 Chr 16:27 instead of "in his sanctuary" (בְּמִקְדָּשׁוֹ) in Ps 96:6; the jussive verb form, "let them say" (וְיֹאמְרוּ) in 1 Chr 16:31 instead of the imperative, "say" (אִמְרוּ) in Ps 96:10. Kalimi observes here that the word order is inverted between 1 Chr 16:30–31 and Ps 96:10–11 (Kalimi, *Reshaping*, 253–54):

people (1 Chr 16:28–30); and praise of the universe (1 Chr 16:31–33). The first subsection emphasizes YHWH's greatness through the praise of the whole earth, indicating that all other gods of the peoples are worthless. In particular, YHWH's characteristics are stressed by a series of nouns, "splendor and majesty" (הוֹד וְהָדָר) and "strength and joy" (עֹז וְחֶדְוָה) in 1 Chr 16:27, passages which showcase rhetorically the accumulation of nouns.[134] The second subsection (1 Chr 16:28–30) concerns the people's praise to YHWH. In particular, the phrase "Ascribe to YHWH" (הָבוּ לַיהוָה) is repeated three times in 1 Chr 16:28–29, which forms an *anaphora* by repeating it at the beginning of two or more lines. The ensuing imperatives "Lift up," "Worship," "Tremble" (שְׂאוּ, הִשְׁתַּחֲווּ, חִילוּ) in 1 Chr 16:29–30 reinforce the peoples' praise towards YHWH. This second subsection is full of the people's praise to YHWH. The third subsection (1 Chr 16:31–33) deals with the cosmic praise to YHWH. The heavens and the earth, the field, and even the trees of the forest are personified in order to praise YHWH, which is rhetorically called *prosopopoeia* (Conformatio).[135] The heavens and the earth rejoice in YHWH and even the trees sing to YHWH as if they were human beings. Thus, the range of praise to YHWH is covered from all the earth even to the universe.

Third, 1 Chr 16:34–36[136] is a summary supplication. It begins with the phrase "Give thanks to YHWH" (1 Chr 16:34), forming an *inclusio* with 1 Chr 16:8, because YHWH's steadfast love is forever. The final supplication (1 Chr 16:35) is for Israel's deliverance, in which David's request is emphasized by repeating the root of ישע twice (הוֹשִׁיעֵנוּ, יִשְׁעֵנוּ). In particular, the phrase "gather us" reflects the scattered situation of the people, and the phrase "deliver us from the nations" might point to David's wars

---

Ps 96:10–11

a. Say among the nations, YHWH reigns
b. The world also is firmly established, it will not be moved. . .
   Let the heavens be glad, and let the earth rejoice. . .

1 Chr 16:30–31

a. . . . The world is firmly established, it will not be moved.
   Let the heavens be glad, and let the earth rejoice,
b. and let them say among the nations, YHWH reigns

Furthermore, it should be noted that Pss 96:10c and 96:13c are omitted: "He will judge the peoples with equity" (יָדִין עַמִּים בְּמֵישָׁרִים); "He will judge the world with righteousness and the peoples with truth" (יִשְׁפֹּט־תֵּבֵל בְּצֶדֶק וְעַמִּים בֶּאֱמוּנָתוֹ).

134. See Bar-Efrat, *Narrative Art*, 216.

135. *Prosopopoeia* means that "an inanimate object is represented as having human attributes." See Lanham, *Handlist*, 123.

136. First Chronicles 16:34–36, which is parallel to Ps 106:1, 47–48, contains two alterations: the two phrases, "our salvation" (in אֱלֹהֵי יִשְׁעֵנוּ הוֹשִׁיעֵנוּ) and "deliver us" (וְהַצִּילֵנוּ), in comparison to Ps 106:47 (הוֹשִׁיעֵנוּ יְהוָה אֱלֹהֵינוּ), are added to 1 Chr 16:35; the verb form is changed from the jussive, "let all the people say" (וְאָמַר כָּל־הָעָם) in Ps 106:48 to the indicative, "all the people said" (וַיֹּאמְרוּ כָל־הָעָם) in 1 Chr 16:36.

in 1 Chr 18–20.[137] Accordingly, YHWH's deliverance of Israel will lead the Israelites to praise YHWH. Finally, David's psalm of praise ends with a blessing of YHWH God of Israel, which is reinforced by the accentuating phrase "from everlasting to everlasting" (1 Chr 16:36). As a response to this blessing, all the people of Israel, who come to join David and transfer the ark of the covenant of YHWH to Jerusalem, praise YHWH God of Israel.

Importantly, the new psalm as David's praise is given to the whole assembly of Israel in the ark-narrative context. Watts claims that the narrative role of this psalm is "to establish continuity between the cult established by David and that of the Chr's own day, and to draw the theological conclusions regarding the status of the Levites and the community as a whole which that community implies."[138] Accordingly, this new psalm shows the role of the temple as a place for the people's worship to YHWH in order to request YHWH's help in the situation of their predicament among the nations and proclaim YHWH's sovereignty to the nations.[139] Thus, although this psalm is eclectically assembled from three different psalms, this psalm as a new creation reveals the Chr's intention.

Rhetorical Situation

The rhetorical situation of 1 Chr 13–16 may be explained by the narrative situation and the Chr's rhetorical situation. The narrative situation expressed by the characters' actions or speeches is related to the preceding event as the narrative constraint so that David's ascension to the throne (1 Chr 11–12) functions as an introduction for 1 Chr 13–16. As Street indicates properly, the preceding two chapters (1 Chr 11–12) "serve as an introduction to the story which sets David apart from his predecessor and portrays him as a strong king who has Yahweh's blessing."[140] David has already ascended the throne and captured Jerusalem as his city in 1 Chr 11–12. In this context, David's kingship will need to be strengthened. The urgent situation of the narrative occurs after the celebration of David's ascension to the throne (1 Chr 12:39–41). David takes the transferring of the ark of the covenant of YHWH to Jerusalem into account, as the ark symbolizes "the dominion of God"[141] and it has been neglected during Saul's reign (1 Chr 13:3). In this situation, David decides to bring the ark to Jerusalem and feels the need to encourage the Israelites to bring the ark to Jerusalem. So, David makes a speech to the assembly of Israel (the narrative audience), urging them to bring the ark to Jerusalem. However, the first try fails. After David is established at Jerusalem after the battle against the Philistines (1 Chr 14), the second attempt to bring the ark to Jerusalem is carried out (1 Chr 15). At the second try, David also makes a speech

137. Klein, *1 Chronicles*, 367.
138. Watts, *Psalm and Story*, 161.
139. Boda, *1–2 Chronicles*, 149–50.
140. Street, *Significance*, 113.
141. Johnstone, *1 and 2 Chronicles*, 1:183.

to the priests, who are about to transfer the ark to Jerusalem (1 Chr 15:12–13). Thus, David's speeches and prayers occur in the narrative situation of the transferring of the ark of the covenant of YHWH to Jerusalem at the two attempts (1 Chr 13:2–3, 14; 1 Chr 15:2, 12–13), the battle against the Philistines (1 Chr 14:10–11; 14–15), and the placement of the ark at Jerusalem (1 Chr 16:8–36).

In particular, various narrative audiences can be identified in this rhetorical unit. For instance, in David's first attempt to transfer the ark, the narrative audience is "all the assembly of Israel" (1 Chr 13:2). In the speeches in the battle accounts, the audience is YHWH since David inquires of YHWH how to fight against the Philistines (1 Chr 14:10–11, 14–15). In the speeches in David's second attempt to transfer the ark, the audience is the priests and the Levites who are about to bring the ark to Jerusalem (1 Chr 15:2, 11–12). In David's psalm of praise and prayer, the narrative audience is YHWH and the Levites who are appointed as the ministers before the ark by David (1 Chr 16:4–7), possibly including those who are participating in David's installment of the ark in a tent at Jerusalem. Thus, the speeches and prayer in this unit are given to various audiences in the narrative context. The texts which speak of the issues of the ark appear to focus attention on proper care for cultic activity, and the new psalm emphasizes a call to the assembly of Israel to praise, reminding them of YHWH's promises.

The narrative situation is closely connected to the Chr's rhetorical situation since the Chr as the implied author ultimately chooses and arranges the speeches and prayers of the characters in the narrative context. In relation to the ark narrative in this unit, the rhetorical situation of the Chr is more embedded in the Persian period. For instance, the term "who remain" (הַנִּשְׁאָרִים) in 1 Chr 13:2 appears to be significant in the situation. In my view, this term is related to not only the narrator's intention to gather those who had not yet presented to David, but also the Chr's intention to gather the scattered people to Jerusalem in the Persian period.[142]

In the battle accounts against the Philistines, the Chr, emphasizing that David shows a faithful attitude towards YHWH in his inquiry of YHWH (1 Chr 14:10–11, 14–15), encourages his audience to have a similar attitude.[143] In the second attempt to transfer the ark, the Chr, focusing on its proper care for cultic activity (1 Chr 15:2, 12–13), encourages the Yehudite community to seek YHWH as David sought YHWH. Thompson points out (fittingly) that the Chr, giving special attention to the events regarding the ark (1 Chr 15), considers the ark "as a holy object even though by the time of the Chr *it had already ceased to exist*."[144]

In the new psalm, the Chr emphasizes that the Yehudite community should praise YHWH, reminding them of YHWH's promises. In this psalm, the Chr gives special attention to the covenantal relationship between YHWH and Israel as an everlasting

---

142. See Knoppers, *I Chronicles*, 584.
143. See Williamson, *1 and 2 Chronicles*, 114.
144. Thompson, *1, 2 Chronicles*, 134.

one, making the implied audience recollect God's covenants with the patriarchs (1 Chr 16:12–22). The Chr underscores that God made an everlasting covenant with Israel, which is strongly reinforced by his appealing to God's covenants with the patriarchs. In 1 Chr 16:34–36, the phrase "gather us and deliver us from the nations" (1 Chr 16:35) reflects the Chr's rhetorical situation, in which the Chr's concern will be how to gather the scattered people to Jerusalem as the worship center.

Myers states that the Chr in this psalm describes "what he believed was the origin and practice in the time of David, by a concrete example from his own time."[145] The Chr appears to have intended to emphasize Jerusalem as the worship center by placing the new psalm in the David narrative. This psalm portrays David as the advocate of the worship in Jerusalem. The Chr will point to the continuity of the worship to YHWH from David's time to the Chr's time. Thus, in the Chr's ark narrative, David is depicted as the great supporter for the worship of YHWH in Jerusalem.

In particular, the Chr's exigence is related to the Jerusalem temple as the center of the worship place in the Yehudite community. In the Chr's view, Jerusalem has competed with Gibeon from the outset of David's reign. Significantly, the Chr, for the first time, refers to the tent of meeting or the tabernacle at Gibeon as a worship center (1 Chr 16:39–42), in which David makes Zadok and the priests minister to the tabernacle in the high place at Gibeon.[146] Even though Jerusalem is already considered to be the worship place that contained the ark of YHWH, David installs Zadok and the priests before the Gibeon sanctuary. In this context, the Chr indicates clearly that there are two worship centers for Israel in the time of David (Gibeon and Jerusalem), demonstrating that David did not neglect "the Mosaic tabernacle."[147] One worship center was in Jerusalem with the ark of the covenant of YHWH, and another worship center was in Gibeon with the tabernacle. Mention of these two worship centers enables the Chr to display David's reorganization of Israel's national worship system while the priests' role at the tabernacle is continuing.[148] Knoppers mentions properly that the Chr arranges "a temporary bifurcation in Israel's national cult."[149] Japhet also indicates that the Chr's main purpose of the reference to the tabernacle at Gibeon is "to present a line of unbroken continuity in the cultic establishment of Israel from its inception by Moses to the kingdom of David and Solomon."[150] In the Chr's view, the Gibeon sanctuary means "the historical and theological continuity between David's

---

145. Myers, *1 Chronicles*, 121.

146. Hill, *1 & 2 Chronicles*, 240; Klein, *1 Chronicles*, 368; Knoppers, *I Chronicles*, 651–52; Boda, *1–2 Chronicles*, 150. For the discussion of the tabernacle tradition in the high place at Gibeon, see Williamson, *1 and 2 Chronicles*, 130–32; Japhet, *I & II Chronicles*, 321–23.

147. Knoppers, *I Chronicles*, 542.

148. See Boda, *1–2 Chronicles*, 150.

149. Knoppers, *I Chronicles*, 651.

150. Japhet, *I & II Chronicles*, 323.

tent-shrine in Jerusalem and the Mosaic tent-shrine in Gibeon."[151] Thus, the Chr's reference to the tabernacle at Gibeon as one worship place during David's reign reveals the continuity of the crucial worship place that will shift from the Gibeon sanctuary to the Jerusalem temple in the Persian period.

Accordingly, the Chr shows that the tabernacle at Gibeon was regarded as a legitimate worship center for the time before the temple was built (2 Chr 1:5–7). Yet, the Chr might consider the temple at Jerusalem, not the tabernacle at Gibeon, to be the united sanctuary in accordance with the demands for centralized worship in Deut 12, in which the ark and the tabernacle also would be united.[152] This concern over the temple at Jerusalem as the worship center is surely reflected in the Chr's presentation. Boda points out that the Chr may be suggesting the necessity of the temple, even though it is not easy to identify why all the shrines could not have been moved from Gibeon to Jerusalem from the start.[153]

Furthermore, as Edelman indicates, in the postexilic period there were certain tensions between the Benjaminites in the non-*golah* community and the Judahites in the *golah* community, one of which was the competition over the worship place (Gibeon or Jerusalem).[154] The Benjaminites claimed Gibeon as the worship center, whereas the Judahites maintained Jerusalem as the center. The tension between the two tribes is reflected in 1 Chr 9:3 (those who live in Jerusalem) and 1 Chr 9:35 (the Benjaminites who live in Gibeon). In this context, the Chr wishes to convey his message to his audience in the Persian period through David's speeches and prayer. The rhetorical problem is the existence of two worship centers. Thus, the Chr tries to draw a fitting response from the Yehudite community through his presentation, reminding them of Jerusalem and Gibeon as the two worshp centers in the time of David— Gibeon is still acknowledged as the place where Zadok served (1 Chr 16:39–42).

In sum, David tries to bring the ark to Jerusalem. At these two attempts, David makes speeches to urge the Israelites, especially the priests and Levites, to bring the ark to Jerusalem. He wishes to achieve the establishment of his kingship. It is the narrative situation which the Chr brings into his own situation to persuade his audience in the Persian period to perceive that the ark, as the symbol of YHWH's presence, is placed in Jerusalem as the sole worship center. In particular, through the speeches and prayers in the ark narrative, the Chr attempts to persuade them to recognize the centrality of Jerusalem as the worship place. In the new psalm, the Chr emphasizes a call to the Yehudites to praise and to pray to YHWH in the Jerusalem temple, reminding them of YHWH's promises. In addition, the Chr stresses that David sought YHWH in his enquiry of God before the battles against the Philistines and that the Levites are legitimate servants who can bring the ark to Jerusalem.

---

151. Hill, *1 & 2 Chronicles*, 240.
152. Knoppers, *I Chronicle*, 660.
153. Boda, *1–2 Chronicles*, 150.
154. Edelman, "Saulide-Davidic Rivalry," 90.

Speeches and Prayers in David's Narrative

Rhetorical Effectiveness

The rhetorical effectiveness of a rhetorical discourse may be assessed by the two levels of audience. We have assumed two layers of audiences from the outset: the narrative audience and the Chr's audience. The former as the addressee of David's speeches and prayers and the latter as the Chr's audience is the Yehudite community who might live in Yehud at a time point in the Persian period.

First, the narrative audience is effectively persuaded by David's speeches in the ark narrative. David, making speeches to his audience who is dwelling in Jerusalem with him, urges them to bring the ark to Jerusalem in the two attempts to transfer the ark (1 Chr 13:2–3, 14; 1 Chr 15:2, 12–13) and they do so according to David's utterances. The first attempt is a failure, but the second is successful by the observance of YHWH's laws regarding the transfer of the ark. In the battles against the Philistines, David's prayers (1 Chr 14:10–11; 14–15) reveal his faithful attitude to YHWH. Through his appeal for YHWH's help, David receives his answer and defeats the Philistines. Thus, David becomes very great among the nations. In this context, David's kingdom will be strengthened. Finally, after the installation of the ark to Jerusalem, David praises YHWH and encourages the people of Israel to praise Him. In his thanksgiving psalm (1 Chr 16:8–36), David invites the Israelites to praise YHWH, appealing to YHWH's everlasting covenant with Israel. Although the people's response was assumed, they praise YHWH according to David's invitation. Thus, David's speeches in the crucial events of the ark narrative function to persuade the Israelites as the narrative audience.

Secondly, in the Chr's own situation, the Chr's audience will be persuaded by the Chr's retelling of the ark narrative. The Chr chooses David's speeches and arranges them in the narrative world in order to convey his message to his audience. David's speeches will influence the Yehudite community in the Persian era even though the Chr looks back on the past of Israel. In the attempts to bring the ark to Jerusalem, the first speech (1 Chr 13:2–3) reveals the Chr's intention to gather the scattered people of Israel to Jerusalem as the worship center. In the speeches in the battle accounts, the Yehudite community will be persuaded by the Chr's portrayal of David who seeks YHWH with his enquiry of YHWH in fighting against the Philistines (1 Chr 14:10–11, 14–15). In the Chr's rhetorical situation, there are certain tensions between Judah and Benjamin, in which the tension of worship place was reflected in the existence of the tabernacle at Gibeon (esp. 1 Chr 16:39–42). Accordingly, even though David makes a speech to the Israelites in his time, the impact of his speech extends to the Chr's audience in the Persian era, legitimizing the priority of Jerusalem as the sole worship place of Israel in the Persian Yehud. If the Chr's rhetorical need is to depict Jerusalem as the sole worship center, the Yehudite community will be effectively persuaded by David's speech in 1 Chr 13:2–3. In particular, the gathering motif, overlapping David's time and the Chr's time, functions to urge the scattered peoples to gather to Jerusalem. Likely, the gathering of the scattered Israelites to Jerusalem is a key issue in the Chr's situation. The Chr reveals his message clearly in this speech. In the second attempt to transfer the ark to Jerusalem, David's speech (1 Chr 15:2, 12–13) points to YHWH's election of the Levites and their duties regarding the transfer of the ark, which emphasizes that the Levites carried the ark and then sang around the ark. This suggests that the Chr wishes to stress the transition of the Levites' duties related to the ark—interestingly, the Levites were the first to minister in Jerusalem in worship while the priestly Zadok family came later. David comes to know YHWH's instructions after the failure of the first try: "we did not seek him [YHWH] according to the ordinances" (1 Chr 15:13). Accordingly, the Chr emphasizes the observance of YHWH's law through David's speech, urging the Yehudite community to seek YHWH, which will result in God's blessing.

Finally, through David's psalm, the Chr attempts to persuade the Yehudite community to praise YHWH. It may be successful since David's psalm will be more effective in a time when the worship of YHWH appears to have been the only way to confirm their identity as God's people under the Persian ruler. In particular, the phrase "Save us. . .And gather us and deliver us from the nations" (1 Chr 16:35) reflects the Chr's situation by showing the people's predicament among the nations. The Chr conveys his purpose and messages through David's speeches. The Yehudite community will request YHWH's help in a time of their predicament, which will be persuasive to those who are living in the Persian Yehud as a provincial district of the Persian Empire, especially those who are dwelling in Jerusalem as the sole worship center in Israel.

SPEECHES AND PRAYERS IN THE DAVIDIC COVENANT (1 CHR 17)

First Chronicles 17 as a rhetorical unit primarily focuses on the Davidic covenant.[155] The entire unit is comprised of speeches, including David's speech (1 Chr 17:1) and Nathan's speech (1 Chr 17:2), the divine speech given to David through Nathan (1

---

155. For studies on the Davidic covenant, see Schniedewind, *Society and the Promise*; Eslinger, *House of God*; Jones, *Nathan Narratives*; Gakuru, *Inter-Biblical Exegetical Study*; Ishida, *Royal Dynasties*, 81–99; Dumbrell, "The Davidic Covenant," 40–47; Kruse, "David's Covenant," 139–64; Levenson, "The Davidic Covenant," 205–10; Grisanti, "The Davidic Covenant," 233–50. For the relationship between the Davidic covenant and the temple in Chronicles, Kelly says, "Most recently, it has been argued that the Chronicler understood the Davidic kingship to be transmuted into and in some sense exercised through the temple" (Kelly, *Retribution*, 158); Mason suggests that "the Chronicler's main interest was not so much the Davidic dynasty *in itself*, but the temple, for the sake of which the dynasty was called into being and in which it found its fulfilment" (Mason, *Preaching*, 32); Riley states, "The Chronicler's interest in the Davidic dynasty can therefore be seen as more concerned with the role of the dynasty in relation to the Temple than with the dynasty's unending rule over Israel . . . For the Chronicler, the centre of the covenant with David is not formed by the dynastic promise but by the task of temple-building, and the fulfilment of the covenant is to be sought in the completed Temple rather than in an unending Davidic rule" (Riley, *King and Cultus*, 75). Interestingly, Mason's and Riley's views were already indicated thirty years ago by Caquot. See Caquot, "Peut-on parler," 110–20. Recently, Boda has discussed covenant in Chronicles ("Reenvisioning the Relationship," 391–408), and he has also dealt with the debate over David and his dynasty in Chronicles with a thorough summary ("Gazing through the Cloud of Incense," 215–45).

Speeches and Prayers in David's Narrative

Chr 17:4–15), and David's prayer (1 Chr 17:16–27). Of these speeches, the divine speech appears to be the most important. Although David intends to build a house for YHWH, YHWH instead says to him that He will build a house for David (the Davidic dynasty), and that David's son will build God's house for Him. Thus, the Chr in this unit utilizes the Davidic covenant regarding the dynasty and one of David's sons building of the temple by the speeches and prayer as his key rhetorical devices.

Rhetorical Unit

This rhetorical unit (1 Chr 17) concerns the Davidic covenant. It is clear cut in terms of its themes in the narrative progression. Most scholars have divided 1 Chr 17 into two (1 Chr 17:1–15, 16–27) or three parts (1 Chr 17:1–2, 3–15, 16–27).[156] However, it does not make any significant distinction since it has been divided into two or three parts according to whether the first part includes the introductory dialogue (1 Chr 17:1–2) or not. Accordingly, it may be divided into two sub-sections. The first sub-unit deals with YHWH's covenant with David (1 Chr 17:1–15),[157] in which a short introductory dialogue between David and Nathan (1 Chr 17:1–2) and Nathan's prophecy as YHWH's speech (1 Chr 17:4–14) are included. The second deals with David's prayer as a response to the divine speech (1 Chr 17:16–23), in which David addresses his praise and supplication to YHWH. This unit, then, consists of a series of the speeches of the characters in the narrative—David's prayer also is his speech to YHWH in this context.

Rhetorical Strategy

The Chr presents YHWH's promise to David in terms of a series of speeches: an introductory dialogue between David and Nathan (1 Chr 17:1–2); Nathan's oracle as the divine speech (1 Chr 17:4–14); and David's responding prayer (1 Chr 17:16–27). Scholars indicate that the Chr presents Nathan's oracle and David's prayer as more closely tied to Solomon's work.[158] Significantly, Nathan's oracle seems to be more focused on the temple builder rather than the Davidic dynasty, which reflects that the Chr's main interest was in the temple at Jerusalem as the worship place. So, the Chr, by using speeches and prayers, describes the Davidic covenant regarding the temple

---

156. For instance, Japhet, (*I & II Chronicles*, 327), Selman (*1 Chronicles*, 181–91), Hill (*1 & 2 Chronicles*, 241), and Boda (*1–2 Chronicles*, 154–57) divide 1 Chr 17 into three: vv. 1–2; vv. 3–15; vv. 16–27; Knoppers divides 1 Chr 17 into two: YHWH's promise to David (vv. 1–15) and David's prayer (vv. 16–27), in which the first part comprises: David's plan to build temple (vv.1–2); Nathan's prophecy of rejection (vv. 3–6); Nathan's prophecy of dynasty (vv. 7–15) (*I Chronicles*, 661–62, 677–78).

157. For the recent study of the comparison between 2 Sam 7:1–16 and 1 Chr 17:1–15, see Schenker, "Die Verheissung Natans," 177–92.

158. For instance, Schniedewind, *Society and the Promise*, 128–34; Williamson, "The Ascension of Solomon," 351–61; "Dynastic Oracle," 305–18; Braun, "Solomonic Apologetic," 503–16; "Chosen Temple Builder," 581–90.

David's Speech and Nathan's Response (1 Chr 17:1–2)

As David dwells in his house (palace) after the transfer of the ark to Jerusalem, he desires to build a house for YHWH. As deliberative rhetoric, David voices his intentions to the prophet Nathan:[159]

1 Chr 17:1	
וַיְהִי כַּאֲשֶׁר יָשַׁב דָּוִיד בְּבֵיתוֹ	And it came to pass when David dwelt in his house,
וַיֹּאמֶר דָּוִיד אֶל־נָתָן הַנָּבִיא	that David said to Nathan the prophet,
הִנֵּה אָנֹכִי יוֹשֵׁב בְּבֵית הָאֲרָזִים	"Behold, I am dwelling in a house of the cedars
וַאֲרוֹן בְּרִית־יְהוָה	but the ark of the covenant of YHWH
תַּחַת יְרִיעוֹת	is under curtains."
1 Chr 17:2	
וַיֹּאמֶר נָתָן אֶל־דָּוִיד	And Nathan said to David,
כֹּל אֲשֶׁר בִּלְבָבְךָ עֲשֵׂה	"Do all that is in your heart,
כִּי הָאֱלֹהִים עִמָּךְ	for God is with you."

In 1 Chr 17:1, David elucidates the contrast between a house of cedars as his dwelling place and a tent (under curtains) as the place of the ark. It is incongruous to David that the ark of the covenant of YHWH resides in a tent, in contrast with his dwelling in a house of the cedars. Accordingly, David voices his intentions to Nathan to build YHWH's house (the temple) as the place for the ark.[160] In particular, 1 Chr 17:1b,

---

159. In 1 Chr 17:1–2, the personal name David is used instead of the title "the king" in the parallel text (2 Sam 7:1–3). The Chr seems to have intended to give a positive impression of the dialogue between David and Nathan to the Chr's audience without any feeling of rejection. Kalimi indicates that this change might have signified "to the reader what the desired attitude toward Nathan's advice was" (Kalimi, *Reshaping*, 181). For the discussion of textual differences between 2 Sam 7 and 1 Chr 17, see Braun, *1 Chronicles*, 196–7.

160. Klein, *1 Chronicles*, 376. Interestingly, 1 Chr 17:1 is parallel to 2 Sam 7:1–2. The phrase "YHWH had given rest to him [David] round about from all enemies" (יְהוָה הֵנִיחַ־לוֹ מִסָּבִיב מִכָּל־אֹיְבָיו) in 2 Sam 7:1b is omitted in 1 Chr 17:1. The reason for this would be the Chr's intention "to avoid a chronological conflict with the later references to David's war" (1 Chr 17:10 and 1 Chr 18–20) (Throntveit, "Idealization," 415). Furthermore, 2 Sam 7:1b is added by the Chr in 1 Chr 22:9, applying it to Solomon. As a result, the Chr forms a chiastic order when compared with that in 2 Samuel (Kalimi, *Reshaping*, 39, 246):

2 Sam 7:1b יְהוָה הֵנִיחַ־לוֹ מִסָּבִיב מִכָּל־אֹיְבָיו
    (YHWH has given rest to him [David] *round about* from all his enemies)
1 Chr 17:1b . . . .
1 Chr 22:9 הֲנִחוֹתִי לוֹ מִכָּל־אוֹיְבָיו מִסָּבִיב
    (I have given rest to him [Solomon] from all his enemies *round about*)

Speeches and Prayers in David's Narrative

beginning with the discourse marker (הִנֵּה) to draw attention of the audience, rhetorically shows an *antithesis* by combining contrasting thoughts,[161] which was expressed by David in the house made of cedars versus the ark of the covenant of YHWH under curtains. In 1 Chr 17:1b, the phrase "and the ark of the covenant of YHWH" (וַאֲרוֹן בְּרִית־יְהוָה) is identified with YHWH's presence.[162] Significantly, the Chr employs the term *covenant* throughout the David-Solomon narrative.[163] The ark of the covenant of YHWH seems to link the ark narrative in the preceding unit (1 Chr 13–16) to David's preparations for building the temple in the following chapters (1 Chr 18–29).[164]

Furthermore, another key word, "house" (בית) used as a metaphoric expression occurs fourteen times in 1 Chr 17 and it implies various meanings: David's house (1 Chr 17:1); the temple that David wants to build (1 Chr 17:4); the dynasty that YHWH will build up (1 Chr 17:10); and the temple that Solomon will build (1 Chr 17:12) and that YHWH will accept (1 Chr 17:14).[165] Of the diverse meanings, the word "house" as the meaning of the temple and the dynasty constitutes the core of the Davidic covenant in 1 Chr 17. David's intention to build a house for YHWH (1 Chr 17:1) is addressed by contrasting his dwelling in the house of cedars with the ark of YHWH under curtains. The speech receives Nathan's positive response.

The Chr here employs the personal name, "David," not the title name (king) in 2 Sam 7:3. Beentjes believes that this is a "functional alteration" because the Chr seems to have used this personal name systematically in 1 Chr 17:1.[166] Kalimi contends that "the name of 'David' is used on purpose instead of the functional designation 'the king' to create an atmosphere of private conversation."[167] In my judgment, this ap-

---

161. Lanham, *Handlist*, 16.

162. The designation of the ark in 1 Chr 17:1b is different from the phrase "and the ark of God" (וַאֲרוֹן הָאֱלֹהִים) in the parallel text (2 Sam 7:2), in which the term "covenant" is not mentioned. It appears to emphasize the significance of Jerusalem as the dwelling place of YHWH by means of the placement of the ark in Jerusalem, as the symbol of YHWH's presence.

163. The various uses of the term "covenant" are identified in Chronicles: "the ark of the covenant of YHWH" (1 Chr 15:25, 26, 28, 29; 16:37; 17:1; 22:19; 28:2, 18; 2 Chr 5:2, 7; 6:11 ["the ark of the covenant of God," 1 Chr 16:6]); "the ark of YHWH" (1 Chr 15:2, 3, 12, 14; 16:4; 2 Chr 8:11); "the ark of God" (1 Chr 13:3, 5, 7, 12, 14; 15:1, 2, 15, 24; 16:1; 2 Chr 1:4); and other uses of "covenant" (a covenant between David and the elders of Israel [1 Chr 11:3], "everlasting covenant" [1 Chr 16:7], "a covenant of salt" [2 Chr 13:5], a covenant between Asa and Benhadad [2 Chr 16:3], the recalling of the Davidic covenant (2 Chr 21:7), a covenant between the whole assembly [Israel] and Joash [2 Chr 23:3], a covenant between Jehoiada and all the people and the king [2 Chr 23:16], a covenant between Hezekiah and YHWH [2 Chr 29:10]) (Japhet, *Ideology*, 76–77). In particular, McKenzie points out that the Chronicler uniquely employs the term "covenant" in Abijah's speech to Jeroboam (2 Chr 13:5) and in Johoram's regnal statement (2 Chr 21:7) (McKenzie, "Typology," 160).

164. This link between the ark and the temple is shown in the Solomon narrative again (2 Chr 5–6).

165. See Klein, *1 Chronicles*, 376; Johnstone, *1 and 2 Chronicles*, 1:200.

166. Beentjes, "Transformations of Space and Time," 37.

167. Kalimi, *Zur Geschichtsschreibung des Chronisten*, 159–60, quoted by Beentjes, "Transformations of Space and Time," 37. According to Beentjes, the Chr employs "the formula 'David, the King' several times, and most of these usages are to be found in *Chronistisches Sondergut*! [1 Chr 21:24;

pellation of the personal name suggests that there was a close relationship between Nathan and David.

According to Kalimi, Nathan's speech, "Do all that is in your heart, for God is with you" in 1 Chr 17:2 is addressed "frankly and spontaneously" to David, and it is not "the words of a 'servant,' a court prophet who was obliged to serve his master and wished to fulfill his king/master's expectations and requests."[168] In this speech, the phrase "all that is in your heart" (כֹּל אֲשֶׁר בִּלְבָבְךָ) is emphasized by being placed in front of the imperative verb, "do" (עֲשֵׂה), which shows the rhetorical device *anastrophe* as an "unusual arrangement of words and clauses within a sentence."[169] Nathan's speech encourages David to do what he has in mind because God is with him. In the past David had become greater since God was with him (1 Chr 11:9). Now, God is with David, so David will be able to perform his plan. YHWH himself says that He has been with David (1 Chr 17:8).[170] Thus, Nathan's speech emphasizes that YHWH has been with David, which leads to His promise to David regarding the temple building and the dynasty. The climax of this rhetorical unit will be the divine speech given to David through Nathan, which is discussed below.

Nathan's Oracle of the Davidic Covenant (1 Chr 17:4–14)

The divine speech is given to David through Nathan. It is a remarkable feature that YHWH's volition is strongly displayed by a series of the first person singular verb forms (e.g., יָשַׁבְתִּי, הֶעֱלֵיתִי, דִּבַּרְתִּי). YHWH's speech (1 Chr 17:4–14) occupies a large section in this rhetorical unit, which can be divided into three parts by the messenger formula (כֹּה אָמַר יְהוָה) and God's declaration of the building of a house for David: 1 Chr 17:4–6 (historical retrospect as *epideictic* rhetoric); 1 Chr 17:7–10a (as deliberative rhetoric); and 1 Chr 17:10b–14 (as deliberative rhetoric):

1 Chr 17:4–6	
⁴לֵךְ וְאָמַרְתָּ אֶל־דָּוִיד עַבְדִּי	"Go and tell David my servant,"
כֹּה אָמַר יְהוָה	Thus says YHWH,
לֹא אַתָּה תִּבְנֶה־לִּי הַבַּיִת לָשָׁבֶת׃	"You shall not build a house for me to dwell in
⁵כִּי לֹא יָשַׁבְתִּי בְּבַיִת מִן־הַיּוֹם	For I have not dwelt in a house from the day
אֲשֶׁר הֶעֱלֵיתִי אֶת־יִשְׂרָאֵל עַד הַיּוֹם הַזֶּה	that I brought up Israel until this day,

---

26:26, 32; 27:32; 28:2; 29:1, 9; 2 Chr 7:6. Only in 1 Chr 18:10, 11; 2 Chr 2:12; 23:9 this formula has been adopted from the *Vorlage*.]" ("Transformations of Space and Time," 37–38). He believes that because the term "the king" does not occur in 1 Chr 17:1ff, this change should be regarded as having "a special *function*." The similar theological backdrop "makes it clear why regarding Solomon in 1 Chr 17:12, reference is made to 'his throne', whereas 2 Sam 7:13 uses 'the throne of his kingdom'" (38).

168. Kalimi, *Reshaping*, 181.
169. Lanham, *Handlist*, 12.
170. See Klein, *1 Chronicles*, 376.

וָאֶהְיֶה מִתְהַלֵּךְ מֵאֹהֶל אֶל־אֹהֶל	and I have been from tent to tent
וּמִמִּשְׁכָּן:	and from a dwelling-place (to another)
⁶ בְּכֹל אֲשֶׁר־הִתְהַלַּכְתִּי בְּכָל־יִשְׂרָאֵל	In all places where I have walked with all Israel,
הֲדָבָר דִּבַּרְתִּי אֶת־אַחַד שֹׁפְטֵי	have I spoken a word with one of the judges
יִשְׂרָאֵל אֲשֶׁר צִוִּיתִי לִרְעוֹת אֶת־עַמִּי	of Israel whom I commanded to feed my people,
לֵאמֹר לָמָּה לֹא־בְנִיתֶם לִי	saying, 'Why have you not built for me
בֵּית אֲרָזִים:	a house of cedars?'"

The first part of the divine speech (1 Chr 17:4–6) begins with the messenger formula, "Thus says YHWH" (כֹּה אָמַר יְהוָה). YHWH first expressed His denial of David as the builder of the temple (1 Chr 17:4), in which the phrase, "You shall not build a house for me to dwell in" shows strong prohibition as a declarative utterance.[171] David provides the reason for this prohibition later (1 Chr 22:8, 28:3). In the Chr's description, the one who will build a house for YHWH is shifted to David's successor Solomon. According to Japhet, the factor of timing is a decisive element from the start: not David but Solomon will build a house for YHWH. When the time of peace and rest comes, which has not yet come, YHWH's house shall be built.[172] For the Chr the concept of God-given rest in the land is the indispensable prerequisite for the building of the temple because it reveals the fulfillment of God's promise to Israel.[173] After examining the importance of the term, "rest," Braun contends that the significance of "rest" is "most apparent from Deut 12, where the unification of the cult is specifically related to Israel's rest in the promised land."[174] Thus, it attests to the close relation of "rest" and the promised land. In this context, the text emphasizes that David is prohibited from building a house for YHWH. Instead of him, his successor will build the house for YHWH (1 Chr 17:4).

YHWH's dwelling place has not been a house (1 Chr 17:5). Rather, it has been "from tent to tent" and "from a dwelling place (to another)." In particular, the latter phrase shows an *ellipsis* in comparison to the former.[175] The Chr reinforces the fact that YHWH has not requested a house for Himself by placing a rhetorical question in 1 Chr 17:6, which forms the climax of the historical retrospect: "In all places where

---

171. The rhetorical question, "Will you build me a house for my dwelling in?" in the parallel text (2 Sam 7:5) is changed to the declarative utterance in 1 Chr 17:4. In 1 Chr 17:4b, the definite article of "the house" would even "be considered to have a *proleptic* function: foreshadowing 1 Chr 22–27, being the most extensive section of *Chronistisches Sondergut* within the entire Book of Chronicles. In these chapters David will undertake all possible preliminary steps for building of the Temple" (Beentjes, "Transformations of Space and Time," 35).

172. Japhet, *I & II Chronicles*, 329–30; Klein, *1 Chronicles*, 377.

173. Throntveit, "Idealization," 415.

174. The term, "rest" is frequently employed in three significant events: Joshua's conquest of the land, David's dynastic promise, and Solomon's building of temple. See Braun, "Chosen Temple Builder," 582–86 (esp. 583).

175. Lanham, *Handlist*, 62.

I have walked with all Israel, have I spoken a word with one of the judges of Israel whom I commanded to feed my people, saying, 'Why have you not build for me a house of cedars?'" The answer to the rhetorical question is self-evident.[176] YHWH never requests a house for Himself. According to Japhet, 1 Chr 17:6 comprises "two elements of direct speech, one within the other, conveying the intention in a rhetorical manner as a hypothetical query, which was *not* directed to the judges."[177] Thus, the Chr closes the first part of the divine speech with this rhetorical question, reinforcing that YHWH has never needed a house for Himself. The Chr, by using the rhetorical question, emphasizes that YHWH has never requested a house of cedars for Himself from the early history of Israel up to now.

This part contains a historical retrospect. In the days of the judges, the ark of the covenant of YHWH did not need a particular location. The ark, as the symbol of YHWH's presence, has broadly affected Israelite life in the early history of Israel. For instance, the ark of the covenant is accompanied by the Israelites when they go up to the land of Canaan (Josh 3:11), and it has been in the land from the days of the judges (Judg 20:27). Thus, David's intention to build a house for YHWH is prohibited by YHWH's word, which is followed by a historical retrospect emphasizing that YHWH has not requested a house and indicating that the ark is YHWH's accompanying presence from the early stage of Israelite history.

1 Chr 17:7–10a	
7 וְעַתָּה כֹּה־תֹאמַר לְעַבְדִּי	"And now thus shall you say to my servant,
לְדָוִיד כֹּה אָמַר יְהוָה צְבָאוֹת	to David," Thus says YHWH of hosts,
אֲנִי לְקַחְתִּיךָ מִן־הַנָּוֶה מִן־אַחֲרֵי הַצֹּאן	"I took you from the pasture, from after the sheep
לִהְיוֹת נָגִיד עַל עַמִּי יִשְׂרָאֵל׃	to be leader over my people Israel
8 וָאֶהְיֶה עִמְּךָ	and I have been with you
בְּכֹל אֲשֶׁר הָלָכְתָּ	in all places where you have gone,
וָאַכְרִית אֶת־כָּל־אוֹיְבֶיךָ	and I have cut off all your enemies
מִפָּנֶיךָ וְעָשִׂיתִי לְךָ שֵׁם	from before you, and I will make you a name
כְּשֵׁם הַגְּדוֹלִים	like the name of the greatest ones
אֲשֶׁר בָּאָרֶץ׃	who are on the earth
9 וְשַׂמְתִּי מָקוֹם לְעַמִּי יִשְׂרָאֵל	And I will appoint a place for my people Israel
וּנְטַעְתִּיהוּ וְשָׁכַן תַּחְתָּיו	and I will plant him and he shall dwell in its place
וְלֹא יִרְגַּז עוֹד	and he shall not be agitated again
וְלֹא־יוֹסִיפוּ בְנֵי־עַוְלָה	and the sons of unrighteousness shall not add

---

176. See Lundbom, *Hebrew Prophets*, 191.

177. Japhet, *I & II Chronicles*, 330–31.

Speeches and Prayers in David's Narrative

לְבַלֹּתוֹ כַּאֲשֶׁר בָּרִאשׁוֹנָה׃	to wear it out as at first
10a וּלְמִיָּמִים אֲשֶׁר צִוִּיתִי שֹׁפְטִים	And from the days when I commanded judges
עַל־עַמִּי יִשְׂרָאֵל	(to be) over my people Israel,
וְהִכְנַעְתִּי אֶת־כָּל־אוֹיְבֶיךָ	and I will subdue all your enemies

The second part of the divine speech (1 Chr 17:7–10a) begins with the messenger formula ("Thus says YHWH of hosts") that is followed by the discourse marker "And now" (וְעַתָּה). YHWH again commands Nathan to address David in 1 Chr 17:7. This second part as another historical retrospect contains YHWH's favor to David (1 Chr 17:7–8a) and to the people of Israel in the past (1 Chr 17:8b–9). YHWH's favor will be continued into the future (1 Chr 17:10a). Johnstone notes that 1 Chr 17 strikingly emphasizes "the people as the ultimate concern of the leaders" (1 Chr 17:7, 9, 10, 21, 22).[178] Accordingly, YHWH's favor will be given to God's people as well as David.

In particular, two promises in the past reverberate within this section. YHWH declares to David that He will make him a great name, echoing Abraham's great name (1 Chr 17:8; cf. Gen 12:2; 1 Chr 14:17) and that He will provide "*a place* for the descendants of Abraham and Moses,"[179] calling them "my people Israel" (1 Chr 17:9; cf. Gen 13:14–17; 15:18–21; Exod 3:8; 6:8; Deut 11:24–25). In this regard, Selman holds that "the Davidic covenant represents a new stage in the fulfillment of the Abrahamic and Mosaic covenants."[180] In my judgment, the Chr appears to have recapitulated the previous covenantal traditions in Israelite history in order to introduce the Davidic covenant in the following part.

One stylistic feature of this part is the use of the first person pronoun (אֲנִי) and the frequent uses of the first person verb forms (אֶהְיֶה, אַכְרִית, עָשִׂיתִי, שַׂמְתִּי, נְטַעְתִּיהוּ, צִוִּיתִי, הִכְנַעְתִּי). It stresses what God Himself has done to David and to Israel. As another stylistic feature, 1 Chr 17:10a contains the verb "subdue" (הִכְנַעְתִּי) in place of the verb "give rest" (הֲנִיחֹתִי) in the parallel text ("and I will give you to rest from all your enemies" וַהֲנִיחֹתִי לְךָ מִכָּל־אֹיְבֶיךָ, 2 Sam 7:11a). As Japhet indicates, the root of both "to give rest" (נוח) and "to subdue" (כנע) frequently occurs in Chronicles.[181] She believes that the Chr changes the verb נוח to כנע in order "to describe more authentically the Lord's actions on behalf of David."[182] Beentjes claims that the rest motif is presented as a remarkably theological theme by clearly connecting 1 Chr 22:6–10 with 1 Chr 28:2,

---

178. Johnstone, *1 and 2 Chronicles*, 1:202.

179. Selman, *1 Chronicles*, 186.

180. Ibid., 186.

181. כנע occurs thirty-six times in the Bible, of which eighteen are in Chronicles; נוח occurs seven times in Chronicles in the meaning of "give rest," especially in mostly unparalleled texts. See Japhet, "Interchanges," 36.

182. Japhet, "Interchanges," 36 (n. 98). Kalimi (*contra* Japhet) asserts that it would be more reasonable "to assume that the Chronicler wanted to harmonize the Lord's promise to David with the actualization of the promise, as expressed in David's victory over the Philistines" (1 Chr 18:1a [cf. 2 Sam 8:1a], "David struck the Philistines and subdued them") (Kalimi, *Reshaping*, 162).

indicating that "only a situation of rest which has been realized *by God* can provide all conditions necessary to start building the Temple."[183] Accordingly, the rest theme contributes to a peaceful time for the temple building, which can be provided only by God Himself. In my judgment, the change of the verb from נוח to בנע has originated from the Chr's intention to link the rest theme to Solomon, not David. It has already been indicated that David is prohibited from building the temple by YHWH's declarative utterance (1 Chr 17:4) and that David's son Solomon will build the temple at a peaceful time.

YHWH's choice of David is emphasized in 1 Chr 17:7–8. YHWH takes David "from the pasture, from after the sheep" in 1 Chr 17:7. The two phrases, representing a semantical repetition, stress that David is chosen by YHWH when he is merely of a humble status as a shepherd. YHWH says to David that He has been with him, referring to His accompanying him in all places, cutting off David's enemies, and YHWH will further make him a great name on the earth (1 Chr 17:8). Accordingly, YHWH's speech in 1 Chr 17:7–8 is entirely related to David.

YHWH also gives special attention to the people of Israel, providing them a place to dwell. YHWH's speech in 1 Chr 17:9–10a emphasizes the safe dwelling of the people of Israel in a place. In 1 Chr 17:9–10a, YHWH says that He will plant His people Israel after appointing a place for them and that the neighboring nations will not oppress them any more from the time when YHWH commanded judges to rule the people of Israel. He will subdue all their enemies. In these verses, the Chr, by comparing the people of Israel to something to plant, has employed the rhetorical device *abusio*, which is a "harsh use of tropes" as a sort of implied metaphor.[184] Accordingly, YHWH, like a gardener taking care of the flowering plant, will look after the people of Israel. Thompson indicates that YHWH's plan is to give David a great name and the Israelites a safe place without any oppression of the neighboring nations.[185]

Japhet states that David's rule will be the turning point in the future of the people (1 Chr 17:8–10): "the beginning of enduring stability."[186] In David's promises, the issue is peace in the land. The Chr links this sort of stability to the establishment of a permanent and centralized temple.[187] In line with this, Hill points out that the building of a permanent temple for the worship of YHWH is linked to Israel's safe position in the promised land (1 Chr 17:9–10).[188] The building of the temple is surely related to the Israelites' secure position in the land. Thus, the Chr emphasizes that YHWH chooses David as the leader of His people, indicating that YHWH is with David. In

---

183. Beentjes, "Transformations of Space and Time," 34.
184. Lanham, *Handlist*, 1; Lundbom, *Hebrew Prophets*, 184.
185. Thompson, *1, 2 Chronicles*, 146.
186. Japhet, *I & II Chronicles*, 332.
187. Knoppers, *I Chronicles*, 669.
188. Hill, *1 & 2 Chronicles*, 243.

the same way, YHWH will give special attention to the people of Israel, subduing all their enemies:

1 Chr 17:10b–14	
וְאַגִּד לָ֑ךְ 10b	and I declare to you
וּבַ֖יִת יִבְנֶה־לְּךָ֥ יְהוָֽה׃	that YHWH will build a house for you
וְהָיָ֗ה 11	And it shall come to pass
כִּי־מָלְא֣וּ יָמֶ֗יךָ	when your days are fulfilled
לָלֶ֣כֶת עִם־אֲבֹתֶ֔יךָ	to go with your fathers,
וַהֲקִֽימוֹתִ֤י אֶֽת־זַרְעֲךָ֙ אַחֲרֶ֔יךָ	and I will raise up your seed after you
אֲשֶׁ֥ר יִהְיֶ֖ה מִבָּנֶ֑יךָ	who will be one of your sons,
וַהֲכִינוֹתִ֖י אֶת־מַלְכוּתֽוֹ׃	and I will establish his kingdom
ה֥וּא יִבְנֶה־לִּ֖י בָּ֑יִת 12	He shall build for me a house,
וְכֹנַנְתִּ֥י אֶת־כִּסְא֖וֹ עַד־עוֹלָֽם׃	and I will establish his throne forever
אֲנִי֙ אֶֽהְיֶה־לּ֣וֹ לְאָ֔ב 13	I will become his father,
וְה֖וּא יִֽהְיֶה־לִּ֣י לְבֵ֑ן	and he will become my son,
וְחַסְדִּי֙ לֹא־אָסִ֣יר	and my steadfast love I will not take away
מֵֽעִמּ֔וֹ	from him
כַּאֲשֶׁ֣ר הֲסִיר֔וֹתִי מֵאֲשֶׁ֥ר הָיָ֖ה לְפָנֶֽיךָ׃	as I took it away from him who was before you
וְהַעֲמַדְתִּ֛יהוּ בְּבֵיתִ֥י 14	But I will set up him in my house
וּבְמַלְכוּתִ֖י עַד־הָעוֹלָ֑ם	and in my kingdom forever,
וְכִסְא֕וֹ יִהְיֶ֥ה נָכ֖וֹן עַד־עוֹלָֽם׃	and his throne shall be established forever."

The third part (1 Chr 17:10b–14) is focused on YHWH's declaration of the building of a house for David. In this part, the first person singular verbs are frequently employed, emphasizing that YHWH Himself speaks. The climactic scene of the divine speech is YHWH's declaration, "YHWH will build a house for you [David]" (1 Chr 17:10b), which is uttered by the third person with the emphasis on "a house."[189] In this declaration, the term, "a house" (בַיִת) represents the rhetorical device, *metonymy*, which is the substitution of a word for another, typically from the abstract to the concrete.[190] The term "house" means a dynasty, and YHWH's declaration indicates that YHWH will establish the Davidic dynasty. It is also supported by the meaning of the verb "build" (יִבְנֶה) in 1 Chr 17:10, which signifies both the establishment of a dynasty and the building of the temple.[191] As Kalimi indicates properly, the Chr's use of the verb

189. The verb "build" (יִבְנֶה) is employed, instead of "make" (יַעֲשֶׂה) in the parallel text (2 Sam 7:11). Throntveit states that in 1 Chr 17:10 the change from "YHWH declares to you. . ." in 2 Sam 7:11 to "I declare to you. . ." is simply to smooth the link between the first person verbs in 1 Chr 17:7–10, 11–14 (Throntveit, "Idealization," 416). See also Mosis, *Untersuchungen*, 82.

190. Lundbom, *Hebrew Prophets*, 186; Lanham, *Handlist*, 102.

191. Throntveit, "Idealization," 417. He also argues for the change of the verb from "make" to

"build" would be for a cohesive arrangement in line with 1 Chr 17:4 ("You shall not build me a house") and 1 Chr 17:12 ("He shall build a house for me"). In this context, YHWH's declaration of the building of a house signifies a dynasty (the house of David), which is more clearly indicated in 1 Chr 17:11, ". . .I will establish his kingdom."[192] Accordingly, the meaning of "house" is secured as dynasty in 1 Chr 17:11 and the Davidic dynasty will be established by YHWH.[193]

YHWH says in 1 Chr 17:11–12 that after David's death, He will establish the Davidic kingdom by raising up one of David's sons, and the throne of the Davidic king will be established forever. In these verses, it is noteworthy that the phrase "I will establish" (the root of the verb, כוּן) is repeated twice as a refrain. It is repeated as the passive form of the verb (נָכוֹן) in 1 Chr 17:14. Accordingly, the text emphasizes that YHWH Himself will establish the Davidic kingdom. YHWH says that one of David's sons shall build a house for YHWH. In this utterance, the phrase "your [David's] seed" (זַרְעֲךָ) that God will raise up is equivalent to the phrase "one of your [David's] sons," which shows *metonymy* as a metaphor.[194] Thus, YHWH proclaims that He will establish the Davidic kingdom.

In 1 Chr 17:13a, YHWH says that He will be a father to David, and he shall be a son to Him. This covenantal adoption formula shows the privilege of David's royal line as the adopted son of YHWH.[195] Furthermore, YHWH will not take His steadfast love away from the Davidic king as He took it away from Saul (1 Chr 17:13b). The word "my steadfast love" (חַסְדִּי) as the object of the verb (אָסִיר) is emphasized by being placed in front of the verb in this verse. YHWH's speech contrasts David with Saul, repeating the same verb as an *antithesis*:[196] "[My steadfast love] I will not take away (לֹא־אָסִיר) from him as I took it away (הֲסִירוֹתִי) from him who was before you." Interestingly, in this phrase, the personal pronoun "him" (מֵעִמּוֹ) is used, avoiding the name of "Saul" (מֵעִם שָׁאוּל) (cf. 2 Sam 7:15). The reason is that the Chr wishes to stress a close relationship between God and the Davidic king by employing the terms,

---

"build." Second Samuel 7:11 is obviously "about the establishment of a family since the verb only appears with 'house' with the idiomatic sense, as, for example, when God promises to 'give' (עשׂה) the midwives Shiphrah and Puah 'families' (בתים) as a reward for their faithful service" (Exod 1:21) (417).

192. Kalimi, *Reshaping*, 192. Kalimi states that it originates from Ps 89, which is based on Nathan's prophecy in Ps 89:4[5] ("I will establish your offspring forever and I will build your throne for all generations"). Johnstone also indicates that the identity of David's son, who would rule over Israel after David's death, "is not divulged at this point (nor was it in Samuel): the fundamental promise is to David's progeny ('seed'). The word includes the immediate heir but also implies the line of heirs ('sons') in perpetuity" (1 Chr 17:11). (Johnstone, *1 and 2 Chronicles*, 1:204).

193. In the Chr's rewriting of Israelite history, "the divine word and its fulfillment" are more often than not changed "from the earlier text into his own work almost in their present form" (Kalimi, *Reshaping*, 159). For instance, "He shall build me a house, and I will establish his throne forever" is quoted in 1 Chr 17:12 (cf. 2 Sam 7:13) (159).

194. Lanham, *Handlist*, 100–102.

195. See Hill, *1 & 2 Chronicles*, 243.

196. Lanham, *Handlist*, 16–17. Antithesis is "an opposition created by contrasting words, phrases, or ideas." See also Lundbom, *Hebrew Prophets*, 188.

"father" and "son," the so-called covenant formula (1 Chr 17:13a). Johnstone points out that the relation of father and son transcends even the bond of covenant, claiming that "it goes beyond the voluntary, contractual status of a mere agreement between two parties and has become the necessary and inescapable tie as between members of the same family."[197] Thus, YHWH's utterance of "father" and "son" clearly stresses the unalterable relationship between God and the Davidic king.

The relationship between YHWH and the Davidic king is further developed in 1 Chr 17:14. In the phrase, "I [YHWH] will set up him [a son of David, that is, Solomon] in my [YHWH's] house and in my kingdom forever" (1 Chr 17:14a), the term "my house" refers to the temple, and the term "my [YHWH's] kingdom" reveals a wordplay with "his kingdom [the Davidic kingdom]" (1 Chr 17:11). This alteration demonstrates that the Chr's depiction of the Davidic covenant regarding dynasty is for the temple, pointing to the relationship between YHWH's kingdom and the Davidic kingdom.[198] This alteration of the phrase from David's kingdom to YHWH's kingdom frequently occurs in Chronicles (1 Chr 28:5; 29:23; 2 Chr 9:8; 13:5, 8), which emphasizes YHWH's reign more than the dynasty.[199] According to Japhet, the Davidic kingdom functions as YHWH's representative on earth. If the Israelites faithfully fulfill YHWH's commands, they will prosper in the land given by YHWH.[200] As an example of this, in the last scene of the David narrative, Solomon sits on "the throne of the kingdom of YHWH" or "the throne of YHWH" (1 Chr 28:5; 29:23).

In the next phrase, "his throne shall be established forever" (1 Chr 17:14b), the text emphasizes that the establishment of the Davidic dynasty will be forever. In this phrase, David's house signifies YHWH's house,[201] pointing out that David's throne is YHWH's throne (1 Chr 28:5). Avioz indicates properly that Nathan's prophecy about the Davidic dynasty (1 Chr 17:14) reflects the building of the temple by: (1) one of David's sons (Solomon); (2) YHWH's kingship; and (3) the throne of the house of David, three of which are more apparently observed in 1 Chr 28:5b–7a: "He [YHWH] has chosen my son Solomon to sit on the throne of the kingdom of YHWH over Israel. And He said to me [David], 'Solomon your son is the one who shall build my house

197. Johnstone, *1 and 2 Chronicles*, 1:205–6.

198. Riley, *King and Cultus*, 70. He also discusses the Chronistic identification of David's kingdom and YHWH's kingdom (175–76).

199. Boda, "Gazing through the Cloud of Incense," 223.

200. Japhet, *Ideology*, 308–20.

201. Beentjes believes that the phrase "my house" (1 Chr 17:14) leads "to at least consider the possibility of whether the noun 'house' in 1 Chr 17:10b could mean 'temple' instead of 'dynasty'" (Beentjes, "Transformations of Space and Time," 39). Riley states, "There is perhaps a fuller connection between Temple and security in Nathan's oracle if the possibility is entertained that the Chronicler saw בית in 1 Chron. 17.10 to pertain to the Temple even more than to the dynasty" (Riley, *King and Cultus*, 183). Cf. Kalimi indicates that the term, "his house" in 1 Chr 10:6 "refers to 'his family' (cf. e.g., Gen 7:1: 'Come, you and *all your house*, into the ark') or 'his dynasty' (cf. 1 Chr 17:10 // 2 Sam 7:11). At any rate, this is a metonymic use of the word; the Chronicler used the name of a dwelling place to mean the people living in it" (Kalimi, *Reshaping*, 309 n. 29).

and my courts because I have chosen him to be a son to me and I will become a father to him. And I will establish his kingdom forever.'"[202]

Selman refers to the nature of the divine kingdom in 1 Chr 17:14, examining the kingdom of God in Chronicles.[203] According to him, the relationship between the Davidic dynasty and God's kingdom is obviously revealed, and the linkage of "my kingdom" and "his kingdom" is confirmed by the fact that YHWH said that the Davidic dynasty and God's kingdom would be permanent. For the Chr, the relationship between the two kingdoms is closely connected with the future temple. YHWH's kingdom is indicated in the two houses of the Davidic covenant: the Davidic dynasty and the temple Solomon built.[204] Thus, David's son Solomon is surely emphasized as YHWH's chosen temple-builder (1 Chr 17:14).

YHWH's volition is emphasized again. In effect, the Chr stresses that God will build a house for David by altering the personal pronoun suffix (from בֵּיתְךָ וּמַמְלַכְתְּךָ to בְּבֵיתִי וּבְמַלְכוּתִי, from כִּסְאֲךָ to כִּסְאוֹ), when compared with the parallel text. One stylistic change of the verb is noticeable. The verb "set up" (hiphil form of עמד) in 1 Chr 17:14 is altered from "to be confirmed" (niphal form of אמן) in 2 Sam 7:16, which instead appears in 1 Chr 17:25, 26 with the emphasis on YHWH himself.[205] Accordingly, the text emphasizes in 1 Chr 17:14 that God will set David up in God's house and kingdom, whereas it is stressed in 2 Sam 7:16 that David's house and kingdom will be confirmed.

In addition, it should be noted that in 1 Chr 17:13 the Chr omits the phrase, "When he commits iniquity, I will reprove him with a rod of men and with the strokes of the sons of Adam" (2 Sam 7:14b). This phrase seems to allude to Solomon's sins, thus the Chr omits it in line with his portrait of Solomon.[206] Beentjes, noting this omission, considers that the Davidic covenant is primarily focused on Solomon as the temple builder. In Beentjes' view, the phrase contains "an *unconditional* promise to the Davidic dynasty" in the context of 2 Sam 7, whereas it was omitted in the context of

---

202. Avioz, "Nathan's Prophecy," 552. Hwang (*contra* Avioz) claims that synoptic study of 2 Sam 7:16 and 1 Chr 17:14 "leads us to conclude that the Temple and its cultus do not replace the Davidic dynasty in Chronicles," arguing that the Chr rather "enhances the role of the Davidic house in the cultic institution of the Temple" (Hwang, "Hope for the Restoration," 194).

203. Selman, "The Kingdom of God," 163–71.

204. Ibid., 164.

205. See Beentjes, "Transformations of Space and Time," 40–43 (esp. 41). The verb אמן in 2 Sam 7:16 "refers to the stability of the Davidic dynasty," and by using the verb עמד in place of אמן, 1 Chr 17:14b significantly alters the sense. The hiphil verb form with a preposition points out official's appointment to a new position. In effect, Solomon is depicted by the Chr as "a Temple official and a governor." Thus, in 1 Chr 17:14, the point is "no longer '*your* house,' the house of David as the royal *dynasty*, or '*your* kingdom,' the kingdom of *David*." By altering possessive suffixes, the Chr emphasizes the term "my house," that is, the house of YHWH as the temple and "my kingdom," that is, God's kingdom. Only the term, "throne," is applied to Solomon (36–7).

206. See Kalimi, *Reshaping*, 94. Kalimi asserts here that the omission of Solomon's sins aims at the glorification of his name.

1 Chr 17 because the David-Solomon narrative in Chronicles concerns "a *conditional* promise relating to the royal dynasty" (1 Chr 22:11–13; 28:9; 2 Chr 7:17–18).[207]

However, the Chr's description of the Davidic covenant seems to hold both conditionality and unconditionality. As Hwang asserts, the two aspects of the Davidic covenant are complementary, not contradictory, in Chronicles.[208] YHWH's promise to David is conditional in that the Davidic kings have been chastised and rebuked. The Davidic kingdom comes to an end when it does not keep YHWH's conditions. On the other hand, the Davidic covenant is unconditional in that YHWH's steadfast love will never be taken away from the Davidic kingdom.[209] He provides an illustration of the complementary relationship of these two aspects: Athaliah's reign (2 Chr 23). Even though Athaliah is a non-Davidic ruler in Judah and reigns for six years, the pause for six years does not signify the abdication of the Davidic covenant because Joash restores the Davidic line.[210] Accordingly, in Hwang's view, the two aspects of the Davidic covenant seem to have been integrated in Chronicles.

Thus, the third part of the divine speech forms the climax of the speech, in which YHWH declares to David that He will build him a house (the Davidic dynasty) and that one of his sons will build the temple. YHWH further says to David that He will establish the Davidic kingdom.

David's Prayer (1 Chr 17:16–27)

David's prayer (1 Chr 17:16–27)[211] is a response to the divine speech conveyed by Nathan, which can be divided into three parts by themes: David's confession of YHWH's mighty act for him in the past (1 Chr 17:16–19); his confession of YHWH's greatness and His mighty act for Israel (1 Chr 17:20–22); and his petition for the fulfillment of God's promise to David (1 Chr 17:23–27).[212] Of the three parts, the first two parts are *epideictic* rhetoric and the last is deliberative rhetoric.

---

207. Beentjes, "Transformations of Space and Time," 38–39.

208. Hwang, "Coexistence," 1–8.

209. Ibid., 1–8. In line with this, the Chr expects further change in the Yehudite community, which is temple-centered, through a restoration of the Davidic kingdom by appealing to the Davidic covenant. For more discussion, see Hwang's dissertation, "Hope for the Restoration."

210. Hwang, "Coexistence," 4.

211. See Beentjes, "Psalms and Prayers," 14–17. For the text-critical discussion of David's prayer in 1 Chr 17:16b–27, see Lynch, *Monotheism*, 222–30. Lynch analyzes David's prayer that responds to Nathan's oracle by a comparison of MT Samuel, MT Chronicles, and 4QSama.

212. Johnstone contends that David's prayer is comprised of three parts, noting frequent occurrences of the past tense (in the first and the third part) and of the jussive form (in the second) (Johnstone, *1 and 2 Chronicles*, 1:206).

1 Chr 17:16–19	
¹⁶ וַיָּבֹא הַמֶּלֶךְ דָּוִיד	And David the king went in
וַיֵּשֶׁב לִפְנֵי יְהוָה	and sat before YHWH,
וַיֹּאמֶר מִי־אֲנִי יְהוָה אֱלֹהִים	and he said, "Who am I, O YHWH God,
וּמִי בֵיתִי כִּי הֲבִיאֹתַנִי	and what (is) my house that you have brought me
עַד־הֲלֹם׃	thus far?
¹⁷ וַתִּקְטַן זֹאת בְּעֵינֶיךָ אֱלֹהִים	And this is small in your eyes, O God,
וַתְּדַבֵּר עַל־בֵּית־עַבְדְּךָ	and you have spoken of your servant's house
לְמֵרָחוֹק וּרְאִיתַנִי	for afar off, and you have seen me
כְּתוֹר הָאָדָם	according to the standard of a man
הַמַּעֲלָה יְהוָה אֱלֹהִים׃	who is on high, O YHWH God
¹⁸ מַה־יּוֹסִיף עוֹד דָּוִיד אֵלֶיךָ לְכָבוֹד	What more can David add to you for the honor
אֶת־עַבְדֶּךָ וְאַתָּה אֶת־עַבְדְּךָ יָדָעְתָּ׃	of your servant? and you know your servant
¹⁹ יְהוָה בַּעֲבוּר עַבְדְּךָ	O YHWH, for your servant's sake,
וּכְלִבְּךָ עָשִׂיתָ	and according to your heart you have done
אֵת כָּל־הַגְּדוּלָּה הַזֹּאת	all this greatness,
לְהֹדִיעַ אֶת־כָּל־הַגְּדֻלּוֹת׃	to make known all the great things

David's prayer is a response to the divine speech (1 Chr 17:4–14). The backdrop of this prayer is implied in the phrase: "David the king went in and sat before YHWH" (1 Chr 17:16a). It implies the tent-shrine in Jerusalem constructed by David after the bringing of the ark (1 Chr 16:1).[213] Likely, David will pray to YHWH in front of the ark in the tent-shrine. In this backdrop, David prays to Him, responding to YHWH's speech.

The first part of David's prayer is his confession of God's mighty acts in the past. This part begins with the rhetorical question (1 Chr 17:16b): "Who am I, O YHWH God, and what (is) my house that you have brought me thus far?" This question apparently expresses David's gratitude to God for his becoming the king of Israel, emphasizing his insignificance. In what follows, David continues to confess God's favor to him and his house, indicating that God has spoken of his house and has seen him as a man highly exalted (1 Chr 17:17).

The Chr, employing another rhetorical question, reinforces the argument of David's prayer (1 Chr 17:18). David says, "What more can David add to you for the honor of your servant?" There is nothing to add to God for David's honor. Interestingly, the Chr immediately provides an answer for the question: "You know your servant." In this verse, the rhetorical device *hypophora* is noticeable in that the speaker answers immediately his own rhetorical question.[214]

---

213. See Hill, *1 & 2 Chronicles*, 244; Knoppers, *I Chronicles*, 681.
214. Lanham, *Handlist*, 87.

David further confesses God's mighty acts in 1 Chr 17:19, mentioning the phrase, "for your servant's sake" (בַּעֲבוּר עַבְדְּךָ) and repeating the phrase, "all this greatness" (כָּל־הַגְּדוּלָּה הַזֹּאת) or "all the great things" (אֵת־כָּל־הַגְּדֻלּוֹת).[215] The latter phrase forms an *epiphora* (*conversio*) that repeats a word or words at the end of two successive lines.[216] These phrases emphasize that God Himself has done great things for David. In particular, one stylistic feature is the vocative frequently used in 1 Chr 17:16–19: "O YHWH God," "O God," "O YHWH." It reflects a close relationship between God and David. Of these vocatives, "O YHWH God" (יְהוָה אֱלֹהִים) is noteworthy in that it is employed in contrast with "O Lord YHWH" (אֲדֹנָי יְהוִה) in the parallel text (2 Sam 7:18–21).[217] The Chr, avoiding the word "Lord" (אֲדֹנָי), seems to intentionally emphasize the close relationship between God and David.

Furthermore, in this part the Chr describes David as the first person pronoun "I" (אֲנִי) and the first person suffix in the phrases: "my house" (בֵּיתִי) and "you have brought me" (הֲבִיאֹתַנִי) in 1 Chr 17:16. David emphasizes that YHWH has brought him thus far. On the other hand, the Chr depicts David as the third person "your servant" (עַבְדְּךָ), repeating the phrase "your servant" four times in 1 Chr 17:17, 18 (x2), 19, which contrasts David's smallness with God's greatness. This clearly demonstrates the relationship between YHWH and David. Accordingly, all these words, emphasizing YHWH's grace and greatness, display David's insignificance in contrast with YHWH's greatness. Japhet indicates that David's insignificance sets the mood of David's prayer most properly: "complete resignation to the will of God, accepting with equanimity both the refusal of his original wish and the promise of what he did not ask."[218]

In this regard, the first part of David's prayer is an expression of his thanksgiving for what God has done for him. The Chr, employing two rhetorical questions, reinforces his argument of YHWH's greatness in contrast with David's smallness. Thus, the Chr emphasizes that YHWH has done great things for David, contrasting David's smallness with YHWH's greatness.

---

215. On the other hand, 2 Sam 7:21 refers to what God has done "for your [God's] word" (בַּעֲבוּר דְּבָרְךָ) and "to cause your servant to know (it)" (לְהוֹדִיעַ אֶת־עַבְדֶּךָ).

216. Lanham, *Handlist*, 69.

217. See Japhet, *I & II Chronicles*, 336; Johnstone, *1 and 2 Chronicles*, 1:207. Japhet points out that in 1 Chr 17:16–27, "the state of great excitement in which the prayer is uttered is reflected in the large number of addresses and invocations, ten in all, in the most variegated of phrase: O Lord God (vv. 16, 17); O God (v. 17); O Lord (vv. 19, 20); and thou, O Lord (22, 27); and now, O Lord (v. 23, 26); for thou, my God (v. 25); for thou, O Lord (v. 27)" (Japhet, *I & II Chronicles*, 336); Johnstone indicates that the divine name occurs six times in 1 Chr 17:16–22, in the form of the vocative, "O LORD, my God," etc., which "well conveys David's wonderment" ("Who am I?") (Johnstone, *1 and 2 Chronicles*, 1:207).

218. Japhet, *I & II Chronicles*, 336.

The Persuasive Portrayal of David and Solomon in Chronicles

1 Chr 17:20–22	
²⁰ יְהוָה אֵין כָּמוֹךָ	O YHWH, there is none like you,
וְאֵין אֱלֹהִים זוּלָתֶךָ	and there is no God besides you,
בְּכֹל אֲשֶׁר־שָׁמַעְנוּ בְּאָזְנֵינוּ:	according to all that we have heard with our ears
²¹ וּמִי כְּעַמְּךָ יִשְׂרָאֵל	and who is like your people Israel,
גּוֹי אֶחָד בָּאָרֶץ	one nation on earth
אֲשֶׁר הָלַךְ הָאֱלֹהִים לִפְדּוֹת לוֹ עָם	whom God went to redeem for himself a people,
לָשׂוּם לְךָ שֵׁם גְּדֻלּוֹת וְנֹרָאוֹת	to make for you a great and fearful name,
לְגָרֵשׁ מִפְּנֵי עַמְּךָ	to cast out nations from before your people
אֲשֶׁר־פָּדִיתָ מִמִּצְרַיִם גּוֹיִם:	whom you redeemed from Egypt?
²² וַתִּתֵּן אֶת־עַמְּךָ יִשְׂרָאֵל	And you made your people Israel
לְךָ לְעָם עַד־עוֹלָם	for yourself for a people forever,
וְאַתָּה יְהוָה הָיִיתָ לָהֶם לֵאלֹהִים:	and you, O YHWH, became their God

The second part of David's prayer (1 Chr 17:20–22) is related to God's greatness and God's mighty acts for Israel. This part includes the main events in Israelite history such as the Exodus and Conquest (1 Chr 17:21), YHWH's election of Israel (1 Chr 17:22) that leads to the covenantal relationship between YHWH and Israel forever.

In 1 Chr 17:20, the text emphasizes that there is none like YHWH by using the negative particle (אֵין) twice. The phrase "all that we have heard with our ears" obviously confirms YHWH's greatness. In 1 Chr 17:21, the rhetorical question emphasizes YHWH's special redemption of the people of Israel in order to make for them a great and fearful name and to cast out other nations from before God's people.²¹⁹ In 1 Chr 17:21, the focus is on God's redemption of Israel, which is expressed by the repetition of the verb "to redeem" (פדה). In particular, it is noteworthy that the Chr uses the phrase "you redeemed from Egypt" (פָּדִיתָ מִמִּצְרַיִם) in this verse. YHWH brings the Israelites out of Egypt.²²⁰ YHWH becomes the God of Israel, and Israel God's people. David's retrospection of Israelite history culminates in his announcement: "And you made your people Israel for yourself for a people forever, and you, O YHWH, became God to them" (1 Chr 17:22). This announcement points to the everlasting covenantal relationship between God and Israel. This relationship cannot be changed. The covenantal relationship is frequently mentioned in the Old Testament by the covenant formula, "I will be your God and you will be my people."²²¹ Thus, the second part of

---

219. In 1 Chr 17:21, one stylistic feature is noticeable. The verb "you made (gave)" (וַתִּתֵּן) is changed from "you established" (וַתְּכוֹנֵן) in 2 Sam 7:24. The verb כון is one of the Chr's favorite words, but at this time the verb נתן, instead of כון, is employed. Why did the Chr not use one of his favorite words? In my judgment, the Chr seems to have intended to employ the verb כון only when it is related to the Davidic dynasty and the temple building.

220. It is not appropriate to say that the Chr had no interest in the Exodus. For the discussion of the Exodus in Chronicles, see Japhet, *Ideology*, 296–301.

221. Martens (*God's Design*, 217–29) states, "The covenant formula, 'I will be your God and you

Speeches and Prayers in David's Narrative

David's prayer emphasizes God's greatness and what God has done for Israel, pointing to the fact that the covenantal relationship between God and Israel would not be altered forever.

1 Chr 17:23–27	
23 וְעַתָּה יְהוָה	And now, O YHWH,
הַדָּבָר אֲשֶׁר דִּבַּרְתָּ	let the word that you have spoken
עַל־עַבְדְּךָ וְעַל־בֵּיתוֹ	concerning your servant and concerning his house
יֵאָמֵן עַד־עוֹלָם	be established forever
וַעֲשֵׂה כַּאֲשֶׁר דִּבַּרְתָּ:	and do as you have spoken
24 וְיֵאָמֵן וְיִגְדַּל שִׁמְךָ עַד־עוֹלָם	and let your name be established and be great forever,
לֵאמֹר יְהוָה צְבָאוֹת אֱלֹהֵי יִשְׂרָאֵל	saying, YHWH of hosts is God of Israel,
אֱלֹהִים לְיִשְׂרָאֵל	God to Israel
וּבֵית־דָּוִיד עַבְדְּךָ	and the house of your servant David
נָכוֹן לְפָנֶיךָ:	is established before you
25 כִּי אַתָּה אֱלֹהַי גָּלִיתָ	For you, O my God, have revealed
אֶת־אֹזֶן עַבְדְּךָ לִבְנוֹת לוֹ בָּיִת	to the ear of your servant, to build him a house.
עַל־כֵּן מָצָא עַבְדְּךָ לְהִתְפַּלֵּל לְפָנֶיךָ:	Therefore your servant has found to pray before you
26 וְעַתָּה יְהוָה אַתָּה־הוּא הָאֱלֹהִים	And now, O YHWH, you are God,
וַתְּדַבֵּר עַל־עַבְדְּךָ	and you have spoken concerning your servant
הַטּוֹבָה הַזֹּאת:	this good thing
27 וְעַתָּה הוֹאַלְתָּ לְבָרֵךְ	And now, you have been pleased to bless
אֶת־בֵּית עַבְדְּךָ לִהְיוֹת לְעוֹלָם לְפָנֶיךָ	the house of your servant, to be forever before you,
כִּי־אַתָּה יְהוָה בֵּרַכְתָּ	because you, O YHWH, have blessed
וּמְבֹרָךְ לְעוֹלָם:	and it is blessed forever

The third part of David's prayer (1 Chr 17:23–27) is his petition for God's mighty act in the future, especially requesting the fulfillment of God's promise.[222] David reminds YHWH of his descendant who will build the temple and the Davidic dynasty, appealing to YHWH's word given to him through Nathan (1 Chr 17:4–14). In particular, David requests that YHWH fulfill His promise to David of the everlasting dynasty, repeating the word "forever" (עוֹלָם) four times (1 Chr 17:23, 24, 27[x2]). Accordingly, David's petition echoes the Davidic covenant concerning the dynasty as a crucial legacy in Israelite history. In this context, it is appropriate that Knoppers states, "If the chosen heir succeeds and Yhwh fulfills the pledges made through Nathan, the

---

shall be my people,' punctuates the Old Testament like a refrain" (Gen 17:7; Exod 6:7; Lev 26:12; Deut 26:16–19; 2 Sam 7:24; Jer 7:23–26; 11:4) (217).

222. First Chronicles 17:23–27 is parallel to 2 Sam 7:25–29.

promises to David will join the Exodus and Conquest as formative events in Israelite history."²²³

This part begins with the discourse marker "now" (עַתָּה). David requests that God's promise will be established forever (1 Chr 17:23).²²⁴ In this verse, the verb "you [God] have spoken" (דִּבַּרְתָּ) points to God's promise to David, forming an *inclusio* by repeating at the end the word occurring at the beginning.²²⁵ In what follows, David's petition for God's name and David's house is mentioned (1 Chr 17:24). In particular, the greatness of God's name is stressed by repeating the name three times: "YHWH of hosts," "God of Israel," "God to Israel." David emphasizes that YHWH is the God of Israel. Based on this repetition, David requests that YHWH establish the Davidic dynasty ("the house of your servant David") forever. In this regard, it is proper that Boda indicates that David's reign is at once linked to the broader concerns over the covenantal relationship between YHWH and Israel.²²⁶ In the following petition, David ascribes his appeal to God's revelation to him ("to build him [one of David's sons] a house," 1 Chr 17:25). In this verse, the phrase "to the ear of your servant" (אֶת־אֹזֶן עַבְדְּךָ), meaning "to David," forms the rhetorical device *synecdoche* that substitutes the whole for a part.²²⁷ Both 1 Chr 17:26 and 17:27 begin with the discourse marker "now" (עַתָּה), which indicates that the two verses function to summarize the third part of David's prayer—1 Chr 17:25–27 appears to boil down the whole chapter (1 Chr 17) with David's petition for God's blessing. In 1 Chr 17:26, David recollects what God has spoken to him by using the verb "you have spoken" (וַתְּדַבֵּר). In 1 Chr 17:27, David admits that YHWH has blessed the house of David, repeating the verb "to bless" (בְּרֵךְ) three times. In this context, Beentjes claims that 1 Chr 17:27 should be regarded "as a *panegyric* establishing that God's blessing on the house of David has already been realized."²²⁸ Accordingly, the third part ends with David's petition for God's blessing. Thus, the Chr, through David's prayer, exhibits that David's heir will build the temple and the dynasty will be forever on the basis of the Davidic covenant.

---

223. Knoppers, *I Chronicles*, 688.

224. In 1 Chr 17:23, the Chr employs the verb "be established" (אָמֵן), instead of "be established" (הָקֵם) in 2 Sam 7:25. Beentjes regards the verb אמן, identifying a new theological inclination, in comparison to the parallel verses (2 Sam 7:25, 26) (Beentjes, "Transformations of Space and Time," 41). According to Beentjes, the Chr has removed the verb אמן from 2 Sam 7:16a, where it points to the Davidic dynasty. Thus, the verb אמן in the new context concerns God's speech and name. The focus is on YHWH himself (42). He also points out that the same pattern is seen in 2 Chr 1:9 and 6:17, in which "the Chronicler diverts from its parent texts with the help of the verb אמן" (42).

225. See Lundbom, *Hebrew Prophets*, 172.

226. Boda, *1–2 Chronicles*, 157.

227. Lanham, *Handlist*, 148.

228. On the other hand, 2 Sam 7:29 is a petition for blessing in the future. First Chronicles 17:27b expresses an utterance relating to YHWH himself, but 2 Sam 7:29b speaks of the Davidic dynasty. Beentjes contends that YHWH was surely exalted in the Chr's depiction (Beentjes, "Transformations of Space and Time," 43).

In sum, the Davidic covenant in 1 Chr 17:1–15 emphasizes that David's successor (Solomon) will build the temple and that the Davidic dynasty will be forever, according to what YHWH has spoken to David (the Davidic covenant). In the Chr's description, the Davidic covenant (cf. 2 Sam 7:1–17) appears to be more related to temple building in the Persian period.[229] In accordance with this, David's prayer (1 Chr 17:16–27) echoes the Davidic covenant and emphasizes God's greatness for the sake of David and the people of Israel. David requests God's blessing for David's house (the Davidic dynasty), appealing to what God has already spoken to David.[230]

Rhetorical Situation

The narrative situation of 1 Chr 17 concerns the ark installed in Jerusalem (1 Chr 16). The urgent situation of the narrative is that David is at his own magnificent palace made of cedar, while the ark is placed in a simple tent (1 Chr 16:1). This makes David uncomfortable, such that he considers building YHWH's house. This urgent narrative situation leads to a series of speeches: David's speech, Nathan's speech, and finally YHWH's speech. David speaks to Nathan of his plan to build a house for YHWH and Nathan responds to it positively (1 Chr 17:1–2). That night, YHWH's words come to Nathan (1 Chr 17:3). YHWH speaks to him of His promise to David (1 Chr 17:4–14), and Nathan conveys YHWH's words to David. Thus, the narrative situation of 1 Chr 17 originates from the placement of the ark in Jerusalem.

The installment of the ark in Jerusalem serves as the foundation of David's preparation for the temple building in the following units.[231] The preceding unit (the ark narrative) functions as a constraint of the narrator's telling of the Davidic covenant. In the preceding unit, David had completed the transferring of the ark to Jerusalem; now, in this unit, he plans to build a house for YHWH (1 Chr 17:1). The preceding unit is closely connected to this rhetorical unit in its narrative progression, providing the narrative situation of the speeches of the characters. With respect to the narrative audience, a variety of audiences of the speeches and prayer are identified in the narrative context. In David's and Nathan's speech, the narrative audience is Nathan and David (1 Chr 17:1–2). In YHWH's speech that follows, the narrative audience is David since the speech is ultimately given to David through Nathan (1 Chr 17:4–14), possibly including Nathan as the conveyer of the divine speech. In David's prayer, the audience is YHWH as the addressee of the prayer (1 Chr 17:16–27).

---

229. Williamson ("Eschatology," 140–42) indicates that the Chr's concern is "to present the reigns of David and Solomon as a single, unified event within the divine economy for the life of the nation, in which the complementary nature of the two kings' functions plays an important role, a feature most marked in the Chronicler's handling of the theme of temple building" (140–41).

230. In the context of 2 Sam 7:18–29, David supplicates God's blessing in the future. Beentjes points out that the time category has been dominated by space category (Beentjes, "Transformations of Space and Time," 43–44).

231. See Hill, *1 & 2 Chronicles*, 241; Williamson, *1 and 2 Chronicles*, 132.

Accordingly, the narrative advances through the speeches and prayer, especially the divine speech. The key issue in these speeches and prayer is the Davidic covenant which YHWH gives to him through Nathan, which is about two houses: one is David's house (the Davidic dynasty) and the other is YHWH's house (the temple as the place which the ark would be finally installed in).

This narrative situation is connected to the rhetorical need of the Chr in his own situation. The Chr, through the speeches and prayer, presents the significance of the Davidic covenant regarding the Davidic dynasty and the temple building to his audience. In the dialogue between David and Nathan, David mentions the phrase "the ark of the covenant of YHWH" (1 Chr 17:1). Significantly, the ark of the covenant of YHWH is linked to the temple as God's dwelling place because the ark stands in the innermost place in the temple.[232] The Chr's use of the personal name "David" possibly indicates a wish to avoid the title "the king" because the title might be misunderstood to refer to the Persian king (1 Chr 17:2).

In the historical retrospect (1 Chr 17:4-6) of YHWH's speech, Johnstone indicates appropriately that during the days of the judges YHWH's accompanying presence is better displayed "by a nomad's movable tent than by the permanent structure of a temple."[233] This statement shows that the Chr's intention is to show that YHWH's dwelling place is being shifted from the nomadic tent to the temple at Jerusalem in David's time. It will further serve to legitimate the temple in Jerusalem as the place of true worship in the Persian period. In YHWH's election of David (1 Chr 17:7-8), the Chr reminds his audience of God's election of Israel as God's people by using the utterance that YHWH has been with David. In YHWH's address (1 Chr 17:9-10a), the Chr is interested in the unification of the scattered Israelites after the exile by the emphasis on the people of Israel. In 1 Chr 17:11-12, the Chr stresses that YHWH will establish the Davidic kingdom by one of David's sons and that his throne will be established forever. This is further emphasized by 1 Chr 17:14. Here, Johnstone states the Chr's purpose in 1 Chr 17:14 as follows:

> It is through this house of human flesh and blood that the LORD is going to actualize his presence among his people and through them in the world. Here the sacramental role of Israel as earthly counterpart to the cosmic forces of the LORD of hosts finds its sharpest focus in the sacramental role of the Davidic king whose rule and status are the living expression of God's own reign.[234]

Thus, Johnstone clearly indicates that the Davidic king plays the sacramental role in revealing God's sovereignty. However, the Chr's message goes beyond Johnstone's statement. The Davidic king will be established in YHWH's house and kingdom by YHWH, functioning as the covenantal partner on behalf of all Israel.

232. See Woudstra, *The Ark of the Covenant*, 55.
233. Johnstone, *1 and 2 Chronicles*, 1:201.
234. Johnstone, *1 and 2 Chronicles*, 1:206.

Speeches and Prayers in David's Narrative

Furthermore, in 1 Chr 17:13, YHWH's reference to "father" and "son" emphasizes the unalterable relationship between God and the Davidic king, which appears to be related to the formation of community identity in the Persian period. The rhetorical need or problem of the Chr is related to the new identity of the Yehudite community based on the Jerusalem temple since the Yehudites in the Persian period needed to reformulate their identity around the temple in Jerusalem as the centralized worship place according to the Deuteronomic law (Deut 12). For this reason, the Chr wishes to describe the Davidic covenant, considering Jerusalem as the worship center according to the Deuteronomic law.

In the Persian period, the question of community identity in Yehud is asked in relation to the Davidic covenant as a key legacy in Israelite history: "Does the Chronicler hope for a revival of the Davidic kingdom in view of the apparently eternally binding (עוֹלָם), unconditional Davidic covenant" (1 Chr 17:11–14; cf. 2 Sam 7:12–16), "or is he satisfied with its replacement by the postexilic cultic society?"[235] This question is whether the Chr hopes for the resurgence of the Davidic dynasty, or if he simply uses the dynasty to legitimize the temple community.[236]

With respect to this question, scholars have proposed two distinct views on the basis of their understanding of the Davidic kingdom in God's promises to David. Some contend that the Chr intended to re-establish the Davidic kingdom, considering the Davidic covenant as still effective for the future restoration of the Davidic kingdom,[237] whereas others maintain that the Chr had no interest in the restoration of the Davidic kingdom, considering that the Davidic covenant could be fulfilled only through the temple and worship in Jerusalem.[238] For instance, Kelly claims that for the Chr, YHWH's eternal kingdom "is still expressed in the personal line of David's descendants and is not simply absorbed in the temple and cult,"[239] whereas Schniedewind contends that the Chr's presentation of the Davidic covenant is to justify the

---

235. Hwang, "Coexistence," 2; "Hope for the Restoration," 194–98.

236. Boda, "Gazing through the Cloud of Incense," 219. Boda argues for the shape of the fulfillment of YHWH's promise to David regarding the dynasty, dividing it into two categories: king versus community (215–45).

237. Keil, *Chronicles*, 223; Rothstein and Hänel, *Das erste Buch der Chronik*, 153; von Rad, *Das Geschichtsbild*, 119–31; Noordtzij, "Les Intentions du Chroniste," 161–8; Noth, *The Chronicler's History*, 105; Brunet, "La Théologie du Chroniste," 1:384–97; Freedman, "The Chronicler's Purpose," 436–42; Stinespring, "Eschatology in Chronicles," 209–19; North, "Theology of the Chronicler," 379–81; Newsome, "Toward a New Understanding," 201–17; Williamson, "Eschatology," 115–54; Im, *Das Davidbild*, 184–5; Sæbø, "Messianism in Chronicles?," 85–109; Kelly, *Retribution*; "Messianic Elements," 249–64; McKenzie, *I & II Chronicles*, 252; Hwang, "Hope for the Restoration," 194–98.

238. Rudolph, *Chronikbücher*; "Problems of the Books of Chronicles," 401–9; Plöger, *Theocracy and Eschatology*; Caquot, "Peut-on parler," 110–20; Ackroyd, "History and Theology," 512–15; Hanson, *Dawn of Apocalyptic*, 273–6; Becker, *Messianic Expectation*, 79–82; De Vries, "Moses and David," 636–9; Riley, *King and Cultus*, 169–85; Pomykala, *Davidic Dynasty Tradition*, 69–111; Sparks, *The Chronicler's Genealogies*, 365; Schniedewind, *Society and the Promise*, 128–34.

239. Kelly, "Messianic Elements," 263–64.

authority of Jerusalem temple as the sole legitimate worship-center.[240] However, these split views among the scholars represent complementary tendencies in Chronicles, as Boda indicates.[241] It seems that these two aspects are reflected in the Davidic covenant regarding dynasty (1 Chr 17). The Chr's concern over the Davidic covenant cannot be easily divided.[242] The Chr may wish to reveal both streams in his presentation although the Davidic covenant appears to have been more related to the temple in Jerusalem in the Persian period. So he may have had a future hope for the Davidic kingdom as well as an idea of a centralized worship for YHWH in Jerusalem. In this context, the Chr felt the need to present the Davidic covenant in the context of the dynasty and the temple building as a crucial legacy of Israelite history. The rhetorical situation of the Chr arises from this exigence in relation to the identity formation of the Yehudite community in the Persian era.

David's prayer occurs as a sort of formal prayer responding to the divine speech (1 Chr 17:4–14). The preceding divine speech constrains David's prayer (1 Chr 17:16–27). In 1 Chr 17:16–19, the Chr presents YHWH's greatness to his audience by describing what God has done for David regardless of David's smallness in contrast with God's greatness. The Chr feels the need to present the significance of Jerusalem as the centralized worship place in the Persian period. In this regard, David's historical reminiscence (1 Chr 17:20–22) is given for the Yehudite community. It leads the Chr to remind the Yehudites of YHWH's covenant with the people of Israel in the past. In 1 Chr 17:23–27, the Chr emphasizes that the Yehudites will praise and pray to YHWH by demonstrating that David requests the fulfillment of YHWH's promise in the future. Significantly, Balentine in his analysis of prose prayers in the Hebrew Bible considers David's prayer as "formal prayer" that is "given their liturgical tone and their focus on issues."[243] If we may accept David's prayer as a formal prayer, the Chr's description of this prayer will serve to highlight the Jerusalem temple as the appropriate place of prayer, which emphasizes the call to worship and prayer by the Yehudites. Thus, the Chr, employing David's prayer, provides a formal prayer in the temple at Jerusalem as the centralized worship place in the Persian period.

The Chr's concern appears to go beyond this description in 1 Chr 17. As Hill indicates, the Davidic covenant "establishes the rule of God on earth in theological principle through the nation of Israel."[244] Selman also states that for the Chr, God's

---

240. Schniedewind, *Society and the Promise*, 128. Interestingly, Pomykala maintains that "neither the text nor the context of Chronicles supports a messianic or royalist interpretation. Instead, in the hands of the Chronicler the Davidic dynasty tradition subserved a particular vision of the Jerusalem cultic community in the late Persian period" (Pomykala, *Davidic Dynasty Tradition*, 111).

241. Boda, "Gazing through the Cloud of Incense," 215–45. Boda concludes then that "an ideal David embedded within a priestly led community and an expectation of a future ideal will arise from and for a community that remains faithful to the priorities already established at the temple" (245).

242. See Pomykala, *Davidic Dynasty Tradition*, 69–111.

243. Balentine, *Prayer*, 19.

244. Hill, *1 & 2 Chronicles*, 245.

kingdom "was still effective despite the depravations of the exile and the foreign imperial rule of his own day."[245] Accordingly, God's kingdom is embedded in the nation of Israel, on which the future hope of the Chr may anchor. Knoppers maintains properly that the Davidic covenant and David's prayer "set the stage for the remainder of David's reign, the tenure of Solomon, and the portrayal of the divided monarchy."[246]

In sum, the narrative situation of 1 Chr 17 occurs when David wishes to build a house for YHWH. At this time, YHWH gives His promises to David regarding the temple building and the dynasty. The Chr, bringing these speeches and prayers into his own context, attempts to persuade the Yehudite community to discern the centrality of Jerusalem as the sole worship place in Israel.

Rhetorical Effectiveness

The rhetorical effectiveness of a discourse functions on two levels. First, it entails the assessment of the rhetorical effectiveness of the discourse in order to persuade the narrative audience. We may evaluate the rhetorical effectiveness of the speeches and prayers since the narrative audience would be the hearers of the speeches and prayers in the narrative context. Second, it considers the possible effectiveness of the discourse, especially the speeches and prayers in the Chr's presentation, in order to persuade the Chr's audience to draw a fitting response.

The installment of the ark in Jerusalem allows David to consider the construction of YHWH's house. The urgent situation of the narrative leads to a series of speeches by the main characters. David's speech to Nathan (1 Chr 17:1) expresses his intention to build a house for YHWH, contrasting him in his cedar house with the ark under curtains. David's speech appears to effectively persuade Nathan in that David draws out Nathan's fitting response (1 Chr 17:2). After that, the divine speech persuades David to understand that: (1) YHWH has never asked any dwelling place for Him from the early history of Israel (1 Chr 17:4–6); (2) YHWH has done great things for David and the Israelites (1 Chr 17:7–10a); (3) YHWH has made his promises to David (1 Chr 17:10b–14), in which YHWH speaks of two houses: David's house (the Davidic dynasty) and YHWH's house (the temple as the place where the ark would be finally installed). The divine speech leads to David's prayer. In his responding prayer, David praises what YHWH has done for David and Israel in the past (1 Chr 17:16–22) and requests that the Davidic kingdom will be established forever, appealing to what God has already spoken to him (1 Chr 17:23–27). In this regard, David's prayer effectively persuades YHWH by appealing to what God has spoken to him. Thus, the Chr, through David's speech and prayer, portrays David as a true worshiper who is eager for the temple building and his praise to YHWH, which leads to YHWH's blessing on him and his kingdom.

---

245. Selman, *1 Chronicles*, 176.
246. Knoppers, *I Chronicles*, 676.

Furthermore, through the divine speech and David's prayer, the Chr attempts to persuade the Yehudites in Persian Yehud to identify the legacy of the Davidic covenant regarding the temple building and the dynasty. In the divine speech (1 Chr 17:4–14), the Chr persuades the Yehudites to recognize YHWH's greatness and His promise to David, in which the Davidic dynasty and the temple are emphasized. In David's prayer (1 Chr 17:16–27), the Chr tells his audience that YHWH hears and answers their prayers, carrying out great things that finally lead to the glory of His name (1 Chr 17:19, 24, 26).[247] It will effectively encourage the Yehudite community to pray to YHWH by appealing to YHWH who surely listens to their prayer. In particular, the Yehudites will come to know YHWH's greatness and His mighty acts for Israel in the past by the historical reminiscence (1 Chr 17:20–22), which will remind them of their previous identity as God's people.

If the Chr's rhetorical need for the Yehudite community is to reformulate their community identity on the basis of the Jerusalem temple as the centralized worship place, his description of the Davidic covenant regarding the temple building and dynasty through the speeches and prayers will be very persuasive to them. In this context, the Chr persuades the Yehudites to recognize the importance of the Davidic covenant in the Persian era. Williamson expresses it well:

> For the Chronicler's first readers, living at a time when prospects of a change in their politically subservient status may well have seemed unlikely, the implications of this message would not have been lost: Israel's kingdom was secure and everlasting, because it was in God's hands, no matter what the present contrary appearance.[248]

The Chr's audience will come to understand their identity in Persian Yehud, anticipating that the Davidic kingdom will be secure and everlasting in YHWH's hand although the Yehudites are living under the Persian Empire. With respect to the Davidic covenant regarding the temple building, Schniedewind summarizes the Chr's retelling of the Davidic covenant properly as follows:

> The Chronicler rewrites and recontextualizes the dynastic oracle so that it justifies the building of the temple and introduces his comprehensive description of the temple and its institutions ... The Chronicler then reappropriates the dynastic oracle within the process of temple building by recalling the dynastic oracle in speeches and narratives.[249]

---

247. See Hill, *1 & 2 Chronicles*, 245.

248. Williamson, *1 and 2 Chronicles*, 136.

249. Schniedewind, *Word of God*, 143–44. He states elsewhere that God's promise to David contributes to three purposes: (1) it justifies David as the usurper over Saul; (2) it ratifies the succession of the Davidic line; and (3) it legitimizes the Davidic monarchy as instituted by YHWH (Schniedewind, *Society and the Promise*, 28). In the same manner, Gakuru investigates the Davidic covenant in 2 Sam 7:1–11, based on his comparison with Neo-Assyrian prophecies of salvation to Esarhaddon (Gakuru, *Inner-Biblical Exegetical Study*). Ishida points out that "the House of David is incorporated as a new

The Yehudite community will comprehend that the Davidic covenant is more related to the temple building, which is reflected in the Chr's depiction of YHWH's promises to David. The rhetorical problem to reformulate the community identity in the Persian period will be resolved by redefining their identity as the temple-centered community on the basis of the temple in Jerusalem as the sole worship place, which will draw out fitting responses from the Yehudites and which will lead them to praise (and pray to) YHWH. Thus, the Chr, through speeches and prayer, persuades the Yehudite community that the Davidic covenant regarding the temple building and the dynasty emphasizes the significance of the Jerusalem temple as the sole worship place and the future hope for the everlasting Davidic kingdom.

SPEECHES IN DAVID'S WARS (1 CHR 18–20)

David's wars (1 Chr 18–20) as a rhetorical unit include several speeches: David's speeches (1 Chr 19:2, 5b); the speech of Hanun's officials (1 Chr 19:3); and Joab's speech (1 Chr 19:12–13). The first two speeches occur in a condolence situation and the last in a battle situation. In this unit, after God's promise to David, the narrative sequence advances to the expansion of David's kingdom with his military successes. In 1 Chr 18–20, the Chr describes David's wars against the Philistines, Moabites, Arameans, Edomites, and Ammonites. As a result of these wars, David's kingdom becomes strongly established. The temple will be built when God gives rest to the land of Israel. At the peaceful time, David's son Solomon will be the temple builder. Thus, this unit describing David's wars helps to establish a time of rest for the building of the temple.

Rhetorical Unit

This rhetorical unit (1 Chr 18–20) concerns David's wars after God's promise to David in 1 Chr 17. The Chr employs discourse markers which show a sequence of time: "It came to pass after this" (1 Chr 18:1, 19:1, 20:4, וַיְהִי אַחֲרֵי־כֵן) and "And it came to pass, at the time of turn of the year—at the time of the going out of the kings" (1 Chr 20:1, וַיְהִי לְעֵת תְּשׁוּבַת הַשָּׁנָה לְעֵת צֵאת הַמְּלָכִים).[250] By these discourse markers, this unit can be divided into four sub-units: 1 Chr 18 comprises David's victories over the Philistines, the Moabites, Arameans, etc; 1 Chr 19 includes the fight against the Ammonites; and 1 Chr 20 includes two sub-units: the siege and capture of Rabbah (1 Chr 20:1–3) and the exploits against the Philistines (1 Chr 20:4–8). Of these sub-units, 1 Chr 19 contains an episode of the Ammonite king Hanun and David, in which there are several short speeches (1 Chr 19:2–3, 5b; 1 Chr 19:12–13).

---

element into the inseparable relationship between Yahweh and Israel" (98), dealing with the threefold nexus between YHWH, Israel and the Davidic dynasty. Thus, the climax of Nathan's oracle is the legitimation of Davidic dynasty towards the Israelites (Ishida, *Royal Dynasties*, 81–99).

250. Boda, *1–2 Chronicles*, 160; Knoppers, *I Chronicles*, 700; Klein, *1 Chronicles*, 49.

The Persuasive Portrayal of David and Solomon in Chronicles
Rhetorical Strategy

David's wars (1 Chr 19:1–19)[251] contain David's speech, which is to console Hanun the king of Ammon upon his father Nahash's death. Yet, Hanun and his officials humiliate David's messengers according to his officials' speech. It results in a battle between Israel and Ammon, in which Joab makes a speech to Abishai, urging him to be strong. Finally, Joab strikes down the Ammonites and the Arameans. As a result, David's kingdom is strongly established. It is appropriate that Hill states that the Chr's presentation of David's wars theologically confirms a partial fulfillment of the Davidic covenant (cf. 1 Chr 17:8–10).[252] David's speeches (1 Chr 19:2, 5b) are deliberative rhetoric, whereas the speech of Hanun's officials (1 Chr 19:3) is *epideictic* rhetoric.

David's Speech and the Speech of Hanun's Officials (1 Chr 19:2–3, 5b)

1 Chr 19:2–3, 5b	
² וַיֹּאמֶר דָּוִיד	And David said,
אֶעֱשֶׂה־חֶסֶד עִם־חָנוּן בֶּן־נָחָשׁ	"I will do kindness with Hanun son of Nahash,
כִּי־עָשָׂה אָבִיו עִמִּי חֶסֶד	for his father did with me kindness,"
וַיִּשְׁלַח דָּוִיד מַלְאָכִים לְנַחֲמוֹ	and David sent messengers to comfort him
עַל־אָבִיו	concerning his father.
וַיָּבֹאוּ עַבְדֵי דָוִיד אֶל־אֶרֶץ	and the servants of David came into the land
בְּנֵי־עַמּוֹן אֶל־חָנוּן לְנַחֲמוֹ:	of the sons of Ammon, to Hanun, to comfort him
³ וַיֹּאמְרוּ שָׂרֵי בְנֵי־עַמּוֹן	But the heads of the sons of Ammon
לְחָנוּן	said to Hanun,
הַמְכַבֵּד דָּוִיד אֶת־אָבִיךָ בְּעֵינֶיךָ	"Is David honoring your father in your eyes,
כִּי־שָׁלַח לְךָ מְנַחֲמִים	for he has sent to you comforters?
הֲלֹא בַּעֲבוּר לַחְקֹר וְלַהֲפֹךְ וּלְרַגֵּל	In order to search, to overturn and to spy out
הָאָרֶץ בָּאוּ עֲבָדָיו אֵלֶיךָ	the land, have not his servants come to you?"
5b וַיֹּאמֶר הַמֶּלֶךְ שְׁבוּ בִירֵחוֹ	The king said, "Dwell in Jericho
עַד אֲשֶׁר־יְצַמַּח זְקַנְכֶם וְשַׁבְתֶּם:	till that your beards grow and (then) return."

In David's speech (1 Chr 19:2–3), the phrase "to Hanun to comfort him" (אֶל־חָנוּן לְנַחֲמוֹ) emphasizes David's intention to send his delegation to the land of Ammon. According to Kalimi, an analogy between the statement of Hanun's officials and the intention of David's servants is shown by some changes in comparison with the parallel text (2 Sam 10:2–3).[253]

---

251. It is parallel to 2 Sam 10:1–19.

252. Hill, *1 & 2 Chronicles*, 258.

253. In 1 Chr 19:2–3, which is parallel to 2 Sam 10:2–3, the Chr employs "the land" (הָאָרֶץ) instead of "the city" (הָעִיר) and "have not his servants come to you" (בָּאוּ עֲבָדָיו אֵלֶיךָ) instead of "has not David sent his servants to you" (שָׁלַח דָּוִד אֶת־עֲבָדָיו אֵלֶיךָ). As a result, the contrast between the statement of

In 1 Chr 19:2, the word "kindness" (חֶסֶד) in David's speech constitutes an *inclusio*, which means that the same word occurring at the beginning is repeated at the end of the speech.[254] It reflects the good relationship between David and Hanun's father Nahash in the past. In the following narration, the phrase "comfort him" (לְנַחֲמוֹ) is repeated twice at the ends of lines (*epiphora*), which emphasizes the reason for David's sending his messengers to Hanun. David's intention is to console Hanun on the death of his father, Nahash. This may have had a political purpose for peace in the future. However, Hanun follows his officials' words (1 Chr 19:3).

The speech of Hanun's officials is comprised of two rhetorical questions. The first positive question emphasizes that David does not come to comfort Hanun, whereas the second negative one underscores that David's coming is to spy out and overturn the land of Ammon. Accordingly, the speech of Hanun's officials reveals their doubt about David's sending his delegation. They think that the delegation's coming to the land of Ammon will be to search and overturn their land. The officials' speech, based on two rhetorical questions, seems to have been effective to evoke Hanun's doubt about David's intention to send the delegation. As a result, Hanun, following his officials' advice, humiliates David's messengers by shaving them and cutting off their garments at the middle of their hips (1 Chr 19:4). This humiliation is an open insult to David as they have come to Hanun on behalf of David as his envoys.[255]

David hears that his messengers were humiliated, and he gives his instructions to them, telling them to dwell in Jericho until their beards grow and then to return (1 Chr 19:5; cf. 2 Sam 10:5b). In this regard, David's speech to his messengers shows his concern over them. Their beards grow, then they return to David. At last, David's battle against the Ammonites begins.

David's speech reveals that he did not want to fight against Hanun, the king of the Ammonites, as David had previously enjoyed a good relationship with Nahash, Hanun's father. As Japhet states, the narrator's purpose is "to indicate by David's restraint that the initiative for the war is the Ammonites.'"[256] David's speech and the officials' speech explain why David's messengers are humiliated and how David's war against the Ammonites takes place. The Chr emphasizes that David wants to comfort Hanun on his father's death, not to fight against the Ammonites.

Hanun's officials and the coming of David's servants is emphasized. See Kalimi, *Reshaping*, 348–49.

254. Lundbom, *Hebrew Prophets*, 172.

255. See Hill, *1 & 2 Chronicles*, 263.

256. Japhet, *I & II Chronicles*, 357. Japhet here says, "David is a man of peace, and even in such grave circumstances he does not seek revenge." However, Japhet's statement seems to be a little overstated because David is a man of war. Rather, his son, Solomon would be a man of peace.

Joab's Speech (1 Chr 19:12–13)

1 Chr 19:12–13	
¹²וַיֹּאמֶר אִם־תֶּחֱזַק מִמֶּנִּי אֲרָם	And he said, "If Aram be stronger than I,
וְהָיִיתָ לִּי לִתְשׁוּעָה ס	then you shall become my salvation,
וְאִם־בְּנֵי עַמּוֹן יֶחֶזְקוּ מִמְּךָ	and if the sons of Ammon be stronger than you,
וְהוֹשַׁעְתִּיךָ:	then I will save you
¹³חֲזַק וְנִתְחַזְּקָה	Be strong, and let us strengthen ourselves,
בְּעַד־עַמֵּנוּ וּבְעַד עָרֵי אֱלֹהֵינוּ	for our people and for the cities of our God,
וַיהוָה הַטּוֹב בְּעֵינָיו יַעֲשֶׂה:	and may YHWH do that which is good in his eyes."

When David's army fights against the Ammonites and the Arameans, Joab makes a speech to Abishai as deliberative rhetoric (1 Chr 19:12–13).[257] In this discourse, Joab encourages Abishai to be strong and courageous, calling on YHWH for help, because the army of Joab and Abishai is outnumbered by that of the Ammonites and the Arameans. In Joab's speech, two conditional clauses are identified. The first protasis-apodosis indicates that if the army of the Arameans is stronger than that of Joab, Abishai's army should come to help Joab's army. The second protasis-apodosis points out that if the army of the Ammonites is stronger than that of Abishai, Joab's army will come to help Abishai's army. Thus, Joab urges Abishai to be strong, strengthening themselves, for the sake of God's people and their cities.

In Joab's speech, two verbs appear to play key roles. First, the verb root of "be strong" (חזק) is repeated four times in 1 Chr 19:12–13, of which the fourth use, "let us strengthen ourselves" (נִתְחַזְּקָה) seems to culminate in its use as *cohortatio* (exhortation).[258] Second, the verb root of "to save" (ישע) is repeated by a cognate noun "salvation" (תְשׁוּעָה) and its verb "save" (ישע) at the ends of two apodoses in 1 Chr 19:12, which form *epiphora*.[259] In 1 Chr 19:13a, the phrase "be strong and let's strengthen ourselves" (חֲזַק וְנִתְחַזְּקָה) reminds the narrative audience of what YHWH has said to Joshua in the Conquest narrative (Josh 1:6–7; cf. 1 Chr 11:10).[260] In 1 Chr 19:13b, it is interesting that Joab requests YHWH's help in this battle just as David does. Joab's speech to Abishai serves to encourage Abishai and himself to fight against the Ammonites and Arameans in order to save God's people and their cities.

In this discourse, what is impressive is that Joab follows what David did, calling on YHWH's help. It reveals that David's warriors also seek YHWH, which provides "a

---

257. First Chronicles 19:12–13 is parallel to 2 Sam 10:11–12, in which the word order of the phrase "If Aram be stronger than I" is changed from אִם־תֶּחֱזַק אֲרָם מִמֶּנִּי to אִם־תֶּחֱזַק מִמֶּנִּי אֲרָם, and the phrase "may YHWH do that which is good in his eyes" from וַיהוָה הַטּוֹב בְּעֵינָיו יַעֲשֶׂה to וַיהוָה הַטּוֹב בְּעֵינָיו יַעֲשֶׂה. See Kalimi, *Reshaping*, 238.

258. Lanham, *Handlist*, 36.

259. Lanham, *Handlist*, 69.

260. Hill, *1 & 2 Chronicles*, 264. Klein, *1 Chronicles*, 405.

model for courageous trust in Yahweh."[261] The battle against the Ammonites and the Arameans ends with the victory of Joab and Abishai. As a result, David's kingdom is strongly established, which provides the peaceful time necessary to build the temple in the reign of Solomon (1 Chr 22:6–16).[262] Furthermore, David's wars and his subduing the surrounding nations is a partial fulfillment of the Davidic covenant (1 Chr 17:8–10). In this unit, David is portrayed as the man of war to prepare for the peaceful time for Solomon's temple building and also as the one who is faithful to YHWH by achieving a partial fulfillment of YHWH's covenant.

Rhetorical Situation

The central narrative situation of the speeches in 1 Chr 19 is the event of Nahash's death (the Ammonite king). David's speech takes place when he is about to send his delegation to Ammon in order to console Hanun the new king of Ammon on his father's death (1 Chr 19:2). David's attitude and speech reflect the previous good relationship between David and Nahash. Yet, David's delegation is not welcomed by Hanun and his officials. Instead, they publicly humiliate David's messengers (1 Chr 19:3). This humiliation is another narrative situation. This event results in the tension between David and Hanun and consequently leads to David's war against the Ammonites. Finally, the narrative situation occurs when David's army fights against the Ammonites and Arameans. Joab discerns that his army is outnumbered by that of the Ammonites and Arameans. So Joab urges Abishai (and himself) to be strong and courageous, making a speech to Abishai (1 Chr 19:12–13). Thus, the narrative situation in this unit is Nahash's death, Hanun's humiliation inflicted upon David's delegation, and David's war against the Ammonites, which leads to the speeches of David, Hanun's officials, and Joab.

The narrative audience is David's officials and his messengers (1 Chr 19:2, 5b), Hanun and his officials (1 Chr 19:3), and Joab and Abishai (1 Chr 19:12–13). Possibly, the narrative audience could be considered to be David's supporters in the strongholds and his advocates in Jerusalem. Both of these dwell in Jerusalem with David after the capture of Jerusalem. They need to understand that David's kingdom was strongly established in order to build a house for YHWH at a peaceful time. Thus, David's battle against the Ammonites is depicted by the speeches of David, Hanun's officials, and Joab in the narrative context.

The narrative constraint is primarily the previous relationship between David and Nahash. They had previously enjoyed a good relationship since Nahash was once the enemy of Saul (1 Sam 11).[263] When David hears the news of Nahash's death, this close relationship leads to David's speech. When his messengers are publicly humili-

---

261. Boda, *1–2 Chronicles*, 167.
262. Ibid., 170.
263. See Knoppers, *I Chronicles*, 718.

ated, David makes another short speech to them. After this, when David's army fights against the Ammonites and Arameans, Joab makes a speech to Abishai.

The Chr, bringing the narrative into his own context, arranges the speeches for his own purpose. The Chr's exigence is the identity formation of the Yehudite community in the Persian era. The temple in Jerusalem will be only a medium to demonstrate their identity in the Persian period. In this context, the Chr wishes to remind the Yehudites as his audience of the origin of the peaceful time for the temple building. The Chr's description of David's war, through the speeches, will lead the Yehudite community to understand their community identity as a temple-centered community in Persian Yehud.

The Chr's constraint will primarily be Persian Yehud as a provincial district of the Persian Empire, which invokes the rhetorical question about their identity as God's people in the Persian period. Thus, the Chr's description of David's wars, through the speeches, will help his audience understand that the peaceful time to build the temple was achieved by David who had strongly established the Davidic kingdom after his wars. This achievement of David was the fulfillment of YHWH's word, echoing the Davidic covenant, since YHWH had said to him that he would make for him a name like the name of great ones (1 Chr 17:8–10).

Rhetorical Effectiveness

The rhetorical effectiveness of the speeches of David, Hanun's officials, and Joab may be traced on two levels. First, the speeches impact the narrative audience. They know that David does not wish to fight against the Ammonites. David's speech (1 Chr 19:2), which legitimizes David's integrity, clearly shows his intention to comfort Hanun. Yet, the speech of Hanun's officials (1 Chr 19:3) reveals their doubts about David's intentions in sending his delegation. Hanun's officials, using rhetorical questions, persuade Hanun to humiliate the delegation. Hanun does so according to his officials' advice. It results in the battle between Israel and Ammon, during which Joab makes a speech to Abishai (1 Chr 19:12–13). Joab's speech encourages Abishai (and himself) to fight for God's people and their cities. In this speech, Joab calls upon YHWH's help, following the example of David who has sought YHWH's aid in fighting against other nations. As a result, Joab and Abishai defeat the Ammonites.

David's speech helps to persuade his audience to recognize that David does not want to fight against the Ammonites, while Joab's speech before the battle shows that David's warriors also seek YHWH's aid as David does. The speeches in this unit serve to establish David's kingdom and the commencement of a peaceful time, in which the building of the temple in the peaceful age of Solomon may commence.

Second, the speeches impact the Chr's audience in the Persian period. The Chr arranges the speeches in the narrative context in such a way as to draw fitting responses from his audience. By the Chr's description of David's wars, the Yehudites will recognize that David faithfully prepares for the temple building. If the Chr's intention is the identity formation of the Yehudite community in the situation of the Persian Yehud as a provincial district under the Persian Empire, the Yehudites, who may be struggling for their new identity formation in the Persian period, will be persuaded by this description of David's wars through the speeches. In this period, the temple will be only a marker to show their identity as God's people. In this context, the Chr may wish to remind his audience of what event led to the peaceful time for Solomon's building of the temple.

The Yehudite community as the Chr's audience will understand that the peaceful time to build the temple is achieved by David (ultimately YHWH Himself) who has strongly established the Davidic kingdom after David's wars against the neighboring nations. Thus, the Yehudite community will be effectively persuaded by the Chr's description of David's wars through these speeches. The Yehudites will come to discern their new identity as a temple-centered community in the Persian period.

SPEECHES AND PRAYERS IN THE CENSUS NARRATIVE (1 CHR 21:1—22:1)

This rhetorical unit, the so-called census narrative (1 Chr 21:1—22:1),[264] contains several speeches: the speeches of David and Joab (1 Chr 21:2–3); David's speech and the divine speech through Gad (1 Chr 21:8–13, 17); dialogue between David and Ornan (1 Chr 21:22–24); David's speech (1 Chr 22:1). These speeches are related to the future temple site. In this unit, God provided David with the future temple site although David's census-taking displeased God. Thus, the Chr, through the speeches in this unit, portrays David as the faithful servant who sought YHWH and prepared the building of the temple by obtaining the location of the altar and temple.

Rhetorical Unit

This rhetorical unit contains David's census narrative, in which a few sub-units are identified. Scholars propose their divisions of the sub-units in the census narrative. Wright divides the census narrative into three parts by the events: the census of the Israelites (1 Chr 21:1–6); the results of the census (1 Chr 21:7–15a); and the acquisition of the future temple site (1 Chr 21:15b—22:1).[265] In a slightly different way, Ristau divides 1 Chr 21:1—22:1 into three parts: 1 Chr 21:1–15; 21:16–27; 21:28—22:1.[266] Boda divides this

---

264. For more discussion of David's census, see Knoppers, "Images of David," 449–70; Adler, "David's Last Sin," 91–95; "David's Census," 255–57; Bailey, "David and God," 337–59; Greenwood, "Labor Pains," 467–77. Johnstone, viewing 1 Chr 21 as the description of "David's climactic failure in the realm of the holy," asserts that "the Chronicler binds the reign of David, and the ensuing rule of the House of David as failure, into his overall schema of guilt and atonement in his presentation of Israel's life" (Johnstone, "Prospective Atonement," 140). Recently, Evans has contended that "the Chronicler's association of this legislation with David's failed census allowed the Chronicler to make the 'crime fit the punishment' regarding the otherwise baffling sin of the census" (80). See Evans, "Let the Crime Fit the Punishment," 65–80.

265. Wright, "Innocence of David," 89.

266. Ristau, "Breaking Down Unity," 203.

unit into four: 1 Chr 21:1–6; 21:7–14; 21:15–27; 21:28—22:1.[267] Interestingly, scholars have different views on the summary statement (1 Chr 21:28—22:1). For instance, De Vries considers it as attached to the next rhetorical unit (1 Chr 21:28—22:19),[268] whereas most scholars attach it to the census narrative (1 Chr 21:1—22:1).[269]

This rhetorical unit begins with David's census as incited by Satan (1 Chr 21:1).[270] David commands Joab to count the Israelites, though Joab advises that this counting will bring guilt upon Israel (1 Chr 21:2–3). Even so, Joab follows David's command and reports the number of the Israelites without the two tribes of Levi and Benjamin.[271] However, God is displeased with David's census.[272] David confesses his sin of the census and requests God's forgiveness (1 Chr 21:8). At this point, Gad the seer conveys God's words to David, asking David to choose among the three options of punishment (1 Chr 21:9-12). David entrusts such a decision to God (1 Chr 21:13). As a result, there is a three-day plague. David humbles himself (1 Chr 21:17), confessing his sin again. He purchases Ornan's threshing floor at full price following a dialogue between David and Ornan (1 Chr 21:22-24), and David erects an altar to God on Ornan's threshing floor according to the direction of the angel of YHWH. This unit ends with David's

---

267. Boda, *1–2 Chronicles*, 171–79.

268. De Vries, *1 and 2 Chronicles*, 178–81.

269. For instance, Braun, *1 Chronicles*, 215; Williamson, *1 and 2 Chronicles*, 143; Knoppers, *I Chronicles*, 743, 759–61.

270. For the discussion of Satan, see Day, *An Adversary in Heaven*, 127–45; Wright, "Innocence of David," 87–104; Knoppers, "Images of David," 449–70; Japhet, *I & II Chronicles*, 373–75; Jarick, *1 Chronicles*, 125–26; Evans, "Divine Intermediaries," 545–58; Kreutzer, "Der Antagonist," 536–44; Hamilton, "Satan," 5:985–89.

271. Some scholars seek to explain why Levi was omitted in the census by indicating that the Levites should not be counted together with other tribes in Num 1:47–49; 2:33, and others have various opinions about why Benjamin was omitted. For instance, Japhet considers the common denominator of Levi and Benjamin as the reason for this omission; both tribes are closely related to Jerusalem: "Jerusalem is included in the territory of Benjamin according to certain geographical concepts (e.g., Josh. 18.28; also Deut. 33.12), while the tribe of Levi is linked to the cultic activity in the Temple" (Japhet, *I & II Chronicles*, 378). Beentjes maintains why Joab did not count the tribes of Levi and Benjamin. First, to number the Levites was prohibited according to Num 1:47–49; 2:33. Second, for why Joab did not count Benjamin, "Joab's non-numbering of the tribe Benjamin prevents Jerusalem, which is a city on the boundary of Benjamin and Judah, from being 'contaminated.' For at the very end of this narrative (1 Chr 22:1) it is precisely Jerusalem that will be pushed forward as the future site of the cult" (Beentjes, "David's Census," 48–9). Knoppers says that "Benjamin may have been omitted because the holy site of Jerusalem was considered to lie within its borders" (Knoppers, *1 Chronicles*, 753). Klein (*contra* Knoppers) states: "It is more likely that it was because the tabernacle was located in Gibeon (1 Chr 16:39; 2 Chr 1:3; cf. 5:5 and Josh 18:25) in Benjaminite territory that the Chronicler had Joab exclude this tribe from the census" (Klein, *1 Chronicles*, 421). See also Tuell, *First and Second Chronicles*, 85; Dirksen, *1 Chronicles*, 258; McKenzie, *I & II Chronicles*, 172–73.

272. With reference to God's displeasure over David's census, Wright maintains that Joab must have caused it, stating that "he did not include Levi and Benjamin in the numbering, for the king's command was abhorrent to Joab" (1 Chr 21:6) (Wright, "Innocence of David," 87–105); Bailey (*contra* Wright), "David's Innocence," 83–90; Beentjes, "David's Census," 45–59. Beentjes claims, following Bailey, that David's confession of sin (1 Chr 21:8) cannot be easily understood if Wright's view is correct (47).

Speeches and Prayers in David's Narrative

announcement that "this shall be the house of YHWH and the altar for burnt-offering for Israel" (1 Chr 22:1). The census narrative includes a few speeches of the characters: the speeches of David and Joab (1 Chr 21:2–3); David's speech and the divine speech through Gad (1 Chr 21:8–13, 17); a dialogue between David and Ornan (1 Chr 21:22–24); and David's speech (1 Chr 22:1). These speeches as key rhetorical devices of the Chr serve to describe how David obtains the location for the future temple site.

Rhetorical Strategy

The Chr presents David's census narrative by employing a few speeches. The census narrative links David's military campaigns against the neighboring nations (1 Chr 18:1—20:8) to David's preparation of the temple building and Solomon's ascension of the throne (1 Chr 22:1—29:30).[273] The major theme in the unit is the chosen place of the future temple. As most scholars admit, the event of David's census in Chronicles is closely related to the founding of the Jerusalem temple and its cult.[274] Through this event, David obtains the location of the altar as the future temple site. Accordingly, the Chr emphasizes that David's sacrificing place for the sin of his census is connected with the future temple site.

The Speeches of David and Joab (1 Chr 21:2–3)

First Chronicles 21:2–3 contains the dialogue between David and Joab. As deliberative rhetoric, David commands Joab to count the number of the Israelites and Joab responds.

1 Chr 21:2–3	
² וַיֹּאמֶר דָּוִיד אֶל־יוֹאָב	And David said to Joab
וְאֶל־שָׂרֵי הָעָם	and to the heads of the people
לְכוּ סִפְרוּ אֶת־יִשְׂרָאֵל	"Go, count the Israelites
מִבְּאֵר שֶׁבַע וְעַד־דָּן	from Beersheba to Dan
וְהָבִיאוּ אֵלַי וְאֵדְעָה אֶת־מִסְפָּרָם:	And bring to me and let me know the number"
³ וַיֹּאמֶר יוֹאָב יוֹסֵף יְהוָה עַל־עַמּוֹ	And Joab said, " May YHWH add to his people
כָּהֵם מֵאָה פְעָמִים הֲלֹא אֲדֹנִי הַמֶּלֶךְ	as they are a hundred times. My lord, O king,
כֻּלָּם לַאדֹנִי לַעֲבָדִים	are they not all of them my lord's servants?
לָמָּה יְבַקֵּשׁ זֹאת אֲדֹנִי	Why does my lord seek this?
לָמָּה יִהְיֶה לְאַשְׁמָה לְיִשְׂרָאֵל:	Why should he be a cause of guilt to Israel?"

---

273. Knoppers, *I Chronicles*, 760. See also Ristau, "Breaking Down Unity," 206.

274. For instance, Duke indicates: "It was necessary to include this transgression of David in order not to omit an event which was crucial in the founding of the Jerusalem cult, for through this event the location for the altar and temple was obtained" (Duke, *Persuative Appeal*, 60). See also Williamson, *1 and 2 Chronicles*, 142–51; Mosis, *Untersuchungen*, 108–22; Braun, *1 Chronicles*, 212–18; Im, *Das Davidbild*,145–53; Japhet, *Ideology*, 109–17; De Vries, *1 and 2 Chronicles*, 177–80; Johnstone, "Guilt and Atonement," 123–24; Hill, *1 & 2 Chronicles*, 291–96; Boda, *1–2 Chronicles*, 173.

The addressee of David's speech in 1 Chr 21:2–3 is Joab and the heads of the people (cf. 2 Sam 24:2–3).²⁷⁵ In 1 Chr 21:2, the Chr seems to employ several rhetorical devices. For instance, the term "Israel" forms the rhetorical device *metonymy* in that it is substitution of the concrete word "the people and the land" for the abstract "Israel."²⁷⁶ The phrase, "from Beersheba to Dan" represents the rhetorical device, *synecdoche* as a type of metonymy, which substitutes the whole land of Israel for that phrase.²⁷⁷ In this verse, David commands Joab to count the Israelites.

Responding to David's command, Joab makes a speech (1 Chr 21:3). Joab's speech is composed of three rhetorical questions. Joab first wishes that YHWH would increase God's people a hundred times and then addresses three questions. The first rhetorical question, "My lord, O king, are they not, all of them to my lord for servants?" emphasizes that all of the Israelites are already David's servants. The second question, "Why does my lord seek this?" stresses that David need not to take a census. The third question, "Why should he be a cause of guilt to Israel?" underscores that taking a census will result in guilt to Israel. Though Joab does not answer the rhetorical questions, the answers are quite obvious. Joab does not wish to follow David's command since he knows that the census is not good in YHWH's eyes. By these three rhetorical questions, Joab indeed reveals his reluctance to take the census David has commanded. In particular, it should be noted that the third rhetorical question, "Why is he [David] a cause of guilt to Israel?" is unique to the book of Chronicles. Probably, the reason is that the word for "guilt" (אַשְׁמָה) is a postexilic Hebrew word (1 Chr 21:3; 2 Chr 24:18; 28:10, 33:23).²⁷⁸ In this speech, the Chr indicates that Joab obviously recognized that taking the census will bring guilt upon Israel.

David's Speech and the Divine Speech through Gad (1 Chr 21:8–13, 17)

First Chronicles 21:8–17 contains David's speech and the divine speech given to David through Gad the seer.²⁷⁹ David confesses his sin of the census-taking and requests God's forgiveness (1 Chr 21:8) and God speaks to David through Gad, who conveys three possibilities of punishment which God has offered (1 Chr 21:9–12):

---

275. Kalimi claims that the Chr changes general expressions to more personal ones in order to make David more prominent in 1 Chr 21. For instance, 1 Chr 21:2 reads "Go and count the Israelites... and bring to me (וְהָבִיאוּ אֵלַי) and let me know the number," whereas 2 Sam 24:2 reads "Number the people and let me know the number of the people" (Kalimi, *Reshaping*, 170). Kalimi concludes, "The numerous examples of almost every point mentioned and their placement in concentrated fashion alongside one another in the census narrative show the Chronicler's efforts to achieve the literary effect described at the onset of this discussion" (Kalimi, *Reshaping*, 170–71).

276. Lanham, *Handlist*, 102.

277. Ibid., 148.

278. See Kellerman, "אַשְׁמָה," in *TDOT* 1:429–37.

279. It is parallel to 2 Sam 24:10–17.

1 Chr 21:8	
⁸ וַיֹּאמֶר דָּוִיד אֶל־הָאֱלֹהִים	And David said to God
חָטָאתִי מְאֹד	"I have sinned greatly
אֲשֶׁר עָשִׂיתִי אֶת־הַדָּבָר הַזֶּה	in that I have done this thing.
וְעַתָּה הַעֲבֶר־נָא	And now please take away
אֶת־עֲוֺן עַבְדְּךָ	the iniquity of your servant
כִּי נִסְכַּלְתִּי מְאֹד׃	for I have acted very foolishly."

First Chronicles 21:8 as *epideictic* rhetoric is David's confession of the sin for his taking the census, requesting God's forgiveness. This speech is composed of two parts: David's confession of the sin (i.e., his taking the census) and his request for God's forgiveness. The two parts are divided by the word "now" (עַתָּה) as a discourse marker (meaning "therefore") that points to "a logical conclusion."[280] Accordingly, David confesses his sin of the census and requests God's forgiveness.

In particular, 1 Chr 21:7 reads: "God was displeased with this thing and he struck Israel."[281] In this verse, one issue is, who does "this thing" (that is, to count the Israelites)? Was it Joab, or David? Some scholars hold that Joab performs "this thing," pointing to the fact that Joab does not count Levi and Benjamin in 1 Chr 21:6,[282] whereas others maintain that David does "this thing," pointing to the fact that the action is confirmed by David's confession, "I have sinned greatly in that I have done this thing" in 1 Chr 21:8.[283] For instance, Wright claims that the divine judgment of David's census is Joab's fault since Joab does not complete David's order to count the Israelites.[284] However, Bailey contends, refuting Wright's view, that the phrase "I am the one who has sinned and done great evil" in 1 Chr 21:17 obviously shows that David confesses himself as the guilty person.[285] Accordingly, "this thing" to number the Israelites may be ascribed to both David and Joab, in that David commands Joab to take the census and Joab carries out the census even though he does not complete it. Of the two persons, David appears to have ultimately been responsible for the census since he has the final authority.

---

280. Van der Merwe et al., *Biblical Hebrew*, 308–9, 333.

281. In 1 Chr 21:7, we read that "God struck Israel," whereas in 2 Sam 24:10 we read that "David was stricken to the heart." The Chr emphasizes that God did it Himself, changing the subject from David to God.

282. See Wright, "Innocence of David," 98–99.

283. See Beentjes, "David's Census," 49; see also Evans, "Divine Intermediaries," 545–58.

284. Wright, "Innocence of David," 90–98. It is noteworthy that after noting the positive role of royal censuses in Chronicles (1 Chr 12:24; 23:3; 2 Chr 2:17; 17:13b–19; 25:5 26:11–13), Wright claims that "the ability of the king to take a census indicates the king's firm control over the army that is necessary to pursue the military interests of the kingdom" (92).

285. Bailey, "David's Innocence," 89.

This being so, why is David's census improper? Johnstone suggests in his study of the use of Exod 30:11–16 in 1 Chr 21 that the reason for the divine judgment of the census is that the proper rituals were not kept.[286] In Exod 30:11–16, YHWH commands Moses to make atonement for the lives of the Israelites when he takes a census. This legislation stipulates that everyone must pay half a shekel as an atonement payment for his/her life to YHWH, which will be used for the maintenance of the tent of meeting. If this legislation was not kept properly, it might result in a plague. Accordingly, in the Chr's census narrative, the plague will come upon the people of Israel since the legislation is not kept when David takes the census. If we consider David's census in this light, we might say that both David and Joab are responsible for the divine judgment of the census since they do not keep the legislation regarding the census-taking. Now we turn to 1 Chr 21:8 in the census narrative.

In 1 Chr 21:8, the Chr frequently uses the first person verbs (חָטָאתִי, עָשִׂיתִי, נִסְכַּלְתִּי), which demonstrates that David recognized his sin of taking the census. The adverb "greatly" or "very" (מְאֹד) at the ends of the first and last clauses reinforces David's confession of the sin and his request of God's forgiveness by stressing the meaning of the verbs ("I have sinned greatly" and "I have acted foolishly"), which rhetorically display an *inclusio*.[287] David's repentance is immediate without any attempt to avoid the responsibility for the census.[288] Japhet indicates that "David's belated recognition of his sin, his repentance and his readiness to admit his failure surely add a certain colour to his image, but they have no consequences in the unfolding of the story."[289] However, there is no image of a character that does not have any consequences in the narrative context. David's recognition and his repentance of the sin serve the portrait of David. So David's faithfulness to YHWH is displayed by his immediate repentance of his sin of taking the census.

Even though David confesses his sin and requests YHWH's forgiveness, YHWH provides three options for punishment. He speaks to David through Gad, David's seer, in order to present these options (1 Chr 21:9–12), and David responds (1 Chr 21:13). First Chronicles 21:9–13 is deliberative rhetoric:

---

286. Johnstone, "Prospective Atonement," 128–40.

287. See Lundbom, *Hebrew Prophets*, 172.

288. As Knoppers indicates, "David is not passive. Unlike Saul, who dies in his rebellion (1 Chr 10:13–14), Ahaz, who stubbornly compounds his guilt (2 Chr 28), David is immediately repentant. He does not attempt to shift the blame to others" (Knoppers, *I Chronicles*, 754).

289. Japhet, *I & II Chronicles*, 378.

Speeches and Prayers in David's Narrative

1 Chr 21:9–13	
⁹ וַיְדַבֵּר יְהוָה אֶל־גָּד חֹזֵה דָוִיד לֵאמֹר	And YHWH said to Gad, David's seer, saying,
¹⁰ לֵךְ וְדִבַּרְתָּ אֶל־דָּוִיד לֵאמֹר	"Go and speak to David, saying
כֹּה אָמַר יְהוָה	'thus says YHWH,
שָׁלוֹשׁ אֲנִי נֹטֶה עָלֶיךָ	three (things) I offer to you,
בְּחַר־לְךָ אַחַת מֵהֵנָּה	choose for yourself one of them,
וְאֶעֱשֶׂה־לָּךְ	that I may do (it) to you'"
¹¹ וַיָּבֹא גָד אֶל־דָּוִיד וַיֹּאמֶר לוֹ	And Gad came to David and said to him,
כֹּה־אָמַר יְהוָה	"thus says YHWH,
קַבֶּל־לָךְ:	take for yourself
¹² אִם־שָׁלוֹשׁ שָׁנִים רָעָב	either three years of famine,
וְאִם־שְׁלֹשָׁה חֳדָשִׁים נִסְפֶּה מִפְּנֵי־צָרֶיךָ וְחֶרֶב אוֹיְבֶךָ לְמַשֶּׂגֶת	or three months to be swept away before your foes and the sword of your enemies to overtake,
וְאִם־שְׁלֹשֶׁת יָמִים חֶרֶב יְהוָה	or three days of the sword of YHWH,
וְדֶבֶר בָּאָרֶץ וּמַלְאַךְ יְהוָה מַשְׁחִית בְּכָל־גְּבוּל יִשְׂרָאֵל	and pestilence in the land, and the angel of YHWH destroying in all the border of Israel.
וְעַתָּה רְאֵה	and now, see
מָה־אָשִׁיב אֶת־שֹׁלְחִי דָּבָר	what word I shall return to Him who sent me"
¹³ וַיֹּאמֶר דָּוִיד אֶל־גָּד	Then David said to Gad,
צַר־לִי מְאֹד	"I am in great distress;
אֶפְּלָה־נָּא בְיַד־יְהוָה	let me fall into the hand of YHWH,
כִּי־רַבִּים רַחֲמָיו מְאֹד	for His mercies are great;
וּבְיַד־אָדָם אַל־אֶפֹּל	but into human hands let me not fall."

In 1 Chr 21:10, as Boda observes, the imperative "choose" (בְּחַר) is employed as "the direct speech of command," and the first person pronoun "I" (אֲנִי) for YHWH and the second person suffix "you" (ךָ) for David, whereas "God is now spoken about in the third person" in the depiction of "Gad's subsequent interaction with David" (1 Chr 21:11–13).²⁹⁰ This speech emphasizes YHWH's sovereignty. YHWH employs Gad the seer as His mouthpiece and Gad conveys YHWH's words to David.

The three options of punishment are: three years of famine, three months of fleeing before the enemies, or three days of pestilence (1 Chr 21:12). The Chr, as Kalimi indicates, reinforces the depiction of retributive measures in the two phrases. For example, the phrase "three months to be swept away before your foes and the sword of your enemies to overtake" (1 Chr 21:12) is longer than the phrase "three months are you fleeing before your foes while they pursue you?" (2 Sam 24:13), and another phrase "three days of the sword of YHWH and pestilence in the land, and the angel

---

290. Boda indicates that this is "an example of the prophetic revelatory process in action" (Boda, *1–2 Chronicles*, 176). See also Boda, "From Complaint to Contrition," 186–97.

of YHWH destroying in all the border of Israel" (2 Chr 21:12) is much longer than the phrase "shall there be three days' pestilence in your land?" (2 Sam 24:13).²⁹¹ Accordingly, three options are provided by YHWH through Gad, and whichever of these three David chooses, God will carry out.

In 1 Chr 21:13, David responds to YHWH's words and chooses to fall into the hands of YHWH rather than human hands, without referring to a specific punishment such as famine or pestilence because God's mercies are great. In this speech, God's mercies are emphasized by placing the clause "for His mercies are great" (1 Chr 21:13) between the two surrounding clauses, which shows a chiasmus in that the clause "let me fall into the hand of YHWH" and the last clause "into human hands let me not fall" *antithetically* forms a chiastic structure. YHWH's mercies are very different from human mercies. Thus, the portrait of David is emphasized in the light of his trust in God's mercy.²⁹²

The humility of David and the elders (1 Chr 21:16) is also noteworthy in 1 Chr 21:7–17.²⁹³ The Chr says that "David and elders, clothed in sackcloth, fell on their faces" (1 Chr 21:16). This stresses dramatically the narrative effect, revealing the nature of the urgent situation.²⁹⁴ First Chronicles 21:17 as deliberative rhetoric shows this attitude of David. It reveals David's prayer in response to pestilence, in which David admits his sin and asks God to spare the people.

1 Chr 21:17	
¹⁷ וַיֹּאמֶר דָּוִיד אֶל־הָאֱלֹהִים	David said to God,
הֲלֹא אֲנִי אָמַרְתִּי לִמְנוֹת בָּעָם	"Did not I say to count the people?
וַאֲנִי־הוּא אֲשֶׁר־חָטָאתִי	and, I am the one who has sinned
וְהָרֵעַ הֲרֵעוֹתִי	and has done great evil.
וְאֵלֶּה הַצֹּאן מֶה עָשׂוּ	and these sheep, what have they done?
יְהוָה אֱלֹהַי	O YHWH my God.
תְּהִי נָא יָדְךָ בִּי	Let your hand be against me
וּבְבֵית אָבִי	and my father's house.
וּבְעַמְּךָ לֹא לְמַגֵּפָה׃	But not against your people for plague"

David prays to God in 1 Chr 21:17. The rhetorical question of David emphasizes his responsibility for the census: "Did not I say to count the people?" and then David blames himself: "I am the one who has sinned and done great evil," answering his own question. Accordingly, the rhetorical device, *hypophora*, is used in this verse.²⁹⁵ David

291. Kalimi, *Reshaping*, 341.
292. Ibid., 342.
293. It is not found in the parallel text (2 Sam 24:10–17).
294. For the Chr's arrangements, the elders appear in significant political (1 Chr 11:3; 2 Chr 10:6, 8, 13) and cultic scenes (1 Chr 15:25; 21:16; 2 Chr 5:2, 4; 34:29). See Beentjes, "David's Census," 52.
295. Lanham, *Handlist*, 87.

continues to seek God using another rhetorical question. The rhetorical question, "and these sheep, what have they done?" with the vocative "O YHWH my God," emphasizes that the Israelites, expressed by "these sheep" as a metaphor, have not sinned. David requests God's hands to be against himself and his father's house, not against the Israelites as God's people. In this request, David contrasts both himself and his father's house with God's people. Beentjes observes here that the narrator puts "the Holy Name ('YHWH') into David's mouth, which is not coincidence of course, since it occurs at a very strategic moment of the story and is also accompanied by the personal address 'my God.'"[296] This means that David appeals to his relationship with God in this request. Interestingly, David's supplication in 1 Chr 21:17 has two more clauses in comparison with the parallel text (2 Sam 24:17): "Did not I say to count the people?" and "But not against your people for plague." These emphasize that David is the one who has commanded the count of the people, and he requests that God not let the plague be on the people, providing a link between God's decision to stop the plague at Jerusalem (1 Chr 21:15) and the sacrifice offered at Ornan's threshing floor (1 Chr 21:22).[297]

Significantly, in this speech, the Chr describes David as a faithful servant who prays on behalf of all Israel. Knoppers states that David's supplication "on behalf of Israel is more pointed."[298] More significantly, the contrite portrait of David is more emphasized,[299] revealing David's faithfulness to God. Boda indicates that the Chr portrays David as "a repentant sinner who seeks atonement through sacrifice."[300] In any case, the Chr emphasizes that David's supplication results in the acquisition of the chosen place of the temple.

Dialogue between David and Ornan (1 Chr 21:22–24)

The angel of YHWH, putting back his sword, commands Gad to tell David that he should go up and erect an altar to YHWH on the threshing floor of Ornan (1 Chr 21:18). So David goes up to the threshing floor and encounters Ornan. The Chr describes the meeting at Ornan's threshing floor as more prominent by being related to the chosen place of the future temple (cf. 2 Sam 24:18–25). The dialogue between David and Ornan (1 Chr 21:22–24) is deliberative rhetoric:[301]

---

296. Beentjes, "David's Census," 52.
297. Japhet, *I & II Chronicles*, 384.
298. Knoppers, *I Chronicles*, 756.
299. See Knoppers, "Images of David," 449–70.
300. Boda, *1-2 Chronicles*, 179.
301. First Chronicles 21:22–24 is parallel to 2 Sam 24:22b–24a.

1 Chr 21:22–24	
²² וַיֹּאמֶר דָּוִיד אֶל־אָרְנָן	And David said to Ornan,
תְּנָה־לִּי מְקוֹם הַגֹּרֶן	"Give to me the place of the threshing floor,
וְאֶבְנֶה־בּוֹ מִזְבֵּחַ לַיהוָה	that I may build on it an altar to YHWH
בְּכֶסֶף מָלֵא תְּנֵהוּ לִי	for full silver give it to me,
וְתֵעָצַר הַמַּגֵּפָה מֵעַל הָעָם׃	and the plague shall be restrained from the people."
²³ וַיֹּאמֶר אָרְנָן אֶל־דָּוִיד	And Ornan said to David,
קַח־לָךְ	"Take (it) for yourself[A]
וְיַעַשׂ אֲדֹנִי הַמֶּלֶךְ הַטּוֹב בְּעֵינָיו	and let my lord the king do what is good in his eyes.
רְאֵה נָתַתִּי הַבָּקָר לָעֹלוֹת	See, I have given the oxen for burnt-offerings,
וְהַמּוֹרִגִּים לָעֵצִים	and the threshing-sledges for the wood,
וְהַחִטִּים לַמִּנְחָה	and the wheat for the grain offering,
הַכֹּל נָתָתִּי׃	the whole I have given."
²⁴ וַיֹּאמֶר הַמֶּלֶךְ דָּוִיד לְאָרְנָן	The king David said to Ornan,
לֹא כִּי־קָנֹה אֶקְנֶה בְּכֶסֶף מָלֵא	"No, for I surely buy for full silver,
כִּי לֹא־אֶשָּׂא אֲשֶׁר־לְךָ לַיהוָה	for I do not lift up that which is yours to YHWH,
וְהַעֲלוֹת עוֹלָה חִנָּם׃	so as to offer a burnt-offering for nothing."

A. The Chr replaces Araunah's (Ornan's) reply to David by the phrase "take (it) for yourself" (קַח־לָךְ) from the word "let... take" (יִקַּח) in 2 Sam 24:22. See Kalimi, *Reshaping*, 311–12.

In the acquisition of Ornan's threshing floor as the future temple site, David wishes to purchase the threshing floor, in order to build an altar of burnt offering. Ornan is willing to provide the floor along with the materials for the burnt offering. Thus, the dialogue between David and Ornan demonstrates how David obtains the future temple site.

In 1 Chr 21:22, the Chr stresses David's strong request to obtain the threshing floor of Ornan by repeating the phrase, "give (it) to me" (תְּנָה־לִּי, תְּנֵהוּ לִי) twice, which forms an *inclusion* that occurs at the beginning and end of this verse. In the latter case, by placing the phrase "for full price" (בְּכֶסֶף מָלֵא) in front of the phrase, "give it to me," David strongly stresses his request to purchase the threshing floor for full price. The reason for his request is to build the altar of burnt offering to YHWH there, so that the plague may be restrained from the people.

Ornan is ready to give David both the place of the threshing floor and the materials for the burnt offering. Ornan responds to David's utterance, urging David to take his threshing floor and even the oxen for burnt-offerings, the threshing-sledges for the wood, and the wheat for the grain offering (1 Chr 21:23). In particular, the Chr mentions that Ornan gives the materials for burnt offering to David, repeating the verb "I have given" (נָתַתִּי) at the beginning and the end of Ornan's speech. In this regard, this verb appears to correspond to the phrase, "give [it] to me" in David's request.

David's request is accepted by Ornan. However, David does not wish to obtain Ornan's threshing floor for nothing, declining Ornan's offer of donation. David intends rather to purchase the floor for full silver as David had at first mentioned (1 Chr 21:22). The verb with infinitive absolute (קָנֹה אֶקְנֶה) emphasizes the fact that David surely wants to buy the threshing floor for the full price.

In this dialogue, the focus is on the determination of the future temple site. It is noteworthy that the word "place" (מָקוֹם), not occurring in the parallel text (2 Sam 24), occurs in 1 Chr 21:22, 25, and 2 Chr 3:1. In particular, the term "the place" in 2 Chr 3:1 means not only Ornan's threshing-floor but also Moriah as the chosen place of the temple.[302] "Moriah" is the place where YHWH tests Abraham's faith. At Moriah, Abraham attempts to offer Isaac as a sacrifice to YHWH according to His command. Confirming the authenticity of Abraham's faith, YHWH spares Isaac and provides a lamb for a burnt offering. Afterwards, YHWH makes a covenant with Abraham (Gen 22:1–19). The focus is on the fact that YHWH appears to Abraham at Moriah. In the Chr's presentation, the sacred place in Israelite history is associated with the chosen place of the future temple.[303] Accordingly, the reference to Moriah in Chronicles appears to stress the significance of the chosen temple site by linking the Abrahamic worship site to the future temple site.

David purchases Ornan's threshing floor (1 Chr 21:25) and builds upon it an altar of the burnt offering (1 Chr 21:26). When David offers burnt offerings, YHWH directly responds to his offering: "He answered him with fire from heaven on altar of burnt offering" (1 Chr 21:26; cf. 2 Chr 7:1).[304] Thus, YHWH provides the new worship place for David. Through David's purchase of the threshing floor and his offering the burnt offering, the future temple site is determined. As a result, David's preparation of the temple building has commenced.

David's Speech (1 Chr 22:1)

First Chronicles 21:28—22:1 exhibits the ultimate result of David's census-taking. The Chr announces the future temple site by employing David's speech (1 Chr 22:1). This speech as *epideictic* rhetoric is the summary statement of David's census narrative.

---

302. See Beentjes, "David's Census," 56.

303. See Williamson, *1 and 2 Chronicles*, 203–205; Japhet, *I & II Chronicles*, 550–52; Boda, *1-2 Chronicles*, 246; Klein, *2 Chronicles*, 45–46; Hill, *1 & 2 Chronicles*, 384. David's purchase of the threshing floor is very similar to the pattern of Abraham's purchase of Machpelah from Ephron (Gen 23). See Williamson, *1 and 2 Chronicles*, 149.

304. This is a parallel to 2 Chr 7:1, in which God responds to Solomon in a similar way when the temple is dedicated.

1 Chr 22:1	
וַיֹּאמֶר דָּוִיד	"And David said,
זֶה הוּא בֵּית יְהוָה הָאֱלֹהִים	"This shall be the house of YHWH God,
וְזֶה־מִזְבֵּחַ לְעֹלָה	and this (shall be) the altar of burnt offering
לְיִשְׂרָאֵל׃	for Israel"

This summary speech of David indicates that Ornan's threshing floor will be the future temple site in Jerusalem. Significantly, the threshing floor is identified with the house of YHWH and the altar of burnt offering for Israel. David's speech stresses the new location of the worship place, referring to the tabernacle of YHWH made by Moses in the wilderness and the altar for burnt offering at Gibeon in 1 Chr 21:29. Accordingly, the Chr intends to make a linkage between the tabernacle at Gibeon and the house of YHWH (the temple) at Jerusalem.

Williamson appropriately indicates that the Chr intentionally contrasts the tabernacle of YHWH and the altar of burnt offering (1 Chr 21:29) with the house of YHWH and the altar of burnt offering (1 Chr 22:1), making the latter verse the conspicuous climax.[305] He holds that the purpose of the Chr is "to establish the divinely-willed continuity of worship between the Mosaic sanctuary and the future Jerusalem temple."[306] The Chr, through David's speech, emphasizes that the Jerusalem temple will be the central worship place in Israel. The Chr portrays David as a faithful servant who seeks YHWH and plays the role of the high priest.

In sum, the Chr, through speeches in the census narrative, explains how the new location of worship came to be. The speeches in this unit contribute to emphasize the temple in Jerusalem as the central worship place in Israel. The Chr portrays David as a faithful worshiper who seeks YHWH and plays the role of the high priest on behalf of the people after David took the census.

Rhetorical Situation

The rhetorical situation of 1 Chr 21 may be traced on two levels: the narrative situation in the narrative context and the Chr's rhetorical situation in the context of Persian Yehud. The narrative situation of 1 Chr 21 is the event of David's census-taking, which leads to the speeches of David and Joab (1 Chr 21:2–3). The census brings about the ensuing urgent situations of the narrative: three options of punishment (1 Chr 21:12) and the angel of YHWH standing with a drawn sword in his hand (1 Chr 21:16). These situations lead to the divine speech and David's speech (1 Chr 21:8–13, 17), the dialogue of David and Ornan (1 Chr 21:22–24), and David's announcement (1 Chr 22:1).

---

305. Williamson, *1 and 2 Chronicles*, 150–51.
306. Ibid., 150.

Speeches and Prayers in David's Narrative

The narrative audiences receive these speeches. In 1 Chr 21:2–3, the narrative audience is Joab and David, possibly including the leaders of Israel standing before David as those overhearing the speeches. In 1 Chr 21:8–13, 17, the narrative audience is YHWH, David and Gad in that David confesses his sin to YHWH and then YHWH gives his words to David through Gad. In 1 Chr 21:22–24, the narrative audience is Ornan and David, possibly including the angel of YHWH and Ornan's four sons as the overhearers of their dialogue (1 Chr 21:20). Although the audience of David's final announcement (1 Chr 22:1) is not clear, they may be those who were at Ornan's threshing floor when YHWH responded to David's offerings in the narrative context.

The census narrative is constrained by the events in the preceding rhetorical units. If we take into account the preceding events as the narrative constraints, the two events could be described as the key constraints of the census narrative: the Davidic covenant (1 Chr 17) and David's victories over the neighboring nations (1 Chr 18–20). In particular, the divine speech in 1 Chr 17 constrains the census narrative. According to the divine speech, Solomon will build a house for YHWH. To this end, David will prepare for his successor's building of the temple. He wishes to know the place of the temple building since YHWH has promised to him that Solomon shall build the temple. David's concern over the temple site may explain why David pronounces that Ornan's threshing floor will be "the house of YHWH" (1 Chr 22:1). Furthermore, the Davidic kingdom is extended and secured by David's victories over the neighboring nations (1 Chr 18–20). In this context, it may be necessary to count the Israelites since David may wish to know how many persons there will be in his army in the secured situation after his victories. The established kingdom of David constrains the census narrative. Thus, we can say that the narrative situation is limited by these two constraints.

The Chr brings the census narrative into his own situation. The Chr, through the speeches of David and Joab and the divine speech and David's speech, portrays David as a faithful worshiper who seeks YHWH. Yet, the census-taking displeased YHWH, emphasizing the significance of the Jerusalem temple in the Persian period. Boda indicates that David's two failures (the first attempt to transfer the ark to Jerusalem and David's census-taking) contribute to "the development of Jerusalem as Israel's central place of worship, and in both cases David emerges as a royal priest who intercedes on behalf of the people."[307] Johnstone further states that "three times David himself, ideally the high-priest of his people, is portrayed as infringing the sphere of the holy: in his attempt to bring the ark into Jerusalem (1 Chron 13); in his proposal to build a Temple (1 Chron. 17); and now, climactically, in the census of the people (1 Chron. 21)."[308] In effect, David builds an altar upon Ornan's threshing floor and offers sacrifices there on behalf of the people (1 Chr 21:26). Knoppers considers 1

---

307. Boda, *1–2 Chronicles*, 173.
308. Johnstone, "Prospective Atonement," 139.

Chr 21:1—22:1 as "a *crux interpretum* in the Chr's depiction of an illustrious reign."[309] He maintains that "David's repentance and intercession are paradigmatic," indicating that David was "a person of confession and supplication par excellence, a human sinner who repents, seeks forgiveness, intercedes on behalf of his people, and ultimately secures the site of the future Temple."[310] Thus, the Chr portrays David as the faithful worshiper who plays the role of the high-priest on behalf of the people.

With respect to the purchase of Ornan's threshing floor in the dialogue of David and Ornan (1 Chr 21:22–24), the Chr emphasizes the determination of the future temple site. The Chr contends that this decision was given by YHWH and that David lays the foundation of the Jerusalem temple. Hill indicates properly that "the purchase of the threshing floor becomes the foundational event for a series of actions by David to make ready for the building of Yahweh's temple."[311] Amit speaks of this acquisition of the threshing floor as follows:[312]

> By turning the story of this acquisition from an almost marginal addendum into a key element in the status of Jerusalem vis-a-vis its rivals, and by loading the story with many allusions to the leading figures of the nation's epic, the Chronicler made a major contribution to the position of Jerusalem in Jewish monotheistic civilization and its inheritors.

Although David's census-taking is his fault, the new location of the altar and temple are determined by the purchase of Ornan's threshing floor. The preparation of the temple building may now commence. Beentjes notes that the census narrative functions as "the introduction to a substantial section of the Book of Chronicles relating to various aspects of the future Temple."[313] He believes that the census narrative has a significant "*programmatic function*,"[314] by showing a conjunction between the threshing floor and the chosen place of the future temple (1 Chr 21:28—22:1).

Through David's announcement as a short speech, the Chr links the threshing floor to the chosen place of the future temple. Japhet regards this speech (1 Chr 22:1) as a climax in the census narrative: "the dénouement of the story: God has chosen the threshing floor as 'the holy place.'"[315] Knoppers says of 1 Chr 22:1 that "the Chronicler construes the mandate to construct an altar at this particular location, not as an ad hominem emergency maneuver to avert divine wrath, but as a decisive turning-point

---

309. Knoppers, *I Chronicles*, 762. Knoppers claims that "David's unequivocal admission of guilt, his mediation on behalf of Israel, his diligent observance of divine instructions, and his securing a site for the future Temple contribute positively to his legacy" (763).

310. Ibid., 764.

311. Hill, *1 & 2 Chronicles*, 291.

312. Amit, "Araunah's Threshing Floor," 142–43.

313. Beentjes, "David's Census," 54.

314. Ibid., 54. Italics Beentjes'.

315. Japhet, *I & II Chronicles*, 390.

in the history of Israelite religion."³¹⁶ Accordingly, this short speech underscores the Jerusalem temple as the house of YHWH by connecting the threshing floor to the future temple site. This summarizes David's census narrative. Thus, the Chr's main concern in this speech appears to be the linkage of the census narrative to the Jerusalem temple.³¹⁷

The Chr's exigence would be to present the Jerusalem temple as the central worship place in Israel. In the Persian period, there were other sanctuaries or shrines in Israel.³¹⁸ For instance, there was the Bethel sanctuary in the Persian era (Hag 2:14; Zech 7:1–3; Jer 41:4–9).³¹⁹ The rivalry between the Jerusalem temple and other temples in the Chr's own time may have led the Chr to describe the Jerusalem temple as the sole worship place in Israel. Probably, some groups in the Persian period had not wished to admit the centrality of the Jerusalem temple—the Benjaminites in Gibeon may not have acknowledged the priority of the Jerusalem temple since they utilized the tabernacle at Gibeon after the exile. In this context, the Chr's rhetorical need is to emphasize the significance of the Jerusalem temple, by indicating that the Gibeon sanctuary as a worship place had been active during the reign of David. Accordingly, the Chr attempts to persuade the Yehudite community to understand the significance of the Jerusalem temple as the central worship place in Israel.

In effect, 1 Chr 21:29, "the tabernacle of YHWH that Moses made in the wilderness and the altar of the burnt-offering were at that time in the high place in Gibeon," reflects the Chr's concern over the Gibeon sanctuary, which was being administered by Zadok and the priests whom David had appointed (1 Chr 16:39). This means that the tabernacle and the altar of the burnt offering were located in Gibeon during the reign of David. In particular, the divine response to David's offering (1 Chr 21:26) paves the way for the tabernacle at Gibeon to be transferred to Jerusalem and then to be united with the ark in the Jerusalem temple, which serves to the Chr's intention of one national cult in Israel.³²⁰ The Chr makes a linkage between the tabernacle at Gibeon and the house of YHWH (the temple) at Jerusalem. This shift from the tabernacle at Gibeon to the temple at Jerusalem may reflect the shift from Benjaminite leadership to Judahite leadership. Significantly, Jonker points out that Gibeon is exclusively referred to in the David narrative and that the Gibeon sanctuary is also mentioned in the Solomon narrative (2 Chr 1).³²¹ All the references to Gibeon (1 Chr

---

316. Knoppers, *1 Chronicles*, 760.

317. See Hill, *1 & 2 Chronicles*, 291.

318. See Amit, "Araunah's Threshing Floor," 141–42. According to Amit, there were various temples or shrines in the post-exilic period: on Mount Gerizim; at Elephantine, Casiphia in Babylonia (Ezra 8:17); at Bethel.

319. Blenkinsopp, "Bethel in the Neo-Babylonian Period," 93–107.

320. Knoppers, *I Chronicles*, 761.

321. Jonker, "Of Jebus, Jerusalem and Benjamin," 87; Day, "Gibeon and the Gibeonites," 113–37.

16:39; 21:29; 2 Chr 1:3) are interestingly identified in the Chr's *Sondergut*.[322] The Chr wishes to stress the close relationship between Benjamin and Gibeon. Thus, the Chr's rhetorical need to present the census narrative arises from this exigence, which also concerns the constraint of the Chr.

The Chr's main constraint is Persian Yehud as a provincial district under the Persian government. For the Chr this constraint is closely related to the identity formation of the Yehudite community under the Persian Empire. The scattered peoples of Israel after the exile experienced an identity crisis in the Persian period. The Chr is well aware of this situation, which raises a question concerning their identity in this context. In this process of the new identity formation, the Chr wishes to contribute to the reestablishment of the identity of the Yehudite community in the Persian period. Thus, the constraint of the Chr's presentation is Persian Yehud under the Persian Empire.

Rhetorical Effectiveness

The rhetorical effectiveness refers to the impact of a rhetorical discourse on the narrative audience and the Chr's audience. First, the narrative audience in the narrative is not persuaded by David's speeches. David's speech to Joab (1 Chr 21:2–3) seems to have been ineffective to Joab and the leaders of Israel standing before David. Rather, Joab's responding speech was more effective, revealing the problem of David's census-taking. The leaders of Israel are persuaded by Joab's speech, recognizing that David's census-taking displeased YHWH from the outset. This census-taking led to the divine speech through Gad and David's speech (1 Chr 21:8–13, 17). As a result, David must choose one of three options of punishment (1 Chr 21:12), a choice which he entrusts to YHWH. David, admitting his fault in the taking of the census, requests YHWH's punishment upon himself and his family, not on the people of Israel (1 Chr 21:17). This speech as a petition is effective in persuading YHWH to stop the plague. As a result, the angel of YHWH gives him the instruction to build an altar to YHWH, which provides David a resolution to stop the plague on the people. In this context, the speeches between David and Ornan (1 Chr 21:22–24) solve the "plague problem" by David's purchase of Ornan's threshing floor as the place of an altar to offer his burnt offering to YHWH. Finally, David's speech (1 Chr 22:1) concludes the census narrative with the announcement of the future temple site as the denouement of the census-taking, on which Solomon will build the temple in Jerusalem in his peaceful time. By this short speech, those who were at Ornan's threshing floor discern that Ornan's threshing floor will become the future temple site. David's repentant speech seems to play a significant role in persuading YHWH to provide the temple site for David. Thus, although David's census-taking displeases YHWH, the speeches of the

---

322. See Jonker, "Revisiting the Saul Narrative," 300–1.

main characters in the census narrative effectively function to persuade the narrative audiences to recognize the acquisition of the future temple site.

The Chr is not merely affected by the rhetorical situation, but also affects his audience, bringing the speeches in the census narrative to his own time, in order to persuade the Yehudite community as his audience to understand that the Jerusalem temple is the sole worship place in Persian Yehud. The Chr impacts his audience by describing how the chosen place of the future temple is obtained through the speeches in the census narrative. As David has announced, the temple will be the house of YHWH and the altar of burnt offering for Israel. The Chr's description of the census narrative is focused on the determination of the temple site. In particular, the temple in Jerusalem will be linked to the tabernacle in the Mosaic covenant (1 Chr 21:29) and Moriah in the Abrahamic covenant (2 Chr 3:1). Thus, the Yehudites may come to understand that the determination of the future temple site is the visual expression of the significance of the Jerusalem temple as the central worship place in Yehud.

In the situation of the rivalry between the Jerusalem temple and other shrines in various places in the Persian era, the Yehudite community is effectively persuaded by the census narrative dealing with the determination of the chosen place of the temple, which will be the site of the Jerusalem temple as the sole worship place in Yehud. However, some Benjaminites in Gibeon did not acknowledge the priority of the Jerusalem temple as they had been with the tabernacle at Gibeon (1 Chr 21:29). Accordingly, the Chr persuades the Yehudite community to consider the Jerusalem temple as the sole worship place, given that the Gibeon sanctuary will be united with the Jerusalem temple to be built by Solomon. The Chr's argument through the speeches in the census narrative is meant to be very persuasive to his audience since he appeals to them by emphasizing that the Jerusalem temple originated from the golden time of David and Solomon. Considering this, the Yehudites should be persuaded by the Chr's contention that the Jerusalem temple has been the central worship place from the early time of Israel. In this regard, it is appropriate that the Chr is speaking to "a community whose key unifying symbol was Jerusalem and its Temple."[323] Thus, in this unit, the Chr through David's speeches attempts to persuade the Yehudites by urging them to recognize the centrality of the Jerusalem temple.

SPEECHES IN DAVID'S PREPARATION FOR THE TEMPLE BUILDING (1 CHR 22:2–19)

David prepares for the building of the temple after the temple site is decided, and he encourages Solomon and the leaders of Israel to build the temple. This unit includes David's speeches to Solomon and the leaders of Israel, which serve to persuade them to build the temple. Through these speeches, the Chr will also attempt to persuade the Yehudite community to comprehend the significance of the Jerusalem temple by the

---

323. Boda, *1–2 Chronicles*, 177.

description of David's preparation for the temple building on the basis of the Davidic covenant. Thus, the Chr, through this portrayal of David as the temple preparer, emphasizes the continuity of the sacred place for worship in the Persian period.

Rhetorical Unit

This rhetorical unit (1 Chr 22:2–19) concerns David's preparation for the building of the temple. Many scholars divide 1 Chr 22:2–19 into three parts: David's preparation for the materials for the temple building (1 Chr 22:2–5); David's speech to Solomon (1 Chr 22:6–16); and David's speech to the leaders of Israel (1 Chr 22:17–19).[324] This unit is primarily comprised of David's speeches, reverberating through the Davidic covenant (1 Chr 17). Thus, the focus is especially on David's speeches, wherein David charges Solomon and his leaders to build the temple.

Rhetorical Strategy

First Chronicles 22:2–19 deals with David's preparation and encouragement for the building of the temple, which is comprised of David's speeches as deliberative rhetoric: David's speech (1 Chr 22:5); his speech to Solomon (1 Chr 22:6–16); and his speech to the leaders of Israel (1 Chr 22:17–19). In this rhetorical unit, the Chr's stylistic features include the repetition of the two verbs: the verb "to build" (בנה) occurs nine times (1 Chr 22:2, 5, 6, 7, 8, 10, 11, 19) and the verb "to provide" (כון) or its hiphil form "to make preparation" five times (1 Chr 22:3, 5, 14).[325] These emphasize that David is very eager to prepare for the temple building.

David's Speech (1 Chr 22:5)

1 Chr 22:5	
5 וַיֹּאמֶר דָּוִיד	And David said,
שְׁלֹמֹה בְנִי נַעַר וָרָךְ	"Solomon my son is young and inexperienced,
וְהַבַּיִת לִבְנוֹת לַיהוָה	but the house to be built for YHWH
לְהַגְדִּיל לְמַעְלָה	is to be made exceedingly great
לְשֵׁם וּלְתִפְאֶרֶת לְכָל־הָאֲרָצוֹת	for name and for beauty to all the lands.
אָכִינָה נָּא לוֹ	Now let me prepare for it."
וַיָּכֶן דָּוִיד לָרֹב לִפְנֵי מוֹתוֹ׃	And David prepared abundantly before his death.

This short speech introduces the reasoning for David's preparation for the building of the temple. Since Solomon is young and inexperienced and the temple will be exceedingly great, David considers preparing for the temple building in advance. In this speech, young Solomon is contrasted with the great task of building the temple.

---

324. Boda, *1–2 Chronicles*, 181–84; Knoppers, *I Chronicles*, 765; Hill, *1 & 2 Chronicles*, 296–301.

325. Hill, *1 & 2 Chronicles*, 296.

Speeches and Prayers in David's Narrative

The phrase, "young and inexperienced" emphasizes Solomon's smallness, whereas the phrase, "exceedingly great for name and for beauty" stresses the excellent magnificence of the temple. Japhet indicates that the Chr's style of phrasing is displayed by the infinitive constructs with לְ (e.g., לִבְנוֹת, לְהַגְדִּיל), stating that "the protasis is a normal clause with a sequence of infinitive constructs with *lamed*."[326] In particular, it is noteworthy that the hiphil form of the verb כון is used twice (אָכִינָה, וַיָּכֶן), of which the *cohortative* form (אָכִינָה), "let me prepare for it," expresses David's strong wish to prepare for the temple building.[327] The phrase "abundantly" (לָרֹב) stresses the magnificence of the task of the temple building, occurring three times (1 Chr 22:3, 4, 5).[328] These features reinforce the fact that David is very eager to prepare for the temple building. David's intention is to help Solomon in building the temple. Thus, David encourages Solomon and the leaders of Israel to build the temple by legitimating his eager preparation for the building task. The reason for this preparation is that Solomon is young and inexperienced, whereas the temple to be built should be exceedingly great. After legitimizing his preparation, David makes a speech to Solomon.

David's Speech to Solomon (1 Chr 22:6–16)

David urges Solomon to build the temple, beginning with "a proleptic statement" (1 Chr 22:6) that summarizes the following speech of David to Solomon (1 Chr 22:7–16).[329] David's speech to Solomon[330] as deliberative rhetoric has three parts: David recounts God's words to Solomon, beginning with the phrase "My son" (1 Chr 22:7–10); David charges Solomon to build the temple, beginning with the phrase "Now my son" (עַתָּה בְנִי, 1 Chr 22:11–13); and David concludes his speech to Solomon with his encouragement to build the temple (1 Chr 22:14–16), by urging Solomon with the phrase, "Arise and do [it], and YHWH be with you" (קוּם וַעֲשֵׂה וִיהִי יְהוָה עִמָּךְ).[331]

---

326. See Japhet, *I & II Chronicles*, 394–95.

327. See Gesenius, *Hebrew Grammar*, §108.

328. Boda, *1–2 Chronicles*, 181; Hill, *1 & 2 Chronicles*, 297.

329. Boda, *1–2 Chronicles*, 182.

330. Mitchell points out, based on Williamson's discussion, that the relationship of David and Solomon is almost identical with that of Moses and Joshua. Mitchell summarizes the similarities between them as follows: "1) David's disqualification as Temple builder linked to Solomon's succession parallels Moses' disqualification from entering the land of Israel linked to Joshua's succession; 2) the installation of Solomon parallels that of Joshua by including encouragement, the description of the task, and the assurance of divine aid; 3) both charges are first given in private and then in public; 4) the obedience of the people is emphasized in both accounts; and 5) Joshua is magnified with respect to Moses, so too Solomon is magnified" (Mitchell, "Transformations in Meaning," §3.1). See also Williamson, "The Ascension of Solomon," 351–61.

331. On the other hand, Johnstone considers that this speech is comprised of two parts: one is a retrospect (1 Chr 22:7–10) and the other is exhortation (1 Chr 22:11–16). Two sub-sections are linked in terms of the word "now" (1 Chr 22:11) (Johnstone, *1 and 2 Chronicles*, 1:240).

1 Chr 22:7–16	
⁷ וַיֹּאמֶר דָּוִיד לִשְׁלֹמֹה	David said to Solomon,
אֲנִי הָיָה עִם־לְבָבִי לִבְנוֹת בַּיִת בְּנִי	"My son, I had intended to build a house
לְשֵׁם יְהוָה אֱלֹהָי:	for the name of YHWH God.
⁸ וַיְהִי עָלַי דְּבַר־יְהוָה לֵאמֹר	But the word of YHWH came to me, saying,
דָּם לָרֹב שָׁפַכְתָּ	'much blood you have shed,
וּמִלְחָמוֹת גְּדֹלוֹת עָשִׂיתָ	and great wars you have made
לֹא־תִבְנֶה בַיִת לִשְׁמִי	You shall not build a house for my name,
כִּי דָמִים רַבִּים שָׁפַכְתָּ אַרְצָה	for you have shed much blood on the earth
לְפָנָי:	before me
⁹ הִנֵּה־בֵן נוֹלָד לָךְ	Behold, a son shall be born to you
הוּא יִהְיֶה אִישׁ מְנוּחָה	who will be a man of rest
וַהֲנִחוֹתִי לוֹ	and I have given rest to him
מִכָּל־אוֹיְבָיו מִסָּבִיב	from all his enemies round about,
כִּי שְׁלֹמֹה יִהְיֶה שְׁמוֹ	for Solomon will be his name
וְשָׁלוֹם וָשֶׁקֶט אֶתֵּן עַל־יִשְׂרָאֵל	and peace and quietness I will give to Israel
בְּיָמָיו:	in his days
¹⁰ הוּא־יִבְנֶה בַיִת לִשְׁמִי	He shall build a house for my name,
וְהוּא יִהְיֶה־לִּי לְבֵן וַאֲנִי־לוֹ לְאָב	and he will be my son, and I will be his father,
וַהֲכִינוֹתִי כִּסֵּא מַלְכוּתוֹ	and I will establish the throne of his kingdom
עַל־יִשְׂרָאֵל עַד־עוֹלָם:	over Israel forever'"
¹¹ עַתָּה בְנִי יְהִי יְהוָה עִמָּךְ	"Now, my son, may YHWH be with you
וְהִצְלַחְתָּ	and may you prosper
וּבָנִיתָ בֵּית יְהוָה אֱלֹהֶיךָ	and build the house of YHWH your God
כַּאֲשֶׁר דִּבֶּר עָלֶיךָ:	as he has spoken concerning you
¹² אַךְ יִתֶּן־לְךָ יְהוָה	Only may YHWH give you
שֵׂכֶל וּבִינָה	wisdom and understanding
וִיצַוְּךָ עַל־יִשְׂרָאֵל	and charge you over Israel,
וְלִשְׁמוֹר אֶת־תּוֹרַת יְהוָה אֱלֹהֶיךָ:	to keep the law of YHWH your God
¹³ אָז תַּצְלִיחַ אִם־תִּשְׁמוֹר לַעֲשׂוֹת	Then you shall prosper if you observe to do
אֶת־הַחֻקִּים וְאֶת־הַמִּשְׁפָּטִים	the statutes and the ordinances
אֲשֶׁר צִוָּה יְהוָה אֶת־מֹשֶׁה עַל־יִשְׂרָאֵל חֲזַק וֶאֱמָץ	that YHWH commanded Moses concerning Israel. Be strong and courageous.
אַל־תִּירָא וְאַל־תֵּחָת:	Do not fear and nor be dismayed"

Speeches and Prayers in David's Narrative

¹⁴ וְהִנֵּה בְעָנְיִי	"And behold with my affliction
הֲכִינוֹתִי לְבֵית־יְהוָה	I have prepared for the house of YHWH
זָהָב כִּכָּרִים מֵאָה־אֶלֶף	a hundred thousand talents of gold,
וְכֶסֶף אֶלֶף אֲלָפִים כִּכָּרִים	and a million talents of silver,
וְלַנְּחֹשֶׁת וְלַבַּרְזֶל אֵין מִשְׁקָל	and of bronze and of iron there is no weighing,
כִּי לָרֹב הָיָה וְעֵצִים וַאֲבָנִים	for they are abundant, and wood and stone
הֲכִינוֹתִי וַעֲלֵיהֶם תּוֹסִיף:	I prepared, and you may add to them.
¹⁵ וְעִמְּךָ לָרֹב עֹשֵׂי מְלָאכָה	And with you there are abundant workmen,
חֹצְבִים וְחָרָשֵׁי אֶבֶן וָעֵץ	stonecutters, and artificers of stone and wood,
וְכָל־חָכָם בְּכָל־מְלָאכָה:	and every skillful man for every work
¹⁶ לַזָּהָב לַכֶּסֶף	Of the gold, the silver,
וְלַנְּחֹשֶׁת וְלַבַּרְזֶל	and the bronze and the iron,
אֵין מִסְפָּר	there is no number.
קוּם וַעֲשֵׂה וִיהִי יְהוָה עִמָּךְ:	Arise and do (it), and YHWH be with you."

In the first part (1 Chr 22:7–10), David recounts God's words to Solomon, explaining why he was disqualified from building the temple and introducing Solomon as the temple builder. In the utterance of his disqualification, the phrase "much blood" (דָּם לָרֹב, דָּמִים רַבִּים; 1 Chr 22:8) emphasizes that David as a man of war has made great wars and has shed much blood.[332] Both phrases constitute an *inclusio* by surrounding the significant clause "You shall not build a house for my name" (1 Chr 22:8).[333] Accordingly, it explains why David cannot become the temple builder. Furthermore, David addresses another word of God to Solomon (cf. 1 Chr 17:12–13), beginning with the word "Behold" (הִנֵּה) in 1 Chr 22:9. In this speech, Solomon is introduced as the temple builder (1 Chr 22:10), stressing the "rest" motif as the prerequisite of the building of the temple (the root of the verb, נוח used twice in 1 Chr 22:9).[334] This motif is reinforced by the wordplay (*paronomasia or pun*) between "Solomon" (שְׁלֹמֹה) and "peace" (שָׁלוֹם), which is to "play upon words which sound alike."[335] In this regard, Solomon as a man of peace is contrasted with David as a man of war. Accordingly, the house for YHWH's name will be built by Solomon, and YHWH himself will provide this rest for Solomon in order to complete the task in his peaceful time. This part

---

332. Dirksen points out in his study of 1 Chr 22:8 that David is disqualified from the temple building due to his shedding blood, which gives the Chronicler's theological explanation about why Solomon would be the temple builder (Dirksen, "Why was David Disqualified," 51–56).

333. In 1 Chr 22:8, Knoppers identifies a chiastic arrangement by the phrase "much blood you have shed" (Knoppers, *I Chronicles*, 772).

334. See the discussion on 1 Chr 17:1, in which the Chr omits the text in 2 Sam 7:1b concerning David, however, in 1 Chr 22:9 the Chr uses these omitted words, applying them to Solomon instead of David.

335. Lanham, *Handlist*, 110; Kalimi, "Paronomasia," 38.

closes with the covenant formula[336] that YHWH will be father and Solomon shall be His son (1 Chr 22:10), which is previously indicated in 1 Chr 17:12–13.[337]

The second part (1 Chr 22:11–13) deals with David's commission to build the temple, on the basis of YHWH's promise to him regarding Solomon (1 Chr 17:7–14). In this part, a stylistic feature is the jussive verb form (יְהִי, 1 Chr 22:11) and the jussive meaning (וְהַצְלַחְתָּ, אַל־תִּירָא, וְאַל־תֵּחָת, 1 Chr 22:13), which functions to express David's wish affirmatively and his warning negatively.[338] David urges Solomon to be strong and courageous, positive, and neither to fear nor to be dismayed. The positive and negative statements, forming an antithetic parallelism, reinforce David's encouragement to Solomon. In 1 Chr 22:12, David requests that YHWH give wisdom and understanding to Solomon, urging him to keep God's law. Many scholars have noted that David's speech to Solomon is similar to both Moses' speech to Joshua (Deut 31:7–8) and YHWH's address to Joshua (Josh 1:6–9), in which we read the same phrase, "Be strong and courageous" and "Do not fear and nor be dismayed" (1 Chr 22:13).[339] Concerning this, Japhet states: "David's discourse as a whole is formulated as an adaption of existing models: Nathan's prophecy to David in the first place and God's words to Joshua in the second."[340]

In particular, David's speech in 1 Chr 22:13 emphasizes that YHWH will prosper Solomon if he observes YHWH's statutes and ordinances. By employing a protasis-apodosis, the Chr stresses the observance of YHWH's law, which will lead Solomon to prosper and to build the temple. In this speech, the verb, "to prosper" (וְהַצְלַחְתָּ, תַּצְלִיחַ) is used twice, and the three kinds of words concerning law (תּוֹרַת, הַחֻקִּים, הַמִּשְׁפָּטִים) are employed. These words emphasize the significance of keeping YHWH's law in seeking YHWH, which will in turn lead Solomon to prosper. Thus, David utters his wish and request to Solomon, based on YHWH's words of the Davidic covenant (1 Chr 17).

Schniedewind points out appropriately that "David's speech borrows heavily from the dynastic oracle."[341] Johnstone summarizes David's speech in this unit: "The

---

336. See, Martens, *God's Design*, 72–76.

337. According to Japhet, four elements of Nathan's oracle are indicated in these verses: "(a) 'he shall build a house'; (b) 'I will establish the throne of his kingdom'; (c) 'I will be his father'; (d) 'he shall be my son.'" 1 Chr 22:10 also contains these four. In effect, David's speeches in 1 Chr 22 are primarily based on the Davidic covenant (Japhet, *I & II Chronicles*, 398).

338. See Gesenius, *Hebrew Grammar*, §109.

339. Williamson, "The Ascension of Solomon," 351–61; Braun, "Chosen Temple Builder," 586–88; Japhet, *I & II Chronicles*, 400, 498–99; Mason, *Preaching*, 24–25; Knoppers, *I Chronicles*, 784; Hill, *1 & 2 Chronicles*, 298–99; Boda, *1-2 Chronicles*, 182.

340. Japhet, *I & II Chronicles*, 400.

341. Schniedewind, *Word of God*, 156. David wishes to build a temple (1 Chr 17:1–2); YHWH's prohibition is expressed as a close paraphrase of 1 Chr 17:4; and the promise of David's heir is followed (1 Chr 17:12, 13). Significantly, the Chr adds to the Davidic covenant, developed from Nathan's oracle in 2 Sam 7, "new justification for the prohibition: David fought many battles and this excluded him from the task of temple building (cf. 1 Chron. 18–20)" (156). The dynastic oracle promises that

centrality and significance of what is done in Jerusalem 'for all lands' is stressed: here continues the exploration of the potentiality of the monarchy to realize God's dominion on earth and thus realize the destiny of Israel at the heart of all humanity—but now through the temple."[342] According to Johnstone, David's speech impacts on the whole world, representing Israel as the representative of all humanity through the temple. However, Johnstone seems to overlook the identity of the primary audience of this speech by generalizing his statement. Johnstone seems to go too far to indicate the effect of David's speech on the whole world.

The last part (1 Chr 22:14–16) contains David's practical preparations for the temple building. Here, David speaks of his numerous preparations, giving a list of building materials in detail: gold, silver, bronze, iron, wood, and stones, which rhetorically forms the accumulation of nouns.[343] The text emphasizes that David has abundantly prepared for the building materials for the temple by using the verb, "to prepare" (הֲכִינוֹתִי)[344] and the word, "abundant" (לָרֹב) each twice in this section. The verb "to prepare," constituting an *inclusio* in 1 Chr 22:14, stresses the enumerated materials, and the word "abundant" in 1 Chr 22:14, 15 shows there were plenty of materials and workers for the temple building. After repeating the materials he has prepared in a summary statement, David charges Solomon to build the temple. The phrase "arise and do [it]" (קוּם וַעֲשֵׂה) closes this section with David's wish, "YHWH be with you" (1 Chr 22:16). This means that the temple project will not succeed without YHWH's accompaniment. Thus, David's speech legitimates David's preparation for the building of the temple, reaffirming Solomon as the temple builder. In sum, the Chr, through David's speech, not only justifies Solomon as the temple builder to Solomon but also emphasizes the observance of God's law by linking the relationship of David and Solomon to that of Moses and Joshua who were the faithful servants of YHWH.

David's Speech to All the Leaders of Israel (1 Chr 22:17–19)

David commands all the leaders of Israel to assist Solomon in the building project of the temple (1 Chr 22:17), making a speech to them as deliberative rhetoric (1 Chr 22:18–19). This speech reveals that seeking YHWH is closely related to the building of the temple:

David's son will follow him, not identifying the person. David's charge especially designates Solomon, which reinforces the choice by the pun between Solomon and peace. Lastly, the Chr adds a promise for peace in Solomon's era. In 2 Sam 7, God gives peace to David from the enemies (2 Sam 7:1, 11), while in the Chr's description, this reference to peace is shifted from David's time to Solomon's.

342. Johnstone, *1 and 2 Chronicles*, 1:240.
343. Bar-Efrat, *Narrative Art*, 216.
344. See Kalimi, *Reshaping*, 288.

1 Chr 22:18–19	
¹⁸ הֲלֹא יְהוָה אֱלֹהֵיכֶם עִמָּכֶם	"Is not YHWH your God with you?
וְהֵנִיחַ לָכֶם מִסָּבִיב	And has he not given to you rest round about?
כִּי נָתַן בְּיָדִי	For he has given into my hand
אֵת יֹשְׁבֵי הָאָרֶץ וְנִכְבְּשָׁה הָאָרֶץ	the dwellers of the land, and the land is subdued
לִפְנֵי יְהוָה וְלִפְנֵי עַמּוֹ:	before YHWH and before his people.
¹⁹ עַתָּה תְּנוּ לְבַבְכֶם וְנַפְשְׁכֶם	Now give your heart and your soul
לִדְרוֹשׁ לַיהוָה אֱלֹהֵיכֶם	to seek YHWH your God,
וְקוּמוּ וּבְנוּ אֶת־מִקְדַּשׁ יְהוָה הָאֱלֹהִים לְהָבִיא	and arise and build the sanctuary of YHWH God,
אֶת־אֲרוֹן בְּרִית־יְהוָה	to bring the ark of the covenant of YHWH
וּכְלֵי קֹדֶשׁ הָאֱלֹהִים לַבַּיִת	and the holy vessels of YHWH to the house
הַנִּבְנֶה לְשֵׁם־יְהוָה: פ	that is to be built for the name of YHWH."

In this speech, David charges the leaders of Israel to help Solomon build the temple. Since YHWH has given rest, David instructs them to seek YHWH and assist Solomon to build the temple. Beginning with two rhetorical questions (1 Chr 22:18), David emphasizes that God has been with Israel and that God has given to them a peaceful time (1 Chr 22:18a) because David had previously conquered the dwellers of the land given by YHWH and the land was subdued before YHWH, and the people of Israel (1 Chr 22:18b). Accordingly, in 1 Chr 22:18, David reminds the leaders of the conquest of the land of Canaan, alluding to the time of Moses-Joshua. At that time, YHWH gave the land to the people of Israel because the land had been subdued before YHWH.

However, the Chr transposes this event of the conquest to David's time. In this context, David is depicted as the one who completes the conquest of the land and who fights with the dwellers of the land. The Chr appears to describe David as the completer of the conquest who achieved a peaceful time for the temple building. Thus, David makes preparation for the building of the temple since the building task will be carried out later in the peaceful time of Solomon.

In 1 Chr 22:19, David encourages the leaders of Israel to seek YHWH and to arise and build the temple. The frequent repetition of "YHWH" (five times) reinforces the theme of seeking YHWH, which forms a prerequisite to build the temple in the Chr's view. The imperative verb forms (וּבְנוּ, וְקוּמוּ, תְּנוּ) are to encourage the leaders to carry out the building task. In this verse, seeking YHWH is linked to the building of the sanctuary of YHWH. The phrase "the house of YHWH" in the preceding speech (1 Chr 22:14) is replaced by the phrase "the sanctuary of YHWH," which clarifies the meaning of the house of YHWH. The house of YHWH is the very sanctuary of YHWH. Interestingly, the purpose of the temple building is referred to in 1 Chr 22:19. David urges the leaders to build the temple and to bring both the ark of the covenant of YHWH signifying YHWH's presence and the holy vessels of YHWH meaning YHWH's holiness to YHWH's house. Thus, the relationship between the temple and the ark of the covenant of YHWH is indicated again. YHWH's house containing the ark of the covenant of YHWH means that the temple itself becomes the symbol of the presence of YHWH.

Rhetorical Situation

The rhetorical situation of 1 Chr 22 may be described by two levels: the narrative situation and the Chr's rhetorical situation. The narrative situation in this rhetorical unit is the commencement of the preparation for the temple building. Since the temple site is now decided, David begins to prepare for the building of the temple (1 Chr 22:2–5), making a speech (1 Chr 22:5) and making speeches to his son Solomon and his leaders concerning the task of the temple building (1 Chr 22:6–19). David's speeches reverberate with the Davidic covenant regarding the building of the temple. These speeches are given to the narrative audiences. In 1 Chr 22:5, the narrative audience is David's officials standing before David as David orders them to assemble the aliens living in Israel (1 Chr 22:2). In David's speech to Solomon (1 Chr 22:6–16), the narrative audience is primarily Solomon and possibly David's officials with David as the overhearers of the speech. In David's speech to his leaders (1 Chr 22:17–19), the audience is the leaders of Israel. Thus, the hearers of David's speeches are Solomon and the leaders of Israel. David encourages them to carry out the building task by his persuasive speeches. In this context, the narrative constraint is the preceding event wherein the temple site had been decided (1 Chr 21:1—22:1). Since the future temple site is given to David by YHWH, David now prepares for the building of the temple. The decision of the future temple site in the preceding unit constrains the narrative situation of David's preparation of the temple building in this unit.

The Chr brings the narrative situation of David's preparation of the temple building to his own situation. Through David's speeches, the Chr attempts to persuade the Yehudite community as his audience. The Chr emphasizes the significance of the Jerusalem temple in the Chr's own context by David's speech (1 Chr 22:5). In David's speech to Solomon (1 Chr 22:6–16), the linkage of the monarchy and the temple may have caused some to raise a question about the legitimacy of the temple, so that the Chr, connecting the monarchy to the previous leadership of Israel (Moses and Joshua), reinforces the argument that both the monarchy and the temple are valid in the Chr's context.[345]

Through David's speech to the leaders of Israel (1 Chr 22:17–19), the Chr emphasizes that YHWH gave rest to David in order to build the temple, which would lead the Yehudites to be reminded of YHWH's faithfulness to Israel in the past and to anticipate YHWH's faithfulness for the Yehudites in the Persian period. Japhet contends that David's speech to the leaders of Israel theologically reflects a significant theme of Deut 12, indicating that "the covenantal terminology of the conquest" in 1 Chr 22:18 shows affinities with that in Deut 12:10, Josh 18:1; 21:44, Exod 23:31, Num

---

345. See Boda, *1–2 Chronicles*, 183–84; Williamson, "The Ascension of Solomon," 351–61.

32:22.³⁴⁶ Thus, the Chr, alluding to YHWH's covenant with Israel, presents the centrality of the Jerusalem temple to his audience in terms of David's speeches.

In this regard, for the Chr's audience, the depiction of David's preparation for the building of the temple (1 Chr 22) is "a reminder of the priority that lay at the core of their community, that is, the maintenance of the Temple and its worship services."³⁴⁷ The temple building is closely related to the Chr's own concern in the Persian period, which presents the centrality of the Jerusalem temple as the sole worship place to the Yehudite community. The existence of many worship places in the Persian period likely raised a question concerning the true worship place in Yehud.³⁴⁸ This rhetorical problem provokes the Chr to present the depiction of David's preparation for the temple building to the Yehudites. In this context, the rhetorical need is to describe David's preparation for the building task of the temple in order to emphasize the Jerusalem temple as the sole worship place in the Persian period. The scattered Israelites, who might worship God in various places after the exile, would need to be united with the Jerusalem temple as the sole worship place given by YHWH. Thus, the Chr appears to have intended to unify the scattered Israelites around the second temple at Jerusalem.

In this situation, Persian Yehud as a provincial district under the Persian government constrains the Chr's description of David's preparation of the temple building. The Chr recognizes the necessity of the identity formation of the Yehudite community on the basis of the Jerusalem temple as the worship place given by YHWH in the Persian period. In effect, there was no monarchical identity in Israel as an independent nation in the Chr's time. Jonker indicates rightly that the Chr represents the new identity that has shifted from a historically-defined identity (the monarchical time to the early postexilic period) to a cultic identity (during the Persian period).³⁴⁹ Thus, the Chr, through David's speeches, presents David's preparation of the temple building in order to persuade the Yehudites to comprehend their identity as the temple-centered community in the Persian period.

Rhetorical Effectiveness

The rhetorical effectiveness of the speeches may be assessed for the two sorts of audiences. First, the narrative audience is Solomon and the leaders of Israel. Through David's speeches, Solomon and the leaders are persuaded to carry out the building task of the temple. David's speech (1 Chr 22:5) legitimizes the preparation for the temple building by appealing to his officials or his leaders by contrasting Solomon's smallness and YHWH's greatness. David's speech to Solomon (1 Chr 22:6–16) is very persuasive

---

346. Japhet, *I & II Chronicles*, 402. First Chronicles 22:18 contains a precise reference to the conquest of the land. In effect, Moses in the past indicated that a rest given by God would be "a precondition for building a sanctuary for the Lord" (Deut 12:10–11). See Hill, *1 & 2 Chronicles*, 300.

347. Boda, *1–2 Chronicles*, 184.

348. See Amit, "Araunah's Threshing Floor," 141–42.

349. Jonker, "Rhetorics of Finding a New Identity," 396–412.

to Solomon, and possibly to David's officials as the overhearers of the speech, since David instructs and encourages Solomon to build the temple by appealing to YHWH's promise to David (1 Chr 17). David further urges Solomon to keep God's law in order to accomplish the building task. Finally, David encourages the leaders of Israel by his speech (1 Chr 22:17–19), in which they are urged to seek YHWH and to help Solomon to build the temple since YHWH already has given them rest on every side. Accordingly, these speeches function to persuade Solomon and the leaders to undertake the construction of the temple.[350]

The Chr brings David's speeches as rhetorical discourses into his own context. The Chr employs the speeches in order to persuade his audience in the Persian period to discern the meaning of David's preparation of the temple building. In this context wherein the scattered Israelites were worshiping YHWH in various shrines, the Chr needs to emphasize the Jerusalem temple as the central worship place. The Chr's emphasis on the Jerusalem temple is depicted by David's speeches, and it significantly affects the Chr's audience. The Yehudite community must be united with the scattered peoples of Israel around the Jerusalem temple. The problem of various worship places in the Persian period is effectively resolved by David's speeches. Accordingly, the Chr persuades the Yehudites to understand that YHWH chooses Solomon as the builder of the central worship place during the reign of David and that He gives Solomon a peaceful time to build the temple. Specifically, the Chr appeals to YHWH's promise to David and employs David's speeches, one of which indicates that the ark of the covenant and the holy vessels of YHWH shall be brought into the temple that will be built by Solomon (1 Chr 22:19). This appeal to the Davidic covenant (1 Chr 17) reinforces the Chr's argument of the centrality of the Jerusalem temple in the Persian period. Thus, the Chr through David's speeches persuades the Yehudites to recognize the significance of the Jerusalem temple, emphasizing the Jerusalem temple as the sole worship place in Yehud.

In sum, David's speeches legitimize his preparations for the building of the temple. In the narrative context, David persuades Solomon and the leaders of Israel to carry out the building project of the temple. In the context of Persian Yehud, the Chr, through David's speeches, effectively persuades the Yehudites to recognize the centrality of the Jerusalem temple in the Persian period.

SPEECH IN DAVID'S ORGANIZATION OF CLERGY AND OTHER LEADERS (1 CHR 23–27)

First Chronicles 23–27 as a rhetorical unit deals with lists of the temple personnel,[351] in which David's speech is identified (1 Chr 23:25–26, 28–32). This speech serves to

---

350. According to Japhet, "The portrayal of David as *the* greatest of Israel's kings and the object of future hopes, the establishment of the Temple as the centre of Israel's religious experience, and the inalienable bond between the house of David and the city of Jerusalem with its Temple—all these had become theological cornerstones" (Japhet, *I & II Chronicles*, 396).

351. Scholars have studied the composition of 1 Chr 23–27 and its sources. Yet, recently their

define a new role for the Levites in the time of the permanent temple. After charging Solomon and his leaders to build the temple (1 Chr 22), David appoints the temple personnel before his death, organizing them into divisions such as priests, musicians, gatekeepers, and civil officials. If the temple is built, they will serve to worship YHWH at the temple. Thus, the Chr portrays David as the organizer of the worship system.

Rhetorical Unit

This rhetorical unit concerns the lists of the Levites and civil officials, which may be outlined as follows:[352] the Levites (1 Chr 23); the priests and non-Aaronic Levites (1 Chr 24); the musicians (1 Chr 25); the gatekeepers and treasurers (1 Chr 26); and the civil officials (1 Chr 27). Knoppers indicates in 1 Chr 23–27 that the temple personnel and administrative officials "all make appearances as an inveterate David makes a series of appointments in anticipation of his successor's reign."[353] Wright points out that David's organization of clergy and leaders of Israel (1 Chr 23–27) "represents David's chief legacy."[354] The lists show those who will serve to worship YHWH at the temple. Accordingly, David prepares for Solomon's building of the temple by appointing the temple personnel.

In this unit, David's speech to all the leaders of Israel (1 Chr 23:25–26, 28–32) is the most significant part that elaborates on the relationship of David and the Levites, which begins with the phrase "for David said" (כִּי אָמַר דָּוִיד).[355] This speech indicates that YHWH has given rest to Israel as the prerequisite of the building of the temple and that the Levites' role will be changed since they will not carry the tabernacle. Instead, they will worship YHWH at the temple and assist the priests there.

---

concerns have shifted to the social, political, and religious aspects in the final composition. For instance, Knoppers states: "One unfortunate consequence of this preoccupation with sources and redactions over the course of the past two centuries is that the larger picture becomes lost as scholars focus on the origins and date of individual textual fragments. I wish to return to the social, political, and religious concerns raised by these chapters, specifically, how the materials relating to administrative appointments made at the close of David's reign contribute to the larger picture of his legacy" (Knoppers, *I Chronicles*, 789; Jonker, "David's Officials," 72–4). See also Wright, "Legacy of David," 229–42; "Those Doing the Work," 361–84; "Guarding the Gates," 69–81; "From Center to Periphery," 20–42; "Origin and Function"; Williamson, "Origins of the 24 Priestly Courses," 126–40; Jonker, "David's Officials," 65–91.

352. See Klein, *1 Chronicles*, 444–45; Hill, *1 & 2 Chronicles*, 301–21; Johnstone, *1 and 2 Chronicles*, 1:244.

353. Knoppers, *I Chronicles*, 788.

354. Wright, "Legacy of David," 241. According to Wright, 1 Chr 23–27 is "not marginal to the Chronicler's Davidic narrative. The passage and its characters do not interrupt the narrative, but complete the story" (233).

355. Jonker, "David's Officials," 77.

Speeches and Prayers in David's Narrative

Rhetorical Strategy

In this unit, David defines the Levites' new duties at the temple by his speech and prepares for the building of the temple by Solomon. David organizes and arranges his kingdom "down to the last detail in preparation for his death and Solomon's accession."[356] Thus, as Wright states, this unit functions to "legitimate the proper order of temple personnel, especially in times of national and cultic renewal."[357]

David's Speech (1 Chr 23:25–26, 28–32)

1 Chr 23:25–26, 28–32	
²⁵ כִּי אָמַר דָּוִיד	For David said,
הֵנִיחַ יְהוָה אֱלֹהֵי־יִשְׂרָאֵל	"YHWH God of Israel has given rest
לְעַמּוֹ וַיִּשְׁכֹּן בִּירוּשָׁלַםִ עַד־לְעוֹלָם׃	to his people, and he dwells in Jerusalem forever
²⁶ וְגַם לַלְוִיִּם	And also to the Levites,
אֵין־לָשֵׂאת אֶת־הַמִּשְׁכָּן	"none (are) to bear the tabernacle
וְאֶת־כָּל־כֵּלָיו לַעֲבֹדָתוֹ׃	and all its vessels for its service"
²⁸ כִּי מַעֲמָדָם לְיַד־בְּנֵי	"For their station (is) at the side of the sons
אַהֲרֹן לַעֲבֹדַת בֵּית יְהוָה	of Aaron for the service of the house of YHWH,
עַל־הַחֲצֵרוֹת וְעַל־הַלְּשָׁכוֹת	over the courts, and over the chambers,
וְעַל־טָהֳרַת לְכָל־קֹדֶשׁ	and over the purifying of all holy things,
וּמַעֲשֵׂה עֲבֹדַת בֵּית הָאֱלֹהִים׃	and the work for the service of the house of God,
²⁹ וּלְלֶחֶם הַמַּעֲרֶכֶת	and for the showbread,
וּלְסֹלֶת לְמִנְחָה	and for fine flour for the grain offering,
וְלִרְקִיקֵי הַמַּצּוֹת	and for the wafers of unleavened bread,
וְלַמַּחֲבַת	and for (what baked in) the pan,
וְלַמֻּרְבָּכֶת	and for that which is mixed,
וּלְכָל־מְשׂוּרָה וּמִדָּה׃	and for all measures of volume and size
³⁰ וְלַעֲמֹד בַּבֹּקֶר בַּבֹּקֶר	and to stand, morning by morning,
לְהֹדוֹת וּלְהַלֵּל לַיהוָה	to give thanks and to give praise to YHWH,
וְכֵן לָעָרֶב׃	and so at evening
³¹ וּלְכֹל הַעֲלוֹת עֹלוֹת לַיהוָה	and to offer all burnt-offering to YHWH

---

356. Wright, "Legacy of David," 233.

357. Ibid., 233–34. In Wright's view, 1 Chr 23–27 "emerges as a pivotal passage within the Chronicler's account of the reign of David" (233).

לְשַׁבָּתוֹת לֶחֳדָשִׁים	for Sabbaths, for new moons,
וְלַמֹּעֲדִים	and for appointed seasons,
בְּמִסְפָּר כְּמִשְׁפָּט	by number, according to the ordinance
עֲלֵיהֶם תָּמִיד לִפְנֵי יְהוָה:	on them continually, before YHWH
³² וְשָׁמְרוּ אֶת־מִשְׁמֶרֶת אֹהֶל־מוֹעֵד	And they shall keep charge of the tent of meeting,
וְאֵת מִשְׁמֶרֶת הַקֹּדֶשׁ	and charge of the holy place,
וּמִשְׁמֶרֶת בְּנֵי אַהֲרֹן אֲחֵיהֶם	and charge of the sons of Aaron, their brethren,
לַעֲבֹדַת בֵּית יְהוָה: פ	for the service of the house of YHWH

David makes a speech to the leaders of Israel (1 Chr 23:25–26, 28–32) as *epideictic* rhetoric. David's instructions to the Levites are "motivated with reference to the rest that YHWH the God of Israel has given to his people, and to the fact that He now dwells (שכן) in Jerusalem forever."³⁵⁸ The Chr employs direct utterances and allusions to legitimize David's act by appealing to Moses' authority.³⁵⁹ For example, the phrase, "according to the ordinance on them [the sons of Aaron]" (כְּמִשְׁפָּט עֲלֵיהֶם) shows that David depends upon the Mosaic law. Japhet states that this speech preliminarily justifies "the extension of the levitical functions beyond what is prescribed in the Pentateuch" (1 Chr 23:25–26) with the depiction of their functions (1 Chr 23:28–32).³⁶⁰ Jonker notes that through David's speech "the Chronicler closely associates the change of duties of the Levites with YHWH's role in the history of his people (giving them rest), and his dwelling in Jerusalem."³⁶¹

David's speech further sheds light on the relationship between the Aaronites and Levites, depicting David's announcement of the Levites' new duties, which are to assist (לְיַד־בְּנֵי אַהֲרֹן, 1 Chr 23:28) and to guard (מִשְׁמֶרֶת, 1 Chr 23:32) the Aaronites in a variety of duties in the temple.³⁶² In this speech, David stipulates that the Levites do not have to bear the tabernacle and all its vessels, and that they will assist the Aaronites at the temple. David gives the Levites the instructions about their new duties at the temple (1 Chr 23:28–32). In particular, the phrase, "for the service of the house of YHWH (or God)" (לַעֲבֹדַת בֵּית יְהוָה, עֲבֹדַת בֵּית הָאֱלֹהִים, 1 Chr 23:28, 32) is used three times, forming an *inclusio* by repeating it at the beginning and at the end of David's instructions. It emphasizes that the service of the Levites will be carried out at the temple, not at the tabernacle. David's appointment of the Levites is obviously for the service of the house of YHWH. In 1 Chr 23:29, the preposition ל at the beginning of words, being repeated six times, displays the rhetorical device *alliteration* that is "the repetition

---

358. Jonker, "David's Officials," 77.

359. See Wright, "Legacy of David," 234. Lundbom points out, "In Hebrew rhetoric, the driving force behind the assertive discourse of one speaking for God is authority, which substitutes for *ethos* in classical rhetoric" (Lundbom, *Hebrew Prophets*, 189).

360. Japhet, *I & II Chronicles*, 418.

361. Jonker, "David's Officials," 79.

362. Ibid., 80–81.

Speeches and Prayers in David's Narrative

of the consonant at the beginning of words."[363] Each word with לְ expounds in detail what the Levites should do at the temple, which indicates that David's instructions to the Levites are concrete and practical. Furthermore, the word, "charge" (מִשְׁמֶרֶת) in 1 Chr 23:32 is employed three times in conjunction with the tent of meeting,[364] the holy place, and the sons of Aaron.[365] It means that the Levites will serve in the temple according to their divisions, as they did at "the tent of meeting." Accordingly, the Levites will not bear the tabernacle and its vessels. Instead, they will serve in the temple in the future, carrying out what they did at the tent of meeting in the past.

In this context, some might raise a question concerning the relationship between the Aaronites and the Levites. One phrase appears to provide an answer to this question. The phrase "at the side of the sons of Aaron" (לְיַד־בְּנֵי אַהֲרֹן) indicates that the Levites will serve YHWH next to Aaronites (1 Chr 23:28). Dirksen considers the phrase as the expression of subordinate relationship, even though he states that the Chr holds that "priests and Levites both have their indispensable function within the order of the cult, while emphasizing only the prerogatives of the priests."[366] Knoppers, on the other hand, points out that the Chr emphasizes "cooperation and complementarity, not competition and hierarchy."[367]

Of the two opinions, Knoppers' view is more persuasive since he indicates that the Levites should thank and praise YHWH (1 Chr 23:30), which means the appointment of Levitical singers as "a case in which the Chr goes beyond Deuteronomic and Priestly precedent."[368] Thus, David's speech links the tent of meeting to the temple by announcing a new role for the Levites. David strongly establishes his kingdom by organizing the temple personnel before Solomon's succession, which contributes to Israel's rest as the prerequisite of the temple building in the peaceful time of Solomon.

Rhetorical Situation

The rhetorical situation of 1 Chr 23–27 may be traced on the narrative situation and the Chr's rhetorical situation. First, the narrative situation of this unit depicts David

---

363. Bar-Efrat, *Narrative Art*, 201; Lanham, *Handlist*, 6–7.

364. There are various views on the phrase, "the tent of meeting." For instance, Japhet asserts that "the anachronistic 'tent of the meeting' is retained and identified as 'the house of the Lord'" (Japhet, *I & II Chronicles*, 421). Allen considers that this phrase is employed metaphorically for the temple (Allen, "The First and Second Books of Chronicles," 437).

365. See Japhet, *I & II Chronicles*, 421.

366. Dirksen, *1 Chronicles*, 286. In line with this, Thompson holds that the Levites seem to "be subordinate to the priests, for they are to stand beside the sons of Aaron, that is, to assist them morning and evening when offerings were presented in the temple" (Thompson, *1, 2 Chronicles*, 170).

367. Knoppers, "Hierodules, Priests, or Janitors?" 70; Welch, *Work of the Chronicler*, 77. Knoppers (*contra* Welch) claims: "There is no firm evidence to suggest that the Chronicler holds to an absolute equality between priests and Levites. Nevertheless, the author does not emphasize hierarchy. Both the priests and the Levites are essential to the success of the temple cultus" (71). Klein also thinks that their relationship is coordinate (Klein, *1 Chronicles*, 455).

368. Knoppers, "Hierodules, Priests, or Janitors?" 67.

about to prepare for Solomon's succession (1 Chr 23:1). David assembles all the leaders of Israel, the priests and the Levites (1 Chr 23:2) and makes a speech to them (1 Chr 23:25–26, 28–32). David's speech occurs when he appoints the temple personnel, wherein he gives instructions to the Levites to assist the priests, the Aaronites at the temple. David wishes to establish worship institutions in Jerusalem by appointing the temple personnel before Solomon's ascension. As David states, YHWH Himself will dwell in Jerusalem forever since YHWH has given rest to his people (1 Chr 23:25) and the Levites' role at the temple will be changed as they need not carry the tabernacle any longer (1 Chr 23:26). Instead, they will assist the Aaronites in the service for the house of YHWH at the Jerusalem temple since the temple has been announced as the permanent dwelling place of YHWH (1 Chr 23:28–32). Accordingly, the narrative situation is the transitional period from the reign of David to that of Solomon.

In the narrative context, the narrative audience of David's speech is all the leaders of Israel, the priests, and the Levites (1 Chr 23:2). The narrative constraint is the preceding speech of David (1 Chr 22:6–19) since this exhortation to Solomon and the leaders of Israel causes David to prepare for the temple building by the appointment of the temple personnel before Solomon's succession. Accordingly, the narrative situation of 1 Chr 23–27 is the transitional period shifting from David's reign to Solomon's. David appoints the temple personnel and civil officials, by which he organizes the worship system in the temple and strengthens his kingdom in order to prepare for Solomon's building of the temple in advance.

Wright contends that 1 Chr 23–27 describes "David's organization of his kingdom in preparation for Solomon's succession."[369] According to him, this rhetorical unit functions as the most important section of the David narrative in that it provides "the narrative basis for the establishment of temple personnel in times of national beginnings and reform throughout Chronicles."[370] However, even though Wright's argument is appropriate in that the organization of the temple personnel is to prepare for Solomon's succession, these chapters do not appear to have functioned as the most important section of the David narrative. Rather, 1 Chr 23–27 appears to point to David's passionate preparation for the temple building, especially functioning as a linking unit between 1 Chr 22 and 1 Chr 28–29. In this context, Knoppers appropriately concludes 1 Chr 23–27 with this statement: "the appointment of various leaders and the assignment of courses to such officials contribute to the larger picture of David's reign as a time of significant change for Israel."[371] David's organization of the temple personnel prepares for the building of the temple in the time of Solomon. In particular, David's speech functions to provide a new order of worship for the Levites, emphasizing the continuity of their service for the tabernacle and for the temple. Thus,

---

369. Wright, "Legacy of David," 241.
370. Ibid., 242.
371. Knoppers, *I Chronicles*, 797.

the narrative situation of David's speech is the transitional period that shifts from the Levites' service for the tabernacle to their new duties in the Jerusalem temple.

The Chr brings the narrative situation of 1 Chr 23–27 into his own context. The Chr uniquely employs 1 Chr 23–27 as a rhetorical unit, which has no parallel in Samuel-Kings. The Chr feels the rhetorical need to describe "the changes in the nature of Levitical service after the establishment of a permanent cult in Jerusalem" (1 Chr 23:26).[372] The linkage of the tent of meeting to the Jerusalem temple by the Levites' duties reflects the significance of the Jerusaelm temple in the Persian period. Accordingly, the Chr attempts to convey this message to the Yehudites as his audience through David's speech in his description of David's organization of the temple personnel and civil officials.

In this context, the Chr's exigence is the identity formation of Jewish community in the Persian period. At that time, Persian Yehud was not an independent nation, merely a provincial district of the Persian Empire, which functions as the Chr's constraint in his retelling of the early history of Israel. The Yehudite community had a need to reformulate their community identity since the previous traditions of Israel seem to have vanished away after the exile. The exile caused the Israelites to be scattered among the nations. As a result, the scattered peoples experience an identity crisis as God's people.

However, this situation changed dramatically with the Cyrus decree (2 Chr 36:22–23). The deportees in Babylonia returned to their homeland. As a result, there were conflicts among various groups in the Yehudite community. In this situation, the Chr feels the need to recount the David narrative regarding the first temple to the Yehudites, to reconstruct their identity in the Persian period. This rhetorical need will lead the Chr to reiterate that David had previously appointed the temple personnel, in order to emphasize the significance of the Jerusalem temple in the Persian period. Jonker points out appropriately that the Chr's presentation of the early history of Israel is reformed in order to be shifted "from the realm of political history to the realm of cultic history" as a part of "identity formation process."[373] Accordingly, in the process of the identity formation of the Yehudite community, the Chr intends to emphasize the significance of the Jerusalem temple by David's appointment of the temple personnel. The Chr through David's speech represents the centrality of the Jerusalem temple in the process of identity formation, pointing to the changes in the Levites' duties in the service for YHWH at the temple.

Rhetorical Effectiveness

The rhetorical effectiveness of David's speech in this unit may be assessed by the impact on the narrative audience and the Chr's audience. First, David's speech to the

---

372. Williamson, *1 and 2 Chronicles*, 162.
373. Jonker, "Reforming History," 34.

leaders of Israel (1 Chr 23:25–26, 28–32) puts forth new duties on the Levites in the service for YHWH at the Jerusalem temple. Since YHWH has given rest to Israel and He dwells in Jerusalem forever, the Levites will not need to bear the tabernacle and its vessels any longer (1 Chr 23:25–26). David assigns new duties to the Levites for the worship in the temple by appealing to Moses' commandments regarding the tabernacle. In this context, David's speech functions to persuade its hearers (the leaders of Israel, the priests and the Levites) to recognize the legitimacy of the organization the temple personnel and civil officials. David's intention is to make preparations for the building of the temple by organizing the temple clergy and civil officials before Solomon's succession. David's speech appears to have been very persuasive to the leaders of Israel, the priests and the Levites. They recognize the shift from the tabernacle to the temple as the place of the Levite service for YHWH since YHWH dwells in Jerusalem forever.

Furthermore, David's speech will affect the Chr's audience who are living in Yehud in the Persian period. At this time, there is no king in Israel since Persian Yehud merely is a provincial district of the Persian Empire. In this situation, they struggle for the rebuilding of the community identity of the Yehudites, raising questions about their identity as God's chosen people. Accordingly, the Chr draws a fitting response from his audience by representing the significance of the Jerusalem temple. In the process of this identity formation, the Chr (through David's speech) emphasizes the centrality of the Jerusalem temple as the sole worship place in Israel, addressing the changes in the Levites' duties of the service for YHWH at the temple. Thus, the Chr effectively persuades the Yehudite community to discern the centrality of the Jerusalem temple as the worship place.

DAVID'S FINAL SPEECHES AND ACTIONS (1 CHR 28–29)

This rhetorical unit contains David's final speeches and actions before Solomon's succession (1 Chr 28–29), which has no parallels in Samuel-Kings. In this unit, David encourages the leaders of Israel to help Solomon to build the temple, stressing Solomon as God's chosen temple-builder. This unit is primarily comprised of David's speeches and prayer throughout: David's speech to the leaders of Israel (1 Chr 28:2–8); David's speech to Solomon (1 Chr 28:9–10); David's final speech to Solomon (1 Chr 28:20–21); David's speech to the assembly of Israel (1 Chr 29:1–5); and David's prayer to YHWH (1 Chr 29:10–19). In this unit, the theme of David's preparations for the temple building continues. Thus, the Chr through David's final speeches and prayer portrays David as the preparer of the temple building, stressing that the building plans of the temple were given by YHWH.

Speeches and Prayers in David's Narrative

Rhetorical Unit

This rhetorical unit (1 Chr 28–29) describes the final scenes of David's reign. This unit begins with David's assembling all the leaders of Israel at Jerusalem (1 Chr 28:1) and ends with Solomon's ascension to the throne in place of his father David (1 Chr 29:22b–25) and the summary statement of David's reign (1 Chr 29:26–30). Scholars identify several parts in 1 Chr 28–29.[374] Although these scholars provide slightly different divisions, this rhetorical unit is clearly divided into several sub-sections by the speech part (David's speech) and other material (narration, the event, or the summary statement).

This unit may be divided into six sub-units: (1) David publicly appoints Solomon as the chosen temple-builder (1 Chr 28:1–10), in which David makes speeches to the leaders (1 Chr 28:2–8) and Solomon (1 Chr 28:9–10); (2) the plans for the temple building are given to Solomon (1 Chr 28:11–21), in which David makes a speech to Solomon (1 Chr 28:19–21); (3) David and the leaders of Israel give their offerings for the temple building (1 Chr 29:1–9), in which David makes a speech to the whole assembly (1 Chr 29:1–5), leading to the assembly's response (1 Chr 29:6–9); (4) David and the whole assembly praise YHWH (1 Chr 29:10–22a), in which David prays to YHWH (1 Chr 29:10–19) and the assembly praises YHWH (1 Chr 29:20–22a); (5) Solomon is anointed as the king over Israel (1 Chr 29:22b–25); and 6) David's reign is summarized (1 Chr 29:26–30). It is noteworthy that David's speech to Solomon (1 Chr 28:19) emphasizes the plan for the building of the temple by YHWH's direction. Accordingly, the rhetorical unit, obviously forming an *inclusio*, seems that David's speeches to the leaders (1 Chr 28:2–8) and the assembly (1 Chr 29:1–5) surround David's speeches to Solomon (1 Chr 28:9–10, 20–21), which also surround David's speech of YHWH's direction (1 Chr 29:19). Thus, this unit is clearly centered on God's initiative.

Rhetorical Strategy

David assembles all the leaders of Israel at Jerusalem (1 Chr 28:1) and he makes a speech to them as deliberative rhetoric (1 Chr 28:2–8). David's speech is very similar to his speech to Solomon in 1 Chr 22, in which YHWH chooses Solomon as the temple builder (1 Chr 22:8–10). In line with this, the Chr emphasizes "Solomon's unique role as temple builder" with his unique election by God in this speech.[375]

---

374. For instance, Williamson divides 1 Chr 28–29 into six parts: 1 Chr 28:1–10, 11–21; 29:1–9, 10–19, 20–25, 26–30 (Williamson, *1 and 2 Chronicles*, 178–89); Japhet identifies 1 Chr 28–29 as six parts: 1 Chr 28:1, 2–10, 11–21; 29:1–9, 10–20, 21–25 (Japhet, *I & II Chronicles*, 482–83); Klein classifies these chapters as eight parts: 1 Chr 28:1–2aα, 28:2aβ–10, 11–19, 20–21; 29:1–9, 10–20, 21–25, 26–30 (Klein, *1 Chronicles*, 517, 531). See also Knoppers, *I Chronicles*, 917–19, 942–44; Boda, *1–2 Chronicles*, 209–23; Hill, *1 & 2 Chronicles*, 322–30, 347–53.

375. Braun, *1 Chronicles*, 269.

The Persuasive Portrayal of David and Solomon in Chronicles
David's Speech to the Leaders (1 Chr 28:2–8)

1 Chr 28:2–8	
² וַיָּקָם דָּוִיד הַמֶּלֶךְ עַל־רַגְלָיו וַיֹּאמֶר	And David the king rises on his feet, and said
שְׁמָעוּנִי אַחַי וְעַמִּי	"Hear me, my brothers and my people
אֲנִי עִם־לְבָבִי לִבְנוֹת בֵּית מְנוּחָה	I had intended to build a house of rest
לַאֲרוֹן בְּרִית־יְהוָה	for the ark of the covenant of YHWH
וְלַהֲדֹם רַגְלֵי אֱלֹהֵינוּ	and for the footstool of our God,
וַהֲכִינוֹתִי לִבְנוֹת:	and I prepared to build.
³ וְהָאֱלֹהִים אָמַר לִי	But God said to me,
לֹא־תִבְנֶה בַיִת לִשְׁמִי	'You shall not build a house for my name
כִּי אִישׁ מִלְחָמוֹת אַתָּה	because you are a man of wars
וְדָמִים שָׁפָכְתָּ:	and you have shed blood.'
⁴ וַיִּבְחַר יְהוָה אֱלֹהֵי יִשְׂרָאֵל בִּי	But YHWH God of Israel chose me
מִכֹּל בֵּית־אָבִי לִהְיוֹת	from all the house of my father
לְמֶלֶךְ עַל־יִשְׂרָאֵל לְעוֹלָם	to be king over Israel forever.
כִּי בִיהוּדָה בָּחַר לְנָגִיד	Because he has chosen Judah to be a leader
וּבְבֵית יְהוּדָה בֵּית אָבִי	and in the house of Judah, my father's house,
וּבִבְנֵי אָבִי	and among the sons of my father
בִּי רָצָה לְהַמְלִיךְ עַל־כָּל־יִשְׂרָאֵל:	he was pleased to make me king over all Israel.
⁵ וּמִכָּל־בָּנַי	And of all my sons
כִּי רַבִּים בָּנִים נָתַן לִי יְהוָה	for YHWH has given to me many sons.
וַיִּבְחַר בִּשְׁלֹמֹה בְנִי לָשֶׁבֶת	He has chosen my son Solomon to sit
עַל־כִּסֵּא מַלְכוּת יְהוָה	on the throne of the kingdom of YHWH
עַל־יִשְׂרָאֵל:	over Israel."
⁶ וַיֹּאמֶר לִי שְׁלֹמֹה בִנְךָ	And He said to me, 'Solomon your son is
הוּא־יִבְנֶה בֵיתִי וַחֲצֵרוֹתָי	the one who shall build my house and my courts
כִּי־בָחַרְתִּי בוֹ לִי לְבֵן	because I have chosen him to be a son to me
וַאֲנִי אֶהְיֶה־לּוֹ לְאָב:	and I will become a father to him.
⁷ וַהֲכִינוֹתִי אֶת־מַלְכוּתוֹ עַד־לְעוֹלָם	And I will establish his kingdom forever
אִם־יֶחֱזַק לַעֲשׂוֹת	if he is strong to do
מִצְוֹתַי וּמִשְׁפָּטַי כַּיּוֹם הַזֶּה:	my commands and my ordinances as at this day.'
⁸ וְעַתָּה לְעֵינֵי כָל־יִשְׂרָאֵל	And now before the eyes of all Israel,
קְהַל־יְהוָה	the assembly of YHWH
וּבְאָזְנֵי אֱלֹהֵינוּ	and in the ears of our God,
שִׁמְרוּ וְדִרְשׁוּ כָּל־מִצְוֹת יְהוָה	keep and seek all the commands of YHWH

אֱלֹהֵיכֶם	your God
לְמַעַן תִּירְשׁוּ אֶת־הָאָרֶץ הַטּוֹבָה	in order that you may possess the good land
וְהִנְחַלְתֶּם לִבְנֵיכֶם אַחֲרֵיכֶם עַד־עוֹלָם: פ	and cause your sons to inherit after you forever."

This speech begins with the imperative "Hear me" (שְׁמָעוּנִי) in 1 Chr 28:2 and ends with the imperatives "keep and seek" (שִׁמְרוּ וְדִרְשׁוּ) in 1 Chr 28:8. David's encouragement is reinforced by these imperatives. In particular, it should be noted that 1 Chr 28:3, 6–7 are the divine speeches quoted by David. In this speech, David depends on YHWH's authority. As YHWH previously chose David, He now chooses Solomon. As God had previously spoken to David, Solomon will be the temple builder.

Interestingly, the imperative plural form, "Hear me" (שְׁמָעוּנִי) betrays a characteristic of the speeches in Chronicles. Specifically, this introductory imperative is found in a number of speech sections in Chronicles (2 Chr 13:4; 15:2; 20:20; 28:11; 29:5). Japhet points out that this term is only found in Gen 23:8 outside Chronicles.[376] Williamson indicates that the introductory imperative "may be related to the tendency of the Chronicler, frequently noticed elsewhere, to involve all the people in the significant events of the nation's life."[377] When all of Israel is concerned with significant national events—such as the transfer of the ark and the building of the temple, the Chr employs the speeches of the characters with this introductory term. Accordingly, the imperative form leads all the people of Israel to give attention to David's speech.

The temple David wishes to build is "a house of rest for the ark of the covenant of YHWH" (1 Chr 28:2). The ark symbolizes YHWH's presence and the temple signifies a place of rest for the ark.[378] Interestingly, the Chr represents the ark as the footstool of God (1 Chr 28:2), language which also refers to the temple in Ps 132:7.[379] As Klein observes, the footstool of God can mean the temple (Pss 99:5; 132:7, 13–14), Zion/Jerusalem (Lam 2:1), or the earth itself (Isa 66:1).[380] Of these meanings, the footstool of God appears to be the equivalent of the temple in Chronicles, which demonstrates the linkage of the ark and the temple. When the ark is installed in the temple, the temple will signify YHWH's presence and footstool by containing the ark within. Thus, the covenantal God would dwell in the temple forever. The Chr emphasizes that the ark is linked to the temple as YHWH's presence.

First Chronicles 28:3–5 explains why David is disqualified for the building of the temple. The reason is that David as a man of wars has shed blood (1 Chr 28:3; cf.

---

376. Japhet, *I & II Chronicles*, 486.

377. Williamson, *1 and 2 Chronicles*, 179.

378. See Klein, *1 Chronicles*, 520.

379. Williamson, *1 and 2 Chronicles*, 179. Schniedewind contends that the Chr develops the meaning of the Davidic covenant by allusions to the temple in Ps 132, pointing to the depiction of the temple images in 1 Chr 28:2. In effect, "the house of rest" and "footstool for the feet of our God," are the same with that of the temple images which the Lord promised to build for David in Ps 132 (esp. 132:7, 8, 13–14) (Schniedewind, *Word of God*, 158–59).

380. Klein, *1 Chronicles*, 520.

1 Chr 22:8). The phrase "You shall not build a temple for my name" is significantly based on 1 Chr 17:4 (cf. 2 Sam 7:5). Regardless of this disqualification, David prepares for the temple building in accordance with God's will. Here, the Chr emphasizes the theme of divine choice. The verb "to choose" (בָּחַר) is repeated four times (1 Chr 28:4–6). YHWH chooses Judah from the tribes, Jesse's house from the tribe of Judah, and David among the brothers of Jesse's house. Accordingly, YHWH chooses David and his son Solomon to sit on the throne and to build the temple. The divine choice is explicitly stressed.[381] This choice concerns Solomon as the builder of the temple, not merely as the king over Israel in place of his father David.[382]

Significantly, Solomon will sit on the throne of the kingdom of YHWH. The Chr uses the phrase "the throne of the kingdom of YHWH over Israel," not the throne of the kingdom over Israel (1 Chr 28:5). The Chr identifies Israel as a nation with the kingdom of God.[383] For the Chr, David and Solomon are merely earthly kings, but the true ruler of Israel is YHWH.[384] The designation for this kingship is also shown in the preceding unit (1 Chr 17), in which we read the phrase, "I will confirm him in my house and in my kingdom forever, and his throne shall be established forever" (1 Chr 17:14). Accordingly, Solomon sits upon YHWH's throne, not merely on the throne of Israel (1 Chr 29:23; 2 Chr 9:8). "The earthly, royal throne is also the throne of Yahweh."[385] Thus, the Chr obviously links the throne of Israel with the throne of YHWH.

First Chronicles 28:6–7, as the divine speech within David's speech, again stresses the divine choice of Solomon, which is based on the Davidic covenant. In this divine speech, the Chr emphasizes that YHWH chose Solomon as his son and He will be his father (cf. 1 Chr 22:10). This covenantal language emphasizes the close relationship between YHWH and Solomon. YHWH's volition is emphatically expressed by the first person verbs and pronoun (בָּחַרְתִּי, וַאֲנִי אֶהְיֶה, וַהֲכִינוֹתִי), yet this divine speech is promised conditionally by the protasis-apodosis.[386] If Solomon keeps YHWH's commands, He will establish his kingdom forever. Because of this, David urges the leaders of Israel to obey YHWH's commands. The observance of the law will result in the

---

381. With respect to the divine choice, McKenzie indicates that the Chr in a most creative way places "his explanation in David's mouth as a quotation from Yahweh—a technique that adds authority to the explanation even though it is not to be found in Nathan's oracle" (McKenzie, *I & II Chronicles*, 213). Japhet also claims that "in Chronicles, Solomon's election is associated with the construction of the Temple and directly linked to Nathan's prophecy that the Temple will be built by one of David's sons (1 Chr 28:5–16)" (Japhet, *Ideology*, 450).

382. Braun, "Chosen Temple Builder," 581–90.

383. Avioz points out that the Chr develops analogies between the Davidic kingdom and God's kingdom in 1 Chr 17:14; 28:5; 29:23; 2 Chr 13:8; 9:8 (Avioz, "Nathan's Prophecy," 552).

384. Klein, *1 Chronicles*, 521. See also Kuntzmann, "Le trône de Dieu dans l'oeuvre du Chroniste," 19–27.

385. Klein, *1 Chronicles*, 521.

386. The conditionality of the Davidic covenant is referred to in Pss 89:29–32; 132:12; 1 Kgs 2:4; 8:25; 9:4–5. See also Dumbrell, *The End of the Beginning*, 50–54.

possession of the land and its inheritance for their descendants forever.[387] Thus, much attention is given to the observance of the law (1 Chr 28:8). The emphasis is on the observance of YHWH's law, which will lead to the possession of the land forever.

The concluding remark of this speech (1 Chr 28:8) is identified by the discourse marker "now" (עַתָּה).[388] The phrases "before the eyes of all Israel" (עֵינֵי כָל־יִשְׂרָאֵל) and "in the ears of our God" (בְּאָזְנֵי אֱלֹהֵינוּ) showcase the rhetorical device *metonymy* by substituting an abstract word for a concrete one.[389] The former phrase means that David's speech is addressed to all the people of Israel or the assembly of YHWH, stressing the observance of the law, and the latter phrase means that David speaks to them before YHWH, urging them to obey YHWH's commands and seek YHWH.

In sum, David's speech to all the leaders of Israel is an encouragement for keeping YHWH's commandments, based on God's choice of the Davidic line to build the temple.[390] Observance of YHWH's law will assure the possession of the land. Indeed, David's speech in 1 Chr 28 appears to develop the Davidic covenant as represented in his charge to Solomon (1 Chr 22),[391] both of which are based on the Davidic covenant in 1 Chr 17. Through David's speech to the leaders of Israel, the Chr depicts Solomon as the chosen temple builder, appealing to the divine choice of Solomon. In addition, the description of the assembling of the Israelite leaders contributes to exhibit the 'all Israel' theme (1 Chr 28:8a).[392] So David's charge to Solomon is somewhat universalized since YHWH searches all hearts (1 Chr 28:9).

David's Speech to Solomon (1 Chr 28:9–10)

David gives his speech to Solomon when all the people of Israel are assembled at Jerusalem. David makes an exhortation to Solomon as deliberative rhetoric, which shows a summary of the Chr's theology with abundant allusions.

---

387. Braun, *1 Chronicles*, 274. Mason, *Preaching*, 30. Mason also says, "The words call for obedience in all ages as the only ground for continuance as God's people in God's land" (30).
388. See van der Merwe et al., *Biblical Hebrew*, 333.
389. Lundbom, *Hebrew Prophets*, 186–87.
390. Mason, *Preaching*, 28.
391. See Schniedewind, *Word of God*, 155–57.
392. See Coggins, *The First and Second Books of the Chronicles*, 137.

1 Chr 28:9–10	
⁹ וְאַתָּה שְׁלֹמֹה־בְנִי	"And you, my son Solomon,
דַּע אֶת־אֱלֹהֵי אָבִיךָ וְעָבְדֵהוּ	know the God of your father and serve him
בְּלֵב שָׁלֵם וּבְנֶפֶשׁ חֲפֵצָה	with a whole heart and with a willing mind
כִּי כָל־לְבָבוֹת דּוֹרֵשׁ יְהוָה	because all hearts YHWH searches[A]
וְכָל־יֵצֶר מַחֲשָׁבוֹת מֵבִין	and all intent of the thoughts he understands.
אִם־תִּדְרְשֶׁנּוּ יִמָּצֵא לָךְ	If you seek him, He will be found to you,
וְאִם־תַּעַזְבֶנּוּ יַזְנִיחֲךָ לָעַד׃	but if you forsake him, He will reject you forever.
¹⁰ רְאֵה עַתָּה כִּי־יְהוָה בָּחַר בְּךָ	See now, because YHWH has chosen you
לִבְנוֹת־בַּיִת לַמִּקְדָּשׁ	to build a house for the sanctuary.
חֲזַק וַעֲשֵׂה׃	Be strong and do (it)."

A. According to McConville ("1 Chronicles 28:9," 105–8), it is appropriate that the phrase "YHWH searches all hearts" is rendered as "Yahweh *seeks out* all hearts" (108, italics McConville's).

First of all, David encourages Solomon to know and serve the God of his father. Japhet indicates that the twofold imperative "know . . . and serve him" (דַּע, וְעָבְדֵהוּ) in 1 Chr 28:9 is "the unique occurrence of this poignant phrase in Chronicles."[393] This twofold imperative at the beginning of the speech is syntactically parallel to another twofold imperative "Be strong and do (it)" (חֲזַק וַעֲשֵׂה) at the end of the speech. The phrase "See now" (עַתָּה רְאֵה) in 1 Chr 28:10, as a discourse marker, stresses Solomon as the chosen temple builder as the logical conclusion of this speech.[394] Accordingly, David's encouragement to Solomon is firstly to know and serve YHWH, and secondly to strengthen himself and carry out the building task. Interestingly, the Chr employs the designation of "God of your father," which occurs once more in a slightly different form in 2 Chr 21:12. The designation reveals the very close relationship between God and David,[395] which also points to the fact that Solomon's authority would be placed in the same relationship.

In particular, David urges Solomon to know and serve the God of his father "with a whole heart and with a willing soul" (1 Chr 28:9), which is very similar to a Deuteronomistic phrase, "with all your heart and will all your soul" (Deut 4:29, 6:5), "a whole heart" (1 Kgs 8:61, 11:4, 15:3, 14; 2 Kgs 20:3). David exhorts Solomon to know and serve God, recognizing YHWH's authority. The Chr employs characteristically "a whole heart" as one of his favorite phrases in Chronicles (1 Chr 12:38; 29:9, 19; 2 Chr 15:17; 16:9; 19:9; 25:2).[396]

---

393. Japhet, *I & II Chronicles*, 491. Japhet indicates here that "the same religious idea is demonstrated in the repentance of Manasseh" (2 Chr 33:13).

394. See van der Merwe et al., *Biblical Hebrew*, 328, 333.

395. See Japhet, *I & II Chronicles*, 491–2.

396. Japhet, *I & II Chronicles*, 492.

Furthermore, the phrase, "God searches all hearts and understands all intent of the thoughts" (1 Chr 28:9) alludes to two verses in Genesis, both within the flood narrative (Gen 6:5; 8:21). It points to YHWH's active searching of all intent of the thoughts in His omniscience.[397] The Chr summarizes his key theology in the next phrase, "If you seek him (תִּדְרְשֶׁנּוּ), He will be found by you, but if you forsake him (תַּעַזְבֶנּוּ), He will reject you forever" (1 Chr 28:9). Significantly, the former verb ("to seek") occurs twenty nine times in Chronicles;[398] whereas, the latter verb ("to forsake") occurs sixteen times in Chronicles.[399] These words mark covenant-makings and covenant-renewals,[400] so that David urges Solomon to seek YHWH and not to forsake Him, charging Solomon to build the temple. In this regard, this protasis-apodosis shows a key theme of the Chr's theology with scriptural allusions to other passages.[401] Through these allusions in this speech, the Chr attempts to persuade his audience to understand that seeking YHWH is the prerequisite of the Judahites' prospering in the Persian period; whereas, forsaking YHWH serves as the major reason for God's rejection (even the exile).[402] Thus, for the Chr, David's speech as an effective rhetorical device leads the Chr's audience to recognize that the exile has resulted from forsaking YHWH, and that prospering in the Persian era will depend upon seeking YHWH.

In 1 Chr 28:10, the Chr emphasizes once more that Solomon has been chosen as the temple builder by YHWH Himself. David encourages Solomon to be strong and to carry out the task of building the temple. In this rhetorical unit (1 Chr 28–29), YHWH's election of Solomon is frequently referred to, which serves to confirm the Davidic covenant (1 Chr 17) and legitimate Solomon's rule after David (1 Chr 28:5, 6, 10; 29:1).[403] David's exhortations to know and serve God thoroughly are "motivated first by the complete knowledge that God possesses of Solomon and second by the conditional character of the dynastic covenant."[404] This is summarized by the phrase, "seek YHWH."

---

397. Boda, *1–2 Chronicles*, 213.

398. McCarthy, "Covenant and Law," 31, in which twenty seven times are related to seeking eagerly YHWH and two times to a prophet's word and the law.

399. Dillard, "Reward and Punishment," 166.

400. The verbs דרש and עזב are central in Asa's covenant-renewal and the verbs (עזב and מעל) in Hezekiah's (McCarthy, "Covenant and Law," 31). For David's charge to Solomon to build the temple, see McCarthy, "Installation Genre," 31–41.

401. Williamson indicates that some prophetic passages seem to be reflected in Deut 4:29; Jer 29:13–14; Isa 55:6 (Williamson, *1 and 2 Chronicles*, 181).

402. Mason points out, "By this device also the original address to Solomon is extended to later generations, to present them with the prophetic call and challenge, but also to assure them that they are to experience the fulfilment of the prophetic promises" (Mason, *Preaching*, 30).

403. Hill, *1 & 2 Chronicles*, 325.

404. Boda, *1–2 Chronicles*, 213.

The Persuasive Portrayal of David and Solomon in Chronicles

David's Final Speech to Solomon (1 Chr 28:20–21)

David gives his final speech to Solomon after David gives Solomon the plan for the temple building. David expresses his preparations for the building of the temple as deliberative rhetoric (1 Chr 28:11–19):[405]

1 Chr 28:20–21	
20 וַיֹּאמֶר דָּוִיד לִשְׁלֹמֹה בְנוֹ	And David said to Solomon his son,
חֲזַק וֶאֱמַץ וַעֲשֵׂה	"Be strong and courageous, and do (it).
אַל־תִּירָא וְאַל־תֵּחָת	Do not fear and do not be dismayed
כִּי יְהוָה אֱלֹהִים אֱלֹהַי עִמָּךְ	because YHWH God, my God is with you.
לֹא יַרְפְּךָ וְלֹא יַעַזְבֶךָּ	He will not fail you and he will not forsake you
עַד־לִכְלוֹת כָּל־מְלֶאכֶת	until all the work
עֲבוֹדַת בֵּית־יְהוָה:	for the service of the house of YHWH is finished.
21 וְהִנֵּה מַחְלְקוֹת הַכֹּהֲנִים וְהַלְוִיִּם	And behold, the divisions of the priests and the Levites
לְכָל־עֲבוֹדַת בֵּית הָאֱלֹהִים	are for all the service of the house of God
וְעִמְּךָ בְכָל־מְלָאכָה לְכָל־נָדִיב	and with you in all the work will be every willing one
בַּחָכְמָה לְכָל־עֲבוֹדָה	with wisdom for every service.
וְהַשָּׂרִים וְכָל־הָעָם	And the officials and all the people will be
לְכָל־דְּבָרֶיךָ:	according to all your words."

First, David urges Solomon to be strong and courageous and neither to be afraid nor dismayed (1 Chr 28:20) since YHWH God is with Solomon. The imperative verbs in 1 Chr 28:20 (חֲזַק וֶאֱמַץ וַעֲשֵׂה, אַל־תִּירָא וְאַל־תֵּחָת) form a contrasting parallelism, drawing special attention to David's encouragement to Solomon. The phrase "for the service of the house of YHWH (or God)" (לְכָל־עֲבוֹדַת בֵּית הָאֱלֹהִים, עֲבוֹדַת בֵּית־יְהוָה) is repeated twice in this speech, which reveals the purpose of David's exhortation.

In 1 Chr 28:21, David refers to his practical preparation for the temple building by beginning with the discourse marker "behold" (הִנֵּה).[406] David prepares the divisions of the priests and the Levites for the building task, indicating that the officials and all the Israelites will help Solomon to build the temple. God will not forsake Solomon until the task of the temple building is completed. Solomon will do all the work for the temple building, and he shall complete it.

This speech alludes to the transition of leadership from Moses to Joshua.[407] The transition of the kingship from David to Solomon is very similar to that from Moses

---

405. Klein states, "David is a second Moses, and the plan itself was revealed to David by God. In carrying out the plan, Solomon will play the role of Bezalel, who constructed the Tabernacle" (Klein, *1 Chronicles*, 528).

406. It draws out special attention from the addressee. See van der Merwe et al., *Biblical Hebrew*, 328–30.

407. McCarthy contends, "The sequence between I Chronicles 22 and I Chronicles 28 is like that

to Joshua. The building project of the temple is begun by David, then completed by Solomon according to YHWH's words, just as the journey to the promise land began under Moses and was completed under Joshua according to God's commands. This speech serves as David's preparation for the building of the temple and Solomon's fulfillment of the task.[408] As Williamson points out, the Chr seems to have intended to showcase "the *complementary* nature of the two kings' functions."[409] If David's preparations had not been completed, Solomon's temple building would not be possible.

Furthermore, the Chr links the relationship of David and Solomon to that of Moses and Joshua. Moses as the representative of Israel stands before YHWH and Joshua as the follower of Moses' covenant conquers the land of Canaan. In the same fashion, David as the representative of Israel stands before YHWH and Solomon as the follower of David's covenant completes the task of the temple building. In this regard, Hill indicates that "the temple is the continuation of all that the tabernacle represented in Israelite religion."[410] Thus, David urges Solomon to build the temple, making an allusion to the relationship between Moses and Joshua in the Sinai tradition, which functions to link the Jerusalem temple to the Mosaic tabernacle as the worship place.

David further urges Solomon to perform the building task, indicating that all the people of Israel are ready to participate in building the temple: the divisions of priests and the Levites for the service of the temple, craftsmen with wisdom for every service, and the officials. David has provided all the necessary preparations for the temple building insofar as he is able. The Chr, through David's words to Solomon, emphasizes that the people of Israel are active partners, and will help Solomon in his task of the building of the temple.

David's Speech to the Assembly (1 Chr 29:1–5)

David again makes a speech to all the assembly of Israel as deliberative rhetoric (1 Chr 29:1–5) and the people of Israel respond to it (1 Chr 29:6–9). In this speech, David conveys to them that Solomon is chosen by YHWH. Yet, Solomon is young and inexperienced, while the building task is great, and David then enumerates the abundant materials he has prepared for Solomon's building of the temple:

---

between Deuteronomy 31 and Joshua 1 and 13" (McCarthy, "An Installation Genre," 36). Due to this similarity, Williamson argues that "the Chronicler modelled the transition of rule from David to Solomon on that from Moses to Joshua at the end of Deuteronomy and the beginning of Joshua" (Williamson, "The Ascension of Solomon," 351). According to Japhet, "in addition to the actual transfer of leadership, there are also other common elements: the first leader is the great founder, who established enduring institutions: Moses—the people, the covenant, the Law; David—the monarchy, the dynasty. The first leader did not live to realize what he regarded as the peak and climax of his mission (for Moses, the conquest of Canaan; for David, the building of the Temple) and had to leave the stage to his successor in obedience to God's command" (Japhet, *I & II Chronicles*, 499).

408. Williamson, "The Ascension of Solomon," 357.
409. Ibid., 357; cf. Braun, "Solomonic Apologetic," 503–16; "Chosen Temple Builder," 586–88.
410. Hill, *1 & 2 Chronicles*, 325.

1 Chr 29:1–5	
¹ וַיֹּאמֶר דָּוִיד הַמֶּלֶךְ לְכָל־הַקָּהָל	And David the king said to all the assembly,
שְׁלֹמֹה בְנִי	"My son Solomon,
אֶחָד בָּחַר־בּוֹ אֱלֹהִים	the one whom God has chosen,
נַעַר וָרָךְ וְהַמְּלָאכָה גְדוֹלָה	is young and inexperienced and the work is great,
כִּי לֹא לְאָדָם הַבִּירָה כִּי לַיהוָה אֱלֹהִים:	for the temple is not for man but for YHWH God.
וּבְכָל־כֹּחִי הֲכִינוֹתִי	² And with all my power I have prepared
לְבֵית־אֱלֹהַי	for the house of my God,
הַזָּהָב לַזָּהָב	the gold for things of gold,
וְהַכֶּסֶף לַכֶּסֶף	and the silver for things of silver,
וְהַנְּחֹשֶׁת לַנְּחֹשֶׁת	and the bronze for things of bronze,
הַבַּרְזֶל לַבַּרְזֶל	and the iron for things of iron,
וְהָעֵצִים לָעֵצִים אַבְנֵי־שֹׁהַם	and the wood for things of wood, onyx stones,
וּמִלּוּאִים אַבְנֵי־פוּךְ	and settings, and stones of antimony
וְרִקְמָה	and of diverse colors,
וְכֹל אֶבֶן יְקָרָה	and all kinds of precious stones,
וְאַבְנֵי־שַׁיִשׁ לָרֹב:	and stones of alabaster in abundance.
³ וְעוֹד בִּרְצוֹתִי בְּבֵית אֱלֹהַי	And again in my delight in the house of my God,
יֶשׁ־לִי סְגֻלָּה זָהָב	the substance I have, a peculiar treasure of gold
וָכֶסֶף נָתַתִּי לְבֵית־אֱלֹהַי	and silver, I have given for the house of my God,
לְמַעְלָה מִכָּל־הֲכִינוֹתִי	over and above all I have prepared
לְבֵית הַקֹּדֶשׁ:	for the house of the sanctuary.
⁴ שְׁלֹשֶׁת אֲלָפִים כִּכְּרֵי זָהָב	Three thousand talents of gold,
מִזְּהַב אוֹפִיר	of the gold of Ophir,
וְשִׁבְעַת אֲלָפִים כִּכַּר־כֶּסֶף מְזֻקָּק	and seven thousand talents of refined silver,
לָטוּחַ קִירוֹת הַבָּתִּים:	to overlay the walls of the houses.
⁵ לַזָּהָב לַזָּהָב	of gold for things of gold
וְלַכֶּסֶף לַכֶּסֶף	and of silver for the things of silver,
וּלְכָל־מְלָאכָה בְּיַד חָרָשִׁים	and for all the work by the hand of the craftsmen,
וּמִי מִתְנַדֵּב	and who is offering willingly
לְמַלֹּאות יָדוֹ הַיּוֹם לַיהוָה:	to consecrate his hand this day to YHWH

In 1 Chr 29:1, God's greatness is stressed in contrast to Solomon's smallness.⁴¹¹ In particular, the term "palatial structure" (הַבִּירָה) is identified with the temple (1 Chr 29:1, 19), which will remind Solomon and the assembly that "the kingdom belongs to

---

411. See Braun, *1 Chronicles*, 279. Braun points out here that David's speeches in 1 Chr 22, 28 are closely related to this speech:

Speeches and Prayers in David's Narrative

God and that he is the only enthroned over Israel."⁴¹² Boda holds that the term seems to contain "a much larger complex of buildings that included the Temple."⁴¹³ In any case, David's utterance here emphasizes the divine choice of Solomon and the temple building for YHWH.

In 1 Chr 29:2–3, David's preparations for the building of the temple are stressed by the repetition of the word, "I have prepared" (הֲכִינוֹתִי), which rhetorically forms an *inclusio*. In particular, the term "a peculiar treasure" (סְגֻלָּה) in 1 Chr 29:3 is distinctively employed to depict Israel as YHWH's "special possession" (Exod 19:5), which is thought of the king's personal property.⁴¹⁴ In these verses, the abundant materials David has prepared (gold, silver, bronze, iron, wood, all kinds of stones) amplify "a general fact or idea by giving all of its details,"⁴¹⁵ which is rhetorically called *enumeratio*.⁴¹⁶ It is indicated in 1 Chr 29:4 that the amount of gold and silver is mentioned in order to overlay the walls of the houses. Thus, the utterance that the temple building is a great task along with David's willing donations made an appeal to the people as a whole.⁴¹⁷

First Chronicles 29:5 contains a sort of consecration, which is literally translated as "to fill his hand" (לְמַלֹּאות יָדוֹ).⁴¹⁸ This phrase actually signifies "to consecrate."⁴¹⁹ More clearly, if it is employed with God, it is always "to consecrate oneself to God's service" as primarily applied to the consecration of the priests (Exod 28:41; 29:9, 29, 33; Lev 8:33, 16:32; Judg 17:5, 12; 1 Kgs 13:33, etc.).⁴²⁰ Accordingly, this phrase is uniquely applied to all the Israelites in Chronicles. This may imply that the nation

Chap. 29		Chaps. 22, 28
29:1	Solomon's election	28:6, 10, cf. 22:9
29:1	Solomon as a ורך נער "inexperienced boy"	22:5
29:1	Greatness of the task	22:5
29:2	David's provisions	22:2–5, 28:3

412. Hill, *1 & 2 Chronicles*, 328. The term often is used in depicting a fortress or a citadel in the OT (Neh 2:8).

413. Boda, *1-2 Chronicles*, 218–19.

414. Hill, *1 & 2 Chronicles*, 328.

415. Lanham, *Handlist*, 55.

416. The rhetorical device also called *denumeratio* or *dinumeratio* (Lanham, *Handlist*, 55, 66).

417. Japhet considers in respect to 1 Chr 29:2–5 that David's donations have two categories: "one prepared in his capacity as king, and the other donated from his private property," so the first category provides a list and the second provides only gold and silver with their quantities (Japhet, *I & II Chronicles*, 506).

418. I translate לְמַלֹּאות as "to consecrate" instead of "to fill" because the phrase "to fill his hand" (לְמַלֹּאות יָדוֹ) is "the technical term for consecrating a priest or Levite, whether by oneself or by another (e.g. Exod. 28.41; 29.29; 32.29 etc.; cf. 2 Chr 13.9; 29.31)" (Johnstone, *1 and 2 Chronicles*, 1:285).

419. See footnote 226.

420. Japhet, *I & II Chronicles*, 508; Boda, *1-2 Chronicles*, 219.

itself is to be regarded as a kingdom of priests (Exod 19:6).[421] It appears to be closely related to the worship in the temple. Thus, in this speech, David's preparation for the temple building is stressed with the list of his donations for the task. David appeals to YHWH's greatness, focusing on the divine election of Solomon as the temple builder.

David's Prayer to YHWH (1 Chr 29:10–19)

David's prayer is to some degree similar to the king's speech in that the king's prayer is a royal speech to YHWH. According to Throntveit, the prayers in Chronicles, composed in the form of prose, are filled with "the same connecting particles that function in the same way and frequently include rhetorical questions," contrasting YHWH's power and greatness and with his people's dependence and weakness.[422] This contrast leads them to pray to YHWH:

1 Chr 29:10–19	
[10] וַיְבָרֶךְ דָּוִיד אֶת־יְהוָה	And David blessed YHWH
לְעֵינֵי כָּל־הַקָּהָל	before the eyes of all the assembly,
וַיֹּאמֶר דָּוִיד	and David said,
בָּרוּךְ אַתָּה יְהוָה אֱלֹהֵי יִשְׂרָאֵל אָבִינוּ מֵעוֹלָם וְעַד־עוֹלָם:	"Blessed are you O YHWH God of Israel our father,
[11] לְךָ יְהוָה הַגְּדֻלָּה וְהַגְּבוּרָה	from everlasting to everlasting
וְהַתִּפְאֶרֶת וְהַנֵּצַח וְהַהוֹד	To you, O YHWH is the greatness and the might,
כִּי־כֹל בַּשָּׁמַיִם וּבָאָרֶץ	and the beauty, and the victory and the honor
לְךָ יְהוָה הַמַּמְלָכָה	because of all in the heavens and in the earth.
וְהַמִּתְנַשֵּׂא לְכֹל לְרֹאשׁ:	To you, O YHWH is the kingdom
[12] וְהָעֹשֶׁר וְהַכָּבוֹד מִלְּפָנֶיךָ	and he who is lifting up himself over all for head.
וְאַתָּה מוֹשֵׁל בַּכֹּל	And the riches and the honor are from before you
וּבְיָדְךָ כֹּחַ וּגְבוּרָה	and you rule over all,
וּבְיָדְךָ לְגַדֵּל	and in your hands is power and might
וּלְחַזֵּק לַכֹּל:	and in your hand to make great,
[13] וְעַתָּה אֱלֹהֵינוּ מוֹדִים אֲנַחְנוּ לָךְ	and to give strength to all.
וּמְהַלְלִים לְשֵׁם תִּפְאַרְתֶּךָ:	And now O our God we give thanks to you
	and praise to your glorious name.

---

421. Japhet, *I & II Chronicles*, 508.
422. Throntveit, *When Kings Speak*, 93.

Speeches and Prayers in David's Narrative

¹⁴ וְכִי מִי אֲנִי וּמִי עַמִּי	But who am I, and who are my people,
כִּי־נַעְצֹר כֹּחַ לְהִתְנַדֵּב כָּזֹאת	that we retain power to offer willingly as this?
כִּי־מִמְּךָ הַכֹּל	for the whole is from you
וּמִיָּדְךָ נָתַנּוּ לָךְ׃	and from your hand we have given to you.
¹⁵ כִּי־גֵרִים אֲנַחְנוּ לְפָנֶיךָ	For sojourners we are before you
וְתוֹשָׁבִים כְּכָל־אֲבֹתֵינוּ	and settlers like all our fathers
כַּצֵּל יָמֵינוּ עַל־הָאָרֶץ	as shadow are our days on the earth
וְאֵין מִקְוֶה׃	and there is no hope
¹⁶ יְהוָה אֱלֹהֵינוּ כֹּל הֶהָמוֹן הַזֶּה	O YHWH our God all this abundance
אֲשֶׁר הֲכִינֹנוּ לִבְנוֹת־לְךָ בַיִת	that we have prepared to build to you a house
לְשֵׁם קָדְשֶׁךָ מִיָּדְךָ הוּא	for your holy name, it is from your hand
וּלְךָ הַכֹּל׃	and the whole belongs to you.
¹⁷ וְיָדַעְתִּי אֱלֹהַי	And I know, O my God,
כִּי אַתָּה בֹּחֵן לֵבָב	that you examine the heart
וּמֵישָׁרִים תִּרְצֶה	and are pleased with uprightness.
אֲנִי בְּיֹשֶׁר לְבָבִי	In uprightness of my heart,
הִתְנַדַּבְתִּי כָל־אֵלֶּה	I have willingly offered all these.
וְעַתָּה עַמְּךָ הַנִּמְצְאוּ־פֹה	And now your people who were found here
רָאִיתִי בְשִׂמְחָה לְהִתְנַדֶּב־לָךְ׃	I have seen with joy to offer willingly to you
¹⁸ יְהוָה אֱלֹהֵי אַבְרָהָם יִצְחָק	O YHWH, God of Abraham, Isaac,
וְיִשְׂרָאֵל אֲבֹתֵינוּ	and Israel, our fathers,
שָׁמְרָה־זֹּאת לְעוֹלָם לְיֵצֶר	keep this forever for the imagination
מַחְשְׁבוֹת לְבַב עַמֶּךָ	of the thoughts of the heart of your people,
וְהָכֵן לְבָבָם אֵלֶיךָ׃	and prepare their heart to you.
¹⁹ וְלִשְׁלֹמֹה בְנִי תֵּן לֵבָב שָׁלֵם לִשְׁמוֹר מִצְוֹתֶיךָ עֵדְוֹתֶיךָ וְחֻקֶּיךָ	And give my son Solomon a perfect heart to keep your commands, your testimonies and your statutes,
וְלַעֲשׂוֹת הַכֹּל וְלִבְנוֹת הַבִּירָה	and to do the whole and to build the temple[A]
אֲשֶׁר־הֲכִינוֹתִי׃ פ	for which I have prepared

A. הַבִּירָה is employed here (cf. 1 Chr 29:1) as the meaning of the temple (lit. palatial structure).

In its structure, this prayer as deliberative rhetoric is comprised of an introductory statement (1 Chr 29:10a) and three subsections (1 Chr 29:10b–12, 13–17; 18–19).[423] Each subsection begins with the vocative, "O YHWH" or "O our God" (1

---

423. Throntveit, *When Kings Speak*, 93. As other prayers in Chronicles, these sub-sections are indicated by a modification of subject such as you (YHWH, 1 Chr 29:10b–12, 18–19) and we (David and the assembly, 1 Chr 29:13–17). Klein, following Throntveit, considers that David's final prayer consists of three sections: praise (1 Chr 29:10b–12), thanksgiving (1 Chr 29:13–17), and petitions (1 Chr 29:18–19) (Klein, *1 Chronicles*, 532). In a slightly different way, Hill divides this prayer into three:

Chr 29:10b, 13, 18), which is repeated seven times (including its occurrences in 1 Chr 29:10, 11, 17). The frequent uses of this vocative indicate that the addressee of David's prayer is YHWH God of Israel, revealing David's thoughtful praise and request to YHWH. Some scholars have noted the significance of this vocative. For instance, Throntveit refers to this vocative as "a highly stylized liturgical formula containing some form of the vocative."[424] Noting the distinctive repetition of the vocative "O YHWH," Balentine maintains, "The rhetorical framework of the prayer serves both to introduce and to promote the major theme" (e.g., 1 Chr 29:10, 18).[425] In Balentine's view, the primary focus of David's prayer is on YHWH. Interestingly, Japhet considers that the second-person vocative reveals the personal relationship between YHWH and the forefathers, which lays a foundation for David's request of the blessing and his supplication. This prayer culminates in 1 Chr 29:18,[426] in which YHWH is called by the appellation, "God of Abraham, Isaac and Israel, our fathers." This epithet, an honorific title,[427] shows the characteristic of the God of Israel as the covenantal God. So this vocative is employed to express the covenantal God who has made covenants with the patriarchs from the early history of Israel. David's final appeal to YHWH is based on the familiar designation of God, "YHWH, God of Abraham, Isaac, and Israel (Jacob)." It means that David prays to the covenantal God, reminding YHWH God of Israel of His covenants with the patriarchs. Thus, the vocative in this prayer emphasizes YHWH God of Israel as the covenantal God who has previously made covenants with the forefathers.

The first subsection begins with an introductory statement (1 Chr 29:10). It points out that YHWH God of Israel is the patriarchs' God as the covenantal God, which is expressed by the rhetorical device *synecdoche* that substitutes the whole forefathers of Israel for its part, "our fathers."[428] Accordingly, it emphasizes that YHWH God of Israel has made covenants with the forefathers from the early history of Israel. In 1 Chr 29:11, YHWH's greatness is extolled by a series of words—such as greatness, might, beauty, victory, and honor, which rhetorically forms *accumulatio* that is to heap up praise.[429] The Chr stresses through David's prayer that all these characteristics belong to YHWH by placing the word "To you" (לְךָ) as the first word in front of the

---

doxology (1 Chr 29:10–12), thanksgiving (1 Chr 29:13–16), and supplication (1 Chr 29:17–19) (Hill, *1 & 2 Chronicles*, 349–50). Boda identifies it as four parts: 1 Chr 29:10b–13, 14–15, 16–17, 18–19 (Boda, *1–2 Chronicles*, 220). Although these divisions do not have significant differences in understanding David's prayer, it seems that Throntveit's view is more appropriate in that he provides the rationale for his division. See also Beentjes, "Psalms and Prayers," 17–21.

424. Throntveit, *When Kings Speak*, 93.
425. Balentine, *Prayer*, 101.
426. Japhet, *I & II Chronicles*, 509.
427. See Lundbom, *Hebrew Prophets*, 186.
428. Lanham, *Handlist*, 148.
429. Ibid., 1. See also Japhet, *I & II Chronicles*, 509.

verse,[430] which forms the rhetorical device *anaphora* in that it is repeated at the beginnings of two successive clauses.[431] David continues to depict God's ways and God's rule generally (1 Chr 29:12). In particular, the phrase "in your hand" (בְּיָדְךָ), meaning God's power as a metaphor, is emphasized by being repeated twice in 1 Chr 29:12. In effect, the phrase "your hand" (God's hand) is twice more repeated in 2 Chr 29:14, 16. Accordingly, YHWH's greatness is metaphorically emphasized. From the description of God's character, David's prayer advances to praise God. Now, the assembly of Israel with David gives thanks and praises to God (1 Chr 29:13).

The second subsection begins with "And now" (וְעַתָּה) in 1 Chr 29:13, which makes the focal point of the prayer move from the description of YHWH's character to the praise of Him. In this subsection, the Chr, through David's prayer, stresses the unworthiness of human beings or human beings' dependence on YHWH for all possessions (1 Chr 29:14–17).[432] This unworthiness is contrasted with God's greatness. Despite the unworthiness of human beings, David and the people, taking upon them a huge building project, made every effort to prepare for the building of the temple. In this regard, Johnstone indicates properly that "their power to give 'free-will offerings,' specifically, to prepare the materials necessary for the construction of the Temple, is simply a reflection of God's power to bestow."[433]

The rhetorical question (1 Chr 29:14) emphasizes the smallness of David and the whole assembly, which is contrasted with God's power to make them offer the materials for the temple building. According to Throntveit, the rhetorical question, "who am I and who are my people" (1 Chr 29:14), which is a tendency in the Chr's depiction (1 Chr 17:16–27, four times; 2 Chr 20:6–12, five times) is a complaint that commenced from 1 Chr 29:13 by the unique use of "the double adversative" (כִּי), and the rhetorical question "functions as a counterpoint to the praise and thanksgiving the people are about to offer."[434] In this context, Klein indicates appropriately that "the Chronicler's David, having praised and thanked God for his power and majesty, now declares on behalf of the whole assembly their own weakness and dependence."[435] In 1 Chr 29:14, YHWH already gave the power to the whole assembly (including David himself), which is emphasized by the causal clause that begins with the causal conjunction (כִּי). In this clause, the words "from you" (מִמְּךָ) and "from your hand" (מִיָּדְךָ) are stressed by being placed in front of the clause. Accordingly, the people's offering originates from YHWH himself, and their willing offering reveals their upright hearts.

---

430. Japhet notes in David's last speech that "the ten-fold repetition of the word" (כֹּל). According to her, the number ten is clearly meaningful from "seemingly unnecessary" phrase, "to do the whole" (וְלַעֲשׂוֹת הַכֹּל), in 1 Chr 29:19 (Japhet, *I & II Chronicles*, 509).

431. Lanham, *Handlist*, 11.

432. Japhet, *I & II Chronicles*, 511.

433. Johnstone, *1 and 2 Chronicles*, 1:288.

434. Throntveit, *When Kings Speak*, 95.

435. Klein, *1 Chronicles*, 538.

In 1 Chr 29:15, David identifies the people of Israel (including himself) with their forefathers, referring to them as sojourners and settlers. He continues by indicating that their days on earth are like a shadow, which rhetorically expresses a *simile* as a metaphor.[436] In particular, David utters at the end of this verse that there is no hope, which reinforces their smallness in contrast with YHWH's greatness. As for 1 Chr 29:15, Estes states, "The fact of sociopolitical sojourning of the previous generations is to the pious mind analogous to the unassimilated character of the righteous individual living in a world estranged from God."[437]

In 1 Chr 29:16, David indicates that they have prepared the temple building for God's holy name, ascribing their preparation to God's hand (God's power). The whole of the project belongs to YHWH himself. First Chronicles 29:17 emphasizes the willing offerings of David and the whole assembly by the repetition of the verb "to offer willingly" (לְהִתְנַדֵּב, הִתְנַדַּבְתִּי), which also occurs in 1 Chr 29:14 (לְהִתְנַדֵּב). These willing offerings originate from the upright heart. The verbal root "to offer willingly" (נדב) is frequently used as a key theme in 1 Chr 29, which indicates that the whole assembly willingly offers their gifts to YHWH with the upright heart (1 Chr 29:5, 6, 9, 14, 17).[438]

The last subsection of this prayer (1 Chr 29:18–19) closes with a petition, which is for the people and Solomon. In particular, the vocative in 1 Chr 29:18 is noteworthy in that it is combined with the patriarchs. As Johnstone indicates appropriately, the Chr exhibits "the immemorial bond between the LORD and his people stretching back to the patriarchal age," referring to Abraham, Isaac, and Israel.[439] The Chr, by using the epithet of God, showcases the relationship between God and the patriarchs from the early history of Israel.

It seems more appropriate that the Chr, by the use of the vocative of God, recalls the relationship between the covenantal God and Israel by appealing to the relationship between YHWH and the patriarchs. Furthermore, the focus is on a "perfect heart" (לֵבָב שָׁלֵם) of the people and Solomon. David requests that God keep the present whole-heart of the people (1 Chr 29:18) and then prays that God will give Solomon a "perfect heart" for the observance of God's law and for the building of the temple (1 Chr 29:19). It is appropriate that Japhet summarizes the last subsection as follows:

> [I]t is a climactic moment in the history of Israel, not in material but in spiritual terms, with the thoughts and hearts of all Israel directed to God. In order to maintain this ideal the people need God's assistance, and this is David's only request. All the rest—success, prosperity, establishment of the kingdom, etc.—are corollaries of this spiritual disposition and will surely follow.[440]

---

436. Lanham, *Handlist*, 140.
437. Estes, "Metaphorical Sojourning," 45–49.
438. See Hill, *1 & 2 Chronicles*, 329.
439. Johnstone, *1 and 2 Chronicles*, 1:288.
440. Japhet, *I & II Chronicles*, 511.

In sum, David's prayer is obviously based on YHWH's greatness in contrast with the unworthiness of human beings. David and the assembly of Israel, depending on YHWH's greatness, can willingly offer the materials for the building project of the temple. Even the materials they offer willingly are given by YHWH Himself. Furthermore, in the last petition, David designates YHWH as the covenantal God who has made covenants with the patriarchs, requesting that YHWH give a perfect heart to the whole assembly and to Solomon.

Rhetorical Situation

The rhetorical situation may be noted on the two levels: the narrative situation and the Chr's situation. The narrative situation is that David's reign is about to end. David needs to encourage the whole assembly of Israel and Solomon to carry out the building task of the temple before Solomon's succession, so David makes speeches to Solomon and the leaders of Israel. Each speech has its own audience in the narrative. For instance, David gives a speech to the leaders of Israel (1 Chr 28:2–8). Also, David gives a speech primarily to Solomon (1 Chr 28:9–10). David gives his final speeches to Solomon (1 Chr 28:20–21) and to the whole assembly of Israel (1 Chr 29:1–5). In the last part of this unit, David addresses his prayer to YHWH (1 Chr 29:10–19). As the narrative advances, the narrative audience of David's speeches extends from the leaders of Israel as David's officials (1 Chr 28:1) to the whole assembly of Israel (1 Chr 29:1).

The construction of the temple is a great task since the temple will be YHWH's dwelling place as the house for YHWH (cf. 1 Chr 22:1). David has already prepared for the temple building (1 Chr 22:2–5, 1 Chr 23–27) and here he will give his plans for the temple building to his son Solomon (1 Chr 29:11–19). It should be noted that 1 Chr 28–29 is connected to 1 Chr 22, although the lists of 1 Chr 23–27 appear to have made a split between 1 Chr 22 and 1 Chr 28–29. Braun indicates that the preceding unit (1 Chr 22) and this unit (1 Chr 28, 29) can be regarded as "a transition unit shaped by the Chr himself to integrate the activities of David and Solomon into a single complex."441 In this regard, the events in the preceding rhetorical unit constrain David's reign in his final days. Thus, David makes speeches to Solomon and the leaders of Israel, including the assembly of Israel, in order to urge them to carry out the building of the temple.

The Chr brings David's speeches in the narrative into his own context. They serve the Chr's purpose. For instance, when the ark is installed in the temple, the temple becomes YHWH's presence and footstool (1 Chr 28:2). In the Persian era, the temple as the place of YHWH's presence and footstool will be regarded as the worship place of the Yehudite community, pointing to the continuity of the relationship between the covenantal God and Israel. In this context, the Chr attempts to persuade the Yehudites

---

441. Braun, "Chosen Temple Builder," 582.

to comprehend the centrality of the Jerusalem temple as the sole worship place in the Persian period, reflecting the relationship between God and Israel as expressed through the temple at the time when the Davidic dynasty no longer exists. Thus, the Chr, through the temple and its worship, emphasizes the relationship between the covenantal God and Israel which continues in the Persian period.

Mason claims that David's speech to the leaders is given to "the representatives of the wider community" (1 Chr 28:2–8),[442] which is also linked to David's speech to Solomon (1 Chr 22:18–19). According to Mason, "there is reference to a much later situation. By their faithfulness they will ensure that the land comes to their successors as their due inheritance, those successors whom the Chronicler is really now addressing."[443] In particular, the phrase "in order that you may possess the good land and cause your sons to inherit after you forever" (1 Chr 28:8) appears to have extended the Chr's audience to the latter generations, including the Yehudite community in the Persian period when the Davidic king did not exist.[444] Thus, Mason extends the Chr's audience to the later generations, reflecting his more concern over the preaching values of the speech.

The Chr's situation relates to the key exigence in the Persian period, that is, the identity reformulation of Persian Yehud. The Chr considers the Yehudites in a provincial district under the Persian Empire and wishes to unite the early traditions of Israel with their current situation. This situation constrains the Chr's retelling of David's final days. The rhetorical need is to present the significance of the Jerusalem temple in the Persian period. Selman holds that for the Chr's audience, the Jerusalem temple will be considered as "the chief symbol of the continuing reality of the kingdom of the Lord."[445] The Yehudite community will want to sustain the temple and its worship in their own time.[446] In this context, the Chr wishes to emphasize the Jerusalem temple as the sole worship place. The Chr legitimizes the centrality of the Jerusalem temple by appealing to the divine origin of the construction of the temple. As Boda indicates well, the two elements may have provoked the Chr's concern over the legitimacy of the temple: one is that the Jerusalem temple is built and bolstered by the Davidic monarchs whose unfaithfulness to YHWH finally led to the demise of Israel as an independent nation with the fall of Jerusalem, and the other is that there is not much concern over the temple in Jerusalem as the sole worship place since the Jerusalem

---

442. Mason, *Preaching*, 28–29. Mason contends that "although in this instance the two are so closely related that it seems better to treat them as one address. But the extension of the address to 'all Israel' again indicates that a wider reference is intended than that suggested merely by its supposed original historical, religious and political context" (29).

443. Ibid., 29.

444. Mason indicates that this is "the real truth behind the historical monarchy, and it remains the truth when the historical incidence of the monarchy has passed away" (Mason, *Preaching*, 29).

445. Selman, *1 Chronicles*, 251.

446. Boda, *1–2 Chronicles*, 212.

temple in the Persian period is one of many sanctuaries in various places—such as the Samaritan temple at Gerizim and the temple built by Egyptian Jews at Elephantine.[447]

In this situation, some might raise a question about the legitimacy of the Jerusalem temple as the sole worship place. As a result, the Chr feels the need to persuade his audience in the Persian period to accept the legitimacy of the Jerusalem temple as the sole worship place chosen by divine initiative. The Chr, linking the tabernacle to the temple and the relationship of Moses-Joshua to that of David-Solomon, makes his strong arguments for the centrality of the Jerusalem temple as "the only true heir of the sanctuary tradition of Israel."[448] Accordingly, the Chr intends to highlight both David and Solomon in order to reconstruct the relationship between the covenantal God and Israel in the Persian period, based on the temple and its worship. Thus, the Chr, by linking the relationship of David-Solomon to that of Moses-Joshua, reminds his audience that YHWH previously made a covenant with Israel at Sinai (Exod 19).

With respect to this unit, Braun indicates that "the Chronicler's primary objective has been to portray Solomon as the divinely chosen temple builder."[449] However, it seems to be more appropriate that McKenzie states as follows:

> The temple, after all, is not just a human project; its very design was delivered by God to David (28:19). The temple and the worship conducted there in the Chronicler's day would have been different in many respects from the original institution. But the Chronicler seeks to demonstrate *continuity* not only with the first temple but also with the traditions about Israel's earliest cultic institutions, the tabernacle and the ark.[450]

The focus is not merely on the continuity of the cultic institution but also on the continuity of relationship between God and Israel with the emphasis on the legitimacy of the Jerusalem temple in the Persian period. Thus, through speeches and prayer of David, the Chr attempts to persuade his audience of the significance of the Jerusalem temple as the sole worship place, which obviously originates from YHWH Himself.

Rhetorical Effectiveness

The rhetorical effectiveness of this rhetorical unit is primarily based on David's speeches and prayer. In a transitional period from David's reign to Solomon's reign, David speaks to the leaders of Israel, Solomon, the assembly of Israel and even to YHWH (David's prayer in 1 Chr 29:10–19) in order to assist Solomon in the building of the temple. These speeches appear to be very persuasive to their audiences. For instance,

---

447. Ibid., 214.

448. Boda, *1-2 Chronicles*, 214.

449. Braun, "Chosen Temple Builder," 590. According to him, the Chr "has accomplished this objective by his use of the concept of rest, by modeling his account after the account of Joshua's commissioning, and by his application of the concept of election to Solomon" (590).

450. McKenzie, *I & II Chronicles*, 223.

David's speech to the leaders (1 Chr 28:2–8) makes the leaders of Israel recognize the divine election of Solomon and the significance of the law-keeping. David's speeches to Solomon (1 Chr 28:9–10, 20–21) lead Solomon to seek YHWH and to focus on his calling to build the temple. David's speech to the assembly (1 Chr 29:1–5) appears to be very effective, such that all the leaders of Israel offer willingly the building materials for the temple (1 Chr 29:6–9). David's prayer (1 Chr 29:10–19) appeals to God's greatness and His faithfulness to the covenants with the patriarchs, in which David effectively requests of YHWH that Solomon keep YHWH's commands with his whole heart and that he complete the building task of the temple.

In this narrative context, David's speeches appear to have been very persuasive to the narrative audiences since David appeals to YHWH's authority as the initiator of the temple building. David depends upon YHWH's faithful character and historical retrospect. By his speeches, David persuades Solomon, the leaders of Israel, and even the whole assembly of Israel as the overhearers of his speeches, to carry out the task of building the temple. It demonstrates one of the key elements in the Chr's portrayal of David, that is, "David as catalyst of faithful worship in Israel."[451] David's prayer also appears to have been very effective as they lead to YHWH's gracious response to David. Thus, by YHWH's sovereign intervention Solomon will complete the building task of the temple.

By bringing David's speeches and prayer into his situation, the Chr makes an argument regarding the Jerusalem temple in the Chr's context. He does this in order to persuade his audience to regard the Jerusalem temple as the focal point of their identity reformulation in the Persian period. David's speeches and prayer have an effect on the Chr's audience, by reminding them of the fact that the golden age of Israel was previously characterized by the temple and its worship in Jerusalem. It is very persuasive to the Yehudite community that needs to reformulate their community identity on the basis of the Jerusalem temple in the Persian era. In particular, the Chr's allusion to the relationship of Moses-Joshua as linked to that of David-Solomon (1 Chr 28:20–21) emphasizes the continuity of the key worship place in Israel by its shift from the tabernacle to the temple. The Chr, through David's speech and prayer, effectively legitimizes the centrality of the Jerusalem temple in the Persian period.

In addition, the Chr's audience is extended to later generations in that David's speech to the assembly (1 Chr 28:2–8, esp. 28:8) is related to their descendants' staying on the land of Israel, which depends on their observance of God's commands and ordinances. It means that the Chr attempted to persuade his contemporaries and later generations to seek YHWH by keeping His commandments and ordinances. The Chr persuasively conveys his message to his audience and even to future readers.

Most significantly, for the Chr, David's speeches and prayer are rooted in the Davidic covenant (1 Chr 17) regarding the temple building. The Chr frequently alludes to the Davidic covenant in encouraging Solomon and the assembly of Israel to carry

---

451. Boda, *1–2 Chronicles*, 223.

out the building task (e.g., 1 Chr 22:9; 28:6; 29:1; cf. 1 Chr 17:11–14). In this unit, the Chr bases David's speeches primarily upon the Davidic covenant (1 Chr 28:6–8; cf. 1 Chr 17:11–14; 22:8–10). Furthermore, the significance of the Davidic covenant is displayed in the ensuing Solomon narrative (2 Chr 1–9), in which Solomon commences the construction of the temple, recalling the Davidic covenant. Even when the temple building was completed, Solomon recalls the Davidic covenant in his speech to the whole assembly of Israel (2 Chr 6).[452]

Thus, David's speeches and prayer in this rhetorical unit serve to persuade the Yehudite community as the Chr's audience, leading them to comprehend that regardless of their present state under the Persian Empire they still belong to the everlasting kingdom of God.[453] For the Chr, YHWH's sovereignty still works in the Persian period. The design of the temple building is given by YHWH to David (1 Chr 28:19). YHWH himself will keep his promises to his people (1 Chr 29:14–16). David's speeches and prayer will lead the Yehudite community to understand that their identity as God's people is based on the Jerusalem temple. Thus, the Chr persuades the Yehudite community to discern their identity as the worship-centered community in the Persian period by portraying David as a true worshiper of YHWH who sought YHWH. Finally, David hands his kingship over to Solomon.

SUMMARY

I have examined the speeches and prayers in David's narrative (1 Chr 11–29), in which the Chr portrays David as the preparer for the building of the temple, a pious worshiper seeking after YHWH, revealing the continuity of the covenantal relationship between YHWH and Israel through the temple in the Persian period. In each rhetorical unit in the David narrative, David's images are portrayed by his speeches and prayers in order to serve to persuade the Chr's audience to recognize the significance of the temple in Jerusalem as the sole worship place in Israel, which echoes the Davidic covenant regarding the temple building.

First Chronicles 11–12 describes David's ascension to the throne, wherein all Israel asks David to be king over Israel (1 Chr 11:1–2). In conquering Jerusalem, the episode of David's mighty warriors demonstrates that all the people of Israel support David (1 Chr 11:10–47). In particular, the dialogue between David and Amasai (1 Chr 12:16[17]–18[19]) indicates that even the Benjaminites support David. The Chr emphasizes that David becomes king over Israel according to YHWH's word (1 Chr 11:3, 10; 12:23[24]). Thus, David is portrayed as the legitimate king of Israel who receives wide support from all Israel.

First Chronicles 13–16 depicts the ark narrative as reformulated by the Chr. David's transfer of the ark of the covenant of YHWH to Jerusalem succeeds on the

---

452. Schniedewind, *Word of God*, 155.
453. See Williamson, *1 and 2 Chronicles*, 136; Ackroyd, *I and II Chronicles*, 90.

second attempt (1 Chr 15:1—16:3) after the failure of the first attempt along with Uzzah's death (1 Chr 13:1-14). Between these two attempts, David's battles against the Philistines are described (1 Chr 14:8-17), in which David requests YHWH's guidance and YHWH answers him positively (1 Chr 14:10). Though the battles appear to have interrupted the narrative flow, they contribute towards the provision of rest for the peaceful time of Solomon in order to build the temple. In particular, David's speech (1 Chr 15:12-13) exhibits the role of the Levites in the second attempt to transfer the ark, which was to carry out the ark of the covenant of YHWH on their shoulders (Num 7:9). After the transfer of the ark, David's prayer emphasizes his praise to the covenantal God (1 Chr 16:8-36). Thus, the Chr portrays David as the pious king of Israel who follows God's law and praises the covenantal God.

First Chronicles 17 describes God's promise to David through Nathan, in which the divine speech (1 Chr 17:11-14) reveals that one of David's sons will be the chosen temple builder, and that YHWH will establish the son of David in YHWH's kingdom forever. Accordingly, David emphasizes his request for God's blessing in relation to the Davidic dynasty, praying to the covenantal God and praising God's mighty acts. Thus, the Chr portrays David as a faithful king of Israel to YHWH.

First Chronicles 18-20 describes David's wars against the Philistines, the Moabites, the Edomites, and the Ammonites. In particular, the episode of David's messengers and the Ammonite king Hanun (1 Chr 19:1-5) reveals that David was a man who seeks peaceful relations with other nations, not who delights in fights against them. Thus, David is portrayed as the king of Israel who loved peace, even though he was a mighty warrior.

First Chronicles 21:1—22:1 describes David's census that provokes God's anger. The census and the ensuing events contribute to the determination of the place of the temple. Though David's census results in a three-day plague on Israel, YHWH elects the temple site for David. Ornan's threshing floor is chosen as the place on which David will build an altar to YHWH. Finally, David announces that this place will be YHWH's house and the altar of burnt-offering for Israel (1 Chr 22:1). Thus, the Chr portrays David as the preparer of the place of the temple according to God's promise to him.

First Chronicles 22:2-19 shows David's eagerness to prepare for the building of the temple, urging Solomon to build the house for YHWH. The emphasis is on David's speech to Solomon (1 Chr 22:6-16), in which David quotes God's words concerning Solomon (2 Chr 22:8-10). In this quotation, the Davidic covenant regarding the chosen temple builder and the everlasting dynasty is manifestly echoed (1 Chr 17:11-14). Thus, the Chr portrays David as an encourager for building the temple according to the Davidic covenant.

First Chronicles 23-27 explains that David is old and that his son Solomon is about to assume his kingship. Accordingly, David organizes the temple clergy and civil officials in order for Solomon to build the temple. The focus is on David's speech to all the leaders of Israel (1 Chr 23:25–32), in which David organizes a new order of worship for the Levites who would carry out their new roles at the temple instead of the tent of meeting. Thus, this portrays David not merely as the temple preparer, but also as the founder of the cultic system at the temple.

First Chronicles 28–29 describes David's final speeches and actions, the purpose of which is to prepare for Solomon's succession and his building of the temple. The focus is on the divine speech (1 Chr 28:6–8), in which the Davidic covenant is apparently echoed (1 Chr 17:11–14; cf. 1 Chr 22:8–10). According to YHWH's words, Solomon will be the temple builder and YHWH would establish his kingdom forever. Thus, the Chr portrays David clearly as a faithful follower of YHWH's words and an eager preparer for the building of the temple.

However, the Chr's portrayal of David goes beyond these images of David. The Chr emphasizes the continuity of the relationship between the covenantal God and Israel, portraying David as the preparer of the building of the temple and echoing the Davidic covenant. Thus, the Chr portrays David as the true worshiper to YHWH who sought YHWH, which serves to persuade the Yehudites to discern their identity as the worship-centered community in the Persian period. Furthermore, the Chr points out that the covenantal relationship between God and Israel still continues through the Jerusalem temple in the Persian period.

5

Speeches and Prayers in Solomon's Narrative

SOLOMON'S NARRATIVE (2 CHR 1–9) follows the pattern of David's narrative.[1] These two narratives are closely connected by the theme of building the temple. David gives Solomon the plans for the temple building, and Solomon completes the construction of the temple as God's chosen temple-builder.[2] The Solomon narrative is distinguished by the two twenty-year periods during the reign of Solomon: in the first twenty years, Solomon builds the temple (2 Chr 1–7) and the second twenty years contains Solomon's reign after the building of the temple (2 Chr 8–9).[3] The construction of the temple leads to some results in the second twenty-year reign of Solomon.[4] God's mercy is obviously stressed during the dedication of the temple (2 Chr 6–7), where the significance of the temple and the Davidic covenant is revealed.

Solomon's narrative begins with Solomon's accession to the throne (2 Chr 1:1–17). His first act as the king of Israel is to visit Gibeon to offer sacrifices. At the Gibeon

---

1. Solomon's narrative, forming a foundation for the ensuing narratives (2 Chr 10–36), follows the same pattern of David's narrative. For instance, 2 Chr 9:29–31 as a concluding remark follows that of the summary statement of David's reign (1 Chr 29:26–30). See Kelly, *Retribution*, 93; Riley, *King and Cultus*, 77.

2. David's narrative is linked to the ensuing Solomon narrative, focusing on establishing kingdom and cult. Second Chronicles 11–29 displays a back and forward pattern. Duke ("Rhetorical Approach," 121) delineates 1 Chr 11–29 as follows:

   1 Chronicles 11–12: kingdom (capturing Jerusalem; support from all Israel)
   1 Chronicles 13: cult (attempt to transport the ark)
   1 Chronicles 14: kingdom (military victories)
   1 Chronicles 15–17: cult (bringing the ark to Jerusalem and David's desire to build a house for it)
   1 Chronicles 18–20: kingdom (military victories)
   1 Chronicles 21–29: cult (preparations for the temple)

3. The Deuteronomist presents two noticeable periods of Solomon. In the first period (1 Kgs 1–10), Solomon is positively portrayed with the emphasis on his obedience; whereas, in the second period (1 Kgs 11), he is negatively portrayed with his apostasy. Solomon's errors (1 Kgs 11) result in the division of his kingdom, which introduces a crucial theme of the following narratives, that is, the failure of the kings in keeping God's covenant.

4. For example, these are faithful worship (2 Chr 8:11–16), prosperity (2 Chr 8:17–18), the Queen of Sheba's visit (2 Chr 9:1–12), and other kings' recognition of Solomon (2 Chr 29:13–28).

sanctuary, God appears to Solomon and gives him riches and honor as well as wisdom and knowledge. The depiction of Solomon's ascension to the throne and his wealth demonstrates that YHWH's promise to David is fulfilled, and confirms that Solomon will be the chosen temple builder of YHWH. The main section of Solomon's narrative deals with the temple building and its dedication, in which Solomon's preparation for the task includes Huram's help to build the temple (2 Chr 2:1–18). This is followed by Solomon's actual building of the temple (2 Chr 3:1—5:1). Solomon then dedicates the temple by bringing the ark to the temple in Jerusalem (2 Chr 5:2—7:22). Finally, Solomon's other achievements and his international fame are described in 2 Chr 8:1—9:31, in which much attention is given to the visit of the queen of Sheba (2 Chr 9:1–12). The Chr mentions Solomon's great wealth (2 Chr 9:13-28) and Solomon's death (2 Chr 9:29–31).

After the completion of the construction of the temple, the dedication ceremony showcases a partial fulfillment of the Davidic covenant (1 Chr 17). In line with David's preparation for the temple building, Solomon completes the building of the temple. The Chr's portrayal of Solomon is also focused on the temple building. In fact, of the nine chapters of the Solomon narrative (2 Chr 1–9), six chapters (2 Chr 2–7) are allocated to the building of the temple and its dedication.[5] The David-Solomon narrative is focused on the building of the temple, especially based on the Davidic covenant regarding the temple (1 Chr 17). This is clearly confirmed in David's speeches and prayers, and it is also frequently recalled in Solomon's speeches and prayers. In this regard, the building of the temple combines David's and Solomon's narrative as a united narrative.

In sum, the Chr, through the speeches and prayers in the Solomon narrative, portrays Solomon as the builder of the central worship place in Israel (the Jerusalem temple). Thus, the Chr emphasizes the centrality of the Jerusalem temple as the sole worship place in the Persian period, which points to the continuity of the covenantal relationship between God and Israel.

SPEECH IN THE NARRATIVE ABOUT SOLOMON'S WISDOM AND WEALTH (2 CHR 1)

The narrative sequence now changes from David's reign to Solomon's.[6] The first act of Solomon as the king of Israel is to worship YHWH as Solomon establishes himself in his kingdom. Solomon summons all Israel, the commanders, judges, and the leaders of Israel. Then he and the whole assembly go to the high place at Gibeon (the tent of meeting or the tabernacle) in order to offer burnt offerings. In this place, God appears to Solomon and speaks to him. Solomon responds to the divine speech, indicating

---

5. See Tuell, *First and Second Chronicles*, 116.

6. David's military strength creates a peaceful time and makes possible his plans for the building of the temple, while Solomon, echoing the Hebrew word for peace, carries out the building project to completion. See McKenzie, *I & II Chronicles*, 227.

that the Davidic covenant is partially fulfilled since Solomon has become the king of Israel according to YHWH's word. Thus, this rhetorical unit emphasizes that Solomon seeks YHWH. As a result, this unit closes by focusing on Solomon's greatness with his wisdom and wealth since God is with him.

Rhetorical Unit

This rhetorical unit (2 Chr 1) begins with Solomon's establishment in his kingdom after David's death. This unit is linked to the previous chapters (1 Chr 22–29). Solomon, as David's successor and as the chosen temple builder, will fulfill the building project, taking over David's preparation for building the temple. In this unit, Solomon is introduced as the completer of the building project in the David-Solomon narrative.

This unit is comprised of four parts: an introduction (2 Chr 1:1); Solomon's visiting the high place at Gibeon with his various leaders of Israel (2 Chr 1:2–6); God's appearance to Solomon with the accompaniment of the divine speech (2 Chr 1:7–13); and, as the conclusion of this unit, Solomon's prosperity since God is with him (2 Chr 1:14–17). Thus, the focus is on Solomon's speech and the divine speech, which portray Solomon as the one who seeks YHWH. Solomon is highly exalted and truly prospers since God is with him.

Rhetorical Strategy

Second Chronicles 1:1 introduces Solomon as the successor of David, linking David's narrative to Solomon's. Significantly, Solomon's first act as king is to seek YHWH. He summons various leaders of Israel (2 Chr 1:2) and then goes to "God's tent of meeting" at Gibeon to worship YHWH (2 Chr 1:3).[7] The tent of meeting (the tabernacle) had been constructed by Moses in the wilderness, and the bronze altar in front of the tabernacle had been made by Bezalel (2 Chr 1:5). Accordingly, the Chr obviously employs the image of the tent of meeting or the tabernacle, and he mentions Moses and Bezalel who played key roles in the building of the tabernacle in the wilderness (Exod 25–31; 35–40). Interestingly, the Chr also refers to another tent which David had previously pitched for the ark of the covenant of YHWH in Jerusalem (2 Chr 1:4). These two tents will be united in the temple which Solomon will build. In any case, Solomon and the assembly seek YHWH at Gibeon (2 Chr 1:5). Thus, Solomon at Gibeon offers a number of burnt-offerings on the bronze altar at the tent of meeting (2 Chr 1:6). That night God appears and speaks to him (2 Chr 1:7–13):

---

7. Johnstone, *1 and 2 Chronicles*, 1:300. He indicates that the phrase, "the tent of meeting" is uniquely given the epithet, "God's tent of meeting."

Speeches and Prayers in Solomon's Narrative

Solomon's Speech and God's Speech to him (2 Chr 1:7–13)

2 Chr 1:7–13	
⁷ בַּלַּיְלָה הַהוּא נִרְאָה אֱלֹהִים לִשְׁלֹמֹה	In that night, God appeared to Solomon
וַיֹּאמֶר לוֹ שְׁאַל מָה אֶתֶּן־לָךְ׃	and said to him, "Ask what I shall give you."
⁸ וַיֹּאמֶר שְׁלֹמֹה לֵאלֹהִים אַתָּה עָשִׂיתָ	And Solomon said to God, "You have treated
עִם־דָּוִיד אָבִי חֶסֶד גָּדוֹל	my father David with great steadfast love,
וְהִמְלַכְתַּנִי תַּחְתָּיו׃	and have made me king instead of him
⁹ עַתָּה יְהוָה אֱלֹהִים	Now, O YHWH God,
יֵאָמֵן דְּבָרְךָ עִם דָּוִיד אָבִי	your promise to David my father is confirmed
כִּי אַתָּה הִמְלַכְתַּנִי עַל־עַם	for you have made me king over a people
רַב כַּעֲפַר הָאָרֶץ׃	numerous as the dust of the earth
¹⁰ עַתָּה חָכְמָה וּמַדָּע תֶּן־לִי	Now, wisdom and knowledge give to me,
וְאֵצְאָה לִפְנֵי הָעָם־הַזֶּה וְאָבוֹאָה	so that I may go out and come in before this people,
כִּי־מִי יִשְׁפֹּט אֶת־עַמְּךָ הַזֶּה הַגָּדוֹל׃	for who can judge this great people of yours?"
¹¹ וַיֹּאמֶר־אֱלֹהִים לִשְׁלֹמֹה	And God said to Solomon,
יַעַן אֲשֶׁר הָיְתָה זֹאת עִם־לְבָבֶךָ	"Because this has been in your heart,
וְלֹא־שָׁאַלְתָּ עֹשֶׁר נְכָסִים וְכָבוֹד	and you have not asked riches, wealth, and honor, and
וְאֵת נֶפֶשׁ שֹׂנְאֶיךָ	the life of those who hate you,
וְגַם־יָמִים רַבִּים לֹא שָׁאָלְתָּ	and also many days you have not asked,
וַתִּשְׁאַל־לְךָ חָכְמָה וּמַדָּע	but you have asked for yourself wisdom and knowledge,
אֲשֶׁר תִּשְׁפּוֹט אֶת־עַמִּי	that you may judge my people,
אֲשֶׁר הִמְלַכְתִּיךָ עָלָיו׃	over whom I have made you king.
¹² הַחָכְמָה וְהַמַּדָּע נָתוּן לָךְ	the wisdom and the knowledge is given to you,
וְעֹשֶׁר וּנְכָסִים וְכָבוֹד אֶתֶּן־לָךְ	and riches and wealth and honor I will give to you
אֲשֶׁר לֹא־הָיָה כֵן לַמְּלָכִים	that there have not been so to the kings
אֲשֶׁר לְפָנֶיךָ	who are before you,
וְאַחֲרֶיךָ לֹא יִהְיֶה־כֵּן׃	and after you it will not be so."
¹³ וַיָּבֹא שְׁלֹמֹה לַבָּמָה	And Solomon came from the high place
אֲשֶׁר־בְּגִבְעוֹן יְרוּשָׁלַ͏ִם	that was at Gibeon to Jerusalem,
מִלִּפְנֵי אֹהֶל מוֹעֵד	from before the tent of meeting,
וַיִּמְלֹךְ עַל־יִשְׂרָאֵל׃	and he reigned over Israel.

Second Chronicles 1:7–13 as deliberative rhetoric concerns God's appearance to Solomon with a dialogue between God and Solomon.[8] This dialogue is divided into two

---

8. Second Chronicles 1:7–13 is parallel to 1 Kgs 3:5–14. There are some differences in 2 Chr 1:7–13. For instance, the phrase, "in that night" (2 Chr 1:7) is employed instead of "in a dream at night" in 1 Kgs 3:5. Klein raises a question about this phrase: "Did the Chronicler omit the reference to the dream for the sake of brevity, or does this represent a critique of the legitimacy of dreams as the source

parts: YHWH's question and Solomon's answer (2 Chr 1:7-10), and God's speech to Solomon (2 Chr 1:11-12). YHWH first says to him, "Ask what I shall give to you" (2 Chr 1:7). Solomon responds to this in 2 Chr 1:8-10. In his response, Solomon mentions God's steadfast love to his father David, indicating that God made Solomon king over Israel instead of his father David (2 Chr 1:8).[9] This utterance is reminiscent of God's promise to David (1 Chr 17) and a partial fulfillment of the Davidic covenant. Accordingly, God has confirmed His promise to David (2 Chr 1:9).[10] In particular, the verb "you [God] have made me king" (הִמְלַכְתַּנִי) is repeated twice in 2 Chr 1:8-9, stressing God's initiative to make Solomon king over Israel. The phrase "numerous as the dust of the earth" (רַב כַּעֲפַר הָאָרֶץ, 2 Chr 1:9) employs the rhetorical device *simile* to emphasize the number of the Israelites, which also seems to allude to a partial fulfillment of God's promise to both Abraham and Jacob (Gen 13:16; 28:14). Solomon refers to his father David twice, pointing to God's steadfast love and His promise to David (2 Chr 1:8-9). Thus, the Chr emphasizes that Solomon becomes king over Israel according to what God had said to David, which is indeed a partial fulfillment of the Davidic covenant (1 Chr 17).[11]

The discourse marker "now" (עַתָּה), pointing to "a logical conclusion," signifies "in the light of" or "therefore" (2 Chr 1:9, 10).[12] Solomon becomes king over Israel due to God's steadfast love to David. In the light of this love, God's promise to David is confirmed, and this confirmation is linked to the Davidic covenant regarding the temple building (1 Chr 17:23-24) by the occurrence of the same verb, "to be confirmed" (יֵאָמֵן) in both discourses.[13] Accordingly, Solomon, reminding God of His steadfast love to his father David, asks God to grant him wisdom and knowledge (2 Chr 1:10).[14] The rhetorical question "who can judge this great people of yours?" (2 Chr 1:10) emphasizes that none can judge and rule God's great people. Accordingly,

---

of revelation (cf. Deut 13:2-6; Jer 23:25-32; 27:9-10; Zech 10:2)?" (Klein, *2 Chronicles*, 23). See also Williamson, *1 and 2 Chronicles*, 195. This omission of the reference to dream appears to have reflected the resistance to dreams in the post-exilic period (Jer 23:25-32 and Zech 10:2).

9. Second Chronicles 1:8 omits the phrase "as he walked before you in truth and in righteousness and in uprightness of heart with you and you kept for him this great lovingkindness" in 1 Kgs 3:6. The phrase "and (you) have made me king instead of him" (2 Chr 1:8) is employed in place of "and you gave to him a son to sit on his throne as (at) this day," omitting "your servant" before David in 1 Kgs 3:6.

10. In 2 Chr 1:9, we read the phrase "your word with David my father is confirmed for you have made me king over a people numerous as the dust of the earth" in place of "you have made your servant king instead of David my father" with the omission of the phrase, "I am a little child I do not know to go out and to come in" (1 Kgs 3:7)—this appears to emphasize God's word given to David, reflecting the Davidic covenant.

11. For a discussion about the relationship between the Davidic covenant and Solomon's reign, see Cross, *Canaanite Myth*, 219-65; Ishida, *Royal Dynasties*, 80-117.

12. Van der Merwe et al., *Biblical Hebrew*, 333.

13. Second Chronicles 6:17 (// 1 Kgs 8:26) employs this verb. See Klein, *2 Chronicles*, 24.

14. Second Chronicles 1:10 abbreviates 1 Kgs 3:8-9, changing the adjective, "great" from הַכָּבֵד to הַגָּדוֹל, omitting 1 Kgs 3:10, "And it was good in the eyes of the Lord that Solomon had asked this thing."

Solomon requests the wisdom and knowledge to judge this people, depending on the Davidic covenant (2 Chr 1:8–10).

In 2 Chr 1:11–12, God answers Solomon's request. The verb "to ask" (שאל) is dominant in this speech as it is repeated three times in 2 Chr 1:11. The three occurrences form a chiastic word-order with its imperative form (שְׁאַל) in 2 Chr 1:7:

> In that night, God appeared to Solomon
> And said to him, "*Ask* (שְׁאַל) what I shall give you" (2 Chr 1:7)
> . . .
> And God said to Solomon
> "Because this has been in your heart,
> and *you have not asked* (לֹא־שָׁאַלְתָּ) riches, wealth, and honor,
> and the life of those who hate you,
> and also many days *you have not asked* (לֹא שָׁאָלְתָּ),
> but *you have asked* (תִּשְׁאַל) for yourself wisdom and knowledge,
> that you may judge my people,
> over whom I have made you king" (2 Chr 1:11)

This emphasizes that YHWH has told Solomon to ask Him what he wants.[15] The first and fourth occurrences are used positively, whereas the second and third are employed negatively. So the four occurrences of this verb constitute a contrasting point. Accordingly, Solomon does not ask for riches, wealth, honor, the life of those who hate Solomon, or many days (2 Chr 1:11)—the accumulation of more or less synonymous nouns creates an effective emphasis.[16] Instead, Solomon asks for the wisdom and knowledge to judge God's great people over whom God has made him king (2 Chr 1:12). The phrase, "wisdom and knowledge" (חָכְמָה וּמַדָּע) which Solomon requests (2 Chr 1:10) is repeated three times in every verse of 2 Chr 1:10–12.[17] Solomon's request obviously pleases God, so that God gives Solomon the riches, wealth, and honor, for which Solomon did not ask (2 Chr 1:11). Thus, God announces that none of the kings who were before Solomon and none after him will be comparable to Solomon.

Finally, 2 Chr 1:13 as a summary statement closes God's appearance to Solomon with his return to Jerusalem from the high place at Gibeon.[18] Accordingly, the focus

---

15. See Carr, *From D to Q*, 105. The verb (שאל) is followed by direct objects and then direct objects are followed by the verb.

16. Bar-Efrat, *Narrative Art*, 216.

17. Second Chronicles 1:11–12 summarizes 1 Kgs 3:11–14, omitting 1 Kgs 3:14, "And if you walk in my ways to keep my statutes and commandment, as David your father walked, then I will prolong your days." In particular, 1 Kgs 3:12–13 emphasizes a "wise and discerning heart," whereas, 2 Chr 1:12 stresses that Solomon's fame refers to his wealth. However, Solomon's request for the wisdom and knowledge in the context of Chronicles is for the building of the temple rather than for the judging of the Israelites in the context of Kings. (Japhet, *I & II Chronicles*, 531–32; Williamson, *1 and 2 Chronicles*, 195; Klein, *2 Chronicles*, 24.) Also, Klein, after noting the alterations from the verbs in the perfect tense in 1 Kgs 3:12–13 to Qal passive participle and the imperfect verb in 2 Chr 1:12, emphasizes that God has already given to Solomon wisdom and knowledge in Chronicles (Klein, *2 Chronicles*, 25).

18. According to Boda, the Chr laid a foundation for Solomon's narrative by the summary notes in

of this rhetorical unit is on the divine speech and Solomon's speech. The former indicates that God makes Solomon king according to God's promise to David (1 Chr 17) and the latter points out that Solomon requests the wisdom and knowledge to judge God's people, especially related to the task of building the temple. Then, as a response to Solomon's request, God grants him more than what he had requested, riches and honor as well as wisdom and knowledge.

In this event of God's appearance to Solomon, the Chr's description of Solomon is further emphasized when compared with his description of David. Solomon in his first act as king of Israel seeks YHWH in the tent of meeting at Gibeon (2 Chr 1:5), and he confirms a partial fulfillment of the Davidic covenant (2 Chr 1:8–9). Even Solomon's wealth and fame will exceed David's (2 Chr 1:12).[19]

Rhetorical Situation

The rhetorical situation of 2 Chr 1 may be traced on two levels. First, the narrative situation is comprised of the urgent situation of the narrative, the narrative audience, and the narrative constraints. Solomon establishes himself in his kingdom as the king of Israel (2 Chr 1:1). The first act he accomplishes as the king of Israel is to go to the tent of meeting (the tabernacle) at Gibeon with the whole assembly in order to offer burnt-offerings (2 Chr 1:3). Accordingly, the urgent narrative situation of 2 Chr 1 is that Solomon and the whole assembly must go to the high place at Gibeon in order to seek YHWH. At Gibeon, God appears and speaks to Solomon (2 Chr 1:7–12). God answers Solomon's request with much more blessing. Solomon's worship at the Gibeon sanctuary and God's appearance legitimizes Solomon's kingship in Israel. In this way, YHWH's theophany functions to ratify Solomon's kingship. After Solomon comes back from the Gibeon sanctuary, he begins his reign over Israel (2 Chr 1:13). The narrative urgent situation is to seek YHWH in the Gibeon sanctuary before Solomon begins to reign over Israel.

The narrative audience of 2 Chr 1 is primarily YHWH and Solomon since YHWH appears to Solomon and speaks with him at night. Possibly, the audience of these speeches may include the leaders of Israel who accompany Solomon to Gibeon (2 Chr 1:2). These leaders are regarded as the whole assembly or all Israel in that they are representative of the entire nation.[20] They may have overheard Solomon's speech and the divine speech in 2 Chr 1:7–13. In this context, Solomon's journey to Gibeon as a major event in this unit is constrained by the preceding events of his ascension to the throne and God's promise to David (1 Chr 17).

In the event at Gibeon, the speeches of Solomon and YHWH call attention to the superiority of Solomon and the Davidic covenant regarding Solomon's enthronement.

---

2 Chr 1:1 and 1:13 (*1–2 Chronicles*, 236).

19. Boda, *1–2 Chronicles*, 236.

20. Boda, *1–2 Chronicles*, 234.

YHWH confirms Solomon's ascension to the throne as a partial fulfillment of the Davidic covenant (1 Chr 17). The Chr's rhetorical situation is related to Solomon's superiority in seeking YHWH. The Chr describes how, as the first act of the king of Israel, Solomon seeks YHWH at the Gibeon sanctuary. This leads the Yehudite community to consider Solomon as the true worshiper who has sought YHWH in the early history of Israel, and to understand YHWH as the covenantal God who has been faithful to the Davidic covenant. Thus, the Chr emphasizes that Solomon seeks YHWH, and that YHWH has been faithful to the Davidic covenant with regard to Solomon's enthronement. The Chr's description of Solomon as the true worshiper in 2 Chr 1 contributes to the process of identity formation of the Yehudite community as a cultic community in the Persian period.

Furthermore, the Chr intentionally stresses the close link between the Gibeon sanctuary and the Jerusalem temple. The Chr describes the building of the temple as lexically and thematically parallel to the building of the tabernacle, portraying Solomon more or less as "a second Bezalel" in applying his wisdom to the building of the temple (cf. Exod 31:1–11).[21] Solomon's first act as the king of Israel is to summon various leaders of Israel and to go to the Gibeon sanctuary to worship YHWH (2 Chr 1:2–3). Solomon's first act closes with his return to Jerusalem from Gibeon (2 Chr 1:13). The references to Gibeon at the beginning and end of this unit reflect the Chr's interest in the tabernacle at Gibeon, which is regarded as another worship place in Israel during the reign of Solomon and David (cf. 1 Chr 16:39; 21:29). David appoints the Levites to minister before YHWH (1 Chr 16:4) after bringing the ark of the covenant of YHWH to Jerusalem, while he leaves Zadok and the priests to minister before the tabernacle of YHWH at the high place in Gibeon (1 Chr 16:39).[22] Hill indicates appropriately that "the Chronicler reminds his audience (and us as later readers of his history) of the importance of Gibeon, a flashback to the account of David's transfer of the ark of the covenant to Jerusalem" (2 Chr 1:3–5; cf. 1 Chr 13–17).[23]

The reference to Gibeon also demonstrates that there was tension between the Judahites and the Benjaminites in the Persian period, as to which city should be the central worship place: the Gibeon sanctuary or the Jerusalem temple, as mentioned above.[24] The Judahites living in Jerusalem (1 Chr 9:3) appear to have competed with the Benjaminites in Gibeon (1 Chr 9:35). The Judahites supported Jerusalem as the worship center, whereas the Benjaminites advocated for Gibeon.[25] Thus, the Chr implicitly reveals that both Judah and Benjamin were the two leading tribes in

---

21. Hill, *1 & 2 Chronicles*, 375.

22. Japhet indicates that the Chr tries to combine the ark traditions in Deuteronomistic history with the tabernacle traditions in the Pentateuch (Japhet, *I & II Chronicles*, 527–29).

23. Hill, *1 & 2 Chronicles*, 378.

24. See chapter 2, "Rhetorical Situation."

25. Berger, "Chiasm and Meaning," 12.

the Yehudite community by indicating that the Gibeon sanctuary and the Jerusalem temple were also the crucial worship places in the time of David-Solomon.

The Yehudite community as the Chr's audience recognized that the Gibeon sanctuary had been regarded as a crucial worship place during the time of David-Solomon, which will come to be united into the Jerusalem temple that will be built by Solomon. The Chr's main constraint is Persian Yehud as a vassal province of the Persian Empire, which constrains the Chr's retelling of the early history of Israel. In this context, the community identity of Persian Yehud has been moved from a monarchical nation to a cultic community. The Chr's main rhetorical purpose is to emphasize the Jerusalem temple as the central worship place in the Persian period.

Rhetorical Effectiveness

The rhetorical effectiveness may be evaluated by two levels of audience: the narrative audience and the Chr's audience. First, in the narrative context, Solomon's speech and God's speech function to prepare for the task of building the temple. In 2 Chr 1:8–9, Solomon expresses his thanks to God for his ascension to the throne, as it is a partial fulfillment of God's promise to David. Solomon's speech is based on the Davidic covenant in 1 Chr 17:11–14 (cf. 1 Chr 22:9–10) regarding the enthronement of Solomon and his building of the temple. Accordingly, Solomon requests God to give him wisdom and knowledge to judge God's people, appealing to the Davidic covenant that God has made with David. In this context, Solomon's request for wisdom and knowledge is for the building of the temple. Solomon's speech is very persuasive to YHWH, since YHWH responds to this request positively. God grants Solomon more than what he had requested, that is, wealth and reputation as well as wisdom and knowledge. Thus, Solomon will be convinced of his reign over Israel by YHWH who has been faithful to His promise to David. In line with this, the whole assembly that may have overheard the speeches of Solomon and YHWH in the Gibeon sanctuary will be convinced of the building of the temple by Solomon.

On the other hand, in the Chr's own context, the Yehudite community as the Chr's audience will comprehend Solomon's superiority in seeking YHWH, which will lead the Yehudite community to consider what true worship will be in the Persian period. The Chr presents Solomon as the true worshiper who seeks YHWH in this context. The Chr's description of Solomon's enthronement was persuasive to the Yehudite community since Solomon's speech appeals to the covenantal God who has kept His promise to David. This means that YHWH will be faithful to the Yehudites who will seek YHWH in the Persian period. The Yehudite community will recognize YHWH's fidelity to His covenant and Solomon's piety through the speeches of Solomon and YHWH in the event at the Gibeon sanctuary, which will in turn lead the Yehudites to seek YHWH.

Furthermore, the Yehudite community will recognize that the Gibeon sanctuary plays a significant role as a crucial worship place in Israel in the time of David-Solomon.

Possibly, some Benjaminites in the Yehudite community would resonate with the Chr's references to Gibeon in 2 Chr 1. The Chr persuades the Yehudite community to understand the centrality of the Jerusalem temple in the Persian period, insinuating that the tabernacle at Gibeon will be united in the Jerusalem temple once Solomon completes the building of the temple. The hearers of Solomon's and YHWH's speeches understand that Solomon's request for the wisdom and knowledge is for the task of the temple building in Chronicles. By placing the speeches of Solomon and YHWH in the scene of God's appearance to Solomon, the Chr persuades his audience that YHWH's fidelity is based on His promise to David, and that Solomon continues to seek YHWH. In line with this, the Chr reveals YHWH's fidelity to His covenant with David through speeches of Solomon and YHWH, anticipating that the Yehudite community in the Persian period will be the temple-centered community. The Chr's audience will come to understand the centrality of the temple in Jerusalem by way of the description of Solomon's temple building, which will be further reinforced by the legitimacy of Solomon's enthronement as the chosen temple builder, as the covenantal God had previously promised to his father David.

SPEECHES IN SOLOMON'S PREPARATION FOR THE TEMPLE BUILDING (2 CHR 2)

Second Chronicles 2 concerns Solomon's actual preparation for the temple building, after deciding to build a house for the name of YHWH and a house for his kingdom (2 Chr 2:1 [1:18]). Solomon, conscripting a number of laborers, sends his message to Huram the king of Tyre in order to obtain his skilled workers and necessary building materials. Huram responds to Solomon's message positively, sending what Solomon had requested. In particular, this rhetorical unit contains two reported speeches as deliberative rhetoric: Solomon's message to Huram (2 Chr 2:2[3]–9[10]) and Huram's letter to Solomon (2 Chr 2:10[11]–15[16]), which highlight Solomon's actual preparation to carry out the construction of the temple. Thus, the Chr emphasizes that Solomon as the chosen temple builder carefully prepared for the building task of the temple.

Rhetorical Unit

This rhetorical unit begins and ends with Solomon's conscription of a number of laborers (2 Chr 1:18–2:1[2:1–2]; 2:16–17[2:17–18]), which forms a clear chiastic structure in this unit.[26] Second Chronicles 2 is primarily comprised of Solomon's words to Huram (2

---

26. Dillard, *2 Chronicles*, 17. Klein (*2 Chronicles*, 31) also indicates that 2 Chr 2 shows a chiastic structure:

  I 1:18 (2:1) Solomon's decision to build the temple and a palace
  II 2:1 (2) Conscription of labourers
  III 2:2–9 (3–10) Solomon's letter to Huram (1 Kgs 5:16, 19–20, 25 [2, 5–6, 11]).
     In vv. 2–5 (3–6) Solomon introduces the temple project to Huram

Chr 2:3–10[2–9]) and Huram's responding letter (2 Chr 2:11–16 [10–15]). In these two reported speeches, the former is Solomon's request for the building materials and skilled workers for the construction, and the latter is Huram's positive answer to Solomon's request. Thus, in this unit, the Chr clearly describes Solomon's actual preparation for building the temple through two reported speeches of Solomon and Huram.

Rhetorical Strategy

Solomon begins his preparation for the building of the temple, in which two letters are contained: Solomon's letter and Huram's letter of response. These two letters emphasize Solomon's preparations for the construction, echoing YHWH's promise to David (1 Chr 17). It is noteworthy that Solomon's actual preparations follow the steps of David's preparation. David in the previous unit has already commanded the assembling of the foreigners in the land of Israel, setting cutters to prepare stones for the temple building (1 Chr 22:2), whereas Solomon in this unit takes a census of all foreigners in the land of Israel, imitating how David had previously acted (2 Chr 2:16). Solomon follows what his father David did with the census and appointment of foreigners for the building of the temple. In terms of this arrangement, the Chr intends to emphasize that the building of the temple launched by David will be completed by Solomon according to God's promise to David (1 Chr 17). Thus, by Solomon's actual preparation for the temple building, as Japhet points out well, the Chr stresses "the *raison d'être* for Solomon's accession and his first priority of action."[27]

Solomon Sent His Message to Huram (2 Chr 2:2[3]–9[10])

2 Chr 2:2[3]–9[10]	
² וַיִּשְׁלַח שְׁלֹמֹה אֶל־חוּרָם מֶלֶךְ־צֹר	And Solomon sent to Huram king of Tyre,
לֵאמֹר	saying,
כַּאֲשֶׁר עָשִׂיתָ עִם־דָּוִיד אָבִי	"As you have dealt with David my father,
וַתִּשְׁלַח־לוֹ אֲרָזִים לִבְנוֹת־לוֹ	and sent to him cedars to build for him
בַיִת לָשֶׁבֶת בּוֹ׃	a house to dwell in.
³ הִנֵּה אֲנִי בוֹנֶה־בַּיִת	Behold, I am about to build a house
לְשֵׁם יְהוָה אֱלֹהָי	for the name of YHWH my God,
לְהַקְדִּישׁ לוֹ	to sanctify (it) to him,
לְהַקְטִיר לְפָנָיו	to make sacrifice before him,
קְטֹרֶת־סַמִּים וּמַעֲרֶכֶת תָּמִיד	the incense of spices, and the continuous row

and in vv. 6–9 (7–10) he makes specific requests of the Phoenician king.
IV 2:10–15 (11–16) Huram's letter to Solomon (1 Kgs 5:21, 23 [7, 9]; 1 Kgs 7:13–14)
V 2:16–17 (17–18) Conscription of labourers (1 Kgs 5:29–30 [15–16])

27. Japhet, *I & II Chronicles*, 536.

וְעֹלוֹת	and whole burnt-offering
לַבֹּקֶר וְלָעֶרֶב לַשַּׁבָּתוֹת	at morning and evening, at Sabbaths,
וְלֶחֳדָשִׁים וּלְמוֹעֲדֵי	and at new moons, and the appointed seasons
יְהוָה אֱלֹהֵינוּ לְעוֹלָם זֹאת עַל־יִשְׂרָאֵל׃	of YHWH our God, this (is) forever for Israel
4 וְהַבַּיִת אֲשֶׁר־אֲנִי בוֹנֶה	And the house that I am about to build
גָּדוֹל	will be great,
כִּי־גָדוֹל אֱלֹהֵינוּ מִכָּל־הָאֱלֹהִים׃	for greater is our God than all the gods
5 וּמִי יַעֲצָר־כֹּחַ לִבְנוֹת־לוֹ בַיִת	and who is able to build a house for him,
כִּי הַשָּׁמַיִם וּשְׁמֵי הַשָּׁמַיִם	for the heavens, even the highest heavens,
לֹא יְכַלְכְּלֻהוּ	cannot contain him?
וּמִי אֲנִי אֲשֶׁר אֶבְנֶה־לּוֹ בַיִת	and who am I that I should build for him a house
כִּי אִם־לְהַקְטִיר לְפָנָיו׃	except to make sacrifices before him?
6 וְעַתָּה שְׁלַח־לִי אִישׁ־חָכָם	And now send me a skilled man
לַעֲשׂוֹת בַּזָּהָב וּבַכֶּסֶף וּבַנְּחֹשֶׁת וּבַבַּרְזֶל וּבָאַרְגְּוָן וְכַרְמִיל וּתְכֵלֶת	to work in gold, silver, bronze, and iron, and in purple, crimson, and violet fabric,
וְיֹדֵעַ לְפַתֵּחַ פִּתּוּחִים	and one who knows (how) to engrave engravings
עִם־הַחֲכָמִים אֲשֶׁר עִמִּי	with the skilled men who (are) with me
בִּיהוּדָה וּבִירוּשָׁלִָם	in Judah and in Jerusalem,
אֲשֶׁר הֵכִין דָּוִיד אָבִי׃	whom David my father prepared
7 וּשְׁלַח־לִי עֲצֵי אֲרָזִים בְּרוֹשִׁים	and send me cedar, cypress,
וְאַלְגּוּמִּים מֵהַלְּבָנוֹן	and algum timber from Lebanon,
כִּי אֲנִי יָדַעְתִּי אֲשֶׁר עֲבָדֶיךָ יוֹדְעִים	for I know that your servants know
לִכְרוֹת עֲצֵי לְבָנוֹן	(how) to cut timber of Lebanon,
וְהִנֵּה עֲבָדַי עִם־עֲבָדֶיךָ	and behold, my servants will be with your servants
וּלְהָכִין לִי עֵצִים לָרֹב	and will prepare for me trees in abundance,
כִּי הַבַּיִת אֲשֶׁר־אֲנִי בוֹנֶה	for the house that I am about to build
גָּדוֹל וְהַפְלֵא׃	will be great and wonderful
9 וְהִנֵּה לַחֹטְבִים לְכֹרְתֵי הָעֵצִים	And behold, to hewers, to those cutting the trees,
נָתַתִּי חִטִּים מַכּוֹת לַעֲבָדֶיךָ	I have given beaten wheat to your servants,
כֹּרִים עֶשְׂרִים אֶלֶף	cors twenty thousand,
וּשְׂעֹרִים כֹּרִים עֶשְׂרִים אָלֶף	and barley, cors twenty thousand,
וְיַיִן בַּתִּים עֶשְׂרִים אֶלֶף	and wine, baths twenty thousand,
וְשֶׁמֶן בַּתִּים עֶשְׂרִים אָלֶף׃ פ	and oil, baths twenty thousand

Solomon's letter to Huram (2 Chr 2:2[3]–9[10]) is divided into three parts by the word "behold" (הִנֵּה)[28] in 2 Chr 2:3, 9. First, an introductory remark (2 Chr 2:2) echoes the

---

28. It primarily functions as a particle to "call special attention either to a certain statement as a

previous relationship between David and Huram, appealing to the fact that Huram sent building materials to David in the past (1 Chr 14:1–2).[29] Second, the body of the letter (2 Chr 2:3–8) as Solomon's direct discourse to Huram deals with Solomon's request for skilled workers and building materials from Huram. The body begins with the discourse marker "Behold" (הִנֵּה), which draws Huram's attention.[30] In particular, the phrase "to make sacrifice before him" (לְהַקְטִיר לְפָנָיו) in 2 Chr 2:3 elucidates more specifically the preceding phrase "to sanctify [the house or temple] to him [YHWH]" (לְהַקְדִּישׁ לוֹ), which rhetorically constitutes an *explanatio* (epexegesis), that is, the addition of some words or phrases to clarify a statement or a reference already made.[31] Significantly, two other phrases obviously display Solomon's intention and plan for the construction of the temple. The one phrase, "I am about to build. . ." (אֲנִי בוֹנֶה) occurs four times (2 Chr 2:3, 4, 5, 8), in which the two successive verses (2 Chr 2:3, 4) reveal the rhetorical device *anaphora* (repeating the same phrase in front of them).[32] The other phrase, "send me" (שְׁלַח־לִי), occurs twice, which also represents an example of *anaphora* in 2 Chr 2:5, 6. The former phrase emphasizes Solomon's intention and plan for the building of the temple, and the latter stresses Solomon's request for the skilled workers and building materials for the task of temple building. Interestingly, the verb form in these two phrases shifts from the participle (בוֹנֶה) to imperative (שְׁלַח). It shows that after expressing his eager intention and plan to build the temple, Solomon requests the skilled workers and the materials from Huram. Third, the list of the wages of the laborers (2 Chr 2:9) enumerates Solomon's provisions for them. This begins with the discourse marker "And behold" (וְהִנֵּה). The enumeration of the provisions rhetorically utilizes the accumulation of nouns.[33] Accordingly, Solomon, sending his message to Huram, tries to persuade Huram to help him to build the temple.

Solomon, in his letter, briefly outlines what he needs for the construction of the temple.[34] The introductory remark (2 Chr 2:2) leads Huram to recall the previous relationship with David, including the fact that Huram sent David cedars to build for David's house in the past. The purpose of the construction of the temple is to worship YHWH, that is, to offer sacrifices before YHWH (2 Chr 2:3).[35] The Chr's

---

whole or to a single word out of the statement" (Waltke and O'Connor, *Biblical Hebrew Syntax*, 300). See also Arnold and Choi, *Hebrew Syntax*, 157–61.

29. For the relationship between Israel and Tyre, see Dillard, *2 Chronicles*, 21; Japhet, *I & II Chronicles*, 546.

30. See van der Merwe et al., *Biblical Hebrew*, 328–30.

31. See Lanham, *Handlist*, 75, 67.

32. Ibid., 11.

33. Bar-Efrat, *Narrative Art*, 216.

34. Solomon's letter to Huram (2 Chr 2:2–9) is much longer than the parallel in 1 Kgs 5:16[2]–20[6]. See Klein, *2 Chronicles*, 31.

35. Second Chronicles 2:2–3 is parallel to 1 Kgs 5:16[2], 19[5], which only mentions that Solomon was chosen as the temple builder by YHWH according to what YHWH had said to David his father.

unique materials (2 Chr 2:4–6, 8)³⁶ portray Solomon as a very eager temple-builder. Here, the Chr emphasizes that the house of YHWH will be exceedingly great and wonderful since "YHWH our God" is greater than all other gods (2 Chr 2:4). Two of Solomon's rhetorical questions highlight YHWH's greatness, pointing out that even the highest heavens cannot contain YHWH (2 Chr 2:5). Solomon indeed underscores that the God of Israel is incomparable. Second Chronicles 2:7 indicates that Solomon's servants will work together with Huram's skilled servants in cutting trees, drawing out Huram's attention again by using the discourse maker "behold" (הִנֵּה).³⁷ In the list of the wages of the laborers (2 Chr 2:9), the wage is enumerated. It is noteworthy that the initiative for the payments of the wages of Huram's servants is taken by Solomon in 2 Chr 2:7, not by Huram as expressed in the phrase, "according to all that you say" (1 Kgs 5:20[6]).³⁸

Solomon's intention and plan to build the temple is persuasively expressed in his letter to Huram. He attempts to obtain the skilled workers and building materials from Huram by appealing to the previous relationship between David and Huram. Solomon comments on the purpose of the temple as a worship place for offering incense, showbread, and burnt-offerings (2 Chr 2:3), displaying important continuity between the tabernacle and the temple, which is also expressed in the phrase "to make sacrifices before him [YHWH]" in the rhetorical questions of Solomon in 2 Chr 2:5. Solomon's intention to build the temple is well expressed, repeating the phrases "I am about to build" and "send me." Thus, Solomon's letter to Huram as his written speech functions to persuade Huram to help him build the temple.

---

36. In 2 Chr 2:8, I translate the infinitive construct (וּלְהָכִין) prefixed by ו as "will prepare." According to Joüon and Muraoka, "The infinitive with ל preceded by ו continues a preceding verb (or nominal clause) and virtually has the value of a finite form" (*Biblical Hebrew*, §124p.).

37. Second Chronicles 2:7 is parallel to 1 Kgs 5:20[6], which mentions the wages of Huram's servants as well as their collaboration with Solomon's servants in cutting the cedars.

38. In this letter, David's disqualification of the building of the temple and the peaceful time only given to Solomon's era (1 Kgs 5:17–18[3–4]) are not mentioned. The reason for this omission would probably be that the Chr has already indicated that David was not able to build the temple (1 Chr 17:4–6; 22:7–10; 28:2–3). See Klein, *2 Chronicles*, 32–33.

The Persuasive Portrayal of David and Solomon in Chronicles

Huram Sent a Letter to Solomon (2 Chr 2:10[11]–15[16])

2 Chr 2:10[11]–15[16]	
10 וַיֹּאמֶר חוּרָם מֶלֶךְ־צֹר בִּכְתָב	And Huram king of Tyre said in writing,
וַיִּשְׁלַח אֶל־שְׁלֹמֹה	and sent to Solomon,
בְּאַהֲבַת יְהוָה אֶת־עַמּוֹ	"In the love of YHWH to his people
נְתָנְךָ עֲלֵיהֶם מֶלֶךְ:	he has made you king over them"
11 וַיֹּאמֶר חוּרָם בָּרוּךְ יְהוָה	And Huram said, "Blessed (is) YHWH,
אֱלֹהֵי יִשְׂרָאֵל	God of Israel,
אֲשֶׁר עָשָׂה אֶת־הַשָּׁמַיִם וְאֶת־הָאָרֶץ	who made the heavens and the earth,
אֲשֶׁר נָתַן לְדָוִיד הַמֶּלֶךְ בֵּן חָכָם	who has given to King David a wise son,
יוֹדֵעַ שֵׂכֶל וּבִינָה	knowing wisdom and understanding,
אֲשֶׁר יִבְנֶה־בַּיִת לַיהוָה	who will build a house for YHWH
וּבַיִת לְמַלְכוּתוֹ:	and a house for his kingdom
12 וְעַתָּה שָׁלַחְתִּי אִישׁ־חָכָם	And now, I am sending a skilled man,
יוֹדֵעַ בִּינָה לְחוּרָם אָבִי:	who has understanding, Huram-abi
13 בֶּן־אִשָּׁה מִן־בְּנוֹת דָּן וְאָבִיו אִישׁ־צֹרִי	the son of a Danite woman and a Tyrian father,
יוֹדֵעַ לַעֲשׂוֹת בַּזָּהָב־וּבַכֶּסֶף	who knows (how) to work in gold, silver,
בַּנְּחֹשֶׁת בַּבַּרְזֶל בָּאֲבָנִים וּבָעֵצִים	bronze, iron, stone and wood,
בָּאַרְגָּמָן בַּתְּכֵלֶת וּבַבּוּץ וּבַכַּרְמִיל	in purple, violet, linen, and crimson fabrics,
וּלְפַתֵּחַ כָּל־פִּתּוּחַ	and to engrave all engravings,
וְלַחְשֹׁב כָּל־מַחֲשָׁבֶת אֲשֶׁר יִנָּתֶן־לוֹ	and to devise every device that is given to him,
עִם־חֲכָמֶיךָ וְחַכְמֵי	with your skilled men and the skilled men
אֲדֹנִי דָּוִיד אָבִיךָ:	of my lord David your father
14 וְעַתָּה הַחִטִּים וְהַשְּׂעֹרִים הַשֶּׁמֶן וְהַיַּיִן	And, now, the wheat and the barley, oil, and wine,
אֲשֶׁר אָמַר	of which he has spoken,
אֲדֹנִי יִשְׁלַח לַעֲבָדָיו:	let my lord send to his servants
15 וַאֲנַחְנוּ נִכְרֹת עֵצִים מִן־הַלְּבָנוֹן	and we will cut trees out of Lebanon,
כְּכָל־צָרְכֶּךָ וּנְבִיאֵם לְךָ	according to all you need, and bring them to you
רַפְסֹדוֹת עַל־יָם יָפוֹ	on rafts by sea to Joppa,
וְאַתָּה תַּעֲלֶה אֹתָם יְרוּשָׁלָםִ:	and you will take them up to Jerusalem"

Huram's letter of response to Solomon (2 Chr 2:10[11]–15[16])[39] is also divided into three parts by the discourse marker, "now" (עַתָּה, 2 Chr 2:12, 14).[40] First, the intro-

---

39. Second Chronicles 2:10–15 is parallel to 1 Kgs 5:21[7]–23[9]. For the differences between the two versions, see Klein, *2 Chronicles*, 32. For the study of Huram's letter to Solomon, see Ben Zvi, "When the Foreign Monarch Speaks," 214–18.

40. In 2 Chr 2:12, although the verb "to send" (שלח) is a *Qal* perfect form (שָׁלַחְתִּי), it could be translated as an "epistolary perfective," which "represents a situation in past time from the viewpoint

226

duction of Huram's letter (2 Chr 2:10–11) contains Huram's references to Solomon's enthronement and his blessing of YHWH.[41] Huram's utterance in 2 Chr 2:11 is reminiscent of the Davidic covenant through Nathan (1 Chr 17:11–12) and David's speech to Solomon concerning it (1 Chr 22:10, 12). Klein indicates that the description of Solomon's wisdom and understanding in 2 Chr 2:11 confirms that "David's prayer-like wish in 1 Chr 22:12 has been fulfilled."[42] The words wisdom and understanding (שֵׂכֶל וּבִינָה), occurring in both 1 Chr 22:12 and 2 Chr 2:11, are related to the prerequisite for the building of the temple.[43] The purpose of Solomon's wisdom and understanding is for the building of the temple in the context of Chronicles.[44]

Second, the body of Huram's letter (2 Chr 2:12–13) depicts Huram-abi as a skillful craftsman, one who could work with the assortment of materials for the building of the temple. Second Chronicles 2:10 refers to Huram's assessment of Solomon's enthronement, that is, God's love for Israel[45] and 2 Chr 2:12 describes Huram-abi as a skilled worker for the building project.[46]

Interestingly, 2 Chr 2:13–14, when compared with the parallel text (1 Kgs 7:13–14), contains very different information about the genealogy of Huram-abi. In Chronicles, Huram-abi's mother is a daughter of Dan and his father is a Tyrian; whereas, in Kings his mother is a widow of Naphtali and his father is a Tyrian. Huram-abi appears to be linked to Oholiab (a Danite) who had previously played a significant role in the building of the tabernacle.[47] In effect, Oholiab with Bezalel had constructed

---

of the recipient of a message," by employing a present progressive form. Waltke and O'Connor, *Biblical Hebrew Syntax*, 489. And the two words יוֹדֵעַ בִּינָה (lit. "knowing understanding") as the case of a noun synonymous with the verb shows an usage of "accusative of the internal object." Joüon and Muraoka, *Biblical Hebrew*, §125q.

41. Second Chronicles 2:11 is parallel to 1 Kgs 5:21[7]. Some words in 1 Kgs 5:21 ("today" and "over this numerous people" with the epithet of YHWH, "God of Israel, who made heavens and earth") are omitted in Huram's blessing in 2 Chr 2:11, while other phrases ("wisdom and understanding" and "who will build a house for YHWH and a house for his kingdom") are contained in 2 Chr 2:11.

42. Klein, *2 Chronicles*, 36.

43. Ben Zvi observes that this collocation ("the wisdom and understanding") does not occur elsewhere in Chronicles or the Hebrew Bible. See Ben Zvi, "When the Foreign Monarch Speaks," 216.

44. See Japhet, *I & II Chronicles*, 544; Klein, *2 Chronicles*, 37.

45. In 2 Chr 9:8, the queen of Sheba also states Solomon's enthronement as given by YHWH. Ben Zvi, "When the Foreign Monarch Speaks," 209–28.

46. With respect to the designation of "Huram-abi," Japhet mentions two possibilities, indicating two elements in this name, Huram and abi (lit. Huram and my father). The first possibility is to understand abi as "a title," not as the possessive suffix in the name, and the second is to conceive abi as "a dialectic form of ab." Accordingly, the former reads Huram as a master craftsman; whereas, the latter reads Huram-abi as an allusion to Oholiab who had the same -ab in his name (Japhet, *I & II Chronicles*, 544). Mosis also asserts that the element, -abi reminds of Oholiab, one of the skilled workers who made the tabernacle (*Untersuchungen*, 137).

47. Dillard believes that the Chr would have intended to make a perfect parallel to Oholiab by assigning Huram-abi a Danite (Dillard, *2 Chronicles*, 20). Tuell also asserts that "it is more likely that the Chronicler has made Huram-abi a Danite to parallel Oholiab, Bezalel's coworker in the construction of the tabernacle and its appurtenances" (Tuell, *First and Second Chronicles*, 124).

the tabernacle, the ark of covenant and all things belonging to the tabernacle (Exod 31:1–11).[48] Furthermore, Huram-abi is primarily depicted as an expert in bronze in 1 Kgs 7:13–14, whereas he is described as an expert in all sorts of materials such as gold, silver, bronze, iron, stone and wood, purple and violet linen, and crimson fabrics, and even all engravings in 2 Chr 2:13. Accordingly, in depicting Huram-abi as a craftsman who has various skills, the Chr appears to have intended to make the description of Huram-abi in Chronicles harmonize with that of Bezalel and Oholiab in the building of the tabernacle (Exod 35:30–35).[49]

Third, the passage includes the wages of the laborers as well as instructions regarding the carrying of the cedars to Jerusalem (2 Chr 2:14–15).[50] Huram confirms the wages of his workers by placing the list of the wages as the first words and before the verb (יִשְׁלַח) in 2 Chr 2:14. Accordingly, Huram's workers, after receiving the wages, cut the trees and bring them to Solomon.

Thus, Huram responds to Solomon's request. In 2 Chr 2:10, Huram declares that Solomon has been made the king of Israel due to YHWH's love of his people. Huram the king of Tyre knows YHWH's character, confirming a partial fulfillment of the Davidic covenant in 1 Chr 17. Furthermore, the depiction of Huram-abi in 2 Chr 2:12–13 echoes that of Bezalel and Oholiab in building the tabernacle in Exod 35:31–35.

Rhetorical Situation

The rhetorical situation of 2 Chr 2 functions on two levels: the narrative situation and the Chr's rhetorical situation. First, the narrative situation is that Solomon, deciding to build the temple, carries out the preparations for its construction. He conscripts a number of laborers, along with overseers. Then, since Solomon needs skilled workers and good timbers for the building task of the temple, he requests that Huram send skilled workers and building materials for the construction. The urgent situation of the narrative is to obtain the human resources and the materials for the building of the temple, which leads to Solomon's reported speech in a written message and the subsequent reported speech of Huram in a responding letter. The narrative audience is Solomon and Huram as the sender and receiver of each letter, and the preceding event at Gibeon (2 Chr 1) constrains Solomon's actual preparations in that he has already received wisdom and knowledge from YHWH to carry out the building project of the temple by seeking YHWH there.

---

48. For the linkage between Solomon in Chronicles and Bezalel in Exodus, see Dillard, "The Chronicler's Solomon," 289–300; *2 Chronicles*, 2–4; Japhet, *I & II Chronicles*, 540–41, 544–46.

49. Japhet indicates that "in view of the author's inclination to create an analogy between this text and Exod. 35, it is most likely that the change was influenced by the figure of 'Oholiab the son of Ahisamach of the tribe of Dan,' Bezalel's chief assistant in building the tabernacle" (Japhet, *I & II Chronicles*, 545). Interestingly, divine inspiration is granted to Bezalel in Exodus; whereas, it is not given to Huram-abi in Chronicles (Klein, *2 Chronicles*, 38).

50. Second Chronicles 2:15 is parallel to 1 Kgs 5:23[9], which explains how to convey the timber to Jerusalem.

On the other hand, the Chr's rhetorical situation is closely related to the Yehudite community. The Chr's audience in this unit would need to hear about the support of the neighboring nations such as Tyre, as they were living under the Persian Empire as a foreign nation. The Chr's exigence underscores the support of the Persian government for the Yehudites as the temple-centered community. Accordingly, the Chr emphasizes that Huram as a foreign king knows YHWH's greatness and faithfulness to David and his son Solomon as expressed in his letter (2 Chr 12–13), alluding to the Persian support for the Yehudite community in the Jerusalem temple and its worship.

In a broader sense, the Chr's exigence would be to explain why the Jerusalem temple is of significance to the Yehudite community as the Chr's audience. His rhetorical need is to provide the rationale for the centrality of the Jerusalem temple in the Persian period. Some in the Yehudite community may have raised a question concerning the legitimacy of the Jerusalem temple as the sole worship place in Yehud. Accordingly, the Chr, responding to the rhetorical need, provides the rationale for the significance of the Jerusalem temple.

The Chr exhibits the continuity of the tabernacle and the temple as the worship place in Israel by connecting the description of Huram-abi in Chronicles to that of Oholi-ab in Exodus.[51] Huram-abi is introduced as the skilled craftsman in the building of the temple, whom is the Chr links to Oholiab as the colleague of Bezalel in the building of the tabernacle. Accordingly, the Chr emphasizes that the Jerusalem temple replaced the tabernacle as the worship place in the past. Thus, in the situation of the Yehudite community under the Persian rule, the Chr attempts to persuade the community to recognize that the Jerusalem temple has the priority over any other shrines in Israel.

Rhetorical Effectiveness

The rhetorical effectiveness of this rhetorical unit may be considered by two levels of audience: the narrative audience and the Chr's audience. The whole assembly as the narrative audience is persuaded by Solomon's passionate preparation for the building of the temple, especially by the reported speeches of Solomon and Huram. The assembly accompanies Solomon to the Gibeon sanctuary and they recognize that God appears to Solomon there (2 Chr 1). Accordingly, when Solomon begins his actual preparations for the construction, the people are ready to help Solomon build the temple.

In his letter to Huram, Solomon requests the skilled workers and building materials from him, appealing to the relationship between David and him in the past and suggests his provisions for the wages of the laborers which Huram had sent to him. Accordingly, the reported speech of Solomon is persuasive to the whole assembly of Israel in that it demonstrates Solomon's careful preparations for the building of the

---

51. Boda indicates that the Chr's strategy is to legitimate the Jerusalem temple as the appropriate successor of the tabernacle (Boda, *1–2 Chronicles*, 242).

temple. In Huram's response letter to Solomon, Huram admits that YHWH, who loves Israel, cannot be compared to other gods, even Tyrian gods. In Huram's view, the people of Israel are God's people. Indeed, Solomon is God's chosen temple-builder.[52] For these reasons, Huram willingly provides Solomon with the skilled workers and the materials to build the temple. Thus, the narrative audience is also persuaded by the reported speech of Huram.

The Chr portrays Huram as a foreign king who knows the God of Israel, emphasizing that Huram recognizes YHWH's greatness as the creator of heaven and earth and His election of Solomon as the temple builder. The Chr conveys his theological intention to the Yehudite community by the mouth of a foreign king. This would have been very persuasive to the Chr's audience.

The Yehudite community in the Persian era needs to understand why the Jerusalem temple as the sole worship place has the priority over any other shrines in Israel. In this context, by linking the skilled worker Huram-abi to Oholiab the coworker of Bezalel, the Chr demonstrates that the tabernacle as the worship place in the past had been merged into the Jerusalem temple in the time of David-Solomon. The link between the Jerusalem temple and the tabernacle would have led the Chr's audience to recollect the continuity of the tabernacle and temple as the worship place in Israel. The Chr's audience would have been persuaded by his presentation of Solomon's actual preparation for the building of the temple, especially through the reported speeches of Solomon and Huram. The Chr legitimizes the centrality of the Jerusalem temple as the sole worship place in the Persian period.

In sum, through the reported speeches of Solomon and Huram, the Chr echoes the Davidic covenant concerning Solomon's enthronement and the building of the temple (1 Chr 17). The Chr emphasizes that Solomon's actual preparation for the building project carefully follows the same direction as David's according to what God had spoken to him previously. The Yehudite community, as a cultic community, will thus come to recognize the significance of the Jerusalem temple in Persian Yehud.

SPEECH AND PRAYER IN THE DEDICATION OF THE TEMPLE (2 CHR 5:2—7:11)

Solomon assembles a variety of the leaders of Israel, and the priests bring the ark of the covenant of YHWH into the house for YHWH in Jerusalem. By transferring the ark into the temple, Solomon completes the dedication of the temple. At this climactic time, Solomon makes a speech and a prayer (2 Chr 6:1–11, 12–42). Through the speech and prayer of Solomon, the Chr wishes to persuade his audience to discern that the Jerusalem temple is a testament to the continuity of the covenantal relationship between God and Israel in the Persian period.

---

52. See Ben Zvi, "When the Foreign Monarch Speaks," 217.

Rhetorical Unit

This rhetorical unit primarily deals with the dedication of the temple, which may be outlined in a seven-fold symmetry according to Dorsey.[53] By placing Solomon's speech concerning the dedication at the center of this unit, the Chr stresses the temple:

> Dedication of the temple (2 Chr 5:2–7:10)
>   a ark dedicated with countless sacrifices (5:2–10); begins: people are assembled
>   b glory of God fills temple (5:11–14); "for he is good; his love is forever"
>   c Solomon's prayer (6:1–2)
>   d CENTER: Solomon's dedicatory speech (6:3–11)
>   c' Solomon's prayer (6:12–42)
>   b' glory of God fills temple (7:1–3); "for he is good; his love is forever"
>   a' temple, court, and altar dedicated with multitude of sacrifices (7:4–10); ends: people are dismissed[54]

Dorsey rightly indicates the importance of the temple, proposing that the Chr arranges a literary *inclusio* in this unit.[55] In particular, the reference to "the glory of YHWH fills the temple" (2 Chr 5:13–14; 7:1–2) surrounds Solomon's prayers with Solomon's dedicatory speech as the center. However, Dorsey does not note the relationship between the ark of the covenant of YHWH and the temple, which is revealed in Solomon's following of David's attempt, showing that the narrative of David and Solomon is a united narrative. This narrative indicates that both of them attempt to transfer the ark of the covenant of YHWH and that they place it either in a tent (David) or in the temple (Solomon) at Jerusalem.[56]

The transfer of the ark of the covenant of YHWH (2 Chr 5:2–14) and the dedication of the temple (2 Chr 6:1–11) are closely linked. Solomon's prayer (2 Chr 6:12–42) follows the dedication of the temple, and it emphasizes the temple as the center of Israelite life.[57] It is noteworthy that Solomon's speech and prayer occupy 2 Chr 6 throughout. The last part summarizes Solomon's dedication of the temple (2 Chr 7:1–11).[58] This rhetorical unit deals with Solomon's successful dedication of the temple through his speeches and prayers.

---

53. Dorsey determines the boundary of this unit (2 Chr 5:2—7:10), excluding 2 Chr 7:11 as a summary statement (Dorsey, *Literary Structure*, 148).

54. Ibid., 148.

55. According to Kalimi, this literary *inclusio* "strengthens the ties among the passages from Kings and Psalms that make up Solomon's prayer in Chronicles. Moreover, the repetitions themselves stress the glory of the Lord in the new Temple and the rejoicing of all strata of the populace at the event (priests, Levites, singers, and all Israel)" (Kalimi, *Reshaping*, 299).

56. In this regard, Begg contends appropriately that 2 Chr 5–7 describes the climax of the ark narrative in Chronicles. In effect, the designation of the ark occurs nine times in 2 Chr 5. Begg, "The Ark in Chronicles," 139–40.

57. Williamson, *1 and 2 Chronicles*, 217.

58. According to Johnstone, there are several striking similarities between the actions of David (1 Chr 15–16) and Solomon (2 Chr 5, 7). Furthermore, 2 Chr 7:1–11 is the resumption of 2 Chr 5:2–14,

Rhetorical Strategy

The Chr primarily presents the rhetorical unit with Solomon's speeches to God and to all the assembly of Israel, describing the dedication of the temple in connection with the transferring of the ark of the covenant of YHWH into the innermost place of the temple (2 Chr 5).[59] Solomon's speech and prayer (2 Chr 6) speak of YHWH (2 Chr 6:3–11) and directly address YHWH (2 Chr 6:12–42),[60] the content of which is largely based on the Davidic covenant of the temple building and the dynasty (1 Chr 17). YHWH has fulfilled what he had previously said to David. As a result, Solomon sits on the throne and completes the building task of the temple. When Solomon finishes his prayer to YHWH, the temple fills with YHWH's glory (2 Chr 7). The Chr emphasizes the significance of the Jerusalem temple as the place of worship and prayer in Israel, and even as the meaning of the continuity of the covenantal relationship between God and Israel in the Persian period.

Solomon's Speech (2 Chr 6:1–11)

2 Chr 6:1–11	
¹ אָז אָמַר שְׁלֹמֹה יְהוָה אָמַר לִשְׁכּוֹן בָּעֲרָפֶל׃	Then Solomon said, "YHWH has said that he would dwell in the thick cloud
² וַאֲנִי בָּנִיתִי בֵית־זְבֻל לָךְ וּמָכוֹן לְשִׁבְתְּךָ עוֹלָמִים׃	and I have built you an exalted house, and a place for your dwelling forever"

---

displaying several similarities between them—"the sacrifices at the altar" (2 Chr 5:6; 7:2), "the inability of the priests to endure the manifestation of the glory of God" (2 Chr 5:14; 7:2), and "the praise of the Lord" (2 Chr 5:13; 7:3) (Johnstone, *1 and 2 Chronicles*, 1:331–32). In my view, the Chr appears to repeat the dedication of the temple intentionally because the Chr's theology culminates in the temple, which is the core of the Davidic covenant in Chronicles and symbolizes the covenantal relationship between God and Israel in the post-exilic period.

59. With respect to the installation of the ark (2 Chr 5:2), Johnstone contends that "the focus is on the vocation of the Israelites to holiness in the world" (Johnstone, *1 and 2 Chronicles*, 1:336).

60. See Beentjes, "Psalms and Prayers," 24.

³ וַיַּסֵּב הַמֶּלֶךְ אֶת־פָּנָיו	And the king turned his face,
וַיְבָרֶךְ אֵת כָּל־קְהַל יִשְׂרָאֵל	and blessed all the assembly of Israel,
וְכָל־קְהַל יִשְׂרָאֵל עֹמֵד:	and all the assembly of Israel was standing
⁴ וַיֹּאמֶר בָּרוּךְ יְהוָה אֱלֹהֵי יִשְׂרָאֵל	And he said, "Blessed be YHWH, God of Israel,
אֲשֶׁר דִּבֶּר בְּפִיו אֵת דָּוִד אָבִי	who spoke by his mouth with David my father,
וּבְיָדָיו מִלֵּא לֵאמֹר:	and by his hands has fulfilled (it), saying,
⁵ מִן־הַיּוֹם אֲשֶׁר הוֹצֵאתִי אֶת־עַמִּי	'From the day that I brought out my people
מֵאֶרֶץ מִצְרַיִם לֹא־בָחַרְתִּי בְעִיר	from the land of Egypt, I have not chosen a city out
מִכֹּל שִׁבְטֵי יִשְׂרָאֵל לִבְנוֹת בַּיִת	of all the tribes of Israel to build a house
לִהְיוֹת שְׁמִי שָׁם וְלֹא־בָחַרְתִּי	for my name being there, and I have not chosen
בְאִישׁ לִהְיוֹת נָגִיד עַל־עַמִּי יִשְׂרָאֵל:	a man to be a leader over my people Israel
⁶ וָאֶבְחַר בִּירוּשָׁלִַם	And I have chosen Jerusalem
לִהְיוֹת שְׁמִי שָׁם	for my name being there,
וָאֶבְחַר בְּדָוִד	and I have chosen David
לִהְיוֹת עַל־עַמִּי יִשְׂרָאֵל:	to be over my people Israel
⁷ וַיְהִי עִם־לְבַב דָּוִד אָבִי	And it was with the heart of David my father
לִבְנוֹת בַּיִת לְשֵׁם יְהוָה	to build a house for the name of YHWH
אֱלֹהֵי יִשְׂרָאֵל:	God of Israel'
⁸ וַיֹּאמֶר יְהוָה אֶל־דָּוִד אָבִי	But YHWH said to David my father,
יַעַן אֲשֶׁר הָיָה עִם־לְבָבְךָ	'because that it was with your heart
לִבְנוֹת בַּיִת לִשְׁמִי	to build a house for my name,
הֱטִיבֹתָ כִּי הָיָה עִם־לְבָבֶךָ:	you did well that it was with your heart
⁹ רַק אַתָּה לֹא תִבְנֶה הַבָּיִת	you surely shall not build the house,
כִּי בִנְךָ הַיֹּצֵא	but your son who shall come forth
מֵחֲלָצֶיךָ	from your loins,
הוּא־יִבְנֶה הַבַּיִת לִשְׁמִי:	he shall build the house for my name'
¹⁰ וַיָּקֶם יְהוָה אֶת־דְּבָרוֹ	And YHWH has established his word
אֲשֶׁר דִּבֵּר	that he spoke
וָאָקֻם תַּחַת דָּוִד אָבִי	and I have risen in place of David my father
וָאֵשֵׁב עַל־כִּסֵּא יִשְׂרָאֵל כַּאֲשֶׁר דִּבֶּר יְהוָה וָאֶבְנֶה	and sat on the throne of Israel, as YHWH spoke,
הַבַּיִת לְשֵׁם יְהוָה	and have built the house for the name of YHWH,
אֱלֹהֵי יִשְׂרָאֵל:	God of Israel
¹¹ וָאָשִׂם שָׁם אֶת־הָאָרוֹן	And there I have set the ark,
אֲשֶׁר־שָׁם בְּרִית יְהוָה	in which is the covenant of YHWH,
אֲשֶׁר כָּרַת עִם־בְּנֵי יִשְׂרָאֵל:	which he made with the sons of Israel

Solomon's speech (2 Chr 6:1–11)[61] as *epideictic* rhetoric may be outlined by his proclamation of the completion of the building of the temple (2 Chr 6:1–2), the praise to YHWH (2 Chr 6:4) with introductory remarks (2 Chr 6:3), God's election of Jerusalem and David (2 Chr 6:5–6), David's intention and Solomon's completion of the building of the temple (2 Chr 6:7–9), and the fulfillment of God's promise to David (2 Chr 6:10) with concluding remarks (2 Chr 6:11).

In this speech, there are repetitions of words and phrases. The temple is frequently referred to as "a house for the name of YHWH" (בַּיִת לְשֵׁם יְהוָה, 2 Chr 6:7, 10) or "a house for my name" (בַּיִת לִשְׁמִי, 2 Chr 6:5, 8, 9).[62] In 2 Chr 6:4–11, the word, "Israel" occurs eight times, "David" five times, and "my people" three times.[63] In particular, it should be noted that Solomon emphasizes God's fulfillment of His promise to David, echoing the Davidic covenant in 1 Chr 17. The fulfillment of the Davidic covenant concerning Solomon is based on divine authority.[64] Thus, the building of the temple is underscored as the fulfillment of YHWH's promise to David.

However, Solomon's speech is more rhetorical. Solomon proclaims that he has built YHWH an exalted house, a place for YHWH's dwelling (2 Chr 6:1–2).[65] In these verses, the thick cloud as YHWH's dwelling place is contrasted with the exalted house as YHWH's permanent dwelling place. This emphasizes Solomon's completion of the temple building as YHWH's new dwelling place.

In 2 Chr 6:3, the phrase, "all the assembly of Israel" forms a chiastic structure.

> And the king turned his face,
> and blessed *all the assembly of Israel* (כָּל־קְהַל יִשְׂרָאֵל),
> and *all the assembly of Israel* (כָּל־קְהַל יִשְׂרָאֵל) was standing

The structure indicates that the narrative audience of Solomon's speech is all of the Israelites. This verse describes the situation of Solomon's speech in the narrative context. Solomon turns to the assembly as they stand before him. Solomon is ready to make his speech to the Israelites.

In 2 Chr 6:4–9, Solomon recollects God's covenant with David, quoting the divine speech in the Davidic covenant regarding the building of the temple. In 2 Chr 6:4, Solomon praises YHWH. The two phrases, "by his mouth" (בְּפִיו) and "by his hand" (בְּיָדָיו) function as anthropomorphisms which stress the fulfillment of YHWH's promise to David by YHWH's actions.[66] Accordingly, when Solomon blesses YHWH,

---

61. Second Chronicles 6:1–11 is parallel to 1 Kgs 8:12–21.
62. Japhet indicates that 2 Chr 6 displays Deuteronomistic style. See Japhet, *I & II Chronicles*, 587.
63. Ibid., 588.
64. In Hebrew rhetoric, YHWH's authority, as the substitution for *ethos* in classical rhetoric, is "the driving force behind the assertive discourse." See Lundbom, *Hebrew Prophets*, 189.
65. In 2 Chr 6:2, the phrase, "I have built" (וַאֲנִי בָנִיתִי) is stressed by the emphatic pronoun "I" (אֲנִי); whereas, the phrase "I have surely built" (בָּנֹה בָנִיתִי) in 1 Kgs 8:13 is stressed by the infinitive absolute (בָּנֹה).
66. See Selman, *2 Chronicles*, 324.

he utters the fulfillment of YHWH's words, based on the Davidic covenant in 1 Chr 17:4–14. This fulfillment is further reinforced by Solomon's quotation of the divine speech (2 Chr 6:5–6), wherein it is stressed that YHWH chooses Jerusalem as the temple site and David as the king over Israel. The verb, "to choose" (לֹא־בָחַרְתִּי, וָאֶבְחַר) occurs four times in 2 Chr 6:5–6, which is arranged in antithetic parallelism (as expressed twice in the negative form and twice in the positive).[67] Since the day that YHWH brought Israel out of the land of Egypt, YHWH had not chosen any city or any person to build a temple (2 Chr 6:5). This recalls the Exodus and Solomon appears to have recognized the continuity between the Mosaic covenant and the Davidic covenant.[68] However, YHWH has anointed Jerusalem as God's chosen place for the temple and David as His chosen king over Israel (2 Chr 6:6). Thus, YHWH's election of Jerusalem and David is stressed in 2 Chr 6:5–6.

Solomon proceeds to speak of YHWH's selection of himself as the temple builder, pointing to David's disqualification as such (2 Chr 6:7–9; cf. 1 Chr 22:8, 28:3). This is irrespective of his father's good intentions for the task with the repetition of the phrase "and it was with the heart of David my father" (וַיְהִי עִם־לְבַב דָּוִיד אָבִי, 2 Chr 6:7) and the phrase "it was with your heart" (הָיָה עִם־לְבָבְךָ, twice in 2 Chr 6:8). Accordingly, Solomon expounds that YHWH has chosen him as the temple builder according to YHWH's word to David (2 Chr 6:9). In this context, Solomon's quotation of the divine speech (2 Chr 6:8–9) echoes Nathan's prophecy in 1 Chr 17:4–14 (cf. 1 Chr 22:7–10; 28:2–7).

Previously, YHWH declared that Solomon, instead of David, would be the builder of the temple. YHWH's word to David is fulfilled by Solomon's sitting upon the throne of Israel and his completion of the temple building. In 2 Chr 6:10, Solomon stresses that YHWH established what He had spoken (twice repeated; דִּבֶּר, דְּבַר), summarizing his speech with the statement that he now sits on the throne of Israel in place of David and has built the house for YHWH's name. In 2 Chr 6:11, the ark of the covenant of YHWH is placed in the temple.[69] The ark signifies the covenant of YHWH which

---

67. Second Chronicles 6:5–6, forming a parallelism, is lengthened from one verse (1 Kgs 8:16) to two verses. As a result, the Chr emphasizes God's choice of Jerusalem and David. Interestingly, Throntveit indicates that most scholars "recognize that the Chronicler's apparent addition of vv. 5b–6a was originally in the Kings account as well. It has been fallen out of the text due to homoioteleuton of להיות שמי שם as suggested by the LXXb" (Throntveit, *When Kings Speak*, 15).

68. Hill, *1 & 2 Chronicles*, 392.

69. In 2 Chr 6:11, the object of the verb "I have set" (שַׂמְתִּי) is "the ark" (הָאָרוֹן) instead of "the place of ark" (מָקוֹם לָאָרוֹן) in 1 Kgs 8:21. It is noteworthy that the omission of "the place" in Chronicles elicits a slightly different meaning, shifting the focal point from "the place of the ark" (the temple) to "the ark" itself. In the same verse, God made his covenant "with the sons of Israel" (עִם־בְּנֵי יִשְׂרָאֵל) in place of "with our fathers" (עִם־אֲבֹתֵינוּ) in 1 Kgs 8:21. Thus, it universalizes the designation of Israel by changing from the specific term "our fathers" to the general one "the sons of Israel." Furthermore, the last temporal clause, "when he brought them out of the land of Egypt" (בְּהוֹצִיאוֹ אֹתָם מֵאֶרֶץ מִצְרָיִם) in 1 Kgs 8:21 is omitted in 2 Chr 6. In this regard, the Chr appears to have stressed the covenantal relationship between God and the sons of Israel by extending the covenantal party of YHWH to the whole Israel, not merely to the ancestors of Israel.

He has made with Israel, beginning with the patriarchs (cf. 1 Kgs 8:21)—the phrase "the sons of Israel" (בְּנֵי יִשְׂרָאֵל) rhetorically shows a *metonymy*, as the substitution of a phrase to another, meaning "the people of Israel."[70] Accordingly, it seems that the covenant does not belong to any time frame, and it becomes a timeless and permanent covenant with the sons of Israel in Chronicles.[71] It is for this reason that the Exodus from Egypt is left out of 2 Chr 6:11.[72] The ark, referred to by the designation of "the ark of the covenant of YHWH," is the symbol of God's covenant, alluding to the previous covenant between God and Israel that was made at Sinai (Exod 19). Thus, it is appropriate that Japhet indicates that the ark containing the covenant tablets "signifies a continuum in Israel's history and the integration of its traditions: the covenant of Sinai represented by the ark is blended with the Jerusalem Temple and the Davidic dynasty."[73] Probably, the emphasis on "the ark" itself in 2 Chr 6:11, not "the place of the ark" in 1 Kgs 8:21, is meant to showcase the relationship between the ark and the temple. In this context, the close link between the ark and the temple is very remarkable in Chronicles, especially in the David-Solomon narrative. By transferring the ark into the temple at Jerusalem, Solomon stresses that the temple has become God's dwelling place. Solomon's speech in 2 Chr 6:10–11 stresses Solomon's fulfillment of the Davidic covenant, revealing God's faithfulness to David. The Chr emphasizes the fulfillment of God's promise to David, shifting from Solomon's ascension to the throne to the building of the temple and the installation of the ark in the temple.

In sum, since the day that YHWH brought Israel from the land of Egypt, He did not choose any city or any person (2 Chr 6:5). YHWH finally elects Jerusalem as His chosen temple site and David as His chosen king over Israel (2 Chr 6:6). YHWH also chooses Solomon as David's successor and confirms His promise to David by causing Solomon to sit upon the throne. Solomon, as the temple builder, has accomplished his role in Nathan's prophecy by completing the building task of the temple (2 Chr 6:9–11). Solomon refers to the fulfillment of Nathan's prophecy twice (2 Chr 6:4, 15). Accordingly, Solomon completes the temple building, recalling the Davidic covenant in 1 Chr 17:4–14. For the Chr, the dedication of the temple substantiates the Davidic covenant of the dynasty (1 Chr 17:11–14) and David's prayer (1 Chr 17:16–27). The installment of the ark of the covenant of YHWH in the temple (2 Chr 6:11) denotes the domiciliation of the ark as the symbol of YHWH's presence since the Exodus. The transfer of the ark into the temple appears to exhibit the link between the Sinaitic covenant and the Davidic covenant via the temple containing the ark of the covenant of YHWH. The Chr displays this link to the Yehudite community through Solomon's

---

70. Lanham, *Handlist*, 102.

71. Japhet points out that in Chronicles, "'covenant' (meaning the laws and commandments stipulated) involves the people in a timeless and eternally-binding commitment" (Japhet, *Ideology*, 82).

72. For the omission of the Exodus account in 2 Chr 6, see North, "Theology of the Chronicler," 377–78; Ackroyd, "History and Theology," 510–12.

73. Japhet, *I & II Chronicles*, 590.

Speeches and Prayers in Solomon's Narrative

speech. Thus, through Solomon's speech (2 Chr 6:1–11), the Chr emphasizes the completion of the temple building as the fulfillment of the Davidic covenant, which in turn portrays Solomon as an ideal king seeking YHWH.

Solomon's Prayer (2 Chr 6:14–42)

Second Chronicles 6:12–13 introduces Solomon's prayer (2 Chr 6:14–42). Solomon stands before the altar of YHWH before the whole assembly of Israel and spreads out his hands. The phrase "in the presence of all the assembly of Israel and spread out his hands" is repeated twice in these verses,[74] which implies that Solomon "has taken on a priestly role as a representative of the people."[75] At this moment, Solomon makes a speech to YHWH as a prayer, which begins with the description of God's character.

2 Chr 6:14–42	
14 וַיֹּאמַר יְהוָה אֱלֹהֵי יִשְׂרָאֵל	And he said, "O YHWH, God of Israel,
אֵין־כָּמוֹךָ אֱלֹהִים בַּשָּׁמַיִם וּבָאָרֶץ	there is no God like you in heaven or on earth,
שֹׁמֵר הַבְּרִית וְהַחֶסֶד	keeping covenant and steadfast love
לַעֲבָדֶיךָ הַהֹלְכִים לְפָנֶיךָ	with your servants who walk before you
בְּכָל־לִבָּם:	with all their heart
15 אֲשֶׁר שָׁמַרְתָּ לְעַבְדְּךָ דָּוִיד אָבִי	who has kept for your servant, David my father,
אֵת אֲשֶׁר־דִּבַּרְתָּ לּוֹ	that which you have spoken to him,
וַתְּדַבֵּר בְּפִיךָ	and you have spoken by your mouth
וּבְיָדְךָ מִלֵּאתָ	and by your hand you have fulfilled (it),
כַּיּוֹם הַזֶּה:	as at this day
16 וְעַתָּה יְהוָה אֱלֹהֵי יִשְׂרָאֵל	Now O YHWH God of Israel,
שְׁמֹר לְעַבְדְּךָ דָוִיד אָבִי	keep for your servant David my father
אֵת אֲשֶׁר דִּבַּרְתָּ לּוֹ לֵאמֹר	that which you have spoken to him, saying,
לֹא־יִכָּרֵת לְךָ אִישׁ מִלְּפָנַי	'there shall not cut off to you a man before me,
יוֹשֵׁב עַל־כִּסֵּא יִשְׂרָאֵל	to sit on the throne of Israel
רַק אִם־יִשְׁמְרוּ בָנֶיךָ אֶת־דַּרְכָּם לָלֶכֶת בְּתוֹרָתִי	if only your sons keep to their way to walk
כַּאֲשֶׁר הָלַכְתָּ לְפָנָי:	in my law as you have walked before me'
17 וְעַתָּה יְהוָה אֱלֹהֵי יִשְׂרָאֵל	And now, O YHWH, God of Israel,
יֵאָמֵן דְּבָרְךָ	let your word be confirmed
אֲשֶׁר דִּבַּרְתָּ לְעַבְדְּךָ לְדָוִיד:	which you have spoken to your servant David

---

74. It is emphasized in 2 Chr 6:12–13 that Solomon stood in front of the whole assembly of Israel and spread out his hands, referring to the same phrase twice (נֶגֶד כָּל־קְהַל יִשְׂרָאֵל וַיִּפְרֹשׂ כַּפָּיו). Between the same phrases, the bronze basin is described. Accordingly, Solomon stood on it and prayed to YHWH.

75. Hill, *1 & 2 Chronicles*, 393.

18 כִּי הַאֻמְנָם יֵשֵׁב אֱלֹהִים אֶת־הָאָדָם עַל־הָאָרֶץ	But will God indeed dwell with humankind on the earth?
הִנֵּה שָׁמַיִם וּשְׁמֵי הַשָּׁמַיִם לֹא יְכַלְכְּלוּךָ אַף כִּי־הַבַּיִת הַזֶּה אֲשֶׁר בָּנִיתִי:	Behold, heaven and the highest heaven cannot contain you, how much less this house which I have built?
19 וּפָנִיתָ אֶל־תְּפִלַּת עַבְדְּךָ	And you turn to the prayer of your servant,
וְאֶל־תְּחִנָּתוֹ יְהוָה אֱלֹהָי	and to his supplication, O YHWH my God,
לִשְׁמֹעַ אֶל־הָרִנָּה וְאֶל־הַתְּפִלָּה	to listen to the cry and to the prayer
אֲשֶׁר עַבְדְּךָ מִתְפַּלֵּל לְפָנֶיךָ:	which your servant prays before you
20 לִהְיוֹת עֵינֶיךָ פְתֻחוֹת אֶל־הַבַּיִת הַזֶּה	to have your eyes open towards this house
יוֹמָם וָלַיְלָה אֶל־הַמָּקוֹם אֲשֶׁר	day and night, toward the place of which
אָמַרְתָּ לָשׂוּם שִׁמְךָ שָׁם	you promised to put your name there,
לִשְׁמוֹעַ אֶל־הַתְּפִלָּה	to listen to the prayer
אֲשֶׁר יִתְפַּלֵּל עַבְדְּךָ אֶל־הַמָּקוֹם הַזֶּה:	which your servant shall pray toward this place
21 וְשָׁמַעְתָּ אֶל־תַּחֲנוּנֵי	And listen to the supplications
עַבְדְּךָ וְעַמְּךָ יִשְׂרָאֵל	of your servant and of your people Israel,
אֲשֶׁר יִתְפַּלְלוּ אֶל־הַמָּקוֹם הַזֶּה	when they pray toward this place,
וְאַתָּה תִּשְׁמַע מִמְּקוֹם שִׁבְתְּךָ	May you indeed hear from your dwelling place,
מִן־הַשָּׁמַיִם וְשָׁמַעְתָּ וְסָלָחְתָּ:	from heaven, and hear and forgive
22 אִם־יֶחֱטָא אִישׁ לְרֵעֵהוּ	If a man sins against his neighbor,
וְנָשָׁא־בוֹ אָלָה	and he takes an oath against him
לְהַאֲלֹתוֹ וּבָא אָלָה	to cause him to swear, and the oath has come in
לִפְנֵי מִזְבַּחֲךָ בַּבַּיִת הַזֶּה:	before your altar in this house
23 וְאַתָּה תִּשְׁמַע מִן־הַשָּׁמַיִם	then may you indeed hear from heaven
וְעָשִׂיתָ וְשָׁפַטְתָּ אֶת־עֲבָדֶיךָ	and act and judge your servants,
לְהָשִׁיב לְרָשָׁע	to give back to the wicked,
לָתֵת דַּרְכּוֹ בְּרֹאשׁוֹ	to put his way on his head
וּלְהַצְדִּיק צַדִּיק	and to declare righteous the righteous,
לָתֶת לוֹ כְּצִדְקָתוֹ: ס	to give to him according to his righteousness

24 וְאִם־יִנָּגֵף עַמְּךָ יִשְׂרָאֵל	And if your people Israel are smitten
לִפְנֵי אוֹיֵב	before an enemy,
כִּי יֶחֶטְאוּ־לָךְ	because they have sinned against you,
וְשָׁבוּ וְהוֹדוּ אֶת־שְׁמֶךָ	and they turn back and confess your name,
וְהִתְפַּלְלוּ וְהִתְחַנְּנוּ	and pray and make supplication
לְפָנֶיךָ בַּבַּיִת הַזֶּה:	before you in this house
25 וְאַתָּה תִּשְׁמַע מִן־הַשָּׁמַיִם	then may you indeed hear from heaven,
וְסָלַחְתָּ לְחַטַּאת עַמְּךָ יִשְׂרָאֵל	and forgive the sin of your people Israel
וַהֲשֵׁיבוֹתָם אֶל־הָאֲדָמָה	and bring them back to the land
אֲשֶׁר־נָתַתָּה לָהֶם וְלַאֲבֹתֵיהֶם:	which you have given to them and to their fathers
26 בְּהֵעָצֵר הַשָּׁמַיִם וְלֹא־יִהְיֶה מָטָר	When the heavens are shut up and there is no rain
כִּי יֶחֶטְאוּ־לָךְ	because they have sinned against you,
וְהִתְפַּלְלוּ אֶל־הַמָּקוֹם הַזֶּה	and they pray toward this place
וְהוֹדוּ אֶת־שְׁמֶךָ מֵחַטָּאתָם יְשׁוּבוּן	and confess your name, and turn from their sin
כִּי תַעֲנֵם:	because you afflict them
27 וְאַתָּה תִּשְׁמַע הַשָּׁמַיִם	then may you indeed hear in heaven
וְסָלַחְתָּ לְחַטַּאת עֲבָדֶיךָ	and forgive the sin of your servants
וְעַמְּךָ יִשְׂרָאֵל	and your people Israel,
כִּי תוֹרֵם אֶל־הַדֶּרֶךְ הַטּוֹבָה	because you teach them the good way
אֲשֶׁר יֵלְכוּ־בָהּ	in which they should walk,
וְנָתַתָּה מָטָר עַל־אַרְצְךָ	and send rain on your land,
אֲשֶׁר־נָתַתָּה לְעַמְּךָ	which you have given to your people
לְנַחֲלָה:	for an inheritance

28 רָעָב כִּי־יִהְיֶה בָאָרֶץ	Famine, if there is in the land,
דֶּבֶר כִּי־יִהְיֶה	pestilence, if there is,
שִׁדָּפוֹן וְיֵרָקוֹן אַרְבֶּה וְחָסִיל	blight and mildew, locust and caterpillar,
כִּי יִהְיֶה	if there is,
כִּי יָצַר־לוֹ אֹיְבָיו בְּאֶרֶץ שְׁעָרָיו	if its enemies besiege it in the land of its cities,
כָּל־נֶגַע וְכָל־מַחֲלָה׃	whatever plague, whatever sickness (there is)
29 כָּל־תְּפִלָּה כָל־תְּחִנָּה אֲשֶׁר יִהְיֶה	whatever prayer, whatever plea that is
לְכָל־הָאָדָם וּלְכֹל עַמְּךָ יִשְׂרָאֵל	for any man and for all your people Israel,
אֲשֶׁר יֵדְעוּ אִישׁ נִגְעוֹ וּמַכְאֹבוֹ	who know each his own plague, and his own pain,
וּפָרַשׂ כַּפָּיו אֶל־הַבַּיִת הַזֶּה׃	and he has spread out his hands toward this house
30 וְאַתָּה תִּשְׁמַע מִן־הַשָּׁמַיִם	then may you indeed hear from heaven,
מְכוֹן שִׁבְתֶּךָ	your dwelling place,
וְסָלַחְתָּ וְנָתַתָּה לָאִישׁ	and forgive and render to each
כְּכָל־דְּרָכָיו אֲשֶׁר תֵּדַע אֶת־לְבָבוֹ	according to all his ways, whose heart you know
כִּי אַתָּה לְבַדְּךָ יָדַעְתָּ אֶת־לְבַב	for you alone know the hearts
בְּנֵי הָאָדָם׃	of the sons of men
31 לְמַעַן יִירָאוּךָ לָלֶכֶת בִּדְרָכֶיךָ	so that they may fear you and walk in your ways,
כָּל־הַיָּמִים אֲשֶׁר־הֵם חַיִּים	all the days that they live
עַל־פְּנֵי הָאֲדָמָה	on the face of the land
אֲשֶׁר נָתַתָּה לַאֲבֹתֵינוּ׃ ס	which you have given to our fathers
32 וְגַם	And also,
אֶל־הַנָּכְרִי אֲשֶׁר לֹא מֵעַמְּךָ	to the stranger who is not of your people
יִשְׂרָאֵל הוּא וּבָא מֵאֶרֶץ רְחוֹקָה	Israel, when he comes from a far land
לְמַעַן שִׁמְךָ הַגָּדוֹל	for the sake of your great name,
וְיָדְךָ הַחֲזָקָה וּזְרוֹעֲךָ הַנְּטוּיָה	and your mighty hand, and your outstretched arm,
וּבָאוּ וְהִתְפַּלְלוּ אֶל־הַבַּיִת הַזֶּה׃	when they come and pray toward this house
33 וְאַתָּה תִּשְׁמַע מִן־הַשָּׁמַיִם	then may you indeed hear from heaven,
מִמְּכוֹן שִׁבְתֶּךָ וְעָשִׂיתָ	your dwelling place and do
כְּכֹל אֲשֶׁר־יִקְרָא אֵלֶיךָ הַנָּכְרִי	according to all that the stranger calls to you for,
לְמַעַן יֵדְעוּ כָל־עַמֵּי הָאָרֶץ	in order that all the peoples of the earth may know
אֶת־שְׁמֶךָ וּלְיִרְאָה אֹתְךָ	your name, and to fear you,
כְּעַמְּךָ יִשְׂרָאֵל	as do your people Israel,
וְלָדַעַת כִּי־שִׁמְךָ נִקְרָא	and to know that your name is called
עַל־הַבַּיִת הַזֶּה אֲשֶׁר בָּנִיתִי׃	on this house that I have built

³⁴ כִּי־יֵצֵא עַמְּךָ לַמִּלְחָמָה	When your people go out to battle
עַל־אוֹיְבָיו	against its enemies
בַּדֶּרֶךְ אֲשֶׁר תִּשְׁלָחֵם וְהִתְפַּלְלוּ	in the way that you shall send them, and they pray
אֵלֶיךָ דֶּרֶךְ הָעִיר הַזֹּאת אֲשֶׁר בָּחַרְתָּ בָּהּ וְהַבַּיִת אֲשֶׁר־בָּנִיתִי לִשְׁמֶךָ:	to you toward this city which you have chosen and the house which I have built for your name
³⁵ וְשָׁמַעְתָּ מִן־הַשָּׁמַיִם	then may you indeed hear from heaven
אֶת־תְּפִלָּתָם וְאֶת־תְּחִנָּתָם	their prayer and their supplication,
וְעָשִׂיתָ מִשְׁפָּטָם:	and maintain their cause
³⁶ כִּי יֶחֶטְאוּ־לָךְ כִּי אֵין אָדָם	When they sin against you, for there is no man
אֲשֶׁר לֹא־יֶחֱטָא וְאָנַפְתָּ בָם	who does not sin, and you are angry with them,
וּנְתַתָּם לִפְנֵי אוֹיֵב	and give them before an enemy,
וְשָׁבוּם שׁוֹבֵיהֶם	and they take them away captive
אֶל־אֶרֶץ רְחוֹקָה אוֹ קְרוֹבָה:	to a land far off or near
³⁷ וְהֵשִׁיבוּ אֶל־לְבָבָם בָּאָרֶץ	and if they turn (it) back to their heart in the land
אֲשֶׁר נִשְׁבּוּ־שָׁם וְשָׁבוּ	where they are taken captive, and repent
וְהִתְחַנְּנוּ אֵלֶיךָ בְּאֶרֶץ	and make supplication to you in the land
שִׁבְיָם לֵאמֹר	of their captive, saying,
חָטָאנוּ הֶעֱוִינוּ	"We have sinned, we have done perversely,
וְרָשָׁעְנוּ:	and have acted wickedly"
³⁸ וְשָׁבוּ אֵלֶיךָ בְּכָל־לִבָּם	if they turn back to you with all their heart
וּבְכָל־נַפְשָׁם	and with all their soul
בְּאֶרֶץ שִׁבְיָם	in the land of their captivity,
אֲשֶׁר־שָׁבוּ אֹתָם	where they have been taken captive,
וְהִתְפַּלְלוּ דֶּרֶךְ אַרְצָם	and pray toward their land
אֲשֶׁר נָתַתָּה לַאֲבוֹתָם	which you have given to their fathers,
וְהָעִיר אֲשֶׁר בָּחַרְתָּ	and the city which you have chosen,
וְלַבַּיִת	and toward the house
אֲשֶׁר־בָּנִיתִי לִשְׁמֶךָ:	which I have built for your name
³⁹ וְשָׁמַעְתָּ מִן־הַשָּׁמַיִם מִמְּכוֹן שִׁבְתְּךָ	then hear from heaven, from your dwelling place,
אֶת־תְּפִלָּתָם וְאֶת־תְּחִנֹּתֵיהֶם	their prayer and supplications,
וְעָשִׂיתָ מִשְׁפָּטָם וְסָלַחְתָּ לְעַמְּךָ	and maintain their cause, and forgive your people
אֲשֶׁר חָטְאוּ־לָךְ:	who have sinned against you
⁴⁰ עַתָּה אֱלֹהַי יִהְיוּ־נָא עֵינֶיךָ פְּתֻחוֹת	Now, O my God, let your eyes be open
וְאָזְנֶיךָ קַשֻּׁבוֹת לִתְפִלַּת	and your ears attentive to the prayer
הַמָּקוֹם הַזֶּה: ס	(from) this place

וְעַתָּה קוּמָה יְהוָה אֱלֹהִים 41	And now, arise, O YHWH God,
לְנוּחֶךָ	to your resting place,
אַתָּה וַאֲרוֹן עֻזֶּךָ	you and the ark of your might
כֹּהֲנֶיךָ יְהוָה אֱלֹהִים	Let your priests, O YHWH God,
יִלְבְּשׁוּ תְשׁוּעָה	be clothed with salvation,
וַחֲסִידֶיךָ יִשְׂמְחוּ בַטּוֹב:	and let your pious ones rejoice in the goodness
יְהוָה אֱלֹהִים 42	O YHWH God,
אַל־תָּשֵׁב פְּנֵי מְשִׁיחֶיךָ	do not turn back the face of your anointed,
זָכְרָה לְחַסְדֵי	remember your steadfast love
דָּוִיד עַבְדֶּךָ:	to your servant David
A. It is literally translated as "gates," but it means "cities."	

Solomon's prayer (2 Chr 6:14–42),[76] as deliberative rhetoric, may be divided into three parts. The first part includes Solomon's praise to YHWH and his supplication for the continuation of the dynasty (2 Chr 6:14–17). The second part comprises Solomon's request for YHWH to listen to the supplications toward the Jerusalem temple (2 Chr 6:18–39), in which there are diverse supplications: a general request for YHWH to listen to the petitions (2 Chr 6:18–21), petitions in the cases of individuals' oath (2 Chr 6:22–23), Israel's defeat in war on account of sin (2 Chr 6:24–25), drought that originated from sin (2 Chr 6:26–27), natural disasters (famine, pestilence, blight and mildew, and locust and caterpillar, 1 Chr 6:28–31), the foreigner (1 Chr 6:32–33), the

---

76. Second Chronicles 6:14–42 is parallel to 1 Kgs 8:23–53. Johnstone points to the significant differences between the two texts: (1) the phrase "walk in my law" in 2 Chr 6:16, instead of "walk before me" in 1 Kgs 8:25, indicates that "[t]he whole system of revelation is in place." Accordingly, "[t]he means of proleptically achieving and experiencing the harmony of the end-time is available to God's people"; (2) the phrase "will God indeed dwell with humankind on the earth" in 2 Chr 6:18, which has no parallel in Samuel-Kings, indicates that "the whole presentation from 1 Chronicles 1 is involved in the function of the Temple"; (3) the phrase "the significance of the Temple is eschatological and stands for all time" in 2 Chr 6:19, as omitted the word "today" in 1 Kgs 8:28; and (4) "God is entreated to hear not statically 'in' heaven, as in Kings, but dynamically as befits the one enthroned invincibly on the ark of the covenant, 'from heaven,' the macrocosmic counterpart of the Temple" in 2 Chr 6:22 and the following supplications. Johnstone, "Solomon's Prayer," 293–94. For the studies of Solomon's prayer in 1 Kgs 8, see Avioz, "The Characterization of Solomon," 19–28; O'Kennedy, "The Prayer of Solomon," 72–88; Knoppers, "Prayer and Propaganda," 229–54; Hurowitz, *I Have Built You*, 285–300; Eslinger, *Into the Hands*, 123–81. For the linguistic study of this prayer, see Talstra, *Solomon's Prayer*, 83–170. For a comparative study of the two versions of Solomon's prayer, see Beentjes, "Psalms and Prayers," 21–28; O'Kennedy, "Twee Weergawes," 155–77.

people of Israel in battle (2 Chr 6:34–35), and the captivity of Israel (2 Chr 6:36–40).[77] The third and the final supplication is a concluding remark (2 Chr 6:41–42).[78]

First, Solomon's supplication in 2 Chr 6:14–17 contains Solomon's praise to the covenantal God and his request for the continuation of the Davidic dynasty.[79] In these verses, it is stressed that God, who has sovereignty over the cosmos, has kept his promise to David. In effect, the verb "to keep" (שָׁמַרְתָּ, שְׁמֹר, יִשְׁמְרוּ) occurs three times (2 Chr 6:15, 16, 17), reinforcing YHWH's character as the covenantal God. YHWH has kept His promise to David (Solomon's succession to the throne and his building of the temple). Furthermore, He keeps the promise regarding the Davidic dynasty. Solomon utters what God has spoken to David (2 Chr 6:15), repeating the same phrase "you have spoken by your mouth and by your hand you have fulfilled (it)" in 2 Chr 6:4. Thus, the Chr depicts YHWH as the one who has kept His covenant in His steadfast love.

Second Chronicles 6:16–17 contains Solomon's prayer related to the Davidic dynasty, quoting the divine speech, which rhetorically forms *epexegesis* (*explanatio*) in that the divine discourse explains what YHWH has spoken to David by adding some words and phrases to clarify Solomon's utterance previously made.[80] Each verse begins with the word, "now" (עַתָּה) as the discourse marker, employing the vocative of the divine name, "O YHWH God of Israel" (יְהוָה אֱלֹהֵי יִשְׂרָאֵל). This invocation emphasizes the relationship between the petitioner and God alongside the urgency for the petition. The Chr provides the conditions of God's promise to David regarding the Davidic dynasty, introducing the promise as dependent upon the observance of the law, "to walk in my law" (2 Chr 6:16).[81] In 2 Chr 6:17, Solomon requests that YHWH's

---

77. Scholars have identified Solomon's prayer in 2 Chr 6:14–42 as having three or four parts, yet there are no significant differences between their divisions. For instance, Hill divides 2 Chr 6:14–42 into four parts: 2 Chr 6:14–17, 18–21, 22–39, 40–42 (Hill, *1 & 2 Chronicles*, 392). Boda views 2 Chr 6:40 as the conclusion of 2 Chr 6:22–39 (Boda, *1–2 Chronicles*, 265). Klein divides 2 Chr 6:34–39 into two sections, 6:34–35 and 6:36–39 (Klein, *2 Chronicles*, 86), but Japhet considers it as one section (Japhet, *I & II Chronicles*, 587).

78. Interestingly, this prayer seems to envisage a progressively downward situation of Israel. The petitions (2 Chr 6:22–25) are possibly in the temple ("in this house"). In the following verses (2 Chr 6:26–33), the petitions are towards the temple ("toward this place or house") as if Israel were driven out from the temple itself. In 2 Chr 6:34–35, Israel appears to be deported from Jerusalem, so they can only pray towards the city and the temple. Finally, Israel in exile can only pray towards the land, the city, and the temple (2 Chr 6:36–39). See Johnstone, "Solomon's Prayer," 293.

79. Second Chronicles 6:14–17 is Solomon's praise to the covenantal God, which is parallel to 1 Kgs 8:23–26. The differences between the two texts are: the words "above" (מִמַּעַל) and "beneath" (מִתָּחַת) in 1 Kgs 8:23 are omitted in 2 Chr 6:14; the phrase, "before me" (לְפָנַי) following "to walk" in 1 Kgs 8:25 is altered into "in my law" (בְּתוֹרָתִי) in 2 Chr 6:16; and the word "my father" (אָבִי) in 1 Kgs 8:26 is omitted in 2 Chr 6:17. Of these modifications, the phrase, "in my law" appears to be more significant than any other changes. As a result, the continuation of the Davidic dynasty depends on the Davidic kings' observance of God's law.

80. Lanham, *Handlist*, 67, 75.

81. In 1 Kgs 8:25, it depends on David's sons "to walk before YHWH." Schniedewind indicates that the Chr "does make fulfillment of the dynastic promise dependent on the obedience to written

word to David be confirmed. Thus, Solomon in 2 Chr 6:14–17 requests God's confirmation of the Davidic covenant, that is, the promise that the one who sits on the throne shall be established forever if he keeps God's commandments and ordinances as David has done.

Second, 2 Chr 6:18–40 is the body of Solomon's prayer; it indicates that the temple functions as the place of prayer. Having blessed YHWH for the fulfillment of His promise to David, Solomon draws YHWH's attention to "the prayer of your servant" (2 Chr 6:19). Solomon requests that God listen to his prayer, justifying why God should do so. It is emphasized that YHWH should take into account "the prayer which your servant prays before you" (2 Chr 6:20). Solomon requests that YHWH heed "day and night" (2 Chr 6:20) to the prayers in this place (the temple). Solomon legitimizes his request on the basis of YHWH's word, "the place of which you have said to put your name there" (2 Chr 6:20). In this supplication, the range of supplicants shifts from king (2 Chr 6:19–20), to king and people (2 Chr 6:21), to people (2 Chr 6:22–39).

The general request that YHWH listen to the petitions (2 Chr 6:18–21)[82] begins with a rhetorical question of YHWH's greatness. This question is a reminder that there is no place to contain YHWH, and that YHWH of Israel is exceedingly great. In this petition, there are a few key words frequently repeated. The noun "prayer" (תְּפִלַּת) and the verb "pray" (פלל) occur six times (2 Chr 6:19, 20, 21), which rhetorically form *multiclinatum* that means "the repetition of verbal roots in succession."[83] The noun "supplication" (תְּחִנָּתוֹ in 2 Chr 6:19, תַּחֲנוּנֵי in 6:21) occurs twice, and the verb "listen" or "hear" (שמע) five times (2 Chr 6:19, 20, 21). The phrase "toward this place" (אֶל־הַמָּקוֹם) occurs three times (2 Chr 6:20, 21), and the phrase "this house" (הַבַּיִת הַזֶּה) twice (2 Chr 6:18, 20), both of which emphasize the temple as the place of prayer. The word, "your servant" (עַבְדְּךָ) as the subject of the supplication occurs three times (2 Chr 6:19, 20, 21). Through these repetitions, Solomon requests that God listen to the prayers of the people when his servant and his people pray toward this place as God's dwelling place.

---

provisions. The command 'to walk before YHWH' was essentially a warning against serving other gods. Yet the injunction 'to walk in my laws' implies a broader set of commandments" (Schniedewind, *Word of God*, 160).

82. Second Chronicles 6:18–21 is parallel to 1 Kgs 8:27–30. The differences between the two are: the prepositional phrase, "with humankind" (אֶת־הָאָדָם) in 2 Chr 6:18 is not found in 1 Kgs 8:27, which makes the rhetorical question more generalized; the word, "today" (הַיּוֹם) in 1 Kgs 8:28 is omitted in 2 Chr 6:19; the phrase, "my name shall be there" (יִהְיֶה שְׁמִי שָׁם) in 1 Kgs 8:29 is changed to "to put my name there" (לָשׂוּם שְׁמִי שָׁם) in 2 Chr 6:20, with the reverse word-order, "night and day" and "day and night"; and the prepositional phrase, "toward your dwelling place, toward heaven" (אֶל) in 1 Kgs 8:30 is altered to "from your dwelling place, from heaven" (מִן־) in 2 Chr 6:21.

83. Lundbom, *Hebrew Prophets*, 178. Instead of the phrase "verbal roots," I will use the phrase "verb and its cognate words."

Speeches and Prayers in Solomon's Narrative

The petition of the oath between individuals (2 Chr 6:22–23)[84] is closely related to the jurisprudence concerning the tabernacle.[85] If one sins against one's neighbor and makes an oath before the altar in this house (protasis), God will judge them (apodosis). There are two words repeated in this petition. In 2 Chr 6:22, the word, "oath" (אָלָה) occurs three times, including its cognate word (לְהַאֲלֹתוֹ). In 2 Chr 6:23, the word "righteousness" (צַדִּיק) occurs three times, including its cognate word (לְהַצְדִּיק). Possibly, these two different terms form a sort of parallelism, indicating that YHWH will judge between the wicked and the righteous, when one makes an oath before the altar in this house. Significantly, this petition alludes to a judicial situation in Exod 22:7–13, wherein the regulations concerning disputes amongst individuals of the community are listed.[86] Solomon requests that God judge between the wicked and the righteous amongst the individuals that have lifted up an oath before the altar in this temple.

The petition of the Israelites (2 Chr 6:24–25) describes a prayer given at a time when Israel was defeated in battle on account of their sins against God.[87] If the people of Israel are defeated due to their sins against God, but then repent, confess God's name, and pray to God in this house (protasis), God will surely hear their prayer, forgive their sins, and bring them back to the land given to the forefathers (apodosis). Accordingly, the petition, which echoes the cyclical pattern of Judges (Judg 2:11–23),[88] emphasizes the repentance of the Israelites when they are defeated by an enemy due to their sins against God. Thus, Solomon requests that when God's people return and pray to God, he will in turn listen to the penitential prayer and forgive the people.

The petition of drought (2 Chr 6:26–27) outlines a prayer given at a time when drought occurs due to the peoples' sin against God.[89] This petition stresses that in the

---

84. Second Chronicles 6:22–23 is parallel to 1 Kgs 8:31–32. There are two differences between them: the word, "if" (אֲשֶׁר אֵת) in 1 Kgs 8:32 is altered to "if" (אִם) in 2 Chr 6:22; the phrase, "to condemn the wicked" (לְהַרְשִׁיעַ רָשָׁע) in 1 Kgs 8:32 is changed to "to give back to the wicked" (לְהָשִׁיב לְרָשָׁע) in 2 Chr 6:23. Japhet indicates, "The Chronicler guards against possible misunderstanding by replacing the juridical term" (לְהַרְשִׁיעַ) in Deut 25:1 and Exod 22:8 with a general one (לְהָשִׁיב) (Japhet, *I & II Chronicles*, 595).

85. See Boda, *1–2 Chronicles*, 261–63.

86. See Klein, *2 Chronicles*, 93; Japhet, *I & II Chronicles*, 594; Boda, *1–2 Chronicles*, 261–63.

87. Second Chronicles 6:24–25 is parallel to 1 Kgs 8:33–34. The differences between the two are: the temporal clause beginning with "when" (בְּ) in 1 Kgs 8:33 is changed to a protasis clause beginning with "if" (אִם) in 2 Chr 6:24; the preposition of the word, "toward you" (אֵלֶיךָ) in 1 Kgs 8:33 is altered to "before" (לְפָנֶיךָ) in 2 Chr 6:24; and the word, "to them" (לָהֶם), which is not found in 1 Kgs 8:34, is included in 2 Chr 6:25. This makes the petition more generalized, showing that the land given by God belongs not merely to ancestors but also to the people of Israel. Interestingly, Johnstone says that the Chr "is "more immanentist" in 2 Chr 6:24–25 in comparison to 1 Kgs 8:33 (Johnstone, *1 and 2 Chronicles*, 1:347).

88. In my judgment, this petition surely echoes the cyclical pattern in Judges: (1) Israel's sin following foreign gods; (2) the oppression of their enemies; (3) their repentance; and (4) salvation by Judges who have been sent by God (Judg 2:11–23).

89. Second Chronicles 6:26–27 is parallel to 1 Kgs 8:35–36. There is no difference between the two except for the word "heavens" (שָׁמַיִם) with or without the definite article ה (2 Chr 6:26 and 1 Kgs 8:35).

case of drought, when the people of Israel pray toward the temple and confess the divine name, God will indeed hear their prayer and forgive their sins. Even God will "teach them the good way" to walk[90] and send rain on their land given to God's people for an inheritance.[91]

The petition of natural disasters (2 Chr 6:28–31) deals with a prayer given at the time when famine, pestilence, blight and mildew, locust and caterpillar occur as a result of sin,[92] echoing the curses of covenantal disobedience in Deut 28.[93] In particular, in 2 Chr 6:31 the phrase "and walk in your ways" (לָלֶכֶת בִּדְרָכֶיךָ) emphasizes the obedience to God's commandments. This phrase reveals the purpose of God's response to the petition, which is to make the sons of men fear God and walk in His ways.[94] There are a few words repeated in this petition: the phrase "if there is" (כִּי־יִהְיֶה) occurs three times (2 Chr 6:28), which introduces each natural disaster in the land, and the word, "all (whatever or any)" (כָּל) occurs six times (2 Chr 6:28, 29 [four times], 30), which covers various sorts of disasters and prayers. These repetitions function to appeal to God. Thus, 2 Chr 6:28–31 emphasizes the sovereignty of God universally,[95] and Solomon requests that God would listen to the petition of God's people.

The petition of the foreigner who comes from a far land (2 Chr 6:32–33)[96] stipulates that when the foreigners come for the sake of YHWH's great name and pray toward this house (the temple), YHWH surely will hear their prayers. The purpose of this petition is to make all the peoples of the earth know God's name and fear God, as the people of Israel do. The phrase, "your [YHWH's] name" (שִׁמְךָ) is repeated three times (2 Chr 6:32, 33[twice]) in this petition, in order to stress YHWH's greatness. Furthermore, this greatness is expressed by some synonymous phrases such as "your

---

90. Japhet indicates that 2 Chr 6:27 has a new element of "the didactic function of divine forgiveness," in that God teaches his people "the good way" to walk (Japhet, *I & II Chronicles*, 596).

91. In particular, Lev 26:3–4 and Deut 11:13–14 indicate that rain is "the reward for obedience"; whereas, Deut 28:23–24, Jer 3:3, and Joel 2:23 point out that drought is "the punishment of disobedience." See Klein, *2 Chronicles*, 94.

92. Second Chronicles 6:28–31 is parallel to 1 Kgs 8:37–40. Differences between the two are: the word "his (own) heart" (לְבָבוֹ) in 1 Kgs 8:38 is changed into "his (own) pain" (מַכְאֹבוֹ) in 2 Chr 6:29; the verb "act (do)" (עָשִׂיתָ) and the word "all" (כָּל) before "the sons of men" in 1 Kgs 8:39 are omitted in 2 Chr 6:30; and the phrase "and walk in your ways" (לָלֶכֶת בִּדְרָכֶיךָ) is added to 2 Chr 6:31.

93. There are various curses of the covenantal disobedience in Deuteronomy—famine (Deut 28:48), pestilence (Deut 28:21), blight and mildew (Deut 28:22), and locust (Deut 28:38). See Klein, *2 Chronicles*, 95.

94. With respect to this phrase, Japhet contends that "God's ultimate purpose in his response is not only the deserved reward of the individual and the people, but to make them 'fear the Lord', know his ways, trust his justice and follow his commandments" (Japhet, *I & II Chronicles*, 597). See also Johnstone, *1 and 2 Chronicles*, 1:349.

95. See Johnstone, *1 and 2 Chronicles*, 1:348.

96. Second Chronicles 6:32–33 is parallel to 1 Kgs 8:41–43. There are a few differences between the two. The Chr incorporates two verses in Kings (1 Kgs 8:41–42) into one verse (2 Chr 6:32). The first clause, "for they will hear of your great name" (כִּי יִשְׁמְעוּן אֶת־שִׁמְךָ הַגָּדוֹל) in 1 Kg 8:42 is omitted except for the adjective "great" (הַגָּדוֹל). The singular verb form (בָּא) in 1 Kgs 8:42 is altered to the plural form (בָאוּ) in 2 Chr 6:32.

great name" (שִׁמְךָ הַגָּדוֹל), "your mighty hand" (יָדְךָ הַחֲזָקָה), and "your outstretched arm" (זְרוֹעֲךָ הַנְּטוּיָה), which place special emphasis on God's character. As the basis of the foreigners' petition, YHWH's greatness is emphasized. This underscores that God will listen to the petition of any foreigners for the sake of YHWH's great name, leading them to know God's name and fear God.

The petition of the people of Israel (2 Chr 6:34–35) deals with the prayer of those that are about to go out into battle against their enemies.[97] It is noteworthy in this petition that Jerusalem and the temple are emphasized. The Chr stresses that in the case of the Israelites' going out to battle, if they pray toward the city (Jerusalem) and the house (the temple), God will surely listen to their petition and maintain their cause (cf. 2 Chr 6:39).

The petition of the Israelites (2 Chr 6:36–39) deals with the case of the captivity of Israel.[98] This petition begins and ends with almost the same phrase, that is, "when they sin against you" (2 Chr 6:36) and "who have sinned against you" (2 Chr 6:39),[99] rhetorically forming an *inclusio*. The root of the verb, "to take captive" (שׁבה) occurs six times (2 Chr 6:36, 37, 38 [twice per each verse]), which seems to presume the situation of Israel's captivity. It is also noticeable that the petition toward the land is reinforced by the previous petitions: the petition toward "this house" or "this place" (2 Chr 6:24, 26), toward "this city" and "the house" (2 Chr 6:34), and toward "their land," "the city," and "the house" (2 Chr 6:38).[100] The Chr goes on to emphasize each of these three places. The people of Israel are meant to pray towards the temple at Jerusalem in Israel. Thus, it will lead to YHWH's listening to their petition and His forgiveness of their sins.

Second Chronicles 6:36 introduces the scenario of the Israelites' captivity, referring to the case of their captivity in an enemy land far off due to their sins against YHWH. The statement "there is no man who does not sin" more or less generalizes the case of the people's committing sin against YHWH. On the basis of this generalization, anyone who has sinned against God has the potential to turn back, pray to God, and confess his/her sin. Furthermore, the conditions of their petitions are comprised of the two protases: in the case of their captivity, "if they turn back. . .repent and make supplication. . ." (2 Chr 6:37) and "if they turn back. . . and pray toward. . ."

---

97. Second Chronicles 6:34–35 is parallel to 1 Kgs 8:44–45. The two versions are almost the same except for a slightly different change, that is, from "to YHWH" (אֶל־יְהוָה) in 1 Kgs 8:44 to "to you" (אֵלֶיךָ) in 2 Chr 6:34.

98. Second Chronicles 6:36–39 is parallel to 1 Kgs 8:46–51. There are some modifications in the two: the noun, "the enemy" (הָאוֹיֵב) in 1 Kgs 8:46 is not found in 2 Chr 6:36; the phrase, "in the land of their enemies" (אֹיְבֵיהֶם בְּאֶרֶץ) in 1 Kgs 8:48 is changed to "in the land of their captivity" (בְּאֶרֶץ שִׁבְיָם) in 2 Chr 6:38. Accordingly, the word, "enemy" was modified twice in this petition. Probably, for the Chr in the Yehudite community under the Persian Empire, the term "enemy" would be an inappropriate word to mention. Furthermore, the phrase, "to you" (אֵלֶיךָ) in 1 Kgs 8:48 is omitted in 2 Chr 6:38.

99. Johnstone, *1 and 2 Chronicles*, 1:350.

100. See Klein, *2 Chronicles*, 97.

(2 Chr 6:38) in the land of their captivity, which show the rhetorical device *anaphora* by repeating the same root word (וְהֵשִׁיבוּ ,וְשָׁבוּ) in front of the successive two verses.[101] The place to pray toward is gradually narrowed down from their land to the city and then to the house (2 Chr 6:38), three of which are clarified further by specific explanation (epexegesis [*explanatio*]).[102] In this context, Boda says that "penitential prayer toward the land, city, and Temple is essential to the resolution of the predicament of the exiled people."[103] It indicates that the Israelites should pray toward the temple at Jerusalem in the land of Israel. The apodosis which follows the protasis provides them with what they would gain from their prayer to YHWH, that is, God's attentiveness to their prayer and supplications, maintaining their cause, and forgiveness of their sin (2 Chr 6:39).[104] If the people of Israel are taken captive, but then turn back to YHWH with all their heart, repent and pray toward their land, YHWH will surely hear their petition, forgive their sin, and turn them back to their land. In addition, the summary of the previous petitions (2 Chr 6:40)[105] begins with a vocative, "Now, O my God" (עַתָּה אֱלֹהַי). The discourse marker, "now" (עַתָּה) functions as a changing marker of the verb form,[106] from the perfect verb form in the previous verse to the imperfect jussive. In this verse, Solomon requests that God would listen to their petitions from this place, using anthropomorphic associations such as God's eyes and ears.

Third, 2 Chr 6:41–42 includes the final supplication of Solomon as a concluding remark, which is composed of Solomon's request for the temple, the priests and people, and the anointed kings of David's house.[107] Second Chronicles 6:41–42 begins with the word "now" (עַתָּה), dealing with Solomon's last supplication (cf. Ps 132:8–10). In these verses, there are three specific supplications: for the temple, for the priests and people, and for the anointed kings of David's house. Significantly, the Chr uses

---

101. Lanham, *Handlist*, 11.

102. Ibid., 67.

103. Boda, *1–2 Chronicles*, 265.

104. Second Chronicles 6:39 abbreviates 1 Kgs 8:49–50.

105. Second Chronicles 6:40 contains the first phrase "your eyes being open" (עֵינֶיךָ פְתֻחוֹת) in 1 Kgs 8:52; whereas, the remainder of 1 Kgs 8:52 and 1 Kgs 8:53 are omitted.

106. According to Arnold and Choi, the word is "typically occurs through the compound form וְעַתָּה and usually indicates a shift in the argument or flow of the discourse without a break in the theme" (Arnold and Choi, *Hebrew Syntax*, 140).

107. Second Chronicles 6:41–42 is parallel to Ps 132:8–10. There are a few differences between the two: the vocative "O YHWH God" (three times) is emphasized in 2 Chr 6:41–42 in comparison to "O YHWH" (only once) in Ps 138:8; the priests put on "salvation" (תְשׁוּעָה) in 2 Chr 6:41 in place of "righteousness" (צֶדֶק) in Ps 132:9; the action of the pious ones is to "rejoice in the goodness" (יִשְׂמְחוּ בַטּוֹב) in 2 Chr 6:41 instead of "shout with joy" (יְרַנֵּנוּ) in Ps 132:9; and 2 Chr 6:42 is reworded with Ps 132:10, changing the phrase, "for the sake of David your servant" into "remember your lovingkindness to David your servant." As a result, 2 Chr 6:42 has two balanced requests with the emphasis on the first negative request, "do not turn back the face of his anointed." With respect to Ps 132, Williamson points out that the major theme of Ps 132 is "a prayer for David, whose appeal is based both upon his faithfulness in caring for the Ark (2 Sam. 6) and upon God's promise to him of an eternal dynasty (2 Sam. 7)" (Williamson, *Israel*, 64–65).

Speeches and Prayers in Solomon's Narrative

the phrase "the ark of your might" (אֲרוֹן עֻזֶּךָ) in 2 Chr 6:41, which is the same with the phrase "the ark in which is the covenant of YHWH" (אֶת־הָאָרוֹן אֲשֶׁר־שָׁם בְּרִית יְהוָה) in 2 Chr 6:11.[108] Solomon's speech and prayer close with the reference to the ark of the covenant of YHWH. The Chr's emphasis is on the covenantal God by closing the reference to the ark installed in the temple. The Chr, via the final supplication, intends to convey that the temple built by Solomon now becomes the dwelling place of the covenantal God by housing the ark of the covenant of YHWH. Solomon requests that God will lead the world to His peaceful reign through the Jerusalem temple, the priests experience God's salvation, the people rejoice in goodness, and the anointed kings of David's house be accepted by God due to His steadfast love to David.[109] The quotation from Ps 132:10 in 2 Chr 6:42 alludes to the everlasting covenant promised to David, and highlights the significant role of the Davidic covenant in the Chr's theology, revealing the covenantal relationship between God and Israel by employing the words, "your steadfast love" and "your servant David" (2 Chr 6:14; cf. 1 Chr 17).[110] In this regard, as McConville states, "prayer is to be the essential instrument in the continuing relationship between God and his people."[111] According to Boda, 2 Chr 6:41–42 summarizes the three key points of the Chr: a continuous desire for God's presence to be experienced in the Chr's day, the restoration of the Davidic line to sit on the throne of Israel as an independent nation, and that until the time when the Davidic dynasty is restored, the priests and the people of Israel would experience God's grace and goodness.[112]

In sum, Solomon alludes to Nathan's prophecy wherein YHWH promises David that his son will sit on the throne and build the temple.[113] The temple functions as a place of prayer, and Solomon's prayer functions to persuade YHWH to listen to the request of the petitioners who pray toward this house (the temple), the city (Jerusa-

---

108. Interestingly, Johnstone maintains that the term "the ark of the covenant" (2 Chr 5:2; 1 Chr 15:25), much more than "the ark of God," stresses "the communal aspect" (Johnstone, *1 and 2 Chronicles*, 1:333).

109. Johnstone indicates in 2 Chr 6:41–42 that Solomon requests three petitions: "for the Temple, that God will indeed express his reign of peace for all the world through it; for the priests and people, that they will appropriate for themselves the new life of harmony with God (key terms from the roots of 'salvation', 1 Chron. 11.14; 'joy', 1 Chron. 12.40; 'good', 1 Chron. 16.34); and for the anointed kings of the house of David (cf. 1 Chron. 11.3), that they may be accepted by God to play their role as his agents on earth" (Johnstone, *1 and 2 Chronicles*, 1:351).

110. See O'Kennedy, "Twee Weergawes," 163–68. Hill indicates, "Both Psalm 132:10–11 and Isaiah 55:3 stress the Lord's promise to continue David's dynasty" (Hill, *1 & 2 Chronicles*, 396). Day indicates that Psalm 132 was considered as reverberating through the two core motifs in 2 Sam 6–7, that is, a procession with the ark of the covenant of YHWH to the innermost place of the temple and the Davidic covenant (Day, *Psalms*, 78, 95–97). See also Hahn, *Kingship by Covenant*, 188–89. In effect, Ps 132 is the only psalm to refer to the ark explicitly. See Begg, "The Ark in Chronicles," 140.

111. McConville, *I & II Chronicles*, 129.

112. Boda, *1–2 Chronicles*, 266.

113. For the echoes of Nathan's oracle in Solomon's prayer in 1 Kgs 8, see Avioz, *Nathan's Oracle*, 87–100.

lem), and the land in the time of their affliction. Miller appropriately asserts that the prayers for help "*have as a primary function the effort to persuade and motivate God to act in behalf of the petitioner who is in trouble and needs God's help.*"[114] The rhetoric of the prayers for help is designed to persuade God to act.[115] Solomon prays to God as the representative of the people of Israel, so that the prayer for help is for all the people. Solomon's prayer functions as a means to lead to God's blessing and forgiveness of sin and it becomes a model for the people's prayer in various situations. The Chr has thus conveyed his message to his audience, encouraging them to pray to YHWH, facing towards the Jerusalem temple in the times of their affliction.

Rhetorical Situation

The Chr's rhetorical strategy is to portray Solomon's dedication of the temple by employing his speech and prayer, wherein the Chr emphasizes the fulfillment of the Davidic covenant (regarding the Davidic dynasty and Solomon's temple building) and the significance of the Jerusalem temple as the place of worship and prayer in the Persian era. This emphasis is closely related to the rhetorical situation, which may be divided into two levels: the narrative situation and the Chr's rhetorical situation.

First, the narrative situation is Solomon's dedication of the temple in the seventh month of a certain year of Solomon's reign (2 Chr 5:3). Solomon is about to complete the construction of the temple by bringing the ark of the covenant of YHWH into the temple. At this point, Solomon makes a speech to YHWH, announcing that "I have built you an exalted house," in front of all the assembly of Israel. He makes supplications to YHWH before the altar of YHWH, providing the people with the place of prayer towards which they could pray to YHWH. Accordingly, YHWH as the first narrative audience will hear Solomon's praise and supplications, and all the assembly of Israel as the second narrative audience will come to recognize that YHWH's promise to David is fulfilled since the building of the temple has been completed by Solomon. The preceding events that YHWH has appeared to David and has promised to him (1 Chr 17) constrain Solomon's speech and prayer in the dedication of the temple.

Second, the Chr's rhetorical situation is closely related to the temple built by Solomon. YHWH confirms His promise to David by causing his son Solomon to sit on the throne. Solomon has accomplished his role in Nathan's oracle by building the temple (2 Chr 6:9–11). Solomon twice mentions the fulfillment of Nathan's prophecy (2 Chr 6:4, 15). For the Chr, the dedication of the temple validates Nathan's prophecy of dynastic oracle (1 Chr 17:11–14) as well as David's prayer (1 Chr 17:16–27). In this context, the Chr's purpose is to emphasize the fulfillment of the Davidic covenant (dynasty) and the significance of the Jerusalem temple as the place of YHWH's

---

114. Miller, "Prayer as Persuasion," 356. Italics Miller's.
115. Ibid., 356–60.

presence, the place of the people's prayer, and even as the rationale of the future hope and renewal of the Davidic kingship.

Solomon's prayer links those who were living in the homeland and the *golah* community that returned to the Persian Yehud. The Chr stresses that the Jerusalem temple provides the scattered people (or the two communities) with the place of worship and prayer toward which they could pray to YHWH. Accordingly, the Chr emphasizes the centrality of the Jerusalem temple as a key factor to unite the scattered people around the Jerusalem temple. Furthermore, Solomon's prayer begins and ends with statements concerning YHWH's presence in the temple, reflecting the future hope and the continuity of the covenantal relationship in the Persian period. Though YHWH's presence cannot be restricted to the temple, the Jerusalem temple as the place of YHWH's presence is still the central place of Israelite worship and prayer toward which the Yehudites can pray. The Yehudite community and the scattered peoples have the ability to be united by the Jerusalem temple, in that both groups may share the temple as the key place of worship and prayer to YHWH.

The Chr's rhetorical situation is reflected in Solomon's petition (2 Chr 6:36–39), as the Chr looks back on the situation of Israel's captivity. In case of captivity due to their sin against YHWH, if the Israelites were to pray to YHWH, facing towards the Jerusalem temple and the land of Israel, YHWH will listen to their prayers and forgive their sin. The Chr emphasizes the key role of the Jerusalem temple as the place of prayer in Persian Yehud. The Chr's exigence is the place of prayer for the Yehudite community in the Persian period. The Chr's rhetorical need is the necessity of a place of worship and prayer within Persian Yehud.[116] Persian Yehud, as a provincial district under the Persian Empire, constrains the Chr's presentation of the significance of the Jerusalem temple. If the Israelites have sinned against YHWH, they will need a place of prayer to YHWH to confess and repent of their sin and thus receive YHWH's forgiveness. In this situation, the Chr stresses that if they pray to YHWH, facing towards the Jerusalem temple and the land of Israel, YHWH will listen to their prayer. Solomon's prayer occupies a large portion of text when compared to the record of the actual construction of the temple in the Solomon narrative, which "substantiates the argument that the Chronicler is making a theological statement to his own audience about the centrality of prayer in the life of the postexilic community."[117] Accordingly, the Jerusalem temple in the Chr's time is to be "a house of prayer like the first temple and so that postexilic Israel may experience God's 'salvation' and 'goodness.'"[118]

Through Solomon's speech and prayer, in this unit the Chr wishes to persuade his audience to recognize a partial fulfillment of the Davidic covenant and the significance of the Jerusalem temple as the place of God's presence and the place of the peoples' prayers. The Chr underscores that Solomon completed the temple building

---

116. See Boda, *1–2 Chronicles*, 265.
117. Hill, *1 & 2 Chronicles*, 393.
118. Ibid., 393.

and dedicated it to YHWH as the place of worship and prayer, and he points to the continuity of the covenantal relationship between God and the people of Israel by indicating that the people can pray to YHWH, towards the Jerusalem temple, as a symbol of this relationship in the Persian period.

Rhetorical Effectiveness

This rhetorical effectiveness of Solomon's speech and prayer in 2 Chr 5:2—7:11 may be assessed according to the two levels of audience, that is, the narrative audience and the Chr's audience. First, the whole assembly as the narrative audience is persuaded by Solomon's speech and prayer. In the narrative situation of the dedication of the temple, the Chr portrays the Jerusalem temple as the place of God's presence, as well as that of the people's prayer. Solomon's speech and prayer function as an indication of a partial fulfillment of the Davidic covenant in the narrative context. According to Williamson, a key theme in 1 Chr 17:22 and 28–29 is the dedication of the temple, revealing a partial fulfillment of God's promise to David regarding his house (dynasty). Furthermore, Solomon requests that God will continue to fulfill the Davidic covenant by establishing the Davidic dynasty forever (2 Chr 6:16–17).[119] It is not surprising that the Chr emphasizes the fulfillment of the Davidic covenant in this unit throughout Solomon's speech and prayer.

Solomon's supplication in dedicating the temple (2 Chr 6:18–39) legitimizes the Jerusalem temple as the place of prayer on the basis of YHWH's word, "the place of which you have said to put your name there" (2 Chr 6:20). Solomon persuades YHWH to listen to the peoples' prayers toward this place (temple), expanding the range of the supplicants from king (2 Chr 6:19-20), to king and God's people (2 Chr 6:21), and to the Israelites as God's people (2 Chr 6:22-39). Solomon encourages the assembly to pray towards the Jerusalem temple and the land of Israel to resolve their petitions. Solomon's supplication functions to exhort the people of Israel in any afflicted times to pray to YHWH, facing towards the Jerusalem temple. In turn, YHWH will surely answer their prayers.

Second, the Yehudite community as the Chr's audience is persuaded by Solomon's speech and prayer in this unit, which reinforces the role of the Jerusalem temple as the place of prayer in the Persian period. In this context, Boda indicates properly that the Chr reminds his audience of "Solomon's role in the development of oral worship," accentuating the temple's function "as a place of prayer for the people of God, as well as for the nations caught in a variety of predicaments."[120] The Jerusalem temple also reveals the continuity of the covenantal relationship between God and Israel, in that the temple contains the ark and the tabernacle as the symbols of the Sinaitic

---

119. Williamson, *1 and 2 Chronicles*, 217. This promise is a significant theme in Ps 132:8–9 (cf. 2 Chr 6:41–42).

120. Boda, *1–2 Chronicles*, 261.

covenant. Hill also states, "Through prayer (whether praise, confession, petition, or intercession) Israel will maintain her covenant relationship with Yahweh."[121]

Through Solomon's speech (2 Chr 6:1–11), the Chr argues for the completion of the temple building as the fulfillment of God's promise to David regarding the dynasty and the temple. Through Solomon's prayer (2 Chr 6:12–42), the Chr contends that YHWH will listen to the requests of the petitioners who pray toward this house (the temple), the city (Jerusalem), and the land of Israel in the time of their affliction, which extends his audience to later generations. In the Chr's description of the dedication of the temple, Solomon prays to YHWH as the representative of the people of Israel, indicating the function of prayer as a means to lead to God's blessing and forgiveness of sin. In this way, Solomon's prayer indeed provides a model supplication for the Yehudites in the Persian period.

Significantly, the Chr arranges Solomon's speech and prayer by ending with the same reference to the ark of the covenant of YHWH installed in the temple (2 Chr 6:11, 41). This reveals the continuity of the covenantal relationship between YHWH and Israel through the Jerusalem temple as the place of prayer in the Persian period. The Chr exhibits this continuity by the Jerusalem temple. Through Solomon's speech and prayer, the Chr glorifies the covenantal God who has made covenants with Israel. Thus, the Chr persuades his audience to trust in the covenantal God in their situation under the Persian Empire, directing them pray to God towards the Jerusalem temple in the time of their affliction.

The dedication of the temple reveals the continuity of the covenantal relationship between God and God's people, despite that such continuity appears to have been broken by the exile. This continuity has already been indicated by the ark of the covenant as the symbol of the Sinaitic covenant being combined with the temple and the Davidic dynasty.[122] Furthermore, the ark is combined with the tent of meeting, which is temporarily set aside by David (1 Chr 16:37–42).[123] Through the emphasis on the temple combined with the ark and the tabernacle, the Chr emphasizes that the covenantal relationship between God and Israel as God's people continues to operate in the Persian period, though the relationship appears to have broken by the exile. The Chr, through Solomon's speech and prayer, portrays Solomon as "the possessor of the tablets of the law"[124] and persuades his audience to recognize that the relationship is still valid through the Jerusalem temple. They must believe that the covenantal God is still working amongst them in the Persian period.

---

121. Hill, *1 & 2 Chronicles*, 392.

122. Japhet in 2 Chr 6:10–11 refers to the integration of these covenant traditions: "the covenant of Sinai represented by the ark is blended with the Jerusalem Temple and the Davidic dynasty" (Japhet, *I & II Chronicles*, 590).

123. According to Johnstone, the ark and tabernacle are "reunited: the ark is fetched from Zion; the tabernacle and all its furnishings are simultaneously collected from Gibeon" (Johnstone, *1 and 2 Chronicles*, 1:333).

124. Widengren, "King and Covenant," 9.

THE DIVINE SPEECH IN GOD'S ACCEPTANCE OF THE TEMPLE (2 CHR 7:12–22)

When Solomon finishes his prayer at the dedication of the temple, fire comes down from the heavens and the glory of YHWH fills the temple. All the Israelites see this and they praise YHWH (2 Chr 7:1–3). Solomon and the Israelites offer sacrifices before YHWH (2 Chr 7:4–7) and celebrate the feast for seven days (2 Chr 7:8–10). Solomon successfully completes all the construction of the temple and his house (2 Chr 7:11). That night, God appears to Solomon and speaks to him (2 Chr 7:12–22). The divine speech as a key discourse in Chronicles is of significance, overshadowing the following narratives (2 Chr 10–36). The focus of the divine speech is on the successive four verbs: "humble themselves, pray, seek God's face, and turn from their wicked ways" (2 Chr 7:14), which indicate that the people of Israel should be faithful to YHWH. The direct discourse of YHWH instructs the Chr's audience to seek YHWH and to keep His commandments and ordinances.

Rhetorical Unit

The rhetorical unit deals with God's appearance to Solomon (2 Chr 7:12–22), which is a response to Solomon's prayer in the dedication of the temple. It is noteworthy that this unit as the divine speech overshadows the following narratives in 2 Chronicles.[125] YHWH's speech is divided into two parts, categorized by those being addressed within the speech: YHWH speaks to Solomon (2 Chr 7:12–18) and then to the people (2 Chr 7:19–22), which may be outlined as follows.[126]

> The Divine Speech (2 Chr 7:12–22)
>
> To Solomon (7:12–18)
>   If they ... God would hear, forgive, and heal (7:13–16)
>   God's covenant with David (7:17–18)
>
> To the People (2 Chr 7:19–22)
>   If they ... God would pluck them from the land and this house (7:19–21)
>   They abandoned God who brought their ancestors

---

125. Dillard, "Reward and Punishment," 164–72.
126. Dillard, "Literary Structure," 86–90. Kalimi also provides a brief outline of the structure of 2 Chr 7:12–22 (Kalimi, *Reshaping*, 224).

> Divine response (7:11–22)
>   God speaks to Solomon (7:12–18)
>   Eyes open; hear and forgive (7:13–16)
>   Promises to David (7:17–18)
>   God speaks to the people (7:19–22)
>   Choice of Jerusalem (7:19–21)
>   Exodus (7:22)

from the land of Egypt (7:22)

This unit demonstrates that God will hear the prayers of the people, facing towards the Jerusalem temple, if God's people follow certain conditions (to humble themselves, pray, seek God's face, and turn from their wicked ways [2 Chr 7:14]); if they do not follow these conditions, they will be plucked from the land.

Rhetorical Strategy

The Chr, through YHWH's speech to Solomon, stresses YHWH's permanent choice of the temple as the worship place (for sacrifice and prayer, 2 Chr 7:12–16) and the everlasting covenant of Davidic dynasty and Israel (2 Chr 7:17–22).[127] The temple exhibits the covenantal relationship between God and Israel in that the people of Israel are called by YHWH's name (2 Chr 7:14) and YHWH will be attentive to their prayer to the temple (2 Chr 7:16).[128] Thus, the Chr legitimizes the centrality of the Jerusalem temple as the sole worship place (for sacrifice and prayer) in the Persian period.

---

127. Boda, *1–2 Chronicles*, 271.
128. Ibid., 273.

The Persuasive Portrayal of David and Solomon in Chronicles
The Divine Speech to Solomon (2 Chr 7:12–22)

2 Chr 7:12–22	
¹² וַיֵּרָא יְהוָה אֶל־שְׁלֹמֹה בַּלָּיְלָה	And YHWH appeared to Solomon in the night
וַיֹּאמֶר לוֹ שָׁמַעְתִּי אֶת־תְּפִלָּתֶךָ	and said to him, "I have heard your prayer
וּבָחַרְתִּי בַּמָּקוֹם הַזֶּה לִי	and I have chosen this place for myself
לְבֵית זָבַח:	as a house of sacrifice
¹³ הֵן אֶעֱצֹר הַשָּׁמַיִם וְלֹא־יִהְיֶה מָטָר	If I shut up the heavens and there is no rain,
וְהֵן־אֲצַוֶּה עַל־חָגָב לֶאֱכוֹל הָאָרֶץ	and if I command the locust to devour the land,
וְאִם־אֲשַׁלַּח דֶּבֶר בְּעַמִּי:	and if I send pestilence among my people,
¹⁴ וְיִכָּנְעוּ עַמִּי אֲשֶׁר נִקְרָא־שְׁמִי עֲלֵיהֶם וְיִתְפַּלְלוּ וִיבַקְשׁוּ פָנַי	and (if) my people who are called by my name humble themselves, and pray, and seek my face,
וְיָשֻׁבוּ מִדַּרְכֵיהֶם הָרָעִים	and turn back from their evil ways
וַאֲנִי אֶשְׁמַע מִן־הַשָּׁמַיִם	then I will hear from heaven,
וְאֶסְלַח לְחַטָּאתָם	and will forgive their sin,
וְאֶרְפָּא אֶת־אַרְצָם:	and will heal their land
¹⁵ עַתָּה עֵינַי יִהְיוּ פְתֻחוֹת	Now, my eyes will be open
וְאָזְנַי קַשֻּׁבוֹת לִתְפִלַּת הַמָּקוֹם הַזֶּה:	and my ears attentive to the prayer of this place
¹⁶ וְעַתָּה בָּחַרְתִּי	And now I have chosen
וְהִקְדַּשְׁתִּי אֶת־הַבַּיִת הַזֶּה	and consecrated this house
לִהְיוֹת־שְׁמִי שָׁם עַד־עוֹלָם	to have my name there forever,
וְהָיוּ עֵינַי וְלִבִּי שָׁם	and my eyes and my heart will be there
כָּל־הַיָּמִים:	all the days
¹⁷ וְאַתָּה אִם־תֵּלֵךְ לְפָנַי	And (as for) you, if you walk before me
כַּאֲשֶׁר הָלַךְ דָּוִיד אָבִיךָ וְלַעֲשׂוֹת	as David your father walked, even to do
כְּכֹל אֲשֶׁר צִוִּיתִיךָ	according to all that I have commanded you,
וְחֻקַּי וּמִשְׁפָּטַי	and my statutes and my ordinances
תִּשְׁמוֹר:	you will keep
¹⁸ וַהֲקִימוֹתִי אֵת כִּסֵּא מַלְכוּתֶךָ	then I will establish the throne of your kingdom,
כַּאֲשֶׁר כָּרַתִּי לְדָוִיד אָבִיךָ	as I covenanted with David your father,
לֵאמֹר לֹא־יִכָּרֵת לְךָ אִישׁ	saying, 'there shall not be cut off to you a man,
מוֹשֵׁל בְּיִשְׂרָאֵל:	a ruler in Israel'

¹⁹ וְאִם־תְּשׁוּבוּן אַתֶּם	But if you turn aside
וַעֲזַבְתֶּם חֻקּוֹתַי וּמִצְוֹתַי	and forsake my statutes and my commandments that I have set before you
אֲשֶׁר נָתַתִּי לִפְנֵיכֶם	and go and serve other gods
וַהֲלַכְתֶּם וַעֲבַדְתֶּם אֱלֹהִים אֲחֵרִים וְהִשְׁתַּחֲוִיתֶם לָהֶם:	and worship them
²⁰ וּנְתַשְׁתִּים מֵעַל אַדְמָתִי	then I will pluck them up from my land
אֲשֶׁר נָתַתִּי לָהֶם וְאֶת־הַבַּיִת הַזֶּה	that I have given to them,
אֲשֶׁר הִקְדַּשְׁתִּי	and this house that I have consecrated
לִשְׁמִי	for my name
אַשְׁלִיךְ מֵעַל פָּנָי	I will cast from my presence,
וְאֶתְּנֶנּוּ לְמָשָׁל וְלִשְׁנִינָה	and I will make it a proverb and a byword
בְּכָל־הָעַמִּים:	among all peoples
²¹ וְהַבַּיִת הַזֶּה אֲשֶׁר הָיָה עֶלְיוֹן	And as for this house that has been exalted,
לְכָל־עֹבֵר עָלָיו יִשֹּׁם	everyone passing by it will be astonished,
וְאָמַר בַּמֶּה עָשָׂה יְהוָה כָּכָה	and he will say, "Why has YHWH done thus
לָאָרֶץ הַזֹּאת וְלַבַּיִת הַזֶּה:	to this land and to this house?"
²² וְאָמְרוּ עַל אֲשֶׁר עָזְבוּ	And they will say, "Because they have forsaken
אֶת־יְהוָה אֱלֹהֵי אֲבֹתֵיהֶם	YHWH God of their fathers,
אֲשֶׁר הוֹצִיאָם מֵאֶרֶץ מִצְרַיִם	who brought them from the land of Egypt,
וַיַּחֲזִיקוּ בֵּאלֹהִים אֲחֵרִים	and they seized other gods,
וַיִּשְׁתַּחֲווּ לָהֶם וַיַּעַבְדוּם	and worshiped them and served them,
עַל־כֵּן	therefore,
הֵבִיא עֲלֵיהֶם אֵת כָּל־הָרָעָה הַזֹּאת:	he has brought all this adversity on them"

The divine speech (2 Chr 7:12–22)[129] as deliberative rhetoric deals with God's appearance to Solomon, which is composed of two parts: God's speech to Solomon (2 Chr 7:12–18) and to the people (2 Chr 7:19–22). The former part focuses on the conditions of prospering (2 Chr 7:12–16)[130] and of the promise of the Davidic dynasty (2

---

129. Second Chronicles 7:12–22 is parallel to 1 Kgs 9:2–9.

130. Second Chronicles 7:12–16 is longer than the parallel text (1 Kg 9:2–3). The differences between them are: the phrase, "a second time, as he had appeared to him at Gibeon" in 1 Kgs 9:2 is briefly changed to "in the night" in 2 Chr 7:12 (Cf. 2 Chr 1:7a has the phrase, "in that night" in the depiction of God's first appearance to Solomon); 1 Kgs 9:3a is taken into 2 Chr 7:12a; the phrase, "and your supplication, which you have made before me" in 1 Kgs 9:3 is omitted in 2 Chr 7:12; the phrase, "I have consecrated this house that you have built to put my name there forever, and my eyes and my heart will be there all the days" in 1 Kgs 9:3b is taken into 2 Chr 7:16, with the addition of the phrase "And now I have chosen." The verb "to put" in 1 Kgs 9:3 is altered to "to be" in 2 Chr 7:16. In particular, it is noticeable that the particle, הֵן "used especially to attract attention (cf. §150 d), is occasionally used with the value of if, as in Aramaic and no doubt under Aramaic influence." Joüon and Muraoka, *Biblical Hebrew*, 631.

Chr 7:17–18), and the latter focuses on the conditions of their destruction (2 Chr 7:19–22).[131]

It is noteworthy that 2 Chr 7:12b–16a reveals the key concepts in Chronicles, among which those in 2 Chr 7:14 are significant in the Chr's theology.[132] These are presented by several key verbs: "humble oneself" (כנע), "pray" (התפלל), "seek YHWH" (דרש/בקש), and "turn" (שוב), which occur repeatedly in Chronicles. Furthermore, they showcase a symmetry with the contrasting verbs: "abandon" or "forsake" (עזב) and "to be unfaithful" or "rebellious" (מעל).[133] It is for this reason that 2 Chr 7:14 not only provides a paradigm in the following narratives of the Davidic kings but also reveals that in the time of disaster, if God's people humble themselves, pray, seek God, and turn back from their wicked ways, God will respond to their prayer.[134] Accordingly, it is necessary to note 2 Chr 7:12b–16a, uniquely composed by the Chr, which shows a chiastic structure. This may be outlined as follows:[135]

> 2 Chr 7:12b A I have heard your prayer
> and I have chosen this place for myself as a house of sacrifice
> 7:13 B If I shut up the heavens and there is no rain,
> and if I command the locust to devour the land
> and if I send pestilence among my people"
> 7:14 C (if) my people who are called by my name <u>humble</u> themselves,
> and <u>pray</u>,
> and <u>seek</u> my face,

---

131. I follow Klein's divisions of 2 Chr 7. See Klein, *2 Chronicles*, 104.

132. Williamson indicates that 2 Chr 7:14 "points the way towards salvation from the paradigmatic 'exilic' situation seen in the Chronicler's comments on the death of Saul, I Chr. 10:13–14," noting several verbs frequently used in describing human responses (Williamson, *1 and 2 Chronicles*, 225–26). He also speaks of the basis of the doctrine of immediate retribution, which "is furnished by 2 Chron. 7:14, which establishes the vocabulary through which its development may be traced in Chr., and shows that it is intended to be generally applicable to the people and not just reserved for certain specific cases" (Williamson, *Israel*, 67).

133. Dillard has extensively examined these key terms in Chronicles. He summarized them as follows: (1) The presence or absence of "seeking God" (דרש, בקש) becomes the essential reason for weal or woe (1 Chr 10:13–14; 22:19; 28:9; 2 Chr 11:16; 12:14; 14:4, 7; 15:2, 4, 12, 13, 15; 16:12; 17:4; 18:4; 19:3; 20:4; 22:9; 25:20; 26:5; 30:19; 31:21; 33:12; 34:3); (2) The presence or absence of "humbling oneself" (כנע) leads to God's response (2 Chr 12:6, 7, 12; 28:19; 30:11; 33:12, 19, 23; 34:27; 36:12); (3) The presence or absence of prayer (1 Chr 4:10; 5:20; 21:26; 2 Chr 13:12–15; 14:11; 18:31; 20:9; 30:18, 27; 32:20, 24; 33:13, 18–19); and (4) "Turning" (שוב) from wickedness (2 Chr 15:4; 30:6, 9; 36:13). On the contrary, there are the antonyms of these terms: (1) The term of "abandon" and "forsake" (עזב) is represented as the opposite terms (1 Chr 28:9, 20; 2 Chr 7:19, 22; 12:1, 5; 13:10–11; 15:2; 21:10; 24:18, 20, 24; 28:6; 29:6; 34:25); (2) The term of "to be unfaithful" or "rebellious" (מעל) is also revealed as the opposite words (1 Chr 2:7; 5:25; 10:13; 2 Chr 12:2; 26:16, 18; 28:19, 22; 29:6; 30:7; 36:14) (Dillard, "Reward and Punishment," 166).

134. Williamson, *1 and 2 Chronicles*, 226. Interestingly, Hill suggests in 2 Chr 7:14 that the four activities of "'humbling, praying, seeking, and turning' should be understood as four facets or aspects of the act (or even process) of biblical repentance" (Hill, *1 & 2 Chronicles*, 400).

135. Kelly, *Retribution*, 51.

>   and <u>turn</u> back from their evil ways,
>   B' then I will hear from heaven
>   and forgive their sin
>   and heal their land
> 7:15–16a A' Now my eyes will be open and ears attentive to the prayer of
>   this place.
>   And now I have chosen and consecrated this house
>   to be my name there forever

In these verses, the temple, frequently called "this place," is now called a "house of sacrifice" (2 Chr 7:12). In 2 Chr 7:13, three protases provide the situation of the people's petition: "if I [YHWH] shut up the heavens," "if I command the locust to devour the land," and "if I send pestilence." In the case of these natural disasters, if God's people "humble themselves, and pray, and seek my [YHWH] face, and turn back from their evil ways," then YHWH will hear, forgive, and heal (2 Chr 7:14).[136] The verbs, "humble themselves," "pray," "and seek" place this prayer in the context of Israel's election and covenantal relationship with YHWH.[137] Second Chronicles 7:15 indicates God's direct response to Solomon's request that "your ears [be] attentive to the prayer of this place" (2 Chr 6:40). Significantly, 2 Chr 7:12b–15 is not found in Kings,[138] and the Chr utilizes a chiastic structure with the verb, "I have chosen" (בָּחַרְתִּי in 2 Chr 7:12 and 7:16a; cf. 1 Kgs 9:3). This verb is one of the Chr's favorite words.[139] The final apodosis of the protasis of 2 Chr 7:14 is the direct discourse of YHWH: "my eyes and my heart will be there all the days" (2 Chr 7:16b). This indicates that YHWH will be attentive to the prayer of this place (the temple). Accordingly, 2 Chr 7:12–16 clearly provides the conditions of prospering: if they will humble themselves, pray, seek, and turn back, God will hear their prayer, forgive their sin, and heal their land.[140]

---

136. According to McKenzie, the verb, "humble themselves" (2 Chr 7:14) is a typical term of the Chr, which expresses one of key concepts of the Chr's theology—"humility before God" (McKenzie, *I & II Chronicles*, 250).

137. Werline, *Pray Like This*, 21. In this covenant framework, "my people" (2 Chr 7:13) is a primary way for YHWH to mention Israel. For instance, in Jeremiah's depiction of a covenantal renewal, YHWH says, "I will be their God, and they shall be my people" (Jer 31:31–37). Accordingly, the section of the "if" clauses "asserts Israel's present standing with YHWH; they *are* YHWH's people, called by YHWH's name" (21).

138. The Chr uniquely employs 2 Chr 7:12b–15 in the divine speech. Dillard stresses the significance of these verses (2 Chr 7:12b–15), in that these verses represent the Chr's theology of "immediate retribution" (Dillard, *2 Chronicles*, 58). According to McKenzie, these verses "draw on Solomon's prayer, especially 6:26–31, and transform the emphasis on obedience that seems directed at the Chronicler's audience," and the primary difference between Solomon's prayer and God's response is that God is depicted "as the source of the envisioned disasters" (McKenzie, *I & II Chronicles*, 250).

139. For instance, 1 Chr 28:6; 2 Chr 6:5, 33:7.

140. With respect to 2 Chr 7:12b–15 as a unique material in Chronicles, Dillard indicates that these verses are "programmatic for the author's presentation of the divided kingdoms (2 Chr 10–36)" and that "the Chronicler specifically enunciates the literary program for his 'theology of immediate retribution'" (2 Chr 7:14). See Dillard, *2 Chronicles*, 58.

Second, 2 Chr 7:17–18 displays the protasis and apodosis regarding the promise of the Davidic dynasty (cf. 1 Chr 17).[141] If Solomon walks before YHWH as David did and if he keeps YHWH's law, which was emphasized with the three-fold word, "all that I [YHWH] have commanded" (כֹּל אֲשֶׁר צִוִּיתִיךָ), "my statutes" (חֻקַּי), "my ordinances" (מִשְׁפָּטַי), then YHWH will establish the Davidic dynasty as He covenanted with David. In particular, Solomon quotes YHWH's direct discourse, "there shall not be cut off a man to you, a ruler in Israel" (2 Chr 7:18), recollecting the Davidic covenant of the dynasty (1 Chr 17:11–14).

With respect to the everlasting dynasty of David, the Chr gives special attention to God's covenant with David. As for the Chr's understanding of the Davidic covenant in the Persian period, McKenzie suggests that the Chr seems to have understood the covenant as both conditional and eternal, depending on the obedience of Solomon and the subsequent Davidic kings.[142] Accordingly, McKenzie asserts that the exile as God's punishment for sin does not contradict God's covenant with David.[143] However, he does not clearly explain why the Davidic covenant is conditional and eternal. Rather, it seems to reflect both the unconditional character of the Davidic covenant and the historical situation to which the covenant was conditionally applied.[144]

Third, 2 Chr 7:19–22 displays the protasis and apodosis of God's address to the people, dealing with the conditions of destruction.[145] The verb forms ("turn aside" [תְּשׁוּבוּן], "forsake" [עֲזַבְתֶּם], "go" [הֲלַכְתֶּם], "serve" [עֲבַדְתֶּם], and "worship" [הִשְׁתַּחֲוִיתֶם]) in 2 Chr 7:19 are changed from the singular to the plural, signifying that the addressee of the divine speech is moving from Solomon to the people. The protasis enumerates the conditions of disasters: if they turn aside, forsake YHWH and serve, worship other

---

141. Second Chronicles 7:17–18 is parallel to 1 Kgs 9:4–5. The differences between the two texts are: the phrase, "in integrity of heart and uprightness" (בְּתָם־לֵבָב וּבְיֹשֶׁר) in 1 Kgs 9:4 is omitted in 2 Chr 7:17; the phrase, "over Israel forever" (עַל־יִשְׂרָאֵל לְעֹלָם) in 1 Kgs 9:5 is omitted in 2 Chr 7:18; the verb "to speak" (דִּבַּרְתִּי) and the word, "throne" (כִּסֵּא) in 1 Kgs 9:5 are changed to "to covenant" (כָּרַתִּי, lit. "to cut") and "ruler" (מוֹשֵׁל, the *Qal* participle form of משׁל). These alterations appear to emphasize God's promise to David in 2 Chr 7:17–18 more intensively than that in 1 Kgs 9:4–5. See Williamson, *1 and 2 Chronicles*, 226; Klein, *2 Chronicles*, 112.

142. McKenzie, *I & II Chronicles*, 252.

143. Ibid., 252. According to him, the exile was "an experience out of which the Chronicler admonishes his audience to learn, for the exile does not abrogate God's covenant. Indeed, the Chronicler finds in the covenant with David a source of hope for the restoration of the Davidic monarchy, for he understands this 'covenant' as a promise" (252).

144. I agree with Dumbrell's view. See Dumbrell, *The End of the Beginning*, 50–51.

145. Second Chronicles 7:19–22 is parallel to 1 Kgs 9:6–9. The differences between the two are: the phrase, "from following me" in 1 Kgs 9:6 is omitted in 2 Chr 7:19, in which the verb, "forsake" (עֲזַבְתֶּם) replaces the phrase, "do not keep" (לֹא תִשְׁמְרוּ) in 1 Kgs 9:6; the verb "cut off" (הִכְרַתִּי אֶת־יִשְׂרָאֵל) with the object, "Israel" in 1 Kgs 9:7 is changed to "pluck" (נְתַשְׁתִּים) with the suffix, "you" in 2 Chr 7:20; the verb, "send away" (אֲשַׁלַּח) in 1 Kgs 9:7 is also altered to "cast" (אַשְׁלִיךְ) in 2 Chr 7:20; the verb, הָיָה with the subject, "Israel" in 1 Kgs 9:7 is changed to אֶתְּנֶנּוּ with the implicit subject in 2 Chr 7:20, which emphasizes God's sovereign action regarding Israel's becoming a proverb and a byword; the verb, "hiss" (שָׁרַק) in 1 Kgs 9:8 is omitted in 2 Chr 7:21 and the divine name, "YHWH" in 1 Kg 9:9 is also omitted in 2 Chr 7:22.

gods. The apodosis that follows the protasis indicates that YHWH will pluck them from the land and this house, and cast them from God's presence (2 Chr 7:20). In particular, the verbs, "pluck" (נְתַשְׁתִּים) and "cast" (אַשְׁלִיךְ) apparently allude to Deut 29:27[28], "YHWH plucked them from their land. . .and cast them into another land." Furthermore, this apodosis includes the reference to YHWH's making of the people into a proverb and a byword, which appears to be a quotation from Deut 28:37 and Jer 24:9.[146]

Second Chronicles 7:21–22 deals with the people's astonishment concerning all the disasters upon the Israelites. These disasters have been brought about on account of forsaking YHWH and following other gods. This motif is also found in Deut 29:23 [24]; Jer 16:10; 22:8–9.[147] The rhetorical question (2 Chr 7:21) and its immediate answer (2 Chr 7:22) form the rhetorical device *hypophora* in that it raises a question concerning the reasons why YHWH has done this to this land and this house, then proceeds to provide an immediate answer to the question.[148] The immediate answer is that the Israelites have forsaken YHWH and followed after other gods. The speakers of this utterance are not the Israelites, who are mentioned in the third person. They say that the Israelites forsook the God of their fathers, who had brought them out of the land of Egypt, and followed other gods. The successive verbs, "seized" (יַחֲזִיקוּ), "and worshipped" (וַיִּשְׁתַּחֲווּ), "and served" (וַיַּעַבְדוּם) reinforce the fact that the Israelites have forsaken YHWH and served other gods. It is for these reasons that YHWH has brought on the Israelites all this adversity (2 Chr 7:22). The peoples' astonishment exhibits the covenantal curse on the Israelites who forsook YHWH and served other gods, reflecting the broken covenantal relationship between God and Israel.

In sum, through the divine speech which employs several protases and apodoses, the Chr shows that YHWH has heard Solomon's prayer and that YHWH has spoken of the conditions of prospering and destruction. Of the two conditions, the condition of the continuation of the Davidic dynasty is underscored. The divine speech provides a paradigm for the following narratives, and the description of Solomon in this speech is also balanced with that of David in 1 Chr 17 regarding the temple, which signifies God's presence among the people of Israel in a new way.[149]

---

146. McKenzie, *I & II Chronicles*, 250.

147. Klein, *2 Chronicles*, 114. Interestingly, McKenzie says that this motif "goes together with the idea of the ruined temple as an object lesson for other people" (McKenzie, *I & II Chronicles*, 250).

148. Lanham, *Handlist*, 87.

149. McKenzie indicates, "God's reply to Solomon's prayer in 7:12–22 balances the promise to David in 1 Chr 17. The balance functions both literally and theologically, as it parallels the Chronicler's two model kings and the accounts about them as well as the two institutions that are key for the Chronicler—the Davidic dynasty and the temple . . . the Chronicler's abridgement of the construction account in Kings and the length of that account in Chronicles in comparison with the one relating the dedication of the temple furnish clues about the Chronicler's theological understanding of the temple" (McKenzie, *I & II Chronicles*, 249–50).

Rhetorical Situation

The rhetorical situation may be traced on the two levels: the narrative situation and the Chr's rhetorical situation. First, the narrative urgent situation in this unit is the time when Solomon's construction of the temple and its dedication is complete (2 Chr 7:11). At this time, YHWH appears and speaks to Solomon (2 Chr 7:12–22). This is a response to the preceding prayer of Solomon (2 Chr 6:14–42). In YHWH's speech, the narrative audience is Solomon, as YHWH speaks with him privately. However, the assembly of Israel (2 Chr 5:2; 7:10) might have overheard the divine speech after the theophany in the dedication of the temple. In this context, the narrative audience may be all the assembly of Israel as overhearers. The ceremony of the dedication of the temple as the preceding main event constrains their understanding of the divine speech regarding God's eternal choice of the temple and the Davidic dynasty.

The Chr's rhetorical situation is related to the rhetorical need in his own time, which is to persuade the Yehudite community to discern the centrality of the Jerusalem temple as the sole worship place in Yehud. The Chr's rhetorical situation in this unit is reflected in the divine speech (2 Chr 7:12–22), which is to emphasize YHWH's election of the temple as the permanent place of sacrifice and prayer and YHWH's everlasting covenant with the Davidic dynasty. Likely, the Chr, through the verbs "forsake," "go," "serve," and "worship" (2 Chr 7:19), intended to provide instruction for the Yehudite community "by recalling the destruction of the first temple brought on by apostasy."[150] Through the verbs "pluck" and "cast" (2 Chr 7:20), he wished to emphasize the continuity of the covenantal relationship between YHWH and the people of Israel, alluding to the blessing and curses of the Sinaitic covenant.[151]

The Chr's exigence in the Persian period is the existence of a number of shrines in various places in Israel.[152] In this context, the Chr's purpose is to underscore YHWH's eternal election of the Jerusalem temple. The Chr's audience, as the Yehudite community who had returned to their homeland and had dwelt in the land, is urged to pray to YHWH toward the Jerusalem temple by the Chr's employment of the divine speech. The Yehudites may pray to YHWH when they confront certain afflictions since YHWH will be attentive to their prayer in the Jerusalem temple or to this place. The temple has functioned as the place of the Israelites' prayer from the first temple built by Solomon. The Jerusalem temple functions as a key institution for the Israelites' repentance after the exile, not only as a tool facilitating the present return from the exile, but also in ensuring that such an exile does not happen again. In their situation under the Persian Empire, the Chr wishes to communicate that the Jerusalem temple will be the key institution of the place for the people's repentance after the exile as the worship center of the Yehudites. The Yehudite community is to be formed as the

---

150. Ibid., 250.
151. See Kelly, *Retribution*, 106.
152. See Knoppers, *I Chronicles*, 940–41.

worship community by collection of all the scattered Israelites around the Jerusalem temple as the sole worship place (for sacrifice and prayer) in the Persian period.

Rhetorical Effectiveness

The rhetorical effectiveness of the divine speech in 2 Chr 7:12–22 may be assessed according to the two levels of audience. The narrative audience understands that the God of Israel will listen to their prayers toward the Jerusalem temple by the divine speech of God's second appearance to Solomon. The people of Israel recognize the significance of the observance of God's commandments and ordinances by the conditions of prospering and destruction (2 Chr 7:12–16; 7:19–22). They comprehend that God's promise of the Davidic dynasty (2 Chr 7:17–18) depends on the Davidic kings' law-keeping, as David and Solomon have demonstrated. More significantly, they identify the Jerusalem temple as the place of sacrifice and prayer.

The Chr, bringing the divine speech into his own time, persuades the Yehudite community that the Jerusalem temple is the central place of worship and prayer. Their situation depends upon their obedience or disobedience of YHWH's commandments and ordinances, through which the covenantal relationship between YHWH and Israel as God's people is still operating. In the Chr's view, both the destruction of Jerusalem and the subsequent exile resulted from the Davidic kings' unfaithfulness to YHWH; that is a crucial aspect of the Chr's arguments in what follows the David-Solomon narrative. The Chr persuades his audience to be faithful to YHWH in the Persian period, and to keep YHWH's commandments and ordinances. The Chr stresses the importance of the faithfulness of God's people towards YHWH.

In particular, 2 Chr 7:12b–15 contains a significant element of the Chr's theology. When God's people meet divinely originated disaster, if they humble themselves, pray to YHWH, seek YHWH, and turn back from evil ways, then YHWH will hear their prayers, forgive their sins, and heal their land (2 Chr 7:14).[153] This reflects the Chr's situation, as he emphasizes the Jerusalem temple as the place of prayer in the time of the Yehudites' affliction. Balentine indicates in 2 Chr 7:14 that the Chr "articulates the charter for Israel's future most succinctly."[154] The Chr emphasizes the Jerusalem temple as a penitential institution, relating to its role in rectifying the present return from the exile, and ensuring that such an exile will not happen again. Furthermore, 2 Chr 7:12b–15 expresses the continuity of the covenantal relationship between God and God's people in that the relationship is still operative through the Jerusalem temple in the Persian period. Boda indicates appropriately that in the Chr's view, the Jerusalem

---

153. According to Kelly, these key vocabularies (2 Chr 7:14) "show the explicit fulfillment of this promise. The validity of such prayer in or toward the Solomonic Temple is, moreover, to be understood as a benefit that Israel derives directly from its constitution by the Davidic covenant as Yahweh's people and the earthly manifestation of his kingdom" (Kelly, "'Retribution' Revisited," 217). For the Chr's theology of retribution, see Williamson, "Eschatology," 149–54; *1 and 2 Chronicles*, 225–26; Dillard, *2 Chronicles*, 76–81.

154. Balentine, "You Can't Pray a Lie," 265.

temple was "not a place for dead ritual, but rather the place for covenantal encounter with Yahweh."[155] The Chr persuades his audience of the centrality of the Jerusalem temple as the place of worship and prayer, and a key institution of repentance, even the place of the continuity of the covenantal relationship between God and Israel in the Persian period.

SOLOMON'S ACHIEVEMENTS (2 CHR 8:1–18)

Second Chronicles 8:1–18 deals with Solomon's achievements, and it records Solomon's other activities such as his building projects and military resources (2 Chr 8:2–10). Solomon makes a speech about his wife, Pharaoh's daughter (2 Chr 8:11). Solomon also offers his burnt-offerings on the altar of YHWH (2 Chr 8:12–15). Through these texts, the Chr records that Solomon has accomplished all the work from the day the foundation of the temple was laid until the temple was completed (2 Chr 8:16).

Rhetorical Unit

This rhetorical unit concerns Solomon's other achievements after the completion of the temple building. Solomon's speech regarding his wife, Pharaoh's daughter (2 Chr 8:11) is placed in the center of this unit. The two summary statements (2 Chr 8:1, 16) surround Solomon's other activities: constructions and military resources (2 Chr 8:3–10) and offering sacrifice (2 Chr 8:12–15). In addition, 2 Chr 8:17–18 contains Solomon's economic achievements with Huram, forming an *inclusio* with 2 Chr 8:2 by the reference to "Huram."

Rhetorical Strategy

Solomon rebuilds the cities which Huram had given him and resettles the Israelites there (2 Chr 8:2). This description is quite different from the parallel text (1 Kgs 9:11–14), wherein Solomon gives twenty cities to Huram as the payment for his support in constructing the temple. Thus, the Chr reverses the direction of the gift between Solomon and Hiram(Huram) depicted in Kings.[156] The Chr likely intends to represent God's blessing to Solomon due to his faithfulness to YHWH.[157]

Solomon in 2 Chr 8:12–16 offers his burnt-offerings, following David's direction that is referred to by the phrases, "according to his father David" and "for so David the man of God had commanded" (2 Chr 8:14). Solomon reveals his faithfulness to YHWH. The Chr stresses that both Solomon and David, as the two model kings, are faithful to YHWH.

---

155. According to Boda, the loss of the covenantal relationship (in the early sixth century BCE) would "signal a serious crisis in the relationship between Yahweh and Israel established at the Exodus; its renewal and restoration signaled for the Chronicler a new day of hope" (Boda, *1–2 Chronicles*, 275).

156. Japhet, *I & II Chronicles*, 621; Hill, *1 & 2 Chronicles*, 402.

157. Boda, *1–2 Chronicles*, 277.

Speeches and Prayers in Solomon's Narrative

Solomon's Speech (2 Chr 8:11b)

2 Chr 8:11b	
אָמַר לֹא־תֵשֵׁב אִשָּׁה לִי	He said, "my wife shall not dwell
בְּבֵית דָּוִיד מֶלֶךְ־יִשְׂרָאֵל	in the house of David king of Israel,
כִּי־קֹדֶשׁ הֵמָּה	for they (the places) are holy
אֲשֶׁר־בָּאָה אֲלֵיהֶם אֲרוֹן יְהוָה:	to which the ark of YHWH has come"

Solomon makes a speech as *epideictic* rhetoric after bringing his wife (Pharaoh's daughter) from the city of David to the house Solomon has built for her. Solomon's marriage to Pharaoh's daughter most likely had political motivations. Possibly, the marriage would have testified to Solomon's position among the neighboring nations.[158] However, this sort of intermarriage was prohibited in Israelite life (Deut 7:3). The Chr would have known this, so he would have tried to create harmony by depicting the house Solomon had built for her. The parallel text in 1 Kgs 9:24, which does not contain Solomon's words (2 Chr 8:11b), indicates simply that Pharaoh's daughter moves from David's city to the house Solomon has built for her.

Solomon's word points out that the house for Pharaoh's daughter could violate the holy temple containing the ark as the symbol of YHWH's presence. The ark is placed in the temple, so the entire temple is holy by the installment of the ark. Accordingly, Pharaoh's daughter would have been prohibited from any access to the temple due to her status as a foreigner (Deut 23:7–8[8–9]).[159] This may have resulted in a problem for the Chr. Some scholars suggest that the real problem is that Pharaoh's daughter was a female.[160] In any case, Solomon builds a house for her and brings her from the city of David to the house. It seems to me that the Chr attempts to harmonize matters by adding Solomon's speech to 2 Chr 8:11. In fact, the Chr does not mention anything about Solomon's intermarriage except for the description of Pharaoh's daughter.

In sum, the key idea for the Chr in this speech is the holiness of the temple, wherein the ark of the covenant of YHWH is placed. Jerusalem also retains the status of the holy city since the temple containing the ark was built in Jerusalem. Accordingly, holiness is a dominant motif, which extends from the ark, displaying the holiness of God's presence, to the temple containing the ark and to Jerusalem where the temple is located. I believe that the holiness motif leads Solomon to mention that "my wife shall not dwell in the house of David king of Israel" (2 Chr 8:11b).

---

158. Klein, *2 Chronicles*, 124; Johnstone, *1 and 2 Chronicles*, 1:365.

159. See Klein, *2 Chronicles*, 124.

160. See Dillard, *2 Chronicles*, 65; Japhet, *I & II Chronicles*, 626. Interestingly, Johnstone indicates that the point of Solomon's building of the house for Pharaoh's daughter is that "it lies outside the city" (Johnstone, *1 and 2 Chronicles*, 1:366).

The Persuasive Portrayal of David and Solomon in Chronicles

Rhetorical Situation

The narrative situation of this unit is the beginning point of the second half of Solomon's reign after the dedication of the temple, which constrains Solomon's achievements in 2 Chr 8:1–18. In this unit, Solomon's other activities are listed with one direct speech of Solomon (2 Chr 8:11). The narrative audience of this speech is not clear, yet they would be Solomon's officers (2 Chr 8:10) or the priests and Levites who are ministering to the temple when Solomon offers burnt offerings to YHWH on the altar of YHWH which Solomon has built (2 Chr 8:12). The narrative situation of Solomon's speech is that the holiness of the temple in Jerusalem will not be defiled by a foreign woman. This speech regarding Pharaoh's daughter links the depiction of Solomon's other activities (2 Chr 8:3–10) to that of Solomon's offering sacrifice and praise to YHWH (2 Chr 8:12–16).

In this context, this short speech, which has no parallel in Kings, has been placed here by the Chr in order to present the holiness of the temple as YHWH's dwelling place to the Chr's audience. The Chr's rhetorical need is to emphasize the holiness of the Jerusalem temple as YHWH's dwelling place in the Persian period. In this context, the Chr's exigence is the concern that the Jerusalem temple not be defiled by Pharaoh's daughter as a foreign woman. The Jerusalem temple as the place of sacrifice and prayer will need to be understood by its holiness as the place of YHWH's presence. Thus, the Chr, through Solomon's speech of Pharaoh's daughter, wishes to persuade the Yehudite community to recognize the holy nature of the Jerusalem temple as YHWH's dwelling place.

Rhetorical Effectiveness

The rhetorical effectiveness of Solomon's speech (2 Chr 8:11b) may be appraised according to the two levels of audience. Solomon's officers (2 Chr 8:10) or the priests and Levites who are ministering to the temple (2 Chr 8:12) as the narrative audience is persuaded by this short speech, discerning the holiness of the Jerusalem temple. Solomon legitimizes his actions, bringing his wife (Pharaoh's daughter) from the city of David to the house he has built for her (likely located outside the city, since she was a foreigner as well as a female).[161] The Chr's audience will come to know the Jerusalem temple as YHWH's holiness and His dwelling place by means of Solomon's speech.

The Chr depicts Solomon as the one who does not want to encroach upon the holiness of the temple in Jerusalem. It is for this reason that the Chr adds this speech to 2 Chr 8:11. Through this speech, the Chr persuades his audience who are living in the Persian period to identify a key aspect of the Jerusalem temple: the dwelling place of YHWH. The Chr portrays Solomon as a faithful king who keeps YHWH's law. Solomon's speech regarding Pharaoh's daughter is very persuasive in that Solomon is

---

161. McKenzie states that this is another example of "the Chronicler's idealization of Solomon" (McKenzie, *I & II Chronicles*, 254).

the one who has sought YHWH by keeping His commandments and ordinances. The Chr wishes to persuade the Yehudite community in the Persian period to comprehend the holiness of the Jerusalem temple and to identify Solomon's image as law-keeper.

SOLOMON'S GREAT WEALTH AND INTERNATIONAL FAME (2 CHR 9:1–31)

The final rhetorical unit in the Solomon narrative deals with the depiction of his great wealth and international fame (2 Chr 9:1–31). When the Queen of Sheba hears of Solomon's fame, she comes to Jerusalem to confirm what she has heard. She asks Solomon difficult questions (2 Chr 9:1), and Solomon answers all her questions without exception (2 Chr 9:2). The Queen of Sheba, noting Solomon's wisdom and his house (2 Chr 9:3–4), makes a speech to him (2 Chr 9:5–8). Solomon's great wealth and international fame are described (2 Chr 9:13–28). This unit closes with a summary statement of Solomon's death (2 Chr 9:29–31). The Chr appears to be describing a partial fulfillment of the Davidic covenant, emphasizing the covenantal God through the Queen's speech.

Rhetorical Unit

This rhetorical unit begins with the visit of the Queen of Sheba, who tests Solomon's wisdom (2 Chr 9:1-12). The Queen's speech is contained within this unit (2 Chr 9:5–8). The speech of the Queen of Sheba confirms Solomon's wisdom, and reveals God's faithfulness to His covenant with David. The Queen's visit is followed in the text by the description of Solomon's great wealth and international reputation (2 Chr 9:13–28). The concluding remarks of this section contain Solomon's death and his son Rehoboam's ascension to the throne (2 Chr 9:29–31).

Rhetorical Strategy

The Queen of Sheba's visit testifies to the greatness of Solomon's wisdom, and the Chr mentions Solomon's wealth and international fame as an indication of Solomon's excellence in riches and wisdom. The Solomon narrative concludes with his death after his forty-year reign (2 Chr 9:29–31). In this unit, the Chr displays the character of YHWH, as the one who has been faithful to His covenant with David and as testified via the mouth of the Queen. Thus, the Queen's speech expresses the Chr's thought concerning the covenantal God.

The Persuasive Portrayal of David and Solomon in Chronicles

The Speech of the Queen of Sheba (2 Chr 9:5–8)

2 Chr 9:5–8	
‎5 וַתֹּאמֶר אֶל־הַמֶּלֶךְ אֱמֶת הַדָּבָר	And she said to the king, "true (is) the word
‎אֲשֶׁר שָׁמַעְתִּי בְּאַרְצִי	that I heard in my land
‎עַל־דְּבָרֶיךָ	concerning your words
‎וְעַל־חָכְמָתֶךָ׃	and concerning your wisdom
‎6 וְלֹא־הֶאֱמַנְתִּי לְדִבְרֵיהֶם	and I did not believe their words
‎עַד אֲשֶׁר־בָּאתִי וַתִּרְאֶינָה עֵינַי	till that I came and my eyes saw it
‎וְהִנֵּה לֹא הֻגַּד־לִי חֲצִי מַרְבִּית	and behold, the half of the greatness
‎חָכְמָתֶךָ	of your wisdom was not told me
‎יָסַפְתָּ עַל־הַשְּׁמוּעָה אֲשֶׁר שָׁמָעְתִּי׃	You added to the report that I had heard
‎7 אַשְׁרֵי אֲנָשֶׁיךָ	Blessed (are) your men,
‎וְאַשְׁרֵי עֲבָדֶיךָ	and blessed your servants,
‎אֵלֶּה הָעֹמְדִים לְפָנֶיךָ תָּמִיד	these (are) standing before you continually
‎וְשֹׁמְעִים אֶת־חָכְמָתֶךָ׃	and hearing your wisdom
‎8 יְהִי יְהוָה אֱלֹהֶיךָ בָּרוּךְ	May YHWH your God be blessed
‎אֲשֶׁר חָפֵץ בְּךָ לְתִתְּךָ עַל־כִּסְאוֹ	who delighted in you, to set you on his throne
‎לְמֶלֶךְ לַיהוָה אֱלֹהֶיךָ	as a king for YHWH your God
‎בְּאַהֲבַת אֱלֹהֶיךָ אֶת־יִשְׂרָאֵל	because your God loved Israel,
‎לְהַעֲמִידוֹ לְעוֹלָם	to establish it forever,
‎וַיִּתֶּנְךָ עֲלֵיהֶם לְמֶלֶךְ	so he made you king over them,
‎לַעֲשׂוֹת מִשְׁפָּט וּצְדָקָה׃	to do justice and righteousness."

Second Chronicles 9:5–8[162] as *epideictic* rhetoric is comprised of three sub-parts: the Queen's confirmation of Solomon's outstanding wisdom (2 Chr 9:5–6); her blessing on Solomon's servants who are standing before him (2 Chr 9:7); and her praise to YHWH who has placed Solomon upon his throne (2 Chr 9:8). In this speech, Solomon's wisdom as a leitmotif is emphasized by the repetitions of the word "your

---

162. Second Chronicles 9:5–8 is parallel to 1 Kgs 10:6–9. There are slight differences between the texts; the verb "to be" (הָיָה) in 1 Kgs 10:6 is omitted in 2 Chr 9:5; the word, "prosperity" (טוֹב) in 1 Kgs 10:7 is also omitted in 2 Chr 9:6, and the word "greatness" (מַרְבִּית) is added to 2 Chr 9:6; and the phrase, "on the throne of Israel" (עַל־כִּסֵּא יִשְׂרָאֵל) in 1 Kgs 10:9 is altered to "on his [YHWH's] throne" (עַל־כִּסְאוֹ) in 2 Chr 9:8. With respect to the phrase "the throne of Israel," Japhet indicates that this phrase appears five times in Kings (1 Kgs 2:4; 8:20, 25; 9:5; 10:9) and twice in Chronicles (2 Chr 6:10, 16); whereas, YHWH's throne "as an expression for rule over Israel is peculiar to Chronicles" (Japhet, *I & II Chronicles*, 636). Furthermore, the phrase, "for a king to YHWH your God" (לְמֶלֶךְ לַיהוָה אֱלֹהֶיךָ) in 2 Chr 9:8, which has no parallel, emphasizes that God made Solomon the king of Israel because God loved Israel, to establish it "forever"; whereas, 1 Kgs 10:9 stresses that God made him the king of Israel because God loved Israel "forever."

wisdom" (חָכְמָתֶךָ, 2 Chr 9:5, 6, 7),[163] and the Queen of Sheba testifies to the blessedness of Solomon's officials by repeating the word "blessed" (אַשְׁרֵי) twice in 2 Chr 9:7, reflecting the faithfulness of the covenantal God.

The Queen of Sheba admits that Solomon's wisdom and wealth are conspicuous indications of YHWH's love for Israel. This implies that Solomon has been faithful to YHWH by the building of the temple, which then led to YHWH's blessing of wisdom, wealth, and fame. The Queen's confirmation (2 Chr 9:5–6) demonstrates the greatness of Solomon's wisdom, which is even greater than what she had previously heard in her land. Her reference to Solomon's wisdom testifies to the greatness of the temple, as the Jerusalem temple reflects his wisdom given by YHWH. In the eyes of the Queen of Sheba, Solomon's servants standing before Solomon are blessed since they can hear Solomon's wisdom continually (2 Chr 9:7).

The last sub-part of the Queen's speech contains her praise to YHWH, who has placed Solomon upon "his throne" [YHWH's throne] (2 Chr 9:8).[164] The Chr previously employs this expression of YHWH's throne in 1 Chr 17:14, wherein David's house and kingdom are referred to as YHWH's house and kingdom.[165] In this regard, the Queen's speech reflects the Davidic covenant in 1 Chr 17. The Queen's words reverberate through Huram's previous speech (2 Chr 2:11), which refers to YHWH's love for Israel and His making Solomon king over Israel.[166] YHWH's love for Israel is precisely referred to only twice by Huram and the Queen of Sheba in Chronicles. In both cases, it was foreign kings who referred to YHWH's love for Israel.[167] Both the Queen of Sheba and Huram as foreign dignitaries echo the Davidic covenant in 1 Chr 17.

Furthermore, the Queen's statement exhibits YHWH's love for Israel and Solomon's sitting on the throne of YHWH instead of David. This represents Solomon as YHWH's representative "on his throne" in connection with the endurance of the Davidic dynasty.[168] Solomon on the throne is a partial fulfillment of the Davidic covenant (1 Chr 17:11; 28:5). The Queen's praise towards YHWH emphasizes the covenantal God who has been faithful to His promise to David. God has made Solomon the king of Israel according to what he has previously said to David (1 Chr 17). Thus, YHWH's love for Israel is emphasized, as it led to Solomon's wisdom, wealth, and fame. Solomon is faithful to YHWH by building the temple, which the Queen of Sheba as a foreign queen admits with her praise to YHWH.

163. See Japhet, *I & II Chronicles*, 636.

164. As the parallel text, 1 Kgs 10:9 contains "the throne of Israel" instead of "his throne."

165. The same phrase occurs in 1 Chr 28:5 ("the throne of the kingdom of YHWH") and 1 Chr 29:23 ("the throne of YHWH"). See Klein, *2 Chronicles*, 139.

166. Ben Zvi points out that the Queen of Sheba, who probably never read Huram's letter to Solomon in Chronicles, repeats Huram's utterance in his letter (2 Chr 9:8) (Ben Zvi, "When the Foreign Monarch Speaks," 215).

167. Ibid., 215.

168. Johnstone, *1 and 2 Chronicles*, 1:370. Johnstone notes that some words in Huram's utterance (2 Chr 2:11–12) are repeated in the Queen's speech.

The Persuasive Portrayal of David and Solomon in Chronicles

Rhetorical Situation

The narrative situation of 2 Chr 9 is the visit of the Queen of Sheba. She comes from Sheba in southern Arabia. According to Johnstone, her visit is placed in "the context of the voyage of Solomon's sailors to Ophir" (2 Chr 8:17–19; 9:10–11),[169] which provides the urgent situation of the narrative. Possibly, Solomon's sailors have made Solomon well-known among the neighboring nations as they set about, collecting various materials for the furnishing of the temple and his house. Thus, the Queen of Sheba visits Solomon in order to test him and to confirm his wisdom. As the narrative audience, Solomon himself (2 Chr 9:5) and Solomon's officials and servants are standing before him (2 Chr 9:7) are very impressed by the foreign queen's speech concerning God's love for Israel.

During her visit, she makes a speech to Solomon, and this speech reveals the Chr's intention to draw his audience's attention to God's fulfillment in what he has spoken to David. The Chr wishes to persuade the Yehudite community, as his audience, to understand a partial fulfillment of the Davidic covenant by the Queen's speech in this unit of the Solomon narrative. The Chr's exigence is the crisis of the covenantal relationship between God and Israel. Although this relationship appears to have been broken after the exile, the Chr may wish to stress that the covenantal relationship is still valid in the Persian period through the Davidic covenant regarding the Jerusalem temple. Thus, the Chr's audience will recognize the continuity of the covenantal relationship between God and Israel through the Jerusalem temple as the place of worship and prayer.

Rhetorical Effectiveness

The rhetorical effectiveness of the Queen of Sheba's speech may be evaluated according to the two kinds of audiences. The narrative audience is Solomon's officials and servants who stand before him. They come to recognize that Solomon's wealth and international fame have originated from YHWH's faithfulness to His covenant with David, as indicated by the Queen's speech. In the narrative context, the Queen of Sheba communicates with Solomon, but then abruptly disappears after playing her literary role. The Queen's speech echoes Huram's letter (2 Chr 2). Both refer to YHWH's selection of Solomon as king over Israel, and these are the only two utterances of YHWH's love for Israel by foreign monarchs in Chronicles.[170] The Queen of Sheba hears of Solomon's wisdom and wealth in her own country, and comes to Solomon to confirm it. The Queen's speech legitimizes Solomon's wisdom, wealth, and fame, and the narrative audience as a result more clearly understands YHWH's blessing of Solomon and his faithfulness to his covenant with David.

---

169. Johnstone, *1 and 2 Chronicles*, 1:369.

170. Ben Zvi, "When the Foreign Monarch Speaks," 218–19. Ben Zvi indicates that their speeches "are similar to those of a pious Israelite in the world of Chronicles" ("When the Foreign Monarch Speaks," 219).

Solomon sits on the throne of YHWH instead of David, as God had previously said to David. As a prerequisite for the building of the temple, the peaceful time of Solomon leads to his wealth and his reputation after the completion of the temple building. Through the Queen's speech, the Chr testifies to the covenantal God who has been faithful to His covenant with David. The speech of the Queen of Sheba stresses Solomon's wisdom and the faithfulness of the covenantal God, reflecting the Davidic covenant (1 Chr 17). The Chr wishes to persuade his audience to recognize that the covenantal God is still working in the Yehudite community. Furthermore, the Chr desires that they understand that the covenantal relationship between God and Israel is still valid in the Persian period through the Jerusalem temple as YHWH's dwelling place. In the Chr's view, Solomon's sitting on the throne as well as his wealth and his reputation originates from the covenantal God. Thus, the Chr persuades the Yehudite community to comprehend YHWH's faithfulness to, and blessing of, Solomon via the Queen's speech, glorifying the covenantal God.

SUMMARY

I have demonstrated above that the speeches and prayers in Solomon's narrative (2 Chr 1–9), wherein the Chr portrays Solomon as the builder of the central worship place in Israel, echo the Davidic covenant regarding Solomon's enthronement and the building of the temple. Furthermore, the Chr emphasizes the continuity of the covenantal relationship between God and Israel through the Jerusalem temple in the Persian period by linking the Jerusalem temple to the tabernacle as the worship place in the past. Thus, the Chr, by emphasizing that Solomon seeks YHWH, portrays Solomon as the builder of the central worship place via speeches and prayers in the Solomon narrative. This functions to persuade the Chr's audience to recognize that the centrality of the Jerusalem temple at the time of the Yehudite community is shifting to a worship community.

In the scene of God's first appearance to Solomon (2 Chr 1:7–13), Solomon sits upon the throne of Israel based upon YHWH's promise to David (1 Chr 17:11). YHWH responds to his request for wisdom and knowledge with many additional blessings. Solomon's actual preparations for the temple building begin in 2 Chr 2. He requests the materials for the construction of the temple from Huram (2 Chr 2:2–9), and Huram responds positively. Accordingly, Huram sends the materials and the skilled workers for the building of the temple to Solomon (2 Chr 2:10–15). These two letters (as reported speech) point to the enthronement of Solomon and the temple building, reverberating throughout the Davidic covenant (1 Chr 17:11–14).

In 2 Chr 5:2—7:11, Solomon successfully completes the construction of the temple by the transfer of the ark of the covenant of YHWH. As part of the dedication, Solomon makes a speech (2 Chr 6:1–11) and a prayer (2 Chr 6:12–42), both of which reveal a partial fulfillment of the Davidic covenant (1 Chr 17:11–14).

The most significant sub-unit in Solomon's narrative is the scene of the dedication of the temple to YHWH, wherein the emphasis is on God's second appearance to Solomon (2 Chr 7:12–22). In this climactic scene, God accepts the temple as the place of prayer and gives a speech to Solomon. The divine speech reveals the role of the Davidic kings, based upon the Davidic covenant (1 Chr 17). God stipulates that, if they are faithful to God's statutes and ordinances, the ruler of Israel shall not be cut off according to His covenant with David (2 Chr 7:17–18).

In the Chr's description of Solomon's achievements and his international fame (2 Chr 8–9), Solomon's speech concerning Pharaoh's daughter (2 Chr 8:11) emphasizes the holiness of the Jerusalem temple. This speech reveals his wish to not violate the holiness of the temple, and the speech of the Queen of Sheba (2 Chr 9:5–8) also demonstrates God's love for Israel. Thus, Solomon is balanced with his father David in order to emphasize the Jerusalem temple as the sole worship place in Israel through the Davidic covenant regarding the Davidic dynasty and the building of the temple.

6

Conclusion

The Chr's portrayal of David and Solomon through the speeches and prayers in the David-Solomon narrative is designed to reformulate the identity of the Yehudite community in the Persian period as a worshipping community based in the Jerusalem temple. The Chr presents David and Solomon as the two kings who seek YHWH; David is the preparer of the temple building and the founder of the cultic system in Israel, and Solomon is YHWH's chosen builder of the temple as the worship center in Israel, which implicitly reveals that the covenantal relationship between God and Israel still continues in the Persian period. In particular, the covenant relationship in the Persian era means a commitment to YHWH through the Jerusalem temple along with a commitment to the worship of YHWH.

David is portrayed as the preparer of the building of the temple as the founder of the cultic system, especially through speeches and prayers based on YHWH's promise to him (1 Chr 17). The speeches and prayers in the David narrative contribute to the portrayal of David as a sincere preparer of the temple building. In the first unit, David's ascension to the throne (1 Chr 11–12) is legitimized by the dialogue between David and Amasai, which encourages all the tribes of Israel to support David. In the second unit, David's transfer of the ark of YHWH to Jerusalem (1 Chr 13–16) is the first step in preparing for the building of the Jerusalem temple, which would lead the Chr's audience to understand why the ark—as the symbol of God's presence—was placed in Jerusalem. As a result, YHWH's promise is given to David (1 Chr 17), which stresses Solomon's election as the temple builder and the Davidic dynasty. The Davidic covenant initiated by YHWH echoes in the Solomon-narrative (1 Chr 1–9). In the third unit, David's wars (1 Chr 18–20) serve to produce a peaceful time in Israel, a prerequisite for the construction of the temple. In the fourth unit, David's census-taking (1 Chr 21:1—22:1) leads to the determination of the future temple site. In the following unit, David's preparation for the temple building (1 Chr 22:2–19) urges Solomon and the leaders of Israel to build the temple. David's speeches to Solomon and the leaders function to legitimize his preparation for the temple building, appealing to YHWH's promise to him. In what follows, David organizes the temple personnel and officials (1 Chr 23–27), which is further preparation for building of the temple. In the last unit,

David's final speeches and actions (1 Chr 28–29) ultimately encourage Solomon and the leaders of Israel to build the temple. Accordingly, the Chr portrays David as the preparer for the building of the temple and the founder of the cultic system in Israel, especially emphasizing the significance of the temple in Jerusalem. Thus, in each rhetorical unit of David's narrative, the Chr's portrayal of David—through the speeches and prayers—serves to persuade his audience of the significance of Jerusalem (the temple) as the worship site in Israel.

Solomon is portrayed as the chosen builder of the temple, based on the Davidic covenant. The speeches and prayers in the Solomon narrative contribute to the portrayal of Solomon as the temple builder chosen according to the Davidic covenant (1 Chr 17). In the first unit, Solomon's request for wisdom and knowledge (2 Chr 1) is for the task of building the temple, which is stressed by Solomon's speech and the divine speech. In the second unit, which contains the letters between Solomon and Huram (2 Chr 2), their reported speeches serve Solomon's actual preparation for the temple building, echoing the Davidic covenant regarding Solomon's enthronement and his building of the temple (1 Chr 17). In the third unit, Solomon begins to build the temple (2 Chr 3) and finishes its construction with furnishings (2 Chr 4). This process exhibits the link of the tabernacle as the symbol of the Mosaic covenant with the temple as the symbol of the Davidic covenant. In the following unit, the dedication of the temple (2 Chr 5:2—7:11) emphasizes the fulfillment of the Davidic covenant regarding the building of the temple through Solomon's speech and prayer. Accordingly, YHWH accepts the temple (2 Chr 7:12–22) and emphasizes the people's obedience to YHWH's laws. Next, Solomon's achievements (2 Chr 8:1–16) are closely related to his law-keeping. Solomon moves Pharaoh's daughter from the city of David, since he did not want to encroach on the holy places in Jerusalem, as expressed by Solomon's speech (2 Chr 8:11b). In the last unit, it is emphasized that Solomon's great wealth and international fame (2 Chr 9) originated from God's faithfulness to His covenant with David. Accordingly, the Chr portrays Solomon as the chosen temple builder, emphasizing that Solomon sought YHWH. In each unit of Solomon's narrative, Solomon's portrayal—through the speeches and prayers—works to persuade the Chr's audience that the Jerusalem temple is the worship place YHWH has chosen, and to elicit the fitting responses at the time when the Yehudite community in the Persian period was shifting to a worship community. In this context, Solomon's portrayal is balanced with that of his father David in order to emphasize the Jerusalem temple and to indicate that the Yehudite community is a worship community centered on the Jerusalem temple. Thus, the Chr's portrayal of David and Solomon serves the identity formation of the Yehudite community.

However, the Chr's portrayal of David and Solomon goes beyond that. Both of them play significant roles as the bearers of God's covenants with Israel, revealing implicitly that the covenantal relationship between God and His people continues through the Jerusalem temple as the sole worship place in the post-exilic period by linking the Jerusalem temple to the ark and the tabernacle. Thus, the Chr portrays David and Solomon as the providers of the central worship place, serving to reformulate the Yehudite community identity in the Persian period.

THE CENTRALITY OF THE JERUSALEM TEMPLE IN CHRONICLES

What is the Chr's purpose in including the speeches and prayers in the David-Solomon narrative? Did the Jerusalem temple and its worship serve to reconstruct the identity of the Yehudite community? Did the Chr resolve the rhetorical needs or problems, responding to the issues of the Persian period? The Chr appears to have intended to resolve these rhetorical needs or problems by the persuasive portrayal of David and Solomon through the speeches and prayers in the David-Solomon narrative.

The Chr's key exigence is the identity crisis of Israel after the exile. Some of the people were deported to Babylonia and others were left in the homeland under the Babylonian occupation of Jerusalem. As time went on, the scattered people of Israel established their own communities in their new locations. Yet, when Cyrus, the king of Persia, announced YHWH's people in Babylonia could return to rebuild the temple in Jerusalem, Cyrus' edict brought a dramatic change to the *golah* community in Babylonia and people living in Yehud. When the *golah* community returned to their homeland, they competed with those living in Yehud—the remainees in Judah after the exile. This competition led to conflict over who would be the leading group in Yehud, a struggle which appears to have continued until the Chr's own time.

In this context, the Chr's rhetorical need is to stress the significance of the Jerusalem temple by presenting the David-Solomon narrative to the Yehudite community. In particular, the Chr appears to have resolved the conflict between the Judahites and the Benjaminites that existed after the exile (as expressed by the reference to the tabernacle at Gibeon [1 Chr 16:39; 21:29; 2 Chr 1:3]) by presenting the two as the leading tribes in the Persian era. Thus, the Chr, pointing to the essential rhetorical problem in the Yehudite community, further emphasizes the community identity formation in the Persian period.

Identity Formation in Persian Yehud

The Yehudite community in the Persian period raised questions about their identity as God's people. Their identity formation was a key issue in the Persian era since the exile challenged their identity; they doubted their identity as God's people. By Cyrus' edict, the deportees came to return to their homeland. In this context, the Yehudites made efforts to reformulate their identity as God's people and move from the previous monarchical nation to a cultic community.[1] Accordingly, the Chr, through the rhetorical devices of speeches and prayers, stresses the temple in the David-Solomon narrative to center the Yehudite community identity around the Jerusalem temple,

---

1. See Jonker, "Rhetorics of Finding a New Identity," 396–412 (esp. 411).

which appears to have implicitly assumed the covenantal relationship between God and Israel from the early history of Israel.

As mentioned above, the Chr's rhetorical problems are summarized by three questions: who should be included in the worship of YHWH; which place should be the location of the worship for YHWH; and who should minister the worship of YHWH?[2] These rhetorical problems are effectively resolved by the Chr's portrayal of David and Solomon through the speeches and prayers in the David-Solomon narrative. The Chr provides his answers for the problems in this presentation.

The Unification of the Scattered People around the Jerusalem Temple

With respect to the rhetorical problem of who should be included in the worship of YHWH, the Chr attempts to unify the scattered people of the exile with the Yehudite community as a cultic community around the Jerusalem temple, which was attested by the Chr's frequent use of the phrase "all Israel" to refer to the whole people (2 Chr 29:24; 30:5; 35:3).[3] In this context, the Chr claims that the scattered people could be gathered around the Jerusalem temple. Accordingly, the Yehudite community is urged to gather the scattered Israelites, including the northern tribes, around the Jerusalem temple as the sole worship center in the Persian period. Regarding the rhetorical need for a location of worship, the Chr indicates that YHWH initiated and determined the location of the future temple, which is depicted in the event of David's census-taking (1 Chr 21). Finally, the Chr resolves his rhetorical problem of who should minister by describing the transfer of the ark of the covenant of YHWH to Jerusalem by the priests and Levites—YHWH's chosen ones (1 Chr 13–16) and the temple personnel whom David appointed (1 Chr 23–27). Thus, the Chr effectively argues that the Yehudites, his audience, should accept the scattered people of Israel, including the northern tribes, and unify around the Jerusalem temple as a worship community in the Persian period.

Convergence of Worship Places on the Jerusalem Temple in Chronicles

The Chr's portrayal of David and Solomon is related to the centrality of the temple in Jerusalem in order to reformulate the identity of the Yehudite community in the Persian period. In the David-Solomon narrative, the Chr portrays David as the sincere preparer of the building of the temple and as the founder of the cultic system, and Solomon as the builder of the worship place. In this context, the covenantal relationship between YHWH and the Yehudites means a commitment to YHWH and their worship of YHWH through the Jerusalem temple.

In effect, the Davidic covenant regarding temple building frequently reverberates through the speeches and prayers in the David-Solomon narrative. In particular, the

---

2. Langston, *Cultic Sites in the Tribe of Benjamin*, 180–200.
3. See chapter 2, "Rhetorical Situation."

Conclusion

David narrative is linked to the Solomon narrative by the ark narrative, with the ark containing the two covenant tablets of Moses. David prepares the resting place of the ark, and Solomon completes the task by building the temple. The ark is finally placed in the Jerusalem temple by Solomon. Accordingly, the ideal age of Israel is the time of David and Solomon "when the ark did receive due attention from king, Levites, and people."[4] Thus, the temple becomes God's dwelling place by containing the ark as the symbol of God's presence in it. In this regard, the ark is closely related to viewing the temple as the worship place and the continuity of the covenantal relationship in the Persian period.

With respect to the worship place, the Chr's connecting of the Davidic covenant to previous covenants—such as the Abrahamic and the Mosaic covenants—further confirms this link. The relationship between the Abrahamic and Davidic covenants is emphasized because of the shared worship place (2 Chr 3:1). In this context, Ornan's threshing floor as the temple site is described as being on Mount Moriah, where YHWH has made his covenant with Abraham (Gen 22). The Jerusalem temple in the Davidic covenant is built upon the significant worship place of Abraham. Thus, the Chr links Abraham's worship place (Moriah) to the temple building in the Davidic covenant.

The Davidic covenant regarding Solomon's temple building is further linked to the Mosaic covenant in that the Jerusalem temple is closely related to the ark of the covenant of YHWH. In the Mosaic covenant, Moses worships YHWH before the ark, which is placed in the innermost place in the tabernacle; in the Davidic covenant, Solomon worships YHWH before the ark in the Jerusalem temple. In particular, the Chr emphasizes the observance of YHWH's laws given through Moses (e.g., 1 Chr 22:13; 28:8; 2 Chr 6:14; 7:17). This attests to another linkage between the two covenants. However, the Mosaic covenant is slightly different from the Davidic covenant in that the former depends on Israel's obedience of God's commandments and the latter does not (2 Sam 7:14b–15a). Interestingly, Levenson claims that the Abrahamic covenant is assimilated into the Mosaic covenant, as proposed by Exod 32:9–14, in which God's promise to Moses focuses on the lineage of Abraham, Isaac, and Jacob.[5] Furthermore, with respect to the worship place, both the Abrahamic and the Mosaic covenants appear to be assimilated into the Davidic covenant in Chronicles. Thus, the worship places in the previous covenants converge on the Jerusalem temple in the Davidic covenant in Chronicles.

The convergence of worship places is attested by the speeches and prayers of major characters in the David-Solomon narrative. Although the speeches and prayers are set in the past in the narrative frame, their main concern is with the present. Thus,

---

4. Begg, "The Ark in Chronicles," 144.
5. Levenson, *Resurrection and Restoration*, 77.

the speeches and prayers convey the Chr's interests and his theology to the Yehudite community.[6]

In sum, the centrality of the Jerusalem temple as the sole worship place in Persian Yehud in the David-Solomon narrative helps answer the Chr's rhetorical needs and problems, which were primarily the identity formation of the Yehudite community, the unification of the scattered people (including the northern tribes) around the Jerusalem temple, and the convergence of worship places on the Jerusalem temple in the Persian period.

CONTRIBUTION AND METHODOLOGICAL IMPLICATION

The purpose of this rhetorical study of the speeches and prayers is to explore the Chr's persuasive portrayal of David and Solomon in Chronicles. The David-Solomon narrative occupies a large part, in relation to the temple and its worship, in Chronicles. This study provides a clearer understanding of the David-Solomon narrative. This study suggests that the Chr's portrayal of David and Solomon, especially through speeches and prayers, serves to construct the new identity of the Yehudite community as a cultic community around the Jerusalem temple in the Persian period, which also reveals implicitly the continuity of the covenantal relationship between YHWH and Israel in the Persian era.

Scholars have studied the speeches and prayers in Chronicles using form criticism. The typical examples are Mason and Throntveit's works.[7] Mason investigates eight speeches in the David-Solomon narrative that have no parallels in Samuel-Kings[8] Mason concludes appropriately that the Davidic kings, in general, show their concern over the temple and its worship.[9] Throntveit's work is considered a major study on the speeches and prayers in Chronicles. According to him, royal speeches are divided into rationales, edicts, and orations in terms of form and content.[10] Royal prayer is analogous to royal speech. The difference between them lies in their addressees. Royal speech is uttered to a human addressee, and royal prayer to God.[11] Royal speech occurs at turning points in the narrative context,[12] and royal prayer occurs in a prose style with the emphasis on YHWH's power and His people's dependence.[13]

---

6. See Kelly, *Retribution*, 187–88.

7. Mason, *Preaching*; Throntveit, *When Kings Speak*.

8. Mason, *Preaching*, 13–122 (1 Chr 12:19[18]; 13:2–3; 15:2, 12–13; 22:6–16; 22:17–19; 28:2–10; 28:20–21; 29:1–5, 20).

9. Ibid., 124.

10. Throntveit, *When Kings Speak*, 20. In particular, David's speeches (1 Chr 22:16, 18–19; 28:2–8, 9–10, 20–21; 29:1–5) and his prayer (1 Chr 29:10–19) link David to Solomon, emphasizing the temple building. See also Braun, "Significance of 1 Chronicles 22, 28, and 29," 225–49 (esp. 228).

11. Throntveit, *When Kings Speak*, 75.

12. Ibid., 50.

13. Ibid., 75.

Conclusion

Thus, Throntveit concludes that the royal speeches and prayers, functioning to structure the Chr's arguments, are represented in the same form.

However, Throntveit examines the royal speeches that are not found in Samuel-Kings, so he does not consider other speeches and dialogues. The speeches and prayers that uniquely belong to the Chr are significant in the Chr's presentation, but other speeches and dialogues also serve to portray David and Solomon as those who seek YHWH and who are eager to build the temple. The divine speeches play the most significant roles in the David-Solomon narrative. Thus, it is unfortunate that Throntveit's study only focuses on royal speeches and prayers that have no parallels in Samuel-Kings, not including the divine speeches.

Throntveit investigates the royal speeches as a separated form of speech.[14] He seems to have not considered the narrative context in which the speeches and prayers are embedded. In effect, the Chr's speeches and prayers are placed in the narrative context. However, Throntveit's study tends to disregard the final form of the text by breaking it into pieces, although he recognizes that the speeches and prayers function to structure the Chr's presentation. Thus, the speeches and prayers detached from the narrative might lead their interpreters in the wrong direction.

We cannot deny the usefulness and fruitfulness of form-critical analysis in biblical studies, especially in Psalms. But this sort of form-critical study appears to be unfit for the study of speeches and prayers in narrative, because it neglects the narrative context in which the speeches and prayers are embedded. Accordingly, the whole text tends to be fragmented by the form-critical study, especially when speeches and prayers are detached from the narrative. If we dismiss the narrative context that the speeches and prayers were placed in, we may not rightly interpret the speeches and prayers. Although the David-Solomon narrative contains David's psalm, it is embedded in the narrative context. As the psalm is placed in the narrative context, we should consider it in the narrative context itself.

Furthermore, Throntveit investigates the idealization of Solomon through the speeches and prayers in Chronicles, considering the idealized Solomon to be intended to glorify YHWH, on the basis of the Davidic covenant (1 Chr 17), David' speeches (1 Chr 22, 28, 29), and Solomon's prayer (2 Chr 6:40–42).[15] Thus, he concludes that Solomon is idealized in order to glorify YHWH. However, the Chr's portrayal of Solomon goes beyond that. Rather, Solomon's image is that of the builder of the Jerusalem temple as the sole worship place.

In addition, David and Solomon's prayers contribute to the Chr's portrayal of them as the true worshipers of YHWH. The previous approaches to biblical prayer were also form-critical studies, focusing on form and content. However, prose prayers in the narrative need to be investigated in their narrative contexts and in their own light. The form-critical approaches to prayer have also neglected the narrative contexts

---

14. Ibid., 20–21.
15. Throntveit, "Idealization," 411–27.

that the prayers are embedded in. In this regard, Balentine and Greenberg rightly note the significance of the narrative context of prayer.[16] Prayers play a part in the argument of the narrative as a means of delivering theological perspectives.[17] In line with it, David and Solomon's prayers in the David-Solomon narrative need to be examined in their narrative context. Thus, I have examined the prayers as well as the speeches in Chronicles with the modified rhetorical method, considering them in their narrative context.

In this regard, rhetorical analysis looks for the author's purpose in a discourse by investigating rhetorical features and the functions of the discourse in the final form of a text. Rhetors do not denounce form-critical studies. Rather, they admit the usefulness of form criticism, considering it as valuable groundwork that can help to discern the larger rhetorical units in the final form. Rhetorical analysis focuses on the biblical text itself, its literary features, and message.[18] For the difference between the two methods, it is noteworthy that Watson and Hauser indicate that form critical approaches underscore "the regularity of the literary pattern or form, and a particular text is then seen as an example of that form"; whereas, rhetorical analysis emphasizes "how a certain form was adapted in order to meet the specific needs of the larger literary unit into which it is expected."[19] Thus, the speeches and prayers need to be considered in their narrative context.

This study has employed a modified version of Kennedy's rhetorical method, focusing on the final text as it appears. I modified the concept of rhetorical situation by dividing it into two levels: the narrative situation and the Chr's rhetorical situation, as based on the two layers of audience—the narrative audience and the Chr's audience in the Persian era. The former is the hearers or addressee(s) of the speeches and prayers within their narrative context and the latter is those to whom the Chr writes. In particular, after I determined the boundaries of the date of the book of Chronicles, I approximated the Chr's audience and his rhetorical situation to be between 425 and 250 BCE. Thus, in this study, I examined the speeches and the prayers in the David-Solomon narrative in terms of the two levels of situations and audiences, regarding the speeches and prayers as the Chr's key rhetorical devices. The Chr's portrayal of David and Solomon through speeches and prayers serves to reformulate the identity of the Yehudite community as a cultic community—especially around the Jerusalem temple as the sole worship place in Israel and as an expression of the continuity of the

---

16. Balentine, *Prayer*, 18; Greenberg, *Biblical Prose Prayer*, 17–18.

17. Balentine, *Prayer*, 29.

18. Watson and Hauser, *Rhetorical Criticism*, 8.

19. Ibid., 8. In line with them, Trible indicates that "the distinction between form criticism and rhetorical criticism does not correspond to a separation between the typical and the individual, with one category assigned to each discipline. Instead, the two categories belong together in each discipline, though they are valued differently" (Trible, *Rhetorical Criticism*, 93).

Conclusion

covenantal relationship between YHWH and Israel under the Persian Empire in the Persian period.

SUGGESTIONS FOR FURTHER STUDY

This study may promote further rhetorical studies on the speeches and prayers in the ensuing narratives (2 Chr 10–36) since the Chr employs speeches and prayers as rhetorical devices to convey his theological intention and message throughout his work. In particular, my modification of Kennedy's rhetorical method would be very useful in interpreting other speeches and prayers as rhetorical discourse in the OT. In effect, Kennedy does not distinguish the narrative situation (as related to the narrative audience) and the Chr's rhetorical situation (as related to the Chr's audience in the Persian era). In Kennedy's view, the concept of the rhetorical situation is not clearly defined, including the author's context and the narrative context. Accordingly, Kennedy's concept of rhetorical situation is more or less obscure.[20] In this regard, the modified rhetorical method employed in this study would provide fruitful results when applied to other texts as well.

The speeches and prayers as the communicative discourse need to be examined by a dialogical process. Bakhtin's dialogism probably would be useful in the study of the direct discourse in narrative.[21] His primary assumption is "the idea that narrative texts are not only composed of a sequence of diegetic events and speech acts, but also–and perhaps even primarily–of the construction of a particular fictional world or chronotope."[22] This method, elaborating on the analysis of the direct discourses in the narrative, would also lead to fruitful results in studies on the speeches and prayers in the biblical text.

Furthermore, the socio-political conflicts in the Yehudite community need to be examined more. The conflicts between some groups in the Persian period would have other complexities. Although I dealt with socio-political backdrop in the Chr's presentation—such as the conflict between Judah and Benjamin, the disagreement over the worship place (Jerusalem or Gibeon), the existence of many shrines in various places, there were other aspects to the Yehudite community in the Persian period.

In particular, the relationship between Yehud and Samaria needs to be examined. Knoppers writes, "The Jerusalem of the Achaemenid era has been described as a village with an administrative center"; whereas, "the Samaria of the Achaemenid era has

---

20. Probably, the problem of the concept of rhetorical situation already originated from Bitzer. Amador indicates that "Bitzer's definition is too simplistic and not critically instrumental" since "the historical and social situation conditioning the rhetorical response is broader and more complex than his understanding of rhetorical situation." See Amador, *Academic Constraints*, 71.

21. See Holquist, *Dialogism*, 13–64 (esp. 62–4). For the studies on Chronicles using Bakhtin's dialogism, see Mitchell, "The Dialogism of Chronicles," 311–26; Evans, "Dialogism in the Chronicler's Ahaz Narrative," 1–24.

22. Bemong et al., *Bakhtin's Theory*, 4. In Bakhtin's theory, *chronotope* means the inherent association of time and space relationship (*Bakhtin's Theory*, 3).

been described as one of ancient Palestine's larger urban areas."[23] Accordingly, Samaria would have been wealthier and larger than Yehud in the Persian era. In this context, the Chr's interest is in unifying the scattered people of Israel around the Jerusalem temple; however, the relationship between Yehud and Samaria cannot be neglected in the study of the Chr's presentation. This sort of study would illuminate more clearly the Chr's rhetorical situation and lead the readers of the book of Chronicles to better comprehend the Chr's intention and message.

In sum, I have examined the speeches and prayers in the David-Solomon narrative in Chronicles and have sought to demonstrate that the Chr's portrayal of David and Solomon attempts to reestablish the Yehudite community identity by arguing that the Jerusalem temple is the sole worship place in Israel in the Persian period and asserting that the covenantal relationship between YHWH and Israel continues even into the Persian period. This study goes beyond the previous form-critical studies of speeches and prayers in Chronicles by examining them in their narrative context and by using a modified rhetorical method. Thus, the Chr's portrayal of David and Solomon through their speeches and prayers serves to persuade his audience of the significance of the Jerusalem temple, reformulating the Yehudite community identity in the post-exilic age by pointing to the continuity of YHWH's covenant with Israel through the Jerusalem temple in the Persian period.

---

23. Knoppers, "Revisiting the Samarian Question," 272–73.

Bibliography

Ackroyd, Peter R. "The Chronicler as Exegete." *JSOT* 2 (1977) 2–32.

———. *The Chronicler in His Age*. JSOTSup 101. Sheffield: Sheffield Academic, 1991.

———. "The Historical Literature." In *The Hebrew Bible and Its Modern Interpreters*, edited by D. A. Knight et al., 297–324. Philadelphia: Fortress, 1985.

———. "History and Theology in the Writings of the Chronicler." *CTM* 38 (1967) 501–15.

———. "The Theology of the Chronicler." *LTQ* 8 (1973) 101–16.

———. *I and II Chronicles, Ezra, Nehemiah*. Torch Bible Commentary. London: SCM, 1973.

Adler, Joshua J. "David's Census: Additional Reflection." *JBQ* 24 (1996) 255–57.

———. "David's Last Sin: Was It the Census?" *JBQ* 23 (1995) 91–95.

Albertz, Rainer. *A History of Israelite Religion in the Old Testament Period, Volume II: From the Exile to the Maccabees*. Translated by John Bowden. Old Testament Library. Louisville: Westminster John Knox, 1994.

———. *Israel in Exile: The History and Literature of the Sixth Century B.C.E.* Translated by David Green. Atlanta: SBL, 2003.

Albright, W. F. "The Date and Personality of the Chronicler." *JBL* 40 (1921) 104–24.

Allen, Leslie C. "The First and Second Books of Chronicles." In *The New Interpreter's Commentary*, edited by L. E. Keck, 3:297–659. Nashville: Abingdon, 1999.

———. "Kerygmatic Units in 1 and 2 Chronicles." *JSOT* 41 (1988) 21–36.

Alter, Robert. *The Art of Biblical Narrative*. New York: Basic Books, 1981.

Amador, J. David Hester. *Academic Constraints in Rhetorical Criticism of the New Testament: An Introduction to a Rhetoric of Power*. Sheffield: Sheffield Academic, 1999.

Amit, Y. "Araunah's Threshing Floor: A Lesson in Shaping Historical Memory." In *What Was Authoritative for Chronicles?* edited by Ehud Ben Zvi et al., 133–44. Winona Lake, IN: Eisenbrauns, 2011.

———. "The Saul Polemic in the Persian Period." In *Judah and the Judeans in the Persian Period*, edited by O. Lipschits et al., 647–61. Winona Lake, IN: Eisenbrauns, 2006.

Aristotle. *Rhetoric*. Translated by Rhys Roberts. New York: Modern Library, 1954.

Arnold, Carroll C. "Oral Rhetoric, Rhetoric, and Literature." *PR* 1 (1968) 191–210.

Arnold, Bill T., and John H. Choi. *A Guide to Biblical Hebrew Syntax*. Cambridge: Cambridge University Press, 2003.

Avioz, Michael. "The Characterization of Solomon in Solomon's Prayer (1 Kings 8)." *BN* 126 (2005) 19–28.

———. *Nathan's Oracle (2 Samuel 7) and Its Interpreters*. Bern: Peter Lang, 2005.

———. "Nathan's Prophecy in II Sam 7 and in I Chr 17: Text, Context, and Meaning." *ZAW* 116 (2004) 542–54.

Bailey, Noel. "David and God in 1 Chronicles 21: Edges with Mist." In *The Chronicler as Author: Studies in Text and Texture*, edited by Steven L. McKenzie et al., 337–59. Sheffield: Sheffield Academic, 1999.

———. "David's Innocence: A Response to J. Wright." *JSOT* 64 (1994) 83–90.

Balentine, Samuel E. *Prayer in the Hebrew Bible: The Drama of Divine-Human Dialogue.* Minneapolis: Augsburg Fortress, 1993.

———. "'You Can't Pray a Lie': Truth *and* Fiction in the Prayers of Chronicles." In *The Chronicler as Historian,* edited by M. Patrick Graham et al., 246–67. JSOTSup 238. Sheffield: Sheffield Academic, 1997.

Bar-Efrat, S. "Die Erzählung in der Bibel." In *Lesarten der Bibel: Untersuchungen zu einer Theorie der Exegese des Alten Testaments,* edited by Helmut Utzschneider et al., 97–116. Stuttgart: Kohlhammer, 2006.

———. *Narrative Art in the Bible.* Sheffield: Almond, 1989.

———. "Some Observations on the Analysis of Structure in Biblical Narrative." *VT* 30 (1980) 154–73.

Barker, Joel. *From the Depths of Despair to the Promise of Presence: A Rhetorical Reading of the Book of Joel.* Siphrut: Literature and Theology of the Hebrew Scriptures 11. Winona Lake, IN: Eisenbrauns, 2014.

Bar-Kochva, Bezalel. *Pseudo-Hecataeus, On the Jews: Legitimizing the Jewish Diaspora.* Berkeley: University of California Press, 1996.

Barstad, Hans M. "After the 'Myth of the Empty Land': Major Challenges in the Study of Neo-Babylonian Judah." In *Judah and the Judeans in the Neo-Babylonian Period,* edited by Oded Lipschits et al., 3–20. Winona Lake, IN: Eisenbrauns, 2003.

Barton, John. "History and Rhetoric in the Prophets." In *The Bible as Rhetoric: Studies in Biblical Persuasion and Credibility,* edited by Martin Warner, 51–64. London: Routledge, 1990.

Becker, Joachim. *Messianic Expectation in the Old Testament.* Translated by David E. Green. Edinburgh: T. & T. Clark, 1980.

Bedford, Peter R. "Diaspora: Homeland Relations in Ezra-Nehemiah." *VT* 52 (2002) 147–65.

Beentjes, Pancratius C. "David's Census and Ornan's Threshing-floor: A Close Reading of 1 Chronicles 21." In *Tradition and Transformation in the Book of Chronicles,* 45–59. Leiden: Brill, 2008.

———. "Jerusalem in the Book of Chronicles." In *The Centrality of Jerusalem,* edited by M. Poorthuis et al., 15–28. Kampen: Kok Pharos, 1996.

———. "Jerusalem: The Very Centre of All the Kingdoms of the Earth." In *Tradition and Transformation in the Book of Chronicles,* 115–27. Leiden: Brill, 2008.

———. "Psalms and Prayers in the Book of Chronicles." In *Psalms and Prayers: Papers Read at the Joint Meeting of the Society of Old Testament Study and Het Oudtestamentisch Werkgezelschap in Nederland en België, Apeldoorn August 2006,* edited by Bob Becking et al., 9–44. OTS 55. Leiden: Brill, 2007.

———. "Transformations of Space and Time: Nathan's Oracle and David's Prayer in 1 Chronicles 17." In *Sanctity of Time and Space in Tradition and Modernity,* edited by Alberdina Houtman et al., 27–44. Leiden: Brill, 1998.

Begg, Christopher T. "The Ark in Chronicles." In *The Chronicler as Theologian: Essays in Honor of Ralph W. Klein,* edited by M. Patrick Graham et al., 133–45. London: T. & T. Clark, 2003.

———. "'Seeking Yahweh' and the Purpose of Chronicles." *LS* 9 (1982) 128–41.

Bemong, Nele, et al. *Bakhtin's Theory of the Literary Chronotope: Reflections, Applications, Perspectives.* Gent: Academic, 2010.

Benzinger, I. *Die Bücher der Chronik.* Tübingen: Mohr Siebeck, 1901.

Ben Zvi, Ehud. "Inclusion in and Exclusion from Israel as Conveyed by the Use of the Term 'Israel' in Postmonarchic Biblical Texts." In *The Pitcher is Broken: Memorial Essays for Gösta W. Ahlström*, edited by S. W. Holloway and L. K. Handy, 95–149. JSOTSup 190. Sheffield: JSOT Press, 1995.

———. "When the Foreign Monarch Speaks." In *The Chronicler as Author: Studies in Text and Texture*, edited by Steven L. McKenzie et al., 209–28. Sheffield: Sheffield Academic, 1999.

Berger, Yitzhak. "Chiasm and Meaning in 1 Chronicles." *JHS* 14 (2014) 1–31.

Berlin, Adele. *Poetics and Interpretation of Biblical Narrative*. Sheffield: Almond, 1983.

Berquist, Jon L., ed. *Approaching Yehud: New Approaches to the Study of the Persian Period*. Atlanta: SBL, 2007

———. "Constructions of Identity in Postcolonial Yehud." In *Judah and Judeans in the Persian Period*, edited by O. Lipschits et al., 53–66. Winona Lake, IN: Eisenbrauns, 2006.

———. *Judaism in Persia's Shadow: A Social and Historical Approach*. Minneapolis: Fortress, 1995.

Bitzer, Lloyd F. "The Rhetorical Situation." *PR* 1 (1968) 1–14.

———. "Functional Communication: A Situational Perspective." In *Rhetoric in Transition: Studies in the Nature and Uses of Rhetoric*, edited by Eugene E. White, 21–38. University Park, PA: Pennsylvania State University Press, 1980.

Black, C. Clifton. "Rhetorical Criticism and Biblical Interpretation." *ET* 100 (1989) 252–58.

Blenkinsopp, Joseph. "Benjamin Traditions Read in the Early Persian Period." In *Judah and Judeans in the Persian Period*, edited by O. Lipschits et al., 629–45. Winona Lake, IN: Eisenbrauns, 2006.

———. "Bethel in the Neo-Babylonian Period." In *Judah and the Judeans in the Neo-Babylonian Period*, edited by O. Lipschits et al., 93–107. Winona Lake, IN: Eisenbrauns, 2003.

———. *David Remembered. Kingship and National Identity in Ancient Israel*. Grand Rapids: Eerdmans, 2013.

———. "Did Saul Make Gibeon His Capital?" *VT* 24 (1974) 1–7.

Boda, Mark J. "Chiasmus in Ubiquity: Symmetrical Mirages in Nehemiah 9." *JSOT* 71 (1996) 55–70.

———. "From Complaint to Contrition: Peering through the Liturgical Window of Jer 14,1–15,4." *ZAW* 113 (2001) 186–97.

———. "Gazing through the Cloud of Incense: Davidic Dynasty and Temple Community in the Chronicler's Perspective." In *Chronicling the Chronicler*, edited by Paul S. Evans et al., 215–45. Winona Lake, IN: Eisenbrauns, 2013.

———. "Identity and Empire, Reality and Hope in the Chronicler's Perspective." In *Community Identity in Judean Historiography: Biblical and Comparative Perspectives*, edited by Gary N. Knoppers et al., 249–72. Winona Lake, IN: Eisenbrauns, 2009.

———. "Prayer as Rhetoric in the Book of Nehemiah." In *A New Perspective on Ezra-Nehemiah: Story and History, Literature and Interpretation*, edited by Isaac Kalimi, 279–96. Winona Lake, IN: Eisenbrauns, 2007.

———. "Reenvisioning the Relationship: Covenant in Chronicles." In *Covenant in the Persian Period: From Genesis to Chronicles*, edited by R. J. Bautch et al., 391–408. Winona Lake, IN: Eisenbrauns, 2015.

———. *1–2 Chronicles*. Cornerstone Biblical Commentary 5. Carol Stream, IL: Tyndale, 2010.

Bodner, Keith. "Ark-elogy: Shifting Emphases in 'Ark Narrative' Scholarship." *CBR* 4 (2006) 169–97.

———. *The Artistic Dimension: Literary Explorations of the Hebrew Bible*. London: Bloomsbury T. & T. Clark, 2013.

Booth, Wayne C. *The Rhetoric of Fiction*. 2nd ed. Chicago: University of Chicago Press, 1983.

Brandt, William J. *The Rhetoric of Argumentation*. Indianapolis: Bobbs-Merrill, 1970.

Braun, Roddy L. *1 Chronicles*. WBC 14. Waco: Word, 1986.

———. "The Message of Chronicles: Rally Round the Temple." *CTM* 22 (1971) 502–14.

———. "Solomon, the Chosen Temple Builder: The Significance of 1 Chronicles 22, 28, and 29 for the Theology of Chronicles." *JBL* 95 (1976) 581–90.

———. "Solomonic Apologetic in Chronicles." *JBL* 92 (1973) 503–16.

———. "The Significance of 1 Chronicles 22, 28, and 29 for the Structure and Theology of the Work of the Chronicler." ThD diss., Concordia Seminary (St. Louis), 1971.

Briant, Pierre. *From Cyrus to Alexander: A History of the Persian Empire*. Winona Lake, IN: Eisenbrauns, 2002.

Brinton, Alan. "Situation in the Theory of Rhetoric." *PR* 14 (1981) 234–48.

Brueggemann, Walter. *David's Truth in Israel's Imagination and Memory*. Minneapolis: Fortress, 1985.

Brunet, A. M. "La Théologie du Chroniste: Théocratie et Messianisme." In *Sacra Pagina: Miscellanea Biblica Congressus Internationalis Catholici de Re Biblica*, edited by J. Coppens et al., 1:384–97. Gemblous: Duculot, 1959.

Burke, Kenneth. *A Rhetoric of Motives*. Berkeley: University of California Press, 1969.

Butler, Trent C. "A Forgotten Passage from a Forgotten Era (1 Chr. XVI 8–36)." *VT* 28 (1978) 142–50.

Callow, John. "Units and Flow in the Song of Songs 1:1–2:6." In *Biblical Hebrew and Discourse Linguistics*, edited by Robert D. Bergen, 462–88. Winona Lake, IN: Eisenbrauns, 1994.

Campbell, Antony F. *The Ark Narrative (1 Sam 4–6; 2 Sam 6): A Form-Critical and Traditio-Historical Study*. SBLDS 16. Missoula, MT: Scholars, 1975.

Caquot, André. "Peut-on parler de messianisme dans l'oeuvre du Chroniste?" *RThP* 16 (1966) 110–20.

Carr, David M. *From D to Q: A Study of Early Jewish Interpretations of Solomon's Dream at Gibeon*. Atlanta: Scholars, 1991.

Carroll, Robert P. "Exile! What Exile? Deportation and the Discourse of Diaspora." In *Leading Captivity Captive: 'The Exile' as History and Ideology*, edited by Lester L. Grabbe, 62–79. JSOTSup 278. Sheffield: Sheffield Academic, 1998.

Carter, Charles E. *The Emergence of Yehud in the Persian Period: A Social and Demographic Study*. JSOTSup 294. Sheffield: Sheffield Academic, 1999.

Cataldo, Jeremiah. "Persian Policy and the Yehud Community During Nehemiah." *JSOT* 28 (2003) 240–52.

———. *A Theocratic Yehud? Issues of Government in a Persian Province*. London: T. & T. Clark, 2009.

Ceresko, Anthony R. "A Rhetorical Analysis of David's 'Boast' (1 Samuel 17:34–37): Some Reflections on Method." *CBQ* 47 (1985) 58–74.

Chang, W. I. "The *Tendenz* of the Chronicler." PhD diss., Hartford Seminary, 1973.

Chatman, Seymour. *Story and Discourse: Narrative Structure in Fiction and Film*. Ithaca, NY: Cornell University Press, 1978.

Clifford, Richard J. *Fair Spoken and Persuading*. New York: Paulist, 1984.

Clines, David J. A. "Deconstructing the Book of Job." In *The Bible as Rhetoric: Studies in Biblical Persuasion and Credibility*, edited by Martin Warner, 65–80. London: Routledge, 1990.
Coats, G. W. "The Ark of the Covenant in Joshua: A Probe into the History of a Tradition." *HAR* 9 (1985) 137–57.
Coggins, R. J. *The First and Second Books of the Chronicles*. CBC. London: Cambridge University Press, 1976.
Consigny, Scott. "Rhetoric and Its Situations." *PR* 7 (1974) 175–86.
Corvin, Jack W. "A Stylistic and Functional Study of the Prose Prayers in the Historical Narratives of the Old Testament." PhD diss., Emory University, 1972.
Cross, F. M. *Canaanite Myth and Hebrew Epic: Essays in the History of the Religion of Israel*. Cambridge, MA: Harvard University Press, 1997.
———. "A Reconstruction of the Judean Restoration." *JBL* 94 (1975) 4–18.
Culley, R. C. "An Approach to the Problem of Oral Tradition. *VT* 13 (1963) 113–25.
Curtis, E. L., and A. A. Madsen. *A Critical and Exegetical Commentary on the Books of Chronicles*. Edinburgh: T. & T. Clark, 1910.
Davies, Philip R. "Exile! What Exile? Whose Exile?" In *Leading Captivity Captive: 'The Exile' as History and Ideology*, edited by Lester L. Grabbe, 128–38. JSOTSup 278. Sheffield: Sheffield Academic, 1998.
———. "The Trouble with Benjamin." In *Reflection and Refraction: Studies in Biblical Historiography in Honour of A. Graeme Auld*, edited by R. Rezetko et al., 93–111. Leiden: Brill, 2007.
Day, Peggy L. *An Adversary in Heaven*: Śāṭān *in the Hebrew Bible*. HSM 43. Atlanta: Scholars, 1988.
Day, John. "Gibeon and the Gibeonites in the Old Testament." In *Reflection and Refraction: Studies in Biblical Historiography in Honour of A. Graeme Auld*, edited by R. Rezetko et al., 113–37. Leiden: Brill, 2007.
———. *Psalms*. OTG. Sheffield: Sheffield Academic, 1992.
———. "Whatever Happened to the Ark of the Covenant?" In *Temple and Worship in Biblical Israel: Proceedings of the Oxford Old Testament Seminar*, edited by John Day, 250–70. London: T. & T. Clark International, 2005.
Dennerlein, N. *Die Bedeutung Jerusalems in den Chronikbüchern*. BEATAJ 46. New York: Peter Lang, 1999.
De Vries, Simon J. *1 and 2 Chronicles*. FOTL 11. Grand Rapids: Eerdmans, 1989.
———. "The Forms of Prophetic Address in Chronicles." *HAR* 10 (1986) 15–36.
———. "Moses and David as Cult Founders in Chronicles." *JBL* 107 (1988) 619–39.
Dillard, Raymond B. *2 Chronicles*. WBC 15. Waco: Word, 1987.
———. "The Chronicler's Solomon." *WTJ* 43 (1980) 289–300.
———. "The Literary Structure of the Chronicler's Solomon Narrative." *JSOT* 30 (1984) 85–93.
———. "Reward and Punishment in Chronicles: The Theology of Immediate Retribution." *WTJ* 46 (1984) 164–72.
Dirksen, Piet B. "Why Was David Disqualified as Temple Builder? The Meaning of 1 Chronicles 22.8." *JSOT* 70 (1996) 51–56.
———. *1 Chronicles*. HCOT. Leuven: Peeters, 2005.
Dorsey, David A. *The Literary Structure of the Old Testament: A Commentary on Genesis—Malachi*. Grand Rapids: Baker, 1999.

Dozeman, T. B. "OT Rhetorical Criticism." In *ABD* 5:712–15.
Driver, S. R. "The Speeches in Chronicles." *The Expositor* I (1895) 241–56.
———. "The Speeches in Chronicles." *The Expositor* II (1895) 286–308.
Duke, Rodney K. "A Rhetorical Approach to Appreciating the Books of Chronicles." In *The Chronicler as Author: Studies in Text and Texture*, edited by Steven L. McKenzie et al., 100–35. JSOTSup 263. Sheffield: Sheffield Academic, 1999.
———. *The Persuasive Appeal of the Chronicler: A Rhetorical Analysis*. JSOTSup 88. Sheffield: Sheffield Academic, 1990.
Dumbrell, William J. "The Davidic Covenant." *RTR* 39 (1980) 40–47.
———. *The End of the Beginning: Revelation 21–22 and the Old Testament*. Reprint, Eugene, OR: Wipf & Stock, 2001.
Dyck, Jonathan E. *The Theocratic Ideology of the Chronicler*. Leiden: Brill, 1998.
Edelman, Diana. "Did Saulide-Davidic Rivalry Resurface in Early Persian Yehud?" In *The Land that I Will Show You: Essays on the History and Archaeology of the Ancient Near East in Honor of J. Maxwell Miller*, edited by J. A. Dearman et al., 69–91. JSOTSup 343. Sheffield: Sheffield Academic, 2001.
———. "Gibeon and Gibeonites Revisited." In *Judah and the Judeans in the Neo-Babylonian Period*, edited by O. Lipschits et al., 153–67. Winona Lake, IN: Eisenbrauns, 2003.
———. "Settlement Patterns in Persian-Era Yehud." In *A Time of Change: Judah and Its Neighbours in the Persian and Early Hellenistic Periods*, edited by Y. Levin, 52–64. LSTS 65. London: T. & T. Clark, 2007.
Engler, Hans. "The Attitude of the Chronicler Toward the Davidic Monarchy." ThD diss., Union Theological Seminary in Virginia, 1967.
Eslinger, Lyle. *House of God or House of David: The Rhetoric of 2 Samuel 7*. JSOTSup 164. Sheffield: Sheffield Academic, 1994.
———. *Into the Hands of the Living God*. JSOTSup 84. Sheffield: Almond, 1989.
———. *Kingship of God in Crisis: A Close Reading of 1 Samuel 1–12*. Sheffield: Almond, 1985.
Eskenazi, T. C. "A Literary Approach to Chronicles' Ark Narrative in 1 Chronicles 13–16." In *Fortunate the Eyes That See: Essays in Honor of David Noel Freedman in Celebration of His Seventieth Birthday*, edited by Astrid B. Beck et al., 258–74. Grand Rapids: Eerdmans, 1995.
Estes, Daniel J. "Metaphorical Sojourning in 1 Chronicles 29:15." *CBQ* 53 (1991) 45–49.
Evans, Paul S. "Divine Intermediaries in 1 Chronicles 21: An Overlooked Aspect of the Chronicler's Theology." *Bib* 85 (2004) 545–58.
———. "Let the Crime Fit the Punishment: The Chronicler's Explication of David's 'Sin' in 1 Chronicles 21." In *Chronicling the Chronicler: The Book of Chronicles and Early Second Temple Historiography*, edited by Paul S. Evans et al., 65–80. Winona Lake, IN: Eisenbrauns, 2013.
———. "Prophecy Influencing History: Dialogism in the Chronicler's Ahaz Narrative." In *Prophets and Prophecy in Ancient Israelite Historiography*, edited by Mark J. Boda and Lyssa Wray Beal, 141–64. Winona Lake, IN: Eisenbrauns, 2013.
Eynikel. E. M. M. "The Relation between the Eli Narrative (1 Sam. 1–4) and the Ark Narrative (1 Sam. 1–6; 2 Sam. 6:1–19)." In *Past, Present, Future: The Deuteronomistic History and the Prophets*, edited by J. C. de Moor et al., 88–106. OTS 44. Leiden: Brill, 2000.
Faust, Avraham. *Judah in the Neo-Babylonian Period. The Archaeology of Desolation*. Atlanta: SBL, 2012.

———. "Settlement Dynamics and Demographic Fluctuations in Judah from the Late Iron Age to the Hellenistic Period and the Archaeology of Persian-Period Yehud." In *A Time of Change: Judah and Its Neighbours in the Persian and Early Hellenistic Periods*, edited by Y. Levin, 23–51. LSTS 65. London: T. & T. Clark, 2007.

Finkelstein, I. "Persian Period Jerusalem and Yehud: A Rejoinder." *JHS* 9 (2009) 2–13.

Flanagan, James W. *David's Social Drama: A Hologram of Israel's Early Iron Age*. Sheffield: Almond, 1988.

Fokkelman, J. P. *Narrative Art and Poetry in the Books of Samuel. A Full Interpretation Based on Stylistic and Structural Analyses. Volume I: King David (II Sam. 9–20 & I Kings 1–2)*. Assen: Van Gorcum, 1981.

Fox, Michael V. "Rhetoric of Ezekiel's Vision of the Bones." *HUCA* 51 (1980) 1–15.

Freedman, David N. "The Chronicler's Purpose." *CBQ* 23 (1961) 436–42.

Fretheim, T. E. "The Ark in Deuteronomy." *CBQ* 30 (1968) 1–14.

———. "The Cultic Use of the Ark of the Covenant in the Monarchical Period." PhD diss., Princeton Theological Seminary, 1967.

Fried, Lisbeth S. "The Land Lay Desolate: Conquest and Restoration in the Ancient Near East." In *Judah and the Judeans in the Neo-Babylonian Period*, edited by Oded Lipschits et al., 21–54. Winona Lake, IN: Eisenbrauns, 2003.

Gakuru, G. *An Inter-Biblical Exegetical Study of the Davidic Covenant and the Dynastic Oracle*. Lewiston, NY: Edwin Mellen, 2000.

Garbini, Giovanni. *History and Ideology in Ancient Israel*. Translated by John Bowden. New York: Crossroad, 1988.

Garret, Mary, and Xiaosui Xiao. "The Rhetorical Situation Revisited." *RSQ* 23 (1993) 3–40.

Garsiel, Moshe. "David's Warfare against the Philistines in the Vicinity of Jerusalem (2 Sam 5,17–25;1 Chr 14,8–16)." In *Studies in Historical Geography and Biblical Historiography Presented to Zecharia Kallai*, edited by G. Galil et al., 150–64. Leiden: Brill, 2000.

Gerstenberger, Erhard S. *Israel in the Persian Period: The Fifth and Fourth Centuries B.C.E.* Atlanta: SBL, 2011.

Gesenius, W. *Gesenius's Hebrew Grammar*. Edited and Enlarged by E. Kautzsch. Oxford: Clarendon, 1910.

Giffone, Benjamin D. "Sit at My Right Hand: The Chronicler's Portrait of the Tribe of Benjamin in the Social Context of Yehud." PhD diss., University of Stellenbosch, 2014.

Gitay, Yehoshua. *Prophecy and Persuasion: A Study of Isaiah 40–48*. Bonn: Linguistica Biblica, 1981.

———. "Reflection on the Poetics of the Samuel Narrative." *CBQ* 54 (1992) 221–30.

Gorrell, Donna. "The Rhetorical Situation Again: Linked Components in a Venn Diagram." *PR* 30 (1997) 395–412.

Grabbe, L. L. "'They Shall Come Rejoicing to Zion'—or Did They? The Settlement of Yehud in the Early Persian Period." In *Exile and Restoration Revisited: Essays on the Babylonian and Persian Periods in Memory of Peter R. Ackroyd*, edited by G. N. Knoppers et al., 116–27. LSTS 73. London: T. & T. Clark, 2009.

Graham, M. Patrick. *The Utilization of 1 and 2 Chronicles in the Reconstruction of Israelite History in the Nineteenth Century*. SBLDS 116. Atlanta: Scholars, 1991.

Grant-Davie, Keith. "Rhetorical Situations and Their Constituents." *RR* 15 (1997) 264–79.

Greenberg, Moshe. *Biblical Prose Prayer: As a Window to the Popular Religion of Ancient Israel*. Berkeley: University of California Press, 1983.

Greenwood, David. "Rhetorical Criticism and Formgeschichte: Some Methodological Considerations." *JBL* 89 (1970) 418–26.

Greenwood, K. R. "Labor Pains: The Relationship between David's Census and Corvée Labor." *BBR* 20 (2010) 467–77.

Grisanti, Michael A. "The Davidic Covenant." *MSJ* 10 (1999) 233–50.

Groom, Sue. *Linguistic Analysis of Biblical Hebrew*. Carlisle, UK: Paternoster, 2003.

Gunkel, Hermann, and Joachim Begrich. *Introduction to Psalms: The Genres of the Religious Lyric of Israel*. Macon, GA: Mercer University Press, 1998.

Gunn, David M. *The Story of King David: Genre and Interpretation*. JSOTSup 6. Sheffield: JSOT, 1978.

Gutmann, Joseph. "The History of the Ark." *ZAW* 83 (1971) 22–30.

Hahn, Scott H. *Kingship by Covenant: A Canonical Approach to the Fulfillment of God's Saving Promises*. New Haven: Yale University Press, 2009.

Hamilton, Victor P. "Satan." In *ABD* 5:985–89.

Hanson, Paul D. *The Dawn of Apocalyptic*. Philadelphia: Fortress, 1979.

Hentschel, Georg. "Der Bruderkrieg zwischen Israel und Benjamin (Ri 20)." *Bib* 98 (2008) 17–38.

Hill, Andrew E. "Patchwork Poetry or Reasoned Verse? Connective Structure in 1 Chronicles XVI." *VT* 33 (1983) 97–101.

———. *1 & 2 Chronicles*. NIVAC. Grand Rapids: Zondervan, 2003.

Hoglund, Kenneth G. *Achaemenid Imperial Administration in Syria-Palestine and the Missions of Ezra and Nehemiah*. Atlanta: Scholars, 1992.

Holquist, M. *Dialogism: Bakhtin and His World*. 2nd ed. London: Routledge. 2002.

Howard, David M. "Rhetorical Criticism in Old Testament Studies." *BBR* 4 (1994) 87–104.

Hurowitz, Victor A. *I Have Built You an Exalted House: Temple Building in the Bible in Light of Mesopotamian and Northwest Semitic Writings*. JSOTSup 115. Sheffield: Sheffield Academic, 1992.

Hwang, Sunwoo. "Coexistence of Unconditionality and Conditionality of the Davidic Covenant in Chronicles." *The Heythrop Journal* (2012) 1–8.

———. "The Hope for the Restoration of the Davidic Kingdom in the Light of the Davidic Covenant in Chronicles." PhD diss., University of Edinburgh, 2011.

Im, Tae-Soo. *Das Davidbild in den Chronikbüchern: David als Idealbild des theokratischen Messianismus für den Chronisten*. Europäische Hochschulschriften 23/263. Frankfurt: Peter Lang, 1985.

Iser, W. *The Implied Reader*. Baltimore: Johns Hopkins University Press, 1974.

———. "The Reading Process: A Phenomenological Approach." *New Literary History* 3 (1972) 279–99.

Ishida, Tomoo. *Royal Dynasties in Ancient Israel: A Study in the Formation and Development of Royal-Dynastic Ideology*. Berlin: de Gruyter, 1977.

Jackson, Jared Judd. "The Ark Narratives: An Historical, Textual, and Form-Critical Study of 1 Samuel 4–6 and 2 Samuel 6." ThD diss., Union Theological Seminary, 1962.

Japhet, Sara. "The Concept of the 'Remnant' in the Restoration Period: On the Vocabulary of Self-Definition." In *From the Rivers of Babylon to the Highlands of Judah: Collected Studies on the Restoration Period*, 432–49. Winona Lake, IN: Eisenbrauns, 2006.

———. "Historical Reliability of Chronicles: The History of the Problem and its Place in Biblical Research." *JSOT* 33 (1985) 83–107.

———. *The Ideology of the Book of Chronicles and Its Place in Biblical Thought.* Translated by Anna Barber. Reprint, Winona Lake, IN: Eisenbrauns, 2009.
———. *I & II Chronicles.* OTL. London: SCM, 1993.
———. "Interchanges of Verbal Roots in Parallel Texts in Chronicles." *HS* 28 (1987) 9–50.
———. "Postexilic Historiography: How and Why?" In *Israel Constructs its History: Deuteronomistic Historiography in Recent Research*, edited by Albert de Pury et al., 144–73. Sheffield: Sheffield Academic, 2000.
———. "The Supposed Common Authorship of Chronicles and Ezra-Nehemiah Investigated Anew." *VT* 18 (1968) 330–71.
Jarick, John. *1 Chronicles.* London: Sheffield Academic, 2002.
Jeon, Young-Ho. *Impeccable Solomon? A Study of Solomon's Faults in Chronicles.* Eugene, OR: Wipf & Stock, 2013.
Johnstone, William. *1 and 2 Chronicles. Vol.1: 1 Chronicles 1–2 Chronicles 9: Israel's Place Among the Nations.* JSOTSup 253. Sheffield: Sheffield Academic, 1997.
———. "Guilt and Atonement: The Theme of 1 and 2 Chronicles." In *Chronicles and Exodus: An Analogy and its Application*, 90–114. JSOTSup 275. Sheffield: Sheffield Academic, 1998.
———. "Prospective Atonement: The Use of Exodus 30.11–16 in 1 Chronicles 21." In *Chronicles and Exodus: An Analogy and Its Application*, 128–40. JSOTSup 275. Sheffield: Sheffield Academic, 1998.
———. "Solomon's Prayer (2 Chronicles 6): Is Intentionalism Such a Fallacy?" In *Chronicles and Exodus: An Analogy and its Application*, 282–97. Sheffield: Sheffield Academic, 1998.
Jones, Gwilym H. *The Nathan Narratives.* JSOTSup 80. Sheffield: Sheffield Academic, 1990.
Jonker, L. "'The Ark of the Covenant of the Lord': The Place of Covenant in the Chronicler's Theology." In *Covenant in the Persian Period: From Genesis to Chronicles*, edited by R. J. Bautch et al., 409–30. Winona Lake, IN: Eisenbrauns, 2015.
———. "David's Officials According to the Chronicler (1 Chronicles 23–27): A Reflection of Second Temple Self-Categorization?" In *Historiography and Identity (Re)Formulation in Second Temple Historiographical Literature*, edited by Louis Jonker, 65–91. LHBOTS 534. London: T. & T. Clark, 2010.
———. "Engaging with Different Contexts: A Survey of the Various Levels of Identity Negotiation in Chronicles." In *Texts, Contexts and Readings in Postexilic Literature: Explorations into Historiography and Identity Negotiation in Hebrew Bible and Related Texts*, edited by Louis Jonker, 63–93. Tübingen: Mohr Siebeck, 2011.
———. "Of Jebus, Jerusalem and Benjamin: The Chronicler's *Sondergut* in 1 Chronicles 21 Against the Background of the Late Persian Era in Yehud." In *Chronicling the Chronicler: The Book of Chronicles and Early Second Temple Historiography*, edited by Paul S. Evans et al., 81–102. Winona Lake, IN: Eisenbrauns, 2013.
———. "Reforming History: The Hermeneutical Significance of the Books of Chronicles." *VT* 57 (2007) 21–44.
———. "The Rhetorics of Finding a New Identity in a Multi-Religious and Multi-Ethnic Society: The Case of the Book of Chronicles." *Verbum et Ecclesia* 24 (2003) 396–416.
———. "Revisiting the Saul Narrative in Chronicles: Interacting with the Persian Imperial Context." *OTE* 23 (2010) 283–305.
———. "Textual Identities in the Books of Chronicles: The Case of Jehoram's History." In *Community Identity in Judean Historiography: Biblical and Comparative Perspectives*, edited by Gary N. Knoppers et al., 197–217. Winona Lake, IN: Eisenbrauns, 2009.

———. "Who Constitutes Society? Yehud's Self-Understanding in the Late Persian Era as Reflected in the Books of Chronicles." *JBL* 127 (2008) 703–24.
Joüon, Paul, and T. Muraoka. *A Grammar of Biblical Hebrew*. Rome: Pontificio Istituto Biblico, 2006.
Kalimi, Isaac. *An Ancient Israelite Historian: Studies in the Chronicler, His Time, Place and Writing*. Assen: Van Gorcum, 2005.
———. "The Capture of Jerusalem in the Chronistic History." *VT* 52 (2002) 66–79.
———. "History of Interpretation: The Book of Chronicles in Jewish Tradition from Daniel and Spinoza." *Revue Biblique* 105 (1998) 5–41.
———. "Jerusalem—The Divine City: The Representation of Jerusalem in Chronicles Compared with Earlier and Later Jewish Compositions." In *The Chronicler as Theologian: Essays in Honor of Ralph W. Klein*, edited by M. Patrick Graham et al., 189–205. London: T. & T. Clark, 2003.
———. "Paronomasia in the Book of Chronicles." *JSOT* 67 (1995) 27–41.
———. *The Reshaping of Ancient Israelite History in Chronicles*. Winona Lake, IN: Eisenbrauns, 2005.
———. *The Retelling of Chronicles in Jewish Tradition and Literature: A Historical Journey*. Winona Lake, IN: Eisenbrauns, 2009.
———. "The View of Jerusalem in the Ethnographical Introduction of Chronicles (1 Chr 1–9)." *Bib* 83 (2002) 556–62.
———. "Was the Chronicler a Historian?" In *The Chronicler as Historian*, edited by M. Patrick Graham et al., 73–89. Sheffield: Sheffield Academic, 1997.
———. *Zur Geschichtsschreibung des Chronisten: Literarisch-historiographische Abweichungen der Chronik von ihren Paralleltexten in den Samuel- und Königsbüchern*. BZAW 226. Berlin: Walter de Gruyter, 1995.
Kang, J. J. *The Persuasive Portrayal of Solomon in 1 Kings 1–11*. Bern: Peter Lang, 2003.
Keil, C. F. *The Books of Chronicles*. Biblical Commentary on the Old Testament. Translated by Andrew Harper. Edinburgh: T. & T. Clark, 1872.
Kellerman, D. "אַשְׁמָה." In *TDOT* 1:429–37.
Kelly, Brian E. "Messianic Elements in the Chronicler's Work." In *The Lord's Anointed: Interpretation of Old Testament Messianic Texts*, edited by P. E. Satterthwaite et al., 249–64. Grand Rapids: Baker, 1996.
———. *Retribution and Eschatology in Chronicles*. JSOTSup 211. Sheffield: Sheffield Academic, 1996.
———. "'Retribution' Revisited: Covenant, Grace and Restoration." In *The Chronicler as Theologian: Essays in Honor of Ralph W. Klein*, edited by M. Patrick Graham et al., 206–27. London: T. & T. Clark, 2003.
Kennedy, G. A. *New Testament Interpretation through Rhetorical Criticism*. Chapel Hill, NC: University of North Carolina Press, 1984.
Kessler, John. "Diaspora and Homeland in the Early Achaemenid Period: Community, Geography and Demography in Zechariah 1–8." In *Approaching Yehud: New Approaches to the Study of the Persian Period*, edited by Jon L. Berquist, 137–66. Atlanta: SBL, 2007.
———. "Persia's Loyal Yahwists: Power Identity and Ethnicity in Achaemenid Yehud." In *Judah and the Judeans in the Persian Period*, edited by Oded Lipschits et al., 91–112. Winona Lake, IN: Eisenbrauns, 2006.
Kessler, M. "Methodological Setting for Rhetorical Criticism." *Semitics* 4 (1974) 22–36.

Kittel, R. *Die Bücher der Chronik übersetzt und erklärt*. Göttingen: Vandenhoeck & Ruprecht, 1902.

Klein, Ralph W. *1 Chronicles: A Commentary*. Hermeneia. Minneapolis: Fortress, 2006.

———. *2 Chronicles: A Commentary*. Hermeneia. Minneapolis: Fortress, 2012.

Kleinig, John W. *The Lord's Song: The Basis, Function and Significance of Choral Music in Chronicles*. JSOTSup 156. Sheffield: JSOT, 1993.

Knoppers, Gary N. *I Chronicles, 10–29: A New Translation with Introduction and Commentary*. AB 12A. New York: Doubleday, 2004.

———. "Greek Historiography and the Chronicler's History: A Reexamination." *JBL* 122 (2003) 627–50.

———. "Hierodules, Priests, or Janitors? The Levites in Chronicles and the History of the Israelite Priesthood." *JBL* 118 (1999) 49–72.

———. "The Images of David in Early Judaism: David as Repentant Sinner in Chronicles." *Bib* 76 (1995) 449–70.

———. "Israel's First King and 'the Kingdom of YHWH in the Hands of the Sons of David.' The Place of the Saulide Monarchy in the Chronicler's Historiography." In *Saul in Story and Tradition*, edited by C. S. Ehrlich et al., 187–213. FAT 47. Tübingen: Mohr Siebeck, 2006.

———. *Jews and Samaritans: The Origins and History of Their Early Relations*. Oxford: Oxford University Press, 2013.

———. "Jerusalem at War in Chronicles." In *Zion: City of Our God*, edited by Richard S. Hess et al., 57–76. Grand Rapids: Eerdmans, 1999.

———. "Prayer and Propaganda: Solomon's Dedication of the Temple and the Deuteronomist's Program." *CBQ* 57 (1995) 229–54.

———. "Revisiting the Samarian Question in the Persian Period." In *Judah and Judeans in the Persian Period*, edited by O. Lipschits et al., 265–90. Winona Lake, IN: Eisenbrauns, 2006.

———. "A Reunited Kingdom in Chronicles?" *Proceedings: Eastern Great Lakes and Midwestern Biblical Societies* 9 (1989) 74–88.

———. *Two Nations under God: The Deuteronomistic History of Solomon and the Dual Monarchies*. Vol. 1, *The Reign of Solomon and the Rise of Jeroboam*. HSM 52. Atlanta: Scholars, 1993.

Kreutzer, F. "Der Antagonist: Der Satan in der Hebräischen Bibel—eine bekannte Größe?" *Bib* 86 (2005) 536–44.

Kruse, Heinz. "David's Covenant." *VT* 35 (1985) 139–64.

Kuhrt, Amélie. *The Persian Empire: A Corpus of Sources from the Achaemenid Period*. London: Routledge, 2007.

Kuntzmann, Raymond. "Le trône de Dieu dans l'oeuvre du Chroniste." In *Le Trône de Dieu*, edited by Marc Philonenko, 19–27. WUNT 69. Tübingen: Mohr Siebeck, 1993.

Langston, Scott M. *Cultic Sites in the Tribe of Benjamin: Benjaminite Prominence in the Religion of Israel*. Frankfurt am Main: Peter Lang, 1998.

Lanham, Richard A. *A Handlist of Rhetorical Terms*. 2nd ed. Berkeley: University of California Press, 1991.

Lenchak, Timothy A. *"Choose Life!": A Rhetorical Critical Investigation of Deuteronomy 28,69–30,20*. Rome: Pontifical Biblical Institute, 1993.

Levenson, Jon D. "The Davidic Covenant and Its Interpreters." *CBQ* 41 (1979) 205–19.

———. *Resurrection and Restoration of Israel*. New Haven: Yale University Press, 2006.

Levin, Yigal. "Joseph, Judah and 'the Benjamin Conundrum.'" *ZAW* 116 (2004) 223–41.

———. "Who Was the Chronicler's Audience? A Hint from His Genealogies." *JBL* 122 (2003) 229–45.

Linafelt, Tod, et al. *The Fate of King David: The Past and Present of a Biblical Icon*. New York: T. & T. Clark, 2010.

Lipschits, Oded. "Achaemenid Imperial Policy, Settlement Process in Palestine, and the Status of Jerusalem in the Middle of the Fifth Century B.C.E." In *Judah and the Judeans in the Persian Period*, edited by Oded Lipschits et al., 19–52. Winona Lake, IN: Eisenbrauns, 2006.

———. "Demographic Changes in Judah between the Seventh and the Fifth Centuries B.C.E." In *Judah and Judeans in the Neo-Babylonian Period*, edited by Oded Lipschits et al., 323–76. Winona Lake, IN: Eisenbrauns, 2003.

———. *The Fall and Rise of Jerusalem: Judah under Babylonian Rule*. Winona Lake, IN: Eisenbrauns, 2005.

———. "Persian Period Finds from Jerusalem: Facts and Interpretations." *JHS* 9 (2009) 2–30.

Lundbom, Jack R. *The Hebrew Prophets: An Introduction*. Minneapolis: Fortress, 2010.

———. *Jeremiah: A Study in Ancient Hebrew Rhetoric*. 2nd ed. Winona Lake, IN: Eisenbrauns, 1997.

Lynch, Matthew. *Monotheism and Institutions in the Book of Chronicles*. Tübingen: Mohr Siebeck, 2014.

Mack, Burton L. *Rhetoric and the New Testament*. Minneapolis: Fortress, 1990.

Macy, Howard Ray. "The Sources of the Books of Chronicles: A Reassessment." PhD diss., Harvard University, 1975.

Martens, Elmer A. *God's Design: A Focus on Old Testament Theology*. 2nd ed. Grand Rapids: Baker, 1994.

Mason, Rex. *Preaching the Tradition: Homily and Hermeneutics after the Exile*. Cambridge: Cambridge University Press, 1990.

McCarthy, D. J. "Covenant and Law in Chronicles–Nehemiah." *CBQ* 44 (1982) 25–44.

———. "An Installation Genre?" *JBL* 90 (1971) 31–41.

McConville, J. G. "1 Chronicles 28:9: Yahweh 'Seeks Out' Solomon." *JTS* 37 (1986) 105–8.

———. *I & II Chronicles*. Philadelphia: Westminster, 1984.

McKenzie, S. M. *The Chronicler's Use of the Deuteronomistic History*. Atlanta: Scholars, 1985.

———. "The Typology of the Davidic Covenant." In *The Land that I will Show You: Essays on the History and Archaeology of the Ancient Near East in Honour of J. Maxwell Miller*, edited by J. Andrew Dearman et al., 152–78. JSOTSup 343. Sheffield: Sheffield Academic, 2001.

———. *I & II Chronicles*. AOTC. Nashville: Abingdon, 2004.

Meyers, M. "Exile and Restoration in Light of Recent Archaeological and Demographic Studies." In *Exile and Restoration Revisited: Essays on the Babylonian and Persian Periods in Memory of Peter R. Ackroyd*, edited by G. N. Knoppers et al., 166–73. LSTS 73. London: T. & T. Clark, 2009.

Miller, Arthur B. "Rhetorical Exigence." *PR* 5 (1972) 111–18.

Miller, Patrick D. "Prayer as Persuasion: The Rhetoric and Intention of Prayer." *WW* 13 (1993) 356–62.

Miller, Patrick D., and J. J. M. Roberts. *The Hand of the Lord: A Reassessment of the "Ark Narrative" of 1 Samuel*. JHNES. Baltimore: Johns Hopkins University Press, 1977.

Mitchell, Christine. "The Dialogism of Chronicles." In *The Chronicler as Author: Studies in Text and Texture*, edited by Steven L. McKenzie et al., 311–26. JSOTSup 263. Sheffield: Sheffield Academic, 1999.

———. "Transformations in Meaning: Solomon's Accession in Chronicles." *JHS* 4 (2002). http://www.jhsonline.org/Articles/article_25.pdf

Mosis, Rudolf. *Untersuchungen zur Theologie des chronistischen Geschichtswerkes*. FTS 92. Freiburg: Herder, 1973.

Möller, Karl. *A Prophet in Debate: The Rhetoric of Persuasion in the Book of Amos*. JSOTSup 372. Sheffield: Sheffield Academic, 2003.

Mowinckel, Sigmund. *The Psalms in Israel's Worship*. Reprint, Grand Rapids: Eerdmans, 2004.

Muilenburg, James. "Form Criticism and Beyond." *JBL* 88 (1969) 1–18.

———. "The Linguistic and Rhetorical Usages of the Particle *kî* in the Old Testament." *HUCA* 32 (1961) 135–60.

Myers, Jacob M. "The Kerygma of the Chronicler: History and Theology in the Service of Religion." *Int* 20 (1966) 259–73.

———. *I Chronicles*. AB 12. Garden City, NY: Doubleday, 1965.

Na'aman, Nadav. "Saul, Benjamin and the Emergence of Biblical Israel (Part 1)." *ZAW* 121 (2009) 211–24.

———. "Saul, Benjamin and the Emergence of Biblical Israel (Part 2)." *ZAW* 121 (2009) 335–49.

Newsome, James D., Jr. "The Chronicler's View of Prophecy." PhD diss., Vanderbilt University, 1973.

———. "Toward a New Understanding of the Chronicler's Purpose." *JBL* 94 (1975) 201–17.

Noll, K. L. *The Faces of David*. JSOTSup 242. Sheffield: Sheffield Academic, 1997.

Noordtzij, A. "Les Intentions du Chroniste." *Revue Biblique* 49 (1940) 161–68.

North, R. "Theology of the Chronicler." *JBL* 82 (1963) 369–81.

Noth, Martin. *The Chronicler's History*. Translated by H. G. M. Williamson. JSOTSup 50. Sheffield: Sheffield Academic, 1987.

Oded, Bustenay. "Where Is 'the Myth of the Empty Land' to Be Found? History versus Myth." In *Judah and Judeans in the Neo-Babylonian Period*, edited by O. Lipschits et al., 55–74. Winona Lake, IN: Eisenbrauns. 2003.

Oeming, M. *Das wahre Israel: Die 'genealogische Vorhalle' 1 Chronik 1–9*. BWANT 128. Stuttgart: Kohlhammer, 1990.

———. "Die Eroberung Jerusalems durch David in deuteronomistischer und chronistischer Darstellung (II Sam 5,6–9 und 1 Chr 11,4–8)." *ZAW* 106 (1994) 404–20.

O'Kennedy, D. F. "The Prayer of Solomon (1 Ki 8:22–53): Paradigm for the Understanding of Forgiveness in the Old Testament." *OTE* 13 (2000) 72–88.

———. "Twee Weergawes van die Gebed van Salomo (1 Kon. 8 en 2 Kron. 6): 'N Vergelykende Studie." *Acta Theologica* 2 (2006) 155–77.

Osborne, W. L. "The Genealogies of 1 Chronicles 1–9." PhD diss., Dropsie College, 1979.

Patrick, Dale, and Allen Scult. *Rhetoric and Biblical Interpretation*. JSOTSup 82. Sheffield: Almond, 1990.

Peltonen, K. "A Jigsaw Without a Model? The Date of Chronicles." In *Did Moses Speak Attic? Jewish History and Historiography in the Hellenistic Period*, edited by Lester L. Grabbe, 225–71. JSOTSup 37. Sheffield: Sheffield Academic, 2001.

Perelman, C. *The New Rhetoric and the Humanities: Essays on Rhetoric and its Applications.* Synthese Library 140. Dordrecht: D. Reidel, 1979.

Perelman, C., and L. Olbrechts-Tyteca. *The New Rhetoric: A Treatise on Argumentation.* Translated by J. Wilkinson and P. Weaver. Notre Dame: University of Notre Dame Press, 1969.

Person, Raymond F. *The Deuteronomistic History and the Book of Chronicles: Scribal Works in an Oral World.* AIL 6. Atlanta: SBL, 2010.

Phelan, James. *Narrative as Rhetoric: Technique, Audiences, Ethics, Ideology.* Ohio: Ohio State University Press, 1996.

Pickering, Wilbur. *A Framework for Discourse Analysis.* Arlington: University of Texas Press, 1980.

Plöger, Otto. "Reden und Gebete im deuteronomistischen und chronistischen Geschichtswerk." In *Festschrift für Guüther Dehn,* edited by Wilhelm Schneemelcher, 35-49. Reprint, Göttingen: Vandenhoeck & Ruprecht, 1975.

———. *Theocracy and Eschatology.* Translated by S. Rudman. Oxford: Blackwell, 1968.

Polzin, Robert. *David and the Deuteronomist: A Literary Study of the Deuteronomic History Part Three: 2 Samuel.* Bloomington: Indiana University Press, 1993.

———. *Late Biblical Hebrew Toward an Historical Typology of Biblical Hebrew Prose.* HSM 12. Missoula: Scholars, 1976.

———. *Moses and the Deuteronomist: A Literary Study of the Deuteronomic History Part 1.* Bloomington: Indiana University Press, 1993.

———. *Samuel and the Deuteronomist: A Literary Study of the Deuteronomic History Part Two: 1 Samuel.* Bloomington: Indiana University Press, 1993.

Pomykala, Kenneth E. *The Davidic Dynasty Tradition in Early Judaism: Its History and Significance for Messianism.* Atlanta: Scholars, 1995.

Porter, John. *The Vertical Mosaic: An Analysis of Social Class and Power in Canada.* Toronto: University of Toronto Press, 1965.

Powell, Mark A. *What is Narrative Criticism?* Minneapolis: Fortress, 1990.

Redditt, Paul L. "The Dependence of Ezra-Nehemiah on 1 and 2 Chronicles." In *Unity and Disunity in Ezra-Nehemiah: Redaction, Rhetoric, and Reader,* edited by Mark J. Boda et al., 216–40. Sheffield: Sheffield Phoenix, 2008.

Renz, Thomas. *The Rhetorical Function of the Book of Ezekiel.* Leiden: Brill, 2002.

Rigsby, R. O. "The Historiography of Speeches and Prayers in the Books of Chronicles." ThD diss., Southern Baptist Theological Seminary, 1973.

Riley, William. *King and Cultus in Chronicles: Worship and the Reinterpretation of History.* JSOTSup 160. Sheffield: Sheffield Academic, 1993.

Rimmon-Kenan, Shlomith. *Narrative Fiction.* 2nd ed. London: Routledge, 2002.

Ristau, Kenneth A. "Breaking Down Unity: An Analysis of 1 Chronicles 21:1—22:1." *JSOT* 30 (2005) 201–21.

———. "Reading and Rereading Josiah: The Chronicler's Representation of Josiah for the Postexilic Community." In *Community Identity in Judean Historiography: Biblical and Comparative Perspectives,* edited by Gary N. Knoppers et al., 219–47. Winona Lake, IN: Eisenbrauns, 2009.

Rom-Shiloni, Dalit. *Exclusive Inclusivity: Identity Conflicts Between the Exiles and the People who Remained (6th–5th Centuries BCE).* London: Bloomsbury T. & T. Clark, 2013.

———. "From Ezekiel to Ezra-Nehemiah: Shifts of Group Identities within Babylonian Exilic Ideology." In *Judah and the Judeans in the Achaemenid Period: Negotiating Identity in an International Context*, edited by Oded Lipschits, et al., 127–51. Winona Lake, IN: Eisenbrauns, 2011.

Rost, Leonhard. *The Succession of the Throne of David*. Sheffield: Almond, 1982.

Rothstein, J. W., and J. Hänel. *Das erste Buch der Chronik*. KAT. Leipzig: Deichertsche, 1927.

Rudolph, Wilhelm. *Chronikbücher*. HAT 21. Tübingen: J. C. B. Mohr, 1955.

———. "Problems of the Books of Chronicles." *VT* 4 (1954) 401–9.

Sæbø, Magne. "Messianism in Chronicles?" *HBT* 2 (1980) 85–109.

Schaefer, G. E. "The Significance of Seeking God in the Purpose of the Chronicler." ThD diss., Southern Baptist Theological Seminary, 1972.

Schaper, Joachim. "The Jerusalem Temple as an Instrument of the Achaemenid Fiscal Administration." *VT* 45 (1995) 528–39.

———. "The Temple Treasury Committee in the Times of Nehemiah and Ezra." *VT* 47 (1997) 200–206.

Schenker, A. "Die Verheissung Natans in 2 Sam 7 in der Septuaginta." In *The Septuagint and Messianism*, edited by M. A. Knibb, 177–92. BETL 195. Louvain: Louvain University Press, 2006.

Schniedewind, William M. *How the Bible Became a Book*. Cambridge: Cambridge University Press, 2004.

———. *Society and the Promise to David: The Reception History of 2 Samuel 7:1–17*. Oxford: Oxford University Press, 1999.

———. *The Word of God in Transition: From Prophet to Exegete in the Second Temple Period*. JSOTSup 197. Sheffield: Sheffield Academic, 1995.

Schmid, Wolf. *Narratology: An Introduction*. Translated by Alexander Starritt. Berlin: de Gruyter, 2010.

Schweitzer, Steven J. *Reading Utopia in Chronicles*. LHBOTS 422. New York: T. & T. Clark, 2007.

Selman, Martin J. "Jerusalem in Chronicles." In *Zion: City of Our God*, edited by Richard S. Hess et al., 43–56. Grand Rapids: Eerdmans, 1999.

———. "The Kingdom of God in Old Testament." *TynBul* 40 (1989) 161–83.

———. *1 Chronicles: An Introduction and Commentary*. TOTC 10a. Downers Grove, IL: InterVarsity, 1994.

———. *2 Chronicles: A Commentary*. TOTC 10b. Downers Grove, IL: InterVarsity, 1994.

Seow, C. L. "The Designation of the Ark in Priestly Theology." *HAR* 8 (1985) 185–98.

Shin, Deuk-il. *The Ark of Yahweh in Redemptive History: A Revelatory Instrument of Divine Attributes*. Eugene, OR: Wipf & Stock, 2012.

Shipp, R. Mark. "'Remember His Covenant Forever': A Study of the Chronicler's Use of the Psalms." *RQ* 35 (1993) 29–39.

Sloan, T., and C. Perelman. "Rhetoric." In *The New Encyclopedia Britannica*, 26:803–10. 15th ed. London: Encyclopaedia Britannica, 1985.

Smend, Rudolf. *Die Entstehung des Alten Testaments*. Stuttgart: Kohlhammer, 1978.

Smith-Christopher, Daniel L. *The Religion of the Landless: A Sociology of the Babylonian Exile*. Bloomington, IN: Meyer-Stone, 1989.

Sparks, James T. *The Chronicler's Genealogies*. Atlanta: SBL, 2008.

Stamps, Dennis L. "Rethinking Rhetorical Situation: The Entextualization of the Situation in New Testament Epistles." In *Rhetoric and the New Testament: Essays from the 1992 Heidelberg Conference*, edited by Stanley E. Porter et al., 193–210. JSNTSup 90. Sheffield: Sheffield Academic, 1993.

Staudt, E. "Prayer and the People in the Deuteronomist." PhD diss., Vanderbilt University, 1980.

Stern, Ephraim, *Archaeology of the Land of the Bible: The Assyrian, Babylonian and Persian Periods (732-332 B.C.E.).* New York: Doubleday, 2001.

Stinespring, W. F. "Eschatology in Chronicles." *JBL* 80 (1961) 209-19.

Street, James M. *The Significance of the Ark Narrative: Literary Formation and Artistry in the Book of Chronicles.* New York: Peter Lang, 2009.

Talstra, E. *Solomon's Prayer: Synchrony and Diachrony in the Composition of I Kings 8, 14-61.* Translated by G. Runia-Deenick. Kampen: Kok Pharos, 1993.

Throntveit, Mark A. "The Chronicler's Speeches and Historical Reconstruction." In *The Chronicler as Historian*, edited by M. Patrick Graham et al., 225-45. Sheffield: Sheffield Academic, 1997.

———. "The Idealization of Solomon as the Glorification of God in the Chronicler's Royal Speeches and Royal Prayers." In *The Age of Solomon: Scholarship at the Turn of the Millennium*, edited by Lowell K. Handy, 411-27. Leiden: Brill, 1997.

———. *When Kings Speak: Royal Speech and Royal Prayer in Chronicles*, SBLDS 93. Atlanta: Scholars, 1987.

Tiňo, Jozef. *King and Temple in Chronicles: A Contextual Approach to Their Relations.* Göttingen: Vandenhoeck & Ruprecht, 2010.

Thompson, J. A. *1, 2 Chronicles.* NAC. Nashville: Broadman & Holman, 1994.

Trible, Phyllis. *Rhetorical Criticism: Context, Method, and the Book of Jonah.* Minneapolis: Fortress, 1994.

Trotter, James M. "Reading, Readers and Reading Readers Reading the Account of Saul's Death in 1 Chronicles 10." In *The Chronicler as Author: Studies in Text and Texture*, edited by M. Patrick Graham et al., 294-310. Sheffield: Sheffield Academic, 1999.

Tuell, Steven S. *First and Second Chronicles.* Louisville: John Knox, 2001.

Van der Merwe, Christo H. J., et al. *A Biblical Hebrew Reference Grammar.* Sheffield: Sheffield Academic, 1999.

Van der Toorn, K., and C. Houtman. "David and the Ark." *JBL* 113 (1994) 209-31.

Vatz, Richard E. "The Myth of the Rhetorical Situation." *PR* 6 (1973) 154-61.

Von Rad, Gerhard. *Das Geschichtsbild des chronistischen Werkes.* BWANT 54. Stuttgart: Kohlhammer, 1930.

———. "The Levitical Sermon in the Books of Chronicles." In *The Problem of the Hexateuch and Other Essays*, 267-80. Translated by E. W. Trueman Dicken. London: Oliver & Boyd, 1966.

———. "The Tent and the Ark." In *The Problem of the Hexateuch and Other Essays*, 103-24. Translated by E. W. Trueman Dicken. London: Oliver & Boyd, 1966.

Walsh, Jerome T. *Old Testament Narrative: A Guide to Interpretation.* Louisville: Westminster John Knox, 2010.

Walters, Stanley D. "Saul of Gibeon." *JSOT* 52 (1991) 61-76.

Waltke, Bruce K., and M. O'Connor. *An Introduction Biblical Hebrew Syntax.* Winona Lake, IN: Eisenbrauns, 1990.

Watson, D. F., and A. J. Hauser. *Rhetorical Criticism of the Bible: A Comprehensive Bibliography with Notes on History and Method.* Leiden: Brill, 1994.

Watts, James W. *Psalm and Story: Inset Hymns in Hebrew Narrative.* JSOTSup 139. Sheffield: Sheffield Academic, 1992.

Weinberg, Joel P. *The Citizen-Temple Community*. Translated by Daniel L. Smith-Christopher. JSOTSup 151. Sheffield: Sheffield Academic, 1992.

Welch, Adam C. *The Work of the Chronicler: Its Purpose and Its Date*. London: Oxford University Press, 1939.

Wellhausen, Julius. *Prolegomena to the History of Israel*. Translated by J. Sutherland Black and Allan Menzies. Reprint, Atlanta: Scholars, 1994.

Welten, P. *Geschichte und Geschichtsdarstellung in den Chronikbüchern*. WMANT 42. Neukirchen-Vluyn: Neukirchener, 1973.

———. "Lade-Tempel-Jerusalem: zur Theologie der Chronikbücher." In *Textgemäss. Aufsätze und Beiträge zur Hermeneutik des Alten Testaments. Festschrift E. Würthwein*, edited by A. J. H. Gunneweg et al., 169–83. Göttingen: Vandenhoeck & Ruprecht, 1979.

Werline, Rodney A. *Pray Like This: Understanding Prayer in the Bible*. London: T. & T. Clark International, 2007.

Westermann, Claus. *Praise and Lament in the Psalms*. Translated by Keith R. Crim and Richard N. Soulen. Atlanta: John Knox, 1981.

White, Hayden V. *Metahistory: Historical Imagination in Nineteenth-Century Europe*. Baltimore: The Johns Hopkins University Press, 1973.

———. "The Structure of Historical Narrative." *Clio* 1 (1972) 5–20.

Widengren, G. "King and Covenant." *JSS* 2 (1957) 1–32.

Willi, Thomas. *Die Chronik als Auslegung: Untersuchungen zur literarischen Gestaltung der historischen Überlieferung Israels*. FRLANT 106. Göttingen: Vandenhoeck & Ruprecht, 1972.

Williamson, H. G. M. *1 and 2 Chronicles*. NCB. Grand Rapids: Eerdmans, 1982.

———. "The Ascension of Solomon in the Books of Chronicles." *VT* 26 (1976) 351–61.

———. "Dynastic Oracle in the Books of Chronicles." In *Isac Leo Seeligmann Volume: Essays on the Bible and the Ancient World*, Volume III: Non-Hebrew Section, edited by A. Rofé et al., 305–18. Jerusalem: E. Rubinstein, 1983.

———. "Eschatology in Chronicles." *TynBul* 28 (1977) 115–54.

———. *Israel in the Books of Chronicles*. Cambridge: Cambridge University Press, 1977.

———. "The Origins of the 24 Priestly Courses: A Study of 1 Chronicles 23–27." In *Studies in Persian Period History and Historiography*, edited by H. G. M. Williamson, 126–40. Tübingen: Mohr Siebeck, 2004.

———. "We are Yours, O David: The Setting and Purpose of 1 Chronicles XII 1–23." *OS* 21 (1981) 164–76.

Wright, John W. "The Innocence of David in 1 Chronicles 21." *JSOT* 60 (1993) 87–104.

———. "The Founding Father: The Structure of the Chronicler's David Narrative." *JBL* 117 (1998) 45–59.

———. "From Center to Periphery: 1 Chronicles 23–27 and the Interpretation of Chronicles in the Nineteenth Century." In *Priests, Prophets, and Scribes: Essays on the Formation and Heritage of Second Temple Judaism in Honor of Joseph Blenkinsopp*, edited by Eugene G. Ulrich et al., 20–42. JSOTSup 149. Sheffield: Sheffield Academic, 1992.

———. "Guarding the Gates. 1 Chronicles 26:1–19 and the Roles of the Gatekeepers in Chronicles." *JSOT* 48 (1990) 69–81.

———. "The Legacy of David in Chronicles: The Narrative Function of 1 Chronicles 23–27." *JBL* 110 (1991) 229–42.

———. "The Origin and Function of 1 Chronicles 23–27." PhD diss., University of Notre Dame, 1989.

———. "'Those Doing the Work for the Service in the House of the Lord': 1 Chronicles 23:6—24:31 and the Socio-Historical Context for the Temple of Yahweh in Jerusalem in the Late Persian/Early Hellenistic Period." In *Judah and the Judeans in the Fourth Century B.C.E*, edited by Oded Lipschits et al., 361–84. Winona Lake, IN: Eisenbrauns, 2007.

Woudstra, M. H. *The Ark of the Covenant from Conquest to Kingship*. Phillipsburg, NJ: Presbyterian and Reformed, 1965.

Wuellner, Wilhelm. "Where is Rhetorical Criticism Taking Us?" *CBQ* 49 (1987) 448–63.

Young, Ian, et al. *Linguistic Dating of Biblical Texts*. London: Equinox, 2008.

Zalewski, Saul. "The Purpose of the Story of the Death of Saul in 1 Chronicles X." *VT* 39 (1989) 449–67.

Zunz, L. *Die gottesdienstlichen Vorträge der Juden historisch entwickelt*. Berlin: A. Asher, 1832. Reprint, Hildersheim: Georg Olms, 1966.

Index of Modern Authors

A

Ackroyd, P. R., 3, 4, 7, 53, 54, 58, 60, 82, 145, 209, 236
Albertz, R., 55
Albright, W. F., 38
Allen, L. C., 93, 104, 185
Amador, J. D. H., 281
Amit, Y., 44, 103, 168, 169, 180
Arnold, B. T., 224, 248
Arnold, C. C., 27
Avioz, M., 135, 136, 192, 242, 249

B

Bailey, N., 155, 156, 159
Bakhtin, M. M, 281
Balentine, S. E., 14, 15, 80, 113, 146, 202, 263, 280
Bar-Efrat, S., 14, 34, 64, 65, 69, 86, 92, 105, 118, 177, 185, 217, 224
Barker, J., 21, 22
Bar-Kochva, B., 46
Barstad, H. B., 42
Barton, J., 18
Becker, J., 145
Bedford, P. R., 48
Beentjes, P. C., 80, 87, 127, 129, 131, 132, 135–37, 142, 143, 156, 159, 162, 163, 165, 168, 202, 232, 242
Begg, C. T., 99, 102, 104, 231, 249, 277
Begrich, J., 14
Bemong, N., 281
Benzinger, I., 6
Ben Zvi, E., 46, 226, 227, 230, 269, 270
Berger, Y., 44, 73, 101, 219
Berlin, A., 64
Berquist, J. L., 41, 42, 48, 49, 50, 61
Bitzer, L. F., 26, 27, 28, 29, 30, 33, 281
Black, C. C., 21
Blenkinsopp, J., 42, 43, 44, 169
Boda, M. J., 2, 9, 39, 40, 54, 55, 59, 61, 70, 74, 100, 102, 103, 104, 107, 108, 119, 121, 122, 124, 125, 135, 142, 145, 146, 149, 153, 155, 156, 157, 161, 163, 165, 167, 171, 172, 173, 176, 179, 180, 189, 195, 199, 202, 206, 207, 208, 217, 218, 229, 243, 245, 248, 249, 251, 252, 255, 263, 264
Bodner, K., 99
Booth, W. C., 16, 17, 27, 34
Brandt, W. L., 24
Braun, R. L., 2, 4, 10, 12, 13, 38, 67, 69, 70, 71, 96, 97, 125, 126, 129, 156, 157, 176, 189, 192, 193, 197, 198, 205, 207, 278
Briant, P., 38, 41
Brinton, A., 33
Brueggemann, W., 6
Brunet, A. M., 145
Burke, K., 27
Butler, T. C., 113

C

Callow, J., 64
Campbell, A. F., 99
Caquot, A., 124, 145
Carr, D. M., 217
Carroll, R. P., 42
Carter, C. E., 43, 50
Cataldo, J., 46, 47, 48, 50
Ceresko, A. R., 18
Chang, W. I., 4
Chatman, S., 17, 34
Clifford, R. J., 18
Clines, D. J. A., 18
Coats, G. W., 99
Coggins, R. J., 7, 8, 193
Consigny, S., 29
Corvin, J. W., 15
Cross, F. M., 3, 216
Culley, R. C., 27
Curtis, E. L., 40, 59, 88

D

Davies, P. R., 42, 43
Day, P. L., 156

Index of Modern Authors

Day, J., 112, 169
Dennerlein, N., 87, 99
De Vries, S. J., 2, 10, 40, 59, 71, 79, 100, 113, 145, 156, 157
Dillard, R. B., 38, 39, 73, 195, 221, 224, 227, 228, 254, 258, 259, 263, 265
Dirksen, P. B., 156, 175, 185
Dorsey, D. A., 64, 71, 72, 73, 74, 76, 231
Dozeman, T. B., 19
Driver, S. R., 10
Duke, R. K., 1, 8, 9, 10, 11, 22, 66, 67, 79, 80, 83, 157, 212
Dumbrell, W. J., 124, 192, 260
Dyck, J. E., 4, 5, 50, 61

E

Edelman, D., 42, 44, 122
Engler, H., 4
Eskenazi, T. C., 99, 101, 104
Eslinger, L., 6, 22, 34, 99, 124, 242
Estes, D. L., 204
Evans, P. S., 155, 156, 159, 281
Eynikel, E. M. M., 99

F

Faust, A., 42
Finkelstein, I., 42
Flanagan, J. W., 85
Fokkelman, J. P., 6
Fox, M. V., 28
Freedman, D. N., 38, 145
Fretheim, T. E., 99
Fried, L. S., 42

G

Gakuru, G., 124, 148
Garbini, G., 46
Garret, M., 27
Garsiel, M., 105
Gerstenberger, E. S., 62
Gesenius, W., 103, 173, 176
Giffone, B. D., 45
Gitay, Y., 18, 99
Gorrell, D., 29
Grabbe, L. L., 42
Graham, M. P., 3
Grant-Davie, K., 40, 58
Greenberg, M., 15, 280
Greenwood, D., 18
Greenwood, K. R., 155
Grisanti, M. A., 124
Groom, S., 16

Gunkel, H., 14, 18
Gunn, D. M., 6
Gutmann, J., 99

H

Hahn, S. H., 249
Hamilton, V. P., 156
Hänel, J., 145
Hanson, P. D., 145
Hauser, A. J., 16, 18, 19, 280
Hentschel, G., 43
Hill, A. E., 79, 100, 113, 121, 122, 125, 132, 134, 138, 143, 146, 148, 150–52, 157, 165, 168, 169, 172, 173, 176, 180, 182, 189, 195, 197, 199, 201, 202, 204, 219, 235, 237, 243, 249, 251, 253, 258, 264
Hoglund, K. G., 41
Holquist, M., 281
Houtman, C., 99
Howard, D. M., 19
Hurowitz, V. A., 242
Hwang, S., 4, 5, 136, 137, 145

I

Im, T-S., 4, 145, 157
Iser, W., 17, 34
Ishida, T., 124, 148, 149, 216

J

Jackson, J. J., 99
Japhet, S., 3, 4, 14, 38, 39, 40, 54, 56, 57, 60, 67, 68, 79, 82, 84, 85, 90, 91, 92, 100, 102, 103, 104, 105, 109, 110, 111, 112, 113, 114, 116, 121, 125, 127, 129, 130, 131, 132, 135, 139, 140, 151, 156, 157, 160, 163, 165, 168, 173, 176, 179, 180, 181, 184, 185, 189, 191, 192, 194, 197, 199, 200, 202, 203, 204, 217, 219, 222, 224, 227, 228, 234, 236, 243, 245, 246, 253, 264, 265, 268, 269
Jarick, J., 156
Jeon, Y-H., 5, 6
Johnstone, W., 46, 54, 71, 102, 103, 110, 111, 112, 113, 119, 127, 131, 134, 135, 137, 139, 144, 155, 157, 160, 167, 173, 176, 177, 182, 199, 203, 204, 214, 231, 232, 242, 243, 245, 246, 247, 249, 253, 265, 269, 270
Jones, G. H., 124
Jonker, L., 8, 14, 44, 45, 49, 50, 52, 58, 99, 169, 170, 180, 182, 184, 187, 275
Joüon, P., 225, 227, 257

Index of Modern Authors

K

Kalimi, I., 3, 4, 6, 7, 8, 40, 59, 61, 84, 85, 87, 88, 91, 106, 107, 108, 109, 110, 111, 113, 116, 117, 126, 127, 128, 131, 133, 134, 135, 136, 150, 151, 152, 158, 161, 162, 164, 175, 177, 231, 254
Kang, J. J., 22, 65
Keil, C. F., 59, 145
Kellerman, D., 158
Kelly, B. E., 1, 60, 124, 145, 212, 258, 262, 263, 278
Kennedy, G. A., 18, 21, 22, 23, 24, 25, 26, 27, 28, 31, 64, 85, 280, 281
Kessler, J., 46, 47
Kessler, M., 18
Kittel, R., 6
Klein, R. W., 38, 39, 40, 45, 54, 55, 59, 70, 79, 84, 86, 88, 90, 94, 95, 96, 97, 100, 104, 105, 106, 107, 117, 119, 121, 126–29, 149, 152, 156, 165, 182, 185, 189, 191, 192, 196, 201, 203, 215, 216, 217, 221, 224, 225, 226, 227, 228, 243, 245, 246, 247, 258, 260, 261, 265, 269
Kleinig, J. W., 113
Knoppers, G. N., 6, 13, 39, 40, 42, 44, 45, 46, 71, 87, 100, 110, 120, 121, 122, 125, 132, 138, 141, 142, 147, 149, 153, 155, 156, 157, 160, 163, 167, 168, 169, 172, 175, 176, 182, 185, 186, 189, 242, 262, 281, 282
Kreutzer, F., 156
Kruse, H., 124
Kuhrt, A., 41
Kuntzmann, R., 192

L

Langston, S. M., 53, 276
Lanham, R. A., 87, 90, 103, 105, 106, 107, 109, 117, 118, 127, 128, 129, 132, 133, 134, 138, 139, 142, 152, 158, 162, 175, 185, 199, 202, 203, 204, 224, 236, 243, 248, 261
Lenchak, T. A., 21, 22, 23, 24, 28
Levenson, J. D., 124, 277
Levin, Y., 43, 50
Lipschits, O., 42, 43, 52
Lundbom, J. R., 18, 104, 130, 132, 133, 134, 142, 151, 160, 184, 193, 202, 234, 244
Lynch, M., 6, 137

M

Mack, B. L., 21
Macy, H. R., 10
Madsen, A. A., 40, 59, 88

Martens, E. A., 140, 176
Mason, R., 10, 11, 14, 80, 92, 93, 124, 176, 193, 195, 206, 278
McCarthy, D. J., 83, 195, 196, 197
McConville, J. G., 1, 194, 249
McKenzie, S. M., 4, 5, 38, 127, 145, 156, 192, 207, 213, 259, 260, 261, 266
Meyers, M., 42
Miller, A. B., 26
Miller, P. D., 99, 250
Mitchell, C., 173, 281
Möller, K., 21, 22, 23, 24, 25, 31, 97
Mowinckel, S., 14
Muilenburg, J., 17, 18, 19, 21, 64, 65
Muraoka, T., 225, 227, 257
Myers, J. M., 4, 38, 121

N

Na'aman, N., 43
Newsome, J. D., 4, 10, 38, 145
Noll, K. L., 6
Noordtzij, A., 145
North, R., 4, 145, 236
Noth, M., 3, 4, 38, 145

O

Oded, B., 42,
Oeming, M., 4, 40, 95
Olbrechts-Tyteca, L., 19, 20, 21, 24, 25, 27, 28, 30
Osborne, W. L., 4
O'Connor, M., 86, 224, 227
O'Kennedy, D. F., 242, 249

P

Patrick, D., 18, 19, 30
Peltonen, K., 39
Perelman, C., 19, 20, 21, 24, 25, 27, 28, 30
Person, R. F., 3
Phelan, J., 16
Pickering, W., 64
Plöger, O., 10, 14, 67, 145
Polzin, R., 6, 28, 33, 38, 99
Pomykala, K. E., 145, 146
Porter, J., 47
Powell, M. A., 30

R

Redditt, P. L., 60
Renz, T., 21, 22
Rigsby, R. O., 4, 10, 11

Riley, W., 4, 83, 124, 135, 145, 212
Rimmon-Kenan, S., 34
Ristau, K. A., 67, 155, 157
Roberts, J. J. M., 99
Rom-Shiloni, D., 46, 55, 56
Rost, L., 99
Rothstein, W., 145

S

Sæbø, M., 145
Schaefer, G. E., 4
Schaper, J., 41
Schenker, A., 125
Schmid, W., 34, 35
Schniedewind, W. M., 10, 42, 83, 93, 95, 124, 125, 145, 146, 148, 176, 191, 193, 209, 243, 244
Schweitzer, S. J., 4, 5
Scult, A., 18, 19, 30
Selman, M. J., 73, 74, 87, 100, 101, 109, 113, 125, 131, 136, 146, 147, 206, 234
Seow, C. L., 99
Shin, D., 112
Shipp, R. M., 113
Sloan, T., 20
Smend, R., 7
Smith-Christopher, D. L., 51
Sparks, J. T., 66, 145
Stamps, D. L., 29, 30
Staudt, E., 15
Stern, E., 42
Stinespring, W. F., 145
Street, J. M., 68, 69, 72, 99, 109, 119

T

Talstra, E., 242
Thompson, J. A. 59, 113, 120, 132, 185
Throntveit, M. A., 1, 10, 12, 13, 14, 38, 79, 126, 129, 133, 200, 201, 202, 203, 235, 278, 279
Tiño, J., 3, 4, 5
Trible, P., 18, 23, 85, 280
Trotter, J. M., 82
Tuell, S. S., 59, 70, 71, 83, 156, 213, 227

V

Van der Merwe, C. H. J., 65, 86, 159, 193, 194, 196, 216, 224
Van der Toorn, K., 99
Vatz, R. E., 28, 29, 33
Von Rad, G., 3, 4, 10, 11, 99, 145

W

Walsh, J. T., 15
Walters, S. D., 44, 60
Waltke, B. K., 86, 224, 227
Watson, D. F., 16, 19, 280
Watts, J. W., 114, 119
Weinberg, J. P., 50, 51
Welch, A. C., 4, 6, 185
Welhausen, J., 6
Welten, P., 38, 95, 99
Werline, R. A., 259
Westermann, C., 14
White, H. V., 8, 9
Widengren, G., 253
Willi, T., 4, 7, 55, 95
Williamson, H. G. M., 1, 3, 4, 38, 39, 40, 59, 60, 61, 67, 71, 83, 84, 88, 95, 103, 104, 108, 109, 110, 113, 120, 121, 125, 143, 145, 148, 156, 157, 165, 166, 173, 176, 179, 182, 187, 189, 191, 195, 197, 209, 216, 217, 231, 248, 252, 258, 260, 263
Woudstra, M. H., 99, 144
Wright, J. W., 70, 83, 155, 156, 159, 182, 183, 184, 186
Wuellner, W., 19, 23, 64

X

Xiao, X., 27

Y

Young, I., 39

Z

Zalewski, S., 74, 82
Zunz, L., 3

Index of Ancient Sources

OLD TESTAMENT

Genesis

1	65
2	86
6:5	195
7:1	135
8:21	195
12:2	131
12:7	116
12:10–20	116
13:14–17	131
13:16	216
15	117
15:17	116
15:18–21	131
17:7	141
20:1–18	116
22	277
22:1–19	165
22:15–18	116, 117
23	165
23:8	191
26:2–5	116, 117
26:7–11	116
27:13–15	116
28:13–15	117
28:14	216
32:24	116
32:29	116
35:9–13	116
35:11–12	117

Exodus

1:21	134
3:8	131
6:7	141
6:8	131
19	207, 236
19:5	199
19:6	200
22:7–13	245
22:8	245
23:31	179
25–31	214
35–40	214
28:41	199
29:9	199
29:29	199
29:33	199
30:11–16	160
31:1–11	219, 228
32:9–14	277
32:29	199
35	228
35:30–35	228
35:31–35	228

Leviticus

8:33	199
16:32	199
26	59
26:3–4	246
26:12	141
26:14–33	59
26:34	59

Numbers

1:47–49	156
2:33	156
4:1–15	111
7:9	111, 210
32:22	180

Deuteronomy

4:29	194, 195
6:5	194
7:3	265
10:8	109
11:13–14	246
11:24–25	131
12	122, 129, 179

Index of Ancient Sources

Deuteronomy (continued)

12:10	179
12:10–11	180
13:2–6	216
17:16–18	5
18:5	110
23:7–8	265
25:1	245
26:16–19	141
28	246
28:21	246
28:22	246
28:38	246
28:48	246
28:23–24	246
28:37	261
29:23	261
29:27	261
31	197
31:7–8	176
33:12	156

Joshua

1	197
1:6–7	152
1:6–9	176
3:11	130
13	197
18:1	179
18:25	156
18:28	156
21:44	179

Judges

2:11–23	245
3:11	65
3:30	65
5:31	65
8:28	65
17:5	199
17:12	199
20:27	130

1 Samuel

16	94
16:4	90
21:1–7	91
22:2	91
27	94
31:1–13	10

2 Samuel

5:1–3	11
5:3	85
5:6–10	10
5:17–25	108
5:19	106
5:19–25	10
5:20	106, 108
5:22	108
5:23	106
5:23–24	107
5:24	107
5:25	108
6	248
6–7	249
6:1–11	10, 102
6:2	111
6:3	111
6:4	111
6:6	111
6:7	111
6:9	105, 111
6:11	111
6:12	111
6:12–19	109, 112
6:13	111
6:15	109, 111
6:17	109, 111
6:17–20	101
6:17–20a	100
7	126, 136, 177, 248
7:1	177
7:1b	126, 175
7:1–2	126
7:1–16	125
7:1–17	143
7:1–29	10
7:2	127
7:3	127
7:5	129, 192
7:11	133, 134, 135, 177
7:11a	131
7:12–16	145
7:13	128
7:14b	136
7:14b–15a	277
7:15	134
7:16	136
7:16a	142
7:18–21	139
7:18–29	143
7:21	139
7:24	140, 141
7:25	142

Index of Ancient Sources

7:25–29	141	8:16	235
7:26	142	8:20	268
7:29	142	8:21	235, 236
8:1a	131	8:22	245
10:1–14	10	8:23	243
10:1–19	150	8:23–26	243
10:2–3	150	8:23–53	242
10:5b	151	8:25	192, 242, 243, 268
10:11–12	152	8:26	216, 243
11	153	8:27	244
19:12–13	86	8:27–30	244
23:13–17	10	8:28	242, 244
23:17	89	8:29	244
24	165	8:30	244
24:1–25	10	8:31	245
24:2	158	8:31–32	245
24:2–3	158	8:32	245
24:10	159	8:33	245
24:10–17	158, 162	8:33–34	245
24:13	161, 162	8:34	245
24:17	163	8:35	245
24:18–25	163	8:35–36	245
24:22	164	8:37–40	246
24:22b–24a	163	8:38	246
		8:39	246
		8:41–42	246
1 Kings		8:41–43	246
1–10	212	8:42	246
2:4	192, 268	8:44	247
2:13	90	8:44–45	247
3:5	215	8:46	247
3:5–14	215	8:46–51	247
3:5–15	10	8:48	247
3:6	216	8:49–50	248
3:8–9	216	8:52	248
3:10	216	8:53	248
3:11–14	217	8:61	194
3:12–13	217	8:66	68
3:14	217	9:1–9	10
5:1–12	11	9:2	257
5:16	221, 224	9:2–3	257
5:16–20	224	9:2–9	257
5:17–18	225	9:3	257, 259
5:19	224	9:3a	257
5:19–20	221	9:3b	257
5:20	225	9:4	260
5:21	222, 227	9:4–5	192, 260
5:21–23	226	9:5	260, 268
5:23	222, 228	9:6	260
5:25	221	9:6–9	260
5:29–30	222	9:7	260
7:13–14	222, 227, 228	9:8	260
8:12–21	234	9:9	260
8:12–52	10	9:11–14	264
8:13	234	9:24	265

Index of Ancient Sources

1 Kings (continued)

10:1–13	10
10:6	268
10:6–9	268
10:7	268
10:9	268, 269
11	212
11:4	194
12:1–24	11
13:33	199
15:3	194
15:14	194
15:17–22	11
18:12–21	13
22:1–40	11

2 Kings

11:4–16	11
12:4–7	10
14:6	10
14:8–14	11
17:26–28	42
18:17–25	11
19:9–13	11
20:3	194
21:2–9	10
22:8–20	10
22:13	57
24:8–17	46
25:27–30	39

1 Chronicles

1	242
1–9	4, 45, 53, 54, 65, 66, 69, 70, 71, 273
1:1–53	66
1:1—9:34	46, 71
2–8	54
2:1–2	66
2:3—4:23	45, 66
2:7	258
3:17	54
3:17–24	39, 54
3:19–20	55
3:24	55
4:10	258
4:14	95
4:24—5:26	66
4:43	56
5:20	258
5:25	258
5:37—6:66	45
6:1–47	66
6:1–80	66
6:1–81	45
6:48–49	66
6:50–53	66
6:54–81	66
7:1–40	66
7:6–12	45, 53, 66
8:1–40	45, 53, 66
8:1—9:1	45
8:29–32	45
8:29–40	44, 66, 67
9:1	54, 59
9:1–35	44
9:1a	66
9:1b	54
9:1b–3	53
9:1b–34	53, 66
9:2	54
9:2–17	54
9:2–44	45
9:3	44, 46, 122, 219
9:3–13	74
9:4–6	54
9:7–9	54
9:10–34	54
9:14–34	74
9:32	46
9:34b	46
9:33–34	46
9:35	44, 122, 219
9:35–40	44
9:35–44	66, 71, 74
9:35—10:14	71
9:35—21:27	71
10	66, 69, 70, 72, 82
10–12	79
10–21	72
10–29	70, 71, 74, 82
10:1	74
10:1–14	10, 71
10:1—11:9	72
10:1—22:1	71, 72, 75
10:1—29:30	75
10:6	135
10:13	54, 106, 258
10:13–14	82, 160, 258
10:14	79, 97, 104, 106
11	84
11–12	35, 36, 37, 75, 76, 80, 82, 83, 84, 94, 95, 96, 97, 119, 209, 212, 273
11–22:1	72
11–29	71, 76, 85, 209, 212
11:1	86, 94, 98

11:1–2	80, 83, 85, 86, 97, 209	12:39	57, 85, 93, 97, 103
11:1–3	11, 75, 76, 84, 94	12:39–41	119
11:1–9	84	12:40	249
11:1—12:40	70	13	102, 167, 212
11:2	87	13–15	72, 104
11:2a	87	13–16	35, 36, 70, 75, 76, 80, 82, 99,
11:2b	87		100, 101, 119, 127, 209, 273,
11:3	85, 88, 94, 97, 127, 162, 209,		276
	249	13–17	70, 79, 219
11:3b	88	13–20	113
11:4–5	83, 97	13:1	102
11:4–9	10, 82, 84, 94	13:1–2	36
11:5a	80, 87, 88, 95	13:1–3	75, 76, 100
11:6	83, 97	13:1–4	101, 102
11:6a	80, 87, 88, 95	13:1–14	82, 100, 101, 104, 111, 210
11:6b	88	13:1—14:17	72
11:7	85, 88	13:1—16:1	101
11:8	56, 88	13:1—21:30	70
11:9	85, 88, 128	13:2	56, 102, 103, 104, 120
11:10	57, 84, 85, 88, 152, 209	13:2a	13
11:10b	89	13:3	13, 102, 104, 111, 119, 127
11:10–47	84, 88, 94, 209	13:2–3	11, 79, 80, 99, 101, 102, 120,
11:10—12:40	72		123, 278
11:10—12:41	84	13:4	103
11:14	249	13:5	57, 85, 127
11:15–19	10	13:5–14	10
11:15–20	89	13:5—15:29	101
11:17	79, 80, 83, 88, 89, 95, 98	13:6	85
11:19	79, 80, 83, 88, 89, 95, 98	13:7	111, 127
12	84, 89, 93	13:8	85
12:1	93	13:9	104
12:1–7	84, 94	13:10	104
12:8–15	84	13:11	104, 111
12:9	92	13:12	80, 102, 104, 105, 109, 127
12:16	36, 92	13:14	99, 101, 104, 105, 120, 123, 127
12:16–18	84, 209	14	112, 119, 212
12:17	11, 79, 90	14:1–2	224
12:17–18	83	14:1–7	105
12:17–19	80, 85, 89, 90, 92, 98	14:1–17	100, 101
12:18	11, 90, 92, 93	14:7	106
12:18–19	98	14:8	85
12:19	80, 90, 91, 92, 93, 95, 278	14:8–12	105
12:19–22	84, 94	14:8–16	82, 108
12:20	83, 93, 98	14:8–17	105, 210
12:20–22	93	14:10	80, 106, 107, 210
12:20b	80, 93	14:10a	79
12:21	92	14:10–11	80, 99, 101, 104, 105, 106, 120,
12:22	93		123
12:23	84, 88, 93, 209	14:10–17	10
12:23–37	84	14:11	79, 104, 106, 107, 108
12:23–38	84	14:13	108
12:24	97, 159	14:13–17	107
12:34	93	14:14	106
12:38	56, 194	14:14–15	80, 99, 101, 107, 120, 123
12:38–40	75, 76, 84	14:15	107

1 Chronicles (continued)

Reference	Pages
14:16	108
14:17	108, 113, 131
15	68, 109, 112, 119, 120
15–16	110, 231
15–17	212
15:1	109, 111, 127
15:1–15	109
15:1–25	100
15:1—16:3	82, 100, 101, 109, 210
15:1—16:43	72
15:2	11, 13, 14, 79, 80, 99, 109, 120, 123, 124, 127, 278
15:3	85, 109, 110, 111, 127
15:3–4	110
15:11	109, 110
15:11–12	120
15:11–13	105
15:12	90, 111, 127
15:12–13	11, 13, 14, 79, 80, 99, 109, 110, 111, 120, 123, 124, 210, 278
15:13	104, 111, 124
15:14	111, 127
15:14–15	111
15:15	111, 127
15:16	69, 109
15:18	109
15:24	127
15:25	111, 112, 127, 162, 249
15:25–29	111
15:25—16:3	100
15:25—16:43	100
15:26	69, 111, 112, 127
15:26–27	110
15:27	112
15:28	69, 85, 111, 112, 127
15:28–29	69
15:29	111, 112, 127
16	100, 110, 113, 143
16:1	101, 109, 127, 138, 143
16:1–43	100, 101
16:1–3	100, 101
16:2	101
16:2–43	101
16:4	100, 113, 127, 219
16:4–6	114
16:4–7	100, 114, 120
16:4–43	82, 100, 101, 114
16:6	127
16:7	100, 114, 127
16:7–36	69
16:8	116, 117, 118
16:8–36	80, 99, 100, 101, 113, 114, 123, 210
16:8–22	116
16:8–11	116
16:9	116, 117
16:10	116
16:10–11	117
16:11	116
16:12	116, 117
16:12–14	117
16:12–22	117, 121
16:13	116, 117
16:14	56
16:15	116, 117
16:15–18	116
16:15–22	116, 117
16:16–17	117
16:17	117
16:18	117
16:19	116
16:19–20	117
16:19–22	116
16:20	117
16:22	117
16:23	117
16:23–33	116, 117
16:23–27	117
16:27	117, 118
16:28–29	118
16:28–30	118
16:29–30	118
16:30–31	117, 118
16:31	117
16:31–33	118
16:34	116, 117, 118, 249
16:34–36	116, 118, 121
16:35	113, 118, 121, 124
16:35–36	116
16:36	118, 119
16:37	100, 127
16:37–42	100, 253
16:37–43	114
16:38–42	100
16:39	52, 156, 169, 170, 219, 275
16:39–42	121, 122, 123
16:43	75, 76, 100, 101, 110
17	13, 35, 36, 70, 73, 75, 77, 80, 82, 110, 124, 125, 126, 127, 137, 142, 143, 146, 147, 149, 166, 172, 176, 181, 192, 193, 195, 208, 210, 213, 216, 218, 219, 222, 228, 230, 232, 234, 249, 250, 260, 261, 269, 271, 272, 273, 274, 279
17–19	113
17–29	73

Index of Ancient Sources

17:1	75, 77, 79, 80, 124, 126, 127, 128, 143, 144, 147, 175	17:20	140
		17:20–22	137, 140, 146, 148
17:1b	126, 127	17:21	131, 140
17:1–2	125, 126, 143, 176	17:22	131, 140, 252
17:1–15	125, 143	17:23	77, 141, 142
17:1–27	10, 72, 82	17:23–24	216
17:2	80, 124, 126, 128, 144, 147	17:23–27	137, 141, 146, 147
17:3	143	17:24	141, 142, 148
17:3–15	125	17:25	136, 142
17:4	127, 129, 132, 134, 176, 192	17:25–27	142
17:4b	129	17:26	77, 136, 142, 148
17:4–6	128, 129, 144, 147, 225	17:27	75, 77, 141, 142
17:4–14	125, 128, 138, 141, 143, 146, 148, 235, 236	17:27b	142
		18	149
17:4–15	80, 125	18–20	35, 36, 70, 75, 77, 80, 82, 113, 119, 126, 149, 166, 176, 210, 212, 273
17:5	129		
17:6	85, 129, 130		
17:7	77, 131, 132	18–21	70, 73
17:7–8	132, 144	18–29	127
17:7–10	133	18:1	75, 77, 149
17:7–10a	128, 130, 131, 147	18:1a	131
17:7–14	176	18:1–17	82
17:8	128, 131, 132	18:1—20:8	72, 157
17:8–10	132, 150, 153, 154	18:10	128
17:8b–9	131	18:11	128
17:9	131	18:14	85
17:9–10	132	19	149, 153
17:9–10a	132, 144	19:1	149
17:10	126, 127, 131, 133, 135	19:1–5	210
17:10a	131	19:1–15	10
17:10b	133, 135	19:1–19	82, 150
17:10b–14	128, 133, 147	19:2	36, 79, 149, 150, 151, 153, 154
17:11	134, 135, 269, 271	19:2–3	80, 149, 150
17:11–12	134, 144, 227	19:3	36, 149, 150, 151, 153, 154
17:11–14	133, 145, 209, 210, 211, 220, 236, 250, 260, 271	19:4	151
		19:5	79, 151
17:12	128, 134, 176	19:5b	80, 149, 150, 153
17:12–13	175	19:12	90, 152
17:13	136, 145, 176	19:12–13	80, 149, 152, 153, 154
17:13a	134, 135	19:13	88
17:13b	134	19:13a	152
17:14	127, 135, 136, 144, 192, 269	19:13b	152
17:14a	135	19:17	85
17:14b	135	20:1	149
17:16	139	20:1–3	149
17:16a	138	20:1–8	82
17:16b	138	20:4	149
17:16–19	137, 138, 139, 146	20:4–8	149
17:16–22	139, 147	20:8	75, 77
17:16–23	125	21	35, 36, 70, 82, 158, 160, 166, 167, 276
17:16–27	11, 79, 80, 125, 137, 139, 143, 146, 148, 203, 236, 250	21–22:1	77, 81
		21–29	70, 212
17:17	138, 139	21:1	75, 77, 79, 156
17:18	138, 139	21:1–6	155, 156
17:19	139, 148		

1 Chronicles (continued)

21:1–15	155
21:1–27	10
21:1—22:1	72, 75, 82, 155, 168, 179, 210, 273
21:2	36, 158
21:2–3	81, 155, 156, 157, 158, 166, 167, 170
21:3	158
21:4	85
21:6	156, 159
21:7	159
21:7–14	156
21:7–15a	155
21:7–17	162
21:8	11, 79, 80, 81, 156, 158, 159, 160
21:8–13	79, 155, 157, 158, 166, 167, 170
21:8–17	158
21:9–12	156, 158, 160
21:9–13	81, 160, 161
21:10	161
21:11	54
21:11–13	161
21:12	161, 162, 166, 170
21:13	54, 156, 160, 162
21:15	163
21:15–27	156
21:15b–22:1	155
21:16	162, 166
21:16–27	155
21:17	11, 79, 80, 81, 155, 156, 157, 158, 159, 162, 163, 166, 167, 170
21:18	163
21:20	167
21:20–21	36
21:22	163, 164, 165
21:22–24	81, 155, 156, 157, 163, 164, 167, 168, 170
21:23	164
21:24	79, 127
21:25	165
21:26	80, 165, 167, 169, 258
21:28—22:1	155, 156, 165, 168
21:28—22:19	79, 156
21:29	52, 166, 169, 170, 171, 219, 275
22	10, 12, 13, 35, 70, 73, 83, 179, 180, 182, 186, 189, 193, 196, 198, 205, 279
22–27	129
22–29	70, 72, 83, 214
22:1	13, 72, 75, 77, 81, 155, 156, 157, 165, 166, 167, 168, 170, 205, 210
22:1—29:30	70, 157
22:2	72, 172, 179, 222
22:2–19	72, 75, 77, 81, 82, 171, 172, 210, 273
22:2–5	75, 77, 172, 179, 199, 205
22:2—29:30	71, 72, 75
22:3	172, 173
22:4	173
22:5	13, 79, 81, 172, 173, 179, 180, 199
22:6	172, 173
22:6–10	131
22:6–16	11, 14, 80, 153, 172, 173, 179, 180, 210, 278
22:6–19	179, 186
22:7	172
22:7–10	173, 175, 225, 235
22:7–13	13, 79
22:7–16	11, 79, 81, 173, 174
22:8	129, 172, 175, 192, 235
22:8–10	189, 209, 210, 211
22:9	126, 175, 100, 209
22:9–10	220
22:10	172, 175, 176, 192, 227
22:11	172, 176
22:11–13	137, 173, 176
22:11–16	173
22:12	176, 227
22:13	176, 277
22:14	172, 177, 178
22:14–16	79, 173, 177
22:15	177
22:16	177, 278
22:17	177
22:17–19	11, 14, 75, 77, 79, 80, 172, 177, 179, 181, 278
22:18	178, 179, 180
22:18a	178
22:18b	178
22:18–19	11, 80, 81, 177, 178, 206, 278
22:19	127, 172, 178, 181, 258
23–27	35, 36, 70, 73, 75, 77, 81, 83, 181, 182, 183, 185, 186, 187, 205, 210, 273, 276
23	182
23:1	72, 75, 77, 186
23:1—26:32	82
23:1—29:30	79
23:2	186
23:2–32	72
23:3	159
23:25	186

Index of Ancient Sources

23:25–26	81, 181, 182, 183, 184, 186, 188	28:20–21	11, 14, 79, 80, 81, 188, 189, 196, 205, 208, 278
23:25–32	79, 211	28:21	196
23:26	186, 187	29	10, 12, 13, 66, 204, 205, 279
23:28	184, 185	29:1	36, 128, 195, 198, 201, 205, 209
23:28–32	81, 181, 182, 183, 184, 186, 188	29:1–5	11, 79, 80, 81, 188, 189, 197, 198, 205, 208, 278
23:29	184	29:1–9	189
23:30	185	29:2	199
23:32	184, 185	29:2–3	199
24	182	29:2–5	199
24:1–19	72	29:3	199
24:20—26:32	72	29:4	199
25	182	29:5	199, 204
26	182	29:6	204
26:26	128	29:6–9	189, 197, 208
26:32	128	29:7	39
27	182	29:9	128, 194, 204
27:1–34	72	29:10	202
27:32	128	29:10–19	11, 79, 80, 81, 113, 188, 189, 200, 205, 207, 208, 278
27:32–34	75, 77	29:10–20	80
28	10, 12, 13, 193, 196, 198, 205, 279	29:10–22a	189
28–29	35, 36, 70, 73, 75, 77, 81, 82, 83, 186, 188, 189, 195, 205, 211, 252, 274	29:10a	201
		29:10b	202
28:1	36, 75, 77, 189, 205	29:10b–12	201
28:1–10	189	29:11	202
28:1—29:30	72	29:11–19	205
28:2	127, 128, 131, 191, 205	29:12	203
28:2–3	13, 225	29:13	202, 203
28:2–8	11, 80, 81, 188, 189, 190, 205, 206, 208, 278	29:14	203, 204
28:2–10	11, 14, 79, 80, 278	29:13–17	201
28:3	129, 191, 199, 235	29:14	203
28:3–5	191	29:14–16	209
28:4	57	29:14–17	203
28:4–6	192	29:15	204
28:5	135, 192, 195, 269	29:16	203, 204
28:5–16	192	29:17	202, 204
28:5b–7a	135	29:18	202, 204
28:6	195, 199, 209, 259	29:18–19	201, 204
28:6–7	13, 191, 192	29:19	189, 194, 198, 203, 204
28:6–8	209, 211	29:20	11, 13, 79, 80, 278
28:8	57, 191, 193, 206, 208, 277	29:20–22a	189
28:8a	193	29:21	85
28:9	36, 90, 108, 137, 193, 194, 195, 258	29:22b–25	189
		29:23	57, 85, 135, 192, 269
28:9–10	11, 13, 80, 81, 188, 189, 193, 194, 205, 208, 278	29:25	57, 85
		29:26	57, 85
28:10	194, 195, 199	29:26–30	75, 76, 77, 79, 189, 212
28:11–19	196		
28:11–21	189		
28:18	127	**2 Chronicles**	
28:19	189, 207, 209	1	35, 36, 75, 76, 81, 169, 213, 214, 218, 221, 228, 229, 274
28:19–21	189		
28:20	36, 196, 258	1–7	71, 212

313

2 Chronicles (continued)

Ref	Pages
1–9	70, 71, 73, 74, 75, 77, 85, 209, 212, 213, 271
1:1	75, 77, 88, 214, 218
1:1–17	71, 73, 74, 77, 212
1:1—9:31	79
1:2	85, 214, 218
1:2–3	219
1:2–6	214
1:3	52, 156, 170, 214, 218, 275
1:3–5	219
1:4	127, 214
1:5	214, 218
1:5–7	122
1:6	214
1:7	80, 81, 215, 216, 217
1:7a	257
1:7–10	216
1:7–12	218
1:7–13	10, 214, 215, 218, 271
1:8	216
1:8–9	216, 218, 220
1:8–10	79, 80, 81, 216, 217
1:9	142, 216
1:10	216, 217
1:11	217
1:11–12	80, 81, 216, 217
1:12	217, 218
1:13	217, 218, 219
1:14–17	214
1:16–17	76, 77
1:18	76, 78, 221
1:18—2:1	221
1:18—2:17	74, 78
2	35, 36, 76, 80, 218, 221, 228, 270, 271, 274
2–7	213
2:1	78, 221
2:1–12	11
2:1–16	74
2:1–18	73, 213
2:1—7:22	71
2:2	223, 224
2:2–3	224
2:2–9	79, 81, 221, 222, 223, 224, 271
2:3	36, 223, 224, 225
2:3–8	224
2:3–10	11, 13, 80, 222
2:4	224, 225
2:4–6	225
2:5	224, 225
2:6	224
2:7	225
2:8	224, 225
2:9	223, 224, 225
2:10	227, 228
2:10–11	227
2:10–15	81, 221, 222, 226, 271
2:11	36, 227, 269
2:11–12	269
2:11–16	11, 80, 222
2:12	128, 226, 227
2:12–13	227, 228, 229
2:13	228
2:13–14	227
2:14	226, 228
2:14–15	228
2:15	228
2:16	222
2:16–17	221, 222
2:17	76, 78, 159
2:17—5:1	74
3	274
3–4	76
3:1	76, 78, 165, 171, 277
3:1—5:1	73, 74, 78, 213
4	274
5	68, 231, 232
5–7	35, 76, 231
5:1	76, 78
5:2	69, 76, 78, 127, 162, 232, 249, 262
5:2–10	37, 231
5:2–14	231
5:2—7:10	73, 74, 231
5:2—7:11	230, 252, 271, 274
5:2—7:22	36, 74, 78, 81, 213
5:3	250
5:4	162
5:5	156
5:6	69, 232
5:7	69, 127
5:11	69
5:11–14	231
5:13	80, 232
5:13–14	231
5:14	232
6	37, 209, 231, 232, 234, 235, 236
6–7	212
6:1–2	79, 231, 234
6:1–11	11, 80, 81, 230, 231, 232, 234, 237, 253, 271
6:1–39	10
6:1—7:11	37
6:2	234
6:2–11	13
6:3	36, 234
6:3–11	37, 80, 231, 232
6:4	234, 235, 243, 250

Index of Ancient Sources

6:4–9	234	6:34	247
6:4–11	79, 234	6:34–39	243
6:5	234, 235, 236, 259	6:36	247
6:5–6	234, 235	6:36–39	243, 247, 251
6:6	235, 236	6:36–40	243
6:7	234, 235	6:37	347
6:7–9	234, 235	6:38	247, 248
6:8	234, 235	6:39	247, 248
6:8–9	235	6:40	243, 248, 259
6:9	234, 235	6:40–42	13, 243, 279
6:9–11	235, 250	6:41	248, 249, 253
6:10	234, 235, 268	6:41–42	243, 248, 249, 252
6:10–11	236, 253	6:42	248, 249
6:11	127, 234, 235, 236, 249, 253	7	231, 232, 258
6:12–13	237	7:1	37, 165
6:12–42	37, 230, 231, 232, 253, 271	7:1–3	231, 254
6:13	36	7:1–11	231
6:14	243, 249, 277	7:2	232
6:14–17	242, 243, 244	7:3	80, 232
6:14–42	11, 36, 79, 80, 81, 237, 242, 243, 262	7:4–7	254
		7:4–10	231
6:15	236, 243, 250	7:6	80, 85, 128
6:16	242, 243, 268	7:8	85
6:16–17	243, 252	7:8–10	254
6:17	142, 216, 243	7:10	68, 262
6:18	242, 244	7:11	231, 254, 262
6:18–21	242, 243, 244	7:11–22	10, 73, 74, 254
6:18–39	242, 252	7:12	257, 259
6:18–40	244	7:12a	257
6:19	242, 244	7:12–16	255, 257, 259, 263
6:19–20	244, 252	7:12b	258
6:20	244, 252	7:12b–15	259, 263
6:21	244, 252	7:12b–16a	258
6:22	242, 245	7:12–18	254, 257
6:22–23	242, 245	7:12–22	36, 76, 78, 80, 81, 254, 256, 257, 261, 262, 263, 272, 274
6:22–25	243		
6:22–39	243, 244, 252	7:13	258, 259
6:23	245	7:13–16	254
6:24	245, 247	7:14	254, 255, 258, 259, 263
6:24–25	242, 245	7:15	259
6:25	245	7:15–16a	259
6:26	245, 247	7:16	255, 257
6:26–27	242, 245	7:16a	259
6:26–31	259	7:16b	259
6:26–33	243	7:17	260, 277
6:27	246	7:17–18	137, 254, 258, 260, 272
6:28	246	7:17–22	255
6:28–31	242, 246	7:18	260
6:29	246	7:19	258, 260, 262
6:30	246	7:19–21	254
6:31	246	7:19–22	254, 257, 258, 260, 263
6:32	246	7:20	260, 261, 262
6:32–33	242, 246	7:21	260
6:33	246	7:21–22	231, 261
6:34–35	243, 247	7:21	261

2 Chronicles (continued)

7:22	254, 255, 258, 260, 261
8	5, 36, 76
8–9	71, 79, 212, 272
8:1	76, 79, 264
8:1–16	71, 74, 79, 274
8:1–18	79, 81, 264, 266
8:1—9:12	73
8:1—9:31	71, 213
8:2	264
8:2–10	264
8:3–10	266
8:10	266
8:11	79, 127, 264, 265, 266, 272
8:11–16	212
8:11b	81, 265, 266, 274
8:12	266
8:12–15	264
8:12–16	264, 266
8:14	264
8:16	76, 79, 264
8:17	76, 79
8:17–18	212, 264
8:17–19	270
8:17—9:12	74
8:17—9:28	74
8:17—9:31	79
9	76, 80, 270, 274
9:1	267
9:1–12	10, 79, 212, 213, 267
9:1–31	81, 267
9:2	267
9:3–4	267
9:5	268, 269, 270
9:5–6	268, 269
9:6	268, 269
9:5–8	11, 37, 80, 81, 267, 268, 272
9:7	268, 269, 270
9:8	135, 192, 227, 268, 269
9:10–11	270
9:13–28	73, 74, 79, 213, 267
9:29	56
9:29–31	76, 79, 212, 213, 267
9:29–34	73
9:30	85
10	5
10–12	67
10–28	71
10–36	14, 50, 66, 67, 69, 70, 71, 212, 254, 259, 281
10—36:23	71
10:1—11:4	11
10:4	1
10:6	162
10:8	162
10:10–11	1
10:13	162
10:14	1
11:1–5	44
11:5–12	44
11:13	57
11:16	258
11:17	68
11:23	44
12:1	57, 258
12:2	258
12:5	258
12:5–8	11
12:6	258
12:7	258
12:12	258
12:13	6, 88
12:14	258
13	67
13:4	57, 191
13:4–12	11, 14
13:5	127, 135
13:7	88
13:8	88, 135, 192
13:9	199
13:10–11	258
13:12–15	258
13:15	57
13:21	88
14–16	67
14:4	258
14:7	11, 14, 258
14:11	11, 258
15:1–7	11
15:2	108, 191, 258
15:4	258
15:12	258
15:13	258
15:15	258
15:17	194
16:1–6	11
16:3	127
16:7–9	11
16:9	88, 194
16:11	59
16:12	258
17–20	67
17:1	88
17:3	67
17:4	258
17:13b–19	159
18:1–34	11
18:4	258
18:31	258

19:1–3	11	28	67, 160
19:3	258	28:1	67
19:6–7	11, 14	28:6	258
19:9	194	28:9–11	11
19:9–11	11, 14	28:10	158
20:4	258	28:11	191
20:6–12	11, 203	28:12–13	11
20:9	258	28:19	258
20:14–17	11	28:22	258
20:20	11, 191	28:23	57
20:34	59	28:26	59
20:37	11	29–32	67
21	67	29–36	71
21:2—22:1	50	29:2	67
21:4	88	29:5	191
21:7	127	29:5–11	11, 14
21:10	258	29:6	258
21:12	194	29:10	127
21:12–15	11	29:13–28	212
21:17	56	29:24	57, 276
22	67	29:31	11, 199
22:9	258	30:1	57
23	137	30:5	57, 276
23–24	67	30:6	56, 57, 258
23:1–15	11	30:6–9	11, 14, 56
23:3	127	30:7	258
23:9	128	30:9	56, 258
23:16	127	30:11	258
24:4–6	10	30:18	258
24:8	57	30:18–19	11
24:14	56	30:19	258
24:18	158, 258	30:27	258
24:20	258	31:10	11
24:20–22	11	31:21	258
24:22	11	32:5	88
24:24	258	32:7–8	11, 14
24:27	59	32:9–17	11
25	67	32:20	258
25:2	194	32:24	258
25:4	10	32:32	59
25:5	159	33	67
25:7–9	11	33:2–9	10
25:15–16	11	33:7	259
25:17–24	11	33:12	258
25:20	258	33:13	194, 258
25:26	59	33:18	59
26	67	33:18–19	258
26:5	258	33:19	258
26:11–13	159	33:23	158, 258
26:16	258	34–35	67
26:17–18	11	34:2–3	67
26:18	258	34:3	258
27	67	34:9	56, 57
27:6	88	34:14–28	10
27:7	59	34:21	56, 57

2 Chronicles (continued)

34:25	258
34:27	258
34:29	162
34:32	44
35:3	57, 68, 276
35:3–6	11
35:4	68
35:27	59
36	67
36:8	59
36:12	258
36:13	258
36:14	258
36:15	11
36:15–20	112
36:17–21	59
36:20	54, 56, 57
36:20–21	60
36:21	59, 112
36:21–22	41
36:22	38
36:22–23	39, 53, 59, 60, 112, 187
36:23	41, 58

Ezra

1:1–3	59, 60
1:2–3	60
1:5	44
2	48, 54
2:6	95
3:8	56
4:1	56, 66
4:1–4	44
6:1–5	59
6:19	56
6:20	56
6:21	56
8:9	95
8:17	169
8:35	56
10:9	44

Nehemiah

1:2	56
1:3	56
7	54
7:11	95
8:17	56
11:3–19	54
11:4	66
11:7–9	66

Psalms

72:18–19	116
89:4	134
89:29–32	192
89:53	116
96	116
96:1	100
96:1–13	116
96:1b	117
96:1b–13a	117
96:6	117
96:10	117
96:10c	118
96:10–11	117, 118
96:13c	118
99:5	191
105	116
105:1	100
105:1–15	116
105:2	100
105:6	116
105:8	116
105:8–11	116
105:8–15	116
105:12	116
105:12–15	116
106:1	116, 118
106:47–48	116, 118
106:48	118
107:1	100, 116
118:1–4	116
118:29	116
132	191, 248, 249
132:7	191
132:8	191, 248
132:8–9	252
132:8–10	248
132:9	248
132:10	249
132:10–11	249
132:12	192
132:13–14	191
136	116

Proverbs

30:15	65
30:18	65
30:21	65
30:29	65

Isaiah

28:21	108

Index of Ancient Sources

44:28	41	Joel	
45:13	61	2:23	246
55:3	249		
55:6	195	Haggai	
66:1	191	1:1	56
66:13–14	61	1:12–14	56
		2:1–4	56
Jeremiah		2:14	169
3:3	246		
3:16	112	Zechariah	
11:4	141	3–4	56
7:23–26	141	6:9–14	56
16:10	261	6:10	56
17:19–27	59	7:1–3	169
22:8–9	261	7:5	56
23:25–32	216	8:6	56
24:9	261	8:7	56
25:11–12	59, 61	8:8	56
27:6–7	61	10:2	216
27:9–10	216		
29:10	59, 61	APOCRYPHA	
29:13–14	195	Sirach	
40:6	46	47:9–10	40
41:4–9	169		
51:11	61	2 Maccabees	
		2:47	112
Lamentation			
2:1	191	2 Esdras	
		10:20–22	112
Ezekiel			
20:1–32	59		

319

www.ingramcontent.com/pod-product-compliance
Lightning Source LLC
Chambersburg PA
CBHW080934300426
44115CB00017B/2818